Interprocess Communications in Linux

John Shapley Gray

PRENTICE
HALL
PTR

Prentice Hall PTR
Upper Saddle River, NJ 07458
www.phptr.com

ISBN 0-13-046042-7

94999

9 780130 460424

Library of Congress Cataloging-in-Publication available

Editorial/production supervision: *Kathleen M. Caren*
Executive Editor: *Greg Doench*
Editorial Assistant: *Brandt Kenna*
Marketing Manager: *Debby vanDijk*
Manufacturing Manager: *Alexis Heydt-Long*
Cover Design Director: *Jerry Votta*
Composition: *G&S Typesetters, Inc.*

© 2003 Pearson Education Inc.
Publishing as Prentice Hall PTR
Upper Saddle River, NJ 07458

Prentice Hall books are widely used by corporations and government agencies for training, marketing, and resale.

For information regarding corporate and government bulk discounts, contact:

Corporate and Government Sales: (800) 382-3419 or corpsales@pearsontechgroup.com

All products mentioned herein are trademarks or registered trademarks of their respective owners.

Printed in the United States of America

10 9 8 7 6 5 4 3 2 1

ISBN 0-13-046042-7

Pearson Education LTD.
Pearson Education Australia PTY, Limited
Pearson Education Singapore, Pte. Ltd.
Pearson Education North Asia Ltd.
Pearson Education Canada, Ltd.
Pearson Educación de Mexico, S.A. de C.V.
Pearson Education—Japan
Pearson Education Malaysia, Pte. Ltd.

To my wife, Marie

CONTENTS

Contents

APPENDIX A Using Linux Manual Pages 551

APPENDIX B UNIX Error Messages 559

APPENDIX C RPC Syntax Diagrams 567

Appendix D Profiling Programs 575

INTRODUCTION

The topic of interprocess communication techniques is broad, challenging and dynamic. All but the most basic operating systems provide methods for processes communication. Early on, UNIX supported a number of rudimentary process communication constructs (such as lock files, signals and pipes). In the early 1980s, facilities such as message queues, semaphores, and shared memory were added to the mix by AT&T with its release of UNIX System V. Somewhat concurrently, the Berkeley Software Distribution added support for Internet protocols (4.3BSD) and the socket interface as a communication construct. By the mid-1990s, threads and multithreaded programming techniques were making significant, permanent inroads into the UNIX mainstream.

Along the way, UNIX spawned innumerable UNIX-like operating systems. One such operating system was MINIX. MINIX, written by Andrew S. Tanenbaum, is a small (about twelve thousand lines) PC version of UNIX. MINIX was presented as a pedagogical tool to permit the user to gain a better understanding of the inner working of a UNIX-like operating system. As all of the operating system source code was provided, the user could tinker with the code and refine its functionality. As a university student, Linus Torvalds' exposure to MINIX led him to develop a more robust UNIX-like operating system called Linux. In brief, Linux is a freely distributed hybrid version of UNIX. Linux system administration is BSD-like while its programming environment has a definite AT&T flavor. A number of commercial versions of Linux populate the market. These versions bundle Linux with a variety of other operating system related utilities and software packages. One of the more widely distributed commercial versions is Red Hat Linux. Red Hat Linux includes Richard Stallman's GNU project C (gcc) and C++ (g++) compilers.

This text explores the intricacies of interprocess communications as supported by Red Hat Linux version 7.3 and 8.0. It is assumed that the reader has a working knowledge of C/C++ programming. It is further assumed that while not being an expert, the reader has worked in a UNIX type environment and is reasonably familiar with generating and editing text using an editor such as vi or pico (available from the University of Washington). This text makes extensive references to specific system calls and predefined library functions. The reader is encouraged to read the manual pages for each system call/library function as it is encountered. As in UNIX, the manual pages in Linux are an unparalleled source of information. Appendix A covers the format and use of manual pages.

All programming references and examples were generated on a PC Pentium-based platform running Red Hat Linux 7.3, using the GNU C/C++ compiler version 2.96. With the release of Red Hat Linux 8.0 and GNU 3.2 the examples were revisited and tweaked where necessary. Many of the examples and most of the exercises have also been compiled and run in a Solaris 2.8 setting using GNU 2.95. Most often, few if any modifications were needed to generate clean, executable code in this alternate environment.

Each example is a complete standalone program. Command line examples, except where noted, are Korn shell based. In any setting, IPC (interprocess communication) support must be available for the user to pursue the materials covered in the chapters on semaphores, message queues, and shared memory. When Linux is installed, usually IPC support is enabled (check the /proc directory for the presence of the sysvipc directory). If it is not present you may need to modify system configuration files and recompile the kernel. There are a number of places that one can peruse for information on how this might be done. One source of information is the Configure.help file that resides in the /usr/src/linuxXXXX/Documentation subdirectory (where XXXX is the version of Linux). A second source is the URL http://www.tldp .org/docs.html. However, unless you are the system administrator, you most likely will want to seek help when doing this. To work with threads, a POSIX compliant thread library (such as LinuxThreads) must be available. Fortunately, most new versions of Linux come with thread libraries that are distributed with the GNU compiler (check the /usr/lib directory for files names containing pthread, e.g., libpthread.a or libpthread.so).

The URL `http://sources.redhat.com/glibc/` provides a web page with additional information on `glibc` the GNU `libc` program.

Works of any complexity are never completely finished. Your comments, suggestions, corrections, and exercise solutions are welcome. I can be contacted at `gray@cs.hartford.edu`. Program examples can be obtained at www.phptr.com/gray.

ACKNOWLEDGMENTS

While my name is on the cover of this text, I would be the first to admit that its creation has not been a singular task. My family—my wife Marie and son Bill—have figured prominently in my efforts. They unfailingly provided me with the moral support when my ardor to complete the task at hand waned and often had to forgo their own activities so that I might pursue mine. Thank you!

I would also like to acknowledge those who helped me in numerous ways to refine my thoughts and class notes into the material that follows. Hoaiphong Truong provided me with numerous helpful comments and suggestions. Outside technical reviewers Robert Lynch and Ryan Caveney (Science Applications International Corporation, NASA Goddard Space Flight Center) provided me with invaluable feedback. My UNIX Internals classes at the University of Hartford continued to serve as a test bed for proposed exercises, and as a springboard for new ideas and topics.

The University of Hartford generously provided me with the sabbatical time to write the bulk of the text. I would like to acknowledge the members of the Math/Physics/Computer Science and Interactive Information Technology departments who offered their ongoing collegial support. Special thanks to my Computer Science department Chair, Joel Kagan, for his continued support in all of my academic endeavors. Personal thanks to Greg Doench, Executive Editor at Prentice Hall who, as always, handled things with a practiced and steady hand. Kathleen M. Caren, my Production Editor, was invaluable in helping to put all the pieces into final form. I am also grateful to the talented Justin Muir of Muir Designs (muirdesigns1790@yahoo.com) who turned my penguin visions into reality. My thanks would not be complete without a mention of my parents and grandparents who instilled in me from the beginning that almost anything is possible if you persevere.

Chapter 1

PROGRAMS
AND
PROCESSES

1.1 Introduction

Fundamental to all operating systems is the concept of a **process**. A process is a dynamic entity scheduled and controlled by the operating system. While somewhat abstract, a process consists of an executing (running) program, its current values, state information, and the resources used by the operating system to manage the process. In a UNIX-based operating system, such as Linux, at any given point in time, multiple processes *appear* to be executing concurrently. From the viewpoint of each of the processes involved, it *appears* they have access to and control of all system resources as if they were in their own standalone setting. Both viewpoints are an illusion. The majority of operating systems run on platforms that have a single processing unit capable of supporting many *active* processes. However, at any point in time, only one process is actually being worked upon. By rapidly changing the process it is currently executing, the operating system gives the appearance of concurrent process execution. The ability of the operating system to multiplex its resources among multiple processes in various stages of execution is called **multiprogramming** (or **multitasking**). Systems with multiple processing units, which by definition can support true concurrent processing, are called **multiprocessing**.

As noted, part of a process consists of the execution of a **program**. A program is an inactive, static entity consisting of a set of instructions and associated data.

If a program is invoked multiple times, it can generate multiple processes. We can consider a program to be in one of two basic formats:

- **source program**—A source program is a series of valid statements for a specific programming language (such as C or C++). The source program is stored in a plain ASCII text file. For purposes of our discussion we will consider a plain ASCII text file to be one that contains characters represented by the ASCII values in the range of 32–127. Such source files can be displayed to the screen or printed on a line printer. Under most conditions, the access permissions on the source file are set as nonexecutable. A sample C++ language source program is shown in Program 1.1.

- **executable program**—An executable program is a source program that, by way of a translating program such as a compiler, or an assembler, has been put into a special binary format that the operating system can execute (run). The executable program is not a plain ASCII text file and in most cases is not displayable on the terminal or printed by the user.

Program 1.1 A source program in C++.

```
File : p1.1.cxx
   |      /*
   |              Display Hello World 3 times
   |       */
   |      #include <iostream>
   +      #include <unistd.h>                      // needed for write
   |      #include <cstring>                       // needed for strcpy
   |      #include <cstdlib>                       // needed for exit
   |      using namespace std;
   |      char          *cptr = "Hello World\n";   // static by placement
  10      char          buffer1[25];
   |      int main( ){
   |        void          showit(char *);          // function prototype
   |        int           i = 0;                    // automatic variable
   |        strcpy(buffer1, "A demonstration\n");   // library function
   +        write(1, buffer1, strlen(buffer1)+1);   // system call
   |        for ( ; i < 3; ++i)
   |          showit(cptr);                        // function call
   |        return 0;
   |      }
  20      void showit( char *p ){
   |        char          *buffer2;
   |        buffer2= new char[ strlen(p)+1 ];
   |        strcpy(buffer2, p);                    // copy the string
   |        cout << buffer2;                       // display string
   +        delete [] buffer2;                     // release location
   |      }
```

1.2 Library Functions

Programs of any complexity make use of functions. A **function** is a collection of declarations and statements that carries out a specific action and/or returns a value. Functions are either defined by the user or have been previously defined and made available to the user. Previously defined functions that have related functionality or are commonly used (e.g., math or graphics routines) are stored in object code format in **library** (archive) **files**. Object code format is a special file format that is generated as an intermediate step when an executable program is produced. Like executable files, object code files are also not displayed to the screen or printed. Functions stored in library files are often called **library functions** or **runtime library routines**.

The standard location for library files in most UNIX systems is the directory /usr/lib. Ancillary library files may also be found in the /usr/local/lib directory. Two basic types of libraries are used in compilations—static libraries and shared object libraries. Static libraries are collections of object files that are used during the linking phase of a program. Referenced code is extracted from the library and incorporated in the executable image. Shared libraries contain relocatable objects that can be shared by more than one application. During compilation the object code from the library is not incorporated in the executable code only a reference to the object is made. When the executable that uses a shared object library is loaded into memory the appropriate shared object library is loaded and attached to the image. If the shared object library is already in memory this copy is referenced. As might be expected shared object libraries are more complex than static libraries. In Linux, by default, shared object libraries are used if present otherwise static libraries are used. Most, but not all, compiler installations include both types of libraries. In the examples below we will focus on the more ubiquitous static libraries.

By convention, the three-letter prefix for a library file is **lib** and the file extension for a static library is **.a**. The UNIX archive utility **ar**, which creates, modifies, and extracts members from an archive, can be used to examine library file contents.[1] For example, the command

```
linux$ ar t /usr/lib/libc.a | pr -4 -t
```

will pipe the table of contents (indicated by the t command-line option) of the standard C library file (libc.a) to the **pr** utility, which will display the output to the screen in a four-column format. The object code in this library is combined by default with all C programs when they are compiled. Therefore, in a C program when a reference is made to **printf**, the object code for

---

[1] The archive utility is one of the many exceptions to the rule that all command-line options for system utilities begin with a hyphen (-).

the **printf** function is obtained from the /usr/lib/libc.a library file. Similarly, the command

```
linux$ ar t /usr/lib/libstdc++-3-libc6.2-2-2.10.0.a | pr -4 -t
```

will display the table of contents of the C++ library file used by the **gcc** compiler. Remember that the versions (and thus the names) of library files can change when the compiler is updated.

Additional information can be extracted from library files using the **nm** utility. For example, the command

```
linux$ nm -C /usr/lib/libstdc++-3-libc6.2-2-2.10.0.a | grep 'bool operator=='
```

will find all the C++ equality operators in the referenced library file. The -C command-line option for **nm** demangles the compiler-generated C++ function names and makes them a bit more readable.

The **ar** command can also be used to create a library. For example, say we have two functions. The first function, called ascii, is stored in a file called ascii.cxx. This function generates and returns an ASCII string when passed the starting and endpoint for the string. The second function, called change_case (stored in the file change_case.cxx), accepts a string and inverts the case of all alphabetic characters in the string. The listing for the two programs is shown in Figure 1.1.

Figure 1.1 Source code for two functions to be stored in archive libmy_demo.a.

```
File : ascii.cxx
  - |     char *
    |     ascii( int start, int finish ){
    |       char *b = new char(finish-start+1);
    |       for (int i=start; i <= finish; ++i)
    +         b[i-start]=char( i );
    |       return b;
    |     }
```

```
File : change_case.cxx
    |     #include <ctype.h>
    |
    |     char *
    |     change_case( char *s ){
    +       char *t = &s[0];
    |       while ( *t ){
    |         if ( isalpha(*t) )
    |           *t += islower(*t) ? -32 : 32;
    |         ++t;
   10       }
    |       return s;
    |     }
```

Each file is compiled into object code, the archive `libmy_demo.a` generated, and the object code added to the archive with the following command sequence:

```
linux$ g++ -c change_case.cxx
linux$ g++ -c ascii.cxx
linux$ ar cr libmy_demo.a ascii.o change_case.o
```

The prototypes for the functions in the `my_demo` library are placed in a corresponding header file called `my_demo.h`. Preprocessor directives are used in this file to prevent it from being inadvertently included more than once. A small C++ program, `main.cxx`, is created to exercise the functions. With the " " notation for the include statement in `main.cxx`, the compiler will look for the `my_demo.h` header file in the current directory. The contents of the `my_demo.h` header file and the `main.cxx` program are shown in Figure 1.2.

Figure 1.2 Header file and test program for `libmy_demo.a`.

```
File : my_demo.h
   |      /*
   |          Prototypes for my_demo library functions
   |       */
   |      #ifndef MY_DEMO_H
   +      #define MY_DEMO_H
   |
   |      char * ascii( int, int );
   |      char * change_case( char * );
   |
  10      #endif
```

```
File : main.cxx
   |      #include <iostream>
   |      #include "my_demo.h"
   |      using namespace std;
   |      int
   +      main( ) {
   |        int start, stop;
   |        char b[20];                              // temp string buffer
   |
   |        cout << "Enter start and stop value for string: ";
  10        cin  >> start >> stop;
   |        cout << "Created string  : " << ascii(start, stop) << endl;
   |        cin.ignore(80,'\n');
   |        cout << "Enter a string  : ";
   |        cin.getline(b,20);
   +        cout << "Converted string: " << change_case( b ) << endl;
   |        return 0;
   |      }
```

The compilation shown below uses the -L command-line option to indicate that when the compiler searches for library files it should also include the current directory. The name of the library is passed using the -l command-line option. As source files are processed sequentially by the compiler, it is usually best to put linker options at the end of the command sequence to avoid the generation of any undefined reference errors.

```
linux$ g++ -o main main.cxx -L. -lmy_demo
```

A sample run of the main.cxx program is shown in Figure 1.3.

Figure 1.3 Sample run testing the archived functions.

```
linux$ main                              ◄──────── If your distribution of Linux does not
Enter start and stop value for string: 56 68    include "." as part of its login path you
Created string  : 89:;<=>?@ABCD          will need to invoke the program as
Enter a string  : This is a TEST!        ./main.
Converted string: tHIS IS A test!
```

If your system supports the **apropos** command, you may issue the following command to obtain a single-line synopsis of the entire set of predefined library function calls described in the manual pages on your system:

```
linux$ apropos '(3'
```

As shown, this command will search a set of system database files containing a brief description of system commands returning those that contain the argument passed. In this case, the '(3' indicates all commands in Section 3 of the manual should be displayed. Section 3 (with its several subsections) contains the subroutine and library function manual pages. The single quotes are used in the command sequence so the shell will pass the parenthesis on to the **apropos** command. Without this, the shell would attempt to interpret the parenthesis, which would then produce a syntax error.

Another handy utility that searches the same database used by the **apropos** command is the **whatis** command. The command

```
linux$ whatis exit
```

would produce a single-line listing of all manual entries for **exit**. If the database for these commands is not present, the command /usr/sbin/makewhatis, providing you have the proper access privileges, will generate it.

A more expansive overview of the library functions may be obtained by viewing the **intro** manual page entry for Section 3. On most systems the command

```
linux$ man 3 intro
```

will return the contents of the **intro** manual page. In this invocation the **3** is used to notify **man** of the appropriate section. For some versions of the **man** command, the option **-s3** would be needed to indicate Section 3 of the manual. Additional manual page information addressing manual page organization and use can be found in Appendix A, "Using Linux Manual Pages."

In addition to manual pages, most GNU/Linux systems come with a handy utility program called **info**. This utility displays documentation written in **Info** format as well as standard manual page documents. The information displayed is text-based and menu-driven. **Info** documents can support limited hypertext-like links that will bring the viewer to a related document when selected. When present, **Info** documentation is sometimes more complete than the related manual page. A few of the more interesting **Info** documents are listed in Table 1.1.

Table 1.1 Partial Listing of Info Documents.

Topic	Description
as	The GNU assembler.
binutils	GNU binary utilities (such as **ar**).
fileutils	GNU file manipulation utilities.
gcc	The **gcc** (and **g++**) compiler. Look here for information on how to use the compiler, special C++ extensions, etc.
gdb	How to use the GNU symbolic debugger.
info	How to use the **info** system. Look here for all the gory details on how to use **info** and write **Info** type documentation.
ipc	System V style interprocess communication constructs: message queues, semaphores, and shared memory.
libc	The C library (as implemented by GNU). A good place to start for an overview on topics such as signals, pipes, sockets, and threads.

The **info** utility should be invoked on the command line and passed the item (a general topic or a specific command—system call, library function, etc.) to be looked up. If an **Info** document exists, it is displayed by the **info** utility. If no **Info** document exists but there is a manual page for the item, then it is displayed (at the top of the Info display will be the string *manpages* to notify you of the source of the information. If neither an **Info** document nor a manual page can be found, then **info** places the user in the **info** utility at the topmost level. When in the **info** utility, use the letter q to quit or a ? to have **info** list the commands it knows. Entering the letter h will direct **info** to display a primer on how to use the utility.

1.3 System Calls

Some previously defined functions used by programs are actually **system calls**. While resembling library functions in format, system calls request the operating system to directly perform some work on behalf of the invoking process. The code that is executed by the operating system lies within the **kernel** (the central controlling program that is normally maintained permanently in memory). The system call acts as a high/mid-level language interface to this code. To protect the integrity of the kernel, the process executing the system call must temporarily switch from **user mode** (with user privileges and access permissions) to **system mode** (with system/root privileges and access permissions). This switch in context carries with it a certain amount of overhead and may, in some cases, make a system call less efficient than a library function that per-

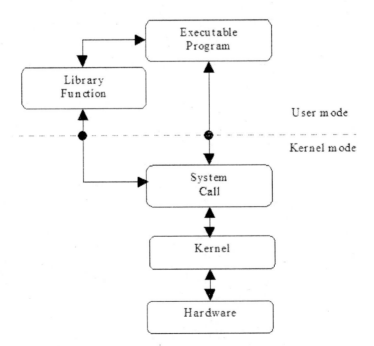

Figure 1.4 Hardware and software layers.

forms the same task. Keep in mind many library functions (especially those dealing with input and output) are fully buffered and thus allow the system some control as to when specific tasks are actually executed.

Section 2 of the manual contains the pages on system calls. Issuing an **apropos** command similar to the one previously discussed but using the value 2 in place of 3 will generate synopsis information on all the system calls defined in the manual pages. It is important to remember that some library functions have embedded system calls. For example, << and >>, the C++ insertion and extraction operators, make use of the underlying system calls **read** and **write**.

The relationship of library functions and system calls is shown in Figure 1.4. The arrows in the diagram indicate possible paths of communication, and the dark circles indicate a context switch. As shown, executable programs may make use of system calls directly to request the kernel to perform a specific function. On the other hand, the executable programs may invoke a library function, which in turn may perform system calls.

1.4 Linking Object Code

Code from library files, predefined or user-defined, is combined with **object code** from the source program at compile time on an as-needed basis. When programming in C/C++, additional library files containing the object code for system calls and library functions not contained in the standard library can be specified at compile time. This is done by using the -1 compiler option, followed by the library name *without* the **lib** prefix and the **.a** extension. For example, the compilation command

```
linux$ gcc prgm.c -lm
```

indicates to the link-loader portion of the **gcc** compiler program that the math library object code found in libm.a should be combined with the object code created from the source program prgm.c. If a special library is needed that does not reside in the standard location, the compiler can be notified of this. The GNU compilers use the -L option, followed by the additional directory (or directories) to be searched. The processing of files passed on the command line to the compiler are done sequentially. Thus, linker options are usually placed at the end of the command sequence to avoid any undefined (unresolved) reference errors.

Be aware that library functions often require the inclusion of additional header files in the source program. The header files contain such information as the requisite function prototypes, macro definitions, and defined constants. Without the inclusion of the proper header files, the program will not compile correctly. Conversely, the program will not compile correctly if you include the proper header file(s) and forget to link in the associated library containing the object code! Such omissions are often the source of cryptic compiler error messages. For example, attempting to compile a C program with gcc that uses a math function (such as pow) without linking in the math library generates the message

```
linux$ gcc m.c
/tmp/ccjKMi3A.o: In function 'main':
/tmp/ccjKMi3A.o(.text+0x15): undefined reference to 'pow'
collect2: ld returned 1 exit status
```

The synopsis section of the manual page (see Appendix A) lists the names of header file(s) if they are required. When multiple inclusion files are indicated, the order in which they are listed in the source program should match the order specified in the manual pages. The order of the inclusion is important, as occasionally the inclusion of a specific header file will *depend upon* the inclusion of the previously referenced header file. This dependency relationship is most commonly seen as the need for inclusion of the <sys/types.h> header file prior to the inclusion of other system header files. The notation <sys/types.h> indicates that the header file types.h can be found in the usual place (most often /usr/include on a UNIX-based system) in the subdirectory sys.

1-1 EXERCISE

Examine the contents of the standard C library (/usr/lib/libc.a). How many **printf**-*related* functions are archived in the standard C library?

1-2 EXERCISE

Are there any library functions/system calls that occur in more than one library? If so, name one and explain why this might be done.

1-3 EXERCISE

Add a **reverse** function to the my_demo library discussed in Section 1.2. This function should reverse the contents of its character string argument. Provide evidence that your function works correctly.

1.5 Managing Failures

In most cases,[2] if a system call or library function is unsuccessful, it returns a value of −1 and assigns a value to an external (global) variable called errno to indicate what the actual error is. The defined constants for all error codes can be found in the header file <sys/errno.h> (or in <asm/errno.h> on some systems). By convention, the defined constants are in uppercase and start with the letter E. It is a good habit to have the invoking program examine the return value from a system call or library function to determine if it was successful. If the invocation fails, the program should take an appropriate action. A common action is to display a short error message and **exit** (terminate) the program. The library function **perror** can be used to produce an error message.

For each system call and library function discussed in detail in the text, a summary table is given. The summary table is a condensed version of manual page information. The format of a typical summary table (in this case the one for **perror**) is shown in Figure 1.5.

The summary table for **perror** indicates the header file <stdio.h> must be included if we are to use **perror**. Notice that the header file <sys/errno.h>, which was mentioned previously, is not referenced in the summary table. The <sys/errno.h> file is included only if the defined constants for specific error codes are to be referenced. The **perror** library function takes a single argument, which is a pointer to a character string constant (i.e., const char *). In addition, the **perror** library function does not return a value (as indicated by the data type void) and will not modify errno if it itself fails.

---

[2] This type of hedging is necessary, since system calls/library functions that return an integer value usually return a −1 on failure, while those that return a pointer return a NULL pointer. However, as these routines are written by a disjointed set of programmers with differing ideas on what should be done, a return value that does not meet this rule of thumb is occasionally encountered.

The header file(s) that must be included when using the library function/system call. These are the ANSI-C header file(s). Note some of these have an ANSI-C++ equivalent.

Manual section where the full description can be found. Some library functions/system calls are found in more than one section of the manual.

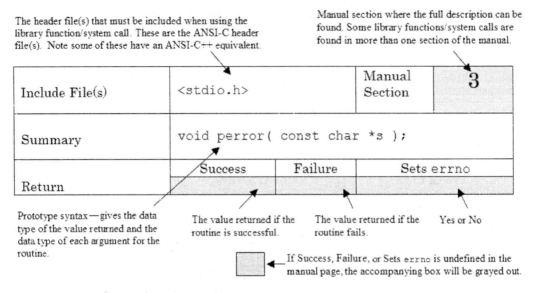

Include File(s)	`<stdio.h>`	Manual Section	3
Summary	`void perror( const char *s );`		

Return	Success	Failure	Sets errno

Prototype syntax—gives the data type of the value returned and the data type of each argument for the routine.

The value returned if the routine is successful.

The value returned if the routine fails.

Yes or No

If Success, Failure, or Sets errno is undefined in the manual page, the accompanying box will be grayed out.

Figure 1.5 Explanation of the summary table format.

A program example using systems calls that provides some error checking by **perror** and errno is shown in Program 1.2.

Program 1.2 Using errno and **perror**.

```
File : p1.2.cxx
  |     /*
  |        Checking errno and using perror
  |      */
  |     #include <iostream>
  +     #include <cstdio>                      // needed for perror
  |     #include <cstdlib>                     // needed for exit
  |     #include <unistd.h>                    // needed for read and write
  |     using namespace std;
  |     extern int errno;
 10     int
  |     main(int argc, char *argv[ ]) {
  |        int n_char = 0,                     // # of chars read
  |        buffer[10];                         // temporary buffer
  |
  +        // Initially n_char is set to 0 and errno is 0 by default
  |
  |        cout << "n_char = " << n_char << "\t errno = " << errno << endl;
  |
  |        // Display a prompt to stdout
```

```
20
 |          n_char = write(1, "Enter a word: ", 15);
 |
 |          // Use the read system call to obtain 10 characters from stdin
 |
 +          n_char = read(0, buffer, 10);
 |          cout << "n_char = " << n_char << "\t errno = " << errno << endl;
 |
 |          if (n_char == -1) {                    // If the read has failed
 |            perror(argv[0]);
30          exit(1);
 |          }
 |
 |          n_char = write(1, buffer, n_char);    // Display the characters read
 |          return 0;
 +        }
```

Notice that to use the errno variable it must first be declared as an external (extern) integer at the top of the program. If this program is run, the initial output indicates that both n_char and errno contain the value 0. Figure 1.6 shows the output if the user enters the word *testing* when prompted.

Figure 1.6 Initial run of Program 1.2 with no errors.

```
linux$ p1.2
n_char = 0      errno = 0
Enter a word: testing
n_char = 8      errno = 0
testing
```

In this case the **read** system call did not fail and has instead, as defined in the manual page, returned the number of characters read from standard input (the keyboard). Note, as we have used **read** in the program, not **cin**, the newline will be one of the characters that is read and counted. As there was no error, the value in errno was not modified and remained at 0. Figure 1.7 shows the output if we run the program again and input more than 10 characters when prompted (in hopes of generating an error).

Figure 1.7 Second run of Program 1.2 with additional keyboard input.

```
$ p1.2
n_char = 0      errno = 0
Enter a word: testing further
n_char = 10     errno = 0
testing fu$rther
rther: Command not found.
```

This time the program reads exactly 10 characters and displays them. The remaining characters are left in the input buffer and end up being processed by the operating system after the program finishes execution. This produces the output of the strange line `testing fu$rther` followed by the line `rther: Command not found`. The characters `testing fu` are displayed by the program. The `Command not found` message is generated by the operating system when it attempts to execute the leftover input `rther` as a command. In this case, providing more input values than needed (i.e., extra characters) does not cause the **read** system call to fail, and as a result `errno` is not changed.

However, if we change the file number for the **read** system call to 3 (a file number that has not been opened versus 0 [standard input] which is automatically opened for us by the operating system when the program runs), the **read** system call will fail. When run, the program output will be as shown in Figure 1.8.

Figure 1.8 Third run of Program 1.2 with an induced error.

```
linux$ p1.2
n_char = 0     errno = 0
Enter a word: n_char = -1     errno = 9
p1.2: Bad file descriptor
```

As expected, this time the return value from the **read** system call is -1. The external variable `errno` now contains the value 9 that is equivalent to the symbolic constant EBADF defined in the `<sys/errno.h>` file.[3] If we call **perror** with a NULL argument, "", the message "Bad file descriptor" will be displayed (the error message the system associates with error code 9). As noted, **perror** does take one argument: a character pointer. If passed a character pointer to a valid string, **perror** will display the referenced string followed by a colon (:) and then append its predefined error message. Programmers often use the argument to **perror** to qualify the error message (e.g., to pass the name of the executing program, as was done in the prior example) or in the case of file manipulation, pass the name of the current file. Unfortunately, **perror** issues a new line following the error message it produces, thus preventing the user from appending additional information to the **perror** display line. There are two ways around this oversight.

Associated with **perror** are two additional external variables. These variables are `extern const char *sys_errlist[ ]` and `extern int sys_nerr`. The external variable `sys_nerr` contains a value that is one

---

[3] Again, in some Linux environments you may find that this constant is actually defined in the `errno.h` include file located in the directory `/usr/include/asm` directory.

greater than the largest error message number value, while `sys_errlist` is a pointer to an external character array of error messages. In place of calling **perror** to return the specific error, we may (if we have provided the proper declarations) use the value in `errno` to index the `sys_errlist[ ]` array to obtain the error message directly.

Another approach to error message generation is to use the library function **strerror** (see Table 1.2).

Table 1.2 Summary of the `strerror` Library Function.

Include File(s)	<string.h>		Manual Section	**3**
Summary	`char *strerror(int errnum);`			
Return		Success	Failure	Sets `errno`
	Reference to error message			

The **strerror** function maps the integer `errnum` argument (which is usually the `errno` value) to an error message and returns a reference to the message. The error message generated by **strerror** should be the same as the message generated by **perror**. If needed, additional text can be appended to the string returned by **strerror**.

Furthermore, Linux provides a command-line utility program called **perror** that returns the error message associated with a specific error code. A sample call of this utility follows:

```
linux$ perror 9
Error code  9: Bad file descriptor
```

Note that the system never clears the `errno` variable (even after a successful system call). It will always contain the value assigned by the system for the last failed call. Appendix B, **"Linux Error Messages,"** contains additional information on error messages.

1-4 EXERCISE

Write a program to display all of the available system error messages in a numbered two-columns-per-line format.

1-5 EXERCISE

The first argument to the **read/write** system call is an integer value indicating the file descriptor. When a program executes, the operating system will automatically open three file descriptors: **stdin** (standard input, which defaults to the keyboard and is referenced by the value 0), **stdout** (standard output, which defaults to the terminal [screen] and is referenced by the value 1), and **stderr** (standard error, which defaults to the console device and is referenced by the value 2). If the last **write** in Program 1.2 is written to 0 (standard input—the keyboard), the program will still compile, run, produce output, and *not* generate an error message. Why is this? One place to start to unravel this mystery might be the command **apropos** stdin.

1-6 EXERCISE

Write your own error messaging function that is called when a file manipulation failure occurs. The function should provide a more descriptive, *user-friendly* interface than **perror**. It might be helpful to examine the header file <sys/errno.h> (as noted previously, an alternate location for this file is the /usr/include/asm directory) and the manual page entry for **intro** in Section 2 (i.e., man 2 intro) prior to starting this assignment.

1.6 Executable File Format

In a Linux environment, source files that have been compiled into an executable form to be run by the system are put into a special format called ELF (Executable and Linking Format). Files in ELF format contain a header entry (for specifying hardware/program characteristics), program text, data, relocation information, and symbol table and string table information. Files in ELF format are marked as executable by the operating system and may be run by entering their name on the command line. Older versions of UNIX stored executable files in a.out format (Assembler OUtpuT Format). While this format is little used today, its name is still tied to the compilation sequence. When

C/C++ program files are compiled, the compiler, by default, places the executable file in a file called a.out.

The layout of the header entry of an ELF format file is defined by the Elf32_Ehdr (or Elf64_Ehdr) structure found in the header file <elf.h>. Write a short C/C++ program that will read the name of a file passed on the command line and determine if the file named is in ELF format and, if so, on what architecture (hardware) type the file will run. You will need to include the header file <libelf/libelf.h> to access predefined ELF header routines, such as elf_begin (used to obtain the ELF descriptor). You must also link the ELF library (i.e., -lelf) when you compile your program. Note that the system utility **file**, which identifies file types, uses the information in the file /usr/share/magic to identify files. An alternate approach to this exercise is to use the /usr/share/magic information to identify an ELF file and the architecture on which it will execute.

1.7 System Memory

In UNIX, when an executable program is read into system memory by the kernel and executed, it becomes a process. We can consider system memory to be divided into two distinct regions or spaces. First is **user space**, which is where user processes run. The system manages individual user processes within this space and prevents them from interfering with one another. Processes in user space, termed **user processes**, are said to be in **user mode**. Second is a region called **kernel space**, which is where the kernel executes and provides its services. As noted previously, user processes can only access kernel space through system calls. When the user process runs a portion of the kernel code via a system call, the process is known temporarily as a **kernel process** and is said to be in **kernel mode**. While in kernel mode, the process will have special (root) privileges and access to key system data structures. This change in mode, from user to kernel, is called a **context switch**.

In UNIX environments, kernels are reentrant, and thus several processes can be in **kernel mode** at the same time. If the system has a single processor, then only one process will be making progress at any given time while the others are blocked. The operating system uses a bit, stored in the program status word (**PSW**), to keep track of the current mode of the process.

1.8 Process Memory

Each process runs in its own private address space. When residing in system memory, the user process, like Gaul, is divided into three segments or regions: **text**, **data**, and **stack**.

- **text segment**—The text segment (sometimes called the instruction segment) contains the executable program code and constant data. The text segment is marked by the operating system as read-only and cannot be modified by the process. Multiple processes can share the same text segment. Processes share the text segment if a second copy of the program is to be executed concurrently. In this setting the system references the previously loaded text segment rather than reloading a duplicate. If needed, shared text, which is the default when using the C/C++ compiler, can be turned off by using the -N option on the compile line. In Program 1.1, the executable code for the functions **main** and **showit** would be found in the text segment.

- **data segment**—The data segment, which is contiguous (in a virtual sense) with the text segment, can be subdivided into initialized data (e.g., in C/C++, variables that are declared as static or are static by virtue of their placement) and uninitialized data.[4] In Program 1.1, the pointer variable cptr would be found in the initialized area and the variable buffer1 in the uninitialized area. During its execution lifetime, a process may request additional data segment space. In Program 1.1 the call to the library routine **new** in the **showit** function is a request for additional data segment space. Library memory allocation routines (e.g., **new**, **malloc**, **calloc**, etc.) in turn make use of the system calls **brk** and **sbrk** to extend the size of the data segment. The newly allocated space is added to the end of the current

---

[4] Some authors use the term BSS segment for the unitialized data segment.

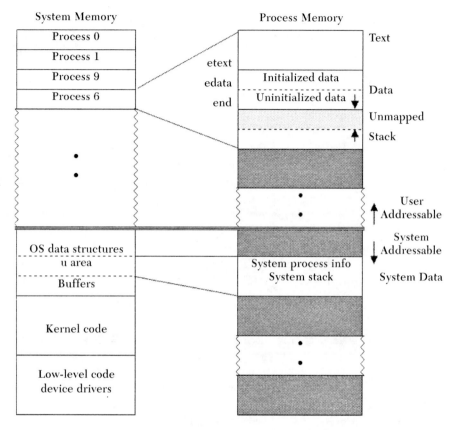

System Memory

| Process 0 |
| Process 1 |
| Process 9 |
| Process 6 |

etext
edata
end

Process Memory

Text

Initialized data
Uninitialized data

Data

Unmapped

Stack

User Addressable

System Addressable

OS data structures

u area

Buffers

Kernel code

Low-level code device drivers

System process info
System stack

System Data

Figure 1.9 System and process memory.

uninitialized data area. This area of available memory is sometimes called the **heap**. In Figure 1.9 this region of memory is labeled as unmapped.

- **stack segment**—The stack segment is used by the process for the storage of automatic identifiers, register variables, and function call information. The identifier i in the function **main**, buffer2 in the function **showit**, and stack frame information stored when the **showit** function is called within the **for** loop would be found in the stack segment. As needed, the stack segment grows toward the uninitialized data segment. The area *beyond* the stack contains the command-line arguments and environment variables for the process. The actual physical location of the stack is system-dependent.

1.9 The u Area

In addition to the text, data, and stack segments, the operating system also maintains for each process a region called the **u area** (user area). The u area contains information specific to the process (e.g., open files, current directory, signal actions, accounting information) and a system stack segment for process use. If the process makes a system call (e.g., the system call to **write** in the function **main** in Program 1.1), the stack frame information for the system call is stored in the system stack segment. Again, this information is kept by the operating system in an area that the process does not normally have access to. Thus, if this information is needed, the process must use special system calls to access it. Like the process itself, the contents of the u area for the process are paged in and out by the operating system.

The conceptual relationship of system and process memory is illustrated in Figure 1.9.

1.10 Process Memory Addresses

The system keeps track of the virtual addresses[5] associated with each user process segment. This address information is available to the process and can be obtained by referencing the external variables etext, edata, and end. The *addresses* (not the contents) of these three variables correspond respectively to the first valid address above the text, initialized data, and uninitialized data segments. Program 1.3 shows how this information can be obtained and displayed.

Program 1.3 Displaying segment address information.

```
File : p1.3.cxx
   |     /*
   |         Displaying process segment addresses
   |      */
   |     #include <iostream>
   +     extern int etext, edata, end;
   |     using namespace std;
   |     int
   |     main( ){
   |       cout << "Adr etext: " << hex << int(&etext) << "\t ";
```

[5] Logical addresses—calculated and used without concern as to their actual physical location.

```
10      cout << "Adr edata: " << hex << int(&edata) << "\t ";
 |      cout << "Adr end: "   << hex << int(&end  ) << "\n";
 |      return 0;
 |   }
```

If we add a few lines of code to our original Program 1.1, we can verify the virtual address location of key identifiers in our program. Program 1.4 incorporates an inline function, SHW_ADR( ), to display the address of an identifier.

Program 1.4 Confirming Program 1.1 address locations.

```
File : p1.4.cxx
 |      /*
 |          Program 1.1 modified to display identifier addresses
 |      */
 |      #include <iostream>
 +      #include <unistd.h>                   // needed for write
 |      #include <cstring>                    // needed for strcpy
 |      #include <cstdlib>                    // needed for exit
 |      using namespace std;
 |      char            *cptr = "Hello World\n"; // static by placement
10      char            buffer1[25];
 |
 |      inline void SHW_ADR(char *ID, int address){
 |      cout << "The id " << ID << "\t is at : "
 |          << hex << address << endl;
 +      }
 |      extern int etext, edata, end;
 |
 |      int main( ){
 |        void          showit(char *);       // function prototype
20        int           i = 0;                // automatic variable
 |                                            // display addresses
 |        cout << "Adr etext: " << hex << int(&etext) << "\t ";
 |        cout << "Adr edata: " << hex << int(&edata) << "\t ";
 |        cout << "Adr end: "   << hex << int(&end ) << "\n";
 +        SHW_ADR("main", int(main));         // function addresses
 |        SHW_ADR("showit", int(showit));
 |        SHW_ADR("cptr", int(&cptr));        // static
 |        SHW_ADR("buffer1", int(&buffer1));
 |        SHW_ADR("i", int(&i));              // automatic
30
 |        strcpy(buffer1, "A demonstration\n"); // library function
 |        write(1, buffer1, strlen(buffer1)+1); // system call
 |        showit(cptr);                       // function call
 |        return 0;
 +      }
```

```
    |    void showit( char *p ){
    |      char          *buffer2;
    |      SHW_ADR("buffer2", int(&buffer2));    // display address
    |
40  |      if ((buffer2= new char[ strlen(p)+1 ]) != NULL){
    |        strcpy(buffer2, p);                  // copy the string
    |        cout << buffer2;                     // display string
    |        delete [] buffer2;                   // release location
    |      } else {
    +        cerr << "Allocation error.\n";
    |        exit(1);
    |      }
    |    }
```

A run of this program produces output (Figure 1.10) that verifies our assertions concerning the range of addresses for identifiers of different storage types. Note the actual addresses displayed by the program are system-dependent. Note that the command-line **nm** utility program can also be used verify the addresses displayed by Program 1.4.

Figure 1.10 Output of Program 1.4.

```
Adr etext: 8048bca       Adr edata: 8049e18       Adr end: 8049ea8
The id main     is at : 8048890
The id showit   is at : 8048a44
The id cptr     is at : 8049c74
The id buffer1  is at : 8049e8c
The id i        is at : bffffc54
A demonstration
The id buffer2  is at : bffffc34
Hello World
```

The output of Program 1.4 is presented pictorially in Figure 1.11.

For those with a further interest in this topic, many versions of Linux have an **objdump** utility that provides additional information for a specified object file.

1-8 EXERCISE

When in the Bourne shell, investigate the commands **ulimit -a** and **size**. How does the information these commands report relate to the values of etext, edata, and end?

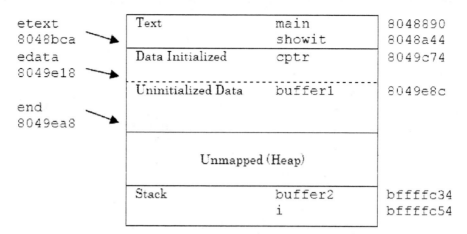

Figure 1.11 Address locations in Program 1.4.

1.11 Creating a Process

It is apparent that there must be some mechanism by which the system can create a new process. With the exception of some special initial processes generated by the kernel during bootstrapping (e.g., **init**), all processes in a Linux environment are created by a **fork** system call, shown in Table 1.3. The initiating process is termed the **parent**, and the newly generated process, the **child**.

Table 1.3 Summary of the **fork** System Call.

Include File(s)	`<sys/types.h>` `<unistd.h>`		Manual Section	2
Summary°	`pid_t fork ( void );`			
Return	Success	Failure	Sets `errno`	
	0 in child, child process ID in the parent	−1	Yes	

° The include file `<sys/types.h>` usually contains the definition of `pid_t`. However, in some environments the actual definition will reside in `<bits/types.h>`. Fortunately, in these environments the `<sys/types.h>` contains an include statement for the alternate definition location, and all remains transparent to the casual user. The include file `<unistd.h>` contains the declaration for the fork system call.

The **fork** system call does not take an argument. If the **fork** system call fails, it returns a -1 and sets the value in errno to indicate one of the error conditions shown in Table 1.4.

Table 1.4 fork Error Messages.[6]

#	Constant	perror Message	Explanation
11	EAGAIN	Resource temporarily unavailable	The operating system was unable to allocate sufficient memory to copy the parent's page table information and allocate a task structure for the child.
12	ENOMEM	Cannot allocate memory	Insufficient swap space available to generate another process.

Otherwise, when successful, **fork** returns the process ID (a unique integer value) of the child process to the parent process, and it returns a 0 to the child process. By checking the return value from **fork**, a process can easily determine if it is a parent or child process. A parent process may generate multiple child processes, but each child process has only one parent. Figure 1.12 shows a typical parent/child process relationship.

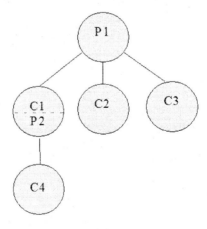

Figure 1.12 The parent/child process relationship.

---

[6] If the library function/system call sets **errno** and can fail in *multiple* ways, an error message table will follow the summary table. This table will contain the error number (#), the equivalent defined constant, the message generated by a call to **perror**, and a brief explanation of the message in the current context.

As shown, process P1 gives rise to three child processes: C1, C2, and C3. Child process C1 in turn generates another child process (C4). As soon as a child process generates a child process of its own, it becomes a parent process.

1-9   EXERCISE

When you check the process status table on a Linux system (see the process status command **ps**), a number of processes with low process IDs (1,2,3, etc.) will be present (for example, **init**, **keventd**, **kswapd**). A search of the file system(s) will show that while there is a system program called **init** (most often found as /sbin/init), there is no system program file for these other processes. Why is this?

When a **fork** system call is made, the operating system generates a copy of the parent process, which becomes the child process. The operating system passes to the child process most of the parent's system information (e.g., open file descriptors, environment information). However, some information is unique to the child process:

- The child has its own process ID (PID).
- The child will have a different parent process ID (PPID) than its parent.
- System-imposed process limits (amount of CPU time the process is allotted) are reset.
- All record locks on files are reset.
- The action to be taken when receiving signals is different.

A program that uses the **fork** system call is shown in Program 1.5.

Program 1.5   Generating a child process.

```
File : p1.5.cxx
  |    /*
  |        First example of a fork system call (no error check)
  |    */
  |    #include <iostream>
  +    #include <sys/types.h>
  |    #include <unistd.h>
  |    using namespace std;
```

25

```
 |      int
 |      main( ) {
10        cout << "Hello\n";
 |        fork( );
 |        cout << "bye\n";
 |        return 0;
 |      }
```

The output of the program is listed in Figure 1.13.

Figure. 1.13 Output of Program 1.5.

```
linux$ p1.5
Hello
bye
bye
```

Notice that the statement cout << "bye\n"; only occurs once in the program at line 12, but the run of the program produces the word "bye" twice—once by the parent process and once by the child process. Once the **fork** system call at line 11 is executed there are two processes each of which executes the remaining program statements. A more detailed description of the **fork** system call and its uses can be found in Chapter 3, "Using Processes."

1.12 Summary

Processes are instances of executable programs that are run and managed by the operating system. Programs make use of predefined functions to implement their tasks. Some of these predefined functions are actually system calls. System calls request the kernel to directly perform a task for the process. Other predefined functions are library functions. Library functions, which may indirectly contain system calls, also perform tasks for the process, but in a less intrusive manner. The object code for system calls and library functions is stored in object code format in library files. The object code for system calls and library functions is included, on an as-needed basis, when a program is compiled.

When a system call or library function fails, the external variable errno can be examined to determine the reason for failure. The library functions **perror** or **strerror** can be used to generate a descriptive error message.

Executing programs are placed in system memory. The executable code and constant data for the program are placed in a region known as the text segment. The initialized and uninitialized program data is placed in the data segment. The program stack segment is used to handle automatic program variables and function call data. In addition, the system will keep process-specific information and system call data in the user area (u area) of memory.

Processes are generated by the **fork** system call. A newly generated process inherits the majority of its state information from its parent.

1.13 Key Terms and Concepts

a.out format
apropos command
ar command
child process
context switch
data segment
ELF format
errno variable
executable program
fork system call
function
heap
info command
kernel
kernel mode
kernel process
kernel space
library file
library function
man command
multiprocessing
multiprogramming

multitasking
nm command
object code
parent process
perror library function
process
program
runtime library routine
source program
stack segment
strerror library function
sys_errlist variable
sys_nerr variable
system call
system mode
text segment
u area
user mode
user process
user space
whatis command

Chapter 2

PROCESSING
ENVIRONMENT

2.1 Introduction

All processes have a processing environment (not to be confused with environment *variables* that are, as we will see, just one part of the processing environment). The processing environment consists of a unique set of information and conditions that is determined by the current state of the system and by the parent of the process. A process can access processing environment information and, in some cases, modify it. This is accomplished either directly or by using the appropriate system calls or library functions.

2.2 Process ID

Associated with each process is a unique positive integer identification number called a process ID (**PID**). As process IDs are allocated sequentially, when a system is booted, a few system processes, which are initiated only once, will always be assigned the same process ID. For example, on a Linux system process 0 (historically known as **swapper**) is created from scratch during the startup process. This process initializes kernel data structures and creates another process called `init`. The `init` process, PID 1, creates a number of special kernel threads[1] to handle system management. These special threads typically have low PID numbers.

Other processes are assigned free PIDs of increasing value until the maximum system value for a PID is reached. The maximum value for PIDs can be found as the defined constant PID_MAX in the header file `<linux/threads.h>` (on older systems check `<linux/tasks.h>`). When the highest PID has been assigned, the system wraps around and begins to reuse lower PID numbers not currently in use.

The system call **getpid** can be used to obtain the PID (Table 2.1). The **getpid** system call does not accept an argument. If it is successful, it will return the PID number. If the calling process does not have the proper access permissions, the **getpid** call will fail, returning a value of -1 and setting `errno` to EPERM (1).

Table 2.1 Summary of the `getpid` System Call.

Include File(s)	`<sys/types.h>` `<unistd.h>`		Manual Section	**2**
Summary	`pid_t getpid( void );`			
Return		Success	Failure	Sets `errno`
		The process ID	-1	Yes

A process can determine its own PID by use of the **getpid** system call, as shown in the following code segment:

```
cout << "My process ID is " << getpid() << endl;
```

The **getpid** system call is of limited use. Usually the PID will be different on each invocation of the program. The manual page entry for **getpid** notes that the most common use for this system call is the generation of unique temporary file names. However, for everyday use, the library function **mkstemp** is much better suited for the production of unique temporary file names.

---

[1] Threads are covered in detail in Chapter 11. Simplistically, a thread is the flow of control through a process. Operating systems vary on how they actually implement a thread. In Linux a thread is a special type of process that shares address space and resources with its parent process. A kernel thread, which runs only in kernel mode, is responsible for a single kernel function, such as flushing buffers to disk or reclaiming returned memory.

2.3 Parent Process ID

Every process has an associated parent process ID (**PPID**). The parent process is the process that forked (generated) the child process. The ID of the parent process can be obtained by using the system call **getppid** (Table 2.2).

Table 2.2 Summary of the `getppid` System Call.

Include File(s)	`<sys/types.h>` `<unistd.h>`		Manual Section	**2**
Summary	`pid_t getppid( void );`			
	Success	Failure	Sets `errno`	
Return	The parent process ID	-1	Yes	

Like the **getpid** system call, **getppid** does not require an argument. If it is successful, it will return the PID number of the parent process. The **getppid** call will fail, returning a value of -1 and setting `errno` to EPERM (1) if the calling process does not have the proper access permissions.

The following code segment displays the PPID:

```
cout << "My Parent Process ID is " << getppid( ) << endl;
```

Unfortunately, there is no system call that allows a parent process to determine the PIDs of all its child processes. If such information is needed, the parent process should save the returned child PID value from the **fork** system call as each child process is created.

2-1 EXERCISE

The manual page entry for the **getppid** system call does not specifically indicate what is returned by **getppid** if the parent process is no longer present when the **getppid** call is made. Write a program that displays the value returned by **getppid** when such an event occurs (the parent predeceases the child). How did you assure that the parent process was not present when the child process made its **getppid** call?

2.4 Process Group ID

Every process belongs to a process group that is identified by an integer process group ID value. When a process generates child processes, the operating system automatically creates a process group. The initial parent process is known as the **process leader**. The process leader's PID will be the same as its process group ID.[2] Additional process group members generated by the process group leader inherit the same process group ID. The operating system uses process group relationships to distribute signals to groups of processes. For example, should a process group leader receive a kill or hang-up signal causing it to terminate, then all processes in its group will also be passed the same terminating signal. A process can find its process group ID from the system call **getpgid**. In some versions of Linux you may find the **getpgid** system call absent. In these versions the system call **getpgrp** (which requires no PID argument) provides the same functionality as the **getpgid** system call. The **getpgid** system call is defined in Table 2.3.

Table 2.3 Summary of the getpgid System Call.

Include File(s)	`<sys/types.h>` `<unistd.h>`		Manual Section	**2**
Summary	`pid_t getpgid( pid_t pid );`			
	Success	Failure	Sets errno	
Return	The process group ID	−1	Yes	

If successful, this call will return the process group ID for the pid that is passed. If the value of pid is 0, the call is for the current process (eliminating the need for a separate call to **getpid**). If the **getpgid** system call fails, a −1 is returned and the value in errno is set to one of the values in Table 2.4 to indicate the source of the error.

Table 2.4 getpgid Error Messages.

#	Constant	perror **Message**	**Explanation**
1	EPERM	Not owner	Invalid access permissions for the calling process.
3	ESRCH	No such process	No such process ID as pid.

[2] Ah-ha—other than generating temporary file names, another use for the **getpid** system call!

A short program using the **getpgid** system call is shown in Program 2.1. Before looking over the program, a brief explanation concerning the compilation of the program is in order. As UNIX has evolved, developers have established a number of standards such as ANSI C, POSIX. 1, POSIX. 2, BSD, SVID, X/Open, and others. On occasion, system calls (such as **getpgid**) and library functions created under one standard (say, BSD) are modified slightly to meet the requirements for another standard (such as POSIX). When using the g++ compiler, defining the constant _GNU_SOURCE instructs the compiler to use the POSIX definition if there is a conflict.

Program 2.1   Displaying process group IDs.

```
File : p2.1.cxx
   |      /*
   |              Displaying process group ID information
   |       */
   |      #define _GNU_SOURCE
   +      #include <iostream>
   |      #include <sys/types.h>
   |      #include <unistd.h>
   |      using namespace std;
   |      int
10        main(  ){
   |        cout << "\n\nInitial process \t PID " << getpid()
   |              << "\t PPID "<< getppid()
   |              << "\t GID " << getpgid(0)
   |              << endl << getpgid(pid_t(getppid())) << endl;
   +
   |        for (int i = 0; i < 3; ++i)
   |          if (fork( ) == 0)                    // Generate some processes
   |            cout << "New process        \t PID " << getpid()
   |                  << "\t PPID "<< getppid()
20                    << "\t GID " << getpgid(0)
   |                  << endl;
   |        return 0;
   |      }
```

Figure 2.1 displays the output of the program.

Figure 2.1   Program 2.1 output.

Initial process	PID 3350	PPID 3260	GID 3350
New process	PID 3351	PPID 3350	GID 3350
New process	PID 3352	PPID 3351	GID 3350

33

New process	PID 3353	PPID 3350	GID 3350
New process	PID 3356	PPID 3353	GID 3350
New process	PID 3355	PPID 3351	GID 3350
New process	PID 3354	PPID 3352	GID 3350
New process	PID 3357	PPID 3350	GID 3350

Note that the actual ID numbers change each time the program is run. The relationship of the processes within the process group is shown in Figure 2.2.

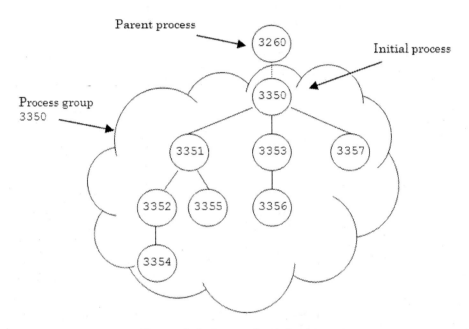

Figure 2.2 Process ID relationships.

All of the processes generated by the program indicate that they belong to the same process group: the process group of the initial process 3350. If the parent of a process dies[3] (terminates) before its child process(es), the process **init** (which is process ID 1) will inherit the child process and become its *foster* parent. The process group ID for a process does not change if this inheritance occurs.

A process may change its process group by using the system call **setpgid**, which sets the process group ID (Table 2.5).

The **setpgid** system call sets the process group pid to that of pgid. If the value for pid is 0, the call refers to the current process. Otherwise, the call

---

[3] There seems to be no end to the anthropomorphic references for parent/child processes, even when they border on the macabre!

Table 2.5 Summary of the `setpgid` System Call.

Include File(s)	`<sys/types.h>` `<unistd.h>`	Manual Section	**2**
Summary	`int setpgid(pid_t pid, pid_t pgid);`		
Return	Success	Failure	Sets `errno`
	0	-1	Yes

refers to the specified PID. The value for `pgid` represents the group to which the process will belong. If the value for `pgid` is 0, the `pid` referenced process will become the process leader. For this call to be successful, the invoking process must have the correct permissions to institute the requested change. The **setpgid** system call returns 0 if successful, or returns a -1 and sets `errno` if it fails. The value `errno` is assigned when **setpgid** fails is given in Table 2.6.

Table 2.6 `setpgid` Error Messages.

#	Constant	`perror` **Message**	**Explanation**
1	EPERM	Operation not permitted	• Process `pid` already a session leader. • Process `pid` is not in same session as calling process. • Invalid process group specified.
3	ESRCH	No such process	No such process ID as `pid`.
22	EINVAL	Invalid argument	The `pgid` value is less than 0 or greater than MAX_PID-1.

For those of us who talk fast or listen casually, it is easy to confuse the *process group* ID with the process's *group* ID. A process's group ID is covered in Section 2.6.

In addition to process groups, UNIX also supports the concept of a **session**. A session is a collection of related and unrelated processes and process groups. As with process grouping, there are a number of system calls (e.g., **setsid**, **getsid**) that can be used to create and manipulate a session. The process calling **setsid** becomes the session leader as well as the process group leader. In this arrangement, there is no controlling tty (terminal device). Keep in mind a process inherits its controlling terminal from its parent. Certain input sequences, such as a quit (CTRL+\) or an interrupt (CTRL+C), received by a controlling terminal are automatically propagated to other processes in the session.

Modify Program 2.1 so that each new process becomes its own group leader.

2.5 Permissions

All UNIX files (executable and otherwise) have an associated set of owner permission bits that are used by the operating system to determine access. The permission bits are grouped into three sets of three bits each. Each bit within a set determines if a file can be read, written to, or executed. The three sets correspond to three classes of users: the file **owner**, those in the file owner's **group** and all **other** users. We can think of the nine permission bits as representing a three-digit octal number, as shown in Figure 2.3. This permission set would indicate that the file owner has read, write, and execute permission; group members have read and write permission; and all others have execute-only permission. The permissions for a file are part of the information stored by the operating system in an **I-list** (with one unique entry per file). When a file is accessed, its attributes are stored in a system **inode** table.

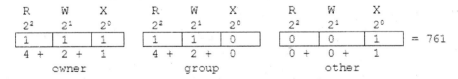

Figure 2.3 File permissions as octal values.

At a system level, the permissions of a file are modified using the **chmod** command. The permissions of a file can be listed with the **ls** command using the **-l** (long format) flag. For example, in the **ls** command output shown in Figure 2.4, the file owner (**root**) of the file (**vi**) has permission to read (**r**), write (**w**), and execute (**x**) the file. Members of the file owner's group can read and execute the file, as can users classified as other. In Linux, the group name for a file is shown by default when issuing the **ls -l** command. In some forms of UNIX (such as *true-blue* BSD), the **-g** flag must be added to the command (i.e., **ls -lg**) to obtain the group name.

The interpretation of the permission bits for directories is slightly different than for files. When the file is a directory, setting the read bit indicates the

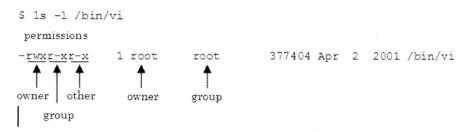

```
$ ls -l /bin/vi
 permissions

-rwxr-xr-x     1 root      root       377404 Apr  2  2001 /bin/vi
```

Figure 2.4 File permissions displayed by `ls`.

directory can be read or displayed. Setting the write bit indicates files or links can be added or removed from the directory, and setting execute permission indicates traversal permission is granted. If traversal permission is *not* set, the directory name can only be used as part of a path name but cannot be examined directly.

2-3 EXERCISE

Is the owner of a file also a member of the class "other"? If the file protections on a file are set so that only those in the class "other" have read/write/execute access, does the owner still have access to the file? Is this reasonable? Why?

When generating files in UNIX, such as by I/O redirection or compiling a source program into an executable, the operating system will assign permissions to the file. The default permissions assigned to the file are determined by a bitwise operation on two three-digit octal mask values. These mask values are the **creation mask** and the **umask**. Unless otherwise specified (such as when creating or opening a file within a program), the creation mask used by the system is 777 for executable and directory files and 666 for text files. The default umask value is set by the system administrator and is most commonly 022. If you want to change the value of umask and would like the value available to all your processes, insert the command **umask** nnn (where nnn is the new value for umask) in your startup `.login` (or `.profile`) file.

At a system level the current umask value may be displayed/modified by using the **umask** command. An example using the **umask** command is shown in Figure 2.5 (notice that leading 0s are displayed on some systems).

37

Figure 2.5 Using the `umask` command.

```
linux$ umask
22
linux$ umask 011
linux$ umask
11
```

When a new file is created, the system will exclusive **OR** (**XOR**) the creation mask for the file with the current umask value. The exclusive **OR** operation acts the same as a subtract (without any borrow) of the umask value from the creation mask. The net result determines the permissions for the new file. For example, generating a text file called `foo` using command-line I/O redirection, as shown in Figure 2.6.

Figure 2.6 Generating a plain text file using I/O redirection.

```
linux$ cat > foo
hello foo
^d
```

This will set the permissions for the text file `foo` to 644 (666 minus 022). This is verified by the output of the **ls** command using the **-l** option, as shown in Figure 2.7.

Figure 2.7 The default permissions of a plain text file.

```
linux$ ls -l foo
-rw-r--r--    1 gray     faculty       10 Jan  1 14:58 foo
```

If we generate a directory (or executable file such as `a.out` using the C/C++ compiler), the default permissions, using the 022 umask, will be 755 (777 minus 022). See Figure 2.8.

Figure 2.8 The default permission of a directory entry.

```
linux$ mkdir bar
linux$ ls -ld bar
drwxr-xr-x    2 gray     faculty     4096 Jan  1 15:00 bar
```

The use of system calls **chmod**, **stat** (file status information), and **umask** that allow a process access to this information is presented in Section 2.7.

2.6 Real and Effective User and Group IDs

In UNIX, with the exception of a few special system processes, processes are generated by users (root and otherwise) who have logged on to the system. During the login process the system queries the password file[4] to obtain two identification (ID) numbers. The numbers the system obtains are in the third and fourth fields of the password entry for the user. These are, respectively, the **real user ID** (**UID**) and **real group ID** (**GID**) for the user. For example, in the sample password file entry

```
ggluck:x:1025:1001:Garrett Gluck:/home/student/ggluck:/bin/tcsh
```

the user login ggluck has a real user ID of 1025 and a group ID of 1001. The real user ID should be (if the system administrator is on the ball) a unique integer value, while the real group ID (also an integer value) may be common to several logins. Group ID numbers should map to the group names stored in the file /etc/group.[5] In general, IDs of less than 500 usually (but not always) indicate user logins with special status.

For every process the system also keeps a second set of IDs called effective IDs, the **effective user ID** (**EUID**) and **effective group ID** (**EGID**). The operating system uses the real IDs to identify the *real user* for things such as process accounting or sending mail, and the effective IDs to determine what additional permissions should be granted to the process. Most of the time the real and effective IDs for a process are identical. However, there are occasions when nonprivileged users on a system must be allowed to access/modify privileged files (such as the password file). To allow controlled access to key files, Linux has an additional set of file permissions, known as **set-user-ID** (**SUID**) and **set-group-ID** (**SGID**), that can be specified by the file's owner. When indicated, these permissions tell the operating system that when the program is run, the resulting process should have the privileges of the owner/group of the program (versus the real user/group privileges associated with the process). In these instances, the effective IDs for the process become those indicated for the file's owner. A listing for an **suid** program follows.

---

[4] In older versions of Linux the complete password file (passwd) was found in the /etc directory. In newer versions, for security reasons, the password file, while still present, may have some of its pertinent information stored elsewhere (such as in the file /etc/shadow). While the /etc/passwd file is readable by the ordinary user, supplemental password files usually are not.

[5] If, for some reason, there is no group name for the assigned group number, the system displays the group number when you issue the **ls -l** command.

```
-r-s--x--x    1 root     root     13536 Jul 12  2000 /usr/bin/passwd
```

As shown, this **passwd** program (the executable for the system-level command **passwd**) has its owner permissions set to **r-s**. The letter **s** in the owner's category, found in place of the letter **x**, indicates that when this program is run, the process should have the privileges of the file owner (which is root). The set-user information is stored by the system in a tenth permission bit and can be modified using the system level command, **chmod**. The **SUID** setting for the **passwd** program allows the non-privileged user running it to temporarily have root (superuser) privileges. In this case, the user running the program will be able to modify the system password files, as the permissions on the password files indicate that they are owned and can only be modified by root. Needless to say, programs that have their **SUID** or **SGID** bit set should be carefully thought out, especially if the programs are owned by the superuser (root).

At a system level, the command **id** (as shown in Figure 2.9) displays the current user, group ID, and group affiliation information. Note that while a file can belong to only one group, a user can belong to many groups.

Figure 2.9 Typical **id** information.

```
linux$ id
uid=500(gray) gid=1000(faculty) groups=1000(faculty)
```

In a programming environment, the system calls that return the user/group real and effective IDs for a process are given in Table 2.7.

Table 2.7 Summary of User/Group Real and Effective ID Calls System.

Include File(s)	`<sys/types.h>` `<unistd.h>`		Manual Section	**2**
Summary	`uid_t getuid( void ); uid_t geteuid ( void );` `gid_t getgid( void ); gid_t getegid ( void );`			
	Success	Failure	Sets errno	
Return	The requested ID			

There are corresponding system calls that can be passed ID values to set (change) the user/group real and effective IDs. Additionally, Linux implements a file system user ID used by the kernel to limit a user's access to a given file system. The file system ID is set with the **setfsuid** system call. The use of **setfsuid** and the calls to set user/group real and effective IDs are beyond the scope of this text.

2.7 File System Information

In addition to process ID information, the process environment contains file system information. Associated with each open file is an integer file descriptor value that the operating system uses as an index to a 1,024-entry **file descriptor table** located in the **u** (user) area for the process. The per-process file descriptor table references a **system file table**, which is located in kernel space. In turn, the system file table maps to a **system inode table** that contains a reference to a more complete internal description of the file.

When a child process is generated, it receives a *copy* of its parent's file descriptor table (this includes the three descriptors—stdin, stdout, and

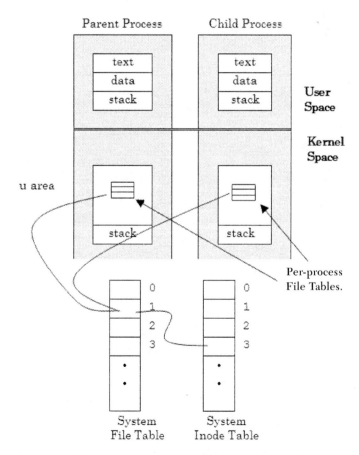

Parent Process   Child Process

text / data / stack

text / data / stack

User Space

Kernel Space

u area

stack   stack

Per-process File Tables.

0 1 2 3

0 1 2 3

System File Table

System Inode Table

Figure 2.10   Process/system file table relationships.

stderr) with the file pointer offset associated with each open file. If a file is marked as shareable, the operating system will need to save each file pointer offset separately. The relationship of process and system tables are shown in Figure 2.10.

2-4 EXERCISE

Write a program that verifies that a parent and child process share the same file pointer and file pointer offset. The parent should **open** a text file and **fork** a child process. The child process should **read** from the text file and display what it has read. When the child terminates, the parent process should then **read** from the same file and display what it has read. At this stage, you may need to use the **sleep** system call to synchronize file access between the parent and child processes.

2-5 EXERCISE

Write a program that determines by *trial and error* the number of files a process can have simultaneously open (is it really 1,024, as mentioned?). Be sure to *remove* (investigate the **unlink** system call) any files that you generate.

2.8 File Information

There are a number of system calls that a process can use to obtain file information. Of these, the **stat** system calls (shown in Table 2.8) provide the process with a comprehensive set of file-related information somewhat analogous to the information that can be obtained by using the system-level **stat** command found in Linux. For example, the command

```
linux$ stat a.out
  File: "a.out"
  Size: 14932      Blocks: 32        Regular File
Access: (0755/-rwxr-xr-x)  Uid: ( 500/ gray)  Gid: (1000/ faculty)
```

```
Device: 815         Inode: 97541      Links: 1
Access: Tue Jan  1 16:05:58 2002
Modify: Tue Jan  1 16:05:57 2002
Change: Tue Jan  1 16:05:57 2002
```

displays information about the file a.out found in the current directory.

Table 2.8 Summary of the stat System Calls.

Include File(s)	`<sys/types.h>` `<sys/stat.h>` `<unistd.h>`		Manual Section	**2**
Summary	`int stat(const char *file_name, struct stat *buf);` `int fstat(int filedes, struct stat *buf);` `int lstat(const char *file_name, struct stat *buf);`			
Return	Success	Failure	Sets errno	
	0	−1	Yes	

As its first argument, the **stat** system call takes a character pointer to a string containing the path for a file. The **lstat** system call is similar to **stat** except when the file referenced is a symbolic link. In the case of a symbolic link, **lstat** returns information about the link entry, while **stat** returns information about the actual file. The **fstat** system call takes an integer file descriptor value of an open file as its first argument.

All three **stat** system calls return, via their second argument, a pointer to a **stat** structure. The **stat** structure is defined in its entirety in the header file `<sys/stat.h>` and the `<bits/stat.h>`. The `<bits/stat.h>` file is automatically included by `<sys/stat.h>` and should not be directly included by the programmer. The **stat** structure normally contains members for

```
struct stat {
dev_t      st_dev;      /* device file resides on */
ino_t      st_ino;      /* this file's number */
u_short    st_mode;     /* protection */
short      st_nlink;    /* number of hard links to the file */
short      st_uid;      /* user ID of owner */
short      st_gid;      /* group ID of owner */
dev_t      st_rdev;     /* the device identifier(special
                           files only)*/
off_t      st_size;     /* total size of file, in bytes */
time_t     st_atime;    /* file data last access time */
```

```
time_t    st_mtime;    /* file data last modify time */
time_t    st_ctime;    /* file data last status change time */
long      st_blksize;  /* preferred blocksize for file system I/O */
long      st_blocks;   /* actual number of blocks allocated */
```

The special data types (e.g., dev_t, ino_t) of individual structure members are mapped to standard data types in the header file <sys/types.h>. If the **stat** system calls are successful, they return a value of 0. Otherwise, they return a value of −1 and set errno. As these system calls reference file information, there are numerous error situations that may be encountered. The value that errno may be assigned and an explanation of the associated **perror** message are shown in Table 2.9.

Table 2.9 stat Error Messages.

#	Constant	perror Message	Explanation
2	ENOENT	No such file or directory	File does not exist (or is NULL).
4	EINTR	Interrupted system call	Signal was caught during the system call.
9	EBADF	Bad file number	The value in fildes is not a valid open file descriptor.
12	ENOMEM	Cannot allocate memory	Out of memory (i.e., kernel memory).
13	EACCES	Permission denied	Search permission denied on part of file path.
14	EFAULT	Bad address	Path references an illegal address.
20	ENOTDIR	Not a directory	Part of the specified path is not a directory.
36	ENAMETOOLONG	File name too long	The path value exceeds system path/file name length.
40	ELOOP	Too many levels of symbolic links	The **perror** message says it all.
67	ENOLINK	The link has been severed	The path value references a remote system that is no longer active.
72	EMULTIHOP	Multihop attempted	The path value requires multiple hops to remote systems, but file system does not allow it.
75	EOVERFLOW	Value too large for defined data type	A value for a member of the structure referenced by buf is too large.

A program showing the use of the **stat** system call is shown in Program 2.2.

Program 2.2 Using the **stat** system call.

```
 |      /*
 |          Using the stat system call
 |      */
 |      #include <iostream>
 +      #include <cstdio>
 |      #include <sys/types.h>
 |      #include <sys/stat.h>
 |      #include <unistd.h>
 |      using namespace std;
10      const int N_BITS = 3;
 |      int
 |      main(int argc, char *argv[ ]){
 |        unsigned int    mask = 0700;
 |        struct stat      buff;
 +        static char     *perm[] = {"---", "--x", "-w-", "-wx",
 |                                   "r--", "r-x", "rw-", "rwx"};
 |        if (argc > 1) {
 |          if ((stat(argv[1], &buff) != -1)) {
 |            cout << "Permissions for " << argv[1] << " ";
20          for (int i=3; i;-i) {
 |            cout << perm[(buff.st_mode & mask) >>
 |            (i-1)*N_BITS];
 |            mask >>= N_BITS;
 |          }
 |          cout << endl;
 +        } else {
 |          perror(argv[1]);
 |          return 1;
 |        }
 |      } else {
30        cerr <<  "Usage: " << argv[0] << "file_name\n";
 |        return 2;
 |      }
 |      return 0;
 |      }
```

When this program is run and passed its own name on the command line, the output is as shown in Figure 2.11.

Figure 2.11 Output of Program 2.2.

```
linux$ p2.2 a.out
Permissions for a.out rwxr-xr-x
```

The system command sequence `ls -l` for the same file produces the same set of permissions as shown in Figure 2.12.

Figure 2.12 Verifying Program 2.2 output with the `ls` command.

```
linux$ ls -l a.out
-rwxr-xr-x    1 gray       faculty       15290 Jan   2 07:26 a.out
```

2-6 EXERCISE

Modify the example **stat** program so that its output is as *close* as possible to the `ls -l` output on your system when passed a file or directory name on the command line. Note, the **stat** call will not return the user's name (only the **UID**). The **UID** can be passed to the **getpwuid** library call. The **getpwuid** call will return the user's name (along with additional password entry information). A description of the **getpwuid** library call is found in Section 3 of the manual. If needed, a second library call, **getgrgid**, can be used to map the **GID** value to the actual group name.

In a programming environment, the access permissions of a file can be modified with the **chmod/fchmod** system calls (Table 2.10).

Table 2.10 Summary of the chmod/fchmod System Calls.

Include File(s)	<sys/types.h> <sys/stat.h>		Manual Section	**2**
Summary	int chmod(const char *path, mode_t mode); int fchmod(int fildes, mode_t mode);			
	Success		Failure	Sets errno
Return	0		−1	Yes

Both system calls accomplish the same action and differ only in the format of their first argument. The **chmod** system call takes a character pointer reference to a file path as its first argument, while **fchmod** takes an integer file descriptor value of an open file. The second argument for both system calls is the mode. The mode can be specified literally as an octal number (e.g., 0755) or by bitwise **OR**ing together combinations of defined permission constants found in the header file <sys/stat.h>. Unless the effective user ID of the process is that of the superuser, the effective user ID and the owner of the file whose permissions are to be changed must be the same. If either system call is successful, it returns a 0. Otherwise, the call returns a −1 and sets the value in errno. As with the **stat** system calls, the number of error conditions is quite extensive (see Table 2.11).

Table 2.11 chmod/fchmod Error Messages.

#	**Constant**	perror **Message**	**Explanation**
1	EPERM	Operation not permitted	Not owner or file or superuser.
2	ENOENT	No such file or directory	File does not exist (or is NULL).
4	EINTR	Interrupted system call	Signal was caught during the system call.
5	EIO	I/O error	I/O error while attempting read or write to file system.
9	EBADF	Bad file number	The value in fildes is not a valid open file descriptor.
12	ENOMEM	Cannot allocate memory	Out of memory (i.e., kernel memory).
13	EACCES	Permission denied	Search permission denied on part of file path.
14	EFAULT	Bad address	path references an illegal address.
20	ENOTDIR	Not a directory	Part of the specified path is not a directory.
30	EROFS	Read-only file system	File referenced by path is on read-only file system.
36	ENAMETOOLONG	File name too long	The path value exceeds system path/file name length.
40	ELOOP	Too many levels of symbolic links	The **perror** message says it all.
67	ENOLINK	The link has been severed	The path value references a remote system that is no longer active.
72	EMULTIHOP	Multihop attempted	The path value requires multiple hops to remote systems but file system does not allow it.

The umask value, which is inherited from the parent process, may be modified by a process with the **umask** system call (Table 2.12).

Table 2.12 Summary of the umask System Call.

Include File(s)	`<sys/types.h>` `<sys/stat.h>`		Manual Section	**2**
Summary	`mode_t umask(mode_t mask);`			
Return	Success	Failure	Sets errno	
	The previous umask			

When invoked, **umask** both changes the umask value to the octal integer value passed and returns the old (previous) umask value.[6] If you use the **umask** system call to determine the *current* umask setting, you should call **umask** a second time, passing it the value returned from the first call, to restore the settings to their initial state. For example,

```
mode_t cur_mask;
cur_mask = umask(0);
cout << "Current mask: " << setfill('0') << setw(4) << oct
    << cur_mask << endl;
umask(cur_mask);
```

2-7 EXERCISE

The **umask** system call will never generate an error or set the value in errno. What happens if you attempt to assign a mask value of −011?

The library function **getcwd** is used to copy the absolute path of the current working directory of a process to an allocated location. The function is defined as shown in Table 2.13. It returns a pointer to the directory pathname. The function expects two arguments. The first is a pointer to the location where the pathname should be stored. If this argument is set to NULL, **getcwd** uses **malloc** to automatically allocate storage space. The second argument is the length of the pathname to be returned (plus 1 for the \0 to terminate the string). The include file `<sys/param.h>` contains the defined constant MAXPATHLEN that can be

---

[6] This system call appears to have been written before such techniques were frowned upon (i.e., both changing the state of the umask and returning its current value).

Table 2.13 Summary of the `getcwd` Library Function.

Include File(s)	`<unistd.h>`	Manual Section	**3**
Summary	`char *getcwd(char *buf, size_t size);`		
Return		Success	Failure	Sets `errno`
	A pointer to the current directory name	NULL	Yes

used to assure a buffer of sufficient size (i.e., MAXPATHLEN+1). In the following code snippet the space allocated to hold the path information will be just what is needed to store the absolute path (most likely less than MAXPATHLEN+1).

```
char *path;
path = getcwd(NULL, MAXPATHLEN+1);
cout << path << endl;
cout << "Path length: " << strlen(path) << endl;   // sufficient to
                                                    hold path
```

If **getcwd** fails, it returns a NULL and sets `errno` (Table 2.14). If **malloc** is used to dynamically allocate storage, the space should be returned with **free** when it is no longer needed.

Table 2.14 `getcwd` Error Messages.

#	Constant	`perror` Message	Explanation
13	EACCES	Permission denied	Search permission denied on part of file path.
22	EINVAL	Invalid argument	The value for `size` is less than or equal to 0.
34	ERANGE	Numerical result out of range	The value for `size` is greater than 0 but less than the length of the path plus 1.

The system call **chdir** is used to change the current working directory (as is the **cd**[7] command at system level). See Table 2.15.

The **chdir** system call takes a character pointer reference to a valid pathname (the process must have search permission for all directories referenced) as its argument. The **fchdir** system call takes an open file descriptor of a directory as its argument. If successful, the system call returns a 0, and the

[7] The **cd** command, unlike many other system-level commands, is not run as a child process, so its change will take effect for the current process.

Table 2.15 Summary of the `chdir/fchdir` System Calls.

Include File(s)	<unistd.h>		Manual Section	**2**
Summary	`int chdir( const char *path );` `int fchdir( int fildes );`			
Return		Success	Failure	Sets errno
		0	−1	Yes

new working directory for the process will be the one specified. If the call fails, a −1 is returned and `errno` is set (Table 2.16).

Table 2.16 chdir/fchdir Error Messages.

#	Constant	perror **Message**	**Explanation**
2	ENOENT	No such file or directory	File does not exist (or is NULL).
4	EINTR	Interrupted system call	Signal was caught during the system call.
5	EIO	I/O error	I/O error while attempting read or write to file system.
9	EBADF	Bad file number	The value in `fildes` is not a valid open file descriptor.
12	ENOMEM	Cannot allocate memory	Out of memory (i.e., kernel memory).
13	EACCES	Permission denied	Search permission denied on part of file path.
14	EFAULT	Bad address	`path` references an illegal address.
20	ENOTDIR	Not a directory	Part of the specified `path` is not a directory.
36	ENAMETOOLONG	File name too long	The `path` value exceeds system path/file name length.
40	ELOOP	Too many levels of symbolic links	The **perror** message says it all.
67	ENOLINK	The link has been severed	The `path` value references a remote system that is no longer active.
72	EMULTIHOP	Multihop attempted	The `path` value requires multiple hops to remote systems, but file system does not allow it.

2-8 EXERCISE

Predict what will happen when a process **fork**s a child process and the child process issues a **chdir** system call—will the current directory for the parent be changed as well? Write a program that substantiates your answer.

2.9 Process Resource Limits

As system resources are finite, every process is restrained by certain operating system-imposed limits. At the command line, the **ulimit** command (which is actually a built-in command found in the Bourne shell [/bin/sh]) provides the user with a means to display and modify current system limits available to the shell and the processes that are started by it.[8]

The command **ulimit -Ha** displays the hard limits for the system. The hard limits can be increased only by the superuser. An example showing the hard limits of a system is shown in Figure 2.13.

Figure 2.13 Typical hard limits on a Linux system.

```
linux$ ulimit -Ha
core file size          (blocks, -c) unlimited
data seg size           (kbytes, -d) unlimited
file size               (blocks, -f) unlimited
max locked memory       (kbytes, -l) unlimited
max memory size         (kbytes, -m) unlimited
open files                     (-n) 1024
pipe size           (512 bytes, -p) 8
stack size              (kbytes, -s) unlimited
cpu time              (seconds, -t) unlimited
max user processes             (-u) 4095
virtual memory          (kbytes, -v) unlimited
```

A soft limit, displayed when **ulimit** is passed the **-Sa** (Soft, all) command-line option, is a limit that can be set by the user. A soft limit is typically lower

---

[8] The C shell (/bin/csh) provides a somewhat similar built-in command called **limit**.

than the established hard limit. Note that the limits for the current process on this system are slightly less for stack size, as shown in Figure 2.14.

Figure 2.14 Individual process resource limits.

```
linux$ ulimit -Sa
core file size          (blocks, -c) unlimited
data seg size           (kbytes, -d) unlimited
file size               (blocks, -f) unlimited
max locked memory       (kbytes, -l) unlimited
max memory size         (kbytes, -m) unlimited
open files                      (-n) 1024
pipe size        (512 bytes, -p) 8
stack size              (kbytes, -s) 8192
cpu time            (seconds, -t) unlimited
max user processes              (-u) 4095
virtual memory          (kbytes, -v) unlimited
```

Resource limit information for a process can be obtained in a programming environment as well. Historically, the **ulimit** system call was used to obtain part of this information. In more recent versions of the operating system the **ulimit** system call has been superseded by the **getrlimit/setrlimit** calls described below. However, **ulimit** still bears a cursory investigation, as it is sometimes found in legacy code (Table 2.17).

Table 2.17 Summary of the **ulimit** System Call.

Include File(s)	<ulimit.h>		Manual Section	**3**
Summary	`long ulimit(int cmd    /* ,` `long newlimit   */ );`			
		Success	Failure	Sets errno
Return		Nonnegative long integer	−1	Yes

The argument cmd can take one of four different values:

1. Obtain file size limit for this process. The value returned is in units of 512-byte blocks.

2. Set the file size limit to the value indicated by `newlimit`. Non-superusers only can decrease the file size limit. This is the only command in which the argument `newlimit` is used.

3. Obtain the maximum break value. This option is not supported by Linux.

4. Return the maximum number of files that the calling process can open.

If **ulimit** is successful, it returns a positive integer value; otherwise, it returns a −1 and sets the value in `errno` (Table 2.18).

Table 2.18 `ulimit` Error Messages.

#	Constant	`perror` Message	Explanation
13	EPERM	Permission denied	Calling process is not superuser.
22	EINVAL	Invalid argument	The value for `cmd` is invalid.

The newer **getrlimit/setrlimit** system calls provide the process more complete access to system resource limits (Table 2.19).

Table 2.19 Summary of the `getrlimit/setrlimit` System Calls.

Include File(s)	`<sys/time.h>` `<sys/resource.h>` `<unistd.h>`		Manual Section	**2**
Summary	`int getrlimit(int resource, struct rlimit *rlim);` `int setrlimit(int resource, const struct rlimit *rlim);`			
	Success	Failure	Sets `errno`	
Return	0	−1	Yes	

The `rlimit` structure:

```
struct rlimit {
        rlimit_t   rlim_cur;    /* current (soft) limit */
        rlimit_t   rlim_max;    /* hard limit           */
};
```

along with a number of defined constants used by the two functions:

```
RLIMIT_CPU              /* CPU time in seconds */
RLIMIT_FSIZE            /* Maximum filesize */
RLIMIT_DATA             /* max data size */
RLIMIT_STACK            /* max stack size */
RLIMIT_CORE             /* max core file size */
RLIMIT_RSS              /* max resident set size */
RLIMIT_NPROC            /* max number of processes */
RLIMIT_NOFILE           /* max number of open files */
RLIMIT_MEMLOCK          /* max locked-in-memory address space*/
RLIMIT_AS               /* address space (virtual memory) limit */
RLIMIT_INFINITY         /* actual value for 'unlimited' */
```

are found in the header file <sys/resource.h> and its associated include files. A program using the **getrlimit** system call is shown in Program 2.3.

Program 2.3 Displaying resource limit information.

```
 |      /*
 |         Using getrlimt to display system resource limits
 |       */
 |      #include <iostream>
 +      #include <iomanip>
 |      #include <sys/time.h>
 |      #include <sys/resource.h>
 |      using namespace std;
 |      int
10      main( ){
 |        struct rlimit plimit;
 |        char   *label[ ]={"CPU time", "File size",
 |                          "Data segment", "Stack segment",
 |                          "Core size","Resident set size",
 +                          "Number of processes", "Open files",
 |                          "Locked-in-memory", "Virtual memory",
 |                          0};
 |        int constant[]= { RLIMIT_CPU    , RLIMIT_FSIZE,
 |                          RLIMIT_DATA   , RLIMIT_STACK,
20                          RLIMIT_CORE   , RLIMIT_RSS,
 |                          RLIMIT_NPROC  , RLIMIT_NOFILE,
 |                          RLIMIT_MEMLOCK, RLIMIT_AS };
 |
 |        for (int i = 0; label[i]; ++i) {
 +          getrlimit(constant[i], &plimit);
 |          cout << setw(20) << label[i] << "\t Current: "
 |               << setw(10) << plimit.rlim_cur << "\t Max: "
 |               << setw(10) << plimit.rlim_max << endl;
 |        }
30        return 0;
 |      }
```

The output sequence from this program (Figure 2.15) is comparable to the output of the system-level **ulimit** command shown earlier.

Figure 2.15 Program 2.3 output.

```
linux$ p2.3
                CPU time    Current: 4294967295    Max: 4294967295
               File size    Current: 4294967295    Max: 4294967295
            Data segment    Current: 4294967295    Max: 4294967295
           Stack segment    Current:    8388608    Max: 4294967295
               Core size    Current: 4294967295    Max: 4294967295
       Resident set size    Current: 4294967295    Max: 4294967295
      Number of processes   Current:      16383    Max:      16383
              Open files    Current:       1024    Max:       1024
         Locked-in-memory   Current: 4294967295    Max: 4294967295
          Virtual memory    Current: 4294967295    Max: 4294967295
```

The **setrlimit** system call, like the **ulimit** call, can be used only by the non-superuser to decrease resource limits. If these system calls are successful, they return a 0; otherwise, they return a −1 and set the value in errno (Table 2.20).

Table 2.20 getrlimit/setrlimit Error Messages.

#	Constant	perror Message	Explanation
13	EPERM	Permission denied	Calling process is not superuser.
22	EINVAL	Invalid argument	The value for resource is invalid.

2-9 EXERCISE

In the Bourne (or BASH /bin/bash) shell issue the command ulimit -u 2 followed by the command ls -l. Explain what happens. How did you correct the situation? If in the C Shell (/bin/csh or /bin/tcsh), replace the ulimit command with limit ma 2).

Additional process limit information can be obtained from the **sysconf** library function (Table 2.21).

Table 2.21 Summary of the `sysconf` Library Function.

Include File(s)	`<unistd.h>`		Manual Section	**3**
Summary	`long sysconf(int name);`			
Return	Success	Failure	Sets `errno`	
	Nonnegative long integer	−1	No (?)	

The **sysconf** function is passed an integer name value (usually in the form of a defined constant) that indicates the limit requested. If successful, the function returns the long integer value associated with the limit or a value of 0 or 1 if the limit is available or not. If the **sysconf** function fails, it returns a −1 and does not set the value in `errno`. The limits that **sysconf** *knows about* are defined as constants in the header file `<unistd.h>`.[9] In past versions of the operating system, some of these limit values were found in the header file `<sys/param.h>`. The constants for some of the more commonly queried limits are listed below:

```
_SC_ARG_MAX        /* space for argv & envp */
_SC_CHILD_MAX      /* max children per process */
_SC_CLK_TCK        /* clock ticks / sec */
_SC_STREAM_MAX     /* max # of data streams per process */
_SC_TZNAME_MAX     /* max # of bytes in timezone name spec. */
_SC_OPEN_MAX       /* max open files per process */
_SC_JOB_CONTROL    /* do we have job control? */
_SC_SAVED_IDS      /* do we have saved uid/gids? */
_SC_VERSION        /* POSIX version supported YYYYMML format*/
```

Program 2.4, which displays the values associated with the limits for a system, is shown below.

Program 2.4 Displaying system limits.

```
File : p2.4.cxx
  |     /*
  |         Using sysconf to display system limits
  |     */
  |     #include <iostream>
  +     #include <iomanip>
```

[9] Actually, this is a bit of a fudge. The include file `<unistd.h>` often includes yet another file that has the constant definitions. There is logic in the `<unistd.h>` file to include the proper file based on the standard being met (POSIX.1, etc.). At present the actual definitions are found in `<bits/confname.h>`—which is never to be included directly by the programmer.

```
     |       #include <cstdio>
     |       #include <unistd.h>
     |       using namespace std;
     |       int
 10       main( ){
     |         char *limits[ ]={"Max size of argv + envp",
     |                          "Max # of child processes",
     |                          "Ticks / second",
     |                          "Max # of streams",
     +                          "Max # of bytes in a TZ name",
     |                          "Max # of open files",
     |                          "Job control supported?",
     |                          "Saved IDs supported?",
     |                          "Version of POSIX supported",
 20                             0};
     |         int constant[ ]={ _SC_ARG_MAX,     _SC_CHILD_MAX,
     |                           _SC_CLK_TCK,     _SC_STREAM_MAX,
     |                           _SC_TZNAME_MAX, _SC_OPEN_MAX,
     |                           _SC_JOB_CONTROL,_SC_SAVED_IDS,
     +                           _SC_VERSION };
     |         for (int i=0; limits[i]; ++i) {
     |           cout << setw(30) << limits[i] << "\t"
     |                << sysconf(constant[i])  << endl;
     |         }
 30       return 0;
     |     }
```

When run on a local system, Program 2.4 produced the output shown in Figure 2.16.

Figure 2.16 Output of Program 2.4.

```
linux$ p2.4
        Max size of argv + envp  131072
      Max # of child processes  999
               Ticks / second  100
             Max # of streams  16
  Max # of bytes in a TZ name  3
           Max # of open files  1024
        Job control supported?  1
          Saved IDs supported?  1
   Version of POSIX supported  199506
```

If the **sysconf** function fails due to an invalid name value, a −1 is returned. The manual page indicates errno will not be set; however, some versions of Linux set errno to ENIVAL, indicating an invalid argument.

2.10 Signaling Processes

When events out of the ordinary occur, a process may receive a signal. Signals are asynchronous and are generated when an event occurs that requires attention. They can be thought of as a software version of a hardware interrupt and may be generated by various sources:

- **Hardware**—Such as when a process attempts to access addresses outside its own address space or divides by zero.
- **Kernel**—Notifying the process that an I/O device for which it has been waiting (say, input from the terminal) is available.
- **Other processes**—A child process notifying its parent process that it has terminated.
- **User**—Pressing keyboard sequences that generate a quit, interrupt, or stop signal.

Signals are numbered and historically were defined in the header file `<signal.h>`. In Linux signal definitions reside in `<bits/signum.h>`. This file is included automatically when you include `<signal.h>`. The `<bits/signum.h>` should not be directly included in your program. The process that receives a signal can take one of three courses of action:

1. **Perform the system-specified default for the signal.** For *most* signals the default action (what will be done by the process if nothing else has been specified) is to (a) notify the parent process that it is terminating, (b) generate a **core** file (a file containing the current memory image of the process), and (c) terminate.

2. **Ignore the signal.** A process can do this with all but two special signals: SIGSTOP (signal 23), a stop-processing signal that was not generated from the terminal, and SIGKILL (signal 9), which indicates the process is to be killed (terminated). The inability of a process to ignore these special signals ensures the operating system the ability to remove errant processes.

3. **Catch the signal.** As with ignoring signals, this can be done for all signals except the SIGSTOP and SIGKILL signals. When a process catches a signal, it invokes a special signal handling routine. After executing the code in the signal handling routine, the process, if appropriate, resumes where it was interrupted.

A child process inherits the actions associated with specific signals from its parent. However, should the child process overlay its process space with another executable image, such as with an **exec** system call (see Chapter 3, "Using Processes"), all signals that were associated with signal catching routines at specific addresses in the process are reset to their default action in the new process. This resetting to the default action is done by the system, as the address associated with the signal catching routine is no longer valid in the new process image. In most cases (except for I/O on slow devices such as the terminal) when a process is executing a system call and a signal is received, the interrupted system call generates an error (usually returning -1) and sets the global errno variable to the value EINTR. The process issuing the system call is responsible for re-executing the interrupted system call. As the responsibility for checking each system call for signal interrupts carries such a large overhead, it is rare that once a signal is caught the process resumes normal execution. More often than not, the process uses the signal catching routine to perform housekeeping duties (such as closing files, etc.) before exiting on its own. Signals sent to a process/session group leader are also passed to the members of the group. Signals and signal catching routines are covered in considerable detail in Chapter 4, "Primitive Communications."

2-10   EXERCISE

The system-specified defaults for signals 1 through 31 are given in the general manual pages on **signal** (Section 7 of the manual). As a default action, how many signals (a) produce core dumps, (b) cause the process to stop (terminate), and (c) are discarded (ignored)?

2.11 Command-Line Values

Part of the processing environment of every process are the values passed to the process in the function **main**. These values can be from the command line or may be passed to a child process from the parent via an **exec** system call. These values are stored in a ragged character array referenced by a character pointer array that, by tradition, is called argv. The number of elements in the argv array is stored as an integer value, which (again by tradition) is referenced by the identifier argc. Program 2.5, which displays command line values, takes advantage of the fact that in newer ANSI standard versions of Linux, the last element of the argv array (i.e., argv[argc]) is guaranteed to be a NULL pointer. However, in most programming situations, especially when backward compatibility is a concern, it is best to use the value in argc as a limit when stepping through argv. If we run the program as p2.5 and place some arbitrary values on the command line, we obtain the output shown in Figure 2.17.

Program 2.5 Displaying command line arguments.

```
File : p2.5.cxx
   |     /*
   |          Displaying the contents of argv[ ] (the command line)
   |     */
   |     #include <iostream>
   +     using namespace std;
   |     int
   |     main(int argc, char *argv[ ]){
   |        for ( ; *argv; ++argv )
   |          cout <<  *argv << endl;
  10        return 0;
   |     }
```

Figure 2.17 Output of Program 2.5.

```
linux$ p2.5 This is a test.
p2.5
This
is
a
test.
```

We can envision the system as storing these command-line values in argc and argv as shown in Figure 2.18.

In this situation (where the system fills the argv array), argc will always be greater than 0, and the first value referenced by argv will be the name of the program that is executing. The system automatically terminates each string with a null character and places a 0 as the last address in the argv array.

In programs, it is a common practice to scan the command line to ascertain its contents (such as when looking for command-line options). At one time programmers wishing to check the contents of the command line for options had to write their own command-line parsing code. However, there is a general-purpose library function called **getopt** that will do this.[10] The **getopt** library function is

---

[10] If you do shell programming, you should find that your system supports a shell version of this library function called **getopt**. The shell version uses the library function version to do its parsing.

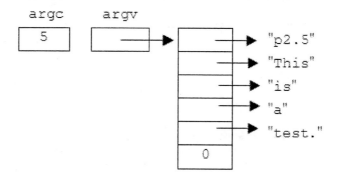

Figure 2.18 Storage of command line values.

somewhat analogous to the Swiss army knife—it can do many things, but to the uninitiated, upon first exposure, it appears unduly complex (Table 2.22).

Table 2.22 Summary of the getopt Library Function.

Include File(s)	<unistd.h>		Manual Section	**3**

Summary	`int getopt( int argc, char * const argv[],`
	`            char *optstring );`
	`extern char *optarg;`
	`extern int   optind, opterr, optopt;`			

	Success		Failure	Sets errno
Return	Next option letter		−1 or ?	

The **getopt** function requires three arguments. The first is an integer value argc (the number of elements in the second argument). The second argument is a pointer to a pointer to an array of characters strings. Usually this is the array of character strings referenced by argv. The third argument is a pointer to a string of valid option letters (characters) that getopt should recognize. As noted, in most settings the values for argc and argv are the same as those for main's first and second arguments. However, nothing prevents users from generating these two arguments to **getopt** on their own.

The format of optstring's content bears further explanation. If an option letter *expects* a following argument, the option letter in optstring is followed by a colon. For example, if the option letter s (which, say, stands for *size*) is to be followed by an integer size value, the corresponding optstring entry would be s:. On the command line, the user would enter -s 200 to indicate a *size* of 200. For a command-line option to be processed properly by **getopt**, it must be preceded with a hyphen(-), while the argument(s) to the option should have no leading hyphen and may or may not be separated by whitespace from the option.

The **getopt** function returns, as an integer, one of three values:

- −1 indicating all options have been processed.
- ? indicating an option letter has been processed that was not in the optstring or an option argument was specified (with the : notation in the optstring) but none was found when processing the command line. When a ? is returned, **getopt** also displays an error message on standard error. The automatic display of the error message can be disabled by changing the value stored in the external identifier opterr to 0 (it is set to 1 by default). The offending character (stored as an integer) is referenced by the optopt variable.
- The next option letter in argv that matches a letter in optstring. If the letter matched in optstring is followed by a colon, then the external character pointer optarg references the argument value. Remember that if the argument value is to be treated as a numeric value (versus a string), it must be converted.

The external integer optind is initialized by the system to 1 before the first call to **getopt**. It will contain the index of the next argument in argv that is not an option. By default **getopt** processes the argument array in a manner that all non-options are placed at the end of the list. A comparison of the value in optind to the value in argc can be used to determine if all items on the command line have been processed. The **getopt** function has a relative called **getopt_long**, which is similar in function to **getopt** but will process long (those with two leading dashes) command-line arguments. Check the manual page on this function for details. A program demonstrating the use of **getopt** is shown in Program 2.6.

Program 2.6 Using the library function getopt.

```
File : p2.6.cxx
   |      /*
   |          Command line using getopt
   |      */
   |      #define _GNU_SOURCE
   +      #include <iostream>
   |      #include <cstdlib>
   |      #include <unistd.h>
   |      using namespace std;
   |      extern char     *optarg;
  10      extern int      optind, opterr, optopt;
```

```
|    int
|    main(int argc, char *argv[ ]){
|      int     c;
|      char    optstring[] = "abs:";
+      opterr = 0;    // turn off auto err mesg
|      while ((c = getopt(argc, argv, optstring)) != -1)
|        switch (c) {
|        case 'a':
|          cout << "Found option a\n";
20         break;
|        case 'b':
|          cout << "Found option b\n";
|          break;
|        case 's':
+          cout << "Found option s with an argument of: ";
|          cout << atoi(optarg) << endl; // convert to integer
|          break;
|         case '?':
|          cout << "Found an option that was not in optstring.\n";
30         cout << "The offending character was " << char(optopt) << endl;
|        }
|      if (optind < argc){
|        cout << (argc—optind) << " arguments not processed.\n";
|        cout << "Left off at: " <<  argv[optind] << endl;
+      }
|      return 0;
|    }
```

A run of the program with some *sample* command-line options is shown in Figure 2.19.

Figure 2.19 Output of Program 2.6.

```
linux$ p2.6 -abc -s 34 -b joe -a student
Found option a
Found option b
Found an option that was not in optstring.
The offending character was c
Found option s with an argument of: 34
Found option b
Found option a
2 arguments not processed.
Left off at: joe
```

As the output shows, **getopt** can process options in groups (e.g., -abc) or as singletons (e.g., -b), and is not concerned with the alphabetic order of options. When processing stops, optind can be checked to determine if any command-line options were not part of the specified options.

Modify Program 2.3 to accept command-line options that will be processed with the library call **getopt**. Where appropriate, allow the user to specify arguments to change values of specific limits (use the **setrlimit** system call). Consider using **getopt_long** to support a --help option that would provide the user with some minimal help about how to run the program.

2.12 Environment Variables

Each process also has access to a list of environment variables. The environment variables, like the command-line values, are stored as a ragged array of characters. Environment variables, which are most commonly set at the shell level,[11] are passed to a process by its parent when the process begins execution. Environment variables can be accessed in a program by using an external pointer called environ, which is defined as

```
extern char **environ;
```

In most older (and in some current) versions of Linux, the environment variables could also be accessed by using a third argument in the function main called envp. When used, the envp argument to main is defined as

```
main(int argc,char *argv[],char **envp /* OR as *envp[]*/)
```

As environ and envp can both be used to accomplish the same thing, and current standards discourage the use of envp, only the use of the external pointer environ will be discussed in detail.

The contents of the environment variables can be obtained in a manner similar to the command-line arguments (Program 2.7).

A *partial* listing of the output of this program run on a local system is show in Figure 2.20.

[11] If at the command-line level you enter the shell command **env** (or **printenv**), the system should display a list of environment variables and their contents.

Program 2.7 Displaying environment variables.

```
File : p2.7.cxx
   |      /*
   |          Using the environ pointer to display the command line
   |      */
   |      #include <iostream>
   +      using namespace std;
   |      extern char **environ;
   |      int
   |      main( ){
   |        for (  ; *environ ; )
  10          cout << *environ++ << endl;
   |        return 0;
   |      }
```

Figure 2.20 Output of Program 2.7.

```
linux$ p2.7
PWD=/home/faculty/gray/revision/02
VENDOR=intel
REMOTEHOST=zeus.cs.hartford.edu
HOSTNAME=kahuna
LOGNAME=gray
SHLVL=2
GROUP=faculty
USER=gray
PATH=/usr/kerberos/bin:/usr/local/bin:/bin:/usr/bin:/usr/X11R6/bin:.
. . .
```

The output shows that all environment variables are stored as strings in the format name=value. Many of the environment variables shown here are common to all Linux systems (e.g., USER, PATH, etc.), while others are system-dependent (e.g., VENDOR). Note that by convention environment variables are normally spelled in uppercase. For the more curious, the manual page on **environ** ($ **man** 5 environ) furnishes a detailed description of the commonly found environment variables and their uses.

The two library calls shown in Tables 2.23 and 2.24 can be used to manipulate environment variables.

The first library call, **getenv**, searches the environment list for the first occurrence of a specified variable. The character string argument passed to **getenv** should be of the format name, where name is the *name* of the environment variable to find *without* an appended =. Note that name is case-sensitive (environment variables are often in uppercase). If **getenv** is successful, it returns a pointer to the string assigned to the environment

Table 2.23 Summary of the `getenv` Library Function.

Include File(s)	`<unistd.h>`		Manual Section	**3**
Summary	`char *getenv( const char *name );`			
Return		Success	Failure	Sets errno
	Pointer to the value in the environment		NULL	

Table 2.24 Summary of the `putenv` Library Function.

Include File(s)	`<stdlib.h>`		Manual Section	**3**
Summary	`int putenv( const char *name );`			
Return		Success	Failure	Sets errno
		0	−1	Yes

variable specified; otherwise, it returns a NULL pointer. If **getenv** fails, it returns a −1 and sets `errno` to ENOMEM (12—"Cannot allocate memory"). In Program 2.8 the output (shown in Figure 2.21) indicates that in this case the environment variable TERM has been found and that its current value is vt220. Notice that only the string to the right of the equals was returned by **getenv**.

Program 2.8 Using `getenv`.

```
File : p2.8.cxx
   |      /*
   |          Displaying the contents of the TERM variable
   |      */
   |     #include <iostream>
   +     #include <cstdlib>
   |     using namespace std;
   |     int
   |     main( ){
   |       char *c_ptr;
```

```
10         c_ptr = getenv("TERM");
|          cout << "The variable TERM is "
|              << (c_ptr==NULL ?  "NOT found" : c_ptr)
|              << endl;
|          return 0;
+      }
```

Figure 2.21   Checking the output of Program 2.8.

```
linux$ echo $TERM
vt220
linux$ p2.8
The variable TERM is vt220
```

Modifying or adding environment variable information, which is usually accomplished with the library function **putenv**, is a little trickier. The environment variables, along with the command-line values, are stored by the system in the area just beyond the stack segment for the process (see Chapter 1, Section 1.8). This area is accessible by the process and can be modified by the process, but it *cannot* be expanded. When environment variables are added or an existing environment variable is modified so it is larger (storage-wise) than its initial setting, the system will move the environment variable information from its stack location to the text segment of the process (the **putenv** function uses **malloc** to allocate additional space). To further complicate the issue in this situation, envp (if supported) will still point to the table on the stack when referencing the original environment variables, but will point to the text segment for the *new* environment variable. This is yet another reason to stay clear of envp!

One last caveat appears in the **putenv** manual page. The argument for **putenv** should not be an automatic variable (such as a variable local to a function), as these variables become undefined once the function in question is exited.

Program 2.9 demonstrates the **putenv** function.

Program 2.9   Using putenv.

```
File : p2.9.cxx
|      /*
|          Using putenv to modify the environment as seen by parent — child
|      */
```

```
  |     #define _GNU_SOURCE
  +     #include <iostream>
  |     #include <cstdlib>
  |     #include <sys/types.h>
  |     #include <unistd.h>
  |     using namespace std;
 10     extern char **environ;
  |     int show_env( char ** );
  |     int
  |     main( ){
  |       int numb;
  +       cout << "Parent before any additions **********" << endl;
  |       show_env( environ );
  |       putenv("PARENT_ED=parent");
  |       cout << "Parent after one addition   **********" << endl;
  |       show_env( environ );
 20       if ( fork( ) == 0 ){                 // In the CHILD now
  |         cout << "Child before any additions *********" << endl;
  |         show_env( environ );
  |         putenv("CHILD_ED=child");
  |         cout << "Child after one addition   *********" << endl;
  +         show_env( environ );
  |         return 0;
  |       }                                    // In the PARENT now
  |       sleep( 10 );                         // Make sure child is done
  |       cout << "Parent after child is done  **********" << endl;
 30       numb = show_env( environ );
  |       cout << "... and at address [" << hex << environ+numb
  |            << "] is ... "
  |            << (*(environ+numb) == NULL ? "Nothing!" : *(environ+numb))
  |            << endl;
  +       return 0;
  |     }
  |     /*
  |        Display the contents of the passed list ... return number found
  |     */
 40     int show_env( char **cp ){
  |       int i;
  |       for (i=0; *cp; ++cp, ++i)
  |         cout << "[" << hex << cp << "] " << *cp << endl;
  |       return i;
  +     }
```

The abridged output (some of the intervening lines of output were removed for clarity) of this program, when run on a local system, is explained in Figure 2.22.

Figure 2.22 Output of Program 2.9.

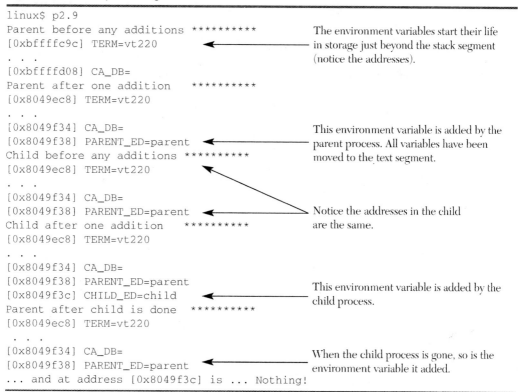

```
linux$ p2.9
Parent before any additions **********
[0xbffffc9c] TERM=vt220
  . . .
[0xbffffd08] CA_DB=
Parent after one addition    **********
[0x8049ec8] TERM=vt220
  . . .
[0x8049f34] CA_DB=
[0x8049f38] PARENT_ED=parent
Child before any additions **********
[0x8049ec8] TERM=vt220
  . . .
[0x8049f34] CA_DB=
[0x8049f38] PARENT_ED=parent
Child after one addition    **********
[0x8049ec8] TERM=vt220
  . . .
[0x8049f34] CA_DB=
[0x8049f38] PARENT_ED=parent
[0x8049f3c] CHILD_ED=child
Parent after child is done    **********
[0x8049ec8] TERM=vt220
  . . .
[0x8049f34] CA_DB=
[0x8049f38] PARENT_ED=parent
... and at address [0x8049f3c] is ... Nothing!
```

The environment variables start their life in storage just beyond the stack segment (notice the addresses).

This environment variable is added by the parent process. All variables have been moved to the text segment.

Notice the addresses in the child are the same.

This environment variable is added by the child process.

When the child process is gone, so is the environment variable it added.

There are several important concepts that can be gained by examining this program and its output. First, it is clear that the addresses associated with the environment variables are changed (from the stack segment to the text segment) when a new environment variable is added. Second, the child process inherits a *copy* of the environment variables from its parent. Third, as each process has its own address space, it is not possible to pass information back to a parent process from a child process.[12] Fourth, when adding an environment variable, the name=value format should be adhered to. While it is not checked in the example program, **putenv** will return a 0 if it is successful and a −1 if it fails to accomplish its mission.

---

[12] I am sure that many *human* children would say this is also true for their parent/child relationship—everything (especially tasks) seems to flow one way.

2-12 EXERCISE

Sam figures he has a way for a child process to communicate with its parent via the environment. His solution is to have the child process modify (without changing the storage size and without using **putenv**) an environment variable that was initially found in the parent. He wrote the following program to test his idea. Will his program work as he thought—why, or why not?

```
File : sam.cxx
   |      /*
   |         Sam's environment program
   |      */
   |      #define _GNU_SOURCE
   +      #include <iostream>
   |      #include <cstdlib>
   |      #include <sys/types.h>
   |      #include <unistd.h>
   |      using namespace std;
  10      int
   |      main( ){
   |         int numb;
   |         char *p;
   |         putenv("DEMO=abcdefghijklmnop");
   +         p = getenv("DEMO");
   |         cout << "1. Parent environment has " << p << endl;
   |
   |         if ( fork( ) == 0 ){              // In the CHILD now
   |            *(p + 9) = 'X';                // Change ref location
  20            p = getenv("DEMO");
   |            cout << "2. Child environment has  " << p << endl;
   |            cout << "3. Exiting child." << endl;
   |            return 0;
   |         }                                 // In the PARENT now
   +         sleep( 10 );                      // Make sure child is done
   |         cout << "4. Back in parent." << endl;
   |         p = getenv("DEMO");
   |         cout << "5. Parent environment has " << p << endl;
   |         return 0;
  30      }
```

2.13 The /proc Filesystem

Linux implements a special virtual filesystem called /proc that stores information about the kernel, kernel data structures, and the state of each process and associated threads. Remember that in Linux a thread is implemented as a special type of process. The /proc filesystem is stored in memory, not on disk. The majority of the information provided is read-only and can vary greatly from one version of Linux to another. Standard system calls (such as **open**, **read**, etc.) can be used by programs to access /proc files.

Linux provides a **procinfo** command that generates a formatted display of /proc information. Figure 2.23 shows the default output of this command. As would be expected, there is a variety of command-line options for **procinfo** (check the manual page $ **man** 8 procinfo for specifics). Additionally, while most of the files in /proc are in a special format, many can be displayed by using the command-line **cat** utility.[13]

Figure 2.23 Typical `procinfo` output.

```
linux$ procinfo
Linux 2.4.3-12enterprise (root@porky) (gcc 2.96 20000731 ) #1 2CPU [linux]

Memory:       Total        Used        Free      Shared     Buffers      Cached
Mem:         512928      510436        2492          84       65996      265208
Swap:       1068284         544     1067740

Bootup: Thu Dec 27 12:31:23 2001    Load average: 0.00 0.00 0.00 <fr>>1/85 10791

user   :        0:12:34.61    0.0%  page in :  7194848
nice   :        0:00:15.34    0.0%  page out:  1714280
system:         0:16:18.81    0.0%  swap in :        1
idle   :    21d 20:49:43.68   99.9% swap out:        0
uptime:     10d 22:39:26.21         context :  31669318

irq  0:  94556622 timer            irq  8:           2 rtc
irq  1:      2523 keyboard         irq 12:       15009 PS/2 Mouse
irq  2:         0 cascade [4]      irq 26:    17046596 e100
irq  3:         4                  irq 28:          30 aic7xxx
irq  4:   6223833 serial           irq 29:          30 aic7xxx
irq  6:         3                  irq 30:      155995 aic7xxx
irq  7:         3                  irq 31:      918432 aic7xxx
```

[13] Do not be put off by the fact that the majority of the files in /proc show 0 bytes when a long listing is done—keep in mind this is a not a true filesystem.

In the /proc file system are a variety of data files and subdirectories. A typical /proc file system is shown in Figure 2.24.

Figure 2.24 Directory listing of a /proc file system.

```
linux$ ls /proc
1        1083   20706   4     684    9228     dma          loadavg      stat
1025     1084   20719   494   7      9229     driver       locks        swaps
1030     1085   20796   499   704    9230     execdomains  mdstat       sys
10457    1086   20797   5     718    9231     fb           meminfo      sysvipc
10458    19947  20809   511   752    9232     filesystems  misc         tty
10459    2      3       526   758    9233     fs           modules      uptime
1057     20268  32463   6     759    9234     ide          mounts       version
10717    20547  32464   641   765    9235     interrupts   mtrr
10720    20638  32466   653   778    9236     iomem        net
10721    20652  32468   655   780    997      ioports      partitions
10725    20680  32469   656   795    bus      irq          pci
10726    20695  32471   657   807    cmdline  kcore        scsi
10731    20696  32473   658   907    cpuinfo  kmsg         self
10736    20704  32474   669   9227   devices  ksyms        slabinfo
```

Numeric entries, such as 1 or 1025, are process subdirectories for existing processes and contain information specific to the process. Nonnumeric entries, excluding the self entry, have kernel-related information. At this point, a full presentation of the kernel-related entries in /proc would be a bit premature, as many of them reflect constructs (such as shared memory) that are covered in detail in later chapters of the text. The remaining discussion focuses on the process-related entries in /proc.

The /proc/self file is a pointer (symbolic link) to the ID of the current process. Program 2.10 uses the system call **readlink** (see Table 2.25) to obtain the current process ID from /proc/self.

Program 2.10 Reading the /proc/self file.

```
File : p2.10.cxx
  |      /*
  |          Determining Process ID by reading the contents of
  |          the symbolic link  /proc/self
  |      */
  +      #define _GNU_SOURCE
  |      #include <iostream>
  |      #include <cstdlib>
  |      #include <sys/types.h>
  |      #include <unistd.h>
 10      using namespace std;
  |      const int size = 20;
```

```
 |      int
 |      main( ){
 |        pid_t proc_PID, get_PID;
 +        char buffer[size];
 |        get_PID = getpid( );
 |        readlink("/proc/self", buffer, size);
 |        proc_PID = atoi(buffer);
 |        cout << "getpid      : " << get_PID  << endl;
20        cout << "/proc/self : " << proc_PID << endl;
 |        return 0;
 |      }
```

Table 2.25 Summary of the readlink System Call.

Include File(s)	<sys/types.h>		Manual Section	2
Summary	int readlink(const char *path, char *buf, size_t bufsiz);			
	Success		Failure	Sets errno
Return	Number of characters read		−1	Yes

The **readlink** system call reads the symbolic link referenced by path and stores this data in the location referenced by buf. The bufsiz argument specifies the number of characters to be processed and is most often set to be the size of the location referenced by the buf argument. The **readlink** system call does not append a null character to its input. If this system call fails, it returns a −1 and sets errno; otherwise, it returns the number of characters read. In the case of error the values that errno can take on are listed in Table 2.26.

A wide array of data on each process is kept by the operating system. This data is found in the /proc directory in a decimal number subdirectory named for the process's ID. Each process subdirectory includes

- cmdline—A file that contains the command-line argument list that started the process. Each field is separated by a null character.
- cpu—When present, this file contains CPU utilization information.
- cwd—A pointer (symbolic link) to the current working directory for the process.
- exe—A pointer (symbolic link) to the binary file that was the source of the process.

73

Table 2.26 `readlink` Error Messages.

#	Constant	`perror` Message	Explanation
2	ENOENT	No such file or directory	File does not exist.
5	EIO	I/O error	I/O error while attempting read or write to file system.
12	ENOMEM	Cannot allocate memory	Out of memory (i.e., kernel memory).
13	EACCES	Permission denied	Search permission denied on part of file path.
14	EFAULT	Bad address	Path references an illegal address.
20	ENOTDIR	Not a directory	Part of the specified path is not a directory.
22	EINVAL	Invalid argument	• Invalid `bufsiz` value. • File is not a symbolic link.
36	ENAMETOOLONG	File name too long	The path value exceeds system path/ file name length.
40	ELOOP	Too many levels of symbolic links	The **perror** message says it all.

- environ—A file that contains the environment variable for the process. Like the `cmdline` file, each entry is separated by a null character.
- fd—A subdirectory that contains one decimal number entry for each file the process has open. Each number is a symbolic link to the device associated with the file.
- maps—A file that contains the virtual address maps for the process as well as the access permissions to the mapped regions. The maps are for various executables and library files associated with the process.
- root—A pointer (symbolic link) to the root filesystem for the process. Most often this is / but can (via the **chroot** system call) be set to another directory.
- stat—A file that contains process status information (such as used by the **ps** command).
- statm—A file with status of the process's memory usage.
- status—A file that contains much of the same information found in stat and statm with additional process (current thread) status

information. This file is stored in a plain text format and is somewhat easier to decipher.

As noted, the `cmdline` file has the argument list for the process. This same data is passed to the function **main** as `argv`. The data is stored as a single character string with a null character \0 separating each entry. On the command line, the **tr** utility can be used to translate the null characters into newlines to make the contents of the file easier to read. For example, the command-line sequence

```
linux$ cat /proc/cmdline | tr "\0" "\n"
```

would display the contents of the `cmdline` file with each argument placed on a separate line. Program 2.11 performs a somewhat similar function. It displays the contents of the command line by accessing the data in the `cmdline` file of the executing process.

Program 2.11 Reading the `cmdline` file.

```
File : p2.11.cxx
    |      #include <iostream>
    |      #include <fstream>
    |      #include <sstream>
    |      #include <sys/types.h>
    +      #include <unistd.h>
    |      using namespace std;
    |      const int size = 512;
    |      int
    |      main( ){
10
    |        ostringstream oss (ostringstream::out);
    |        oss  << "/proc/" << getpid( ) << "/cmdline";
    |        cout << "Reading from file: " << oss.str() << endl;
    |
    +        static char buffer[size];
    |        ifstream i_file;
    |        i_file.open(oss.str().c_str());        // open to read
    |        i_file.getline(buffer, size, '\n');
    |
20      char *p = &buffer[0];                       // ref 1st char of seq
    |        do {
    |          cout << "[" << p << "]" << endl;
    |          p += strlen(p)+1;                     // move to next location
    |        } while ( *p );                         // still ref a valid char
    +        return 0;
    |      }
```

In line 11 of the program, a new output stream descriptor for a string (oss) is declared. In line 12 the name of the file (using a call to **getpid** to obtain the process ID) is constructed and written to the string. The specified file is opened and read into buffer. The contents of buffer is parsed and displayed. The processing loop uses the fact that the command-line arguments are separated by a null character to divide the data into its separate arguments. Figure 2.25 shows the output of the program when several arguments are passed on the command line.

Figure 2.25 Program 2.11 output.

```
linux$ p2.11 this is 1 test
Reading from file: /proc/12123/cmdline
[p2.11]
[this]
[is]
[1]
[test]
```

2-13 EXERCISE

The file environ stores the process's environment variables in a format similar to the content of the cmdline file. Modify Program 2.11 to read and display the contents of the environ file.

2-14 EXERCISE

In most versions of Linux the statm file contains a series of integer values separated by blanks. For Red Hat Linux there are seven values in the file. In order, from left to right, these values are (a) program size in KB, (b) memory portion of program in KB, (c) number of shared pages, (d) number of code pages, (e) number of pages of data/stack, (f) number of pages of library, and (g) number of dirty pages. In operating system parlance, a dirty page is one that has been modified (and thus will need to be written back at some time for updating). Write a program that performs an activity that causes a *verifiable* increase in the number of dirty pages for the process.

2.14 Summary

The framework in which a process carries on its activities is its processing environment. The processing environment consists of a number of components. A series of identification numbers—process ID, parent process ID, and process group ID—are used to reference the individual process, its parent, and the group with which the process is affiliated. In its environment a process has access to resources (i.e., files and devices). Access to these resources is determined by permissions that are initially set when the resource is generated. When accessing files, a process can obtain additional system information about the resource. All processes are constrained by system-imposed resource limits. A process can obtain limit information using the appropriate system call or library function. Processes may receive signals that in turn may require a specific action. The values passed via the command line to the process can be obtained. In addition, the process has access to, and may modify (in some settings), environment variables. Linux also supports a /proc directory that contains special files with information about the kernel, its data structures, and all active processes.

2.15 Key Terms and Concepts

/proc filesystem
argc
argv
chdir system call
chmod system call
cmdline file
command-line values
cpu file
creation mask
cwd pointer
effective group ID (EGID)
effective user ID (EUID)
environ
environ command
environ file
environment variable
fchdir system call

fchmod system call
fd subdirectory
file descriptor table
file permissions
getcwd library function
getenv library function
getgrgid system call
getopt library function
getpgid system call
getpid system call
getppid system call
getpwuid system call
getrlimit system call
init process
inode
lstat system call
maps file

process group

process group ID (GID)

process ID (PID)

process leader

procinfo command

putenv library function

readlink system call

real group ID (GID)

real user ID (UID)

root pointer

session

set-group-ID (SGID)

setpgid system call

setrlimit system call

set-user-ID (SUID)

signal

stat file

stat system call

statm file

status file

sysconf library function

system file table

system inode table

ulimit command

ulimit system call

umask command

umask system call

Chapter 3

USING PROCESSES

3.1 Introduction

Processes are at the very heart of the operating system. As we have seen, all but a very few special processes are generated by the **fork** system call. If successful, the **fork** system call produces a child process that continues its execution at the point of its invocation in the parent process. In this chapter, we explore the generation and use of child processes in detail. In Chapter 11, "Threads," the creation of threads will be discussed.

3.2 The fork System Call Revisited

The **fork** system call is unique in that while it is called once, it returns twice—to the child and to the parent processes. As noted in Chapter 1, "Programs and Processes," if the **fork** system call is successful, it returns a value of 0 to the child process and the process ID of the child to the parent process. If the **fork** system call fails, it returns a −1 and sets the global variable errno. The failure of the system to generate a new process can be traced, by examination of the errno value, to either exceeding the limits on the number of processes (systemwide or for the specific user) or to the lack of available swap space for the new process. It is interesting to note that in theory the operating system is always supposed to leave room in the process table for at least one superuser process, which could be used to remove (kill) hung or runaway processes. Unfortunately, on many systems it is still relatively easy to write a program (sometimes euphemistically called a **fork** bomb) that will fill the system with dummy processes, effectively locking out system access by anyone, including the superuser.

After the **fork** system call, both the parent and child processes are running and continue their execution at the next statement after the **fork**. The return from the **fork** system call can be examined, and the process can make a decision as to what code is executed next. The process receiving a 0 from the **fork** system call *knows* it is the child, as 0 is not valid as a PID. Conversely, the parent process will receive the PID of the child. An example of a **fork** system call is shown in Program 3.1.

Program 3.1   Generating a child process.

```
File : p3.1.cxx
   |      /*
   |          Generating a child process
   |       */
   |      #include <iostream>
   +      #include <sys/types.h>
   |      #include <unistd.h>
   |      using namespace std;
   |      int
   |      main( ){
  10        if (fork( ) == 0)
   |           cout << "In the CHILD process" << endl;
   |        else
   |           cout << "In the PARENT process" << endl;
   |        return 0;
   +      }
```

There is no guarantee as to the output sequence that will be generated by this program. For example, if we issue the command-line sequence

```
linux$ p3.1 ; echo DONE ; p3.1 ; echo DONE ; p3.1
```

numerous times, sometimes the statement In the CHILD process will be displayed before the In the PARENT process, and other times it will not. The output sequence is dependent upon the scheduling algorithm used by the kernel. Keep in mind that commands separated by a semicolon on the command line are executed sequentially, with the shell waiting for each command to terminate before executing the next. The effects of process scheduling are further demonstrated by Program 3.2.

Program 3.2 Multiple activities parent/child processes.

```
File : p3.2.cxx
  |       /*
  |              Multiple activities PARENT -- CHILD processes
  |        */
  |       #include <iostream>
  +       #include <cstring>
  |       #include <sys/types.h>
  |       #include <unistd.h>
  |       using namespace std;
  |       int
 10       main( ) {
  |         static char buffer[10];
  |         if (fork( ) == 0) {              // In the child process
  |           strcpy(buffer, "CHILD...");
  |         } else {                         // In the parent process
  +           strcpy(buffer, "PARENT..");
  |         }
  |         for (int i=0; i < 3; ++i) {      // Both processes do this
  |           sleep(1);                      // 3 times each.
  |           write(1, buffer, sizeof(buffer));
 20         }
  |         return 0;
  |       }
```

Figure 3.1 shows the output of this program when run twice on a local system.

Figure 3.1 Output of Program 3.2.

```
linux$ p3.2
PARENT..CHILD...CHILD...PARENT..PARENT..CHILD...linux$
linux$ p3.2
PARENT..CHILD...PARENT..CHILD...PARENT.. $ CHILD...
```

There are several interesting things to note about this program and its output. First, the **write** (line 19) system call, not the cout object, was used in the program. The cout object (an instance of the ostream class defined in <iostream>) is buffered and, if used, would have resulted in the three-message output from each process being displayed all at one time without any interleaving of messages. Second, the system call **sleep** (sleep a specified number of seconds) was used to prevent the process from running to completion within one time slice (which again would produce a homogenous output sequence). Third, one process will always end before the other. If there is sufficient intervening time before the second process ends, the system will redisplay the prompt, thus producing the last line of output where the output from the child process is appended to the prompt (i.e., linux$ CHILD...).

Keep in mind the system will *flush* an output stream (write its data to the physical media) in a variety of circumstances. This synchronization occurs when (a) a file is closed, (b) a buffer is full, (c) in C++ the flush or endl manipulators are placed in the output stream, or (d) a call is made to the **sync** system call.

3-1 EXERCISE

When the following program is compiled and run,

```
File : funny.cxx
   |      /*
   |            A very funny program ...
   |       */
   |      #include <iostream>
   +      #include <sys/types.h>
   |      #include <unistd.h>
   |      using namespace std;
   |      int
   |      main( ) {
 10        fork( );    cout << "hee " << endl;
   |        fork( );    cout << "ha " << endl;
   |        fork( );    cout << "ho " << endl;
   |        return 0;
   |      }
```

assuming all **fork** system calls are successful, how many lines of output will be produced? Is it ever possible for a ho to be output before a hee? Why is this? Would the number of hees, has and hos be different if the << endl was left out of each of the cout statements? Why?

3.3 exec's Minions

Processes generate child processes for a number of reasons. In a Linux environment, there are several long-lived processes, which run continuously in the background and provide system services upon demand. These processes, called daemon processes, frequently generate child processes to carry out the requested service. Some daemon processes commonly found in a Linux environment are **lpd**, the line printer daemon; **xinetd**, the extended Internet services daemon; and **syslogd**, the system logging daemon. Some problems (such as with databases) lend themselves to concurrent type solutions that can be effected via multiple child processes executing the same code. More commonly, such as when the shell processes a command, a process procreates a child process because it would like to transform the child process by changing the program code the child process is executing.

In Linux, any one of five library functions and one system call can be used to replace the current process image with a new image.[1] The library functions act as a front end to the system call. The library functions are discussed in the **exec** manual pages (Section 3), while the system call (**execve**) warrants its own manual page entry in Section 2. Any of these can be directly invoked by the programmer. For ease of comparison, the library functions and the system call are discussed as a group. The phrase **exec** call will reference this group.

It is important to remember that when a process issues any **exec** call, if the call is successful, the existing process is overlaid with a new set of program code. The text, data (initialized and uninitialized), and stack segment of the process are replaced and only the **u** (user) area of the process remains the same. The new program code (if a C/C++ binary) begins its execution at the function **main.** Since the system is now executing a different set of code for the same process, some things, by necessity, must change:

- Signals that were specified as being caught by the process (i.e., associated with a signal-catching routine) are reset to their default action. This is necessary, as the addresses for the signal-catching routines are no longer valid.

- In a similar vein, if the process was profiling (determining how much time is spent in individual routines), the profiling will be turned off in the overlaid process.

- If the new program has its **SUID** bit set, the effective **EUID** and **EGID** are set accordingly.

The program to be executed can be a script. In this case, the script should have its execute bit set and start with the line # ! *interpreter* [*arg(s)*], where *interpreter* is a valid executable (but not another script). If successful, the

---

[1] In some versions of UNIX, such as Solaris, all the **exec** calls are system calls and are grouped together as library functions and discussed in one section of the manual. Linux has a more historic approach to things.

exec calls do *not* return, as the initial calling image is lost when overlaid with a new image.

Before we delve into these calls, we should take a quick look at what normally transpires when a valid command is issued at the system (shell) level, as this process will reflect the functionality available in a program. If the command issued is

```
linux$ cat file.txt > file2.txt
```

the shell parses the command line and divides it into valid tokens (e.g., **cat**, `file.txt`, etc.). The shell (via a call to **fork**) then generates a child process. After the **fork**, the shell closes standard output and opens the file `file2.txt`, mapping it to standard output in the child process. Next, by calling **execve**, the shell overlays the current program code with the program code for the command (in this case, the code for **cat**). When the command is finished, the shell redisplays its prompt. Figure 3.2 shows the process creation and command execution sequence.

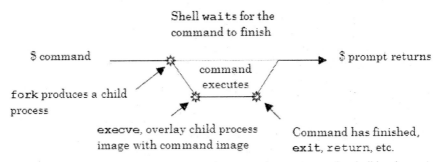

Figure 3.2 Process creation and command execution at the shell level.

While the command is executing, the shell, by default, waits in the background. As we will see, there is a **wait** system call that allows the shell or any other process to wait. Should the user place an & at the end of the command (to indicate to the shell that the command be placed in background), the shell will not wait and will return immediately with its prompt. When the command is finished, it may perform a call to **exit** or return when in the function `main`. The integer value passed to these calls is made available to the parent process via an argument to the **wait** system call. When on the command line, the returned value is stored in the system variable named **status**. If in the Bourne or BASH shell you issue the command

```
linux$ echo $?
```

the system will display the value returned by the last command executed. As the mapping of standard output to the file `file2.txt` was done in the child process and not in the shell, the I/O redirection has no further impact on ensuing command sequences.

We should note that it is possible for a user at the command line to issue an **exec** call. The syntax would be

```
linux$ exec command [arguments]
```

However, most users would *not* do this. The current process (the shell) would be overlaid with the program code for the command. Once the command was finished, the user would be logged out, as the original shell process would no longer exist!

In a programming environment, the **exec** calls can be used to execute another program. The prototypes for the **exec** calls are listed in Table 3.1.

Table 3.1 The exec Call Prototypes.

```
#include <unistd.h>

extern char **environ;

int execl (const char *path, const char *arg, ...);
int execv (const char *path, char *const argv[]);

int execle(const char *path, const char *arg , ..., char * const envp[]);
int execve(const char *path, char *const argv[],    char * const envp[]);

int execlp(const char *file, const char *arg, ...);
int execvp(const char *file, char *const argv[]);
```

The naming convention for these system calls reflects their functionality. Each call starts with the letters **exec**. The next letter in the call name indicates if the call takes its arguments in a list format (i.e., literally specified as a series of arguments) or as a pointer to an array of arguments (analogous to the `argv` structure discussed earlier). The presence of the letter **l** indicates a list arrangement (a variable argument list—see the manual page on **stdarg** for details); **v** indicates the array or vector arrangement. The next letter of the call name (if present) is either an **e** or a **p**. The presence of an **e** indicates the programmers will construct (in the array/vector format) and pass their own environment variable list. The passed environment variable list will become the third argument to the function `main` (i.e., **envp**). As noted in the section on environment variables, **envp** is of limited practical value. When the programmer is responsible for the environment, the current environment variable list is *not* passed. The presence of a **p** indicates the current environment PATH variable should be used when searching for a file whose name does not contain a slash.[2] In the four calls, where the PATH string is not used (**execl**, **execv**, **execle** and **execve**), the path to the program to be executed must be fully specified.

The functionality of the **exec** system calls is best summarized by Table 3.2.

Table 3.2 exec Call Functionality.

Library Call Name	Argument Format	Pass Current Set of Environment Variables?	Search of PATH Automatic?
execl	list	yes	no
execv	array	yes	no
execle	list	no	no
execve	array	no	no
execlp	list	yes	yes
execvp	array	yes	yes

Of the six variations, **execlp** and **execvp** calls are used most frequently (as automatic environment passing and path searching are usually desirable) and will be explained in detail.

3.3.1 **execlp**

The **execlp** library function (Table 3.3) is used when the number of arguments to be passed to the program to be executed is known in advance.

When using **execlp**, the initial argument, file, is a pointer to the file that contains the program code to be executed. If this file reference begins with a /, it is assumed that the reference is an absolute path to the file. In this circumstance, it would appear that the **p** specification (**execlp**) is superfluous; however, the PATH string is still used if other arguments are file names or if the code to be executed contains file references. If no / is found, each of the directories specified in the PATH variable will be, in turn,

---

[2] If the executable file is a script, the Bourne shell (**/bin/sh**) is invoked to execute the script. The shell is then passed the specified argument information.

Table 3.3 Summary of the `execlp` Library Function.

Include File(s)	`<unistd.h>` `extern char **environ;`		Manual Section	**3**
Summary	`int execlp(const char *file, const char *arg, . . .);`			
	Success	Failure	Sets `errno`	
Return	Does not return	−1	Yes	

preappended to the file name specified, and the *first* valid program reference found will be the one executed. It is a good practice to fully specify the program to be executed in all situations to prevent a program with the same name, found in a prior PATH string directory, from being inadvertently executed. For the **execlp** call to be successful, the file referenced must be found and be marked as executable. If the call fails, it returns a −1 and sets errno to indicate the error. As the overlaying of one process image with another is very complex, the possibilities for failure are numerous (as shown in Table 3.4).

Table 3.4 exec Error Messages.

#	**Constant**	`perror` **Message**	**Explanation**
1	EPERM	Operation not permitted	• The process is being traced, the user is not the superuser, and the file has an SUID or SGID bit set. • The file system is mounted nosuid, the user is not the superuser, and the file has an SUID or SGID bit set.
2	ENOENT	No such file or directory	One or more parts of path to new process file does not exist (or is NULL).
4	EINTR	Interrupted system call	Signal was caught during the system call.
5	EIO	Input/output error	
7	E2BIG	Argument list too long	New process argument list plus exported shell variables exceed the system limits.
8	ENOEXEC	Exec format error	New process file is not in a recognized format.

Continued

Table 3.4 (Continued)

#	Constant	perror **Message**	**Explanation**
11	EAGAIN	Resource temporarily unavailable	Total system memory while reading raw I/O is temporarily insufficient.
12	ENOMEM	Cannot allocate memory	New process memory requirements exceed system limits.
13	EACCES	Permission denied	• Search permission denied on part of file path. • The new file to process is not an ordinary file. • No execute permission on the new file to process.
14	EFAULT	Bad address	path references an illegal address.
20	ENOTDIR	Not a directory	Part of the specified path is not a directory.
21	EISDIR	Is a directory	An ELF interpreter was a directory.
22	EINVAL	Invalid argument	An ELF executable had more than one interpreter.
24	EMFILE	Too many open files	Process has exceeded the maximum number of files open.
26	ETXTBSY	Text file busy	More than one process has the executable open for writing.
36	ENAMETOOLONG	File name too long	The path value exceeds system path/file name length.
40	ELOOP	Too many levels of symbolic links	The **perror** message says it all.
67	ENOLINK	Link has been severed	The path value references a remote system that is no longer active.
72	EMULTIHOP	Multihop attempted	The path value requires multiple hops to remote systems, but file system does not allow it.
80	ELIBBAD	Accessing a corrupted shared library	An ELF interpreter was not in a recognized format.

The ellipses in the **execlp** function prototype can be thought of as argument 0 (arg0) through argument n (argn). These arguments are pointers to the null-terminated strings that would be normally passed by the system to the program if it were invoked on the command line. That is, argument 0, by convention, should be the name of the program that is executing. This is usually the same as the value in `file`, although the program referenced by `file` may include an absolute path, while the value in argument 0 most often would not. Argument 1 would be the first parameter to be passed to the program (which, using `argv` notation, would be `argv[1]`), argument 2 would be the second, and so on. The last argument to the **execlp** library call must be a NULL that is, for portability reasons, cast to a character pointer. Program 3.3, which invokes the **cat** utility program, demonstrates the use of the **execlp** library call.

Program 3.3 Using the `execlp` system call.

```
File : p3.3.cxx
   |      /*
   |            Running the cat utility via an exec system call
   |      */
   |      #include <iostream>
   +      #include <cstdio>
   |      #include <unistd.h>
   |      using namespace std;
   |      int
   |      main(int argc, char *argv[ ]){
  10        if (argc > 1) {
   |          execlp("/bin/cat", "cat", argv[1], (char *) NULL);
   |          perror("exec failure ");
   |          return 1;
   |        }
   +        cerr <<  "Usage: " << *argv << " text_file" << endl;
   |        return 2;
   |      }
```

When passed a text file name on the command line, this program displays the contents of the file to the screen. The program accomplishes this by overlaying its own process image with the program code for the **cat** utility program. The program passes the **cat** utility program the name (referenced by `argv[1]`) of the file to display. If the **execlp** system call fails, the call to **perror** is made and the program exits and returns the value 1 to the system. If the call is successful, the **perror** and return statements are never reached, as they are replaced with the program code for the **cat** utility.

A sample run of the program is shown in Figure 3.3.

Figure 3.3 Output of Program 3.3.

```
linux$ p3.3 test.txt
This is a sample text
file for the program to
display!
```

3-2 EXERCISE

Harley wondered what value is used by the system to generate a system process table entry when the **execlp** call is issued. Is it the value referenced by `file` or the value referenced by `arg0`? Further, what happens if `arg0` is set to NULL ("") , or if `arg0` is omitted entirely (e.g., the `file` value is immediately followed with `(char *)NULL`)? Is it possible, in a case like this, for the value of `argc` to be 0? To test things she wrote, and compiled, the `count.cxx` program below. She then modified Program 3.3 to call her `count` executable by changing "/bin/cat" in line 11 of Program 3.3 to ". /count". What did she find?

```
File : count.cxx
   |      #include <iostream>
   |      #include <cstdlib>
   |      #include <unistd.h>
   |      using namespace std;
   +      int
   |      main(int argc, char *argv[]){
   |         cerr << "argc = " <<  argc  << endl;
   |         cerr << "Processes running" << endl;
   |         system("ps -f");                       // issue a shell
   |                                                //    ps cmd
  10         if ( argc > 1 ) {                      // value passed?
   |            int limit = atoi(argv[1]);          // convert to #
   |            for(int i=limit; i ;--i){           // count
   |               cerr << i << endl;
   |               sleep( 1 );
   +            }
   |         } else {
   |            cerr << "Nothing to count" << endl;
   |            return 2;
   |         }
  20         return 0;
   |      }
```

3.3.2 execvp

If the number of arguments for the program to be executed is dynamic, then the **execvp** call can be used (Table 3.5). As with the **execlp** call, the initial argument to **execvp** is a pointer to the file that contains the program code to be executed. However, *unlike* **execlp**, there is only one additional argument that **execvp** requires. This second argument, defined as

```
char *const argv[ ]
```

specifies that a reference to an array of pointers to character strings should be passed. The format of this array parallels that of argv and, in many cases, is argv. If the reference is not the argv values for the current program, the programmer is responsible for constructing and initializing a *new* argv-like array. If this second approach is taken, the last element of the new argv array should contain a NULL address value. If **execvp** fails, it returns a value of −1 and sets the value in errno to indicate the source of the error (see Table 3.5).

Table 3.5 Summary of the execvp System Call.

Include File(s)	<unistd.h> <extern char **environ;		Manual Section	**3**
Summary	int execvp(const char *file, char *const argv[]);			
Return		Success	Failure	Sets errno
	Does not return		−1	Yes

Program 3.4 makes use of the argv values for the current program.

Program 3.4 Using **execvp** with argv values.

```
File : p3.4.cxx
   |      /*
   |          Using execvp to execute the contents of argv
   |      */
   |      #include <iostream>
   +      #include <cstdio>
   |      #include <unistd.h>
   |      using namespace std;
   |      int
   |      main(int argc, char *argv[ ]) {
 10        if ( argc > 1 ) {
   |          execvp(argv[1], &argv[1]);
   |          perror("exec failure");
   |          return 1;
   |        }
   +        cerr << "Usage: " << *argv << " exe [arg(s)]" << endl;
   |        return 2;
   |      }
```

The program will execute, via **execvp**, the program passed to it on the command line. The first argument to **execvp**, argv[1], is the reference to the program to execute.

The second argument, &argv[1], is the reference to the remainder of the command-line argv array. Notice that both of these references began with the second element of argv (that is, argv[1]), as argv[0] is the name of the current program (e.g., p3.4). The output in Figure 3.4 shows that the program does work as expected.

Figure 3.4 Output of Program 3.4 when passed the cat command.

```
linux$ p3.4 cat test.txt
This is a sample text
file for a program to
display!
```

If we place additional information on the command line when running Program 3.4, we find the program will pass the information on, as demonstrated in Figure 3.5.

Figure 3.5 Output of Program 3.4 when passed the cat command with the -n option.

```
linux$ p3.4 cat -n test.txt
     1  This is a sample text
     2  file for a program to
     3  display!
```

If command-line argv values of the current program are not used with **execvp**, then the programmer must construct a new argv to be passed. An example of how this can be done is shown in Program 3.5.

Program 3.5 Using **execvp** with a programmer-generated argument list.

```
File : p3.5.cxx
  |     /*
  |          Generating our own argv type list for execvp
  |      */
  |     #include <iostream>
  +     #include <cstdio>
  |     #include <unistd.h>
  |     using namespace std;
  |     int
  |     main( ){
 10     char    *new_argv[ ] = {"cat",
  |                              "test.txt",
  |                              (char *) 0
  |                             };
```

```
    |           execvp("/bin/cat", new_argv );
    +           perror("exec failure ");
    |           return 1;
    |       }
```

When compiled and run as p3.5, the output of this program will be the
same as the output from the first run of Program 3.4.

3.4 Using fork and exec Together

In most programs, the **fork** and **exec** calls are used in conjunction with one
another (in some operating systems, the **fork** and **exec** calls are packaged as
a single **spawn** system call). The parent process generates a child process,
which it then overlays by a call to **exec**, as in Program 3.6.

Program 3.6 Using fork with execlp.

```
File : p3.6.cxx
    |       /*
    |            Overlaying a child process via an exec
    |        */
    |       #include <iostream>
    +       #include <sstream>
    |       #include <cstdio>
    |       #include <unistd.h>
    |       using namespace std;
    |       int
10          main( ){
    |          char  *mesg[ ] = {"Fie", "Foh", "Fum"};
    |          int   display_msg(char *);
    |          for (int i=0; i < 3; ++i)
    |             display_msg(mesg[i]);
    +          return 0;
    |       }
    |       int
    |       display_msg(char *m){
    |          ostringstream oss(ostringstream::out);
20          switch (fork( )) {
    |          case 0:
    |             sleep(1);
    |             execlp("/bin/echo", "echo", m, (char *) NULL);
    |             oss << m << " exec failure";       // build error msg string
    +             perror(oss.str().c_str());
    |             return 1;
```

```
  |      case -1:
  |        perror("Fork failure");
  |        return 2;
30         default:
  |        return 0;
  |      }
  |    }
```

Program 3.6 displays three messages (based on the contents of the array mesg). This action is accomplished by calling the display_msg function three times. Once in the display_msg function, the program **fork**s a child process and then overlays the child process code with the program code for the **echo** command. The output of the program is shown in Figure 3.6.

Figure 3.6 Output of Program 3.6.

```
linux$ p3.6
Foh
Fie
Fum
```

Due to scheduling, the order of the messages may change when run multiple times.

It is interesting to observe what happens if the **execlp** call in display_msg fails (line 23). If we purposely sabotage the **execlp** system call by changing it to

```
execlp("/bin/no_echo", "echo", m , (char *) NULL );
```

and assuming there is not an executable file called no_echo to be found in /bin, the output[3] of the program becomes that shown in Figure 3.7.

Figure 3.7 Output of Program 3.6 when **execlp** fails.

```
linux$ p3.6
Foh exec failure: No such file or directory
Fie exec failure: No such file or directory
Fum exec failure: No such file or directory
Fum exec failure: No such file or directory
Foh exec failure: No such file or directory
Fum exec failure: No such file or directory
Fum exec failure: No such file or directory
```

---

[3] The program uses a common programming *trick* to create a message string on-the-fly to pass to the **perror** routine.

Surprisingly, when the **execlp** call fails, we end up with a total of *eight* processes—the initial process and its seven children. Most likely this was not the intent of the original programmer. One way to correct this is within the display_msg function: In the case 0: branch of the switch statement, replace the return statement in line 26 with a call to **exit**.

3-3 EXERCISE

In its current implementation, Program 3.6 does not make use of the value returned by the display_msg function. Modify the program so that in line 14 the returned value is used. Compare and contrast the output of this modification to the suggested modification in the previous paragraph (replacing the return statement in line 26 with a call to **exit**).

Combining what we have learned so far, we can produce, in relatively few lines of code, a shell program that restricts the user to a few basic commands (in this example, **ls**, **ps**, and **df**). The code for our shell program[4] is shown in Program 3.7.

This program could be considered a *very* stripped-down version of a restricted[5] shell. The main thrust of the program is pedagogical, and improvements and expansions (of which there can be many) will be addressed in ensuing sections of the text and in a number of exercises.

Program 3.7 The huh shell.

```
File : p3.7.cxx
   |      /*
   |           A _very_ limited shell program
   |      */
   |      #include <iostream>
   +      #include <cstdio>
   |      #include <cstring>
   |      #include <cstdlib>
```

---

[4] For reasons that become obvious when the program is run, this is nicknamed the **huh** shell.

[5] Many UNIX environments come with a predefined restricted shell (which is different from the remote shell **/bin/rsh**). A restricted shell is sometimes specified as a login shell for users (such as **ftp**) that require a more controlled environment. Linux does not come with a specific restricted shell for users, but some of the standard shells (such as **bash** and **ksh**) can be passed a command-line option (−r) that will run the shell in restricted mode. Linux does come with a restricted shell for **sendmail** (**smrsh**).

```
 |       #include <unistd.h>
 |       using namespace std;
10
 |       const int MAX    =256;
 |       const int CMD_MAX=10;
 |       char *valid_cmds = " ls  ps  df ";
 |       int
 +       main( ){
 |         char  line_input[MAX], the_cmd[CMD_MAX];
 |         char  *new_args[CMD_MAX], *cp;
 |         int   i;
 |         while (1) {
20         cout << "cmd> ";
 |           if (cin.getline(line_input, MAX, '\n') != NULL) {
 |             cp = line_input;
 |             i  = 0;
 |             if ((new_args[i] = strtok(cp, " ")) != NULL) {
 +               strcpy(the_cmd, new_args[i]);
 |               strcat(the_cmd, " ");
 |               if ((strstr(valid_cmds, the_cmd)-valid_cmds) % 4 == 1) {
 |                 do {
 |                   cp = NULL;
30                 new_args[++i] = strtok(cp, " ");
 |                 } while (i < CMD_MAX && new_args[i] != NULL);
 |                 new_args[i] = NULL;
 |                 switch (fork( )) {
 |                 case 0:
 +                   execvp(new_args[0], new_args);
 |                   perror("exec failure");
 |                   exit(1);
 |                 case -1:
 |                   perror("fork failure");
40                 exit(2);
 |                 default:
 |                   // In the parent we should be waiting for
 |                   // the child to finish
 |                   ;
 +                 }
 |               } else
 |                 cout << "huh?" << endl;
 |             }
 |           }
50      }
 |       }
```

The commands the user is permitted to issue when running our shell
are found in the global character string called valid_cmds. In the
valid_cmds string, each two-letter command is preceded and followed by

a space. By delimiting the commands in this manner, a predefined C string searching function **strstr** can be used to determine if a user has entered a *valid* command. While this technique is simplistic, it is effective when a limited number of commands need to be checked. The program then issues a shell-like prompt, cmd>, and uses the C++ input function **getline** to store user input in a character array buffer called line_input. The **getline** function will read a line of input, including intervening whitespace that is terminated by a newline. If the **getline** function fails (such as when the user just presses return), the program loops back around and reprompts the user for additional input. Upon entry of input, the program uses the C string function **strtok** to obtain the first valid token from the line_input array. The **strtok** function, which will divide a referenced character string into tokens, requires a pointer to the array it is to parse and a list of delimiting characters that delimit tokens (in this case only a blank " " has been indicated). The **strtok** function is a wonderful example of the idiosyncratic nature of some functions in C/C++. When **strtok** is called successive times and passed a reference to NULL, it will continue to parse the initial input line starting each time where it left off previously. The **strcat** function is used to add a trailing blank to this first token (assumed to the command), and the resulting sequence is stored in a character array called the_cmd.

The next line of the program checks for the presence of the command in the valid_cmds string at a modulus-4-based offset (see Figure 3.8).

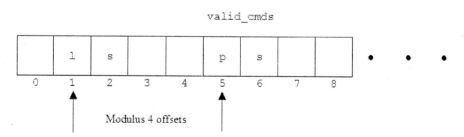

Figure 3.8 Character offsets in the valid_cmds string.

If the command is found, a do-while loop is used to obtain the remaining tokens (up to the limit CMD_MAX). These tokens are stored in successive elements of the previously declared new_args array. Upon exiting the loop, we assure that the last element of the new_args array contains the requisite NULL value. A switch statement, in concert with **fork** and **execvp** system calls, is used to execute the command.

3-4 EXERCISE

In Program 3.7, why was `new_args[0]`, rather than the reference `the_cmd`, passed to the **execvp** system call?

3-5 EXERCISE

When running Program 3.7, we can specify options to commands. For example,

```
df -t
```

will work just as if we were running the regular shell. However, if we indicate that the output of a command is to be redirected to a file, say, `df -t > /tmp/ps_out`, the command no longer works as expected. Why is this?

3-6 EXERCISE

Restructure Program 3.7 into functional units. Add (as part of the `valid_cmds` string) the **pwd** (print working directory), **lo** (logout), and **cd** (change directory) commands. Submit evidence that these *new* commands have been implemented successfully.

3.5 Ending a Process

Eventually all things must come to an end. Now that we have generated processes, we should take a closer look at how to end a process. Under its own power (assuming the process does not receive a terminating signal and the system has not crashed) a process normally terminates in one of three ways.[6] In order of preference, these are

---

[6] Of course, the library function **abort** can also be used to end a process, but its call will result in an abnormal termination of the process.

1. It issues (at any point in its code) a call to either **exit** or **_exit**.
2. It issues a `return` in the function `main`.
3. It *falls off the end* of the function `main` ending implicitly.

Programmers routinely make use of the library function **exit** to terminate programs. This function, which does not return a value, is defined as shown in Table 3.6.

Table 3.6 Summary of the `exit` Library Function.

Include File(s)	`<stdlib.h>`		Manual Section	3
Summary	`void exit(int status);`			
Return		Success	Failure	Sets `errno`
		Does not return	No return	

In earlier versions of C the inclusion of a specific header file was not required when using **exit**. More recent versions of C (and C++) require the inclusion of the file `<stdlib.h>` (or `<cstdlib>` if going the full ANSI-C++ route) that contains the **exit** function prototype. The **exit** function accepts a single parameter, an integer **status** value that will be returned to the parent process.[7] By convention, a 0 value is returned if the program has terminated normally; otherwise, a nonzero value is returned.[8] For those who wish to standardize the value returned by **exit** when terminating, the header file `<stdlib.h>` contains two defined constants, EXIT_SUCCESS and EXIT_FAILURE, which can be used to indicate program success and failure respectively. If we somehow are able to slip by the compiler a call to **exit** without passing an exit status value (i.e., **exit( );**) or issue a `return;` in `main` without specifying a value, then what is returned to the parent process is *technically* undefined.

Upon invocation, the **exit** function performs several actions. Figure 3.9 shows the relationship of the actions taken.

First, **exit** will call, in *reverse* order, all functions that have been registered using the **atexit** library function. The **atexit** function is relatively new. Some older BSD-based versions of C (as well as some version of GNU)

---

[7] I know, I know—what if the parent is no longer around? Remember that **init** inherits processes whose parents are gone. The handling of status values is discussed further in Section 3.6.

[8] Only the low-order eight bits are returned, thus values range from 0 to 255. (Hmm, I wonder ... would **exit(-1)** actually return a 255?)

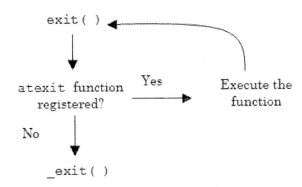

Figure 3.9 Actions taken by library function `exit`.

supported a library function called **on_exit** that offered a similar functionality. As future support for **on_exit** looks to be a bit sketchy; it might be best to stay clear of it. The **atexit** function should provide similar functionality.

A brief description of the **atexit** function is in order. The definition of **atexit**, shown in Table 3.7, indicates that functions to be called (when the process terminates normally)[9] are registered by passing the **atexit** function the address of the function. The registered functions should not have any parameters. If **atexit** is successful in registering the function, **atexit** returns a 0; otherwise, it returns a −1 but will not set `errno`.[10]

Program 3.8 demonstrates the use of **atexit**.

When run, the output of the program shows that the registered functions are called in inverse order (Figure 3.10).

In older versions of C, once all **atexit** functions were called, the standard I/O library function **_cleanup** would be called. Newer versions of GNU C/C++ do not support the **_cleanup** function. Now when all **atexit** functions have been processed, **exit** calls the system call **_exit** (passing on

Table 3.7 Summary of the `atexit` Library Function.

Include File(s)	`<stdlib.h>`		Manual Section	**3**
Summary	`int atexit(void (*function)(void));`			
	Success	Failure	Sets errno	
Return	0	−1	No	

[9] A normal termination is considered a call to **exit** or a return in main. On our system, **atexit** registered functions will be called even if the program ends implicitly (without a `return` in main).

[10] This is one of the rare cases where no explanation of `errno` values is provided by system designers.

Program 3.8 Using the `atexit` library function.

```
File : p3.8.cxx
     |      #include <iostream>
     |      #include <cstdlib>
     |      using namespace std;
     |      int
     +      main( ){
     |        void       f1( ), f2( ), f3( );
     |        atexit(f1);
     |        atexit(f2);
     |        atexit(f3);
    10        cout << "Getting ready to exit" << endl;
     |        exit(0);
     |      }
     |      void
     |      f1( ){
     +        cout << "Doing F1" << endl;
     |      }
     |      void
     |      f2( ){
     |        cout << "Doing F2" << endl;
    20      }
     |      void
     |      f3( ){
     |        cout << "Doing F3" << endl;
     |      }
```

Figure 3.10 Output of Program 3.8.

```
linux$ p3.8
Getting ready to exit
Doing F3
Doing F2
Doing F1
```

3-7 EXERCISE

Explore the **atexit** function. What happens if one of the functions registered with **atexit** contains a call to **exit**? What if the registered function (with the **exit** call) is called directly rather than having the program **exit** in main—are things handled correctly?

to it the value of status). Programmers may call **_exit** directly if they wish to circumvent the invocation of **atexit** registered functions and the flushing of I/O buffers. See Table 3.8.

Table 3.8 Summary of the _exit System Call.

Include File(s)	<unistd.h>		Manual Section	**2**
Summary	void _exit(int status);			
	Success	Failure	Sets errno	
Return	Does not return	Does not return		

The **_exit** system call, like its relative, **exit**, does not return. This call also accepts an integer status value, which will be made available to the parent process. When terminating a process, the system performs a number of housekeeping operations:

- All open file descriptors are closed.
- The parent of the process is notified (via a SIGCHLD signal) that the process is terminating.
- Status information is returned to the parent process (if it is waiting for it). If the parent process is not waiting, the system stores the status information until a **wait** by the parent process is affected.
- All child processes of the terminating process have their parent process ID (PPID) set to 1—they are inherited by **init**.
- If the process was a group leader, process group members will be sent SIGHUP/ SIGCONT signals.
- Shared memory segments and semaphore references are readjusted.
- If the process was running accounting, the accounting record is written out to the accounting file.

3.6 Waiting on Processes

They also serve who only stand and wait.
John Milton 1608–1674
On His Blindness [1652]

More often than not, a parent process needs to synchronize its actions by waiting until a child process has either stopped or terminated its actions. The **wait** system call allows the parent process to suspend its activity until one of these actions has occurred (Table 3.9).

Table 3.9 Summary of the **wait** System Call.

Include File(s)	`<sys/types.h>` `<sys/wait.h>`		Manual Section	**2**
Summary	`pid_t wait(int *status);`			
Return	Success	Failure	Sets `errno`	
	Child process ID or 0	−1	Yes	

The activities of `wait` are summarized in Figure 3.11.

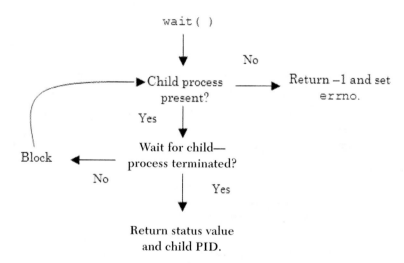

Figure 3.11 Summary of `wait` activities.

The **wait** system call accepts a single argument, which is a pointer to an integer, and returns a value defined as type `pid_t`. Data type `pid_t` is found in the header file `<sys/types.h>` and is most commonly a `long int`. If the calling process does not have any child processes associated with it, **wait** will return immediately with a value of −1 and `errno` will be set to `ECHILD` (10). However, if *any* child processes are still active, the calling process will block (suspend its activity) until a child process terminates. When a waited-for

103

child process terminates, the status information for the child and its process ID (PID) are returned to the parent. The status information is stored as an integer value at the location referenced by the pointer `status`. The low-order 16 bits of the location contain the actual status information, and the high-order bits (assuming a 32-bit machine) are set to zero. The low-order bit information can be further subdivided into a low- and high-order byte. This information is interpreted in one of two ways:

1. If the child process terminated normally, the low-order byte will be 0 and the high-order byte will contain the exit code (0–255):

byte 3	byte 2	byte 1	byte 0
		exit code	0

2. If the child process terminated due to an uncaught signal, the low-order byte will contain the signal number and the high-order byte will be 0:

byte 3	byte 2	byte 1	byte 0
		0	signal #

In this second situation, if a core file has been produced, the leftmost *bit* of byte 0 will be a 1. If a NULL argument is specified for **wait**, the child status information is *not* returned to the parent process, the parent is only notified of the child's termination.

Here are two programs, a parent (Program 3.9) and child (Program 3.10), that demonstrate the use of **wait**.

Program 3.9 The parent process.

```
File : p3.9.cxx
    |     /*
    |         A parent process that waits for a child to finish
    |     */
    |     #include <iostream>
    +     #include <cstdlib>
    |     #include <iomanip>
    |     #include <unistd.h>
    |     #include <sys/types.h>
    |     #include <sys/wait.h>
   10     using namespace std;
    |     int
    |     main(int argc, char *argv[] ){
    |       pid_t   pid, w;
    |       int     status;
```

```
  +        if ( argc < 4 ) {
  |          cerr << "Usage " << *argv << " value_1 value_2 value_3\n";
  |          return 1;
  |        }
  |        for (int i = 1; i < 4; ++i)               // generate 3 child processes
 20          if ((pid = fork( )) == 0)
  |            execl("./child", "child", argv[i], (char *) 0);
  |          else                                   // assuming no failures here
  |            cout << "Forked child " << pid << endl;
  |      /*
  +          Wait for the children
  |      */
  |        while ((w=wait(&status)) && w != -1)
  |          cout << "Wait on PID: " << dec <<  w << "  returns status of  "
  |              << setw(4) << setfill('0') << hex
 30              << setiosflags(ios::uppercase) << status << endl;
  |        return 0;
  |      }
```

The parent program forks three child processes. Each child process is over-laid with the executable code for the child (found in Program 3.10). The parent process passes to each child, from the parent's command line, a numeric value. As each child process is produced, the parent process displays the child process ID. After all three processes have been generated; the parent process initiates a loop to wait for the child processes to finish their execution. As each child process terminates, the value returned to the parent process is displayed.

Program 3.10 The child process.

```
File : p3.10.cxx
  |      /*
  |          The child process
  |      */
  |      #define _GNU_SOURCE
  +      #include <iostream>
  |      #include <cstdlib>
  |      #include <iomanip>
  |      #include <sys/types.h>
  |      #include <unistd.h>
 10      #include <signal.h>
  |      using namespace std;
  |      int
  |      main(int argc, char *argv[ ]){
  |        pid_t      pid = getpid( );
  +        int        ret_value;
  |        srand((unsigned) pid);
  |        ret_value = int(rand( ) % 256);           // generate a return value
  |        sleep(rand( ) % 3);                       // sleep a bit
```

105

```
 |        if (atoi(*(argv + 1)) % 2) {          // assuming argv[1] exists!
 20            cout << "Child " << pid << " is terminating with signal 0009" <<
 |             endl;
 |             kill(pid, 9);                     // commit hara-kiri
 |         } else {
 |             cout << "Child " << pid << " is terminating with   exit("
 |                 << setw(4) << setfill('0') << setiosflags(ios::uppercase)
 +                 << hex  << ret_value << ")" << endl;
 |             exit(ret_value);
 |         }
 |     }
```

In the child program, the child process obtains its own PID using the
getpid call. The PID value is used as a *seed* value to initialize the **srand**
function. A call to **rand** is used to generate a unique value to be returned
when the process exits. The child process then sleeps a random number of
seconds (0–3). After sleeping, if the argument passed to the child process
on the command line is odd (i.e., not evenly divisible by 2), the child process
kills itself by sending a signal 9 (SIGKILL) to its own PID. If the argument on
the command line is even, the child process exits normally, returning the previously calculated return value. In both cases, the child process displays a
message indicating what it will do before it actually executes the statements.

The source programs are compiled and the executables named parent and
child respectively. They are run by calling the parent program. Two sample
output sequences are shown in Figure 3.12.

Figure 3.12 Two runs of Programs 3.9 and 3.10.

```
linux$ parent 2 1 2         ◄──────── Two even values and one odd
Forked child 8975
Forked child 8976
Child 8976 is terminating with signal 0009
Forked child 8977
Wait on PID: 8976  returns status of  0009
Child 8977 is terminating with   exit(008F)
Wait on PID: 8977  returns status of  8F00
Child 8975 is terminating with   exit(0062)
Wait on PID: 8975  returns status of  6200

linux$ parent 2 2 1         ◄──────── Two even values and one odd but in
Forked child 8980                      a different order.
Forked child 8981
Forked child 8982
Child 8982 is terminating with signal 0009
Wait on PID: 8982  returns status of  0009
Child 8980 is terminating with   exit(00B0)
```

```
Wait on PID: 8980   returns status of   B000
Child 8981 is terminating with    exit(00D3)
Wait on PID: 8981   returns status of   D300
```

There are several things of interest to note in this output. In the first output sequence, one child processes (PID 8976) has terminated before the parent has finished its process generation. Processes that have terminated but have not been **wait**ed upon by their parent process are called **zombie** processes. Zombie processes occupy a slot in the process table, consume no other system resources, and will be marked with the letter Z when a process status command is issued (e.g., ps -alx or ps -el). A zombie process cannot be killed[11] even with the standard Teflon bullet (e.g., at a system level: **kill -9** process_id_ number). Zombies are put to rest when their parent process performs a **wait** to obtain their process status information. When this occurs, any remaining system resources allocated for the process are recovered by the kernel. Should the child process become an orphan before its parent issues the **wait**, the process will be inherited by **init**, which, by design, will issue a **wait** for the process. On some very *rare* occasions, even this will not cause the zombie process to "die." In these cases, a system reboot may be needed to clear the process table of the entry.

Both sets of output clearly show that when the child process terminates normally, the exit value returned by the child is stored in the second byte of the integer value referenced by argument to the **wait** call in the parent process. Likewise, if the child terminates due to an uncaught signal, the signal value is stored in the first byte of the same referenced location. It is also apparent that **wait** will return with the information for the first child process that terminates, which may or may not be the first child process generated.

3-8 EXERCISE

Add the **wait** system call to the **huh** shell program (Program 3.7).

3-9 EXERCISE

Write a program that produces three zombie processes. Submit evidence, via the output of the **ps** command, that these processes are truly generated and are eventually destroyed.

---

[11] This miraculous ability is the source of the name *zombie*.

In Program 3.10 if the child process uses a signal 8 (versus 9) to terminate, what is returned to the parent as the signal value? Why?

It is easy to see that the interpretation of the status information can be cumbersome, to say the least. At one time, programmers wrote their own macros to interrogate the contents of status. Now most use one of the predefined status macros. These macros are shown in Table 3.10.

Table 3.10 The `wstat` Macros.

Macro	Description
WIFEXITED(status)	Returns a true if the child process exited normally.
WEXITSTATUS(status)	Returns the **exit** code or `return` value from `main`. Should be called only if `WIFEXITED(status)` has returned a true.
WIFSIGNALED(status)	Returns a true if the child exited due to uncaught signal.
WTERMSIG(status)	Returns the signal that terminated the child. Should be called only if `WIFSIGNALED(status)` has returned a true.
WIFSTOPPED(status)	Returns a true if the child process is stopped.
WSTOPSIG(status)	Returns the signal that stopped the child. Should be called only if WIFSTOPPED(status) has returned a true.

The argument to each of these macros is the integer status value (not the pointer to the value) that is returned to the **wait** call. The macros are most often used in pairs. The **WIF** macros are used as a test for a given condition. If the condition is true, the second macro of the pair is used to return the specified value. As shown below, these macros could be incorporated in the wait loop in the parent Program 3.9 to obtain the child status information:

```
. . .
while ((w = wait(&status)) && w != -1)
  if (WIFEXITED(status))                          // test with macro
    cout << "Wait on PID: " << dec << w << " returns a value of "
        << hex << WEXITSTATUS(status) << endl;    // obtain value
  else if (WIFSIGNALED(status))                   // test with macro
    cout << "Wait on PID: " << dec << w << " returns a signal of "
        << hex << WTERMSIG(status) << endl;       // obtain value
. . .
```

3-11 EXERCISE

Some systems support a WCOREDUMP macro. This macro is only called if the WIFSIGNALED macro returns a true. WCOREDUMP returns a true if the offending signal generates a core dump. Write your own version of the WCOREDUMP macro (inline function). You may need to check the signal manual page (Section 7) to determine what signals generate a core dump or do a bit of bit manipulation (see earlier discussion). Show that your macro works when a process receives a terminating signal that generates or does not generate a core image file.

While the **wait** system call is helpful, it does have some limitations. It will always return the status of the *first* child process that terminates or stops. Thus, if the status information returned by **wait** is not from the child process we want, the information may need to be stored on a temporary basis for possible future reference and additional calls to **wait** made. Another limitation of **wait** is that it will always block if status information is not available. Fortunately, another system call, **waitpid**, which is more flexible (and thus more complex), addresses these shortcomings. In most invocations, the **waitpid** call will block the calling process until one of the specified child processes changes state. The **waitpid** system call summary is shown in Table 3.11.

Table 3.11 Summary of the `waitpid` System Call.

Include File(s)	`<sys/types.h>` `<sys/wait.h>`		Manual Section	2
Summary	`pid_t waitpid(pid_t pid, int *status, int options);`			
	Success		Failure	Sets `errno`
Return	Child PID or 0		−1	Yes

The first argument of the **waitpid** system call, `pid`, is used to stipulate the set of child process identification numbers that should be waited for (Table 3.12).

Table 3.12 Interpretation of `pid` Values by `waitpid`.

pid Value	Wait for
< -1	Any child process whose process group ID equals the absolute value of `pid`.
-1	Any child process—in a manner similar to **wait**.
0	Any child process whose process group ID equals the caller's process group ID.
> 0	The child process with this process ID.

The second argument, `*status`, as with the **wait** call, references an integer status location where the status information of the child process will be stored if the **waitpid** call is successful. This location can be examined directly or with the previously presented **wstat** macros.

The third argument, `options`, may be 0 (don't care), or it can be formed by a bitwise OR of one or more of the flags listed in Table 3.13 (these flags are usually defined in the `<sys/wait.h>` header file). The flags are applicable to the specified child process set discussed previously.

Table 3.13 Flag Values for `waitpid`.

FLAG Value	Specifies
WNOHANG	Return immediately if no child has exited—do not block if the status cannot be obtained; return a value of 0, not the `PID`.
WUNTRACED	Return immediately if child is blocked.

If the value given for `pid` is -1 and the option flag is set to 0, the **waitpid** and **wait** system call act in a similar fashion. If **waitpid** fails, it returns a value of –1 and sets `errno` to indicate the source of the error (Table 3.14).

Table 3.14 `waitpid` Error Messages.

#	Constant	perror Message	Explanation
4	EINTR	Interrupted system call	Signal was caught during the system call.
10	ECHILD	No child process	Process specified by `pid` does not exist, or child process has set action of SIGCHILD to be SIG_IGN (ignore signal).
22	EINVAL	Invalid argument	Invalid value for `options`.
85	ERESTART	Interrupted system call should be restarted	WNOHANG not specified, and unblocked signal or SIGCHILD was caught.

We can modify a few lines in our current version of the parent process (Program 3.9) to save the generated child PIDs in an array. This information can be used with the **waitpid** system call to coerce the parent process into displaying status information from child processes in the order of child process generation instead of their termination order. Program 3.11 shows how this can be done.

Program 3.11   A parent program using `waitpid`.

```
File : p3.11.cxx
    |        #include <iostream>
    |        #include <cstdlib>
    |        #include <iomanip>
    |        #include <unistd.h>
    +        #include <sys/types.h>
    |        #include <sys/wait.h>
    |        using namespace std;
    |        int
    |        main(int argc, char *argv[] ){
  10          pid_t   pid[3], w;
    |          int     status;
    |          if ( argc < 4 ) {
    |            cerr << "Usage " << *argv << " value_1 value_2 value_3\n";
    |            return 1;
    +          }
    |          for (int i=1; i < 4; ++i)              // generate 3 child processes
    |            if ((pid[i-1] = fork( )) == 0)
    |              execl("./child", "child", argv[i], (char *) 0);
    |            else                                 // assuming no failures here
  20            cout << "Forked child " << pid[i-1] << endl;
    |          /*
    |             Wait for the children
    |          */
    |          for (int i=0;(w=waitpid(pid[i], &status,0)) && w != -1; ++i){
    +            cout << "Wait on PID " << dec << w << " returns ";
    |            if (WIFEXITED(status))                         // test with macro
    |              cout << " a value of  " << setw(4) << setfill('0') << hex
    |                   << setiosflags(ios::uppercase) << WEXITSTATUS(status)
    |                   << endl;
    |            else if (WIFSIGNALED(status))                  // test with macro
  30            cout << " a signal of " << setw(4) << setfill('0') << hex
    |                   << setiosflags(ios::uppercase) << WTERMSIG(status)
    |                   << endl;
    |            else
    |              cout << " unexpectedly!" << endl;
    |          }
    +          return 0;
    |        }
```

A run of this program (using the same child process—Program 3.10) confirms that the status information returned to the parent is indeed ordered based on the sequence of child processes generation, not the order in which the processes terminated. Also, note that the status macros are used to evaluate the return from **waitpid** system call (Figure 3.13).

Figure 3.13 Output of Program 3.11.

```
linux$ p3.11  2  2  1
Forked child 9772                               Order of creation: 9772, 9773, 9774
Forked child 9773
Child 9773 is terminating with   exit(008B)     Order of termination: 9773, 9772, 9774
Forked child 9774
Child 9772 is terminating with   exit(00CD)
Wait on PID 9772 returns  a value of  00CD      Order of wait: 9772, 9773, 9774
Wait on PID 9773 returns  a value of  008B
Child 9774 is terminating with signal 0009
Wait on PID 9774 returns  a signal of 0009
```

3-12 EXERCISE

The discussion in the text centers on a parent process *waiting* for a child process to terminate or stop. We already have the tools necessary for a child process to determine if its parent process has terminated. Show how this can be done. What are the advantages and disadvantages of your implementation?

On some occasions, the information returned from **wait** or **waitpid** may be insufficient. Additional information on resource usage by a child process may be sought. There are two BSD compatibility library functions, **wait3** and **wait4**,[12] that can be used to provide this information (Table 3.15).

---

[12] It is not clear if these functions will be supported in subsequent versions of the GNU compiler, and they may limit the portability of programs that incorporate them. As these are BSD-based functions, _USE_BSD must be defined in the program code or defined on the command line when the source code is compiled.

Table 3.15 Summary of the `wait3`/`wait4` Library Functions.

Include File(s)	`#define _USE_BSD`
	`#include <sys/types.h>`
	`#include <sys/resource.h>`
	`#include <sys/wait.h>`
		Manual
		Section
			3

Summary	`pid_t wait3(int *status, int options,`
	`          struct rusage *rusage);`
	`pid_t wait4(pid_t pid, int *status,`
	`          int options, struct rusage *rusage);`		

Return	Success	Failure	Sets `errno`
	Child PID or 0	−1	Yes

The **wait3** and **wait4** functions parallel the **wait** and **waitpid** functions respectively. The **wait3** function waits for the first child process to terminate or stop. The **wait4** function waits for the specified PID (`pid`). In addition, should the `pid` value passed to the **wait4** function be set to 0, **wait4** will wait on the first child process in a manner similar to **wait3**. Both functions accept option flags to indicate whether or not they should block and/or report on stopped child processes. These option flags are shown in Table 3.16.

Table 3.16 Option Flag Values for `wait3`/`wait4`.

FLAG Value	Specifies
WNOHANG	Return immediately if no child has exited—do not block if the status cannot be obtained; return a value of 0 not the PID.
WUNTRACED	Return immediately if child is blocked.

Both functions contain an argument that is a reference to a `rusage` structure. This structure is defined in the header file `<sys/resource.h>`.[13]

```
struct rusage {
          struct timeval ru_utime;  /* user time used */
          struct timeval ru_stime;  /* system time used */
          long ru_maxrss;           /* maximum resident set size */
          long ru_ixrss;            /* integral shared memory size */
          long ru_idrss;            /* integral unshared data size */
```

[13] On some systems, you may need the header file `<sys/rusage.h>` instead of `<sys/resource.h>`, and you may need to explicitly link in the BSD library that contains the object code for the **wait3**/**wait4** functions.

```
        long ru_isrss;          /* integral unshared stack size */
        long ru_minflt;         /* page reclaims */
        long ru_majflt;         /* page faults */
        long ru_nswap;          /* swaps */
        long ru_inblock;        /* block input operations */
        long ru_oublock;        /* block output operations */
        long ru_msgsnd;         /* messages sent */
        long ru_msgrcv;         /* messages received */
        long ru_nsignals;       /* signals received */
        long ru_nvcsw;          /* voluntary context switches */
        long ru_nivcsw;         /* involuntary context switches */
};
```

If the rusage argument is non-null, the system populates the rusage structure with the current information from the specified child process. See the **getrusage** system call in Section 2 of the manual pages for additional information. The status macros (see previous section on **wait** and **waitpid**) can be used with the status information returned by **wait3** and **wait4**. See Table 3.17.

Table 3.17 wait3/wait4 Error Messages.

#	Constant	perror Message	Explanation
4	EINTR	Interrupted system call	Signal was caught during the system call.
10	ECHILD	No child process	Process specified by pid does not exist, or child process has set action of SIGCHILD to be SIG_IGN (ignore signal).
22	EINVAL	Invalid argument	Invalid value for options.
85	ERESTART	Interrupted system call should be restarted	WNOHANG not specified, and unblocked signal or SIGCHILD was caught.

3-13 EXERCISE

Modify Program 3.11 to use the **wait4** library function. After each child terminates, have the parent process display the number of page faults the child process incurred. A page fault occurs when a program requests data that is not currently in memory. To satisfy the request the operating system must locate the data and load it into memory. As loading data from a device takes time and slows down processing the fewer page faults generated the better.

3.7 Summary

Processes are generated by the **fork** system call. The process that issues the **fork** system call is known as the parent, and the new process as the child. Child processes may have their executable code overlaid with other executable code via an **exec** system call. When a process finishes executing its code, performs a return in the function main, or makes an **exit** system call, the process terminates. Parent processes may **wait** for their child processes to terminate. Terminating child processes return status information that can be examined by the parent process.

3.8 Key Terms and Concepts

_exit system call
atexit system call
daemon
exec
execl library function
execle function call
execlp library function
execv library function
execve system call
execvp library function
exit code
exit library function
flush
rand library function
restricted shell
rusage structure

srand library function
status information
strstr library function
strtok library function
wait system call
wait3 library function
wait4 library function
waitpid system call
WEXITSTATUS macro
WIFEXITED macro
WIFSIGNALED macro
WIFSTOPPED macro
wstat macros
WSTOPSIG macro
WTERMSIG macro
zombie

Chapter 4

PRIMITIVE COMMUNICATIONS

4.1 Introduction

Now that we have covered the basics of process structure and generation, we can begin to address the topic of interprocess communications. It is common for processes to need to coordinate their activities (e.g., such as when accessing a non-shareable system resource). Conceptually, this coordination is implemented via some form of passive or active communication between processes. As we will see, there are a number of ways in which interprocess communications can be carried out. The remaining chapters address a variety of interprocess communication techniques. As the techniques become more sophisticated, they become more complex, and hopefully more flexible and reliable. We begin by discussing primitive communication techniques that, while they get the job done, have certain limitations.

4.2 Lock Files

A lock file (which should not be confused with file/record locking, an I/O technique covered in Section 4.3) can be used by processes as a way to communicate with one another. The processes involved may be different programs or multiple instances of the same program. The use of lock files has a long history in UNIX. Early versions of UNIX (as well as some current versions) use lock files as a means of communication. Lock files are sometimes found in line printer and **uucp** implementations. In some systems the coordination of access to password and mail files also rely on lock files and/or the locking of a specific file.

The theory behind the use of a lock file as an interprocess communication technique is rudimentary. In brief, by using an agreed-upon file-naming convention, a process examines a prearranged location for the presence or absence of a lock file. Often the location is a temporary directory (e.g., /tmp) where the files are automatically cleared when the system reboots (or by periodic housecleaning by the system administrator) and where all users normally have read/write/execute permission. In its most basic form, if the file is present, the process takes one set of actions, and if the file is missing, it takes another. For example, suppose we have two processes, Process_One and Process_Two, that seek access to a single non-shareable resource (e.g., a printer or disk). A lock file-based communication convention for the two processes could be as shown in Figure 4.1.

Process_One checks for the presence of the lock file. If no lock file is found, Process_One creates the lock file using the agreed-upon naming convention. Process_One then uses the resource. When Process_One is done with the resource, it releases the resource and removes the lock file. However, if upon inspection the lock file was present (indicating, in this case, that Process_Two has access to the resource), Process_One would repeatedly *wait* a specified amount of time and then check again for the presence of the lock file, and so on. Process_Two would act in a manner similar to Process_One.

Figure 4.1 Using a lock file for communication with two processes.

It is clear that communication implemented in this manner only conveys a minimal amount of information from one process to another. In essence, the processes are using the presence or absence of the lock file as a binary semaphore. The file's presence or absence communicates, from one process to another, the availability of a resource.

Such a communication technique is fraught with problems. The most apparent problem is that the processes must agree upon the naming convention for the lock file. However, additional, perhaps unforeseen, problems may arise as well. For example,

1. What if one of the processes fails to remove the lock file when it is finished with the resource?

2. Polling (the constant checking to determine if a certain event has occurred) is expensive (CPU-wise) and is to be avoided. How does the process that does not obtain access to the resource wait for the resource to become free?

3. Race conditions whereby both processes find the lock file absent at the same time and, thus, both attempt to simultaneously create it should not happen. Can we make the generation of the lock file atomic (non-divisible, i.e., non-interruptible)?

As we will see, we will be able to address some of these concerns and others we will only be able to limit in scope. A program that implements communications using a lock file is presented below. The code for the main portion of the program is shown in Program 4.1.

Program 4.1 Using a lock file—the main program.

```
File : p4.1.cxx
    |      /*
    |            Using a lock file as a process communication technique.
    |      */
    |      #include <iostream>
    +      #include <unistd.h>
    |
    |      #include "lock_file.h"              ←——————————— This header resides locally.
    |      using namespace std;
    |      int
   10      main(int argc, char *argv[ ]){
    |        int   numb_tries, i = 5;
    |        int   sleep_time;
    |        char *fname;
    |        /*
    +            Assign values from the command line
    |        */
    |        set_defaults(argc, argv, &numb_tries, &sleep_time, &fname);
    |        /*
    |            Attempt to obtain lock file
   20        */
```

```
|       if (acquire(numb_tries, sleep_time, fname)) {
|         while (i--) {                          // simulate resource use
|           cout << getpid( )<< " " << i << endl;
|           sleep(sleep_time);
+         }
|         release(fname);                        // remove lock file
|         return 0;
|       } else
|         cerr << getpid( ) << " unable to obtain lock file after "
30             << numb_tries << " tries." << endl;
|       return 1;
|     }
```

At line 7 of the program, the local header file `lock_file.h` is included. This file (Figure 4.2) contains the prototypes for the three functions `set_defaults`, `acquire`, and `release`, that are used to manipulate the lock file. Preprocessor statements are used in the header file to prevent the file from being inadvertently included more than once.

In line 17 of the main program the `set_defaults` function is called to establish the default values. Once these values have been assigned, the program attempts to obtain the lock file by calling the function `acquire` (line 21). If the program is successful in creating the lock file, it then accesses the non-shareable resource. In the case of Program 4.1 the resource involved is the screen. When access to the screen is acquired, the program displays a series of integer values. Once the program is finished with the resource (all values have been displayed), the lock file is removed using the `release` function.

Figure 4.2 The `lock_file.h` header file.

```
File : lock_file.h
|       #ifndef LOCK_FILE_H
|       #define LOCK_FILE_H
|       /*
|          Lock file function prototypes
+       */
|       void  set_defaults(int, char *[], int *, int *, char **);
|       bool  acquire(int, int, char *);
|       bool  release(char *);
|       #endif
```

The `set_defaults` function accepts five arguments. The first two arguments (an integer and an array of character pointers) are the `argc` and `argv` values passed to the main program (Program 4.1). As written, the program will allow the user to change some or all of the default values by passing alternate values on the command line when the program is invoked. The remaining three arguments for set_defaults are the number of tries to be made when attempting to generate the lock file, the amount of time to wait in seconds between attempts, and a reference to the name of the lock file.

The acquire function takes three arguments. The first is the number of times to attempt to create the lock file, the second the sleep interval between tries, and the third a reference to the lock file name. The acquire function returns a boolean value indicating its success.

The function release removes the lock file. This function is passed a reference to the lock file and returns a boolean value indicating whether or not it was successful. The code for these functions, which are stored in a separate file, is shown in Figure 4.3.

Figure 4.3 Source code for the set_defaults, acquire, and release functions.

```
File : lock_file.cxx
   |      /*
   |         Source code for using lock file. Compile using -c and
   |         -D_GNU_SOURCE options. Link object code as needed.
   |      */
   +      #include <iostream>
   |      #include <cstring>
   |      #include <cstdlib>
   |      #include <cerrno>
   |      #include <limits.h>
  10      #include <fcntl.h>
   |      #include <unistd.h>
   |      const int  NTRIES = 5;                   // default values
   |      const int  SLEEP  = 5;
   |      const char *LFILE = "/tmp/TEST.LCK";
   +      using namespace std;
   |      void
   |      set_defaults(int ac, char *av[ ],
   |                  int *n_tries, int *s_time, char **f_name){
   |        static char full_name[PATH_MAX];
  20        *n_tries = NTRIES;                     // Start with defaults
   |        *s_time  = SLEEP;
   |        strcpy(full_name, LFILE);
   |        switch (ac) {
   |        case 4:                                // File  name was specified
   +          full_name[0] = '\0';                 // "clear" the string
   |          strcpy(full_name, av[3]);            // Add the passed in file
   |        case 3:
   |          if ((*s_time = atoi(av[2])) <= 0)    //  Seconds of sleep time
   |            *s_time = SLEEP;
```

121

```
30        case 2:
 |          if ((*n_tries = atoi(av[1])) <= 0)   // Number of times to try
 |            *n_tries = NTRIES;
 |          case 1:                              // Use the defaults
 |            break;
 +        default:
 |          cerr << "Usage: " << av[0] <<
 |                  " [[tries][sleep][lockfile]]" << endl;
 |          exit(1);
 |        }
40        *f_name = full_name;
 |      }
 |
 |      bool
 |      acquire(int numb_tries, int sleep_time, char *file_name){
 +        int    fd, count = 0;
 |        while ((fd = creat(file_name, 0)) == -1 && errno == EACCES)
 |          if (++count < numb_tries)           // If still more tries
 |            sleep(sleep_time);                // sleep for a while
 |          else
50            return (false);                   // Unable to generate
 |        close(fd);                            // Close (0 byte in size)
 |        return (bool(fd != -1));              // OK if actually done
 |      }
 |
 +      bool
 |      release(char *file_name){
 |        return bool(unlink(file_name) == 0);
 |      }
```

At the top of the `lock_file.cxx` file, the default values are assigned. The `set_defaults` function examines the number of arguments passed on the command line (which has been passed to it as the variable `ac`). A cascading `switch` statement is used to determine if changes in the default assignments should be made. The `set_defaults` function assumes the command-line arguments, if present, are arranged as

```
linux$ program_name  numb_of_tries  sec_to_sleep  lck_file_name
```

The value for `numb_of_tries` and the `sec_to_sleep` should be nonzero. The `lck_file_name` is the name to be used for the lock file. As written, the `set_defaults` function does not validate the passed-in lock file location/name but does attempt to disallow values of zero or less for the number of tries and the sleep interval.

The function `acquire` relies on the system call **creat** (note there is no trailing **e**) to generate the lock file (Table 4.1).

Table 4.1 Summary of the `creat` System Call.

Include File(s)	`<sys/types.h>` `<sys/stat.h>` `<fcntl.h>`		Manual Section	**2**
Summary	`int creat(const char *pathname,mode_t mode);`			
Return	Success		Failure	Sets `errno`
	Lowest available integer file descriptor		−1	Yes

By definition, **creat** is used to create a new file or rewrite a file that already exists (first truncating it to 0 bytes). The **creat** system call will open a file for writing only.

creat requires two arguments. The first argument, `pathname`, is a character pointer to the file to be created, and the second argument, `mode`, is a value of type **mode_t** (in most cases defined as type `int` in the `<sys/types.h>` file), which specifies the mode (access permissions) for the created file. The header file `<fcntl.h>` contains a number of predefined constants that may be bitwise ORed to specify the `mode` for the file. The **creat** system call in the program function `acquire` creates a file whose access mode is 0. If **creat** is successful, the file generated will not have read, write, or execute permission for any user groups (this excludes the superuser root).[1]

An alternate approach to creating the file would be to use the **open**[2] system call. The equivalent statement using `open` would be:

```
open( path, O_WRONLY | O_CREAT | O_TRUNC, 0 );
```

If the **creat** call is successful, it will return an integer value that is the lowest available file descriptor. If **creat** fails, it returns/sets a −1 and sets `errno`. Table 4.2 contains the errors that may be encountered when using the **creat** system call.

As shown, a number of things can cause **creat** to fail, including too many files open, an incorrectly specified file and/or path name, and so on. The failure we test for in the `while` loop of the `acquire` function is EACCES.[3] The failure of **creat** and the setting of `errno` to EACCES indicates the file to be

---

[1] As the superuser has special privileges, the lock file implementation shown here would not work for the superuser.

[2] At one time the **open** system call did not support the O_CREAT (create) option.

[3] EACCES is a defined constant found in the `<sys/errno.h>` header file.

Table 4.2 `creat` Error Messages.

#	Constant	`perror` **Message**	Explanation
2	ENOENT	No such file or directory	One or more parts of the path to new file do not exist (or is NULL).
6	ENXIO	No such device or address	`O_NONBLOCK	O_WRONLY` is set, the named file is a pipe, and no process has the file open for reading.
12	ENOMEM	Cannot allocate memory	Insufficient kernel memory was available.
13	EACCES	Permission denied	• The requested access to the file is not allowed. • Search permission denied on part of file path. • File does not exist.
14	EFAULT	Bad address	`pathname` references an illegal address space.
17	EEXIST	File exists	`pathname` (file) already exists and `O_CREAT` and `O_EXCL` were specified.
19	ENODEV	No such device	`pathname` refers to a device special file, and no corresponding device exists.
20	ENOTDIR	Not a directory	Part of the specified path is not a directory.
21	EISDIR	Is a directory	`pathname` refers to a directory, and the access requested involved writing.
23	ENFILE	Too many open files in system	System limit on open files has been reached.
24	EMFILE	Too many open files	The process has exceeded the maximum number of files open.
26	ETXTBSY	Text file busy	More than one process has the executable open for writing.
28	ENOSPC	No space left on device	Device for pathname has no space for new file (it is out of inodes).
30	EROFS	Read-only file system	The `pathname` refers to a file on a read-only filesystem, and write access was requested.
36	ENAMETOOLONG	File name too long	The `pathname` value exceeds system path/file name length.
40	ELOOP	Too many levels of symbolic links	The **perror** message says it all.

created already exists and write permission to the file is denied (remember, the file was generated with a mode of 0).

As noted, the while loop in the acquire function tests to determine if a file can be created. If the file can be created, the loop is exited and the file descriptor is closed (leaving the file present and 0 bytes in length). When the file cannot be created and the error code in errno is EACCES, the if statement in the body of the loop is executed. In the if statement the value for count is tested against the designated number of tries for creating the file. If insufficient tries have been made, a call to **sleep**, to suspend processing, is made.

sleep is a library function that suspends the invoking process for the number of seconds indicated by its argument seconds.[4] See Table 4.3. If **sleep** is interrupted (such as by a signal), the number of unslept seconds is returned. If the amount of time slept is equal to the argument value passed, **sleep** will return a 0. Using **sleep** in the polling loop to have the process wait is a compromise. It is not an elegant way to reduce CPU-intensive code but, at this point, is better than no built-in wait or running some sort of throwaway calculation loop. In later chapters, we discuss alternate solutions to this problem.

Table 4.3 Summary of the **sleep** Library Function.

Include Files(s)	<unistd.h>	Manual Section	3
Summary	unsigned int sleep(unsigned int seconds);		
	Success	Failure	Sets errno
Return	Amount of time left to sleep.		

If, in the program function acquire, the number of tries has been exceeded, a FALSE value, indicating a failure, is returned. A boolean TRUE type value is returned if the while loop is exited because the **creat** call was successful. Additionally, if the **creat** fails for any other reason, a FALSE type value is returned.

The release function attempts to remove the file using the system call **unlink** (Table 4.4). This call deletes a file from the filesystem if the reference is the last link to the file and the file not currently in use. If the reference is a symbolic link, the link is removed. In the program the release function is coded to return the success or failure of **unlink**'s ability to accomplish its task. As written, the main program discards the value returned by the release function.

---

[4] If smaller intervals are needed, there is a usleep (unsigned sleep) library function that suspends execution of the calling process for a specified number of microseconds.

Table 4.4 Summary of the `unlink` System Call.

Include Files(s)	`<unistd.h>`		Manual Section	**2**
Summary	`int unlink(const char *pathname);`			
	Success		Failure	Sets `errno`
Return	0		−1	Yes

If the **unlink** system call fails it returns a value of −1 and sets `errno` to one of the values found in Table 4.5. If **unlink** is successful, it returns a value of 0.

Table 4.5 `unlink` error messages.

#	Constant	`perror` **Message**	**Explanation**
1	EPERM	Operation not permitted	• Not owner of file or not superuser. • The filesystem (in Linux) does not allow the unlinking of files.
2	ENOENT	No such file or directory	One or more parts of `pathname` to the file to process does not exist (or is NULL).
4	EINTR	Interrupted system call	A signal was caught during the system call.
5	EIO	I/O error	An I/O error has occurred.
12	ENOMEM	Cannot allocate memory	Insufficient kernel memory was available.
13	EACCES	Permission denied	• Search permission denied on part of file path. • The requested access to the file is not allowed for this processes EUID.
14	EFAULT	Bad address	`pathname` references an illegal address space.
16	EBUSY	Device or resource busy	The referenced file is busy.
20	ENOTDIR	Not a directory	Part of the specified path is not a directory.

Table 4.5   (Continued)

#	Constant	`perror` **Message**	**Explanation**
21	EISDIR	Is a directory	`pathname` refers to a directory (not a file).
26	ETXTBSY	Text file busy	More than one process has the executable open for writing.
30	EROFS	Read-only file system	`pathname` refers to a file that resides on a read-only filesystem.
36	ENAMETOOLONG	File name too long	`pathname` is too long.
40	ELOOP	Too many levels of symbolic links	The **perror** message says it all.
67	ENOLINK	The link has been severed	The path value references a remote system that is no longer available.
72	EMULTIHOP	Multihop attempted	The path value requires multiple hops to remote systems, but file system does not allow it.

A sample compilation run of the program is shown in Figure 4.4.

Figure 4.4   Output of Program 4.1.

```
linux$ g++ p4.1.cxx lock_file.o -o p4.1          ◄────────── Compile the program linking in
                                                              the lock_file object code.
linux$ p4.1 1 5 & p4.1 2 2 &
24347 4                                           ◄────────── Run the program twice, placing
[1] 24347                                                     each in the background.
[2] 24348
linux$ 24348 unable to obtain lock file after 2 tries.
24347 3
24347 2
24347 1
24347 0                                                      Second instance of the program
[2]  + Exit 1                  p4.1 2 2          ◄────────── failed, returning a value of 1. The
[1]  + Done                    p4.1 1 5                       first instance completed normally.
```

The program p4.1 is invoked twice. To allow the two processes to execute concurrently, the program invocations are placed in the background (via the trailing &). The first process creates the lock file and gains access to the screen. This process is responsible for generating the five values (4, 3, 2, 1, 0) that are displayed on the screen. The second process, after two tries with a two-second interval between tries, exits and produces the message Unable to obtain lock file after 2 tries. When each process finishes, the operating system

127

displays the exit/return value. The process that was unable to gain access to the resource exits with a value of 1. It is informative to run the program several times using varying settings. When doing so, you should be able to ascertain whether the lock file really does allow rudimentary communication between the processes involved.

Our example uses the **creat** system call as the base for its atomic file locking. Unfortunately, **creat** may generate race conditions on NFS filesystem (network mounted filesystem). The Linux manual page for **creat** recommends using the **link** system call as the atomic file locking operation (which it indicates should not cause race conditions in an NFS setting). The **link** system call is used to generate a hard link to the lock file, giving it new name. With a hard link, the link and the file being linked must reside on the same filesystem. If the **stat** system call for the file returns a link count of two, then the lock has been successfully implemented (acquired). See Exercise 4-1 for more on using **link** versus **creat**.

4-1 EXERCISE

Hillary wrote the following program code for an acquire function that uses the **link** and **stat** system calls.

```
File : hillary.cxx
    |       #include <cstdio>                            ←——— Needed for sprintf call.
    |       bool
    |       acquire(int numb_tries, int sleep_time, char *file_name){
    +         char      my_link[512];
    |         sprintf( my_link, "%s.%d", file_name, getpid());
    |         int count = 0;                              ↖ Generate a unique link file name.
    |         struct stat buf;
    |         while ( ++count < numb_tries) {
   50           creat(my_link,0);
    |           link( my_link, file_name );  ←——— Generate a hard link.
    |           if (!stat(my_link, &buf) && buf.st_nlink == 2){
    |             unlink(my_link);           ←——— If the file has two links, then this
    |             return true;                        process has control.
    +           }
    |           sleep(sleep_time);
    |         }
    |         return false;
    |       }
```

Does her function work correctly? Why or why not? Provide output that supports your answer.

4-2 EXERCISE

Write a program where a parent process **fork**s three child processes. The child processes are to be similar to the example program just given (p4.1.cxx). Each child process should be passed the name of a text file to display on the screen. Show output whereby all processes eventually gain access to the file, and show output when at least one of the processes fails. The parent process should remove any *leftover* lock files that may have existed from previous invocations before forking the child processes.

4-3 EXERCISE

A classic operating system problem is that of coordinating a producer and consumer process. The producer *produces* a value and stores the value (such as in a common buffer or file) that can *hold only one* of the items produced. The consumer obtains (in a nondestructive manner) the value from the storage location and *consumes* it. The producer and consumer work at different rates. To guarantee integrity, each value *produced* must be *consumed* (not lost via overwriting by a speedy producer with a slow consumer), and no value should be consumed twice (such as when the consumer is faster than the producer). Write a producer/consumer process pair that uses a lock file communication technique to coordinate their activities. To ensure that no data is lost or duplicated, the producer process should produce its values by reading them one-by-one from an input file and in turn storing them in the common location. The consumer should append the values it consumes (reads from the common location) to an output file. After processing, say, 100, unique values, both the input file for the producer and the output file for the consumer should be identical. Use the **sleep** library call with small random values to simulate the producer and consumer working at different rates.

One way to solve the problem is to use *two* lock files. When using two lock files, one file would indicate whether or not the number has been produced, and the second file would indicate if the number has been consumed. The activities of the two processes to be coordinated can be summarized as follows:

```
Producer
do
   sleep random amount
   read a number from input file
   if # has been consumed
      write number to common buffer
      indicate new # produced
until 100 numbers produced

Consumer
do
   sleep random amount
   if a new # produced
      read number from common buffer
      indicate # was consumed
      append number read to output file
until 100 numbers produced
```

Hint: When using lock files, we test whether or not we can create a lock file. Thus, we could use the successful creation of the lock file as an indication of access and the inability to create the lock file as a prohibition of access. Using this approach initially, the lock file indicating a number has been consumed would be absent, and the lock file indicating a new number has been produced would be present.

4.3 Locking Files

A second basic communication technique, similar in spirit to using lock files, can be implemented by using some of the standard file protection routines found in UNIX. UNIX allows the locking of records. As there is no real record structure imposed on a file, a record (which is sometimes called a segment or section) is considered to be a specified number of contiguous bytes of storage starting at an indicated location. If the starting location for the record is the beginning of a file, and the number of bytes equals the number found in the file, then the entire file is considered to be the record in question. Locking routines can be used to impose **advisory** or **mandatory** locking. In advisory locking the operating system keeps track of which processes have locked files. The processes that are using these files cooperate and access the record/file only when they determine the lock is in the appropriate state. When advisory locking is used, outlaw processes can still ignore the lock, and if permissions permit, modify the record/file. In mandatory locking the operating system will check lock information with every **read** and **write** call. The operating system will ensure that the proper lock protocol is being followed. While mandatory locking offers added security, it is at the expense of additional system overhead. Locks become mandatory if the file being locked is a plain file (not executable) and the set-group-ID is on and the group execution bit is off.

At a system level the **chmod** command can be used to specify a file support mandatory locking. For example, in Figure 4.5, the permissions on the data file x.dat are set to support mandatory file locking. The **ls** command will display the letter S in the group execution bit field of a file that supports a mandatory lock. Notice that in the example absolute mode was used with the **chmod** command to establish locking. The first digit of the mode value should be a 2 and the third digit a 6, 4, 2, or 0 (but not a 1).

Figure 4.5 Specifying mandatory locking with **chmod**.

```
linux$ echo hello > x.dat                                          ◄——— Create a small text file.

linux$ ls  -l  x.dat
-rw-r--r--  1 gray      faculty    6 Jan 30 12:06 x.dat   ◄——— Default protections.

linux$ chmod  2644  x.dat                                          ◄——— Set the execution bit
$ ls  -l  x.dat                                                              for the group.
-rw-r-Sr--  1 gray      faculty    6 Jan 30 12:06 x.dat
```

The topic of record locking is expansive. We focus on one small aspect of it. We use file locking routines to place and remove an advisory lock on an entire file as a communication technique with cooperating processes.

There are several ways to set a lock. The two most common approaches are presented: the **fcntl** system call and the **lockf** library function. We begin with **fcntl** (Table 4.6).

Table 4.6 Summary of the **fcntl** System Call.

Include File(s)	`<unistd.h>` `<fcntl.h>`		Manual Section	**2**
Summary	`int fcntl(int fd, int cmd /* , struct` `flock *lock */);`			
		Success	Failure	Sets `errno`
Return	Value returned depends upon the cmd argument passed.		-1	Yes

As its first argument the **fcntl** system call is passed a valid integer file descriptor of an open file. The second argument, cmd, is an integer command value that specifies the action that **fcntl** should take. The command values for locking are specified as defined constants in the header file <bits/fcntl.h> that is included by the <fcntl.h> header file. The lock specific constants are shown in Table 4.7.

Table 4.7 Lock-Specific Defined Constants Used with the fcntl System Call.

Defined Constant	Action Taken by fcntl
F_SETLK	Set or remove a lock. Specific action is based on the contents of the flock structure that is passed as a third argument to **fcntl**.
F_SETLKW	Same as F_SETLK, but block (wait) if the indicated record/segment is not available—the default is not to block.
F_GETLK	Return lock status information via the flock structure that is passed as the third argument to **fcntl**.

The third argument for **fcntl** is optional for some invocations (as indicated by it being commented out in the function prototype). However, when working with locks, the third argument is specified and references a flock structure, which is defined as

```
struct flock  {
      short int l_type;    /* Type of lock: F_RDLCK, F_WRLCK, or F_UNLCK. */
      short int l_whence;  /* Where 'l_start' is relative to.             */
      #ifndef __USE_FILE_OFFSET64
      __off_t l_start;     /* Offset where the lock begins.              */
      __off_t l_len;       /* Size of the locked area; (0 == EOF).       */
      #else
      __off64_t l_start;   /* For systems with 64 bit offset.            */
      __off64_t l_len;
      #endif
      __pid_t l_pid;       /* PID of process holding the lock.           */
};
```

The flock structure is used to pass information to and return information from the **fcntl** call. The type of lock, l_type, is indicated by using one of the defined constants shown in Table 4.8.

The l_whence, l_start, and l_len flock members are used to indicate the starting location (0, the beginning of the file; 1, the current location; and 2, the end of the file), relative offset, and size of the record (segment). If these values are set to 0, the entire file will be operated upon. The l_pid member is used to return the PID of the process that placed the lock.

Table 4.8 Defined Constants Used in the `flock l_type` Member.

Defined Constant	Lock Specification
F_RDLCK	Read lock
F_WRLCK	Write lock
F_UNLCK	Remove lock

When dealing with locks, if **fcntl** fails to carry out an indicated command, it will return a value of −1 and set `errno`. Error messages associated with locking are shown in Table 4.9.

Table 4.9 `fcntl` Error Messages Relating to Locking.

#	Constant	`perror` **Message**	**Explanation**
4	EINTR	Interrupted system call	A signal was caught during the system call.
9	EBADF	Bad file number	`fd` does not reference a valid open file descriptor.
11	EAGAIN	Resource temporarily unavailable	Lock operation is prohibited, as the file has been memory mapped by another process.
13	EACCES	Permission denied	Lock operation prohibited by a lock held by another process.
14	EFAULT	Bad address	`*lock` references an illegal address space.
22	EINVAL	Invalid argument	• cmd invalid. • cmd is F_GETLK or F_SETLK and `*lock` or data referenced by `*lock` is invalid. • fd does not support locking.
35	EDEADLK	Resource deadlock avoided	cmd is F_SETLKW and requested lock is blocked by a lock from another process. If **fcntl** blocks the calling process waiting for lock to be free, deadlock would occur.
37	ENOLCK	No locks available	System has reached the maximum number of record locks.

Program 4.2 demonstrates the use of file locking.

Program 4.2 Using `fcntl` to lock a file.

```
File : p4.2.cxx
    |      /* Locking a file with fcntl
    |       */
    |      #include <iostream>
    +      #include <cstdio>
    |      #include <cerrno>
    |      #include <fcntl.h>
    |      #include <unistd.h>
    |      using namespace std;
    |      const int MAX = 5;
   10      int
    |      main(int argc, char *argv[ ]) {
    |        int           f_des, pass = 0;
    |        pid_t         pid = getpid();
    |        struct flock  lock;                  // for fcntl info
    +        if (argc < 2) {                      // name of file to lock missing
    |          cerr << "Usage " << *argv << " lock_file_name" << endl;
    |          return 1;
    |        }
    |        sleep(1);                            // don't start immediately
   20        if ((f_des = open(argv[1], O_RDWR)) < 0){
    |          perror(argv[1]);                   // could not access file
    |          return 2;
    |        }
    |        lock.l_type   = F_WRLCK;             // set a write lock
    +        lock.l_whence = 0;                   // start at beginning
    |        lock.l_start  = 0;                   // with a 0 offset
    |        lock.l_len    = 0;                   // whole file
    |        while (fcntl(f_des, F_SETLK, &lock) < 0) {
    |          switch (errno) {
   30          case EAGAIN:
    |          case EACCES:
    |            if (++pass < MAX)
    |              sleep(1);
    |            else {                           // run out of tries
    +              fcntl(f_des, F_GETLK, &lock);
    |              cerr << "Process " << pid << " found file "
    |                   << argv[1] << " locked by " << lock.l_pid << endl;
    |              return 3;
    |            }
   40            continue;
    |          }
    |          perror("fcntl");
    |          return 4;
    |        }
```

```
+        cerr << endl << "Process " << pid << " has the file" << endl;
|        sleep(3);                          // fake processing
|        cerr << "Process " << pid << " is done with the file" << endl;
|        return 0;
|     }
```

In this program the name of the file to be locked is passed on the command line. A call to **sleep** is placed at the start of the program to slow down the processing (for demonstration purposes only). The designated file is opened for reading and writing. In lines 24 through 27 the lock structure is assigned values that indicate a **write** lock is to be applied to the entire file. In the while loop that follows, a call to **fcntl** requests the lock be placed. If **fcntl** fails and errno is set to either EAGAIN or EACCES (values that indicate the lock could not be applied), the process will **sleep** for one second and try to apply the lock again. To be safe, the EACCES constant is grouped with EAGAIN, as in some versions of UNIX this is the value that is returned when a lock cannot be applied. If the MAX number of tries (passes) has been exceeded, another call to **fcntl** (line 35) is made to obtain information about the process that has locked the file. In this call the address of the lock structure is passed to **fcntl**. The PID of the locking process is displayed, and the program exits. If an error other than EAGAIN or EACCES is encountered when attempting to set the lock, **perror** is called, a message is displayed, and the program exits. If the process successfully obtains the lock, the process prints an informational message, sleeps three seconds (to simulate some sort of processing), and prints a second message as it terminates. When the process terminates, the system automatically removes the lock on the file. If the process were not to terminate, the process would need to set the l_type member to F_UNLCK and reissue the **fcntl** call to clear the lock.

If we run three copies of Program 4.2 in rapid succession, using the file x.dat as the lock file, their output will be similar to that shown in Figure 4.6.

Figure 4.6 Running multiple copies of Program 4.2—locking a file.

```
linux$ p4.2 x.dat & p4.2 x.dat &  p4.2 x.dat &      All three processes
[1] 28392                                           will use the same
[2] 28393                                           file: x.dat.
[3] 28394
$
Process 28392 has the file
Process 28392 is done with the file
```

```
Process 28393 has the file
Process 28394 found file x.dat locked by 28393
Process 28393 is done with the file

[3]  — Exit 3                        p4.2 x.dat
[2]  — Done                          p4.2 x.dat
[1]  + Done                          p4.2 x.dat
```

Notice that the last process, PID 28394 in this example, is unable to place a lock on the file and returns the process ID of the process that currently has the lock on the file. The second process, PID 28393, through repeated retries (with intervening calls to **sleep**) is able to lock the file once the first process is finished with it.

4-4 EXERCISE

Change the F_SETLK constant in Program 4.2 to F_SETLKW. Recompile the program and rerun it as shown in Figure 4.6. What sequence of messages are produced now? Why?

The **lockf** library function may also be used to apply, test, or remove a lock on an open file. Beneath the covers this library function is an alternate interface for the **fcntl** system call. The **lockf** library function is summarized in Table 4.10.

Table 4.10 Summary of the **lockf** Library Call

Include File(s)	<sys/file.h> <unistd.h>		Manual Section	3
Summary	int lockf(int fd, int cmd, off_t len);			
	Success	Failure	Sets errno	
Return	0	−1	Yes	

The fd argument is a file descriptor of a file that has been opened for either writing (O_WRONLY) or for reading and writing (O_RDWR). The cmd argument for **lockf** is similar to the cmd argument used with **fcntl**. The cmd value indicates the action to be taken. The action that **lockf** will take for each cmd value (as specified in the include file <unistd.h>) is summarized in Table 4.11.

Table 4.11 Defined cmd Constants.

Defined Constant	Lock Specification
F_ULOCK	Unlock a previously locked file.
F_LOCK	Lock a file (or a section of a file) for exclusive use if it is available. If unavailable, the **lockf** function will block.
F_TLOCK	Test and, if successful, lock a file (or section of a file) for exclusive use. An error is returned if no lock can be applied; with this option the **lockf** function will not block if the lock cannot be applied.
F_TEST	Test a file for the presence of a lock. A 0 is returned if the file is unlocked or locked by the current process. If locked by another process, −1 is returned and errno is set to EACCES.

The len argument of **lockf** indicates the number of contiguous bytes to lock or unlock. A value of zero indicates the section should be from the present location to the end of the file.

If the **lockf** call is successful, it returns a value of 0. If the call fails, it sets errno and returns the value −1 (Table 4.12).

Table 4.12 lockf error messages.

#	Constant	perror **Message**	Explanation
9	EBADF	Bad file number	fd is not a valid open file descriptor.
11	EAGAIN	Resource temporarily unavailable	• The cmd is F_TLOCK or F_TEST, and the specified section is already locked. • File is memory mapped by another process.
13	EACCES	Permission denied	Lock operation prohibited by a lock held by another process.
22	EINVAL	Invalid argument	Invalid operation specified for fd.
35	EDEADLK	File locking deadlock	Requested lock operation would cause a deadlock.
37	ENLOCK	No locks available	Maximum number of system locks has been reached.

Of the two techniques, `lockf` is simpler but less flexible than using `fcntl`. Note that when using the `lockf` call, the user must issue a separate `lseek` system call to position the file pointer to the proper location in the file prior to the call. Also, when generating parent/child process pairs, each shares the same file pointer. If locks are to be used in both processes, it is sometimes best to close and reopen the file in question so that each process has its own separate file pointer.

A final note—Linux supports a `shlock` command that can be used in shell scripts. The `shlock` command creates a lock file that contains an identifying PID.

4-5 EXERCISE

Write Exercise 4.3 using the `lockf` system call. Verify that your solution works.

4.4 More About Signals

A second primitive interprocess communication technique involves the use of signals. As previously indicated, signals occur asynchronously (with no specified timing or sequencing). Signals, which can be sent by processes or by the kernel, serve as notification that an event has occurred. Signals are generated when the event first occurs and are considered to be delivered when the process takes action on the signal. The delivery of most signals can be blocked so the signal can be acted upon later. Blocked signals, and those sent to processes in a non-running state are commonly called pending signals.

The symbolic name for each signal can be found in several places. Usually, the manual pages for **signal** (try man 7 signal) or the header file `<asm/signal.h>` will contain a list of each signal name. Signals, as described in Section 7 of the manual, are shown in Table 4.13. The definition of a signal (its symbolic name, the associated integer value, and the event signaled) has evolved over time. Signals defined by the POSIX 1 standard have the letter P in the **Def** column; those defined by SUS v2 (Single UNIX Specification, version 2) have a letter S. The letter O indicates signals not defined by either of these standards. Furthermore, keep in mind that some signals are architecture-dependent. To denote this if three numbers are listed in the **Value** column for a signal, the first number is the signal for alpha and sparc platforms; the middle number is for i386 and ppc platforms; while the last number is for mips platforms. A dash (−) indicates the signal is missing platform. A single value indicates all platforms use the same signal ....ber. The default action associated with the signal is defined by one or more letters in the Action column of the table. The letter A indicates the recipient process will terminate; B, the process will ignore the signal; C, the process will terminate and produce a core file; and D, the process will stop (suspend) execution. Additionally, the letter E indicates the signal cannot be caught (trapped), and the letter F, that the signal cannot be ignored.

Table 4.13 Signal Definitions.

Symbolic Name	Def	Value	Action	Description
SIGABRT	P	6	C	Abort signal from **abort**.
SIGALRM	P	14	A	Timer signal from **alarm**.
SIGBUS	S	10,7,10	C	Bus error (bad memory access).
SIGCHLD	P	20,17,18	B	Sent to parent when child is stopped or terminated.
SIGCLD	O	−,−,18	B	A synonym for SIGCHLD.
SIGCONT	P	19,18,25	B	Resume if process is stopped.
SIGEMT	O	7,−,7	C	Emulation trap.
SIGFPE	P	8	C	Floating-point exception.
SIGHUP	P	1	A	A hangup was detected on the controlling terminal or the controlling process has died.
SIGILL	P	4	C	Illegal instruction.
SIGINFO	O	29,−,−		A synonym for SIGPWR.
SIGINT	P	2	A	Interrupt from keyboard.
SIGIO	O	23,29,22	A	I/O now possible.
SIGIOT	O	6	C	IOT trap—equivalent to SIGABRT.
SIGKILL	P	9	A,E,F	Kill signal—force process termination.
SIGLOST	O	−,−,−	A	File lock lost.
SIGPIPE	P	13	A	Broken pipe; write to pipe with no readers.

Continued

Table 4.13 (Continued)

Symbolic Name	Def	Value	Action	Description
SIGPOLL	S	23	A	A pollable event has occurred—synonymous with SIGIO (also 23).
SIGPROF	S	27,27,29	A	Profiling timer expired.
SIGPWR	O	29,30,19	A	Power supply failure.
SIGQUIT	P	3	C	Quit from keyboard.
SIGSEGV	P	11	C	Invalid memory reference (segmentation violation).
SIGSTKFLT	O	-,16,-	A	Coprocessor stack error.
SIGSTOP	P	17,19,23	D,E,F	Stop process—not from tty.
SIGSYS	S	12,-,12	C	Bad argument to system call.
SIGTERM	P	15	A	Termination signal from **kill**.
SIGTRAP	S	5	C	Trace/breakpoint trap for debugging.
SIGTSTP	P	18,20,24	D	Stop typed at a tty.
SIGTTIN	P	21,21,26	D	Background process needs input.
SIGTTOU	P	22,22,27	D	Background process needs to output.
SIGUNUSED	O	-,31,-	A	Unused signal (will be SIGSYS).
SIGURG	S	16,23,21	B	Urgent condition on I/O channel (socket).
SIGUSR1	P	30,10,16	A	User-defined signal 1.
SIGUSR2	P	31,12,17	A	User-defined signal 2.
SIGVTALRM	S	26,26,28	A	Virtual alarm clock.
SIGWINCH	O	28,28,20	B	Window resize signal.
SIGXCPU	S	24,24,30	C	CPU time limit exceeded.
SIGXFSZ	S	25,25,31	C	File size limit exceeded.

Some additional caveats to consider include the following:

- For some S signals (SUS v2), the default action is listed as A (terminate) but by their actual action should be C (terminate the process and generate a core file).

- Signal 29 is SIGINFO/SIGPWR on an alpha platform but SIGLOST on a sparc platform.

Note that all signals begin with the prefix SIG and end with a semi-mnemonic suffix. For the sake of portability when referencing signals, it is usually best to use their symbolic names rather than their assigned integer values. The defined constants SIGRTMIN and SIGRTMAX are also found in <asm/signal.h> and allow the generation of additional real-time signals. Real-time signals, usually the values 32 to 63, can be queued. The queuing of signals ensures that when multiple signals are sent to a process, they will not be lost. At present, the Linux kernel does not make use of real-time signals.

For each signal, a process may take one of the following three actions:

1. **Perform the default action.** This is the action that will be taken unless otherwise specified. The default action for each signal is listed in the previous table. Specifically these actions are

   - **Terminate (Abort)**—Perform all the activities associated with the **exit** system call.

   - **Core (Dump)**—Produce a core image (file) and then perform termination activities.

   - **Stop**—Suspend processing.

   - **Ignore**—Disregard the signal.

2. **Ignore the signal.** If the signal to be ignored is currently blocked, it is discarded. The SIGKILL and SIGSTOP signals cannot be ignored.

3. **Catch the signal.** In this case, the process supplies the address of a function (often called a **signal catcher**) that is to be executed when the signal is received. In most circumstances, the signal catching function will have a single integer parameter. The parameter value, which is assigned by the system, will be the numeric value of the signal caught. When the signal catcher function finishes, the interrupted process will, unless otherwise specified, resume its execution where it left off.

A discussion of the implementation details for ignoring and catching signals are covered in Section 4.5.

Signals are generated in a number of ways:

1. By the kernel, indicating

   - **Hardware conditions,** the most common of which are SIGSEGV, when there has been an addressing violation by the process, and SIGFPE, indicating a division by zero.

   - **Software conditions,** such as SIGIO, indicating I/O is possible on a file descriptor or the expiration of a timer.

141

2. By the user at a terminal:

- **Keyboard**—The user produces keyboard sequences that will interrupt or terminate the currently executing process. For example, the interrupt signal, SIGINT, is usually mapped to the key sequence CTRL+C and the terminate signal, SIGQUIT, to the key sequence CTRL+\. The command **stty -a** will display the current mappings of keystrokes for the interrupt and quit signals.

- **kill command**—By using the **kill** command, the user, at the command line, can generate any of the previously listed signals for any process that has the same effective ID. The syntax for the **kill** command is

```
$ kill [ -signal ] pid . . .
```

When issued, the **kill** command will send the specified signal to the indicated PID. The signal can be an integer value or one of the symbolic signal names with the SIG prefix removed. If no signal number is given, the default is SIGTERM (terminate). The PID(s) (multiple PIDs are separated with whitespace) are the IDs of the processes that will be sent the signal. If needed, the **ps** command can be used to obtain current PIDs for the user.

It is possible for the pid value to be less than 1 and/or for the signal value to be 0. In these cases, the **kill** command will carry out the same actions as specified for the **kill** system call described in the following section. As would be expected, the **kill** command is just a command-line interface to the **kill** system call.

3. By other processes:

- By the **kill** system call (Table 4.14). The **kill** system call is used to send a signal to a process or a group of processes.

Notice that the argument sequence for the **kill** system call is the *reverse* of that of the **kill** command. The value specified for the pid argument indicates

Table 4.14 Summary of the **kill** System Call.

Include File(s)	`<sys/types.h>` `<signal.h>`		Manual Section	**2**
Summary	`int kill( pid_t pid, int sig );`			
	Success	Failure	Sets `errno`	
Return	0	−1	Yes	

which process or process group will be sent the signal. Table 4.15 summarizes how to specify a process or process group.

Table 4.15 Interpretation of `pid` values by the `kill` System Call.

pid	Process(es) Receiving the Signal
>0	The process whose process ID is the same as `pid`
0	All the processes in the same process group as the sender
-1	Not superuser: All processes whose real ID is the same as the effective ID of the sender Superuser: All processes excluding special processes
<-1	All the processes whose process group is absolute_value (-pid)

The value for `sig` can be any of the symbolic signal names (or the equivalent integer value) found in the signal header file. If the value of `sig` is set to 0, the **kill** system call will perform an error check of the specified PID, but will not send the process a signal. Sending a signal of 0 to a PID and checking the return value of the **kill** system call is sometimes used as a way of determining if a given PID is present. This technique is not foolproof, as the process may terminate on its own immediately after the call to check on it has been made. Remember that UNIX will reuse PID values once the maximum PID has been assigned. The statement

```
kill(getpid(),sig);
```

can be used by a process to send itself the signal specified by `sig`.[5]

If the **kill** system call is successful, it returns a 0; otherwise, it returns a value of −1 and sets `errno` as indicated in Table 4.16. In Linux, for security reasons, it not possible to send a signal to process one—**init**. Signals are passed to **init** via `telinit`.

Table 4.16 `kill` Error Messages.

#	Constant	perror Message	Explanation
1	EPERM	Operation not permitted	• Calling process does not have permission to send signal to specified process(es). • Process is not superuser and its effective ID does not match real or saved user ID.
3	ESRCH	No such process	No such process or process group as `pid`.
22	EINVAL	Invalid argument	Invalid signal number specified.

[5] ANSI C also defines a `raise` library function that can be used by a process to send itself a signal.

4-6 EXERCISE

The **kill** command also accepts the option **-l** (the letter L in lower-case), which lists the defined signals that **kill** knows about. At the system level, issue the command

```
$ kill -l
```

Find the (a) integer value, (b) default action, and (c) the event signaled for at least two signals that are known by the **kill** command but were not described in the previous signal table (Table 4.13).

4-7 EXERCISE

Write a parent program that **fork**s several child processes that each **sleep** a random number of seconds. The parent process should then **wait** for the child processes to terminate. Once a child process has terminated, the parent process should terminate the remaining children by issuing a SIGTERM signal to each. Be sure to verify (via the **wait** system call) that each child process terminated received the SIGTERM signal.

- By the **alarm** system call (Table 4.17).

The **alarm** system call sets a timer for the issuing process and generates a SIGALRM signal when the specified number of real-time seconds have passed.

Table 4.17 Summary of the **alarm** System Call.

Include File(s)	<unistd.h>		Manual Section	**2**
Summary	`unsigned int alarm(unsigned int seconds);`			
	Success	Failure	Sets `errno`	
Return	Amount of time remaining			

If the value passed to **alarm** is 0, the timer is reset. Processes generated by a **fork** have their alarm values set to 0, while processes created by an **exec** inherit the **alarm** with its remaining time. **alarm** calls cannot be stacked—multiple calls will reset the alarm value. A call to **alarm** returns the amount of time remaining on the alarm clock. A "sleep" type arrangement can be implemented for a process using **alarm**. However, mixing calls to **alarm** and **sleep** is not a good idea.

Program 4.3 demonstrates the use of an **alarm** system call.

Program 4.3 Setting an **alarm**.

```
File : p4.3.cxx
    |      #include <iostream>
    |      #include <iomanip>
    |      #include <cstdlib>
    |      #include <sys/types.h>
    +      #include <sys/wait.h>
    |      #include <unistd.h>
    |      using namespace std;
    |      int
    |      main(int argc, char *argv[] ) {
   10        int w, status;
    |        if ( argc < 4 ) {
    |          cerr << "Usage: " << *argv << " value_1 value_2 value_3 "
    |               << endl;
    |          return 1;
    +        }
    |        for(int i=1; i <= 3; ++i)
    |          if ( fork( ) == 0 ) {
    |            int t = atoi(argv[i]);
    |            cout << "Child " << getpid( ) << " waiting to die in "
   20                  << t << " seconds." << endl;
    |            alarm( t );
    |            pause( );
    |            cout << getpid( ) << " is done." << endl;
    |          }
    +        while (( w=wait(&status)) && w != -1)
    |          cout << "Wait on PID: " << dec << w << " returns status of  "
    |               << setw(4) << setfill(48) << hex
    |               << setiosflags(ios::uppercase) << status << endl;
    |        return 0;
   30      }
```

When the program is invoked, three integer values are passed to the program. The parent process generates three child processes using the command-line values to set the **alarm** in process. In line 22 the **pause** library function is called. This function causes the child process to wait for the receipt of a signal. In the example, this will be the receipt of the SIGALRM signal. When the signal is received, the child process takes the default action for the signal. The default for SIGALRM is for the process to exit and return the value of the signal to its waiting parent. The parent process waits for all of the child processes to finish. As each finishes, the parent displays the child PID and its return status information. It is important to note that the **cout** statement in line 23 is never executed, as the child process exits before reaching this statement. This can be verified by the output shown in Figure 4.7.

Figure 4.7 Setting an **alarm** in multiple child processes.

```
linux$ p4.3  3  1  5
Child 17243 waiting to die in 3 seconds.
Child 17244 waiting to die in 1 seconds.
Child 17245 waiting to die in 5 seconds.
Wait on PID: 17244 returns status of  000E
Wait on PID: 17243 returns status of  000E
Wait on PID: 17245 returns status of  000E
```

The child processes end in the order specified by their alarm times. Each passes back the SIGALRM value (14 an E in hexadecimal).

A call to **pause** suspends a process (causing it to sleep) until it receives a signal that has not been ignored (Table 4.18).

Table 4.18 Summary of the **pause** Library Function.[6]

Include File(s)	<unistd.h>		Manual Section	2
Summary	int pause (void);			
Return		Success	Failure	Sets errno
	If the signal does not cause termination then –1 returned	Does not return	Yes	

pause returns a −1 if the signal received while pausing does not cause process termination. The value in errno will be EINTR (4). If the received signal causes termination, **pause** will not return (which is to be expected!).

---

[6] While in Section 2 of the manual, the manual page indicates this is a library function.

4.5 Signal and Signal Management Calls

In the previous section we noted that a process can handle a signal by doing nothing (thus allowing the default action to occur), ignoring the signal, or catching the signal. Both the ignoring and catching of a signal entail the association of a signal-catching routine with a signal. In brief, when this is done the process automatically invokes the signal-catching routine when the stipulated signal is received. There are two basic system calls that can be used to modify what a process will do when a signal has been received: **signal** and **sigaction**. The **signal** system call has been present in all versions of UNIX and is now categorized as the ANSI C version signal-handling routine (Table 4.19). The **sigaction** system call (Table 4.20) is somewhat more recent and is one of a group of POSIX signal management calls.

Table 4.19 Summary of the **signal** System Call.

Include File(s)	`<signal.h>`		Manual Section	**2**
Summary	`void (*signal(int signum,` `        void (*sighandler)(int)))(int);`			
	Success	Failure	Sets errno	
Return	Signal's previous disposition	SIG_ERR (defined as −1)	Yes	

Table 4.20 Summary of the **sigaction** System Call.

Include File(s)	`<signal.h>`		Manual Section	**2**
Summary	`int sigaction(int signum, const` `                struct sigaction *act,` `                struct sigaction *oldact);`			
	Success	Failure	Sets errno	
Return	0	−1	Yes	

The most difficult part of using **signal** is deciphering its prototype. In essence, the prototype declares **signal** to be a function that accepts two arguments—an integer signum value and a pointer to a function—which are called when the signal is received. If the invocation of **signal** is successful, it returns a pointer to a function that returns nothing (**void**). This is the previous disposition for the signal. The mysterious (**int**), found at the far right of the prototype, indicates the referenced function has an integer argument. This argument is automatically filled by the system and contains the signal number. Either system call fails and returns the value -1, setting the value in errno to EINTR (4), if it is interrupted or to EINVAL (22) if the value given for signum is not valid or is set to SIGKILL or SIGSTOP. Further, **sigaction** returns EFAULT (14) if the act or oldact arguments reference an invalid address space.

While both **signal** and **sigaction** deal with signal handling, the functionality of each is slightly different. Let's begin with the **signal** system call.

The first argument to the **signal** system call is the signal that we intend to associate with a new action. The signal value can be an integer or a symbolic signal name. This value cannot be SIGKILL or SIGSTOP. The second argument to **signal** is the address of the signal-catching function. The signal-catching function can be a user-defined function or one of the defined constants SIG_DFL or SIG_IGN. Specifying SIG_DFL for a signal resets the action to be taken to its default action when the signal is received. Indicating SIG_IGN for a signal means the process will ignore the receipt of the indicated signal.

An examination of the signal header files shows that SIG_DFL and SIG_IGN are defined as integer values that have been appropriately cast to address locations that are invalid (such as -1, etc.). The declaration most commonly found for SIG_DFL and SIG_IGN is shown below. With these definitions is another defined constant that can be used—SIG_ERR. This constant is the value that is returned by **signal** if it fails. See Figure 4.8.

Figure 4.8 Defined constants used by signal and sigset.

```
/* Fake signal functions.   */

#define SIG_ERR ((__sighandler_t) -1)      /* Error return.   */
#define SIG_DFL ((__sighandler_t)  0)      /* Default action.  */
#define SIG_IGN ((__sighandler_t)  1)      /* Ignore signal.   */
```

Program 4.4 uses the **signal** system call to demonstrate how a signal can be ignored.

Program 4.4 Pseudo nohup—ignoring a signal.

```
File : p4.4.cxx
    |       /* Using the signal system call to ignore a hangup signal
    |        */
    |       #include <iostream>
    +       #include <cstdio>
    |       #include <cstdlib>
    |       #include <signal.h>
    |       #include <fcntl.h>
    |       #include <unistd.h>
    |       using namespace std;
   10       const char   *file_out = "nohup.out";
    |       int
    |       main(int argc, char *argv[]){
    |         int         new_stdout;
    |         if (argc < 2) {
    +           cerr << "Usage: " << *argv << " command [arguments]" << endl;
    |           return 1;
    |         }
    |         if (isatty( 1 )) {
    |           cerr <<  "Sending output to " << file_out << endl;
   20           close( 1 );
    |           if ((new_stdout = open(file_out, O_WRONLY | O_CREAT |
    |                             O_APPEND, 0644)) == -1)             {
    |             perror(file_out);
    |             return 2;
    +           }
    |         }
    |         if (signal(SIGHUP, SIG_IGN) == SIG_ERR) {
    |           perror("SIGHUP");
    |           return 3;
   30         }
    |         ++argv;
    |         execvp(*argv, argv);
    |         perror(*argv);                        // Should not get here unless
    |         return 4;                             // the exec call fails.
    +       }
```

Program 4.4 is a *limited* version of the **/usr/bin/nohup** command
found on most UNIX-based systems. The **nohup** command can be used to
run commands so they will be immune to the receipt of SIGHUP signals. If
the standard output for the current process is associated with a terminal, the
output from **nohup** will be sent to the file nohup.out. The **nohup** command is often used with the command-line background specifier & to allow
a command to continue its execution in the background even after the user
has logged out.

Like the real **nohup**, our pseudo **nohup** program (Program 4.4) will execute the command (with optional arguments) that is passed to it on the command line. After checking the number of command-line arguments, the file descriptor associated with stdout is evaluated. The assumption here is that the file descriptor associated with stdout is 1. However, if needed, there is a standard I/O function named **fileno** that can be used to find the integer file descriptor for a given argument stream. The library function **isatty** (Table 4.21) is used to determine if the descriptor is associated with a terminal device.

Table 4.21 Summary of the isatty Library Function.

Include File(s)	<unistd.h>		Manual Section	**3**
Summary	int isatty(int desc);			
	Success	Failure	Sets errno	
Return	1	0		

The **isattty** library function takes a single integer desc argument. If desc is associated with a terminal device, **isatty** returns a 1; otherwise, it returns a 0. In the program, if the **isatty** function returns a 1, an informational message is displayed to standard error to tell the user where the output from the command passed to the pseudo **nohup** program can be found. Next, the file descriptor for stdout is closed. The **open** statement that follows the close returns the first free file descriptor. As we have just closed stdout, the descriptor returned by the **open** will be that of stdout. Once this reassignment has been done, any information written to stdout (cout) by the program will in turn be appended to the file nohup.out. Notice that the call to **signal** to ignore the SIGHUP signal is done within an if statement. Should the **signal** system call fail (return a SIG_ERR), a message would be displayed to standard error and the program would exit. If the **signal** call is successful, the argv pointer is incremented to step past the name of the current program. The remainder of the command line is then passed to the **execvp** system call. Should the **execvp** call fail, **perror** will be invoked and a message displayed. If **execvp** is successful, the current process will be overlaid by the program/command passed from the command line.

The output in Figure 4.9 shows what happens when the pseudo **nohup** program is run on a local system and passed a command that takes a long time to execute. In the example the long-running command is a small Korn shell script called count that counts from 1 to 100, sleeping one second after the display of each value. As written, the output from the script would normally be displayed on the screen.

Figure 4.9 Output of Program 4.4 when passed a command that takes a long time to execute.

```
linux$ cat count
#!  /bin/ksh
c=1
while (( $c <= 100 ))
do
  echo "$c"
  sleep 1
  (( c = c + 1 ))
done

linux$ ./p4.4 ./count &
Sending output to nohup.out
[1] 19481
linux$ jobs
[1]  + Running                p4.4 count
linux$ kill -HUP %1
linux$ jobs
[1]  + Running                p4.4 count
linux$ kill -KILL %1
linux$
[1]     Killed                p4.4 count
linux$ jobs
linux$
```

The script count from 1 to 100, sleeping one second in between the display of each number. If run on the command line, it will take approximately 100 seconds to count from 1 to 100.

Pass the count script to our pseudo nohup program—place it in the background.

The operating system returns the PID of the background process.

Sending a hangup signal to the process does not cause it to terminate.

When the program was placed in the background, the system reported the job number (in this case [1]) and the PID (19481). The **jobs** command confirms that the process is still running. As can be seen, the **kill** -HUP %1 command (which sends a hangup signal to the first job in the background) did not cause the program to terminate. This is not unexpected, as the SIGHUP signal was being ignored. The command **kill** -KILL %1 was used to terminate the process by sending it a SIGKILL signal.

4-8   EXERCISE

If a **find** command (e.g., **find** / -name * -print) is run by Program 4.4, the error messages from **find** (such as it not having permission to read certain directories), which are written to stderr, are still displayed. Modify Program 4.4 so that error messages from the program being run are discarded (written to /dev/null). What are the pros and cons of such a modification?

As noted, if a signal-catching function name is supplied to the **signal** system call, the process will automatically call this function when the process receives the signal. However, prior to calling the function, if the signal is not SIG-KILL, SIGPWR, or SIGTRAP, the system will reset the signal's disposition to its default. This means that if two of the same signals are received successively, it is entirely possible that before the signal-catching routine is executed, the second signal may cause the process to terminate (if that is the default action for the signal). This behavior reduces the reliability of using signals as a communication device. It is possible to reduce, but not entirely eliminate, this window of opportunity for failure by resetting the disposition for the signal in the catching routine. Program 4.5 catches signals and attempts to reduce this window of opportunity.

Program 4.5 Catching SIGINT and SIGQUIT signals.

```
File : p4.5.cxx
    |      /* Catching a signal
    |       */
    |      #include <iostream>
    +      #include <cstdlib>
    |      #include <cstdio>
    |      #include <signal.h>
    |      #include <unistd.h>
    |      using namespace std;
    |      int
   10      main( ) {
    |        void            signal_catcher(int);
    |        if (signal(SIGINT , signal_catcher) == SIG_ERR) {
    |          perror("SIGINT");
    |          return 1;
    +        }
    |        if (signal(SIGQUIT , signal_catcher) == SIG_ERR) {
    |          perror("SIGQUIT");
    |          return 2;
    |        }
   20        for (int i=0;  ; ++i) {                 // Forever ...
    |          cout << i << endl;                    // display a number
    |          sleep(1);
    |        }
    |        return 0;
    +      }
    |      void
    |      signal_catcher(int the_sig){
    |        signal(the_sig, signal_catcher);        // reset immediately
    |        cout << endl << "Signal " << the_sig << " received." << endl;
```

```
30        if (the_sig == SIGQUIT)
 |            exit(3);
 |        }
```

In an attempt to avoid taking the default action (which in this case is to terminate) for either of the two caught signals, the first statement (line 28) in the program function `signal_catcher` is a call to **signal**. This call reestablishes the association between the signal being caught and the signal-catching routine.

Figure 4.10 shows the output of the program when run on a local system.

Figure 4.10 Output of Program 4.5.

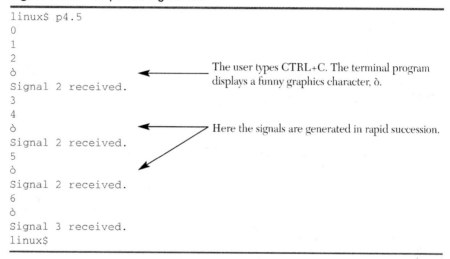

```
linux$ p4.5
0
1
2
ò                                      The user types CTRL+C. The terminal program
Signal 2 received.                     displays a funny graphics character, ò.
3
4
ò                                      Here the signals are generated in rapid succession.
Signal 2 received.
5
ò
Signal 2 received.
6
ò
Signal 3 received.
linux$
```

From this output we can see that each time CTRL+C was pressed, it was echoed back to the terminal as ò. If CTRL+C was struck twice in quick succession, the program responded with the `Signal 2 received` message for each keyboard sequence. On this system it appears as if some of the signals were queued if they were received in rapid succession. However, this is somewhat misleading, as the mechanics of terminal I/O come into play. Say we were (via a background process) to deliver to the process, in very rapid succession, multiple copies of the same signal. In this setting we would find most often that only one copy of the signal would be delivered to the process, while the others are discarded. Most systems do not queue the signals 1 through 31. When a SIGQUIT signal was generated, a message was displayed and the program exited.

4-9 EXERCISE

Lad wrote the program below in an attempt to determine what keystrokes generate a signal that can be caught.

```
File : lad.cxx
    |       /* Lad's signal catching program
    |        */
    |       #include <iostream>
    +       #include <cstdlib>
    |       #include <cstdio>
    |       #include <signal.h>
    |       #include <unistd.h>
    |       using namespace std;
    |       int
   10       main( ) {
    |         void  signal_catcher(int);
    |         char  a_num[5];
    |         for (int i=1; i < _NSIG; ++i)
    |           switch( i ){
    +           case SIGKILL: case SIGSTOP:
    |             break;
    |           default:
    |             if (signal(i , signal_catcher) == SIG_ERR) {
    |               sprintf( a_num, "%d", i );
   20               perror(a_num);
    |               return 1;
    |             }
    |           }
    |         for (int i=0;  ; ++i) {              // Forever ...
    +           cout << i << endl;                 // display a number
    |           sleep(1);
    |         }
    |         return 0;
    |       }
   30       void
    |       signal_catcher(int the_sig){
    |         signal(the_sig, signal_catcher);     // reset
    |         cout << endl << "Signal " << the_sig << " received." << endl;
    |         if (the_sig == SIGQUIT)
    +           exit(3);
    |       }
```

The constant _NSIG is the upper bound for signal numbers. On some systems, this constant does not have the leading underscore.

Catch all signals that can be caught—map each to the signal-catching function.

When running his program, how many signals did Lad find he could generate from the keyboard? What are they? Describe what happens (and why) when the following keystrokes are entered? CTRL+S, CTRL+Q, and CTRL+R.

4-10 EXERCISE

Remove the statement

```
if (the_sig == SIGQUIT)
    exit(3);
```

from Program 4.5. Recompile the program and run it in the background (i.e., p4.5 &). How did you stop the program from displaying numbers on the screen?

4-11 EXERCISE

Write a program that **fork**s a child process. The parent and child processes should generate and send random signals to each other. In each process, display the signal being sent and the signal that is caught. Be sure both processes **exit** gracefully and that neither remains active if the other has terminated due to the receipt of a SIGKILL signal. *Hint*: Remember that you can, with **kill**, determine if a process is present.

The **sigaction** system call, like the **signal** system call, can be used to associate an alternate action with the receipt of a signal. This system call has three arguments. The first is an integer value that specifies the signal. As with the **signal** system call, this argument can be any valid signal except SIGKILL or SIGSTOP. The second and third arguments are references to a sigaction structure. Respectively these structures store the new and previous action for the signal. The full definition of the sigaction structure is found in the file sigaction.h. This file is automatically included by signal.h. Basically, the sigaction structure is

```
struct sigaction {
    void (*sa_handler)(int);                      // 1
    void (*sa_sigaction)(int, siginfo_t *, void *); // 2
    sigset_t sa_mask;                             // 3
    int sa_flags;                                // 4
    void (*sa_restorer)(void);                    // 5
}
```

Both sa_handler and sa_sigaction can be used to reference a signal handling function. Only one of these should be specified at any given time, as

155

on most systems this data is often stored in a union within the sigaction structure. By definition, a union can hold only one of its members at a time. Our discussion centers on using the sa_handler member. The sa_mask member specifies the signals, which should be blocked when the signal handler is executing. Each signal is represented by a bit. If the bit in the mask is on, the signal is blocked. By default the signal that triggered the handler is blocked. The sa_flags member is used to set flags that modify the behavior of the signal-handling process. Flag constants, shown in Table 4.22, can be combined using a bitwise OR.

Table 4.22 sa_flags Constants.

Flag	Action
SA_NOCLDSTOP	If the signal is SIGCHILD, then the calling process will not receive a SIGCHILD signal when its child processes exit.
SA_ONESHOT or SA_RESETHAND	Restore the default action after the signal handler has been called once (similar to the default of the **signal** call).
SA_RESTART	Use BSD signal semantics (certain interrupted system calls are restarted after the signal has been caught).
SA_NOMASK or SA_NODEFER	Undo the default whereby the signal triggering the handler is automatically blocked.
SA_SIGINFO	The signal handler has three arguments—use sa_sigaction, not sa_handler.

The remaining structure member, sa_restorer, is obsolete and should not be used.

Unlike **signal**, a **sigaction** installed signal-catching routine remains installed even after it has been invoked. Program 4.6, which is similar to Program 4.5, shows the use of the **sigaction** system call.

Again, notice that in the program function signal_catcher, it is no longer necessary to reset the association for the signal caught to the signal-catching routine.

Program 4.6 Using the sigaction system call.

```
File : p4.6.cxx
   |       /* Catching a signal using sigaction
   |        */
   |       #define_GNU_SOURCE
   +       #include <iostream>
   |       #include <cstdlib>
   |       #include <cstdio>
```

```
 |      #include <signal.h>
 |      #include <unistd.h>
 |      using namespace std;
10      int
 |      main( ) {
 |        void   signal_catcher(int);
 |        struct sigaction new_action;
 |        new_action.sa_handler = signal_catcher;
 +        new_action.sa_flags   = 0;
 |
 |        if (sigaction(SIGINT,  &new_action, NULL) == -1) {
 |          perror("SIGINT");
 |          return 1;
20        }
 |        if (sigaction(SIGQUIT, &new_action, NULL) == -1) {
 |          perror("SIGQUIT");
 |          return 2;
 |        }
 +        for (int i=0;  ; ++i) {           // Forever ...
 |          cout << i << endl;             // display a number
 |          sleep(1);
 |        }
 |        return 0;
30      }
 |      void
 |      signal_catcher(int the_sig){
 |        cout << endl << "Signal " << the_sig << " received." << endl;
 |        if (the_sig == SIGQUIT)
 +          exit(3);
 |      }
```

A sigaction structure is allocated.

The signal catching function is assigned and the sa_flags member set to 0.

A new action is associated with each signal.

Three other POSIX signal-related system calls that can be used for signal management are shown in Table 4.23.

Table 4.23 Summary of the `sigprocmask, sigpending,` and `sigsuspend` System Call.

Include File(s)	<unistd.h>		Manual Section	2

Summary	`int sigprocmask (int how, const sigset_t *set,`
	`                 sigset_t *oldset);`
	`int sigpending(sigset_t *set);`
	`int sigsuspend(const sigset_t *mask);;`			

	Success		Failure	Sets errno
Return	0		−1	Yes

Each function returns a 0 if it is successful; otherwise, it returns a −1 and sets the value in errno (Table 4.24).

Table 4.24 sigprocmask, sigpending, and sigsuspend Error Messages.

#	Constant	perror Message	Explanation
4	EINTR	Interrupted system call	A signal was caught during the system call.
14	EFAULT	Bad address	set or oldset references an invalid address space.

The process's signal mask can be manipulated with the **sigprocmask** system call. The first argument, how, indicates how the list of signals (referenced by the second argument, set) should be treated. The action that **sigprocmask** will take, based on the value of how, is summarized in Table 4.25.

Table 4.25 Defined how Constants.

Signal	Action
SIG_BLOCK	Block the signals specified by the union of the current set of signals with those specified by the set argument.
SIG_UNBLOCK	Unblock the signals specified by the set argument.
SIG_SETMASK	Block just those signals specified by the set argument.

If the third argument, oldset, is non-null, the previous value of the signal mask is stored in the location referenced by oldset.

The use of the **sigprocmask** system call is shown in Program 4.7.

Program 4.7 Using sigprocmask.

```
File : p4.7.cxx
    |    /* Demonstration of the sigprocmask call */
    |    #define_GNU_SOURCE
    |    #include <iostream>
    |    #include <cstdio>
    +    #include <signal.h>
    |    #include <unistd.h>
    |    using namespace std;
    |    sigset_t new_signals;
```

```
   |     int
  10     main( ) {
   |        void    signal_catcher(int);              ◄————— Empty (clear) the set of signals.
   |        struct  sigaction new_action;
   |                                                   ◄—————Add the SIGUSR1 signal to
   |        sigemptyset(&new_signals);                        this set.
   +        sigaddset(&new_signals,SIGUSR1);
   |
   |        sigprocmask(SIG_BLOCK, &new_signals, NULL);
   |        new_action.sa_handler = signal_catcher;
   |        new_action.sa_flags   = 0;
  20        if (sigaction(SIGUSR2, &new_action, NULL) == -1) {
   |          perror("SIGUSR2");
   |          return 1;
   |        }
   |        cout << "Waiting for signal" << endl;
   +        pause( );
   |        cout << "Done" << endl;
   |        return 0;
   |     }
   |     void
  30     signal_catcher( int n ) {
   |        cout << "Received signal " << n << " will release SIGUSR1" << endl;
   |        sigprocmask(SIG_UNBLOCK, &new_signals, NULL);
   |        cout << "SIGUSR1 released!" << endl;
   |     }
```

The example makes use of the SIGUSR1 and SIGUSR2 signals. These are two user-defined signals whose default action is termination of the process. In lines 14 and 15 of the example are two signal-mask manipulation library functions (**sigemptyset** and **sigaddset**) that are used to clear and then add a signal to the new signal mask. A signal mask is essentially a string of bits—each set bit represents a signal. The signal-mask manipulation library functions are covered in detail in Chapter 11, "Threads." In Program 4.7, the **sigprocmask** system call in line 17 *holds* (blocks) incoming SIGUSR1 signals. The **sigaction** system call (line 20) is used to associate the receipt of SIGUSR2 with the signal-catching routine. Following this, an informational message is displayed, and a call to **pause** is made. In the program function signal_catcher, the **sigprocmask** system call is used to release the pending SIGUSR1 signal. Notice that a **cout** statement was placed *before* and *after* the **sigprocmask** call. A sample of this program run locally is shown in Figure 4.11.

When run, the program is placed in background so the user can continue to issue commands from the keyboard. The system displays the job number for the process and the PID. The program begins by displaying the Waiting for signal message. The user, via the **kill** command, sends the process a SIGUSR1 signal. This signal, while received by the process, is not acted upon,

---

Figure 4.11 Output of Program 4.7.

```
linux$ ./p4.7 &
Waiting for signal
[1] 21895
linux$ kill -USR1 21895
linux$ kill -USR2 21895
Received signal 12 will release SIGUSR1
linux$
[1]    User signal 1              ./p4.7
```

SIGUSR1 would normally cause the process to exit—but it has been blocked.

SIGUSR2 has been mapped to the signal-catching routine. In this routine, SIGUSR1 is unblocked; consequently, the process exits without executing the second cout statement in the signal catcher.

---

as the process has been directed to block this signal. When the SIGUSR2 signal is sent to the process, the process catches the signal, and the program function **signal_catcher** is called. The initial **cout** statement in the signal-catching routine is executed, and its message about receiving signals is displayed. The following **sigprocmask** call then unblocks the pending SIGUSR1 signal that was issued earlier. As the default action for SIGUSR1 is termination, the process terminates and the system produces the trailing information indicating the process was terminated via user signal 1. As the process terminates abnormally, the second **cout** statement in the signal-catching routine and the **cout** in the main of the program are not executed.

The **sigsuspend** system call is used to pause (suspend) a process. It replaces the current signal mask with the one passed as an argument. The process suspends until a signal is delivered whose action is to execute a signal-catching function or terminate the process. Program 4.8 demonstrates the use of the **sigsuspend** system call.

Program 4.8 Using `sigsuspend`.

```
File : p4.8.cxx
    |       /* Pausing with sigsuspend */
    |       #define_GNU_SOURCE
    |       #include <iostream>
    |       #include <cstdio>
    +       #include <signal.h>
    |       #include <unistd.h>
    |       using namespace std;
    |       int
    |       main( ){
   10       void      signal_catcher(int);
    |       struct    sigaction new_action;
    |       sigset_t  no_sigs, blocked_sigs, all_sigs;
```

```
|      sigfillset ( &all_sigs    );       // turn all bits on
+      sigemptyset( &no_sigs     );       // turn all bits off
|      sigemptyset( &blocked_sigs );
|                                          // Associate with catcher
|      new_action.sa_handler = signal_catcher;
|      new_action.sa_mask    = all_sigs;
20     new_action.sa_flags   = 0;
|      if (sigaction(SIGUSR1, &new_action, NULL) == -1) {
|        perror("SIGUSR1");
|        return 1;
|      }
+      sigaddset( &blocked_sigs, SIGUSR1 );
|      sigprocmask( SIG_SETMASK, &blocked_sigs, NULL);
|      while ( 1 ) {
|        cout << "Waiting for SIGUSR1 signal" << endl;
|        sigsuspend( &no_sigs );          // Wait
30     }
|      cout << "Done." << endl;
|      return 0;
|    }
|    void
+    signal_catcher(int n){
|      cout << "Beginning important stuff" << endl;
|      sleep(10);                          // Simulate work ....
|      cout << "Ending important stuff" << endl;
|    }
```

In main, the signal-catching function is established. Lines 14 to 16 create three signal masks. The **sigfillset** call turns all bits on, while the **sigemptyset** turns all bits off. The filled set (all bits on, denoting all signals) becomes the signal mask for the signal-catching routine. Thus specified, this directs the signal-catching routine to block all signals. In line 21 the receipt of signal SIGUSR1 is associated with the signal-catching function signal_catcher. In lines 25 and 26 the process is directed to block any SIGUSR1 signals. While at first glance this might seem superfluous, as receipt of this signal has been mapped to signal_catcher, it allows duplicate SIGUSR1 signals to be pending rather than discarded. Then, in an endless loop, the program pauses when the **sigsuspend** statement is reached, waiting for the receipt of the SIGUSR1 signal. Once the SIGUSR1 signal is received (caught), the signal-catching function is executed. While in the signal-catching function, all signals that can be blocked are held. A set of messages indicating the beginning and end of an *important* section of code are displayed. When the signal-catching routine is exited, any blocked signals are released. In summary, the program defers the execution of an interrupt-protected section of code until it receives a SIGUSR1 signal. A run of the program produces the output shown in Figure 4.12.

Figure 4.12 Output of Program 4.8.

```
linux$ p4.8 &
Waiting for SIGUSR1 signal
[1] 6277
linux$ kill -USR1 %1
Beginning important stuff
linux$ kill -INT %1
linux$ jobs
[1]  + Running                          p4.8
linux$ Ending important stuff
[1]    Interrupt                        p4.8
```

The process was first sent a SIGUSR1 signal that caused it to begin the program function `signal_catcher`. While it was in the `signal_catcher` function, an interrupt signal was sent to the process. This signal did not cause the process to immediately terminate, as the process had indicated that all signals were to be blocked (held). The **jobs** command confirms that the process is still active after the interrupt command was sent. However, once the blocked signals are released (when the signal-catching routine is exited), the pending SIGINT signal is acted upon and the process terminates.

4-12 EXERCISE

Examine Figure 4.12 carefully. Run program p4.8 and place it in the background. Experiment with issuing multiple `kill -USR1 %1` commands before you issue the `kill -INT %1` command (note, you may need to increase the sleep time from 10 to something more if you type slowly and want to issue the signals when the process is in the signal-catching routine). Does the system process all the blocked SIGUSR1 signals before it responds to the SIGINT signal. Why or why not?

Write a program that generates a parent and child process that solves the producer/consumer problem presented in Exercise 4-3. Make the parent process the producer and the child process the consumer. In place of a lock file, use signals to coordinate the activities of the processes. One approach would be to use SIGUSR1 to indicate the resource is available to be accessed and use signal SIGUSR2 to indicate a new value is available. Do signals provide a reliable way of solving the problem? What problems are inherent in their use?

4.6 Summary

As we have seen, lock files, the locking of files and signals, can be used as a basic means of communication between processes. Lock files require the participating processes to agree upon file names and locations. The creation of a lock file carries with it a certain amount of system overhead characteristic of all file manipulations. In addition, the problems associated with the removal of "leftover" invalid lock files and the implementation of nonsystem-intensive polling techniques must be addressed. On the positive side, lock file techniques can be used in any UNIX environment that supports the **creat** system call, and cooperating processes do not need to be related.

UNIX has predefined routines that can be used to lock a file. We can use the presence of a lock on a file to indicate that a resource is unavailable. Advisory locking is less system-intensive than mandatory locking and is thus more common. As with lock files, the participating processes using advisory locking must cooperate to effectively communicate.

Signals provide us with another basic communication technique. While signals do not carry any information content, they can be, as we have seen, used to communicate from one process to another. From a system implementation standpoint, signals are more efficient than using lock files. However, participating processes must have access to each other's PIDs (in most cases the processes will be parent/child pairs). In most environments, the number of user-designated signals is limited. Cooperating processes must agree upon the "meaning" of each signal. When a signal is sent from one process to another, unless the receiving process acknowledges the receipt of the signal, there is no way for the sending process to know if its initial signal was received. Signal manipulation can be tricky, and its implementation from one version of UNIX to another may vary (this is one of the last areas of UNIX to be standardized). All of these techniques are easy to understand and to implement but are often difficult to implement well. However, all approaches have a number of limitations that remove them from serious consideration when reliable communication between processes is needed.

4.7 Key Terms and Concepts

aborting a process
advisory locking
alarm system call
asynchronous
atomic
consumer process
core image
creat system call
fcntl system call
file locking
flock structure
ignoring a signal
interrupt
isatty library function
kill command
kill system call
link system call
lock file
lockf library call
mandatory locking
nohup command

pause library function
polling
producer process
race condition
raise library function
real-time signals
shlock command
sigaction structure
sigaction system call
signal blocking
signal catcher
signal delivery
signal generation
signal system call
signals
sigpending system call
sigprocmask system call
sigsuspend system call
sleep library function
stopping a process
unlink system call

Chapter 5

PIPES

READ   WRITE

We have discussed . . .   the previous chapter . . .

5.1 Introduction

We have discussed the nature and generation of processes. In the previous chapter we addressed primitive techniques for communicating between two or more processes. These techniques were limited in scope and suffered from a lack of reliable synchronization. Beginning with this chapter, we explore interprocess communication techniques using system-designed interprocess facilities. We start with **pipes**, which provide processes with a simple, synchronized way of passing information. By the early 1970s pipes became a standard part of UNIX.

We can think of the pipe as a special file that can store a limited amount of data in a first in, first out (FIFO) manner. On most systems, pipes are limited to a specific size. In Linux, the defined constant PIPE_SIZE (which is usually equivalent to the PAGE_SIZE for the system) establishes the total number of bytes allocated for a pipe. The defined constant PIPE_BUF (found in <linux/limits.h>, which is included by <limits.h>) sets the block size for an atomic write to a pipe. On our system the value for PIPE_BUF is 4096. Generally, one process writes to the pipe (as if it were a file), while another process reads from the pipe.

As shown in Figure 5.1, conceptually we can envision the pipe as a conveyor belt composed of data blocks that are continuously filled at (written to) the "write end" and emptied (read) from the "read end." The system keeps track of the current location of the last read/write location. Data is written to one end of the pipe and read from the other. From an implementation standpoint, an actual file pointer (as associated with a regular file) is not defined for a pipe, and as such no seeking is supported.

Figure 5.1 Conceptual data access using a pipe.

The operating system provides the synchronization between the writing and reading processes. By default, if a writing process attempts to **write** to a full pipe, the system automatically blocks the process until the pipe is able to receive the data. Likewise, if a **read** is attempted on an empty pipe, the process blocks until data is available. In addition, the process blocks if a specified pipe has been opened for reading, but another process has not opened the pipe for writing.

In a program, data is written to the pipe using the unbuffered I/O **write** system call (Table 5.1).

Table 5.1 Summary of the **write** System Call.

Include File(s)	<unistd.h>		Manual Section	**2**
Summary	`ssize_t write(int fd, const void *buf, size_t count);`			
	Success	Failure	Sets errno	
Return	Number of bytes written	−1	Yes	

Using the file descriptor specified by fd, the **write** system call attempts to write count bytes from the buffer referenced by buf. If the **write** system call is successful, the number of bytes actually written is returned. Otherwise,

Table 5.2 `write` Error Messages.

#	Constant	`perror` **Message**	**Explanation**
4	EINTR	Interrupted system call	Signal was caught during the system call.
5	EIO	I/O error	Low-level I/O error while attempting **read** from or **write** to file system.
6	ENXIO	No such device or address	O_NONBLOCK ∣ O_WRONLY is set, the named file is a FIFO, and no process has the file open for reading.
9	EBADF	Bad file descriptor	fd is an invalid file descriptor or is not open for writing.
11	EAGAIN	Resource temporarily unavailable	• O_NDELAY or O_NONBLOCK is set and the file is currently locked by another process. • System memory for raw I/O is temporarily insufficient. • Attempted a **write** to pipe of count bytes, but less than count bytes is available.
14	EFAULT	Bad address	buf references an illegal address.
22	EINVAL	Invalid argument	fd associated with an object unsuitable for writing.
27	EFBIG	File too large	Attempt to **write** to a file that exceeds the current system limits.
28	ENOSPC	No space left on device	Device with file has run out of room.
32	EPIPE	Broken pipe	• Attempt to write to a pipe that is not opened for reading on one end (in this case a SIGPIPE signal also generated). • Attempt to write to a FIFO that is not opened for reading on one end. • Attempt to **write** to a pipe with only one end open.
34	ERANGE	Numerical result out of range	count value is less than 0 or greater than system limit.
35	EDEADLK	Resource deadlock avoided	The **write** system call would have gone to sleep generating a deadlock situation.
37	ENOLCK	No locks available	• Locking enabled, but region was previously locked. • System lock table is full.
63	ENOSR	Out of streams resources	Attempt to **write** to a stream, but insufficient stream memory is available.
67	ENOLINK	The link has been severed	The buf value references a remote system that is no longer active.

a –1 is returned and the global variable errno is set to indicate the nature of the error. As shown in Table 5.2, the number of ways in which **write** can fail is impressive indeed!

writes to a pipe are similar to those for a file except that

- Each file **write** request is always *appended* to the end of the pipe.
- **write** requests of PIPE_BUF size or less are guaranteed to not be interleaved with other **write** requests to the same pipe.[1]
- When the O_NONBLOCK and O_NDELAY flags are clear, a **write** request may cause the process to block. The defined constants O_NONBLOCK and O_NDELAY are included by the header file <sys/fcntl.h> and can be set with the **fcntl** system call. By default, these values are considered to be cleared, thus **write** blocks if the device is busy and **write**s are delayed (written to an internal buffer, which is written out to disk by the kernel at a later time). Once the **write** has completed, it returns the number of bytes successfully written.
- When the O_NONBLOCK or O_NDELAY flags are set and the request to **write** PIPE_BUF bytes or less is not successful, the value returned by the **write** system call can be summarized as

O_NONBLOCK	O_NDELAY	Value Returned
set	clear	–1
clear	set	0

If both O_NONBLOCK and O_NDELAY flags are set, **write** will not block the process.

- If a **write** is made to a pipe that is not open for reading by any process, a SIGPIPE signal is generated and the value in errno is set to EPIPE (broken pipe). The default action (if not caught) for the SIGPIPE signal is termination.

Data is read from the pipe using the unbuffered I/O **read** system call summarized in Table 5.3.

[1] While **write** may still work if the number of bytes is greater than PIPE_BUF, it is best to stay within this limitation to guarantee the integrity of data.

Table 5.3 Summary of the read System Call.

Include File(s)	<unistd.h>		Manual Section	**2**
Summary	`ssize_t read(int fd, void *buf,` `                size_t count);`			
Return		Success	Failure	Sets errno
	Number of bytes read		−1	Yes

The **read** system call reads count bytes from the open file associated with the file descriptor fd into the buffer referenced by buf. If the **read** call is successful, the number of bytes actually read is returned. If the number of bytes left in the pipe is less than count, the value returned by **read** will reflect this. When at the end of the file, a value of 0 is returned. If the **read** system call fails, a −1 is returned and the global variable errno is set. The values that errno may take when **read** fails are shown in Table 5.4.

Table 5.4 read Error Messages.

#	Constant	perror **Message**	**Explanation**
4	EINTR	Interrupted system call	Signal was caught during the system call.
5	EIO	I/O error	Background process cannot **read** from its controlling terminal.
6	ENXIO	No such device or address	File descriptor reference is invalid.
9	EBADF	Bad file descriptor	fd is an invalid file or is not open for reading.
11	EAGAIN	Resource temporarily unavailable	• O_NDELAY or O_NONBLOCK is set, and the file is currently locked by another process. • System memory for raw I/O is temporarily insufficient. • O_NDELAY or O_NONBLOCK is set, but there is no data waiting to be **read**.
14	EFAULT	Bad address	buf references an illegal address.
22	EINVAL	Invalid argument	fd associated with an unsuitable object for reading.

Continued

169

Table 5.4 *(Continued)*

#	Constant	`perror` **Message**	Explanation
35	EDEADLK	Resource deadlock avoided	The **read** system call would have gone to sleep generating a deadlock situation.
37	ENOLCK	No locks available	• Locking enabled, but region was previously locked. • System lock table is full.
67	ENOLINK	Link has been severed	The `buf` value references a remote system that is no longer active.
74	EBADMSG	Not a data message	Message to be **read** is not a data message.

In other aspects, **read**s performed on a pipe are similar to those on a file except that

- All **reads** are initiated from the current position (i.e., no seeking is supported).
- If both O_NONBLOCK and O_NDELAY flags are clear, then a **read** system call blocks (by default) until data is written to the pipe or the pipe is closed.
- If the pipe is **open** for writing by another process, but the pipe is empty, then a **read** (in combination with the flags O_NDELAY and O_NONBLOCK) will return the values

O_NONBLOCK	O_NDELAY	Value Returned
set	clear	−1
clear	set	0

- If the pipe is not opened for writing by another process, **read** returns a 0 (indicating the end-of-file condition). Note, this is the same value that is returned when the O_NDELAY flag has been set, and the pipe is open but empty.

Pipes can be divided into two categories: **unnamed** pipes and **named** pipes. Unnamed pipes can be used only with related processes (e.g., parent/child or child/child) and exist only for as long as the processes using them exist. Named pipes actually exist as directory entries. As such, they have file access permissions and can be used with unrelated processes.

5.2 Unnamed Pipes

An unnamed pipe is constructed with the **pipe** system call (see Table 5.5).

Table 5.5   Summary of the **pipe** System Call.

Include File(s)	`<unistd.h>`		Manual Section	**2**
Summary	`int pipe(int filedes[2]);`			
Return	Success	Failure	Sets `errno`	
	0	–1	Yes	

If successful, the **pipe** system call returns a pair of integer file descriptors, `filedes[0]` and `filedes[1]`. The file descriptors reference two data streams. Historically, pipes were unidirectional, and data flowed in one direction only. If two-way communication was needed, two pipes were opened: one for reading and another for writing. This is still true in Linux today. However, in some versions of UNIX (such as Solaris) the file descriptors returned by **pipe** are full duplex (bidirectional) and are both opened for reading/writing.

In a full duplex setting, if the process writes to `filedes[0]`, then `filedes[1]` is used for reading; otherwise, the process writes to `filedes[1]`, and `filedes[0]` is used for reading. In a half duplex setting (such as in Linux) `filedes[1]` is *always* used for writing, and `filedes[0]` is *always* used for reading—an attempt to **write** to `fildes[0]` or **read** from `filedes[1]` will produce an error (i.e., bad file descriptor).

If the **pipe** system call fails, it returns a –1 and sets `errno` (Table 5.6).

Table 5.6   pipe Error Messages.

#	Constant	perror **Message**	**Explanation**
23	ENFILE	File table overflow	System file table is full.
24	EMFILE	Too many open files	Process has exceeded the limit for number of open files.
14	EFAULT	Bad address	`filedes` is invalid.

As previously noted, data in a pipe is read on a FIFO basis. Program 5.1 shows a pair of processes (parent/child) that use a pipe to send the first

argument passed on the command line to the parent as a *message* to the child.
Notice that the pipe is established prior to forking the child process.

Program 5.1 Parent/child processes communicating via a pipe.

```
File : p5.1.cxx
 |      /* Using a pipe to send data from a parent to a child process
 |       */
 |      #include <iostream>
 |      #include <cstdio>
 +      #include <unistd.h>
 |      #include <string.h>
 |      using namespace std;
 |      int
 |      main(int argc, char *argv[ ]) {
10         int           f_des[2];
 |         static char   message[BUFSIZ];
 |         if (argc != 2) {
 |           cerr << "Usage: " << *argv << " message\n";
 |           return 1;
 +         }
 |         if (pipe(f_des) == -1) {              // generate the pipe
 |           perror("Pipe");      return 2;
 |         }
 |         switch (fork( )) {
20         case -1:
 |           perror("Fork");      return 3;
 |         case 0:                               // In the child
 |           close(f_des[1]);
 |           if (read(f_des[0], message, BUFSIZ) != -1) {
 +             cout << "Message received by child: [" << message
 |                  << "]" << endl;
 |             cout.flush();
 |           } else {
 |             perror("Read");      return 4;
30         }
 |           break;
 |         default:                              // In the Parent
 |           close(f_des[0]);
 |           if (write(f_des[1], argv[1], strlen(argv[1])) != -1) {
 +             cout << "Message sent by parent    : [" <<
 |                  argv[1] << "]" << endl;
 |             cout.flush();
 |           } else {
 |             perror("Write");    return 5;
40         }
 |         }
 |         return 0;
 |      }
```

In the parent process the "read" pipe file descriptor f_des[0] is closed, and the message (the string referenced by argv[1]) is written to the pipe file descriptor f_des[1]. In the child process the "write" pipe file descriptor f_des[1] is closed, and pipe file descriptor f_des[0] is **read** to obtain the message. While the closing of the unused pipe file descriptors is not required, it is a good practice. Remember that for **read** to be successful, the number of bytes of data requested must be present in the pipe or all the **write** file descriptors for the pipe must be closed so that an end-of-file can be returned. The pipe file descriptors f_des[0] in the child and f_des[1] in the parent will be closed when each process exits. The output of Program 5.1 is shown in Figure 5.2.

Figure 5.2 Output of Program 5.1.

```
linux$ p5.1 Once_upon_a_starry_night
Message sent by parent    : [Once_upon_a_starry_night]
Message received by child: [Once_upon_a_starry_night]
```

5-1 EXERCISE

Modify Program 5.1 so the child, upon receipt of the message, changes its case and returns the message (via a pipe) to the parent, where it is then displayed. On a system that does not support duplex pipes, you will need to generate two pipes prior to forking the child process.

At a command-line level, a pipe is specified by the | symbol. As shown in Figure 5.3, pipes are used to tie the standard output of one command to the standard input of another to create a command pipeline.

Figure 5.3 Using pipes on the command line.

For example, the command line sequence

```
linux$ ps -ef  | grep $USER | cat -n
```

will execute the **ps** -ef command (which displays, in full form, the process status of all users) and pipe its output to the **grep** $USER command. The **grep** command prints those lines that contain the contents of the variable $USER—that is, the user's login. A second pipe passes the output of the **grep** command to the **cat**, which (with option –n) displays its output as a numbered list. The redirection of the output of the **ps** command to be the input to the **grep** command and the output of the **grep** command to be the input of the **cat** command is accomplished with the inclusion of the command-line specification of a pipe. To achieve a similar arrangement with our parent/child pair, we need a way to associate standard input and standard output with the pipe we have created. This can be done either by using the **dup** or the **dup2** system call (Tables 5.7 and 5.8).

The **dup2** call supersedes the **dup** system call, but both bear discussion. The **dup** system call duplicates an original open file descriptor. The *new* descriptor references the system file table entry for the next available

Table 5.7 Summary of the dup System Call.

Include File(s)	<unistd.h>		Manual Section	**2**
Summary	int dup(int oldfd);			
	Success	Failure	Sets errno	
Return	Next available nonnegative file descriptor	–1	Yes	

Table 5.8 Summary of the dup2 System Call.

Include File(s)	<unistd.h>		Manual Section	**2**
Summary	int dup2(int oldfd, int newfd);			
	Success	Failure	Sets errno	
Return	newfd as a file descriptor for oldfd	–1	Yes	

nonnegative file descriptor. The new descriptor will share the same file pointer (offset), have the same access mode as the original, and share locks. Both will remain open across an **exec** call, but they do not, however, share the close-on-exec flag. An important point to consider is that when called, **dup** will *always* return the next lowest available file descriptor.

A code sequence of

```
int f_des[2];
pipe(f_des);
close( fileno(stdout) );   // close standard output
dup(f_des[1]);             // duplicate 1st free descriptor
                           //    as write end of pipe
.
.
.
```

declares and generates a pipe. The file descriptor for standard output (say, file descriptor 1) is closed. The following **dup** system call returns the next lowest available file descriptor, which in this case should be the previously closed standard output file descriptor (i.e., 1). Thus, any data written to standard output in following statements would now be written to the pipe. Notice that there are two steps in this sequence: closing the descriptor and then **dup**-ing it. There is an outside chance that the sequence will be interrupted and the descriptor returned by **dup** will not be the one that was just closed. This could happen if a signal was caught and the signal-catching routine closed a file.

Enter the **dup2** system call. The **dup2** system call closes and duplicates the file descriptor as a single *atomic* action. When calling **dup2**, there is no time at which newfd is closed and oldfd has not yet been duplicated. If the file referenced by newfd is already open, it will be closed before the duplication is performed. For those more stout of heart, both the **dup** and **dup2** calls can be implemented with the **fcntl** system call (when passed the proper flag values).

A short program that mimics the last | sort command-line sequence is shown in Program 5.2. The files/pipes for the two processes, once Program 5.2 successfully executes the **fork** system call in line 17, are shown in Figure 5.4.

	parent	child	
0	stdin	stdin	0
1	stdout	stdout	1
2	stderr	stderr	2
3	f_des[0]	f_des[0]	3
4	f_des[1]	f_des[1]	4
5	. . .	. . .	5
6			6

Figure 5.4 Initial entries for files/pipes.

175

Assuming a fairly standard setting (i.e., stdin = 0, stdout = 1, stderr = 2) with both stdout and stderr mapped to the same device (most likely the terminal), initially both the parent and child processes reference the same entries in the system file table. After the child process is generated, we use the **dup2** call to close standard output and duplicate it. The system returns the previous reference for standard output, which is now associated with the file table entry for f_des[1]. Once this association has been made, the file descriptors f_des[0] and f_des[1] are closed, as they are not needed by the child process.

Program 5.2 A last | sort pipeline.

```
File : p5.2.cxx
    |     /* A home grown last | sort cmd pipeline
    |      */
    |     #define_GNU_SOURCE
    |     #include <iostream>
    +     #include <cstdio>
    |     #include <unistd.h>
    |     using namespace std;
    |     enum { READ, WRITE };
    |
 10     int
    |     main( ) {
    |        int      f_des[2];
    |        if (pipe(f_des) == -1) {
    |          perror("Pipe");
    +          return 1;
    |        }
    |        switch (fork( )) {
    |        case -1:
    |          perror("Fork");
 20          return 2;
    |        case 0:                                   // In the child
    |          dup2( f_des[WRITE], fileno(stdout));
    |          close(f_des[READ] );
    |          close(f_des[WRITE]);
    +          execl("/usr/bin/last", "last", (char *) 0);
    |          return 3;
    |        default:                                  // In the parent
    |          dup2( f_des[READ], fileno(stdin));
    |          close(f_des[READ] );
 30          close(f_des[WRITE]);
    |          execl("/bin/sort", "sort", (char *) 0);
    |          return 4;
    |        }
    |        return 0;
    +     }
```

In the parent process the **dup2** call closes standard input and duplicates it as the reference f_des[0]. The entries for the files/pipes would now look like those shown in Figure 5.5. In the parent process, stdout and stderr have not been modified. However, stdin is now the read end of the pipe shared with the child. In the child process, stdout and stderr are their default values. However, stdout has been associated with the write end of pipe shared with the parent.

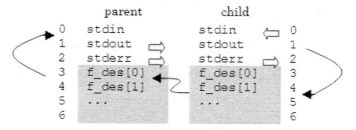

Figure 5.5 End entries for files/pipes.

When running Program 5.2, the two processes (parent and child) are running concurrently (at the same time). The sequence in which these processes will be executed is not guaranteed. For the processes involved, this is not a concern, since the pipe allows both processes to write/read at the same time.

We can summarize the steps involved for communication via unnamed pipes:

1. Create the pipe(s) needed.

2. Generate the child process(es).

3. Close/duplicate file descriptors to properly associate the *ends* of the pipe.

4. Close the unneeded ends of the pipe.

5. Perform the communication activities.

6. Close any remaining open file descriptors.

7. If appropriate, wait for child processes to terminate.

If either **dup** or **dup2** fail, they return a −1 and set errno. The error codes for **dup** and **dup2** are shown in Table 5.9.

Table 5.9 dup/dup2 Error Messages.

#	Constant	perror Message	Explanation
4	EINTR	Interrupted system call	Signal was caught during the system call.
9	EBADF	Bad file descriptor	The file descriptor is invalid.
24	EMFILE	Too many open files	Process has exceeded the limit for number of open files.
67	ENOLINK	The link has been severed	The file descriptor value references a remote system that is no longer active.

5-2 EXERCISE

Most UNIX-based systems include a utility program called **tee** that copies standard input to standard output and to the file descriptor passed on the command line. Thus, the command sequence

```
linux$ cat x.c | tee /dev/tty | wc
```

would **cat** the contents of the file x.c and pipe the standard output to **tee**. The **tee** program would copy its standard input (from the **cat** command) to the file /dev/tty and to its standard output, where it would be piped to the **wc** (word count) program. Using unnamed pipes, write your own version of **tee** called **my_tee**. *Hint:* If you do not know your terminal device, on most systems the command **stty** will display the device. If **stty** does not work, try the **who** command. When passing the name of the terminal device to your **my_tee** program, be sure to include the full path for the device.

5-3 EXERCISE

Modify Program 5.2 so a variable number of commands can be passed to the program. Each command passed to the program should be *connected* to the next command via a pipe. When using this new program, a three-command sequence such as

```
linux$ last | sort | more
```

would be indicated as

```
linux$ my_p5.2  last  sort  more
```

5-4 EXERCISE

Rework the program written for Exercise 4.3 (the producer/consumer problem in Chapter 4) so the producer and consumer now use a pipe to communicate with one another.

Since the sequence of generating a pipe, forking a child process, duplicating file descriptors, and passing command execution information from one process to another via the pipe is relatively common, a set of standard library functions is available to simplify this task: **popen** and **pclose**. See Tables 5.10 and 5.11.

Table 5.10 Summary of the **popen** Library Function.

Include File(s)	<stdio.h>		Manual Section	3
Summary	FILE *popen(const char *command, const, char *type)			
	Success	Failure	Sets errno	
Return	Pointer to a FILE	NULL pointer	Sometimes	

Table 5.11 Summary of the **pclose** Library Function.

Include File(s)	<stdio.h>		Manual Section	3
Summary	int pclose(FILE *stream);			
	Success	Failure	Sets errno	
Return	Exit status of command	−1	Sometimes	

When successful, the **popen** call returns a pointer to a file stream (not an integer file descriptor). The arguments for **popen** are a pointer to the shell command[2] that will be executed and an I/O mode type. The I/O mode type

---

[2] This can be any valid Bourne shell command, including those with I/O redirection. Most often, the command is placed in a doubly quoted string.

(read or write) determines how the process will handle the file pointer returned by the **popen** call.

When invoked, the **popen** call automatically generates a child process. The child process **exec**s a Bourne shell (**/bin/sh**), which will execute the passed shell command. Input to and output from the child process is accomplished via a pipe. If the I/O mode type for **popen** is specified as w the parent process can **write** to the standard input of the shell command. In other terms, writing to the file pointer reference generated by the **popen** in the parent process will enable the child process running the shell command to **read** the data as its standard input. Conversely, if the I/O type is r, using the **popen** file pointer, the parent process can **read** from the standard output of the shell command (run by the child process). By default, the I/O stream generated by **popen** is fully buffered.

If **popen** fails due to an inability to allocate memory, errno will not be set. However, if the mode type is specified incorrectly, **popen** sets errno to EINVAL.

The **pclose** call is used to close a data stream opened with a **popen** call. If the data stream being closed is associated with a **popen**, **pclose** returns the exit status of the shell command referenced by the **popen**. If the data stream is not associated with a **popen** call, the **pclose** call returns a value of –1. If **pclose** is unable to obtain the status of the child process, errno is set to ECHILD.

Program 5.3 shows one way the **popen** and **pclose** calls can be used to pipe the output of one shell command to the input of another.

Program 5.3 Using popen and pclose.

```
File : p5.3.cxx
    |      /* Using the popen and pclose I/O commands
    |       */
    |      #define_GNU_SOURCE
    |      #include <iostream>
    +      #include <cstdio>
    |      #include <limits.h>
    |      #include <unistd.h>
    |      using namespace std;
    |      int
  10       main(int argc, char *argv[ ]) {
    |        FILE    *fin, *fout;
    |        char    buffer[PIPE_BUF];
    |        int     n;
    |        if (argc < 3) {
    +          cerr << "Usage " << argv << "cmd1 cmd2" << endl;
    |          return 1;
    |        }
```

```
  |        fin  = popen(argv[1], "r");
  |        fout = popen(argv[2], "w");
 20        fflush(fout);
  |        while ((n = read(fileno(fin), buffer, PIPE_BUF)) > 0)
  |          write(fileno(fout), buffer, n);
  |        pclose(fin);
  |        pclose(fout);
  +        return 0;
  |     }
```

As written, Program 5.3 requires two command-line arguments: two shell commands whose standard output/input is *redirected* via pipes generated when using the **popen** call. The first **popen** call, with the I/O option of r, directs the system to **fork** a child process that will execute the shell command referenced by argv[1]. The output of the command will be redirected so it can be **read** by the parent process when using the file pointer reference fin. In a similar manner, the second **popen**, with the I/O option of w directs the system to **fork** a second child process. As this child process executes its shell command (referenced by argv[2]), its standard input will be the data written to the pipe by the parent process, and its output will go the standard output. The parent process writes data to the second pipe using the file pointer reference fout and reads data from the first pipe using the file pointer reference fin. The **while** loop in the program is used to copy the data from the output end of one pipe to the input end of the other. The call to **fflush** in line 20 of the program is used to clear buffered output so that it will not be interleaved with data in the pipe.

Figure 5.6 depicts the arrangement when the shell command **last** and **more** are passed on the command line to Program 5.3.

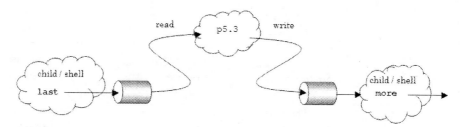

Figure 5.6 Program 5.3 relationships when invoked as p5.3 last more.

Using *just* the **popen** call to generate pipes, can we create a pipeline consisting of *three* separate shell commands (e.g., a program that when passed three shell commands on the command line, would *pipe* the commands together in the manner cmd1 | cmd2 | cmd3)? If yes, write a program that shows how this can be done. If no, give the reason(s) why.

5.3 Named Pipes

UNIX provides for a second type of pipe called a named pipe, or FIFO (we will use the terms interchangeably). Named pipes are similar in spirit to unnamed pipes but have additional benefits. When created, named pipes have a directory entry. With the directory entry are file access permissions and the capability for unrelated processes to use the pipe file. Although the FIFO has a directory entry, keep in mind the data written to the FIFO is passed to and stored by the kernel and is not directly written to the file system.

Named pipes can be created at the shell level (on the command line) or within a program. It is instructive to look at the generation of a named pipe at the shell level before addressing its use in a program. At the shell level the command used to make a named pipe is **mknod**. Officially, **mknod** is a utility command designed to generate special files. It is most commonly used by the superuser to generate special device files (e.g., the block, character device files found in the /dev directory). For nonprivileged users, **mknod** can only be used to generate a named pipe. The syntax for the **mknod** command to make a named pipe is

```
linux$ mknod PIPE p
```

The first argument to the **mknod** command is the file name for the FIFO (this can be any valid UNIX file name; however, it is common to use an uppercase file name to alert the user to the *special* nature of the file). The second argument is a lowercase p, which notifies **mknod** that a FIFO file is to be created. If we issue the command shown above and check the directory entry for the file that it has created, we will find a listing similar to that shown below:

```
linux$ ls -l PIPE
prw-r--r--    1 gray       faculty        0 Feb 26 07:18 PIPE
```

The lowercase letter p at the start of the permission string indicates the file called PIPE is a FIFO. The default file permissions for a FIFO are assigned using the standard **umask** arrangement discussed previously. The number of bytes in the FIFO is listed as 0. As soon as all the processes that are using a named pipe are done with it, any remaining data in the pipe is released by the system and the byte count for the file reverts to 0. If we wish to, we can, on the command line, redirect the output from a shell command to a named pipe. If we do this, we should place the command sequence in the background to prevent it from hanging. We could then redirect the output of the same FIFO to be the input of another command.

For example, the command

```
linux$ cat test_file > PIPE &
[1] 27742
```

will cause the display of the contents of file test_file to be redirected to the named pipe PIPE. If this command is followed by

```
linux$ cat < PIPE
This is test
file to use
with our pipe.
[1]  + Done                        cat test_file > PIPE
```

the second **cat** command will read its input from the named pipe called PIPE and display its output to the screen.

5-6 EXERCISE

As long as there is one active reader and/or writer for a FIFO, the system will maintain its contents. Is it possible to produce a command sequence that proves this is so? Try issuing a command that generates a large amount of outpt (e.g., cat p5.2.cxx) and redirect the output to the FIFO, placing the command in the background. Follow this command with ls -l to see if the pipe actually has contents. Now try the following command sequence:

```
linux$ cat p5.2.cxx > PIPE & more < PIPE & ls -l PIPE
```

How do you explain the differences in output you observe?

While the previous discussion is instructive, it is of limited practical use. Under most circumstances, FIFOs are created in a programming environment, not on the command line. The system call to generate a FIFO in a program has the same name as the system command equivalent: **mknod** (Table 5.12).

Table 5.12 Summary of the mknod System Call.

Include File(s)	`<sys/types.h>` `<sys/stat.h>` `<fcntl.h>` `<unistd.h>`		Manual Section	**2**
Summary	`int mknod(const char *pathname, mode_t mode, dev_t dev);`			
	Success	Failure	Sets `errno`	
Return	0	−1	Yes	

The **mknod** system call creates the file referenced by `pathname`. The type of the file created (FIFO, character or block special, directory[3] or plain) and its access permissions are determined by the `mode` value. Most often the `mode` for the file is created by **OR**ing a symbolic constant indicating the file type with the file access permissions (see the section on **umask** for a more detailed discussion). Permissible file types are listed in Table 5.13.

Table 5.13 File Type Specification Constants for mknod.

Symbolic Constant	File Type
S_IFIFO	FIFO special
S_IFCHR	character special
S_IFDIR	directory
S_IFBLK	block special
S_IFREG	ordinary file

The `dev` argument for **mknod** is used only when a character or block special file is specified. For character and block special files, the `dev` argument is used to assign the major and minor number of the device. For nonprivileged users, the **mknod** system call can only be used to generate a FIFO. When generating a FIFO, the `dev` argument should be left as 0. If **mknod** is successful, it returns a value of 0. Otherwise, `errno` is set to indicate the error, and a value of −1 is returned.

---

[3] While most versions of **mknod** can also be used to generate a directory (if you are the superuser), the version found in Linux cannot (use the **mkdir** system call instead).

Table 5.14 mknod Error Messages.

#	Constant	`perror` **Message**	**Explanation**
1	EPERM	Operation not permitted	The effective ID of the calling process is not that of the superuser.
4	EINTR	Interrupted system call	Signal was caught during the system call.
12	ENOMEM	Cannot allocate memory	Insufficient kernel memory was available.
13	EACCES	Permission denied	Parent directory (or one of the directories in `pathname`) lacks write permission.
14	EFAULT	Bad address	`pathname` references an illegal address.
17	EEXIST	File exists	`pathname` already exists.
20	ENOTDIR	Not a directory	Part of the specified `pathname` is not a directory.
22	EINVAL	Invalid argument	Invalid `dev` specified.
28	ENOSPC	No space left on device	File system has no inodes left for new file generation.
30	EROFS	Read-only file system	Referenced file is (or would be) on a read-only file system.
67	ENOLINK	The link has been severed	The `pathname` value references a remote system that is no longer active.
72	EMULTIHOP	Multihop attempted	The `pathname` value requires multiple hops to remote systems, but file system does not allow it.
36	ENAMETOOLONG	File name too long	The `pathname` value exceeds system path/file name length.
40	ELOOP	Too many levels of symbolic links	The `perror` message says it all.

In many versions of UNIX, a C library function called **mkfifo** simplifies the generation of a FIFO. The **mkfifo** library function (Table 5.15) uses the **mknod** system call to generate the FIFO. Most often, unlike **mknod**, **mkfifo** does not require the user have superuser privileges.

Table 5.15 Summary of the `mkfifo` Library Function.

Include File(s)	`<sys/types.h>` `<sys/stat.h>`		Manual Section	**3**
Summary	`int mkfifo (const char *pathname,` `                mode_t mode)`			
	Success	Failure	Sets `errno`	
Return	0	−1	Yes	

If **mkfifo** is used in place of **mknod**, the mode argument for **mkfifo** refers only to the file access permission for the FIFO, because the file type, by default, is set to S_IFIFO. If the **mkfifo** call fails, it returns a –1 and sets the value in errno. When generating a FIFO, the errors that may be encountered with **mkfifo** are similar to those previously listed for the **mknod** system call (Table 5.14). In our examples, we use the more universal **mknod** system call when generating a FIFO.

Our next example is somewhat more grand in scope than some of the past examples. We combine the use of unnamed and named pipes to produce a **client–server** relationship. Both the client and server processes will run on the same platform. The single-server process is run first and placed in the background. Client processes, run subsequently, are in the foreground. The client processes accept a shell command from the user. The command is sent to the server via a *public* FIFO (known to all clients and the server) for processing. Once the command is received, the server executes it using the **popen-pclose** sequence (which generates an unnamed pipe in the process). The server process returns the output of the command to the client over a *private* FIFO where the client, upon receipt, displays it to the screen. Figure 5.7 shows the process and pipe relationships.

More succinctly, the steps taken by the processes involved are as follows:

- Server generates the public FIFO (available to all participating client processes).
- Client process generates its own private FIFO.
- Client prompts for, and receives, a shell command.
- Client writes the name of its private FIFO and the shell command to the public FIFO.
- Server reads the public FIFO and obtains the private FIFO name and the shell command.

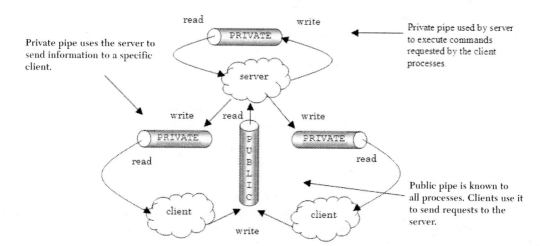

Figure 5.7 Client–server process relationships.

- Server uses a **popen–pclose** sequence to execute the shell command. The output of the shell command is sent back to the client via the private FIFO.
- Client displays the output of the command.

To ensure that both server and client processes will use the same public FIFO name and have the same message format, a local header file is used. This header file is shown in Figure 5.8.

Figure 5.8 Header file for client–server example.

```
File : local.h
    |      /*
    |          local header file for pipe client-server
    |      */
    |      #include <cstdio>
    +      #include <sys/types.h>
    |      #include <sys/stat.h>
    |      #include <fcntl.h>
    |      #include <unistd.h>
    |      #include <string.h>
   10      #include <linux/limits.h>
    |      #include <stdlib.h>
    |      using namespace std;
    |      const char *PUBLIC = "/tmp/PUBLIC";        Establish the name
    |      const int   B_SIZ  = (PIPE_BUF / 2);       of the common
    +      struct message {                           public FIFO.
```

187

```
|        char    fifo_name[B_SIZ];
|        char    cmd_line[B_SIZ];
|     };
```

In this file, a constant is used to establish the name for the public FIFO as /tmp/PUBLIC. The format of the message that will be sent over the public FIFO is declared with the struct statement. The message structure consists of two character array members. The first member, called fifo_name, stores the name of the private FIFO. The second structure member, cmd_line, stores the command to be executed by the server.

Program 5.4 shows the code for the client process.

Program 5.4 The client process.

```
File : client.cxx
|       /* The client process */
|       #define _GNU_SOURCE
|
|       #include "local.h"
+       int
|       main( ){
|         int            n, privatefifo, publicfifo;
|         static char    buffer[PIPE_BUF];
|         struct message  msg;
10
|         sprintf(msg.fifo_name, "/tmp/fifo%d", getpid( ));
|
|         if (mknod(msg.fifo_name, S_IFIFO | 0666, 0) < 0) {
|           perror(msg.fifo_name);
+           return 1;
|         }
|         if ((publicfifo = open(PUBLIC, O_WRONLY)) == -1) {
|           perror(PUBLIC);
|           return 2;
20        }
|         while ( 1 ) {
|           write(fileno(stdout), "\ncmd>", 6);
|           memset(msg.cmd_line, 0x0, B_SIZ);
|           n = read(fileno(stdin), msg.cmd_line, B_SIZ);
+           if (!strncmp("quit", msg.cmd_line, n-1))
|             break;
|           write(publicfifo, (char *) &msg, sizeof(msg));
|           if ((privatefifo = open(msg.fifo_name, O_RDONLY)) == -1) {
|             perror(msg.fifo_name);
30          return 3;
|         }
```

Build a unique name for the *private* FIFO for this process.

Generate the *private* FIFO.

Open the *public* FIFO for writing.

Prompt for command; clear space to hold command.

Write command to public pipe for server to process.

```
|        while ((n = read(privatefifo, buffer, PIPE_BUF)) > 0) {
|            write(fileno(stderr), buffer, n);
|        }
+        close(privatefifo);
|    }
|    close(publicfifo);
|    unlink(msg.fifo_name);
|    return 0;
40   }
```

Open *private* FIFO;
read what is returned.

Using the `sprintf` function, the client creates a unique name for its private FIFO by incorporating the value returned by the **getpid** system call. The **mknod** system call is used next to create the private FIFO with read and write permissions for all. The following **open** statement opens the public FIFO for writing. If for some reason the public FIFO has not been previously generated by the server, the **open** will fail. In this case the **perror** call produces an error message and the client process exits. If the **open** is successful, the client process then enters an endless loop. The client first prompts the user for a command.[4] Prior to obtaining the command, the structure member where the command will be stored is set to all NULLs using the C library function **memset**. This action assures that no extraneous characters will be left at this storage location. Note that using **memset** is preferable to using the deprecated **bzero** library function for clearing a string. The **read** statement in line 24 obtains the user's input from standard input and stores it in `msg.cmd_line`. The input is checked to determine if the user would like to quit the program. The check is accomplished by comparing the input to the character string `quit`. We use `n-1` as the number of characters for comparison to avoid including the `\n` found at the end of the user's input. If `quit` was entered, the `while` loop is exited via the `break` statement, the private FIFO is removed, and the client process terminates. If the user does not want to quit, the entire message structure, consisting of the private FIFO name and the command the user entered, is written to the public FIFO (thus sending the information on to the server). The client process then attempts to **read** its private FIFO to obtain the output that will be sent to it from the server. At this juncture, if the server has not finished with its execution of the client's command, the client process will block (which is the default for **read**). Once data is available from the private FIFO, the `while` loop in the client will **read** and **write** its contents to standard error. The code for the server process is shown in Program 5.5.

---

[4] Notice that all the I/O in the program is done with **read/write** to avoid buffer flushing problems associated with standard I/O library calls.

Program 5.5 The server process.

```
File : server.cxx
    |       /* The server process */
    |       #define _GNU_SOURCE
    |
    |       #include "local.h"
    +       int
    |       main( ){
    |         int             n, done, dummyfifo, publicfifo, privatefifo;
    |         struct message  msg;
    |         FILE            *fin;
  10        static char     buffer[PIPE_BUF];
    |
    |         mknod(PUBLIC, S_IFIFO | 0666, 0);
    |
    |         if ((publicfifo = open(PUBLIC, O_RDONLY)) == -1 ||
    +             (dummyfifo  = open(PUBLIC, O_WRONLY | O_NDELAY)) == -1 ) {
    |           perror(PUBLIC);
    |           return 1;
    |         }
    |
  20        while (read(publicfifo, (char *) &msg, sizeof(msg)) > 0) {
    |           n = done = 0;
    |           do {
    |             if ((privatefifo=open(msg.fifo_name,
    |                               O_WRONLY|O_NDELAY)) == -1)
    +               sleep(3);
    |             else {
    |               fin = popen(msg.cmd_line, "r");
    |               write(privatefifo, "\n", 1);
    |               while ((n = read(fileno(fin), buffer, PIPE_BUF)) > 0) {
  30              write(privatefifo, buffer, n);
    |                 memset(buffer, 0x0, PIPE_BUF);
    |               }
    |               pclose(fin);
    |               close(privatefifo);
    +               done = 1;
    |             }
    |           } while (++n < 5 && !done);
    |           if (!done) {
    |             write(fileno(stderr),
  40            "\nNOTE: SERVER ** NEVER ** accessed private FIFO\n", 48);
    |             return 2;
    |           }
    |         }
    |         return 0;
    +       }
```

Generate *public* FIFO and open for reading and writing.

Read message (command) from *public* FIFO.

Open the child's *private* FIFO.

Server executes the command using **popen**.

Command output is read and sent to the child.

The server process is responsible for creating the public FIFO. Once created, the public FIFO is opened for both reading and writing. This may appear to be a little odd, as the server process only needs to **read** from the public FIFO. By opening the public FIFO for writing as well, the public FIFO always has at least one writing process associated with it. Therefore, the server process will never receive an end-of-file on the public FIFO. The server process will block on an empty public FIFO waiting for additional messages to be written. This technique saves us from having to close and reopen the public FIFO every time a client process finishes its activities.

Once the public FIFO is established, the server attempts to **read** a message from the public FIFO. When a message is **read** (consisting of a private FIFO name and a command to execute), the server tries to **open** the indicated private FIFO for writing. The attempt to **open** the private FIFO is done within a do-while loop. The O_NDELAY flag is used to keep the **open** from generating a deadlock situation. Should the client, for some reason, not open its end of the private FIFO for reading, the server would, without the O_NDELAY flag specification, block at the **open** of the private FIFO for writing. If the attempt to open the private FIFO fails, the server sleeps three seconds and tries again. After five unsuccessful attempts, the server displays an informational message to standard error and continues with its processing. If the private FIFO is successfully opened, a **popen** is used to execute the command that was passed in the message structure. The output of the command (which is obtained from the unnamed pipe) is written to the private FIFO using a while loop. When all of the output of the command has been written to the unnamed pipe, the unnamed pipe and private FIFO are closed. A sample run of the client-server programs is shown in Figure 5.9.

Figure 5.9 Typical client-server output.

```
linux$ server &                    ◀─────── Place the server in the background.
[1] 27107
$ client                           ◀─────── Run a client process in the foreground.
cmd>ps
  PID TTY          TIME CMD
14736 pts/3    00:00:00 csh
27107 pts/3    00:00:00 server
27108 pts/3    00:00:00 client
27109 pts/3    00:00:00 6
cmd>who
gray      pts/3    Feb 27 11:28
cmd>quit                           ◀─────── The server process must be removed by
linux$ kill -9 27107                        sending it a kill signal.
[1]    Killed            server
$
```

The server process is placed in the background. The client process is then run, and shell commands (**ps** and **who**) are entered in response to the cmd> prompt. The output of each command (after it is executed by the server process and its output sent back to the client) is shown. The client process is terminated by entering the word quit. The server process, which remains in the background even after the client has been removed, is terminated by using the **kill** command.

5-7 EXERCISE

There are a number of additions that can be made to the client program to make it more robust. For example, if the client exits due to the receipt of an interrupt signal (CTRL+C), the private FIFO is not removed. Use a signal-catching routine to correct this oversight. When the client process is initiated, it will fail if the server process is not available. Correct this by having the client start the server process if it is not active.

5-8 EXERCISE

As written, the server program will process each command request in turn. Should one of these requests require a long time to execute, all other client processes must wait to be serviced. Rewrite the server program so that when the server process receives a message, it **forks** a child process to carry out the task of executing the command and returning the output of the command to the client process.

5.4 Summary

Pipes provide the user with a more reliable, synchronized means of inter-process communication. Unnamed pipes can be used only with related processes. The **popen** system call provides the user with an easy way to generate an unnamed pipe to execute a shell command. Named pipes (FIFOs), which exist as actual directory entries, can be shared by unrelated processes. The amount of data a pipe can contain is limited by the system. When a pipe is no longer associated with any processes, its contents are flushed by the system. The **read** and **write** system calls, which can be used with pipes, provide the user with an easy means of coordinating the flow of data in a pipe. Care must be taken when using pipes to prevent deadlock situations. Deadlock can occur when one process opens one end of a pipe for writing and another process opens the other end of the same pipe for writing. Each process in turn is waiting for the other to complete its action.[5] Pipes can be used only by processes that are running on the same platform. Unfortunately, pipes provide no easy way for a reading process to determine who the writing process was. All processes involved with using pipes must have forehand knowledge of their existence.

5.5 Key Terms and Concepts

bzero library function	**pclose** library function
dup system call	pipe
dup2 system call	**pipe** system call
FIFO	PIPE_BUF
memset library function	PIPE_SIZE
mkdir library function	**popen** I/O function
mkfifo library function	private FIFO
mknod command	public FIFO
mknod system call	**read** system call
named pipe	**tee** command
O_NDELAY flag	unnamed pipe
O_NOBLOCK flag	**write** system call

---

[5] As the unnamed pipe generated by **popen** is done without the user's direct use of the **open** system call, should the O_NDELAY or O_NBLOCK flags need to be set, the **fcntl** system call must be used.

Chapter 6

MESSAGE QUEUES

6.1 Introduction

The designers of UNIX found the types of interprocess communications that could be implemented using signals and pipes to be restrictive. To increase the flexibility and range of interprocess communication, supplementary communication facilities were added. These facilities, added with the release of System V in the 1970s, are grouped under the heading IPC (Interprocess Communication). In brief, these facilities are

- **Message queues**—Information to be communicated is placed in a predefined message structure. The process generating the message specifies its type and places the message in a system-maintained message queue. Processes accessing the message queue can use the message type to *selectively* read messages of specific types in a first in first out (FIFO) manner. Message queues provide the user with a means of asynchronously multiplexing data from multiple processes.

- **Semaphores**—Semaphores are system-implemented data structures used to communicate small amounts of data between processes. Most often, semaphores are used for process synchronization.

- **Shared memory**—Information is communicated by accessing shared process data space. This is the fastest method of interprocess communication. Shared memory allows participating processes to randomly access a shared memory segment. Semaphores are often used to synchronize the access to the shared memory segments.

All three of these facilities can be used by related and unrelated processes, but these processes must be on the same system (machine).

Like a file, an IPC **resource**[1] must be generated before it can be used. Each IPC resource has a creator, owner, and access permissions. These attributes, established when the IPC is created, can be modified using the proper system calls. At a system level, information about the IPC facilities supported by the system can be obtained with the **ipcs** command. For example, on our system the **ipcs** command produces the following output shown in Figure 6.1.

Figure 6.1 Some `ipcs` output.

```
linux$ ipcs                                              One shared memory
                                                         segment attached (shared)
------ Shared Memory Segments ------                     by three processes.
key         shmid      owner      perms      bytes     nattch    status
0x00000000 25198594   root        666        247264    3


------ Semaphore Arrays ------
key         semid      owner      perms      nsems     status
0x00000000 65537      root        666        4                    Four sets of semaphores
0x00000000 98306      root        666        16                   all owned by root.
0x00000000 131075     root        666        16
0x00000000 163844     root        666        16                   No message queues
                                                                  are currently allocated.
------ Message Queues ------
key         msqid      owner      perms      used-bytes messages
```

The **ipcs** utility supports a variety of options for specifying a specific resource and the format of its output. The meaning of each is shown in Table 6.1.

Additionally, `-s`, `-q`, or `-m` can be used to indicate semaphore, message queue, or shared memory, and can be followed by `-i` and a valid decimal ID to display additional information about a specific IPC resource (Figure 6.2).

[1] In the context of IPC facilities, the term resource indicates an instance of the facility.

Table 6.1 `ipcs` Command Line Options.

Resource Specification		Output Format	
-a	All (default)	-c	Creator
-m	Shared memory	-l	Limits
-q	Message queues	-p	Process ID
-s	Semaphores	-t	Time
		-u	Summary

Figure 6.2 Using `ipcs` to display the details on a specific resource.

```
linux$ ipcs -s -i 65537                          Specifics of the four-element
                                                  semaphore.
Semaphore Array semid=65537
uid=0    gid=1002         cuid=0  cgid=1002
mode=0666, access_perms=0666
nsems = 4
otime = Wed Feb 27 23:00:00 2002
ctime = Fri Jan  4 13:18:00 2002
semnum    value    ncount    zcount    pid
0         1        0         0         0
1         1        0         0         20719
2         1        0         0         20797
3         1        0         0         0
```

The limits for each facility are established when the kernel is generated. The command

```
linux$ /sbin/sysctl -a
```

displays all the configurable kernel parameters. On our system, this command generates a large amount of output. The IPC related information from this command is as follows:

```
. . .
kernel.sem     = 250        32000   32        128
kernel.msgmnb = 16384
kernel.msgmni = 16
kernel.msgmax = 8192
kernel.shmmni = 4096
kernel.shmall = 2097152
kernel.shmmax = 33554432
. . .
```

A comparison of this output with that of the **ipcs** -1 (limits) command easily establishes the role of each value—for example, kernel.msgmni is the maximum number of message queues systemwide.

IPC resources exist and maintain their contents even after the process that created them has terminated. An IPC resource can be removed *by its owner*, using the appropriate system call within a program or by using the system-level command **ipcrm**. The message queue, shown in the output of the previous **ipcs** command, could be removed by its owner issuing the command

```
linux$ ipcrm sem 65537
```

The sem[2] command-line option tells **ipcrm** that a semaphore is to be removed, and the argument 65537 is the ID number of the semaphore. As there are per-user and systemwide limits to the number of IPC resources available, users should make a conscientious effort to remove unneeded allocated IPCs. Note that as superuser, it is unwise to capriciously remove root owned IPC resources.

6.2 IPC System Calls: A Synopsis

A set of similar system calls are used to create an IPC resource and manipulate IPC information.[3] Due to their flexibility, the syntax for these calls is somewhat arcane (the calls appear, like the camel, to have been designed by a committee). The System V IPC calls are summarized in Table 6.2.

Table 6.2 Summary of the System V IPC Calls.

Functionality	Message Queue	System Call Semaphore	Shared Memory
Allocate an IPC resource; gain access to an existing IPC resource.	msgget	semget	shmget
Control an IPC resource: obtain/modify status information, remove the resource.	msgctl	semctl	shmctl
IPC operations: send/receive messages, perform semaphore operations, attach/free a shared memory segment.	msgsnd msgrcv	semop	shmat shmdt

[2] Use shm to indicate a shared memory segment or msg for a message queue.

[3] Note Linux also supports a nonstandard, nonportable system call called **ipc** that can be used to manipulate IPC resources. As this is a Linux-specific call, its use is best left to Linux system developers.

The *get* system calls[4] (**msgget**, **semget**, and **shmget**) are used either to allocate a new IPC resource (which generates its associated system IPC structure) or gain access to an existing IPC. Each IPC has an owner and a creator, which under most circumstances are usually one and the same. When a new resource is allocated, the user must specify the access permissions for the IPC. Like the **open** system call, the *get* system calls return an integer value called an IPC identifier, which is analogous to a file descriptor. The IPC identifier is used to reference the IPC. From a system standpoint, the IPC identifier is an index into a system table containing IPC permission structure information. The IPC permission structure is defined in <bits/ipc.h> that is included by the header file <sys/ipc.h>. This structure is defined as

```
struct ipc_perm  {
      __key_t __key;                         /* Key                 */
      __uid_t uid;                           /* Owner's user ID.    */
      __gid_t gid;                           /* Owner's group ID.   */
      __uid_t cuid;                          /* Creator's user ID.  */
      __gid_t cgid;                          /* Creator's group ID. */
      unsigned short int mode;               /* Access permission.  */
      unsigned short int __pad1;
      unsigned short int __seq;              /* Sequence number.    */
      unsigned short int __pad2;
      unsigned long int __unused1;
      unsigned long int __unused2;
};
```

The type definitions for __uid_t, __gid_t, and so on can be found in the header file <sys/types.h>. In general, all programs that use the IPC facilities should include the <sys/types.h> and <sys/ipc.h> files. As will be explained in the discussion of *ctl* system calls, some members of the permission structure can be modified by the user.

There are two arguments common to each of the three *get* system calls. Each *get* system call takes an argument of defined type __key_t (of base type integer). This argument, known as the key value, is used by the *get* system call to generate the IPC identifier. There is a direct, one-to-one relationship between the IPC identifier returned by the *get* system call and the key value. While the key can be generated in an arbitrary manner, there is a library function called **ftok** that is commonly used to standardize key production.[5] By calling **ftok** with the same arguments, unrelated processes can be assured

---

[4] The term *get* (in *italics*) will be used to reference the group of system calls.

[5] In all honesty, the **ftok** library function is superfluous, but is presented for historical and continuity reasons. As long as processes that wish to access a *common* IPC resource have a method to communicate the key value for the IPC (such as in a common header file), **ftok** can be avoided.

of producing the same **key** value and thus reference the same IPC resource. The **ftok** function is summarized in Table 6.3.

Table 6.3 Summary of the ftok Library Function.

Include File(s)	`<sys/types.h>` `<sys/ipc.h>`		Manual Section	**3**
Summary	`key_t ftok ( char *pathname, char proj );`			
	Success	Failure	Sets errno	
Return	Returns a **key_t** value for IPC *get* system call	−1	As in **stat** system call	

The **ftok** function takes two arguments. The first, `path`, is a reference to an existing accessible file. Often the value "." is used for this argument, since in most situations the self-referential directory entry "." is always present, accessible, and not likely to be subsequently deleted. The second argument for **ftok**, `proj`, is a single-character project identifier most commonly represented as a literal. The value returned by a successful call to **ftok** is of defined type `key_t`. **ftok**'s underlying algorithm, which uses data returned by the **stat** system call for the specified `pathname` as well as the `proj` argument value, does not guarantee a unique key value will be returned. If **ftok** fails, it returns a −1 and sets `errno` in a manner similar to the **stat** system call (the **stat** system call is discussed in Section 2.8, "File Information."

As demonstrated in Program 6.1, the most significant byte of the value returned by **ftok** is the character `proj` value, which is passed as the second argument.

Program 6.1 Generating some key values with ftok.

```
File : p6.1.cxx
   |      /*
   |          Using ftok to generate key values
   |       */
   |      #include <iostream>
   +      #include <sys/types.h>
   |      #include <sys/ipc.h>
   |      using namespace std;
   |      int
```

```
  |      main( ) {
 10        key_t key;
  |        for (char i = 'a'; i <= 'd'; ++i) {
  |          key = ftok(".", i);
  |          cout << "proj = " << i << " key = [" << hex << key
  |               << "] MSB = " << char(key >> 24) << endl;
  +        }
  |        return 0;
  |      }
```

Figure 6.3 shows the output of Program 6.1 when run on a local 32-bit system.

Figure 6.3 Output of Program 6.1.

```
linux$ p6.1                                      The proj argument becomes
proj = a key = [61153384] MSB = a  ◄────         the most significant byte of the
proj = b key = [62153384] MSB = b                value returned by ftok.
proj = c key = [63153384] MSB = c
proj = d key = [64153384] MSB = d
```

6-1 EXERCISE

As shown in Program 6.1, the most significant byte of ftok's returned key value is the character value passed as the second argument i.e., the value assigned to proj. The remaining parts of the key are obtained from information returned by the **stat** system call (using pathname as its argument). What **stat** information is used by **ftok**, and what is ftok's underlying algorithm? Write a short program that supports your answer.

The key value for the *get* system calls may also be set to the defined constant IPC_PRIVATE. Beneath the covers, IPC_PRIVATE is defined as having a value of 0. Note that regardless of its argument values, the **ftok** library function will *not* return a value of 0. Specifying IPC_PRIVATE instructs the *get* system call to create an IPC resource with a unique IPC identifier. Thus, no other process creating or attempting to gain access to an IPC resource will receive this same IPC identifier.

An IPC resource created with IPC_PRIVATE is normally shared between related processes (such as parent/child or child/child) or in client–server settings. In the related process settings, the parent process creates the IPC resource. When is performed, an **exec**, the associated IPC identifier is passed to the child process by way of the environment or as a command-line parameter. In client–server relationships, the server process usually creates the IPC using IPC_PRIVATE. The IPC identifier is then made available to the client via a file. Note that in either scenario, the child/client process would not specify IPC_PRIVATE when issuing its *get* system call to gain access to the existing private resource. Finally, using IPC_PRIVATE does not prohibit other processes from gaining access to the resource; it only makes it a bit more difficult for a process to determine the identifier associated with the resource.

The second argument common to all of the IPC *get* system calls is the message flag. The message flag, an integer value, is used to set the access permissions when the IPC resource is created. The lower nine bits of the message flag argument define the access permissions. Table 6.4 summarizes the subsequent types of permissions required for each of the IPC system calls[6] to perform their functions. The execute bit is not relevant for IPC facilities.

Table 6.4 Required Permissions for IPC System Calls.

Permissions Required	Message Queues	Semaphores	Shared Memory
write (alter)	**msgsnd** place message in the queue	**semop** increase or decrease a semaphore value	**shmat** to write to the shared memory segment
	msgctl write out modified IPC status information	**semctl** set the value of one semaphore or a whole set; write out modified IPC status information	**shmctl** write out modified IPC status information
read	**msgrcv** obtain message from queue	**semop** block until a semaphore becomes 0	**shmat** read from the shared memory segment
	msgctl to retrieve IPC status information	**semctl** to retrieve IPC status information	**shmctl** to retrieve IPC status information

[6] The header files for each of the IPC facilities (i.e., <sys/msg.h>, <sys/sem.h>, and <sys/shm.h>) contain defined constants for read/write (access) permissions for the facility. As noted previously, using defined constants does increase the portability of code. However, there is no free lunch, as the programmer must often take the time to look up the correct *spelling* of infrequently used defined constants.

In addition to setting access modes, there are two defined constants, found in <sys/ipc.h>, that can be ORed with the access permission value(s) to modify the actions taken when the IPC is created. The constant IPC_CREAT directs the *get* system call to create an IPC resource if one does not presently exist. When IPC_CREAT is specified, if the resource is already present and it was not created using IPC_PRIVATE, its IPC identifier is returned. In conjunction with IPC_CREAT, the creator may also specify IPC_EXCL. Using these two constants together (i.e., IPC_CREAT | IPC_EXCL) causes the *get* system call to act in a *no clobber* manner. That is, should there already be an IPC present for the specified key value, the *get* system call will fail; otherwise, the resource is created. Using this technique, a process can be assured that it is the creator of the IPC resource and is not gaining access to a previously created IPC. In this context, specifying IPC_EXCL by itself has no meaning.

The *ctl* system calls (**msgctl**, **semctl**, and **shmctl**) act upon the information in the system IPC permission structure described previously. All of these system calls require an IPC identifier and an integer command value to stipulate their action. The values the command may take are represented by the following defined constants (found in the header file <sys/ipc.h>):

- **IPC_STAT**—Return the referenced IPC resource status information. When specifying IPC_STAT, the *ctl* system call must pass a pointer to an allocated structure of the appropriate type to store the returned information.

- **IPC_SET**—Change the owner, group, or mode for the IPC resource. In addition, as with IPC_STAT, a pointer to a structure of the appropriate type (with the changed member information) must be passed.

- **IPC_RMID**—Destroy the contents of the IPC resource and remove it from the system.

A process can specify IPC_SET or IPC_RMID only if it is the owner or creator of the IPC (or if it has superuser privileges). Some of the *ctl* system calls have additional functionality, which will be presented in later sections.

The remaining IPC system calls are used for IPC *operations*. The **msgsnd** and **msgrcv** calls are used to send and receive a message from a message queue. By default, the system blocks on an **msgsnd** if a message queue is full, or on an **msgrcv** if the message queue is empty. The process will remain blocked until the indicated operation is successful, a signal is received, or the IPC resource is removed. A process can specify to not block by ORing in the IPC_NOWAIT flag with the specified operation flag. The **semop** system call performs a variety of operations on semaphores (such as setting and testing). Again, the default is to block when attempting to decrement a semaphore that is currently at 0 or if the process is waiting for a semaphore to become 0. The **shmat** and **shmdt** system calls are used with shared memory to map/ attach and unmap/detach shared memory segments. These calls do not block.

For some reason known only to those who authored the documentation, the **msgsnd** and **msgrcv** manual pages (found in Section 2) contain a reference to **msgop**. However, there is no system call **msgop**. Likewise, the **shmat** and **shmdt** manual pages make reference to **shmop**, which also is not a system call. The manual page for **semop** only makes reference to **semop** (which is indeed a system call). One must only conclude that the initial intent was to group all of these calls under the general heading of IPC operations.

We address each set of IPC system calls in detail as we cover message queues, semaphores, and shared memory.

6.3 Creating a Message Queue

A message queue is created using the **msgget** system call (Table 6.5).

Table 6.5 Summary of the msgget System Call.

Include File(s)	<sys/types.h> <sys/ipc.h> <sys/msg.h>		Manual Section	**2**
Summary	int msgget (key_t key,int msgflg);			
Return		Success	Failure	Sets errno
	Nonnegative message queue identifier associated with key		−1	Yes

If the **msgget** system call is successful, a nonnegative integer is returned. This value is the message queue identifier and can be used in subsequent calls to reference the message queue. If the **msgget** system call fails, the value −1 is returned and the global variable errno is set appropriately to indicate the error (see Table 6.6). The value for the argument key can be specified directly by the user or generated using the **ftok** library function (as covered in the previous discussion). The value assigned to key is used by the operating system to produce a unique message queue identifier. The low-order bits of the msgflg argument are used to determine the access permissions for the message queue. Additional flags (e.g., IPC_CREAT, IPC_EXCL) may be **OR**ed with the permission value to indicate special creation conditions.

A new message queue is created if the defined constant IPC_PRIVATE is used as the key argument or if the IPC_CREAT flag is **OR**ed with the access permissions and no previously existing message queue is associated with the key value. If IPC_CREAT is specified (without IPC_EXCL) and the message queue already exists, **msgget** will *not* fail but will return the message queue identifier that is associated with the key value (Table 6.6).

Table 6.6 msgget Error Messages.

#	Constant	perror Message	Explanation
2	EOENT	No such file or directory	Message queue identifier does not exist for this key and IPC_CREAT was not set.
12	ENOMEM	Cannot allocate memory	Insufficient system memory to allocate the message queue.
13	EACCES	Permission denied	Message queue identifier exits for this key, but requested operation is not allowed by current access permissions.
17	EEXIST	File exists	Message queue identifier exists for this key, but the flags IPC_CREAT and IPC_EXCL are both set.
28	ENOSPC	No space left on device	System imposed limit (MSGMNI) for the number of message queues has been reached.
43	EIDRM	Identifier removed	Specified message queue is marked for removal.

Program 6.2 generates five message queues with read/write access, uses the **ipcs** command (via a pipe) to display message queue status, and then removes the message queues.

Program 6.2 Generating message queues.

```
File : p6.2.cxx
    |     /*  Message queue generation
    |      */
    |     #define _GNU_SOURCE
    |     #include <cstdio>
    +     #include <unistd.h>
    |     #include <linux/limits.h>
    |     #include <sys/types.h>
    |     #include <sys/ipc.h>
    |     #include <sys/msg.h>
   10     using namespace std;
    |     const int MAX=5;                              ←—— Create five message queues.
    |     int
    |     main( ){
    |       FILE *fin;
    +       char  buffer[PIPE_BUF], proj = 'A';
    |       int   i, n, mid[MAX];
    |       key_t key;
    |       for (i = 0; i < MAX; ++i, ++proj) {
    |         key = ftok(".", proj);
   20         if ((mid[i] = msgget(key, IPC_CREAT | 0660)) == -1) {
    |           perror("Queue create");
    |           return 1;
    |         }                                          ←—— Use a named pipe to execute
    |       }                                                 the ipcs command.
    +       fin = popen("ipcs", "r");
    |       while ((n = read(fileno(fin), buffer, PIPE_BUF)) > 0)
    |         write(fileno(stdout), buffer, n);          ←—— Remove the five message
    |       pclose(fin);                                      queues.
    |       for (i = 0; i < MAX; ++i )
   30         msgctl(mid[i], IPC_RMID, (struct msqid_ds *) 0);
    |       return 0;
    |     }
```

When run on our system, this program produces the output in Figure 6.4, indicating that five message queues have been generated.

Figure 6.4 Output of Program 6.2.

```
linux$ p6.2

------ Shared Memory Segments ------
```

key	shmid	owner	perms	bytes	nattch	status
0x00000000	25198594	root	666	247264	3	

```
------ Semaphore Arrays ------
```

key	semid	owner	perms	nsems	status
0x00000000	65537	root	666	4	
0x00000000	98306	root	666	16	
0x00000000	131075	root	666	16	
0x00000000	163844	root	666	16	

```
------ Message Queues ------
```

key	msqid	owner	perms	used-bytes	messages
0x41153384	2260992	gray	660	0	0
0x42153384	2293761	gray	660	0	0
0x43153384	2326530	gray	660	0	0
0x44153384	2359299	gray	660	0	0
0x45153384	2392068	gray	660	0	0

6-2 EXERCISE

Run Program 6.2 several times in rapid succession. Look at the message queue identifiers that are produced. What appears to be the numbering scheme the system is using? *Hint*: Look in the header file <linux/msg.h>. Can you find any rationale for this approach? Now add the statement sleep(5); after the statement pclose(fin); on line 28. Recompile the program and invoke the program twice, placing it in the background each time. Assuming the program is still called p6.2, this can be accomplished by

```
linux$ p6.2 & p6.2 &
```

Count the number of message queues generated and explain why there are not 10 present.

When a message queue is created, a system message-queue data structure called msqid_ds is generated. This structure, maintained by the system, is defined in the system-dependent header file <bits/msq.h>, which in turn is included by the header file <sys/msg.h>. The msqid_ds structure for Linux is defined as

```
struct msqid_ds {
  struct ipc_perm msg_perm;        /* structure describing operation
                                      permission */
  __time_t msg_stime;              /* time of last msgsnd command */
  unsigned long int __unused1;
  __time_t msg_rtime;              /* time of last msgrcv command */
  unsigned long int __unused2;
  __time_t msg_ctime;              /* time of last change */
  unsigned long int __unused3;
  unsigned long int __msg_cbytes;  /* current number of bytes on queue */
  msgqnum_t msg_qnum;              /* number of messages currently on queue */
  msglen_t msg_qbytes;             /* max number of bytes allowed on queue */
  __pid_t msg_lspid;               /* pid of last msgsnd() */
  __pid_t msg_lrpid;               /* pid of last msgrcv() */
  unsigned long int __unused4;
  unsigned long int __unused5;
};
```

However, conceptually (and in keeping with its original definition), the `msqid_ds` structure is considered to be as found in the header file `<linux/msg.h>`:

```
struct msqid_ds {
  struct ipc_perm msg_perm;
  struct msg *msg_first;           /* first message on queue, unused  */
  struct msg *msg_last;            /* last message in queue, unused */
  __kernel_time_t msg_stime;       /* last msgsnd time */
  __kernel_time_t msg_rtime;       /* last msgrcv time */
  __kernel_time_t msg_ctime;       /* last change time */
  unsigned long  msg_lcbytes;      /* Reuse junk fields for 32 bit */
  unsigned long  msg_lqbytes;      /* ditto */
  unsigned short msg_cbytes;       /* current # of bytes on queue */
  unsigned short msg_qnum;         /* number of messages in queue */
  unsigned short msg_qbytes;       /* max number of bytes on queue */
  __kernel_ipc_pid_t msg_lspid;    /* pid of last msgsnd */
  __kernel_ipc_pid_t msg_lrpid;    /* last receive pid */
};
```

But, if we investigate even further, we find that what is actually implemented by the kernel is different still. A check of the kernel source code `msg.c` (usually found in `/usr/src/linux-XX.XX.XX/ipc` where XX are the version numbers for the particular operating system) for message queue implementation defines a kernel structure called `msg_queue`:

```
struct msg_queue {
    struct kern_ipc_perm q_perm;
    time_t q_stime;                     /* last msgsnd time */
    time_t q_rtime;                     /* last msgrcv time */
    time_t q_ctime;                     /* last change time */
    unsigned long q_cbytes;             /* current number of bytes on queue */
    unsigned long q_qnum;               /* number of messages in queue */
    unsigned long q_qbytes;             /* max number of bytes on queue */
    pid_t q_lspid;                      /* pid of last msgsnd */
    pid_t q_lrpid;                      /* last receive pid */
    struct list_head q_messages;
    struct list_head q_receivers;
    struct list_head q_senders;
};
```

While this all may seem a bit confusing at first, there is some commonality (e.g., the permission structure and reference to the message queue list). The discussion that follows is based on the conceptual definition as found in the header file `<linux/msg.h>`.

The first member of the `msqid_ds` structure is the IPC permission structure discussed earlier. When the resource is allocated, the system sets, respectively, the `msg_perm.cuid`, `msg_perm.uid`, `msg_perm.cgid`, and `msg_perm.gid` members to the effective user and group ID of the invoking process. The low-order nine bits of `msgflg` (taken from the **msgget** call) are used to set the value in `msg_perm.mode`.

Next, in the `msqid_ds` structure are two pointers to the first and last messages in the queue. From a conceptual standpoint, the individual messages in the queue are structures of type `msg`, defined as

```
struct msg {
    struct msg    *msg_next;       /* ptr to next message on q */
    long          msg_type;        /* message type */
    ushort        msg_ts;          /* message text size */
    short         msg_spot;        /* address of text message */
};
```

Individual messages are placed in a linked list by the system. Each `msg` structure contains four members: a reference to the next `msg` in the list, a long integer, user-assigned value denoting the message type, a short integer value indicating the size in bytes of the message (maximum 8192 bytes), and a reference to the actual message. When the message queue is created the system sets the `msqid_ds` members `msg_qnum`, `msg_lspid`, `msg_lrpid`,

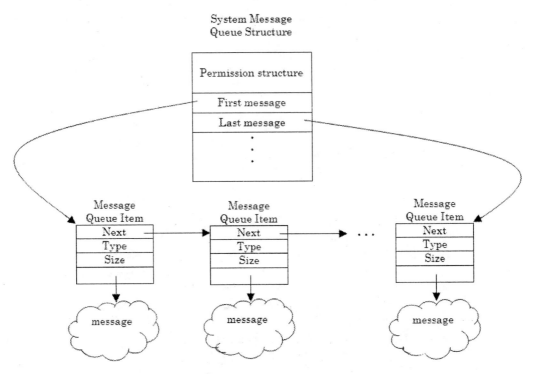

Figure 6.5 A message queue with *N* items.

msg_stime, and msg_rtime to 0. The member msg_ctime is set to the current time, and msg_qbytes is set to the system limit. Thus, *conceptually*, we can envision a message queue with *N* items as being similar to Figure 6.5.

6.4 Message Queue Control

The ownership and access permissions, established when the message queue was created, can be examined and modified using the **msgctl** system call (see Table 6.7).

The **msgctl** system call references the message queue indicated by the msqid argument. The value of the cmd argument is used to indicate the action that **msgctl** should take. The following defined constants/actions can be specified:

Table 6.7 Summary of the `msgget` System Call.

Include File(s)	`<sys/types.h>`
	`<sys/ipc.h>`
	`<sys/msg.h>`
			Manual
			Section
				2

Summary	`int msgget (int msqid,int cmd, struct` `msqid_ds *buf);`			
	Success	Failure	Sets `errno`	
Return	0	-1	Yes	

- **IPC_STAT**—Return the current values for each member of the `msqid_ds` data structure (remember that this also contains the permission structure). When using the IPC_STAT flag, the user *must* provide a location to store the returned information. The address of the storage location for the information is passed as the third argument to the **msgctl** system call. Of course, the calling process must have read-access privileges for the message queue.

- **IPC_SET**—With this flag, the user (creator, owner, or superuser) can modify a limited number of `msqid_ds` structure member values. The following members can be modified:

  `msg_perm.uid`, `msg_perm.gid`, `msg_perm.mode`, and `msg_qbytes`

  Similar to IPC_STAT, the user must first generate a structure of type msqid_ds, modify the appropriate structure members, and then call **msgctl** with the IPC_SET flag and pass the address of the modified structure. A successful update will also update the `msg_ctime` member.

- **IPC_RMID**—Immediately removes all associated message queue structures. When specifying IPC_RMID, the third argument to **msgctl** is not considered and thus may be left out. However, wanting to leave nothing to chance, most programmers enter the third argument as a NULL value cast to be a pointer to an `msqid_ds` structure.

If the **msgctl** system call fails, it returns a -1 and sets `errno`; otherwise, it returns a 0 indicating success. The value that `errno` may be assigned when **msgctl** fails is given in Table 6.8.

Program 6.3 creates a message queue, uses the **msgctl** system call to obtain the message queue structure information, and displays pertinent data to the screen.

Table 6.8 `msgctl` Error Messages.

#	Constant	perror **Message**	**Explanation**
1	EPERM	Operation not	• `cmd` is IPC_RMID and the calling process permitted is not the owner or superuser. • `cmd` is IPC_SET and non-superuser process is attempting to increase `msg_qbytes` beyond the system limit (MSGMNB).
13	EACCES	Permission denied	`cmd` is IPC_STAT, but operation is forbidden by the current access permissions (i.e., lacks read access).
14	EFAULT	Bad address	`cmd` is set to IPC_SET or IPC_STAT, but `buf` references a bad address.
22	EINVAL	Invalid argument	• Message queue identifier is invalid. • `cmd` is invalid. • `cmd` is IPC_SET, but `msg_perm.uid` or `msg_perm.gid` value is invalid.
43	EIDRM	Identifier removed	The message queue was removed.
75	EOVERFLOW	Value too large for defined data type	`cmd` is IPC_STAT and location referenced by `buf` is too small to hold the `uid` or `gid` values.

Program 6.3 Using `msgctl`.

```
File : p6.3.cxx
   |    /*
   |        Displaying message queue status information
   |     */
   |    #include <iostream>
   +    #include <cstdio>
   |    #include <sys/types.h>
   |    #include <sys/ipc.h>
   |    #include <sys/msg.h>
   |    using namespace std;
```

```
10    int
 |    main( ){
 |      int              mid;
 |      key_t            key;
 |      struct msqid_ds buf;
 +
 |      key = ftok(".", 'z');
 |      if ((mid = msgget(key, IPC_CREAT | 0660)) == -1) {
 |        perror("Queue create");
 |        return 1;
20    }
 |      msgctl(mid, IPC_STAT, &buf);
 |      cout << "Message Queue *Permission* Structure Information" << endl;
 |      cout << "Owner's user ID   \t" << buf.msg_perm.uid  << endl;
 |      cout << "Owner's group ID  \t" << buf.msg_perm.gid  << endl;
 +      cout << "Creator's user ID \t" << buf.msg_perm.cuid << endl;
 |      cout << "Creator's group ID\t" << buf.msg_perm.cgid << endl;
 |      cout << "Access mode in HEX\t" << hex <<   buf.msg_perm.mode << endl;
 |      cout << "\nAdditional Selected Message Queue Structure Information\n";
 |      cout << "Current # of bytes on queue  \t" << dec
30                                         << buf.__msg_cbytes << endl;
 |      cout << "Current # of messages on queue\t" << buf.msg_qnum   << endl;
 |      cout << "Maximum # of bytes on queue  \t" << buf.msg_qbytes << endl;
 .|      msgctl(mid, IPC_RMID, (struct msqid_ds *) 0 );
 |      return 0;
 +    }
```

The structure buf will store the returned information on the message queue.

Generate the message queue.

Run locally, Program 6.3 produces the output shown in Figure 6.6.

Figure 6.6 Output of Program 6.3.

```
linux$ p6.3
Message Queue *Permission* Structure Information
Owner's user ID         500
Owner's group ID        1000
Creator's user ID       500
Creator's group ID      1000
Access mode in HEX      1b0

Additional Selected Message Queue Structure Information
Current # of bytes on queue     0
Current # of messages on queue  0
Maximum # of bytes on queue     16384
```

As shown, when first generated, the creator of the message queue and the owner are the same. If we convert the displayed hexadecimal access mode value to binary:

$1B0_{16} \equiv 110\ 110\ 000_2$

213

and examine the lower nine bits of the binary number, we see the access permissions are indeed 0660 as we specified. The value for the maximum number of bytes on the message queue, shown here as 16384, is one of several system-imposed message queue limits. Additional message queue limit information can be found in the header file <linux/msg.h>.

It is not possible to create and initialize message queue members atomically. Is this a design flaw or a feature? Support your answer with an example.

6.5 Message Queue Operations

Message queues are used to send and receive messages. An actual message, from the system's standpoint, is defined by the msgbuf structure found in the header file <sys/msg.h> as

```
struct msgbuf {
    long int mtype;        /* type of received/sent message */
    char mtext[1];         /* text of the message */
};
```

This structure is used as a *template* for the messages to be sent to and received from the message queue.

The first member of the msgbuf structure is the message type. The message type, mtype, is a long integer value and is normally greater than 0. The message type, generated by the process that originates the message, is used to indicate the kind (category) of the message. The type value is used by the **msgrcv** system call to selectively retrieve messages falling within certain boundary conditions. Messages are placed in the message queue in the order they are sent and *not* grouped by their message type.

Following mtype is the reference to the body of the message. As shown, this is defined as a character array with one element: mtext[1]. In actuality, any valid structure member(s), character arrays or otherwise, that make up a message can be placed after the requisite mtype entry. The system assumes a valid message always consists of a long integer followed by a series of 0 or

more bytes (the organization of the data bytes is the programmer's preroga-
tive). It is the address of the first structure member after `mtype` that the
system uses as its reference when manipulating the `msg` structure (discussed
in Section 6.3). Therefore, users can generate their own message structures to
be placed in the message queue so long as the first member (on most systems
this is the *first* four bytes) is occupied by a long integer.

Messages are placed in the message queue (sent) using the system call
msgsnd (Table 6.9).

Table 6.9 Summary of the `msgsnd` System Call.

Include File(s)	`<sys/types.h>`
	`<sys/ipc.h>`
	`<sys/msg.h>`
			Manual
			Section
				2

Summary	`int msgsnd (int msqid, struct msgbuf *msgp,` `                size_t msgsz,        int msgflg);`			
Return		Success	Failure	Sets `errno`
		0	−1	Yes

The **msgsnd** system call requires four arguments. The first argument,
`msqid`, is a valid message queue identifier returned from a prior **msgget**
system call. The second argument, `msgp`, is a pointer to the message to be sent.
As noted, the message is a structure with the first member being of the type
long integer. The message structure must be allocated (and hopefully initialized) prior to its being sent. The third argument, `msgsz`, is the size (number
of bytes) of the message to be sent. The size of the message is the amount of
storage allocated for the message structure minus the storage used for the
message type (stored as a long integer). The message size can be from 0 to the
system-imposed limit. The fourth argument to **msgsnd**, `msgflg`, is used to
indicate what action should be taken if system limits for the message queue
(e.g., the limit for the number of bytes in a message queue) have been reached.
The `msgflg` can be set to IPC_NOWAIT or to 0. If set to IPC_NOWAIT and
a system limit has been reached, **msgsnd** will not send the message and will
return to the calling process immediately with `errno` set to EAGAIN. If
`msgflg` is set to 0, **msgsnd** will block until the limit is no longer at system
maximum (at which time the message is sent), the message queue is removed,
or the calling process catches a signal. The system uses the `msgsz` argument

215

to **msgsnd** as its msg.msg_ts value, the msgbuf.mtype value as its msg.msg_type, and the msgbuf.mtext reference as msg.msg_spot.

If **msgsnd** is successful, it returns a value of 0; otherwise, it returns a value of −1 and sets errno to indicate the nature of the error. See Table 6.10.

Table 6.10 msgsnd Error Messages.

#	Constant	perror **Message**	**Explanation**
4	EINTR	Interrupted system call	When sleeping on a full message queue, the process received an interrupt.
11	EAGAIN	Resource temporarily unavailable	Message cannot be sent (msg_qbyte limit exceeded) and IPC_NOWAIT was specified.
12	ENOMEM	Cannot allocate memory	Insufficient system memory to copy message.
13	EACCES	Permission denied	Calling process lacks write access for the message queue.
14	EFAULT	Bad address	msgp references a bad address.
22	EINVAL	Invalid argument	• Message queue identifier is invalid. • mtype is nonpositive. • msgsz is less than 0 or greater than system limit.
43	EIDRM	Identifier removed	Message queue has been removed.

Messages are retrieved from the message queue using the system call **msgrcv**, summarized in Table 6.11.

Table 6.11 Summary of the msgrcv System Call.

Include File(s)	<sys/types.h> <sys/ipc.h> <sys/msg.h>		Manual Section	**2**
Summary	ssize_t msgrcv (int msqid, struct msgbuf *msgp, size_t msgsz, long msgtyp, int msgflg);			
Return		Success	Failure	Sets errno
		Number of bytes actually received	−1	Yes

The **msgrcv** system call takes five arguments. The first, as for the **msgsnd** system call, is the message queue identifier. The second, msgp, is a pointer to the location (structure) where the received message will be placed. The receiving location should have as its first field a long integer to accommodate the message type information. The third argument, msgsz, is the maximum size of the message in bytes. This value should be equal to the longest message to be received. Truncation of the message will occur if the size value is incorrectly specified, and depending upon the value for msgflg (see following section), an error may be generated. The fourth argument, msgtyp, is the type of the message to be retrieved. The message type information is interpreted by the **msgrcv** system call, as shown in Table 6.12.

Table 6.12 Actions for msgrcv as Indicated by msgtyp Values.

When msgtyp value is	msgrcv takes this action
0	Retrieve the first message of **any** msgtyp.
> 0	Retrieve the first message **equal** to msgtyp if MSG_EXCEPT is not specified. If MSG_EXCEPT is specified, the first message that is not equal to the msgtyp.
< 0	Retrieve the first message of the **lowest** type less than or equal to absolutevalue of msgtyp.

Using the type argument judiciously, a user can, with minimal effort, implement a priority-based messaging arrangement whereby the message type indicates its priority.

The fifth and final argument, msgflg, is used to indicate what actions should be taken if a given message type is not in the message queue, or if the message to be retrieved is larger in size than the number of bytes indicated by msgsz. There are three predefined values that msgflg can take. IPC_NOWAIT is used to indicate to **msgrcv** that it should not block if the requested message type is not in the message queue. If MSG_EXCEPT is specified and the msgtyp value is greater than 0, **msgrcv** returns the first message not equal to msgtyp. MSG_NOERROR directs **msgrcv** to silently truncate messages to msgsz bytes if they are found to be too long. If MSG_NOERROR is not specified and **msgrcv** receives a message that is too long, it returns a −1 and sets the value in errno to E2BIG to indicate the error. In don't-care situations, the value for msgflg can be set to 0. When **msgrcv** is successful, it returns the number of bytes actually retrieved. See Table 6.13.

Table 6.13   `msgrcv` Error Messages.

#	Constant	`perror` Message	Explanation
4	EINTR	Interrupted system call	When sleeping on a full message queue, the process received an interrupt.
7	E2BIG	Argument list too long	`mtext` is greater than `msgsz` and MSG_NOERROR is not specified.
13	EACCES	Permission denied	Attempt made to read a message, but the calling process does not have permission.
14	EFAULT	Bad address	`msgp` references a bad address.
22	EINVAL	Invalid argument	• Message queue identifier is invalid. • `msgsz` is less than 0 or greater than the system limit.
42	ENOMSG	No message of desired type	Message queue does not have a message of type `msgtyp`, and IPC_NOWAIT is set.
43	EIDRM	Identifier removed	Message queue has been removed.

6.6 A Client–Server Message Queue Example

At this point we can use what we have learned about message queues to write a pair of programs that establish a client–server relationship and use message queues for bidirectional interprocess communication. The client process obtains input from the keyboard and sends it via a message queue to the server. The server reads the message from the queue, manipulates the message by converting all alphabetic text in the message to uppercase, and places the message back in the queue for the client to read. By mutual agreement, the client process identifies messages designated for the server by placing the value 1 in the message type member of the message structure.[7] In addition, the client includes its process ID (PID) number in the message. The server uses the PID number of the client to identify messages it has processed and placed back in the queue. Labeling the processed messages in this manner allows the server to handle messages from multiple clients.

[7] This works nicely, as in multiple client situations, because not every client has initial access to the PID of the server.

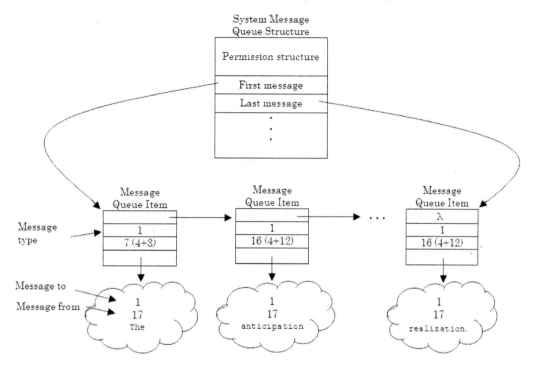

Figure 6.7 Conceptual view of message queue after the client has sent all seven messages

For example, if the client process with a PID of 17 placed each word in the statement "The anticipation is greater than the realization." into separate messages, the current state of the message queue would be as depicted in Figure 6.7. As shown, the messages placed in the queue by the client (PID 17) are labeled as a message type of 1 (for the server).

When the server reads the queue, it obtains the first message of type 1. In our example this is the message containing the word The. The server processes the message, changes the message type to that of the client, and puts the message back on the queue. This leaves the message queue in the state shown in Figure 6.8.

To accomplish this task, both the client and server programs need to access common include files and data structures. These items are placed in a local header file called local.h, whose contents are shown in Figure 6.9. An examination of this file reveals that the messages placed in the queue consist of a structure with three members. The first member (which must be of type long if things are to work correctly) acts as the message type (mtype) member. Here we call this member msg_to, since it contains a value that

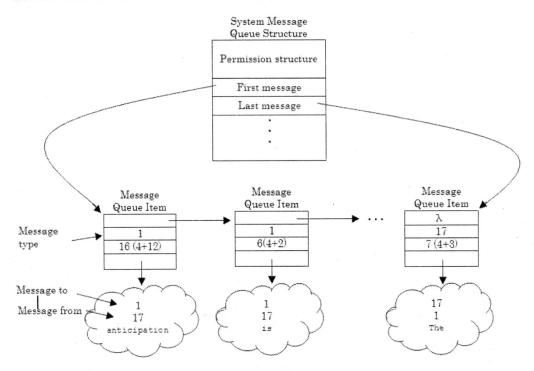

Figure. 6.8 Conceptual view of message queue after the first client message has been processed.

indicates the process to whom we are addressing the message. We use the value of 1 to designate a message for the server process, and other positive PID values to indicate a message for a client. The second member of the message structure, called `msg_fm` (which is also a long integer), contains the ID of the process that is sending the message. In the program example, if the message is sent by a client, this value will be the client PID. If the message is sent by the server, this value will be set to 1. The third member of the message structure is an array of a fixed size that will contain the text of the actual message.

Figure 6.9 Local header file for message queue example.

```
File : local.h
  |      /*
  |            Common header file for 2nd Message Queue Example
  |      */
  |      #define _GNU_SOURCE
  +      #include <cstdio>
  |      #include <cstring>
  |      #include <sys/types.h>
```

```
  |      #include <sys/ipc.h>
  |      #include <sys/msg.h>
 10      #include <unistd.h>
  |      const char     SEED  ='M';        // Common seed for ftok
  |      const long int SERVER=1L;         // Message type for server
  |      typedef struct {
  |        long int msg_to;                // Message in queue for this type
  +        long int msg_fm;                // Placed in the queue by this type
  |        char buffer[BUFSIZ];            // The actual message
  |      }MESSAGE;
  |      using namespace std;
```

The client program, shown as Program 6.4, begins by obtaining its PID. This value is used later to mark messages sent to the server, identifying them as coming from a particular client process. The **ftok** library function is used to produce a key. When the client process is invoked, we want it to create the message queue if one does not already exist. Further, if the server process is not present, we want the client to start it. We will assume that if the message queue is not present, the server process is not present as well. To accomplish this the initial call to **msgget**, mid=msgget(key, 0) in line 19, is tested to determine if the call has failed. If the message queue is not found (the call fails), the message queue is created by the second call to **msgget**. If this occurs, the client process **fork**s a child process and overlays it with a call to **exec** to run the server process. The server is passed the message queue identifier via the command line. As all command-line arguments are strings, the **sprintf** string function is used to put the message queue identifier in the correct format.

Once the message queue is created, the client program enters an endless loop, prompting for user input, placing the input in the message queue for the server to process, retrieving the processed input, and displaying the results to standard output. If the user enters a message of 0 bytes (i.e., enters CTRL+D from the keyboard), the client exits its loop and sends the server a special 0-byte-length message (see line 47) indicating it is done.

Program 6.4 The client.

```
File : client.cxx
  |      /*
  |           CLIENT ... sends messages to the server
  |       */
  |      #include "local.h"
  +      #include <cstdio>
  |      using namespace std;
  |      int
  |      main( ){
  |        key_t        key;
```

```
10      pid_t       cli_pid;
 |      int         mid, n;
 |      MESSAGE     msg;
 |      static char m_key[10];
 |      cli_pid = getpid( );
 +      if ((key = ftok(".", SEED)) == -1) {
 |        perror("Client: key generation");
 |        return 1;
 |      }
 |      if ((mid=msgget(key, 0 )) == -1 ) {
20        mid = msgget(key,IPC_CREAT | 0660);
 |        switch (fork()) {
 |        case -1:
 |          perror("Client: fork");
 |          return 2;
 +        case 0:
 |          sprintf(m_key, "%d", mid);
 |          execlp("./server", "server", m_key, "&", 0);
 |          perror("Client: exec");
 |          return 3;
30        }
 |      }
 |      while (1) {
 |        msg.msg_to = SERVER;
 |        msg.msg_fm = cli_pid;
 +        write(fileno(stdout), "cmd> ", 6);
 |        memset(msg.buffer, 0x0, BUFSIZ);
 |        if ( (n=read(fileno(stdin), msg.buffer, BUFSIZ)) == 0 )
 |          break;
 |        n += sizeof(msg.msg_fm);
40        if (msgsnd(mid, &msg, n, 0) == -1 ) {
 |          perror("Client: msgsend");
 |          return 4;
 |        }
 |        if( (n=msgrcv(mid, &msg, BUFSIZ, cli_pid, 0)) != -1 )
 +          write(fileno(stdout), msg.buffer, n);
 |      }
 |      msgsnd(mid, &msg, 0, 0);
 |      return 0;
 |    }
```

Generate a key for the message queue.

If the message queue is not present, create the queue.

Turn message queue ID into a string to pass to the server via the command line.

Label message as to receiving and originating process.

The message size is the size of the second member (the first is assumed) of the structure plus the number of bytes in the message.

Server will pause, waiting for messages to be added to the message queue. Once a message is retrieved, it is written to standard output.

The server process (shown as Program 6.5) begins by checking the number of command-line arguments. If three command-line arguments are not found, an error message is generated and the server program exits. Otherwise, the contents of argv[1] are converted to an integer value to be used as the message queue identifier. The server then enters into a loop. It first attempts to receive a message of type SERVER (1) from the queue. If the number of bytes returned by **msgrcv** is 0, the server assumes that the client process is done. In this case, the

Program 6.5 The server.

```
File : server.cxx
    |       /*
    |             SERVER-receives messages from clients
    |        */
    |       #include "local.h"
    +       #include <iostream>
    |       #include <cstdio>
    |       #include <ctype.h>
    |       #include <stdlib.h>
    |       using namespace std;
  10        int
    |       main(int argc, char *argv[ ]) {
    |         int     mid, n;
    |         MESSAGE msg;
    |         void    process_msg(char *, int);
    +         if (argc != 3) {
    |           cerr << "Usage: " << argv[0] << " msq_id &" << endl;
    |           return 1;
    |         }
    |         mid = atoi(argv[1]);
  20          while (1) {
    |           memset( msg.buffer, 0x0, BUFSIZ );
    |           if ((n=msgrcv(mid, &msg, BUFSIZ, SERVER, 0)) == -1 ) {
    |            perror("Server: msgrcv");
    |            return 2;
    +           } else if (n == 0) break;
    |           process_msg(msg.buffer, strlen(msg.buffer));
    |           msg.msg_to = msg.msg_fm;
    |           msg.msg_fm = SERVER;
    |           n += sizeof(msg.msg_fm);
  30            if (msgsnd(mid, &msg, n, 0) == -1 ) {
    |             perror("Server: msgsnd");
    |             return 3;
    |           }
    |         }
    +         msgctl(mid, IPC_RMID, (struct msqid_ds *) 0 );
    |         exit(0);
    |       }
    |       /*
    |          Convert lowercase alphabetics to uppercase
  40         */
    |       void
    |       process_msg(char *b, int len){
    |         for (int i = 0; i < len; ++i)
    |           if (isalpha(*(b + i)))
    +             *(b + i) = toupper(*(b + i));
    |       }
```

Check number of command-line arguments.

Retrieve message from queue; wait if no messages are present.

If a zero-length message, exit the loop.

Reassign the to and from fields for the message. Process the message and put it back in the message queue.

Remove the message queue.

loop is exited and the server removes the message queue with a **msgctl** system call (line 35) and exits. However, if a message is successfully retrieved from the message queue, it is processed (in the function process_msg) and placed back on the queue so the client process can retrieve it.

Entering the name of the client program on the command line executes the program. The client creates the message queue and invokes the server process (which must reside locally). A prompt is placed on the screen, requesting input. Each time the user enters a string of characters and presses return, the client places the input in the message queue for processing. After the message has been processed, the client retrieves the message from the message queue and displays it to the screen. Entering CTRL+D from the keyboard terminates the client process. As implemented, multiple copies of the client process can run/communicate with the server at the same time. One way to try this is to open multiple windows and run multiple copies of the client. An alternate approach is to place the executable version of the client and server programs in /tmp (be sure to change the permissions so that all users have access to them). Then **cd** to /tmp and run the client program. Ask another user to do the same (again, remember this is all done on the same machine). Each of you should be able to run the client program and receive processing service. In either scenario, just one message queue will be generated.

6-4   EXERCISE

As written, the server program removes the message queue when any client sends a message of length 0. Modify the server program so that it only removes the message queue after *all* client processes are done with it. One approach might be for the server to keep track of the client processes using the message queue and exit only when the last one sends a message of length 0.

6.7 Message Queue Class

As the functionality of and syntax for message queues is somewhat complex, they are ideal candidates for incorporation into a C++ class. A message queue class would define the relationships between message queue data and the functions (methods) that manipulate this data. A declaration of a simplified message queue class called Message_que is shown in Figure 6.10.

Figure 6.10 Header file for a basic message queue class.

```
File : Message_que.h
  |       /*
  |          A VERY simplified message queue class for use in a std UNIX
  |          environment.  See the text for instructions on how to use
  |          this class.  Copyright (c) 2002  J. S. Gray
  +
  |          Exit codes for class operations:
  |
  |          1 - Unable to create queue    2 - Cannot access queue
  |          3 - Enque has failed          4 - Deque has failed
 10          5 - Unable to remove queue
  |       */
  |       #ifndef Message_que_h
  |       #define Message_que_h
  |       #define _GNU_SOURCE
  +       #include <iostream>
  |       #include <cstring>
  |       #include <sys/types.h>
  |       #include <sys/ipc.h>
  |       #include <sys/msg.h>
 20       #include <stdlib.h>
  |       #include <unistd.h>
  |
  |       class Message_que {
  |         public:
  +           Message_que (const char ='M');    // Constructor
  |           void Remove( );                   // Remove the queue
  |           void Enque( void *, int );        // Place a message in the queue
  |           int  Deque( void *, int, int );   // Obtain a message from queue
  |           bool Exist( const char ='M' );    // True if the queue exists
 30           void Create( );                   // Create the queue
  |           void Acquire( );                  // Acquire access to the queue
  |         private:
  |           int      msqid;                   // ID of message queue
  |           key_t    ipckey;                  // Key from ftok
  +       };
  |       #endif
```

As defined, the Message_que class has seven public methods and three private data members. The functionality of each method is shown in Table 6.14.

The C++ code that implements the message queue class is found in the program file Message_que.cxx (Program 6.5). As shown, the code is bare bones—little is done to handle errors, and only basic message queue functionality is addressed.

Table 6.14 Message_que Class Methods.

Method name	Explanation
Message_que	This is the class constructor. This method takes one argument, which, if specified, defaults to the value M. The constructor generates the message queue ID.
Remove	This method removes the message queue from the system.
Enque	Enque is used to add a message to the message queue. This method is passed a reference to the message and the message size (in bytes).
Deque	The Deque method removes a single message from the message queue. This method has three arguments: a reference to a structure to store the returned data, the maximum size of a returned message, and the message type.
Exist	This method returns a true or false as to whether or not the message queue exists.
Create	Create (generate) a new message queue.
Acquire	Gains access to the existing message queue.

Program 6.5 Program code for the Message Queue Class.

```
File : Message_que.cxx
   |      /*
   |          Message queue implementation—Copyright (c) 2002   J. S. Gray
   |      */
   |      #include "Message_que.h"
   +      #include <cstdio>
   |
   |      // Message queue constructor.
   |      Message_que::Message_que( const char the_key ){
   |        ipckey = ftok( ".", the_key );
  10        msqid  = -1;
   |      }
   |      // Remove the message queue (if this process created it)
   |      void
   |      Message_que::Remove( ) {
   +        if ( msgctl( msqid, IPC_RMID, (struct msqid_ds *) 0 ) == -1 )
   |          exit( 5 );
   |      }
   |      // Place a message in the message queue.
   |      void
  20      Message_que::Enque( void *msg, int msg_size ){
   |        if ( msgsnd( msqid, msg, msg_size, 0 ) == -1 )
   |          exit( 3 );
   |      }
```

```
  |       // Return a message from the message queue.
  +       int
  |       Message_que::Deque( void *msg, int msg_size, int msg_type ){
  |         int n;
  |         memset( msg, 0x0, msg_size );          // clear space
  |         if ( (n=msgrcv( msqid, msg, msg_size, msg_type, IPC_NOWAIT)) == -1 )
 30           exit( 4 );
  |         return n;
  |       }
  |       //   True if message queue exists else false.
  |       bool
  +       Message_que::Exist( const char the_key ){
  |         return (msgget(ipckey, 0) != -1);
  |       }
  |       //   Generate a new message queue.
  |       void
 40       Message_que::Create( ){
  |         if ( (msqid=msgget(ipckey, IPC_CREAT|0660)) == -1 )
  |           exit( 1 );
  |       }
  |       //   Acquire (gain access to) existing message queue.
  +       void
  |       Message_que::Acquire( ){
  |         if ( (msqid=msgget(ipckey, 0)) == -1 )
  |           exit( 2 );
  |       }
```

To use this class, the files `Message_que.h` and `Message_que.cxx` should reside locally. The `Message_que` class is compiled into object code with the command line

```
linux$  g++ Message_que.cxx -c
```

At the top of the source file that will use a `Message_que` object, add the statement

```
#include "Message_que.h"
```

to make the class definition available to the compiler. When compiling the source file, include the message queue object code file

```
linux$  g++ your_file_name.cxx   Message_que.o
```

Program 6.6 demonstrates the use of a message queue object. This program allows command-line manipulation of a message queue. As such, the message queue could be used as a drop off and retrieval site for messages.

227

Program 6.6 A command-line message queue manipulation utility.

```
File : p6.6.cxx
  |      /*
  |            A message queue manipulation utility
  |       */
  |      #include "Message_que.h"
  +      #include <iostream>
  |      #include <cstdlib>
  |      #include <unistd.h>
  |      using namespace std;
  |
 10      typedef struct {
  |        long int m_type;
  |        char m_text[1024];
  |      } MESSAGE;
  |      extern char    *optarg;
  +      extern int        optind, opterr, optopt;
  |      int
  |      main(int argc, char *argv[ ]){
  |        int      c;
  |        char     optstring[] = "sri:m:";
 20      opterr = 0;
  |        bool    snd_msg=false, get_msg=false, rmv_que=false;
  |        char    *the_message;
  |        //                               Allocate msg - clear text
  |        MESSAGE my_msg;
  +        memset( my_msg.m_text, 0x0, 1024 );
  |        //                               Allocate - acquire msg queue
  |        Message_que MQ('M');
  |        if ( !MQ.Exist('M') )
  |          MQ.Create( );
 30      else
  |          MQ.Acquire( );
  |        //                               Process command line args
  |        while ((c = getopt(argc, argv, optstring)) != -1)
  |          switch (c) {
  +          case 's':
  |            snd_msg=true;
  |            break;
  |          case 'r':
  |            get_msg=true;
 40          break;
  |          case 'i':
  |            my_msg.m_type=atol(optarg);
  |            break;
  |           case 'm':
  +            strcpy(my_msg.m_text,optarg);
  |          }
```

Include the `Message_que` class definition.

Acceptable command-line options: -s send, -r read, -i xx set message ID type to xx, and -m my_message (follow -m with the message).

Use the `optarg` reference to obtain the actual command-line data.

228

```
   |          if ( snd_msg && my_msg.m_type > 0  ){
   |            MQ.Enque( &my_msg, strlen(my_msg.m_text)+1);
   |            cerr << "Added   : " << my_msg.m_text << endl;
  50          } else  if ( get_msg &&  my_msg.m_type > 0 ){
   |            MQ.Deque(&my_msg, 1024, my_msg.m_type);
   |            cerr << "Message: " << my_msg.m_text << endl;
   |          } else
   |            cerr << "Invalid command line option(s)" << endl;
   +          return 0;
   |        }
```

In line 4 of the program, the definition of the Message_que class is included. At line 10, the format of a message queue message is defined. Within the function main, the acceptable command-line options are assigned to the optstring array. The program accepts two standard-format command-line options. The -s option indicates a message is to be sent to the message queue, while -r means a message should be read from the message queue. The remaining two options of the program require arguments. The -i option is to be followed with the message queue ID (type), and the -m option is to be followed with an actual message. If the message is more than one word, it should be surrounded with quotes.

A while loop and the **getopt** library function are used to parse command-line options. If the user indicates a message is to be sent, the message type (-i) and the actual message (-m) must be specified. If a message is to be retrieved, then just the message type (-i) must be indicated. The program informs the user of its activity, including a message that indicates when an improper set of command-line options has been passed. Figure 6.11 demonstrates the use of Program 6.6.

Figure 6.11 Manipulating a message queue from the command line.

```
linux$ ipcs -q                                              At the start, no message
------ Message Queues ------                          ◄———  queues in the system.
key        msqid      owner      perms      used-bytes messages

linux$ p6.6 -i 98 -s -m "Don't forget the fish!"
Added  : Don't forget the fish!
                                                             Add some messages to the
linux$ p6.6 -i 98 -s -m "See you Wednesday -jg            ╱► message queue.
Added  : See you Wednesday -jg

linux$ p6.6 -s -i 72 -m "Paper due on the 16th"
Added  : Paper due on the 16th

                                                            Three messages now in
linux$ ipcs -q                                        ◄———  the queue.
------ Message Queues ------
key        msqid      owner      perms      used-bytes messages
0x4d15ae86 4718592    gray         660         67         3
```

229

```
linux$ p6.6 -r -i 98
Message: Don't forget the fish!                    ◄──────   Retrieve the first two
                                                             messages of type 98.

linux$ p6.6 -r -i 98
Message: See you wednesday -jg

linux$ ipcs -q
------ Message Queues ------
key         msqid       owner       perms      used-bytes  messages
0x4d15ae86  4718592     gray        660        22          1

linux$ ipcs -q -i 4718592                                    What the system knows
Message Queue msqid=4718592        ──          ◄──────       about this message queue.
uid=500          gid=1000          cuid=500       cgid=1000       mode=0660
cbytes=22        qbytes=16384      qnum=1         lspid=17306     lrpid=17309
send_time=Sun Mar 10 17:06:40 2002
rcv_time=Sun Mar 10 17:06:40 2002
change_time=Sun Mar 10 17:06:40 2002
```

6-5 EXERCISE

Program 6.6 has a great deal of room for improvement. For example, when a message is retrieved, it is removed from the message queue. In addition, the user is unable to remove the message queue (without resorting to the **ipcrm** command). Modify Program 6.6 to support the nondestructive reading of messages and the removal of the message queue from the system.

6-6 EXERCISE

Modify the client–server programs to implement a *rudimentary chat* program that allows users to interactively talk to one another (sort of a poor man's **talk**). One way to do this is to have the server examine the first character of the text portion of a SERVER message. If the character is, say, a ".", then the message is assumed to be a command the server should act on. For example, if the sequence is .lo, then the server records the PID of the client as logged in. If the sequence is .who, the server returns the list of the PIDs of all logged-in (attached) clients. The PID information can then be used to *connect* the two processes so that interactive communication can occur.

6.8 Summary

Message queues are one of three interprocess communication facilities added
to UNIX with the release of System V. Once created, a message queue is maintained by the system. Unrelated processes, executing at different times, can use
a message queue to pass information. Each message has an associated type that
can be used to implement a rudimentary form of data multiplexing when multiple producers are involved. Message queues are created and accessed using
the **msgget** system call. Messages are placed in the message queue with the
msgsnd system call and retrieved from the queue with the **msgrcv** system
call. Additional message queue manipulations are carried out with the **msgctl**
system call. The **msgctl** system call returns information about the message
queue, permits modification of access permissions, and allows the owner to
remove the message queue facility.

6.9 Key Terms and Concepts

ftok library function
IPC facility
IPC key
IPC resource
IPC_CREAT
IPC_EXCL
IPC_NOWAIT
ipc_perm structure
IPC_PRIVATE
IPC_RMID
IPC_SET
IPC_STAT
ipcs command
iprm command
message queue class

message queues
message type
msg structure
MSG_EXCEPT
MSG_NOERROR
msgbuf structure
msgget system call
MSGMNB
MSGMNI
msgrcv system call
msgsnd system call
msqid_ds structure
semaphore
shared memory

Chapter 7

SEMAPHORES

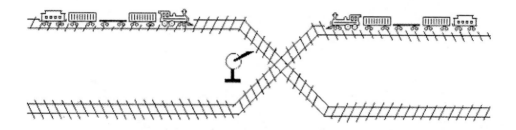

7.1 Introduction

Conceptually, a semaphore is a data structure that is shared by several processes.[1] Semaphores are most often used to synchronize operations when multiple processes access a common, non-shareable resource. By using semaphores, we attempt to avoid **starvation** (which occurs when a process is habitually denied access to a resource it needs) and **deadlock** (which occurs when two or more processes each hold a resource that the other needs while waiting for the other process to release its resource). When used to synchronize the access to a resource, a semaphore is initially set to the number of available resources. Each time a process wants to obtain the resource, the associated semaphore is tested. A positive, nonzero semaphore value indicates the resource is available. To indicate it has gained access to the resource, the process decrements the semaphore. For events to progress correctly, the test and decrement operation on the semaphore must be **atomic** (i.e., noninterruptible/indivisible). If the tested semaphore is zero, indicating the resource is not available, the requesting process must wait. When a process is finished with

---

[1] In this chapter we concentrate on semaphores as they relate to processes. In Chapter 11, we revisit semaphores and address their use with threads.

a semaphore-associated resource, the process indicates the return of the resource by incrementing the semaphore. Once a resource is returned, other processes that have been waiting for the resource are notified by the system. Semaphores that control access to a single resource, taking the value of 0 (resource is in use) or 1 (resource is available), are often called **binary** semaphores.[2] Semaphores controlling access to multiple resources, thus assuming a range of nonnegative values, are frequently called **counting** semaphores.

E. W. Dijkstra (1965) did much of the early work describing the use of semaphores to coordinate access to shared resources. Most college-level operating systems textbooks—for example, Silberschatz and Peterson (1989), Tanenbaum (2001), Nutt (2002), Stallings (2001), and Deitel (1990)—contain excellent discussions on the theory and use of semaphores for process synchronization.

Implementation-wise, a semaphore is a nonnegative integer that is stored in the kernel. Access to the semaphore is provided by a series of semaphore system calls. The semaphore system calls assure the user the test and decrement operations on the semaphore will be atomic. Likewise, the semaphore system calls, by default, cause the invoking process to block if the semaphore value indicates the resource is not available (i.e., the semaphore is a 0). When the resource becomes available and the semaphore becomes nonzero, the system notifies the queued, waiting processes of this event. To increase their flexibility, in UNIX semaphores are generated as sets (arrays) consisting of one or more semaphores. Operations acting upon individual semaphores within the set or upon the entire semaphore set are provided.

7.2 Creating and Accessing Semaphore Sets

Before a semaphore set can be used, it must be created. The creation of the semaphore set generates a unique data structure that the system uses to identify and manipulate the semaphores. The definition of system semaphore data structure is found in the system-dependent include file `<bits/sem.h>`. This file is not directly referenced by the programmer, since the standard include file `<sys/sem.h>` includes this file.

---

[2] In function, binary semaphores are similar to the lock files discussed in Chapter 4. Unfortunately, semaphores can only be used by processes residing on the same system, while, with some stretching, lock files can be implemented in a networked environment. Of course, semaphores are much faster and more reliable than lock files.

```
struct semid_ds {
    struct ipc_perm sem_perm;            /* operation permission struct */
    __time_t sem_otime;                  /* last semop() time */
    unsigned long int __unused1;
    __time_t sem_ctime;                  /* last time changed by semctl() */
    unsigned long int __unused2;
    unsigned long int sem_nsems;         /* number of semaphores in set */
    unsigned long int __unused3;
    unsigned long int __unused4;
};
```

In keeping with its origins, and for System V compatibility, the `semid_ds` structure is also defined in `<linux/sem.h>` as

```
struct semid_ds {
    struct ipc_perm sem_perm;             /* permissions .. see ipc.h */
    __kernel_time_t sem_otime;            /* last semop time */
    __kernel_time_t sem_ctime;            /* last change time */
    struct sem        *sem_base;          /* ptr to first semaphore in array */
    struct sem_queue *sem_pending;        /* pending operations to be processed */
    struct sem_queue **sem_pending_last;  /* last pending operation */
    struct sem_undo *undo;                /* undo requests on this array */
    unsigned short    sem_nsems;          /* no. of semaphores in array */
};
```

As with message queues, there is a bit of a disconnect between the way we view and discuss semaphores and the way they may actually be implemented at a system level. Additional system-specific details can be found in the source code for semaphore implementation in the kernel source directory `/usr/src/linux-XX.XX.XX/ipc` (where XX is the appropriate version number). On our system the files `sem.c` and `util.h` contain additional semaphore implementation details.

Using the `<linux/sem.h>` definition as our reference, the system semaphore data structure `semid_ds` contains a permission structure of type `ipc_perm`, which is used to specify the access permissions for the semaphore set. The access permission structure is followed by two time members. These store the time of the last operation on the semaphore (`sem_otime`) and the time of its last modification (`sem_ctime`). The next member is a reference, `sem_base`, to an array (set) of structures of type `sem`. The `sem` structure contains the semaphore value and the ID of the last process to operate on the semaphore. Here is the definition of a `sem` structure:

```
struct sem {
        int     semval;       /* current value        */
        int     sempid;       /* pid of last operation */
};
```

Following the pointer to the base of the semaphore array are three additional pointers. The `sem_pending` member references a linked list (treated as a queue) of pending semaphore operations. Normally, semaphore operations are done immediately, so requests are only added to this list if for some reason the request cannot processed immediately. The `sem_pending_last` member references the end of the same list. The `sem_undo` member references a list of undo operations. These operations, stored when a semaphore operation sets the SEM_UNDO flag, can be used to undo requested semaphore operations to return the semaphore to its previous state. The kernel uses the undo list information to reverse semaphore operations when a process exits without releasing its allocated semaphores. This action helps reduce the chance of deadlock. The system semaphore data structure also keeps track of the number of semaphores in the set (`sem_nsems`).

A conceptual arrangement of a system semaphore structure for a newly allocated set of three semaphores is shown in Figure 7.1.

To create a semaphore or gain access to one that exists, the **semget** system call, shown in Table 7.1, is used.

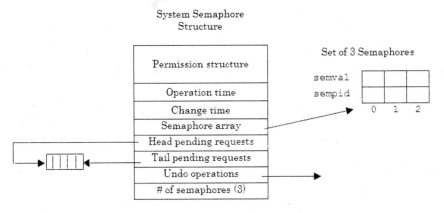

Figure 7.1 Data structures for a set of three semaphores.

Table 7.1 Summary of the `semget` System Call.

Include File(s)	`<sys/types.h>` `<sys/ipc.h>` `<sys/sem.h>`	Manual Section	**2**
Summary	`int semget (key_t key, int nsems, int semflg);`		

	Success	Failure	Sets `errno`
Return	The semaphore identifier	−1	Yes

The **semget** system call takes three arguments. The first argument, `key`, is used by the system to generate a unique semaphore identifier. The second argument, `nsems`, is the number of semaphores in the set. The system uses the `nsems` value when allocating the array of `sem` structures. Remember, as with all arrays in C/C++, the array of `sem` structures that represents the set of semaphores is indexed starting at 0. The `nsems` value should be less than or equal to the SEMMSL value, which sets the upper boundary for the number of semaphores for a given semaphore ID. The third argument, `semflg`, is used to specify access permission and/or special creation conditions. The low-order bits of the `semflg` value are used to specify the access permissions for the owner, group, and other. Read and write permissions control reading and alteration of the semaphore; execute permission settings are ignored. The flags IPC_CREAT and IPC_EXCL may be **OR**ed with the permission value.

If the **semget** system call is successful, a nonnegative integer, the semaphore identifier, is returned. If the value for `key` is IPC_PRIVATE or the value for `key` does not have a semaphore identifier associated with it, and IPC_CREAT has been specified, a new set of semaphores is created. When created, the semaphore set represented by the array of `sem` structures is not initialized. If IPC_CREAT is specified (but not IPC_EXCL) and the semaphore set for the indicated key value already exists, the **semget** system call returns the associated semaphore identifier. When using **semget** to access an established semaphore set (such as in a client process), the value of `nsems` can be set to 0 (a don't-care value).

When the semaphore is created, the system sets, respectively, the `semid_ds` members `sem_perm.cuid`, `sem_perm.uid`, `sem_perm.cgid`, and `sem_perm.gid` to the effective user and group ID of the invoking process. The member `sem_otime` is set to 0, and `sem_ctime` is assigned the current time. The `nsems` member stores the number of semaphores in the semaphore set.

If the **semget** system call fails, it returns a -1 and sets the value stored in `errno`. Error messages for **semget** are shown in Table 7.2.

Table 7.2 semget Error Messages.

#	**Constant**	`perror` **Message**	**Explanation**
2	EOENT	No such file or directory	Semaphore identifier does not exist for this key, and IPC_CREAT was not set.
12	ENOMEM	Cannot allocate memory	Insufficient system memory to allocate the semaphore set.

Continued

237

Table 7.2   *(Continued)*

#	Constant	`perror` **Message**	**Explanation**
13	EACCES	Permission denied	Semaphore identifier exists for this key, but requested operation is not allowed by current access permissions.
17	EEXIST	File exists	Semaphore identifier exists for this key, but the flags IPC_CREAT and IPC_EXCL are both set.
28	ENOSPC	No space left on device	System-imposed limit (SEMMNI) for the number of semaphore sets or systemwide maximum number of semaphores (SEMMNS) has been reached.
43	EIDRM	Identifier removed	Specified semaphore set is marked for removal.

Program 7.1 attempts to create several semaphore sets, each containing three semaphores.

Program 7.1   Creating semaphore sets.

```
File : p7.1.cxx
   |     /* Creating sets of semaphores */
   |     #include <iostream>
   |     #include <cstdio>
   |     #include <sys/types.h>
   +     #include <sys/ipc.h>
   |     #include <sys/sem.h>
   |     using namespace std;
   |     int
   |     main( ){
  10       int      sem1, sem2, sem3;
   |        key_t    ipc_key;
   |        ipc_key = ftok(".", 'S');
   |        if ((sem1 = semget(ipc_key, 3, IPC_CREAT | 0666)) == -1) {
   |          cerr << "semget: IPC_CREAT | 0666" << endl;
   +        }
   |        cout << "sem1 identifier " << sem1 << endl;
   |        if ((sem2 = semget(ipc_key, 3, IPC_CREAT|IPC_EXCL|0666)) == -1) {
   |          cerr << "semget: IPC_CREAT | IPC_EXCL | 0666" << endl;
   |        }
  20       cout << "sem2 identifier " << sem2 << endl;
   |        if ((sem3 = semget(IPC_PRIVATE, 3, 0600)) == -1) {
```

```
|        cerr << "semget: IPC_PRIVATE" << endl;
|      }
|      cout << "sem3 identifier " <<  sem3 <<  endl;
+      return 0;
|    }
```

The first call to **semget**, provided the system limits have not been reached, creates a set of three semaphores. The permissions for the set are **read** and **alter** (write) for the owner, group, and others (world). The value of the semaphore identifier is tied to the key value that is produced by the call to **ftok**. The second call to **semget** attempts to create a second set of three semaphores. The call uses the same key value as the first but includes the specification IPC_EXCL. With the IPC_EXCL flag set and the previous successful creation of the semaphore set using the same key value, this invocation of **semget** will fail. The third call to **semget** creates a three-semaphore set used by specifying IPC_PRIVATE instead of using the **ftok** key value. The semaphore identifier generated for this set will be private to this process.

When the program is run twice consecutively, the output generated will be similar to that shown in Figure 7.2.

Figure 7.2   Two consecutive runs of Program 7.1.

```
linux$ p7.1
sem1 identifier 9797637
semget: IPC_CREAT | IPC_EXCL | 0666: File exists
sem2 identifier -1
sem3 identifier 9830406

linux$ p7.1
sem1 identifier 9797637
semget: IPC_CREAT | IPC_EXCL | 0666: File exists
sem2 identifier -1
sem3 identifier 9863175
```

Notice that when the program is run the second time, the same semaphore identifier (9797637) is returned from the initial call to **semget**. Without the IPC_EXCL flag, the **semget** system call will not fail if the semaphore set has already been created, but will instead return the associated semaphore identifier. The creation of a second private semaphore set by the second invocation of the program produces another unique semaphore identifier (9863175), which is different from the first private semaphore identifier (9830406). The output of the **ipcs** command, shown in Figure 7.3, verifies the presence and permissions of the three semaphore sets that were created by the user gray. Notice that the key for each of the private semaphore sets is 0.

Figure 7.3 `ipcs` output.

```
linux$ ipcs -s
-----Semaphore Arrays------
key        semid     owner     perms     nsems     status
0x53157f08 9797637   gray      666       3
0x00000000 9830406   gray      600       3
0x00000000 9863175   gray      600       3
```

As written, Program 7.1 does not remove the semaphore sets it creates. Semaphores, like message queues, are a limited resource. In a programming setting, semaphores can be removed with the **semctl** system call (see the following section). Semaphores may also be removed at the command-line level using the **ipcrm** command (as discussed in Chapter 6, Section 6.1). If there are several semaphores to remove, a shell script, such as that shown in Program 7.2, can be used to automate the removal process.

Program 7.2 A Korn shell script to remove all semaphores for a user.

```
File : clean
  |      #!/bin/ksh
  |      #
  |      #  Korn Shell script to remove all existing semaphores for a user
  |      #
  +      list=$(ipcs -s | grep "$USER" | cut -d' ' -f2)
  |      count=0
  |      for semaphore in $list
  |      do
  |       ipcrm sem $semaphore > /dev/null
 10       ((count=count+1))
  |      done
  |      print "$count semaphore(s) for $USER removed"
```

7-1 EXERCISE

Rewrite the shell script shown as Program 7.2 to permit the user to specify four command-line options: -q to remove message queues, -s to remove semaphores, -m to remove shared memory segments, and -a to remove all IPC facilities. If the script is run by root, a warning message and request for verification should be included.

Write a program that determines by trial and error the maximum number of semaphores per `semid` and semaphore sets. If you completed Exercise 7-1, you may find your script to be of help in removing allocated semaphores.

7.3 Semaphore Control

The **semget** system call (Table 7.3) is used to create or gain access to a set of semaphores. The **semctl** system call allows the user to perform a variety of generalized control operations on the system semaphore structure, on the semaphores as a set, and on individual semaphores. Additional manipulative operations on specific semaphores within a set are covered in the following section on semaphore operations (Section 7.4).

Table 7.3 Summary of the `semctl` System Call.

Include File(s)	`<sys/types.h>`
	`<sys/ipc.h>`
	`<sys/sem.h>`
		Manual Section	**2**

Summary	`int semctl(int semid, int semnum, int cmd,` `union semun arg);`		
	Success	Failure	Sets `errno`
Return	0 or the value requested	-1	Yes

The **semctl** system call takes four arguments. The first argument, `semid`, is a valid semaphore identifier that was returned by a previous **semget** system call. The second argument, `semnum`, is the number of semaphores in the semaphore set. In most cases, this value is greater than 0 but less than the system limit. However, we will see occasions when the value for `semnum` is set to 0. These occasions arise when we ask **semctl** to perform an operation for which the number of semaphores in the set is not relevant. The third argument to **semctl**, `cmd`, is an integer command value (usually expressed as one of the symbolic constants found in the header files `<sys/ipc.h>` or `<sys/sem.h>`). As discussed in detail in Section 7.3.1, "Semaphore Control Details," the `cmd` value directs

semctl to take one of several control actions. Each action requires specific access permissions to the semaphore control structure (i.e., **read** or **alter**). The fourth argument to **semctl**, arg, is a union of type semun. Given the action specified by the preceding cmd argument, the data in arg can be one of any of the following four values:

1. An integer used with SETVAL to indicate a specific value for a particular semaphore within the semaphore set.
2. A reference to a semid_ds structure where information is returned when IPC_STAT or IPC_SET is specified.
3. A reference to an array of type unsigned short integers; the array is used either to initialize the semaphore set (such as when stipulating SETALL) or as a return location when specifying GETALL.
4. A reference to a seminfo structure when IPC_INFO is requested.

In some versions of UNIX the definition of the semun union is found in the include files required by **semctl**. However, technically the user should define the union. To this end, the manual page for **semctl** contains the following cryptic reference.

```
#if defined(__GNU_LIBRARY__) && !defined(_SEM_SEMUN_UNDEFINED)
/* union semun is defined by including <sys/sem.h> */
#else
/* according to X/OPEN we have to define it ourselves */
union semun {
        int val;                     /* value for SETVAL */
        struct semid_ds *buf;        /* buffer for IPC_STAT, IPC_SET */
        unsigned short int *array;   /* array for GETALL, SETALL */
        struct seminfo *__buf;       /* buffer for IPC_INFO */
};
#endif
```

This sequence of preprocessor directives determines whether the programmer defines the semun union. If __GNU_LIBRARY__ has been defined (is nonzero), and _SEM_SEMUN_UNDEFINED has not been defined, the definition of the union semun is found in the include file <sys/sem.h>. Otherwise, the user defines the union. To be safe, this set of preprocessor directives should be placed at the top any program that will make use of the fourth argument of the **semctl** call. Its omission may cause the **semctl** system call to fail, returning the value EFAULT (bad address). Further, when specifying arg as the fourth argument to **semctl**, the value for arg should be explicitly assigned (e.g., arg.buf=ptr_to_my_structure). This assignment must be done prior to the calling of **semctl** (see Program 7.3).

7.3.1 Semaphore Control Details

The following cmd values cause **semctl** to act upon the system semaphore structure (semid_ds):

- **IPC_STAT**—Return the current values of the semid_ds structure for the indicated semaphore identifier. The returned information is stored in a user-generated structure referenced by the fourth argument to **semctl**. To specify IPC_STAT, the process must have **read** permission for the semaphore set associated with the semaphore identifier.
- **IPC_SET**—Modify a restricted number of members in the semid_ds structure. The members sem_perm.uid, sem_perm.gid and sem_perm.mode (in the permissions structure within semid_ds) can be changed if the effective ID of the accessing process is that of the superuser or is the same as the ID value stored in sem_perm.cuid or sem_perm.uid. To make these changes, a structure of the type semid_ds must be allocated. The appropriate members' values are then assigned, and a reference to the modified structure is passed as the fourth argument to the **semctl** system call.
- **IPC_RMID**—Remove the semaphore set associated with the semaphore identifier.

When specifying IPC_STAT, IPC_SET, or IPC_RMID, the value for semnum (the number of semaphores in the set) is not considered and can be set to 0.

The following cmd values cause **semctl** to act upon the entire set of semaphores:

- **GETALL**—Return the current values of the semaphore set. The values are returned via the array reference passed as the fourth argument to **semctl**. The user is responsible for allocating the array of the proper size and type prior to passing its address to **semctl**. **Read** permission for the semaphore set is required to specify GETALL. When specifying GETALL, the argument semnum is ignored.
- **SETALL**—Initialize all semaphores in a set to the values stored in the array referenced by the fourth argument to **semctl**. Again, the user must allocate the initializing array and assign values prior to passing the address of the array to **semctl**. The process must have **alter** access for the semaphore set to use SETALL. When specifying SETALL, the sem_ctime member of the system semaphore data structure is updated.

243

The last set of **semctl** cmd values acts upon individual semaphores or upon specific members in the semid_ds structure. All of these commands require **read** permission except for SETVAL, which requires **alter** permission:

- **GETVAL**—Return the current value of the individual semaphore referenced by the value of the semnum argument (remember, arrays in C/C++ are zero-based; thus, the first semaphore of a set is at index 0).
- **SETVAL**—Set the value of the individual semaphore referenced by the semnum argument to the value specified by the fourth argument to **semctl** (e.g., the value stored in arg.val).
- **GETPID**—Return the PID from the sem_perm structure within the semid_ds structure.
- **GETNCNT**—Return the number of processes waiting for the semaphore referenced by the semnum argument to increase in value.
- **GETZCNT**—Return the number of processes waiting for the semaphore referenced by the semnum argument to become 0.

If **semctl** is successfully issues any of these commands, the requested integer value is returned: the value of semncnt for GETNCNT, the value of sempid for GETPID, the value of semval for GETVAL, or the value of semzcnt for GETZCNT. If **semctl** fails, it returns a value of −1 and sets errno to indicate the specific error. The errors returned by **semctl** with an explanation of their meaning are shown in Table 7.4.

Table 7.4 semctl Error Messages.

#	Constant	perror Message	Explanation
1	EPERM	Operation not permitted	Value for cmd is IPC_RMID or IPC_SET and the calling process in not the owner or superuser.
13	EACCES	Permission denied	The requested operation is not allowed by the current access permissions for this process.
14	EFAULT	Bad address	The fourth argument to semctl contains a reference to an illegal address (the union semun may not have been declared).
22	EINVAL	Invalid argument	• The semaphore identifier is invalid.

Table 7.4 (Continued)

#	Constant	perror Message	Explanation
			• The number of semaphores specified is less than 0 or greater than the number in the semaphore set. • The value for cmd is invalid. • The value for cmd is IPC_SET, but the value for sem_perm.uid or sem_perm.gid is invalid.
34	ERANGE	Numerical result out of range	The value for cmd is SETVAL or SETALL, and the value to be assigned is greater than the system maximum or less than 0.
43	EIDRM	Identifier removed	Specified semaphore set is marked for removal.

Program 7.3 uses the **semctl** system call to perform a number of semaphore control operations.

Program 7.3 Using semctl.

```
File : p7.3.cxx
   |     /*
   |           Using the semctl system call
   |      */
   |     #include <iostream>
   +     #include <cstdio>                        Do we need to define semun union?
   |     #include <sys/ipc.h>
   |     #include <sys/sem.h>
   |     #include <time.h>
   |     #define  NS    3
  10     #if defined(__GNU_LIBRARY__) && !defined(_SEM_SEMUN_UNDEFINED)
   |                                     // definition in <sys/sem.h>
   |     #else
   |     union semun {                   // We define:
   |       int val;                      // value  for SETVAL
   +       struct semid_ds *buf;         // buffer for IPC_STAT, IPC_SET
   |       unsigned short int *array;    // array  for GETALL, SETALL
   |       struct seminfo *__buf;        // buffer for IPC_INFO
   |     };
   |     #endif
  20     using namespace std;
   |     int
   |     main( ){
```

245

```
  |        int            sem_id, sem_value, i;
  |        key_t          ipc_key;
  +        struct semid_ds sem_buf;
  |        unsigned short int  sem_array[NS] = {3, 1, 4};
  |        union semun    arg;
  |        ipc_key = ftok(".", 'S');
  |
 30        if ((sem_id = semget(ipc_key, NS, IPC_CREAT | 0660)) == -1) {
  |          perror("semget: IPC_CREAT | 0660");
  |          return 1;
  |        }
  |        cout << "Semaphore identifier " << sem_id << endl;
  +        arg.buf = &sem_buf;
  |        if (semctl(sem_id, 0, IPC_STAT, arg) == -1) {
  |          perror("semctl: IPC_STAT");
  |          return 2;
  |        }
 40        cout << "Created " <<  ctime(&sem_buf.sem_ctime) << endl;
  |        arg.array = sem_array;
  |        if (semctl(sem_id, 0, SETALL, arg) == -1) {
  |          perror("semctl: SETALL");
  |          return 3;
  +        }
  |        for (i = 0; i < NS; ++i) {
  |          if ((sem_value = semctl(sem_id, i, GETVAL, 0)) == -1) {
  |            perror("semctl: GETVAL");
  |            return 4;
 50        }
  |          cout << "Semaphore " << i << " has value of " << sem_value << endl;
  |        }
  |        if (semctl(sem_id, 0, IPC_RMID, 0) == -1) {
  |          perror("semctl: IPC_RMID");
  +          return 5;
  |        }
  |        return 0;
  |      }
```

Set arg to be the address of the storage for the returned values.

Set arg to be the address of the initializing vector.

Program 7.3 creates a set of three semaphores. The semaphore identifier for the set is printed. In line 35, the address of sem_buf is assigned to the appropriate member of arg. The union arg now contains the location where the returned data will be stored. Then, by specifying IPC_STAT and passing the proper address, **semctl** obtains the current values of the system semaphore structure. The date and time the semaphore was created are displayed using the library function **ctime**. Using similar syntax, other members of the semid_ds structure could be displayed. However, there is another way to obtain the entire contents of the semid_ds structure (albeit on a temporary basis). To do this, compile Program 7.3 with the -g option and then use the debugger, **gdb**, to examine the semid_ds structure. This can be accomplished by invoking

gdb with the executable program name, such as `linux$ gdb p7.3`. When in **gdb**, direct **gdb** to stop at the correct line (say, `break 40`). The program is then run, and when **gdb** stops at line 40, it is asked to print the contents of the structure using the **gdb** command: `print sem_buf`. The output of such a sequence will display the contents of the entire `sem_buf` structure. On our system, Program 7.3 run in **gdb** produces the output shown in Figure 7.4:

Figure 7.4   dbx output of Program 7.3.

```
linux$ g++ -g -o p7.3 p7.3.cxx              ◄─────────── Compile the program with
linux$ gdb p7.3                                          the −g option.
GNU gdb 5.0rh-5 Red Hat Linux 7.1
Copyright 2001 Free Software Foundation, Inc.
GDB is free software, covered by the GNU General Public License, and you are
welcome to change it and/or distribute copies of it under certain conditions.
Type "show copying" to see the conditions.
There is absolutely no warranty for GDB.  Type "show warranty" for details.
This GDB was configured as "i386-redhat-linux"...
(gdb) break 40                               ◄─────────── Stop at line 40 of the
Breakpoint 1 at 0x8048890: file p7.3.cxx, line 40.       program.
(gdb) run
Starting program: /home/faculty/gray/revision/07/p7.3
Semaphore identifier 10027013
Breakpoint 1, main () at p7.3.cxx:40
40          cout << "Created " << ctime(&sem_buf.sem_ctime) << endl;
Current language:  auto; currently c++
(gdb) print sem_buf
$1 = {sem_perm = {__key = 1393917704, uid = 500, gid = 1000, cuid = 500,
      cgid = 1000, mode = 432, __pad1 = 0, __seq = 306, __pad2 = 0,
      __unused1 = 0, __unused2 = 0}, sem_otime = 0, __unused1 = 0,
      sem_ctime = 1016545082, __unused2 = 0, sem_nsems = 3, __unused3 = 0,
      __unused4 = 0}
(gdb)
```

Notice, as would be expected, that the number of semaphores in the set, three, has been stored in the `sem_nsems` member.

Program 7.3 uses the **semctl** system call to initialize the three-semaphore set to the values stored in the array `sem_array`. Again, notice that prior to calling **semctl** the address of the initializing vector (see line 41) is assigned to the proper member of `arg`. Once the values are assigned to the semaphore set, the program uses a loop to display to the screen the value stored in each semaphore. The last action of Program 7.3 is to use the **semctl** system call with the IPC_RMID flag to remove the semaphore set.

When run outside of **gdb**, the output of Program 7.3 should be similar to that shown in Figure 7.5.

Figure 7.5 Output of Program 7.3.

```
linux$ p7.3
Semaphore identifier 10027013
Created Tue Mar 19 08:38:02 2002

Semaphore 0 has value of 3
Semaphore 1 has value of 1
Semaphore 2 has value of 4
```

7-3 EXERCISE

After generating a set of, say, three semaphores, can **semctl** be used to alter the values of sem_nsems to indicate an increase or decrease in the number of semaphores in a set? Is this a bug or a feature? Provide a program segment that supports your answer

7-4 EXERCISE

In earlier IPC implementations, the base address of the semaphore set was stored in the member sem_base. In current versions, the user does not have access to this address. Why do you suppose the developers removed the ability to access the semaphore set directly?

7.4 Semaphore Operations

Additional operations on individual semaphores are accomplished by using the **semop** system call, shown in Table 7.5.

The **semop** system call requires three arguments and returns an integer value. If successful, **semop** returns a 0; otherwise it returns a −1 and sets errno to indicate the source of the error (see Table 7.9 for details). The first argument for **semop**, semid, is the semaphore identifier returned by a previous successful call to **semget**. The second argument, sops, is a reference to the base address of an array of semaphore operations that will be performed on the semaphore set associated with by the semid value. The **semop** system call will attempt to perform, in an all-or-nothing manner, all of the semaphore

Table 7.5 Summary of the `semop` System Call.

Include File(s)	`<sys/types.h>` `<sys/ipc.h>` `<sys/sem.h>`	Manual Section	**2**
Summary	`int semop(int semid, struct sembuf *sops,` `unsigned nsops);`		
	Success	Failure	Sets `errno`
Return	0	−1	Yes

operations indicated by `sops`. The third argument, `nsops`, is the number of elements in the array of semaphore operations.

Each element of the semaphore operation array is a structure of type `sembuf`.

```
/*
    User semaphore template for semop system calls.
 */

struct sembuf {
  unsigned short int sem_num;   // semaphore #: 0 = first
  short int sem_op;             // semaphore operation
  short int sem_flg;            // operation flags
};
```

The first member of the `sembuf` structure, `sem_num`, is the semaphore number (remember, the first semaphore is 0, the second 1, etc.). The second member of `sembuf`, `sem_op`, is the operation to be performed on the semaphore. A positive integer value means to increment the semaphore (in general, indicating a release or return of a resource), a negative value for `sem_op` means to decrement the semaphore (an attempt to acquire a resource), and a value of 0 means to test if the semaphore is currently at 0 (in use, all resource(s) allocated). Additional details on semaphore operations will be provided in a subsequent section. The third member of `sembuf` is an operation flag. These flags are

- **IPC_NOWAIT**—If the semaphore operation cannot be performed (such as when attempting to decrement a semaphore or test if it is equal to 0), the call returns immediately. No other semaphores in the set are modified if one of the specified semaphore operations fails with the IPC_NOWAIT flag.
- **SEM_UNDO**—If IPC_NOWAIT has not been indicated, the SEM_UNDO flag allows an operation to be undone if a blocked operation (one waiting for a specific condition) subsequently fails. The system keeps track of the adjustment values needed for each semaphore set. The

249

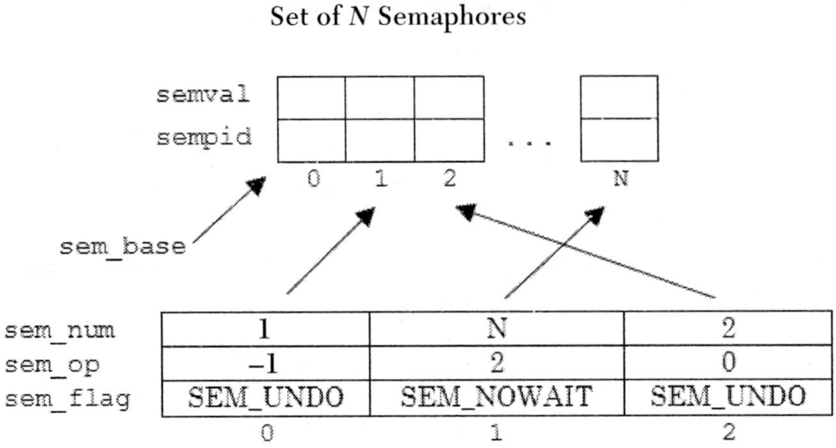

Set of *N* Semaphores

Figure 7.6 Three-semaphore operations for an *N* element set of semaphores.

adjustment values are kept on a per-process basis and actually indicate how many resources are being held, while the systemwide semaphore value indicates how many resources are currently free.

Figure 7.6 shows a relationship of an arbitrary three-element semaphore operation array to an *N* element set of semaphores.

7.4.1 Semaphore Operation Details

When the `sem_op` value is *negative*, the process specifying the operation is attempting to decrement the semaphore. The decrement of the semaphore is used to record the acquisition of the resource affiliated with the semaphore. When a semaphore value is to be modified, the accessing process must have **alter** permission for the semaphore set. The actions taken by the **semop** system call when the value for `sem_op` is negative are summarized in Table 7.6.

When the `sem_op` value is *positive*, the process is adding to the semaphore value. The addition is used to record the return (release) of the resource affiliated with the semaphore. Again, when a semaphore value is to be modified, the accessing process must have **alter** permission for the semaphore set. The actions taken by the **semop** system call when the value for `sem_op` is positive are summarized in Table 7.7.

When the `sem_op` value is *zero*, the process is testing the semaphore to determine if it is at 0. When a semaphore is at 0, the testing process can

Table 7.6 Actions Taken by `semop` when the Value for `sem_op` is Negative.

Condition	Flag Set	Action Taken by `semop`
`semval >= abs(semop)`		Subtract `abs(sem_op)` from `semval`.
`semval >= abs(semop)`	SEM_UNDO	Subtract `abs(sem_op)` from `semval` and update the undo counter for the semaphore.
`semval < abs(semop)`		Increment `semncnt` for the semaphore and wait (block) until • `semval >= abs(semop)`, then adjust `semncnt` and subtract as noted in the previous two rows of table. • `semid` is removed, then return −1 and set `errno` to EIDRM. • A signal is caught, then adjust `semncnt` and set `errno` to EINTR.
`semval < abs(semop)`	IPC_NOWAIT	Return −1 immediately and set `errno` to EAGAIN.

Table 7.7 Actions Taken by `semop` when the Value for `sem_op` Is Positive.

Condition	Flag Set	Action Taken by `semop`
		Add `sem_op` to `semval`.
	SEM_UNDO	Add `sem_op` to `semval` and update the undo counter for the semaphore.

assume that all the resources affiliated with the semaphore are currently allocated (in use). For a semaphore value to be tested, the accessing process must have **read** permission for the semaphore set. The action taken by the **semop** system call when the value for `sem_op` is 0 is summarized in Table 7.8.

The errors returned by **semop**, with an explanation of their meaning, are shown in Table 7.9.

If **semop** is successful, for each of the semaphores modified/referenced, **semop** sets the value of `sempid` to that of the calling process for each semaphore specified in the array referenced by `sops`. Additionally, both the `sem_otime` and `sem_ctime` members are set to the current time.

Program 7.4 demonstrates the use of the **semop** system call. Two semaphores are used to coordinate concurrent producer and consumer

251

Table 7.8 Actions Taken by `semop` when the Value for `sem_op` is Zero.

Condition	Flag Set	Action Taken by `semop`
`semval == 0`		Return immediately.
`semval != 0`	IPC_NOWAIT	Return -1 immediately and set `errno` to EAGAIN.
`semval != 0`		Increment `semzcnt` for the semaphore and wait (block) until • `semval == 0`, then adjust `semzcnt` and return. • `semid` is removed, then return -1 and set `errno` to EIDRM. • A signal is caught, then adjust `semzcnt` and set `errno` to EINTR.

Table 7.9 `semop` Error Messages.

#	Constant	`perror` Message	Explanation
4	EINTR	Interrupted system call	While in a wait queue for the semaphore, a signal was received by the calling process.
7	E2BIG	Argument list too long	The value for `nsops` is greater than the system limit.
11	EAGAIN	Resource temporarily unavailable	The requested operation would cause the calling process to block, but IPC_NOWAIT was specified.
12	ENOMEM	Cannot allocate memory	The limit for number of processes requesting SEM_UNDO has been exceeded.
13	EACCES	Permission denied	The requested operation is forbidden by the current access permissions.
14	EFAULT	Bad address	The value for `sops` references an illegal address.
22	EINVAL	Invalid argument	• The semaphore identifier is invalid. • The number of semaphores requesting SEM_UNDO is greater than the system limit.
27	EFBIG	File too large	The value for `sem_num` is < 0 or $>=$ to the number of semaphores in the set.

Table 7.9   (Continued)

#	Constant	`perror` Message	Explanation
34	ERANGE	Numerical result out of range	The requested operation would cause the system semaphore adjustment value to exceed its limit.
43	EIDRM	Identifier removed	The semaphore set associated with `semid` value has been removed.

processes. The producer process generates (at its own pace) an integer value. The value is stored in a non-shareable resource (in this case a file in the local directory). The consumer process, once a new value has been generated, retrieves the value from the same file and displays the value to the screen. Two semaphores are used by the producer process to prevent it from overwriting a previously stored integer value before the consumer process has retrieved it (should the producer process be speedier than the consumer process). The consumer process uses the two semaphores to prevent it from retrieving the same value multiple times (should the producer process be slow in generating new values). The semaphores, which we will arbitrarily call READ and MADE, are treated in a binary manner. By convention, the MADE semaphore is set to 1 by the producer process once the producer has stored its newly created integer value in the file. The READ semaphore is set to 1 by the consumer process once the consumer has read the value stored in the file by the producer. If the number has yet to be made by the producer or the number has not been read by the consumer, the corresponding semaphore value will be 0. The producer will gain access to the file to store the generated number only if the number currently in the file has been consumed. Likewise, the consumer can gain access to the file to read the stored number only if a new value has been made. Figure 7.7 shows the contents of the two semaphores in the producer and consumer processes and their relationship to one another. At the start we indicate that the current stored number has been read (we set READ to 1) and that a new number has not been generated (we set MADE to 0).

	Producer		Consumer		
	READ	MADE	READ	MADE	
Acquire READ	1	0	0	1	Acquire MADE
Critical Region	0	0	0	0	Critical Region
Release MADE	0	1	1	0	Release READ

Figure 7.7 Semaphore values in the producer and consumer processes.

253

A high-level algorithm for the producer and consumer processes would be as follows:

Producer

While 10 new numbers not generated

- Generate a new number
- If the current stored number has not been read, then wait
- Store the new number in the file
- Indicate that a new number has been made

Consumer

Forever

- If a new number has not been made, then wait
- Retrieve the new number from the file
- Indicate new number has been read
- Display the retrieved number

For discussion purposes, the program (which actually resides in a single file) has been divided into three sections, shown as Programs 7.4A, 7.4B, and 7.4C. The first part of the program, which establishes the operations that will be performed on the semaphores, creates the set of two semaphores and initializes them, is shown in Program 7.4A.

Program 7.4A The first section of the producer/consumer problem.

```
File : p7.4.cxx
    |      /*
    |             The producer/consumer problem
    |       */
    |      #include <iostream>                     // Section ONE
    +      #include <cstdio>
    |      #include <unistd.h>
    |      #include <stdlib.h>
    |      #include <sys/types.h>
    |      #include <sys/ipc.h>
  10       #include <sys/sem.h>
    |      #define BUFFER "./buffer"
    |      #if defined(__GNU_LIBRARY__) && !defined(_SEM_SEMUN_UNDEFINED)
    |                                              // definition in <sys/sem.h>
    |      #else
    +      union semun {                           // We define:
    |        int val;                              // value  for SETVAL
    |        struct semid_ds *buf;                 // buffer for IPC_STAT, IPC_SET
    |        unsigned short int *array;            // array  for GETALL, SETALL
    |        struct seminfo *__buf;                // buffer for IPC_INFO
```

```
20    };
 |    #endif
 |    using namespace std;
 |    int
 |    main(int argc, char *argv[ ]) {
 +       FILE            *fptr;
 |       static struct sembuf acquire = {0, -1, SEM_UNDO},
 |                            release = {0,  1, SEM_UNDO};
 |       pid_t           c_pid;
 |       key_t           ipc_key;
30       static unsigned short   start_val[2] = {1, 0};
 |       int             semid, producer = 0, i, n, p_sleep, c_sleep;
 |       union semun     arg;
 |       enum { READ, MADE };
 |       if (argc != 2) {
 +          cerr << argv[0] <<  " sleep_time" << endl;
 |          return 1;
 |       }
 |       ipc_key = ftok(".", 'S');
 |       if ((semid=semget(ipc_key, 2, IPC_CREAT|IPC_EXCL|0660)) != -1) {
40          producer = 1;
 |          arg.array = start_val;
 |          if (semctl(semid, 0, SETALL, arg) == -1) {
 |             perror("semctl--producer--initialization");
 |             return 2;
 +          }
 |       } else if ((semid = semget(ipc_key, 2, 0)) == -1) {
 |          perror("semget--consumer--obtaining semaphore");
 |          return 3;
 |       }
50       cout << (producer==1 ? "Producer" : "Consumer" )
 |            << " starting" << endl;
```

Define the two operations that can be done on a semaphore.

The program uses the symbolic constant BUFFER to reference a local file named ./buffer. This file acts as the non-shareable resource to be accessed by the producer and consumer processes. Following this definition is the declaration of the union semun as an argument of type semun is required for the **semctl** system call.

Using the sembuf structure as a template, the program defines two operations—acquire and release—that can be used with either of the semaphores. For both operations the value for the member sem_num has been set to 0. This value acts as a placeholder and will be changed dynamically to indicate which of the two semaphores within the set we are referencing. The sem_op member of each is set to −1 and 1 for acquire and release respectively. The value of −1 is used when we want to acquire a resource that is associated with a semaphore (indicated by decrementing the semaphore). The value 1 is used when we want to indicate the return of the resource (thus incrementing the associated semaphore). In either case, we set the value for sem_flg to SEM_UNDO to allow rollback. The variable arg, of type union semun, is declared and used as the fourth argument to the **semctl** system call. The values in the array start_val (1, 0) are used to set the initial values for the two semaphores. The enumerated constants READ and MADE act as indices to reference which of the two semaphores we are using.

The program begins by checking the command line to determine if an argument has been passed. The program expects a small integer value to be passed. This value is used to indicate the number of seconds the process should **sleep** in its processing cycle. The inclusion of **sleep** allows the producer and consumer process to progress at different rates, thus providing the user with an easy way to check the integrity of the semaphore arrangement.

The **semget** system call is used to create/gain access to the semaphore set. The flag combination IPC_CREAT | IPC_EXCL insures that the first time the program is run it will create the two-semaphore set. As written, the first invocation of the program is considered to be the producer (the process that will generate the integer values). The variable producer is set to 1 in the producer process to indicate this. Once the semaphore set is successfully created, the program uses the **semctl** system call to initialize the semaphore set to the values stored in start_val.[3] When the program is run a second time, the resulting process is considered to be a consumer (a process that will obtain the stored integer value). In the second program invocation, the initial **semget** system call, which is within the if statement, fails, as the semaphore set has already been generated by the producer. The else-if branch of the same if statement invokes **semget** a second time without any flags set. This second invocation of **semget** allows the consumer process to gain access to the previously generated semaphore set.

The second section of the program, which contains the logic executed by the producer, is shown in Program 7.4B.

Program 7.4B The second section of the producer/consumer problem—the producer logic.

```
|                                            // Section TWO
|        switch (producer) {
|        case 1:                             // The PRODUCER
|          p_sleep = atoi(argv[1]);
+          srand((unsigned) getpid());
|          for (i = 0; i < 10; i++) {
|            sleep(p_sleep);
|            n = rand() % 99 + 1;
|            cout << "A. The number [" << n << "] generated by producer" << endl;
```

[3] Notice that the union member arg.array is assigned the base address of the array start_val prior to invoking **semctl**.

```
60              acquire.sem_num = READ;
 |              if (semop(semid, &acquire, 1) == -1) {
 |                perror("semop -producer- waiting for consumer to read number");
 |                return 4;
 |              }
 +              if ((fptr = fopen(BUFFER, "w")) == NULL ){
 |                perror(BUFFER);
 |                return 5;
 |              }
 |              fprintf(fptr, "%d\n", n);
70              fclose(fptr);
 |              release.sem_num = MADE;
 |              cout << "B. The number [" << n << "] deposited by producer" << endl;
 |              if (semop(semid, &release, 1) == -1) {
 |                perror("semop -producer- indicating new number has been made");
 +                return 6;
 |              }
 |            }
 |            sleep(5);
 |            if (semctl(semid, 0, IPC_RMID, 0) == -1) {
80             perror("semctl -producer-");
 |             return 7;
 |            }
 |            cout << "Semaphore removed" << endl;
 |            break;
```

Critical Region

As noted, the first time the program is run, the value of the variable producer is set to 1. When producer contains a 1, the case 1: section of program code, the producer logic, is executed. The small integer value passed on the command line to indicate the number of seconds the process should sleep is converted by the library function **atoi** and stored for future reference in the variable p_sleep. Following this, the random number generator is initialized using the value of the current PID. A for loop that produces 10 random integer values in the range 1 to 99 is entered. After the program sleeps, a random number is generated and displayed to the screen (this allows the user to verify the activity of the program). Following this, the sem_num member of the acquire operation is set to the value READ. This directs the following **semop** system call to reference the READ semaphore, which is the first semaphore of the set. We use a value of 1 for the READ semaphore to indicate the current stored number has been read (consumed) and a value of 0 to indicate the number has not been read. As the initial value for the READ semaphore is 1, the very first time the producer tests the READ semaphore with the **semop** system call, the producer can acquire the semaphore. Once this occurs, the producer continues on to the next section of code where it opens the file, stores the generated value, and closes the file. In later passes through this code, the producer may or may not find the READ semaphore at 1. If the semaphore is at 0 (indicating the consumer has not read the value), the producer, by default, blocks (waits) for this event to occur. Once the produced value has been written to the file, the producer process, using the `release` operation, increments the MADE semaphore. By incrementing the MADE semaphore, the producer indicates a new number is now available for the consumer. When all 10 numbers have been generated, the producer exits the `for` loop and, after sleeping 5 seconds to allow for the consumption of the last produced value, it removes the semaphore set with the **semctl** system command. If needed, the **unlink** call can be used to remove the temporary file.

The logic for the consumer is shown in Program 7.4C.

Program 7.4C The third section of the producer/consumer problem—the consumer logic.

```
+           case 0:                              // Section THREE
|             c_sleep = atoi(argv[1]);           // The CONSUMER
|             c_pid = getpid();
|             while (1) {
|               sleep(c_sleep);
90              acquire.sem_num = MADE;
|               if (semop(semid, &acquire, 1) == -1) {
|                 perror("semop -consumer- waiting for new number to be made");
|                 return 8;
|               }
+               if ( (fptr = fopen(BUFFER, "r")) == NULL ){
|                 perror(BUFFER);
|                 return 9;
|               }                                              Critical Region
|               fptr = fopen(BUFFER, "r");
100             fscanf(fptr, "%d", &n);
|               fclose(fptr);
|               release.sem_num = READ;
|               if (semop(semid, &release, 1) == -1) {
|                 perror("semop -consumer- indicating number has been read");
+                 return 10;
|               }
|             cout << "C. The number [" << n <<] obtained  by consumer "
|                 << c_pid << endl;
|             }
110         }
|         return 0;
|       }
```

The consumer process, like the producer, converts the value passed on the command line into an integer value by using the library function **atoi**. The consumer then obtains its PID using the **getpid** system call. The PID is used to identify individual consumer processes when more than one consumer process is present. The consumer then enters an endless loop. It sleeps `c_sleep` seconds and then tests the MADE semaphore. To accomplish this, the sem_num member of the acquire operation structure is set to MADE. The call to **semop**, which is passed the reference to acquire, causes the consumer to block (wait) if the semaphore is at 0. Once the MADE semaphore becomes 1, the consumer opens the file where the number was written, reads the number, and closes the file. The consumer then indicates that it has read the number. The release structure member, sem_num, is set to READ to reference the second semaphore of the set. The following **semop** system call causes the contents of the READ semaphore to be incremented. The consumer then displays a short message to the screen indicating the value retrieved and its PID value. The consumer continues to consume values until the call to **semop** fails due to the removal of the semaphore set by the producer.

We can run the program to simulate a number of conditions. We begin by making the producer process slower than a single consumer process. The output in Figure 7.8 shows how this is accomplished.

Figure 7.8 A single slow producer with a single consumer.

```
linux$ p7.4 2 & p7.4 0
Producer starting
[1] 31223
Consumer starting
A. The number [79] generated by producer
B. The number [79] deposited by producer
C. The number [79] obtained  by consumer 31224
A. The number [17] generated by producer
B. The number [17] deposited by producer
C. The number [17] obtained  by consumer 31224
       .
       .
       .
C. The number [53] obtained  by consumer 31224
A. The number [15] generated by producer
B. The number [15] deposited by producer
C. The number [15] obtained  by consumer 31224
Semaphore removed
semop -consumer- waiting for new number to be made: Identifier removed
[1]  + Done                       p7.4 2
```

In this example the program p7.4 is run twice on the command line. The first invocation of the program, which will be the producer,[4] is passed the value 2. This directs the producer process to sleep 2 seconds each time it cycles through the for loop. The producer process is placed in the background by specifying

---

[4] This may be an invalid assumption on some systems, as process scheduling may allow the program invoked second to be run first and thus become the producer. If your output indicates this is happening, enter the two commands on separate lines—do not forget to add the & after the first command to place it in the background.

& after the command-line sleep value. In the second invocation of the program, the consumer is passed the value 0 as the sleep value. The system responds to the command sequence by displaying the PID of the commands that were placed in background. The display of

```
[1] 31223
```

means that, for this invocation, the producer PID is 31223. As the two processes execute, we can clearly see from the output that the producer must first generate and deposit the value in the file before the consumer can obtain it. As the producing process is slower than the consuming process, the consumer process spends a portion of its time waiting for the producer to deposit a number. When all of the numbers have been produced, the producer process removes the semaphore set. When this happens, the consumer process exits. If we run this command sequence several times, we should find it behaves in a consistent manner. Although the consumer process is faster than the producer process, the consumer should never read the same value twice from the file (unless, by chance, the same number was generated twice by the producer).

We can reverse the conditions and make the producer process faster than the consumer process. The output shown in Figure 7.9 shows how this can be accomplished.

Figure 7.9 A producer with a single slow consumer.

```
linux$ p7.4 0 & p7.4 2
[1] 31229
Producer starting
A. The number [28] generated by producer
B. The number [28] deposited by producer
A. The number [69] generated by producer
Consumer starting
C. The number [28] obtained  by consumer 31230
B. The number [69] deposited by producer
A. The number [83] generated by producer
C. The number [69] obtained  by consumer 31230
  .
  .
A. The number [29] generated by producer
C. The number [65] obtained  by consumer 31230
B. The number [29] deposited by producer
C. The number [29] obtained  by consumer 31230
Semaphore removed
semop -consumer- waiting for new number to be made: Identifier removed
[1]   + Done                      p7.4 0
```

This output sequence is slightly different from the previous one. Notice, as before, the producer generates and deposits the number. The producer, being faster than the consumer, then goes on to generate another number. However, this number is not deposited until the slower consumer process has read the existing stored value. If we run this command sequence several times, we should again be able to confirm that the producer process never overwrites the existing stored value until the consumer process has read it.

7-5 EXERCISE

What if there are several competing consumer processes? Will the current set of semaphores handle things correctly? Will competing consumer processes alternate their access to the produced values? Will some consumer processes starve? Try the following command sequences (several times each) and explain *what happens* and *why* for each.

```
A) linux$ p7.4 2 & p7.4 1 & p7.4 0

B) linux$ p7.4 0 & p7.4 1 & p7.4 1 & p7.4 1

C) linux$ p7.4 2 & p7.4 1 & p7.4 0 & p7.4 1
```

7-6 EXERCISE

As shown by the code listed below, we can add another operation for **semop** (called `zero`) that can be used to determine if a specified semaphore is at 0 (see Table 7.8 for the actions taken by **semop** when the value for sem_op is zero).

```
static struct sembuf
     acquire = {0, -1, SEM_UNDO},
     release = {0,  1, SEM_UNDO},
     zero    = {0,  0, SEM_UNDO};
```

Modify Program 7.4, incorporating the `zero` operation, so the producer can use this operation on the appropriate semaphore to determine if it should continue its processing. To verify that your solution is not rapidly passing through the producer loop, comment out the producer's call to **sleep** (line 78). Once you are positive your implementation is solid, uncomment the call to `sleep`. Generate sufficient output to assure the user that the producer process never overwrites a value that has not been consumed and that a consumer process never consumes the same value twice.

7-7 EXERCISE

Modify Program 7.4 to support multiple producers as well as multiple consumers accessing a single non-shareable resource. *Hint*: You may need additional semaphores to coordinate activities.

7.5 Semaphore Class

As with message queues, the syntax and manipulation of semaphores is somewhat complex, making them a prime candidate for incorporation into a C++ class. A semaphore class would define the relationships between semaphore data and the functions (methods) that manipulate this data. A declaration of a simplified semaphore class called `SSemaphore`[5] is shown in Figure 7.10.

Figure 7.10 Header file for a basic semaphore class.

```
File : SSemaphore.h
  |      /*
  |         A VERY simplified semaphore class for use in a std UNIX
  |         environment.  See the text for instructions on how to use
  |         this class.  Copyright (c) 2002 J. S. Gray
  +
  |         Exit codes for class operations:
  |
  |         1 - Semaphore allocation failure   2 - Unable remove semaphore
  |         3 - Unable to LOCK semaphore       4 - Unable to UNLOCK semaphore
 10         5 - Failure on wait for ZERO       6 - Unable to assign value
```

---

[5] The name `SSemaphore` (with the extra `'S'`) was chosen to minimize any conflicts with existing semaphore definitions.

```
 |        7 - Unable to return value
 |      */
 |
 |      #ifndef SSemaphore_h
 +      #define SSemaphore_h
 |      #define _GNU_SOURCE
 |      #include <iostream>
 |      #include <cstdio>
 |      #include <sys/types.h>
20      #include <sys/ipc.h>
 |      #include <sys/sem.h>
 |      #include <stdlib.h>
 |      #include <unistd.h>
 |      using namespace std;
 +
 |      class SSemaphore {
 |        public:
 |          SSemaphore ( );                    // Constructor
 |          ~SSemaphore( );                    // Destructor - remove semaphore
30          int  P( );                         // LOCK (decrement semaphore)
 |          void V( );                         // UNLOCK (increment semaphore)
 |          int  Z( );                         // WAIT while semaphore is NOT 0
 |          void Put( const int );             // Assign a value to semaphore
 |          int  Get( );                       // Return value of the semaphore
 +        private:
 |          #if defined(__GNU_LIBRARY__) && !defined(_SEM_SEMUN_UNDEFINED)
 |                                             // definition in <sys/sem.h>
 |          #else
 |          union semun {                      // We define:
40            int val;                         // value   for SETVAL
 |            struct semid_ds *buf;            // buffer for IPC_STAT, IPC_SET
 |            unsigned short int *array;       // array   for GETALL, SETALL
 |            struct seminfo *__buf;           // buffer for IPC_INFO
 |          };
 +          #endif
 |          union  semun  arg;                 // For semctl call
 |          struct sembuf zero,lock, unlock;   // hoo ha's for P,V & Z operations
 |          int    semid;                      // ID of semaphore
 |          pid_t my_pid;                      // PID of creator
50      };
 |      #endif
```

As defined, the SSemaphore class creates a private semaphore set with a
single element. There are seven public methods and six private data members
in the class. The functionality of each method is shown in Table 7.10.

Table 7.10 SSemaphore Class Methods.

Method Name	Explanation
SSemaphore	This is the class constructor. This method assigns the proper values to the zero, lock, and unlock sembuf structures and saves the PID of the calling process. Additionally, it generates the private, single element semaphore and sets it to 0.
~SSemaphore	This method removes the semaphore from the system if the calling function is the process that generated the semaphore.
P	This method atomically tests and decrements the semaphore. It blocks if the semaphore is 0.
V	This method increments the semaphore.
Z	This method tests whether or not the semaphore is at 0. If it is not at 0, it blocks.
Put	Put assigns a value to a semaphore.
Get	Get returns the current value of a semaphore.

The C++ code that implements the semaphore class is found in the program file SSemaphore.cxx (Program 7.5). As shown, the code is bare bones—little is done to handle errors, and only basic semaphore functionality is addressed.

Program 7.5 Program code for the semaphore class.

```
File : SSemaphore.cxx
  |     /*
  |         SSemaphore implementation - Copyright (c)  2002  J. S. Gray
  |     */
  |     #include "SSemaphore.h"
  +                                               // Generate a private semaphore
  |     SSemaphore::SSemaphore(  ){
  |       zero.sem_num   = 0, zero.sem_op   =  0, zero.sem_flg   = SEM_UNDO;
  |       lock.sem_num   = 0, lock.sem_op   = -1, lock.sem_flg   = SEM_UNDO;
  |       unlock.sem_num = 0, unlock.sem_op =  1, unlock.sem_flg = SEM_UNDO;
 10       my_pid = getpid( );
  |       if((semid = semget( IPC_PRIVATE, 1, 0660 )) == -1 ){
  |           exit( 1 );
  |       }
  |       Put( 0 );                               // Default - set to zero @ start
  +     }
  |                                               // Remove semaphore if creator
  |     SSemaphore::~SSemaphore( ) {
  |       if ( getpid( ) == my_pid )
  |         if ( semctl( semid, 0, IPC_RMID ) == -1 )
```

```
20                exit( 2 );
  |           }
  |                                         // LOCK semaphore
  |           int                           // Atomic test & decrement
  |           SSemaphore::P( ){
  +             if ( semop( semid, &lock, 1 ) == -1 )
  |               exit( 3 );
  |             return 0;
  |           }
  |                                         // UNLOCK semaphore
30          void                            // Increment semaphore
  |           SSemaphore::V( ){
  |             if ( semop( semid, &unlock, 1 ) == -1 )
  |               exit( 4 );
  |           }
  +
  |           int                           // Wait for semaphore to be 0
  |           SSemaphore::Z( ){
  |             if ( semop( semid, &zero, 1 ) == -1 )
  |               exit( 5 );
40            return 0;
  |           }
  |                                         // Assign value to the semaphore
  |           void
  |           SSemaphore::Put( int const value ){
  +             arg.val = value;
  |             if ( semctl(semid, 0, SETVAL, arg ) == -1 )
  |               exit( 6 );
  |           }
  |                                         // Return value of the semaphore
50          int
  |           SSemaphore::Get( ){
  |             int sem_value;
  |             if ((sem_value=semctl(semid, 0, GETVAL, 0)) == -1 )
  |               exit( 7 );
  +             return sem_value;
  |           }
```

To use this class, the files `SSemaphore.h` and `SSemaphore.cxx` should reside locally. The `SSemaphore` class is compiled into object code with the command line

```
linux$  g++ SSemaphore.cxx -c
```

At the top of the source file that uses a `SSemaphore` object, add the statement

```
#include "SSemaphore.h"
```

to make the class definition available to the compiler. When compiling the source file, include the message queue object code file

```
linux$  g++  your_file_name.cxx   SSemaphore.o
```

In 1965 Dijkstra presented what is now considered to be a classic synchronization problem involving a group of dining philosophers. In brief, the group of philosophers is sitting around a table. Each engages in the activity of thinking and eating. To eat, the philosopher must obtain the forks on his or her left and right. Both forks are needed for dining, and once obtained, neither fork is released until the philosopher is done. For N philosophers, there are N forks (not $2 \times N$). Clearly, if all the philosophers are to eat, some sort of synchronization of their activities is needed.

We can use the recently presented SSemaphore class to implement a naive solution to the dining philosophers' problem. In essence, each fork will be represented by a single binary semaphore. If a philosopher can obtain both the left and right fork (think semaphore), he or she will eat for a random number of seconds, and when done, return the forks. If either instrument is not available, he or she will wait. Keep in mind that this solution has a very basic flaw. Should all the philosophers pick up their left fork at the same time, we would have deadlock. This could occur, as each left fork is also the right fork of the philosopher to the left. With every philosopher waiting for his or her right fork (the left fork of the philosopher on his or her right), no progress can be made. Program 7.6 implements our less-than-perfect solution.

Program 7.6 A rudimentary dining philosophers' solution using semaphore objects.

```
File : p7.6.cxx
   |      /*
   |           The dining philosophers
   |      */
   |      #include <iostream>
   +      #include "SSemaphore.h"                 // Our basic semaphore class
   |      const int MAX = 5;
   |      SSemaphore Forks[MAX];
   |      void Philosopher( int );
   |      void Eat_It( const int,const int, const int );
  10      int
   |      main(int argc, char *argv[] ) {
   |        int i;
   |        if ( argc < 2 ) {
   |          cerr << "Usage: " << argv[0] << " secs_to_wait " << endl;
   +          return 1;
   |        }
   |        for( i=0; i < MAX; ++i )
   |          Forks[i].Put(true);
   |        for(i = 0; i < MAX; ++i )
  20          Philosopher( i );
   |        sleep(atoi(argv[1]));                 // Parent process waits a bit
```

```
 |        return 0;
 |      }
 |      void
 +      Philosopher(int number ){
 |        if (fork() == 0) {                      // Run in the child
 |          int left, right;
 |          srand(getpid( ));
 |          left = number;
30        right= (number+1) % MAX;
 |          do {
 |            cout << "A. P" << number << " is thinking\n";
 |            sleep(rand( ) % 3 + 1);             // Take a while to THINK
 |            cout << "B. P" << number << " ASKS to eat with forks "
 +                 << left << " & " << right << endl;
 |            Forks[left].P( );                   // Acquire left fork
 |              Forks[right].P( );                // Acquire right fork
 |                Eat_It(number, left, right);
 |              Forks[right].V( );
40          Forks[left].V( );
 |          } while( true );
 |        }
 |      }
 |      void
 +      Eat_It(const int number, const int left, const int right) {
 |        cout << "C. P" << number << " is EATING   with forks "
 |             << left << " & " << right << endl;
 |        sleep(rand( ) % 3 + 1);                 // Take a while to EAT
 |        cout << "D. P" << number << " is now DONE with forks "
50           << left << " & " << right << endl;
 |      }
```

As written, the program expects the user to pass an integer command-line value that will be used for the number of seconds the program should run. A value of 10 seems to produce a reasonable amount of output. In line 7 of the program, an array of five private semaphore objects is instantiated. This array represents the five forks. The loop at line 17 sets each of the semaphores to true (fork available). This is followed by a second loop that calls the Philosopher function MAX times. Upon each invocation, the Philosopher function generates a child process to carry on the activities of the philosopher. The philosopher's activities consist of thinking for a random amount of time and eating. To eat, the left and right fork (semaphore) must be acquired. When both semaphores have been procured, the Eat_It function is called where, for a random amount of time, the eating activity is carried out. While the child processes carry on their activities, the parent process sleeps for a period (see line 21). When the parent process exits, the destructor for the semaphore objects is called. The child processes exit as they encounter an error condition when the attempt to access a removed semaphore.

Figure 7.11 shows a typical run when the value 10 is passed to the program. To save space, the output is displayed as two columns.

Figure 7.11 10 seconds of output from the dining philosophers' program.

```
linux$ g++ p7.6.cxx SSemaphore.o -o p7.6    A. P2 is thinking
                                            D. P0 is now DONE with forks 0 & 1
linux$ p7.6 10                              A. P0 is thinking
A. P0 is thinking                           B. P1 ASKS to eat with forks 1 & 2
A. P1 is thinking                           C. P1 is EATING   with forks 1 & 2
A. P2 is thinking                           B. P3 ASKS to eat with forks 3 & 4
A. P3 is thinking                           C. P4 is EATING   with forks 4 & 0
A. P4 is thinking                           B. P2 ASKS to eat with forks 2 & 3
B. P1 ASKS to eat with forks 1 & 2          D. P4 is now DONE with forks 4 & 0
C. P1 is EATING   with forks 1 & 2          A. P4 is thinking
B. P3 ASKS to eat with forks 3 & 4          C. P3 is EATING   with forks 3 & 4
C. P3 is EATING   with forks 3 & 4          B. P0 ASKS to eat with forks 0 & 1
B. P0 ASKS to eat with forks 0 & 1          D. P1 is now DONE with forks 1 & 2
B. P2 ASKS to eat with forks 2 & 3          A. P1 is thinking
B. P4 ASKS to eat with forks 4 & 0          C. P0 is EATING   with forks 0 & 1
D. P1 is now DONE with forks 1 & 2          D. P3 is now DONE with forks 3 & 4
A. P1 is thinking                           C. P2 is EATING   with forks 2 & 3
D. P3 is now DONE with forks 3 & 4          A. P3 is thinking
A. P3 is thinking                           B. P1 ASKS to eat with forks 1 & 2
C. P0 is EATING   with forks 0 & 1          B. P4 ASKS to eat with forks 4 & 0
C. P2 is EATING   with forks 2 & 3          D. P0 is now DONE with forks 0 & 1
D. P2 is now DONE with forks 2 & 3          D. P2 is now DONE with forks 2 & 3
                                            B. P3 ASKS to eat with forks 3 & 4
```

7-8 EXERCISE

As presented, the SSemaphore class generates a private semaphore. Private semaphores are fine for use with related processes but are difficult to use with unrelated processes. Modify the SSemaphore class to allow for the generation of a nonprivate semaphore. Rewrite the producer/consumer program (Program 7.4) using this newly defined class. Be sure to provide output to show that your class works and that it removes all semaphores when done.

7-9 EXERCISE

What if in Program 7.6 (the dining philosophers), odd-number philosophers acquired their forks as right and then left, and even-number philosophers acquired their forks as left and then right. Would this prevent deadlock? Modify Program 7.6 to implement this approach. Run your program a sufficient number of times to reasonably assure yourself that this approach does or does not work. *Hint*: Here is a command sequence to collect some summary information for a 100-second period:

```
linux$  p7.6 100 | sort | uniq -c
```

7.6 Summary

Semaphores are specialized data structures used to coordinate access to a non-shareable resource (section of code). Cooperating (or possibly competing) processes use the semaphore(s) to determine if a specific resource is available. If the resource is unavailable, by default the system places the requesting process in an associated queue. The system notifies the waiting process when the resource is available. This alleviates the process from using polling to determine the availability of the resource. Semaphores can be categorized as binary or counting. Binary semaphores are used to synchronize access to a single instance of a non-shareable resource, while counting semaphores are used with multiple instances of a non-shareable resource.

The actions needed to manipulate semaphores are provided by a series of system calls. The **semget** system call is used to generate a new semaphore/semaphore set (array) or to gain access to an existing semaphore. The **semctl** system call allows the user to set initial semaphore values, obtain their current value, and remove the semaphore. Operations on semaphores are performed with the **semop** system call. These operations (which are atomic) are used to decrement (obtain), increment (release), and test for zero-specific semaphores. Sets of operations can be specified if several semaphores are needed to coordinate access to a specific resource. The sets of operations may also be marked as being atomic.

While the syntax for using semaphores is somewhat complex, they do provide a standardized way of implementing classic primitive semaphore

269

operations referenced in most operating system texts. As with many of the previous communication techniques, controlling access to a resource by using semaphores implies all involved processes will follow the rules. Semaphores cannot prevent processes from accessing a controlled resource.

7.7 Key Terms and Concepts

binary semaphore	IPC_RMID
counting semaphore	IPC_SET
critical region	IPC_STAT
ctime library function	sem structure
deadlock	SEM_UNDO
dining philosophers	semaphore class
GETALL	**semctl** system call
GETNCNT	**semget** system call
GETVAL	semid_ds structure
GETZCNT	**semop** system call
IPC_CREAT	semun union
IPC_EXCL	SETALL
IPC_NOWAIT	SETVAL
IPC_PRIVATE	starvation

Chapter 8

SHARED MEMORY

8.1 Introduction

Shared memory allows multiple processes to share virtual memory space. This is the fastest but not necessarily the easiest (synchronization-wise) way for processes to communicate with one another. In general, one process creates or allocates the shared memory segment. The size and access permissions for the segment are set when it is created. The process then attaches the shared segment, causing it to be mapped[1] into its current data space. If needed, the creating process then initializes the shared memory. Once created, and if permissions permit, other processes can gain access to the shared memory segment and map it into their data space. Each process accesses the shared memory relative to its attachment address. While the data that these processes are referencing is in *common*, each process uses different attachment address values. For each process involved, the mapped memory appears to be no different from any other of its memory addresses. Figure 8.1 presents a diagrammatic way to envision three processes sharing a common memory segment. As there are no intrinsic shared memory synchronization

[1] The actual mapping of the segment to virtual address space is dependent upon the memory management (MMU) hardware for the system.

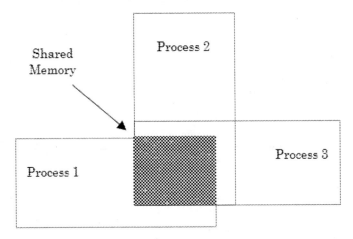

Figure 8.1 Envisioning three processes sharing a common memory segment.

constructs, semaphores are normally used to coordinate access to a shared memory segment. When a process is finished with the shared memory segment, it can detach from it. Additionally, the creator of the segment may grant ownership of the segment to another process. When all processes are finished with the shared memory segment, the process that created the segment is usually responsible for removing it.

8.2 Creating a Shared Memory Segment

The **shmget** system call is used to create the shared memory segment and generate the associated system data structure or to gain access to an existing segment. The shared memory segment and the system data structure are identified by a unique shared memory identifier that the **shmget** system call returns (see Table 8.1).

Providing no system parameters are exceeded, the **shmget** system call creates a *new* shared memory segment if

- The value for its first argument, key, is the symbolic constant IPC_PRIVATE, or
- the value key is *not* associated with an existing shared memory identifier and the IPC_CREAT flag is set as part of the shmflg argument

Table 8.1 Summary of the shmget System Call.

Include File(s)	`<sys/ipc.h>` `<sys/shm.h>`		Manual Section	**2**
Summary	`int shmget(key_t key, int size,int shmflg);`			
	Success	Failure	Sets `errno`	
Return	Shared memory identifier.	−1	Yes	

(otherwise, the existing shared memory identifier associated with the key value is returned), or

- the value key is *not* associated with an existing shared memory identifier and the IPC_CREAT along with the IPC_EXCL flag have been set as part of the shmflg argument. With IPC_CREAT and IPC_EXCL set, the user can be assured of creating a unique shared memory segment without inadvertently gaining access to a preexisting segment.

As with previous IPC system calls for message queues and semaphores, the **ftok** library function can be used to generate a key value.

The argument size determines the size in bytes of the shared memory segment. If we are using **shmget** to access an existing shared memory segment, size can be set to 0, as the segment size is set by the creating process. Common overall default system maximums, as related to shared memory, are shown in Table 8.2.

Table 8.2 Shared Memory Limits.

Shared Memory Segment Defaults	**Constant**	**Value**
Maximum segment size	SHMMAX	4 MB
Minimum segment size	SHMMIN	1 byte
Systemwide maximum number of segments	SHMMNI	4096
Maximum number of segments per process	SHMSEG	Not specified

The last argument for **shmget**, shmflg, is used to indicate segment creation conditions (e.g., IPC_CREAT, IPC_EXCL) and access permissions (stored in the low order 9 bits of shmflg). At this time the system does not use the execute permission settings. To specify creation conditions along with access permissions, the individual items are bitwise **OR**ed (e.g., 0660 | IPC_CREAT).

The **shmget** system call does not entitle the creating process to actually use the allocated memory; it merely reserves the requested memory. To be used by the process, the allocated memory must be attached to the process using a separate system call. The technique for accomplishing this is discussed in Section 8.4.

If **shmget** is successful in allocating a shared memory segment, it returns an integer shared memory identifier. At creation time, the system data structure shmid_ds, defined in the <bits/shm.h> header file, is generated and initialized. As with other System V IPC facilities, the user does not directly include <bits/shm.h> but instead includes the standard header file for shared memory <sys/shm.h>, which in turn includes the <bits/shm.h>. The standard definition for the shmid_ds data structure follows:

```
struct shmid_ds {
    struct ipc_perm shm_perm;       /* operation permission struct    */
    size_t shm_segsz;               /* size of segment in bytes       */
    __time_t shm_atime;             /* time of last shmat()           */
    unsigned long int __unused1;
    __time_t shm_dtime;             /* time of last shmdt()           */
    unsigned long int __unused2;
    __time_t shm_ctime;             /* time of last change by shmctl() */
    unsigned long int __unused3;
    __pid_t shm_cpid;               /* pid of creator                 */
    __pid_t shm_lpid;               /* pid of last shmop              */
    shmatt_t shm_nattch;            /* number of current attaches     */
    unsigned long int __unused4;
    unsigned long int __unused5;
};
```

The source files for the kernel for System V IPC (found in /usr/src/ linux-XX.XX.XX/ipc where XX are the version numbers of the operating system) defines a similar private kernel shared memory structure called shmid_kernel.

The shmid_ds structure contains an ipc_perm permission structure called shm_perm. When created, the shm_perm.cuid and shm_perm.uid members are assigned the effective user ID of the calling process, and the shm_perm.cgid and shm_perm.gid members are set to the group ID of the calling process. The access permission bits, stored in the shm_perm.mode member, are set according to the value specified by the shmflg value. The shm_segsz member is set to the specified size from the **shmget** system call. The shm_lpid, shm_nattch, shm_atime, and shm_dtime members are each set to 0, while the shm_ctime member is set to the current time. The shm_cpid member stores the ID of the creating process.

If **shmget** fails, it returns a value of −1 and sets the value in `errno` to indicate the specific error condition. The values that `errno` may be assigned and their interpretations are shown in Table 8.3.

Table 8.3 `shmget` Error Messages

#	Constant	`perror` Message	Explanation
2	EOENT	No such file or directory	The shared memory identifier does not exist for this `key`, and IPC_CREAT was not set.
12	ENOMEM	Cannot allocate memory	When creating a shared memory segment, insufficient memory is available.
13	EACCES	Permission denied	The shared memory identifier exists for this `key`, but the requested operation is not allowed by the current access permissions.
17	EEXIST	File exists	Shared memory identifier exists for this `key`, but IPC_CREAT and IPC_EXCL are both set.
22	EINVAL	Invalid argument	• The value of `size` is less than system minimum or greater than system maximum. • The shared memory identifier exists, but the requested `size` is too large.
28	ENOSPC	No space left on device	System-imposed limit for number of shared memory segments has been reached.
43	EIDRM	Identifier removed	Memory segment is marked as removed.

Program 8.1 attempts to create two shared memory segments of differing sizes.

Program 8.1 Creating shared memory segments.

```
File : p8.1.cxx
   |     /*
   |           Allocating a shared memory segment
   |      */
   |     #include <iostream>
   +     #include <cstdio>
   |     #include <sys/ipc.h>
   |     #include <sys/shm.h>
   |     using namespace std;
   |     int
  10     main( ) {
   |        key_t  key = 15;
   |        int    shmid_1, shmid_2;
```

275

```
 |        if ((shmid_1=shmget(key, 1000, 0640|IPC_CREAT)) == -1){
 |          perror("shmget shmid_1");
 +          return 1;
 |        }
 |        cout << "First shared memory identifier is : " << shmid_1 << endl;
 |        if ((shmid_2=shmget(IPC_PRIVATE, 20, 0640)) == -1){
 |          perror("shmget shmid_2");
20          return 2;
 |        }
 |        cout << "Second shared memory identifier is: " <<  shmid_2 << endl;
 |        return 0;
 |      }
```

Figure 8.2 shows the output of Program 8.1 when invoked twice in succession.

Figure 8.2 Output of Program 8.1.

```
linux$ p8.1                                               ◄──────── Run the program.
First shared memory identifier is : 40665091
Second shared memory identifier is: 40697860

linux$ ipcs -m                                            ◄──────── Check with ipcs.
------ Shared Memory Segments --------
key        shmid       owner     perms     bytes     nattch     status
0x0000000f 40665091    gray      640       1000      0
0x00000000 40697860    gray      640       20        0

linux$ p8.1                                               ◄──────── Run the program
First shared memory identifier is : 40665091                        again.
Second shared memory identifier is: 40730629

linux$ ipcs -m
                                                          ◄──────── Recheck with ipcs.
------ Shared Memory Segments --------
key        shmid       owner     perms     bytes     nattch     status
0x0000000f 40665091    gray      640       1000      0
0x00000000 40697860    gray      640       20        0
0x00000000 40730629    gray      640       20        0
```

Examination of the output shows the first invocation created two shared memory segments with the identifier values of 40665091 and 40697860. The first segment, with the shared memory identification value of 40665091, was created by the first call to **shmget**, as the key value (15) coded in the program was not associated with any other previously allocated memory segment. The second segment, identified by the 40697860, was created by **shmget**, since IPC_PRIVATE was specified. However, when the program was invoked the second time, the results were slightly different. The first call to **shmget** returned the shared memory identifier from the first invocation of the program, as the shared memory segment already existed for the key value of 15. The second call to **shmget**, since it uses IPC_PRIVATE, produced another unique shared memory segment (40730629). Notice that the output for the **ipcs** command shows that the key value entries for both of the unique shared memory segments generated with IPC_PRIVATE are set to zero.

8-1 EXERCISE

Write a program that determines by trial and error if the maximum shared memory segment size is or is not the 4 MB noted. If the maximum is not this value, what is the maximum (to the nearest 1K)? *Note*: Please be sure to *remove* any shared memory segments you generate for this exercise. You may want to look ahead to Section 8.3 to obtain the proper syntax to accomplish the removal of the shared memory segment within your program (versus using the **ipcrm** command on the command line). Of course, if you modified the cleanup script (Exercise 7.1), you could use it to remove your shared memory segments.

8.3 Shared Memory Control

The **shmctl** system call permits the user to perform a number of generalized control operations on an existing shared memory segment and on the system shared memory data structure (see Table 8.4).

Table 8.4 Summary of the shmctl System Call.

Include File(s)	`<sys/ipc.h>` `<sys/shm.h>`		Manual Section	**2**
Summary	`int shmctl(int shmid, int cmd, struct shmid_ds *buf);`			
	Success		Failure	Sets `errno`
Return	0		-1	Yes

There are three arguments for the **shmctl** system call. The first, shmid, is a valid shared memory segment identifier generated by a prior **shmget** system call. The second argument, cmd, specifies the operation **shmctl** is to perform. The third argument, buf, is a reference to a structure of the type shmid_ds.

The operations that **shmctl** will perform, which are specified by the following defined constants, consist of

- **IPC_STAT**—Return the current values of the shmid_ds structure for the memory segment indicated by the shmid value. The returned information is stored in a user-generated structure, which is passed by reference as the third argument to **shmctl**. To specify IPC_STAT, the process must have **read** permission for the shared memory segment.

- **IPC_SET**—Modify a limited number of members in the permission structure found within the shmid_ds structure. The permission structure members that can be modified are shm_perm.uid, shm_perm.gid, and shm_perm.mode. The accessing process must have the effective ID of the superuser or have an ID that is equivalent to either the shm_perm.cuid or shm_perm.uid value. To modify structure members, the following steps are usually taken. A structure of the type shmid_ds is allocated. The structure is initialized to the current system settings by calling **shmctl** with the IPC_STAT flag set and passing the reference to the *new* shmd_ds structure. The appropriate members of the structure are then assigned their *new* values. Finally, with the cmd argument set to IPC_SET, the **shmctl** system call is invoked a second time and passed the reference to the *modified* structure. To carry out this modification sequence, the accessing process must have **read** and **write** permissions for the shared memory segment. When IPC_SET is specified, the shm_ctime member is automatically updated with the current time.

- **IPC_RMID**—Remove the system data structure for the referenced shared memory identifier (shmid). When specifying IPC_RMID, an address value of 0 is used for buf. The 0 address value is cast to the proper type, with (shmid_ds *). Once all references to the shared memory segment are eliminated (i.e., shm_nattch equals 0), the system will remove the actual segment. If a **shmctl** system call, specifying IPC_RMID, is not done, the memory segment will remain active and associated with its key value.

- **SHM_LOCK**—Lock, in memory, the shared memory segment referenced by the shmid argument. A locked shared segment is not swapped out by the system thus avoiding I/O faults when referenced. Locking can only be specified by processes that have an effective ID equal to that of the superuser.

- **SHM_UNLOCK**—Unlock the shared memory segment referenced by the shmid argument. Once unlocked the shared segment can be swapped out. Again, this can only be specified by processes that have an effective ID equal to that of the superuser.

If **shmctl** is successful, it returns a value of 0; otherwise, it returns a value of −1 and sets the value in errno to indicate the specific error condition. The values that errno may be assigned and their interpretation are shown in Table 8.5.

Table 8.5 shmctl Error Messages

#	Constant	perror **Message**	**Explanation**
1	EPERM	Operation not permitted	• The value for cmd is IPC_RMID or IPC_SET, and the calling process is not the owner, creator, or superuser. • The value for cmd is SHM_LOCK or SHM_UNLOCK, and the calling process is not the superuser.
13	EACCES	Permission denied	The requested operation is not allowed by current access permissions.
12	ENOMEM	Cannot allocate memory	The cmd is SHM_LOCK, but there is insufficient memory available.
14	EFAULT	Bad address	The third argument to **shmctl**, buf, contains a reference to an illegal address.
22	EINVAL	Invalid argument	• The shared memory identifier is invalid. • The value for cmd is invalid. • The value for cmd is IPC_SET, but the value for shm_perm.uid or shm_perm.gid is invalid.
43	EIDRM		Memory segment is marked as removed.

8-2 EXERCISE

Justin could not understand all the brouhaha over shared memory. Why not, he reasoned, just use variables that were global to say parent/child processes and control their access with semaphores? Using the SSemaphore object from the previous chapter, he wrote the program below to test his theory:

```
File : justin.cxx
  |     #include <iostream>
  |     #include <sys/types.h>
  |     #include <sys/wait.h>
  |     #include "SSemaphore.h"
  +     using namespace std;
  |     char c = 0;                           // 'global' variable
  |     int
  |     main( ){
  |       SSemaphore S;                       // SSemaphore object
 10       S.Put(1);                           // Start it at 1
  |       switch(fork( )){
  |         case -1:
  |           perror("fork failure");
  |           return 1;
  +         case 0:                           // Child - lowercase
  |           srand(getpid( ));
  |           for (int i=0; i < 10; ++i){
  |             S.P( );                        // Obtain semaphore
  |             cout << char(c+'a'); cout.flush( );
 20             ++c;
  |             S.V( );                        // Release semaphore
  |             sleep(rand( ) % 3 + 1);
  |           }
  |           break;
  +         default:                          // Parent - uppercase
  |           srand(getpid( ));
  |           for (int i=0; i < 10; ++i){
  |             S.P( );                        // Obtain semaphore
  |             cout << char(c+'A'); cout.flush( );
 30             ++c;
  |             S.V( );                        // Release semaphore
  |             sleep(rand( ) % 3 + 1);
  |           }
  |           break;
  +       }
  |       wait(0);
  |       return 0;
  |     }
```

Before he ran his program, Justin expected his output to be similar to `AbcDefGhiJ` (ten characters with alternating case). He was quite taken back when his output looked more like the following: `AabBcCdDeEFfGgHhIiJj`. Why did Justin get the output he did—what was the flaw in his reasoning?

8.4 Shared Memory Operations

There are two shared memory operation system calls. The first, **shmat**, is used to attach (map) the referenced shared memory segment into the calling process's data segment. See Table 8.6.

Table 8.6 Summary of the `shmat` System Call.

Include File(s)	`<sys/types.h>` `<sys/shm.h>`		Manual Section	**2**
Summary	`void *shmat(int shmid, const void` `            *shmaddr, int shmflg);`			
Return		Success	Failure	Sets `errno`
	Reference to the data segment		-1	Yes

The first argument to **shmat**, `shmid`, is a valid shared memory identifier. The second argument, `shmaddr`, allows the calling process *some* flexibility in assigning the location of the shared memory segment. If a nonzero value is given, **shmat** uses this as the attachment address for the shared memory segment. If `shmaddr` is 0, the system picks the attachment address. In most situations (especially if portability is of concern), it is advisable to use a value of 0 and have the system pick the address. The third argument, `shmflg`, is used to specify the access permissions for the shared memory segment and to request special attachment conditions, such as an aligned address or a read-only segment. The values of `shmaddr` and `shmflg` are used by the system to determine the attachment address, using the algorithm shown in Figure 8.3.

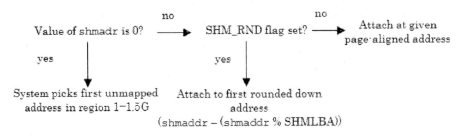

Figure 8.3 Determining the attachment address.

By default, attached segments are accessible for reading and writing. If needed, the SHM_RDONLY flag can be bitwise ORed with the shmflg value to indicate a read-only segment. There is no flag to specify a write-only memory segment. The SHM_RND flag is used to specify whether or not the attachment address should be aligned on a page boundary. The value in the defined constant SHMLBA (found in <bits/shm.h>) is used by the system as the page size. For reference, a page is a unit of virtual address space. When a page is mapped to physical memory it is called a page frame.

When **shmat** is successful, it returns the address of the actual attachment. It also sets shm_atime to the current time, shm_lpid to the ID of the calling process, and increments shm_nattch by one. If **shmat** fails, it returns a value of −1 and sets errno to indicate the source of the error. Table 8.7 lists the error codes generated and their interpretation when the **shmat** system call fails. Remember that after a **fork**, the child inherits the attached shared memory segment(s). However, after an **exec** or an **exit** attached, shared memory segment(s) are detached but are not destroyed.

Table 8.7 shmat Error Messages.

#	Constant	perror Message	Explanation
12	ENOMEM	Cannot allocate memory	There is insufficient memory available to accommodate the shared memory segment.
13	EACCES	Permission denied	The requested operation is not allowed by current access permissions.
22	EINVAL	Invalid argument	• The shared memory identifier is invalid. • Illegal address.
24	EMFILE	Too many open files	Number of attached memory segments has exceeded system limits.

8-3 EXERCISE

Create three 1-byte shared memory segments. Specify a shmaddr of 0 when attaching the segments. Does the system place the segments at contiguous locations? Why? Will the system allow reference to or modification of an address just "outside" the segment size (say, segment size +1 [or 2]) without generating an error? Why? Does the system respond the same way if the segment size is 4096? Why?

The second shared memory operation, **shmdt**, is used to detach the calling process's data segment from the shared memory segment. See Table 8.8.

Table 8.8 Summary of the shmdt System Call

Include File(s)	`<sys/types.h>` `<sys/shm.h>`		Manual Section	**2**
Summary	`int shmdt ( const void *shmaddr);`			
	Success	Failure	Sets errno	
Return	0	−1	Yes	

The **shmdt** system call has one argument, shmaddr, which is a reference to an attached memory segment. If **shmdt** is successful in detaching the memory segment, it returns a value of 0. It also sets shm_atime to the current time, shm_lpid to the ID of the calling process, and decrements shm_nattch by one. If shm_nattch becomes 0 and the memory segment is marked for deletion by the operating system, it is removed. If the **shmdt** call fails, it returns a value of −1 and sets errno. Table 8.9 gives the error code that is generated when **shmdt** fails.

Table 8.9 shmdt Error Message

#	**Constant**	perror **Message**	**Explanation**
22	EINVAL	Invalid argument	The value in shmaddr does not reference a valid shared memory segment.

In Program 8.2, a private shared memory segment, 30 bytes in length, is created at line 18. The shared memory segment is mapped to the process's data space (line 22) using the first available address (as picked by the system). The actual attachment address along with the addresses for **etext**, **edata**, and **end** are displayed for reference. A character pointer is set to reference the shared memory segment, and then a sequence of uppercase alphabetic characters is written to the referenced location (lines 31–33). A **fork** system call is used to generate a child process. The child process redisplays the contents of the shared memory segment. The child process then modifies the contents of the shared memory by converting the uppercase alphabetics to lowercase (line 49). After it converts the alphabetics, the child process detaches the shared memory segment and exits. The parent process, after waiting for the child to exit, redisplays the contents of shared memory (which now is in lowercase), detaches the shared memory segment, and removes it.

Program 8.2 Creating, attaching, and manipulating shared memory.

```
File : p8.2.cxx
   |      /*
   |             Using shared memory
   |      */
   |      #include <iostream>
   +      #include <cstdio>
   |      #include <unistd.h>
   |      #include <sys/types.h>
   |      #include <sys/ipc.h>
   |      #include <sys/shm.h>
  10      #include <sys/wait.h>
   |      #define SHM_SIZE 30
   |      using namespace std;
   |      extern int etext, edata, end;
   |      int
   +      main( ) {
   |         int    shmid;
   |         char   c, *shm, *s;
   |         if ((shmid=shmget(IPC_PRIVATE,SHM_SIZE,IPC_CREAT|0660))< 0) {
   |           perror("shmget fail");
  20           return 1;
   |         }
   |         if ((shm = (char *)shmat(shmid, 0, 0)) == (char *) -1) {
   |           perror("shmat : parent");
   |           return 2;
   +         }
   |         cout << "Addresses in parent"  << endl;
   |         cout << "shared mem: " << hex << int(shm) << " etext: "
   |              << &etext << " edata: "   << &edata
   |              << " end: " << &end << endl << endl;
```

```
30        s = shm;                          // s now references shared mem
 |        for (c='A'; c <= 'Z'; ++c)        // put some info there
 |           *s++ = c;
 |        *s='\0';                          // terminate the sequence
 |        cout << "In parent before fork, memory is: " << shm << endl;
 +        switch (fork( )) {
 |        case -1:
 |          perror("fork");
 |          return 3;
 |        default:
40          wait(0);                        // let the child finish
 |          cout << "In parent after fork, memory is : " << shm << endl;
 |          cout << "\nParent removing shared memory" << endl;
 |          shmdt(shm);
 |          shmctl(shmid, IPC_RMID, (struct shmid_ds *) 0);
 +          break;
 |        case 0:
 |          cout << "In child after fork, memory is  : " << shm << endl;
 |          for ( ; *shm; ++shm)            // modify shared memory
 |            *shm += 32;
50          shmdt(shm);
 |          break;
 |        }
 |        return 0;
 |      }
```

When Program 8.2 is run (output shown in Figure 8.4), we find that the address the system picks for the shared memory segment is not in the text or data segment address space for the process. In addition, the child process, via the **fork** system call, obtains access to the shared memory segment without having to make its own calls to **shmget** and **shmat**. As shown, the modifications to the shared memory segment made by the child process are *seen* by the parent even after the child process has detached its reference to the shared memory segment and terminated.

Figure 8.4 Output of Program 8.2.

```
linux$ p8.2
Addresses in parent
shared mem: 40018000 etext: 0x8048c6e edata: 0x8049f6c end: 0x8049fb4

In parent before fork, memory is: ABCDEFGHIJKLMNOPQRSTUVWXYZ
In child after fork, memory is  : ABCDEFGHIJKLMNOPQRSTUVWXYZ
In parent after fork, memory is : abcdefghijklmnopqrstuvwxyz

Parent removing shared memory
```

Run Program 8.2 on your system and record the addresses it displays. Modify the program by adding a variety of static and automatic variable declarations. Does the first free address the system picks for the shared memory segment remain constant? If not, is there a consistent set distance the system uses as an offset from the **etext**, **edata**, or **end** values? Why might this be? If the shared memory segment is not in the text or data segment of the process, is it actually found in the stack segment of the process? How did you determine this?

Using our previous producer/consumer example from Program 7.4 as a base, we can implement a producer/consumer relationship that uses shared memory in place of a file to convey information from one process to another. In our example, the producing process generates a series of random messages that are stored in a shared memory segment for the consumer process to read. To facilitate communication between the two processes, which may operate at differing rates, an array with six message buffers (slots) is used. The message buffer array is treated as a queue, whereby new messages are added to the tail of the list and messages to be processed are removed from the head of the list. The two integer indices, referencing the head and tail of the list respectively, are also stored in the shared memory segment. The basic configuration of the shared memory segment is shown in Figure 8.5.

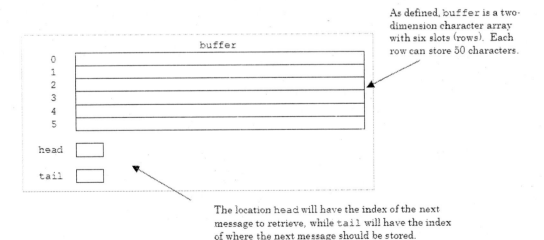

As defined, buffer is a two-dimension character array with six slots (rows). Each row can store 50 characters.

The location head will have the index of the next message to retrieve, while tail will have the index of where the next message should be stored.

Figure 8.5 Conceptual configuration of memory.

We will use two semaphores to coordinate access to the shared memory segment. The first semaphore, treated as a counting semaphore, will contain the number of available slots that can be written to. As long as this semaphore is nonzero, the producing process can continue to write its messages to the shared memory segment. Initially, this semaphore is set to indicate that six slots are available. The second semaphore, also treated as a counting semaphore, indicates the number of slots available for consumption (reading). Both the producer and consumer processes execute concurrently and reference the same shared memory segment. The activities of the processes are shown in Figure 8.6 with the areas within the boxes indicating access to the shared memory segment.

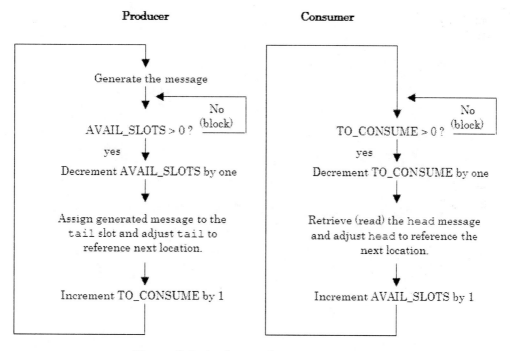

Figure 8.6 Producer and consumer activities.

To reduce the amount of coding and to provide programming consistency, a common local header file, called `local.h`, is generated. The `local.h` file contains the `include` statements and variable declarations needed by each of the programs that make up this example. Each program references this file in its first lines of program code via the preprocessor statement `#include` "local.h". The contents of the local.h file are shown in Figure 8.7. Lines 35 through 38 define the makeup of the shared memory segment.

Figure 8.7 The common header file.

```
File : local.h
  |     /*
  |         Common header file: parent, producer and consumer
  |     */
  |     #ifndef LOCAL_H
  +     #define LOCAL_H
  |     #define _GNU_SOURCE
  |     #include <iostream>
  |     #include <cstdio>
  |·    #include <unistd.h>
 10     #include <stdlib.h>
  |     #include <string.h>
  |     #include <sys/types.h>
  |     #include <sys/ipc.h>
  |     #include <sys/sem.h>
  +     #include <sys/shm.h>
  |     #include <signal.h>
  |     #include <wait.h>
  |     #define ROWS 5                         // Establish some common values
  |     #define COLS 3
 20     #define SLOT_LEN 50
  |     #define N_SLOTS  6
  |     using namespace std;
  |     #if defined(__GNU_LIBRARY__) && !defined(_SEM_SEMUN_UNDEFINED)
  |                                            // definition in <sys/sem.h>
  +     #else
  |     union semun {                          // We define:
  |       int val;                             // value   for SETVAL
  |       struct semid_ds *buf;                // buffer for IPC_STAT, IPC_SET
  |       unsigned short int *array;           // array   for GETALL, SETALL
 30       struct seminfo *__buf;               // buffer for IPC_INFO
  |     };
  |     #endif
  |     enum {AVAIL_SLOTS, TO_CONSUME};
  |                                            // Layout for shared memory
  +     struct MEMORY {
  |       char buffer[N_SLOTS][SLOT_LEN];
  |       int  head, tail;
  |     };
  |                                            // Actions for semaphores
 40     struct sembuf acquire = { 0, -1, SEM_UNDO},
  |                   release = { 0,  1, SEM_UNDO};
  |     #endif
```

In this example, a parent process is responsible for creating and initializing the shared memory segment and the two semaphores that control access to it. Once this has been done, the parent process will **fork** two child processes. The first process will be the producing process and the second, the consuming process. The code for the parent process is shown in Program 8.3.

Program 8.3 The parent process.

```
File : parent.cxx
   |      /*
   |         The PARENT
   |      */
   |      #include "local.h"
   +      int
   |      main(int argc, char *argv[ ]) {
   |        static struct MEMORY    memory;
   |        static unsigned int short   start_val[2] = {N_SLOTS, 0};
   |        int              semid, shmid, croaker;
  10        char             *shmptr;
   |        pid_t            p_id, c_id, pid = getpid( );
   |        union semun      arg;
   |        memory.head = memory.tail = 0;
   |                                         // Check command line arguments
   +        if ( argc != 3 ) {
   |          cerr << argv[0] << " producer_time  consumer_time" << endl;
   |          return 1;
   |        }
   |                                         // Create, attach, clear segment
  20        if ((shmid=shmget((int)pid, sizeof(memory),
   |                           IPC_CREAT | 0600 )) != -1){
   |          if ((shmptr=(char *)shmat(shmid, 0, 0)) == (char *) -1){
   |            perror("shmptr -- parent -- attach ");
   |            return 2;
   +          }
   |          memcpy(shmptr, (char *)&memory, sizeof(memory));
   |        } else {
   |          perror("shmid -- parent -- creation ");
   |          return 3;
  30        }
   |                                         // Create & initialize semaphores
   |        if ((semid=semget((int)pid, 2, IPC_CREAT | 0666)) != -1) {
   |          arg.array = start_val;
   |          if (semctl(semid, 0, SETALL, arg) == -1) {
   +            perror("semctl -- parent -- initialization");
   |            return 4;
   |          }
   |        } else {
   |          perror("semget -- parent -- creation ");
```

```
40              return 5;
 |          }
 |                                          // Fork PRODUCER process
 |          if ( (p_id=fork( )) == -1) {
 |            perror("fork -- producer");
 +            return 6;
 |          } else if ( p_id == 0 ) {
 |            execl( "producer", "./producer", argv[1], (char *) 0);
 |            perror("execl -- producer");
 |            return 7;
50          }
 |                                          // Fork CONSUMER process
 |          if ( (c_id =fork( )) == -1) {
 |            perror("fork -- consumer");
 |            return 8;
 +          } else if ( c_id == 0 ) {
 |            execl( "consumer", "./consumer", argv[2], (char *) 0);
 |            perror("execl -- consumer");
 |            return 9;
 |          }                               // Wait for 1 to die -
60          croaker = (int) wait( (int *) 0 );   // kill remaining process
 |          kill( ((croaker == p_id ) ? c_id : p_id), SIGKILL);
 |          shmdt( shmptr );
 |          shmctl(shmid,IPC_RMID,(struct shmid_ds *)0);
 |          semctl( semid, 0, IPC_RMID, 0);
 +          return 0;
 |      }
```

The parent process expects two integer values to be passed via the command line (program lines 15–18). These values indicate a maximum time, in seconds, for a process to sleep during its execution cycle. The first value is passed to the producing process and the second to the consuming process. By specifying differing values on the command line, we can easily simulate producer/consumer relationships that operate at different speeds. In lines 20 through 25, we create and attach the shared memory segment. Once this is done, we copy the contents of our memory structure (which has been set to its initial values) to the shared memory segment using the library function **memcpy**. The **memcpy** function is one of a group of functions that work with sequences of bytes bounded by a byte count value rather than by a terminating NULL character. See Table 8.10.

The **memcpy** function copies n number of bytes from the location referenced by src to the location referenced by dest. Upon completion, a pointer to the dest location is returned. Be careful: The **memcpy** function does not check for overflow.

In lines 32 through 41 of the parent program, the two semaphores that control access to the shared memory segment are created and set to their

Table 8.10 Summary of the memcpy Library Function.

Include File(s)	<string.h>		Manual Section	3
Summary	void *memcpy(void *dest, const void *src,size_t n);			
	Success	Failure	Sets errno	
Return	A pointer to dest			

initial values. The AVAIL_SLOTS semaphore is set to 6 to reflect the six available slots, and the TO_CONSUME semaphore is set to 0. A child process is then forked and overlaid with the producer process code (line 47). The producing process is passed a single integer argument to be used as its sleep time. Following this, the parent process forks a second child process, which it then overlays with the consumer process code (line 56). The consumer process is also passed an integer sleep value as its first argument. Once this is done, the parent process waits for one of its child processes (either the producer or consumer) to terminate. When this occurs, the PID is returned and stored in the program variable croaker. The parent process then checks the contents of this variable to determine which child process remains. The remaining process is removed with a call to **kill**, and the shared memory segment is detached and removed. The code for the producer process is shown in Program 8.4.

Program 8.4 The producer process.

```
File : producer.cxx
    |       /*
    |               The PRODUCER ...
    |       */
    |       #include "local.h"
    +       int
    |       main(int argc, char *argv[]) {
    |         static char    *source[ROWS][COLS] = {
    |                           {"A", "The", "One"},
    |                           {" red", " polka-dot", " yellow"},
   10                          {" spider", " dump truck", " tree"},
    |                           {" broke", " ran", " fell"},
    |                           {" down", " away", " out"}
    |         };
```

291

```
 |        static char     local_buffer[SLOT_LEN];
 +        int             i, r, c, sleep_limit, semid, shmid;
 |        pid_t           ppid = getppid( );
 |        char            *shmptr;
 |        struct MEMORY   *memptr;
 |                                            // Check command line
20        if ( argc != 2 ) {
 |          cerr << argv[0] << " sleep_time" << endl;
 |          return 20;
 |        }
 |                                            // Access, attach & ref mem
 +        if ((shmid=shmget((int) ppid, 0, 0)) != -1 ){
 |          if ((shmptr=(char *)shmat(shmid,(char *)0,0))==(char *)-1){
 |            perror("shmat -- producer -- attach ");
 |            return 21;
 |          }
30          memptr = (struct MEMORY *) shmptr;
 |        } else {
 |          perror("shmget -- producer -- access ");
 |          return 22;
 |        }
 +                                            // Access semaphore set
 |        if ( (semid=semget((int) ppid, 2, 0)) == -1 ) {
 |          perror("semget -- producer -- access ");
 |          return 23;
 |        }
40        sleep_limit = atoi(argv[1]) % 20;
 |        i = 20 - sleep_limit;
 |        srand((unsigned)getpid());
 |        while( i-- ) {
 |          memset(local_buffer, '\0', sizeof(local_buffer));
 +          for (r = 0; r < ROWS; ++r) {       // Make a random string
 |            c = rand() % COLS;
 |            strcat(local_buffer, source[r][c]);
 |          }
 |          acquire.sem_num = AVAIL_SLOTS;
50          if (semop(semid, &acquire, 1 ) == -1 ){
 |            perror("semop -- producer -- acquire ");
 |            return 24;
 |          }
 |          strcpy(memptr->buffer[memptr->tail], local_buffer);
 +          cout << "P: [" << memptr->tail << "] "
 |               << memptr->buffer[memptr->tail] << endl;
 |          memptr->tail = (memptr->tail +1) % N_SLOTS;
 |          release.sem_num = TO_CONSUME;
 |          if (semop( semid, &release, 1 ) == -1 ) {
60            perror("semop -- producer -- release ");
 |            return 25;
 |          }
```

Once the random string is generated, acquire the **AVAIL_SLOTS** semaphore, store the string, update the tail index, and increment the **TO_CONSUME** semaphore.

```
|        sleep( rand( ) % sleep_limit + 1 );
|      }
+      return 0;
|    }
```

The producer process allocates a two-dimensional array, source, that contains a series of strings used to generate random messages to store in the shared memory segment. A storage location, local_buffer, is created that temporarily holds the message. Next, the PID of the parent is obtained via the **getpid** system call. The parent PID is used as the key value for the **shmget** system call. This enables the producer process to reference the shared memory segment that was created by the parent process. Another approach would be to pass the shared memory identifier from the parent process to the producer via the command line. If this were done, the parent process would convert the integer shared memory identifier to a character string before passing it, and the producing process would convert the string back to its original integer format.

In program lines 25 through 29, the producer process gains access to the shared memory segment and attaches it. The producer uses a local pointer, memptr, to assign the shared memory address at program line 30 in order to reference the shared memory location. The producer process then gains access to the semaphore set (again using the parent PID as the **semget** key value). After this is done, the limit for the time to **sleep** during its processing cycle is obtained (line 40), and the maximum number of messages to be generated is calculated.

The program then loops through the following steps. It clears the local_buffer by filling it with null characters. A short random message is produced and stored in the local_buffer. The producer then evaluates the AVAIL_SLOTS semaphore. Once the producer can acquire the semaphore (which by definition will occur only if the semaphore is nonzero),[2] the message in local_buffer is copied to the shared memory location using the value in the memory->tail location as an offset index. The message that is stored is displayed to the screen for reference. The memory->tail value is then incremented in a modular fashion so as to reference the next valid storage location. The TO_CONSUME semaphore is incremented next to indicate the addition of another message. The producer then sleeps a maximum of sleep_limit seconds and continues its processing loop. The producer exits when all messages have been produced and written to the shared memory segment or when it receives a termination signal (such as from its parent process). The code for the consumer process is shown in Program 8.5.

---

[2] The contents of the AVAIL_SLOTS semaphore is decremented when it is acquired.

Program 8.5 The consumer process.

```
File : consumer.cxx
    |       /*
    |                   The CONSUMER
    |        */
    |       #include "local.h"
    +       int
    |       main(int argc, char *argv[]) {
    |         static char    local_buffer[SLOT_LEN];
    |         int            i, sleep_limit, semid, shmid;
    |         pid_t          ppid = getppid( );
   10         char           *shmptr;
    |         struct MEMORY  *memptr;
    |                                              // Check command line
    |         if ( argc != 2 ) {
    |           cerr << argv[0] << " sleep_time" << endl;
    +           return 30;
    |         }
    |                                              // Access, attach & ref memory
    |         if ((shmid=shmget((int) ppid, 0, 0)) != -1 ){
    |           if ( (shmptr=(char *)shmat(shmid,(char *)0,0)) == (char *) -1){
   20             perror("shmat -- consumer -- attach");
    |             return 31;
    |           }
    |           memptr = (struct MEMORY *) shmptr;
    |         } else {
    +           perror("shmget -- consumer -- access");
    |           return 32;
    |         }
    |                                              // Access semaphore set
    |         if ( (semid=semget((int) ppid, 2, 0)) == -1 ) {
   30           perror("semget -- consumer -- access ");
    |           return 33;
    |         }
    |         sleep_limit = atoi(argv[1]) % 20;
    |         i = 20 - sleep_limit;
    +         srand((unsigned)getpid());
    |         while( i ) {
    |           acquire.sem_num = TO_CONSUME;
    |           if (semop(semid, &acquire, 1 ) == -1 ){
    |             perror("semop -- consumer -- acquire ");
   40             return 34;
    |           }
    |           memset(local_buffer, '\0', sizeof(local_buffer));
    |           strcpy(local_buffer, memptr->buffer[memptr->head]);
    |           cout << "C: [" << memptr->head << "] "
    +                << local_buffer << endl;
    |           memptr->head = (memptr->head +1) % N_SLOTS;
```

```
 |          release.sem_num = AVAIL_SLOTS;
 |          if (semop( semid, &release, 1 ) == -1 ) {
 |            perror("semop -- consumer -- release ");
50            return 35;
 |          }
 |          sleep( rand( ) % sleep_limit + 1 );
 |        }
 |      return 0;
 +    }
```

In most aspects, the logic for the consumer process is similar to that of the producer process. However, the consumer will be allowed access to the shared memory segment via the TO_CONSUME semaphore. If this semaphore is nonzero, it indicates there are messages available for the consumer to read. When a message is available, the consumer copies the message to its local_buffer array from the shared memory location using the value in memory->head as an offset index. The local_buffer contents are then displayed on the screen for reference. As in the producer process, the value referenced by memory->head is incremented in a modular fashion to reference the next valid location. The AVAIL_SLOTS semaphore is incremented, and the consumer continues its processing.

When viewing the output of a run of the program, note that if the parent process is passed a set of values that allow the producer process to be faster than the consumer process, the shared memory location will eventually become full. When this occurs, the producer must block and wait[3] for the consumer to read a message. Only after a message has been read by the consumer is a slot released and a new message stored by the producer. See Figure 8.8.

Figure 8.8 Output when the producer process works faster than the consumer process.

```
linux$ parent 1 3
P: [0] The yellow tree broke out
C: [0] The yellow tree broke out
P: [1] One yellow spider broke away
C: [1] One yellow spider broke away
P: [2] One red dump truck fell away
P: [3] The polka-dot dump truck broke away      The producer is working
P: [4] One red spider broke away                faster than the consumer.
C: [2] One red dump truck fell away
P: [5] The yellow dump truck ran out
P: [0] A red dump truck broke away
 . . .
```

[3] The default action when attempting to acquire a zero value semaphore.

If values are passed to the producer/consumer that permit them to work at similar rates, we should find the six-element message array sufficient to allow both processes to continue their work without each having an inordinate amount of waiting for the other process to finish its task. However, the consumer process will still wait should no new messages be available. See Figure 8.9.

Figure 8.9 Output when the consumer process works at the same rate the producer process.

```
linux$ parent 3 3
P: [0] One yellow spider fell away
C: [0] One yellow spider fell away
P: [1] One yellow spider fell away
C: [1] One yellow spider fell away
P: [2] One yellow tree broke out
P: [3] A yellow dump truck ran away
C: [2] One yellow tree broke out
C: [3] A yellow dump truck ran away
P: [4] The polka-dot dump truck broke out
C: [4] The polka-dot dump truck broke out
. . .
```

8-5 EXERCISE

In this producer/consumer example, the code to display the message to the screen and the adjusting of the head/tail indices was done within the critical regions bounded by the two semaphores. Is this actually necessary? Why, why not? If both the producer and consumer *know* there are six buffer slots, are two semaphores actually needed? Why?

8-6 EXERCISE

Modify the producer/consumer example to support multiple consumers. Can this be done without adding another semaphore? Support your findings with output.

Modify the producer/consumer example to support multiple producers. Is yet another semaphore needed to coordinate process activity? Supply output to support your findings.

8.5 Using a File as Shared Memory

Most versions of Linux-UNIX also support the **mmap** system call, which can be used to map a file to a process's virtual memory address space. In many ways **mmap** is more flexible than its shared memory system call counterpart. Once a mapping has been established, standard system calls rather than specialized system calls can be used to manipulate the shared memory object (Table 8.11). Unlike memory, the contents of a file are nonvolatile and will remain available even after a system has been shut down (and rebooted).

Table 8.1 Summary of the **mmap** System Call. If _POSIX_MAPPED_FILES has been defined.

Include File(s)	<unistd.h> <sys/nman.h>		Manual Section	2

Summary	`#ifdef _POSIX_MAPPED_FILES`
	`void *mmap(void *start, size_t length, int prot,`
	`        int flags, int fd, off_t offset);`
	`#endif`			

	Success	Failure	Sets errno	
Return	A pointer to the mapped area	MAP_FAILED ((void *) -1)	Yes	

The **mmap** system call requires six arguments. The first, start, is the address for attachment. As with the **shmat** system call, this argument is most often set to 0, which directs the system to choose a valid attachment address. The number of bytes to be attached is indicated by the second argument, length. While the call will allow the user to specify a number of bytes for length that will extend beyond the end of the mapped file, an actual reference to these locations will generate an error (a SIGBUS signal). The third argument, prot, is used to set the type of access (protection) for the segment. The specified access should not be in conflict with the access permissions for the associated file descriptor. The prot argument uses the defined constants found in the include file <sys/mman.h>. These constants are shown in Table 8.12.

Table 8.12 Defined Protection Constants.

Defined Constant	Access
PROT_READ	Read access to specified region.
PROT_WRITE	Write access to specified region.
PROT_EXEC	Execute access to specified region.
PROT_NONE	No access.

Constants can be ORed to provide different combinations of access. The manual page for **mmap** notes that on some systems PROT_WRITE is implemented as PROT_READ | PROT_WRITE, and PROT_EXEC as PROT_READ | PROT_EXEC. In any case, PROT_WRITE must be set if the process is to write to the mapped segment. The fourth argument, flags, specifies the type of mapping. Mapping types are also indicated using defined constants from the <sys/mman.h> include file. These constants are shown in Table 8.13.

Table 8.13 Defined Mapping Type Constants.

Defined Constant	Mapping Type
MAP_SHARED	Share all changes.
MAP_PRIVATE	Do not share changes.
MAP_FIXED	Interpret the value for the start argument exactly.

The first two constants specify whether **write**s to the shared memory will be shared with other processes or be private. MAP_SHARED and MAP_PRIVATE are exclusionary. When specifying MAP_PRIVATE, a private copy is not generated until the first **write** to the mapped object has occurred. These specifications are retained across a **fork** system call but not across a call to **exec**. MAP_FIXED directs the system to *explicitly* use the address value in start.

When MAP_FIXED is indicated, the values for `start` and `length` should be a multiple of the system's page size. Specifying MAP_FIXED greatly reduces the portability of a program, and its use is discouraged. When specifying the flags argument, either MAP_SHARED or MAP_PRIVATE must be indicated. Linux also supports the flags shown in Table 8.14.

Table 8.14 Linux-Specific Defined Mapping Type Constants.

Defined Constant	Mapping Type
MAP_GROWSDOWN	Treat the segment as a stack.
MAP_EXECUTABLE	Mark the segment as executable.
MAP_DENYWRITE	Do not allow writing.
MAP_NORESERVE	Do not check for reservations.
MAP_LOCKED	Lock the mapped segment.

The fifth argument, `fd`, is a valid **open** file descriptor. Once the mapping is established, the file can be closed. The sixth argument, `offset`, is used to set the starting position for the mapping.

If the **mmap** system call is successful, it returns a reference to the mapped memory object. If the call fails, it returns the defined constant MAP_FAILED (which is actually the value -1 cast to a `void *`). A failed call will set the value in `errno` to reflect the error encountered. The errors for **mmap** are shown in Table 8.15.

Table 8.15 mmap Error Messages.

#	Constant	`perror` Message	Explanation
6	ENXIO	No such device or address	The values for `off` or `off + len` are illegal for the specified device.
9	EBADF	Bad file descriptor	The file referenced by `fd` is invalid.
11	EAGAIN	Resource temporarily unavailable	• Insufficient swap space for the mapping. • Mapping could not be locked in memory. • Mapped file is already locked.
12	ENOMEM	Cannot allocate memory	Insufficient address space to implement the mapping.

Continued

Table 8.15 (Continued)

#	Constant	`perror` **Message**	**Explanation**
13	EACCES	Permission denied	• MAP_PRIVATE indicated and file descriptor is not open for reading. • File descriptor is not open for writing, and PROT_WRITE was indicated with a mapping type of MAP_SHARED.
19	ENODEV	No such device	`fd` references an invalid device (such as a terminal).
22	EINVAL	Invalid argument	• MAP_FIXED specified, and value for `start` or `offset` are not multiples of the system's page size. • Illegal `flag` value. • Argument `length` is less than 1.
26	ETXTBSY	Text file busy	MAP_DENYWRITE was set but `fd` is open for writing.

While the system will automatically unmap a region when a process terminates, the system call **munmap**, shown in Table 8.16, can be used to explicitly unmap pages of memory.

Table 8.16 Summary of the `munmap` System Call.

Include File(s)	`<unistd.h>` `<signal.h>`		Manual Section	**2**

Summary	`#ifdef _POSIX_MAPPED_FILES`
	`int munmap(void *start, size_t length);`
	`#endif`			

	Success	Failure	Sets `errno`	
Return	0	−1	Yes	

The **munmap** system call is passed the starting address of the memory mapping (argument `start`) and the size of the mapping (argument `length`). If the call is successful, it returns a value of 0. Future references to unmapped addresses generate a SIGVEGV signal. If the **munmap** system call fails, it returns the value −1 and sets the value in errno to EINVAL. The interpretation of **munmap**-related error is given in Table 8.17.

Table 8.17 munmap Error Messages.

#	Constant	perror **Message**	Explanation
22	EINVAL	Invalid argument	• Argument length is less than 1. • Argument start is not a multiple of the system page size. • Argument start or start + length is outside the process's address space.

The **msync** system call is used in conjunction with **mmap** to synchronize the contents of mapped memory with physical storage (Table 8.18). A call to **msync** will cause the system to write all modified memory locations to their associated physical storage locations. If MAP_SHARED is specified with **mmap**, the storage location is a file. If MAP_PRIVATE is specified, then the storage location is the swap area.

Table 8.18 Summary of the msync Library Function.

Include File(s)	`<unistd.h>` `<sys/mman.h>`		Manual Section	**2**

Summary	`#ifdef _POSIX_MAPPED_FILES`
	`#ifdef _POSIX_SYNCHRONIZED_IO`
	`int msync(const void *start, size_t length,`
	`            int flags);`
	`#endif`
	`#endif`			

Return	Success	Failure	Sets errno	
	0	−1	Yes	

The start argument for **msync** specifies the address of the mapped memory; the length argument specifies the size (in bytes) of the memory. The flags argument directs the system to take the actions shown in Table 8.19.

Table 8.19 Defined Flag Constants for msync.

Defined Constant	Action
MS_ASYNC	Return immediately once all writes have been scheduled.
MS_SYNC	Return once all writes have been performed.
MS_INVALIDATE	Invalidate cached copies of memory—system reloads memory from the associated storage location.

If **msync** fails, it returns a −1 and sets errno (Table 8.20). If the call is successful, it returns a value of 0.

Table 8.20 mmap Error Messages.

#	Constant	perror **Message**	Explanation
1	EPERM	Operation not permitted	MS_INVALIDATE indicated but some of the referenced locations are locked in memory.
14	EFAULT	Bad address	Invalid address reference.
16	EBUSY	Device or resource busy	MS_SYNC and MS_INVALIDATE specified but some of the referenced addresses are currently locked.
22	EINVAL	Invalid argument	• Argument addr is not a multiple of the page size. • Argument flags not a combination of MS_ASYNC | MS_INVALIDATE | MS_SYNC.

Program 8.6 demonstrates the use of the **mmap** system call.

Program 8.6 Using mmap.

```
File : p8.6.cxx
    |    /*
    |         Using the mmap system call
    |    */
    |    #define _GNU_SOURCE
    +    #include <iostream>
    |    #include <cstdio>
    |    #include <sys/types.h>
```

```
   |      #include <sys/mman.h>
   |      #include <sys/stat.h>
  10      #include <fcntl.h>
   |      #include <stdlib.h>
   |      #include <unistd.h>
   |      #include <signal.h>
   |      #include <string.h>
   +      using namespace std;
   |      int
   |      main(int argc, char *argv[]){
   |        int        fd, changes, i, random_spot, kids[2];
   |        struct stat  buf;
  20        char        *the_file, *starting_string="ABCDEFGHIJKLMNOPQRSTUVWXYZ";
   |        if (argc != 3) {
   |          cerr << "Usage " << *argv << " file_name #_of_changes" << endl;
   |          return 1;
   |        }
   +        if ((changes = atoi(argv[2])) < 1) {
   |          cerr << "# of changes < 1" << endl;
   |          return 2;
   |        }
   |        if ((fd = open(argv[1], O_CREAT | O_RDWR, 0666)) < 0) {
  30          perror("file open");
   |          return 3;
   |        }
   |        write(fd, starting_string, strlen(starting_string));
   |                                          // Obtain size of file
   +        if (fstat(fd, &buf) < 0) {
   |          perror("fstat error");
   |          return 4;
   |        }
   |                                          // Establish the mapping
  40        if ((the_file = (char *) mmap(0, (size_t) buf.st_size,
   |                         PROT_READ | PROT_WRITE, MAP_SHARED,
   |                         fd, 0)) == (void *) - 1) {
   |          perror("mmap failure");
   |          exit(5);
   +        }
   |        for (i = 0; i < 2; ++i)
   |          if ((kids[i] = (int) fork()) == 0)
   |            while (1) {
   |              cout << "Child " << getpid() << " finds: " << the_file << endl;
  50              sleep(1);
   |            }
   |        srand((unsigned) getpid());
   |        for (i = 0; i < changes; ++i) {
   |          random_spot = (int) (rand() % buf.st_size);
   +          *(the_file + random_spot) = '*';
   |          sleep(1);
   |        }
```

```
  |        cout << "In parent, done with changes" << endl;
  |        for (i = 0; i < 2; ++i)
 60            kill(kids[i], 9);
  |        cout << "The file now contains: " << the_file << endl;
  |        return 0;
  |      }
```

Program 8.6 uses a parent/two-child process arrangement to demonstrate the use of **mmap**. The parent process modifies the contents of a memory-mapped file. Each child process repetitively displays the contents of the mapped files to allow verification of the changes. The program is passed two command-line arguments. The first argument is the name of a file that it will use for mapping. The second argument indicates the number of modifications that should be made to the file. Upon execution of the program, the validity of the command-line arguments is checked. If problems are encountered, an appropriate error message is generated and the program exits. If the command-line arguments are good, the program opens, for reading and writing, the file whose name was passed as the first command-line argument. As the O_CREAT flag is specified, if the file does not exist, it will be created. Next, the string "ABCDEFGHIJKLMNOPQRSTUVWXYZ" is written to the first part of the file. Following this, the **fstat** call is used to determine the size of the file.

In our example, if we start with an empty file, the size of the file is actually the length of the string that is written to the file. However, this would not be true if the file contained previous data. In many cases we will want to know the full size of the file to be mapped—**fstat** provides us with a handy way of determining the file's size (it is returned as part of the stat structure). The call to **mmap** (line 40) establishes the actual mapping. We allow the system to pick the address and indicate that we want to be able to read from and write to the mapped memory region. We also specify the region be marked as shared, be associated with the open file descriptor fd, and have an offset (starting position within the file) of 0. Two child processes are then generated. Each child process displays the contents of the memory-mapped file using the the_file reference which was returned from the initial call to **mmap**. It is important to note that a call to **read** was not needed. The child process then **sleep**s one second and repeats the same sequence of activities until a terminating signal is received. The parent process loops for the number of times specified by the second command-line argument. Within this loop the parent process randomly picks a memory-mapped location and changes it to an asterisk (*). Again, this is done by direct reference to the location using the the_file reference; notice **no write** function is used. Between changes, the parent sleeps one second to slow down the processing sequence. Once the parent process is done, it displays the final contents of the memory-mapped file, removes the child processes, and exits. A sample run of the program is shown in Figure 8.10.

Figure 8.10 A sample run of Program 8.6.

```
linux$ p8.6 demo 7
Child 16592 finds: ABCDEFGHIJKLMNOPQRSTUVWXYZ
Child 16593 finds: ABCDEFGHIJKLMNOPQRSTUVWXYZ
Child 16592 finds: ABCDEFG*IJKLMNOPQRSTUVWXYZ
Child 16593 finds: ABCDEFG*IJKLMNOPQRSTUVWX*Z
Child 16592 finds: ABCDEFG*IJKLMNOPQRSTUVWX*Z
Child 16593 finds: ABCDEF**IJKLMNOPQRSTUVWX*Z
Child 16592 finds: ABCDEF**IJKLMNOPQRSTUVWX*Z
Child 16593 finds: ABCDEF**IJ*LMNOPQRSTUVWX*Z
Child 16592 finds: ABCDEF**IJ*LMNOPQRSTUVWX*Z
Child 16593 finds: ABCDEF**I**LMNOPQRSTUVWX*Z
Child 16592 finds: ABCDEF**I**LMNOPQRSTUVWX*Z
Child 16593 finds: ABCDEF**I**LMNOPQRS*UVWX*Z
Child 16592 finds: ABCDEF**I**LMNOPQRS*UVWX*Z
Child 16593 finds: ABCDEF**I**L*NOPQRS*UVWX*Z
Child 16592 finds: ABCDEF**I**L*NOPQRS*UVWX*Z
In parent, done with changes
The file now contains: ABCDEF**I**L*NOPQRS*UVWX*Z
```

In this invocation the child processes, PIDs 16592 and 16593, initially find the mapped location to contain the unmodified starting string. A second check of the mapped location shows that each child now *sees* the string with a single '*' replacing the letter H. Additional passes reveal further modifications. When all of the processes have terminated, we will find that the file demo will contain the fully modified string.

8-8 EXERCISE

If we replace MAP_SHARED with MAP_PRIVATE, will the output from Program 8.6 remain the same? Why, why not? Will the file test contain the * modified string or the original string? Why, why not? Why is the MAP_SHARED specification retained across a **fork** but not an **exec** system call?

What if the file that we map resides on a shared file system? Can we then have unrelated processes residing on different workstations use this file as a means of communication? Support your answer with a program example.

8.6 Shared Memory Class

A shared memory class is shown in Figure 8.11. As defined, this class can be used only with processes that have access to the same shared memory ID.

Figure 8.11 Header file for a basic shared memory class.

```
File : Shared_mem.h
   |      /*
   |         A VERY simplified shared memory class for use in a std UNIX
   |         environment.  See the text for instructions on how to use
   |         this class.  Copyright (c) 2002 J. S. Gray
   +
   |         Exit codes for class operations:
   |
   |         1 - Unable to allocate memory      2 - Unable map memory
   |         3 - Could not remove shared memory
  10      */
   |      #pragma interface            ◄──────────── This notifies the compiler that
   |      #ifndef Shared_mem_h                       a template class is being declared.
   |      #define Shared_mem_h
   |      #define _GNU_SOURCE
   +      #include <iostream>
   |      #include <cstdio>
   |      #include <sys/types.h>
   |      #include <unistd.h>
   |      #include <stdlib.h>
  20      #include <sys/ipc.h>
   |      #include <sys/shm.h>
   |      using namespace std;
   |      template <class S_type>          // Allow for different data types
   |      class Shared_mem {
   +        public:
   |          Shared_mem ( );              // Constructor
   |          ~Shared_mem( );              // Destructor - remove shared memory
```

```
  |        void    Put ( const S_type ); // Assign value to shared memory
  |        S_type Get (  );              // Return value from shared memory
30
  |     private:
  |        int    shmid;                 // ID of shared memory
  |        S_type *shm_ptr;              // Reference to shared memory
  |        pid_t  my_pid;                // Hang on to originator PID
  +     };
  |     #endif
```

The shared memory class is templated to allow the passing of a data type. The shared memory class generates a private shared memory segment of the appropriate size for the data type. There are four public methods and three private data members in the shared memory class. The public methods and their functionality are described in Table 8.21.

Table 8.21 Shared_mem Class Methods.

Method name	Explanation
Shared_mem	This is the class constructor. This method generates the shared memory segment. The size of the segment is set by the data type. Once created, the segment is attached. The creating PID is saved in the my_pid data member.
~Shared_mem	The class destructor. This method removes the shared memory segment from the system if the calling function is the process that created the segment.
Put	Put assigns a value to the shared memory segment.
Get	Get retrieves the current value stored in the memory segment.

The C++ code that implements the shared memory methods is found in Program 8.7, Shared_mem.cxx. Again, as with the previously defined System V IPC classes (Message_que and SSemaphore), this is a very rudimentary implementation.

Program 8.7 Program code for the shared memory class.

```
File : Shared_mem.cxx                          This notifies the compiler that
  |     #pragma implementation      ◄──────    a template class is being defined.
  |     /*
  |         Shared memory implementation -  Copyright (c) 2002 J. S. Gray
  |         Compile with: -fexternal-templates
  +     */
```

```
 |      #include "Shared_mem.h"
 |                                           // Generate private mem segment
 |      template <class S_type>              // Generalize data type
 |      Shared_mem<S_type>::Shared_mem(  ){
10        my_pid = getpid( );              // Save PID of creating process
 |        if ((shmid = shmget(IPC_PRIVATE, sizeof(S_type),
 |            IPC_CREAT | 0660)) < 0)
 |          exit(1);
 |        if ((shm_ptr = (S_type *) shmat(shmid, NULL, 0)) == NULL)
 |          exit(2);
 +      }
 |                                           // Remove memory if creator
 |      template <class S_type>
 |      Shared_mem<S_type>::~Shared_mem(  ) {
 |        if ( getpid( ) == my_pid ) {
20        shmdt( (char *) shm_ptr );
 |          if ( shmctl(shmid, IPC_RMID, (struct shmid_ds *) 0) == -1 )
 |            exit( 3 );
 |        }
 |      }
 +                                           // Assign value to this location
 |      template <class S_type>
 |      void
 |      Shared_mem<S_type>::Put( const S_type stuff  ){
 |        *shm_ptr = stuff;
30      }
 |                                           // Retrieve value from location
 |      template <class S_type>
 |      S_type
 |      Shared_mem<S_type>::Get(  ){
 +        static S_type stuff;
 |        stuff = *shm_ptr;
 |        return stuff;
 |      }
 |                                           // Force instantiation
40      typedef Shared_mem<int>    Shared_int;
 |      typedef Shared_mem<char>   Shared_char;
 |      typedef Shared_mem<float>  Shared_float;
 |      typedef Shared_mem<double> Shared_double;
```

Note that since templates are involved, a few more gymnastics are called for if we want to keep our class declaration and definition code in separate files. To accomplish this, using the **g++** compiler, the directive #pragma interface must be placed at the top of the code in the header file containing the class declaration, while the directive #pragma implementation is placed in the file with the class definition (the corresponding .cxx file). At the bottom of the class definition, a typedef is used to coerce the compiler into generating object code for each specified data type. Lastly, when we compile the shared memory class into object code, the command-line compile option `-fexternal-templates` (generate external templates) must be specified along with the `-c` option. As if this were not enough, newer versions of the compiler may notify the user that the external templates option is deprecated (may not be supported in future versions). The compiler switch: `-Wno-deprecated` can be used to silence these warnings. The compilation of code containing templates can be somewhat daunting. The latest information on the **g++** compiler can be obtained from the site `http://www.gnu.org`.

To use the shared memory class, the files `Shared_mem.h` and `Shared_mem.cxx` should reside locally. The `Shared_mem` class is compiled into object code with the command line

```
linux$  g++ Shared_mem.cxx -c -fexternal-templates
```

At the top of the source file that uses a `Shared_mem` object, add the statement

```
#include "Shared_mem.h"
```

to make the class definition available to the compiler. When compiling the source file, include the message queue object code file

```
linux$  g++  your_file_name.cxx   Shared_mem.o
```

Program 8.8 uses the `Shared_mem` class. This program is passed a small integer value (1–6) on the command line. It goes on to generate a number of child processes. The first process generated is considered to be process 0, the next 1, and so on. As each process is generated, it displays its number in the sequence. To make things a bit more interesting, the output is displayed in a tree-like format. The height of the tree being the value passed in on the command line. Common information, such as the process sequence number, the width of field for output, etc. are stored in a shared memory which is available to the parent and all child processes. The source for the program is shown as in Program 8.8.

Program 8.8 Using the shared memory class.

```
File : p8.8 .cxx
   |      #include <iostream>
   |      #include <iomanip>
   |      #include <sys/types.h>
   |      #include <sys/wait.h>
   +      #include "Shared_mem.h"
```

309

```
 |     int
 |     main(int argc, char *argv[]) {              Instantiate an array of shared memory
 |       int    n;                                 objects—each to hold an integer value.
 |       Shared_mem<int> s[4];
10     if (argc < 2 || (n = atoi(argv[1])) > 6 || n < 1 ) {
 |         cerr << "Usage: " << argv[0] << " value 1-6" << endl;
 |         return 1;
 |       }
 |       setbuf(stdout, NULL);                   // Standard output is unbuffered
 +                                               // Starting values
 |       s[0].Put(0);                            // Process counter
 |       s[1].Put(1);                            // Process # when @ end of line
 |       s[2].Put(64);                           // Output width
 |       s[3].Put(0);                            // Process # that starts new line
20     cout <<  "\t\t\tTree of level " << n << endl << endl;
 |       for (int i=0; i < n; ++i) {
 |         if ( !fork() ) {                      // in the child
 |           int temp_width = s[2].Get();        // get output width
 |           if ((s[0].Get()) == s[3].Get())     // if @ start of line use 1/2
 +              temp_width /= 2;
 |           cout << setiosflags(ios::uppercase) << hex
 |                << setw(temp_width) << (s[0].Get()) % 16;
 |           s[0].Put(s[0].Get()+1);             // count the process
 |         }
30     if ( s[0].Get() == s[1].Get() ){          // If at the end of line
 |         s[1].Put( s[1].Get() * 2 + 1 );       // update end of line process #
 |         s[2].Put( s[2].Get() / 2 );           // decrease output width
 |         s[3].Put( s[0].Get() );               // new sart of line process #
 |         cout << endl << endl;
 +       }
 |       wait(0);                                // wait for the child to finish!
 |     }
 |     return 0;
 |   }
```

In line 9 of the program, a four-element array of shared memory objects is instantiated. In line 14 the **setbuf** library function is used to turn off line buffering of standard out. Data streams can be block buffered, line buffered, or unbuffered. With block buffering, the operating system saves data in a temporary location until it has a block, at which time it performs the I/O operation. File I/O is normally block buffered. With line buffering, data is saved until a newline is encountered, while unbuffered data is made available immediately. The **fflush** library function can also be used to force the system to transfer data, as will the closing of a stream (**fclose**). By default, standard output (stdout, cout) is line buffered, while standard error (stderr, cerr) is not. Setting I/O to unbuffered causes the standard library I/O functions to call the underlying I/O system call for each character of data, which in turn increases the amount of CPU time the process requires. Beneath the covers, **setbuf** is actually an alias to the **setvbuf** library call. As used in the program example, the first argument of **setbuf** references the file stream, while second argument references the buffer where data is to be stored. If the second argument is set to NULL (as is our case), only the mode of the stream is affected.

Lines 16 through 20 establish the initial contents of the shared memory segments. The `for` loop is driven by the value passed on the command line. Each pass through the loop generates one level of the output display. The call to **fork** generates a child process. Each child process announces its presence by displaying a hexadecimal sequence value at a specific location. Back in the parent, a check is made to determine if the current shared memory values need to be adjusted (such as when at the end of a line of output). The parent process waits for the child to terminate (line 36).

Figure 8.12 shows the output generated when the program is run and passed the value 4. Note the dotted lines were not produced by the program.

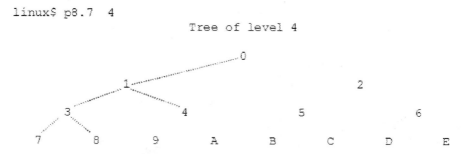

Figure 8.12 A run of program p8.7 when passed the value 4.

8-10 EXERCISE

Program 8.8 will fail if the call to **wait** (line 36) is removed (verify this by commenting it out and recompiling the program). Why is this? Modify Program 8.8 so that it will produce correct output without using the call to **wait** in line 36. *Hint*: Consider using a semaphore to synchronize the access to the shared memory segment(s).

As presented, the shared memory class allocates a segment to hold a single occurrence of the specified data type. While this is fine for a small number of individual values, it is not a good solution for, say, long sequences of character data. Rewrite the shared memory class to support the passing of an integer value to the class constructor to indicate a repetition number. For example, passing a 3 would allocate a segment large enough to store 3 of the specified data type (the default would be 1). Rewrite Program 8.8 using your modified shared memory class. Keep in mind that you may need to adjust other methods in the class to accommodate this change.

8.7 Summary

Shared memory provides the user with an efficient means of communication via the sharing of data that resides in memory. Unlike pipe-based communications, this data can be accessed in a nonserial (random) manner. To prevent inconsistencies, semaphores are often used to coordinate access to shared memory segments. When using System V-based shared memory techniques, shared memory segments are generated with the **shmget** system call. If a shared memory segment has already been created, the **shmget** call provides the process with access to the segment. The **shmctl** system call is used to obtain the status of a memory segment, set permissions, and remove a shared memory segment. The **shmat** and **shmdt** system calls are used to attach (map the segment into the process's address space) and detach memory segments.

The **mmap** system call may also be used to map the virtual memory space of a process to a file. As files remain after a process has terminated, **mmap**ed files provide a means for communicating information between processes that exist at different times. Overall, **mmap**-based techniques are less complex and somewhat more portable than their System V-based counterparts.

8.8 Key Terms and Concepts

`#pragma implementation`	PROT_READ
`#pragma interface`	PROT_WRITE
MAP_DENYWRITE	**setbuf** library function
MAP_EXECUTABLE	Shared memory
MAP_FIXED	SHM_LOCK
MAP_GROWSDOWN	SHM_RND
MAP_LOCKED	SHM_UNLOCK
MAP_NORESERVE	**shmat** system call
MAP_PRIVATE	**shmctl** system call
MAP_SHARED	**shmdt** system call
memcpy library function	**shmget** system call
mmap system call	SHMLBA
msync system call	SHMMAX
munmap system call	SHMMIN
PROT_EXEC	SHMMNI
PROT_NONE	SHMSEG

Chapter 9

REMOTE
PROCEDURE CALLS

9.1 Introduction

So far, the examples we have worked with have been run on the same work-station or host. However, as we gain expertise with interprocess communication techniques, it becomes evident that there will be many occasions when we will want to communicate with processes that may reside on different workstations. These workstations might be on our own local area network or part of a larger wide area network. In a UNIX-based, networked computing setting, there are several ways that communications of this nature can be implemented. This chapter examines the techniques involved with remote procedure calls (RPC).[1] As a programming interface, RPCs are designed to resemble standard, local procedure (function) calls. The *client* process (the process *making* the request) invokes a local procedure commonly known as a **client stub** that contains the network communication details and the actual RPC. The *server* process (the process *performing* the request) has a similar **server stub**, which contains its network communication details. Neither the client nor the server needs to be aware of the underlying network transport

---

[1] The word *remote* in RPC is somewhat misleading. RPCs can also be used by processes residing on the same host (indeed, this approach is often used when debugging routines that contain RPCs).

protocols. The programming stubs are usually created using a protocol compiler, such as Sun Microsystems **rpcgen**. This chapter is based on Sun's RPC implementation as ported to Linux. The protocol compiler is passed a protocol definition file written in a C-like language. For **rpcgen**, the language used is called RPC language. The protocol definition file contains a definition of the remote procedure, its parameters with data types, and its return data type.

When the client invokes an RPC (generates a request), the client waits for the server to reply. Since the client must wait for a response, several coordination issues are of concern:

- How long should a client wait for a reply from the server (the server could be down or very busy)? In general, RPCs address this problem by using a default timeout to limit the client's wait time.

- If the client makes multiple, identical requests, how should the server handle it? The resolution of this problem proves to be program-specific. Depending upon the type of processing (such as a **read** request), the requested activity may indeed be done several times. In other settings, such as transaction processing, the request must be done only once. In these settings, the software must implement its own management routines. By definition, RPCs are independent of transport protocols; however, if an RPC runs on top of a reliable transport (such as TCP), the client can infer from receiving a *reply* from the server process that its request will be executed.

- How can call-by-reference (the passing of address pointers) be implemented when the processes reside in separate process spaces? Further, it is entirely possible that the client and server processes, while not being on the same system, may even be executing on different platforms (e.g., Sun, VAX, IBM, etc.). To resolve these issues and to ensure that client and server processes can communicate using RPC, the data that is passed between the processes is converted to an architecture-independent representation. The data format used by Sun is known as XDR (e**X**ternal **D**ata **R**epresentation). The client and server program stubs are responsible for translating the transmitted data to and from the XDR format. This process is known as **serialization** and **deserialization**. The high-level relationships of client and server processes using an RPC are shown in Figure 9.1.

We will find that, while hidden from the casual user, RPC uses socket-based communication. The details of socket-based communication are covered in Chapter 10, "Sockets."

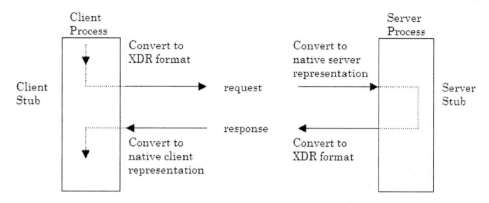

Figure 9.1 An RPC client–server communications overview.

At a system level, the **rpcinfo** command can be used to direct the system to display all of the currently registered RPC services. When the -p flag is passed to **rpcinfo**, the services for the current host are displayed. The **rpcinfo** command is often located in /usr/sbin. If this is the case on your system, /usr/sbin should be part of the search path (so you will not have to fully qualify the path for each invocation). Some versions of **rpcinfo** require the host name to be specified. If you do not know the host name, the **hostname** command will display the name of the host upon which you are working.

9.2 Executing Remote Commands at a System Level

Before delving into the fine points of RPCs from a programming standpoint, it is instructive to look at the execution of remote commands at a system (command-line) level. Most UNIX systems offer several commands that allow the user to execute commands on a remote system. Historically, the most commonly supported remote execution command is **rsh** (the **r**emote **sh**ell command).

The **rsh** command connects to a specified host and executes the indicated command. Standard input from the local host is copied to standard input on the remote host. The remote host's standard output and error will be copied to the local host's standard output and error respectively. Signals such as interrupt, quit, and terminate are passed on to the remote host. As the **rsh** command has proven to be a security risk, users are encouraged to use, in its place, the **ssh** command found in the OpenSSH suite of tools. The **ssh** command provides secure encrypted communication between two hosts and supports more secure methods for authenticating a user (more on this will follow in a bit).

The general syntax for the **ssh** command is

```
linux$ ssh remote_host_name the_command
```

Figure 9.2 demonstrates using **ssh** on a system called linux to run the **who** command on the remote system called morpheus.

Figure 9.2 A typical ssh command.

```
linux$ ssh morpheus who                          No echo of password
gray@morpheus's password:        ◄——————————     when entered.
root       console      Feb 18 11:54     (:0)
root       pts/6        Mar 28 14:03     (:0.0)
gray       pts/2        Apr  8 11:29     (zeus)
root       pts/7        Apr  5 12:37     (:0.0)
root       pts/8        Mar 28 13:02     (:0.0)
root       pts/3        Mar 14 12:11     (:0.0)
root       pts/9        Apr  4 12:10     (:0.0)
root       pts/10       Apr  4 12:15     (:0.0)
```

The remote system (in this case morpheus) prompts for the user's password (as required for the remote system). The output of the command is displayed on the local host linux. It is possible to redirect the output produced by the remote command. However, there are some interesting wrinkles that we should be aware of when we specify I/O redirection with the command to be remotely executed. For example, the two command sequences that follow *appear* to be very similar:

```
linux$ ssh morpheus who > /tmp/whoosie
linux$ ssh morpheus who ">" /tmp/whoosie
```

The first command sequence places the output of the **who** command in the file whoosie in the tmp directory of the local host linux. The second command sequence places the output of the **who** command in the file whoosie in the tmp directory of the remote host morpheus! This occurs because in the second command sequence the redirection, which has been placed in quotes, is passed as part of the remote command and is not acted upon by the local host. If **ssh** is passed just the host name and not passed a command to execute, it will log into the specified host and provide the shell specified in the user's password entry. All communications with the remote shell are encrypted.

For **ssh** to execute a remote command, the user issuing the command must be authenticated.[2] This can be accomplished in a number of ways. Similar to **rsh**, if the host the user is logging in from is listed in the remote host's /etc/hosts.equiv (or /etc/shosts.equiv) file, and the user's login name is the same on both systems, the user is permitted access. Failing this, if the user's $HOME/.rhosts (or $HOME/.shosts) file on the remote host has the name of the local host and user's login name, then the user is are granted access. However, as this sort of authentication is inherently insecure (due to IP, DNS, and routing spoofing), it is normally combined with public–private key encryption authentication.

For **ssh** public–private authentication can be specified in a number of ways (the following is an overview—see the manual page on **ssh** for the all the gory details). The configuration file sshd_config (which is most often in the /etc/ssh directory) designates the authentication method. While four different approaches are available, most system administrators opt to let the system authenticate a request either by checking the user's public key or by prompting the user for his or her normal login password (the default).

The public–private key approach deserves some additional discussion. A user generates a public–private key pair by running the **ssh-keygen** utility. Newer versions of this utility permit the user to specify the type (-t) of key to be created. The choices are protocol version 1 (specified as rsa1) or protocol version 2 (specified as rsa or dsa). If rsa1 is specified, the keys are placed in separate files (usually called identity and identity.pub for private and public keys respectively) in the $HOME/.ssh directory. While permission-wise the identity.pub file is accessible to all, the identity file should not be readable by anyone other than its owner. The first time **ssh** is used to access a remote system, authentication information is added by **ssh** to the user's $HOME/.ssh/known_hosts file. Figure 9.3 shows the process of generating a public–private key and then using **ssh** to connect from a remote host back to the author's base system (linux.hartford.edu).

Figure 9.3 Creating a public–private key and using **ssh** to access a system for the first time.

```
[gray@remote_sys ~]$ ssh-keygen -t rsa1          ◄──────   Create a rsa1 type public and
                                                           private key pair.
Generating public/private rsa1 key pair.
Enter file in which to save the key (/home/gray/.ssh/identity):
Enter passphrase (empty for no passphrase):
Enter same passphrase again:
```

[2] The need for system security today is much different than it was, say, even 5 years ago. An in-depth discussion of security is beyond the scope of this text.

```
Your identification has been saved in /home/gray/.ssh/identity.
Your public key has been saved in /home/gray/.ssh/identity.pub.
The key fingerprint is:
6b:8d:a5:32:7d:8e:cc:66:56:c2:60:5b:a3:76:23:10 gray@remote_sys.somewhere.edu

[gray@remote_sys ~] ssh linux.hartford.edu        ◄──────   From remote system, use ssh to
                                                            access home system.
The authenticity of host 'linux.hartford.edu(137.49.6.1)' can't be established.
RSA key fingerprint is 4b:a4:ac:a6:4f:22:43:e1:1a:35:6d:b9:19:41:fd:ba.
Are you sure you want to continue connecting (yes/no)? yes
Warning:Permanently added 'linux.hartford.edu,137.49.6.1' (RSA) to the list of
known hosts.
gray@linux.hartford.edu's password:
Last login: Tue Apr  9 08:20:26 2002 from remote_sys.somewhere.edu
Red Hat Linux Thu Mar 29 18:44:10 CST 2001
[gray@linux ~]$
```

9.3 Executing Remote Commands in a Program

The library function **rexec** can be used in a program to execute a system-level command on a remote host. In many ways we can think of the **rexec** library function as a *remote* version of the system call **system** that was discussed earlier, as it allows us to request the execution of a command on a remote system. The syntax for **rexec** is summarized in Table 9.1.

Table 9.1 Summary of the rexec Library Call.

Include File(s)	`<netdb.h>`		Manual Section	**3**
Summary	`int rexec( char **ahost,` `char *user,` `char *cmd,` `unsigned short inport,` `char *passwd,` `int *fd2p );`			
	Success	Failure	Sets errno	
Return	A stream socket file descriptor	-1		

The **rexec** library call takes six arguments. The first is a reference to the name of the remote host. This reference is passed by **rexec** to the **gethostbyname** network call for authentication (the details of the **gethost-**

byname function are covered in Chapter 10). The second argument, inport, is an integer value that indicates the port to be used for the connection. Most often, the port number used with **rexec** is 512 (the port associated with the execution of remote commands, using TCP protocol). The port argument is followed by two character-string reference arguments that indicate the user's name and password respectively. If these entries are set to NULL, the system checks the contents of the file .netrc that resides in the user's home directory for machine (host), login (user name), and password information. If the $HOME/.netrc file does not exist or it contains only partial information, the user is prompted for his or her name and/or password. The sixth argument to **rexec** is a reference to an integer. If this value is not 0, **rexec** assumes it is a reference to a valid file descriptor and maps a standard error from the execution of the remote command to the indicated file descriptor. If the **rexec** command is successful, it returns a valid stream socket file descriptor that is mapped to the local host's standard input and output. If the **rexec** function fails, it returns a −1.

Program 9.1 demonstrates the use of the **rexec** library call.

Program 9.1   Using rexec in a program.

```
File : p9.1.cxx
   |      /*
   |          Using rexec
   |      */
   |      #define _GNU_SOURCE
   +      #include <iostream>
   |      #include <cstdio>
   |      #include <sys/types.h>
   |      #include <unistd.h>
   |      #include <netinet/in.h>
  10      #include <netdb.h>
   |      using namespace std;
   |      int
   |      main(int argc, char *argv[]) {
   |        int    fd, count;
   +        char   buffer[BUFSIZ], *command, *host;
   |        if (argc != 3) {
   |          cerr << "Usage " << argv[0] << " host command" << endl;
   |          return 1;
   |        }
  20        host   = argv[1];
   |        command= argv[2];
   |        if ((fd=rexec(&host,htons(512),NULL,NULL,command,(int *)0)) == -1) {
   |          perror("rexec ");
   |          return 2;
   |        }
   +      }
```

Note that on some systems you may need to install the nfs-utils, rsh, and rsh-server packages to run this program. The package manager **rpm** can be used to check if these packages have been installed, e.g.,

```
$ /bin/rpm -qv nfs-utils
```

Additionally, the rexec server service may need to be turned on. This can be accomplished with the **chkconfig** utility:

```
# /sbin/chkconfig --level 5 rexec on
```

```
|      while ((count = read(fd, buffer, BUFSIZ)) > 0)
|        fwrite(buffer, count, 1, stdout);
|      return 0;
|    }
```

In Program 9.1 the first command-line argument is the host on which the remote command will be executed. The second command-line argument is the command that will be passed to the remote host. The invocation of the **rexec** function (line 22) uses the **htons** network call on its second argument to ensure the proper network byte ordering when specifying the port number.[3] The prototype for **htons** resides in the include file <netinet/in.h>. The arguments for the user name and password are set to NULL. This directs **rexec** to first check the .netrc file in the owner's home directory for user name and password information. If the .netrc file is not present or is incomplete, **rexec** prompts the user for this information. Note that while this is technically how things should work, on our system (running Red Hat Linux version 7.1) unless the .netrc file is present and its contents complete (includes the host and the user's login and password), the **rexec** call will fail. In a weak attempt to gain at least a semblance of security, **rexec** will read .netrc files whose permissions are read only for the file's owner. If the **rexec** call completes without error, the output from the execution of the command on the remote host is read and displayed to standard output on the local host. Figure 9.4 shows a compilation and run of Program 9.1. Note in some versions of the OS the library -lnsl and/or -lsocket may need to be included as the object code for the network functions may reside in these separate libraries.

Figure 9.4 Using Program 9.1.

```
linux$ g++ p9.1.cxx -o p9.1
linux$ p9.1 morpheus df
/                (/dev/dsk/c0t0d0s0 ): 1066026 blocks   241598 files
/usr             (/dev/dsk/c0t0d0s4 ): 3538746 blocks   384628 files
/proc            (/proc            ):       0 blocks     3768 files
/dev/fd          (fd               ):       0 blocks        0 files
/etc/mnttab      (mnttab           ):       0 blocks        0 files
. . .
```

The **rexec** function communicates with **rexecd** (the remote execution daemon) on the host system. While the **rexec** function is interesting and does

---

[3] On i80x86 platforms the host byte order is LSB (least significant byte first), while on the Internet the byte order is MSB (most significant byte first).

provide a somewhat painless (but generally insecure) way to execute commands on a remote host, we more frequently will want to write our own client–server pairs that will perform specific, directed tasks.

To round out the discussion, a command-line version of **rexec** can also be found in Linux. Usually, it resides in the /usr/bin directory. Its general syntax is

```
linux$ rexec [options] -l user_name -p password host the_command
```

Unlike its library function counterpart, the command-line version of **rexec** does not seem to choke if the user's .netrc file is not fully qualified, and it will know enough to prompt if a user's login or password are omitted.

9.4 Transforming a Local Function Call into a Remote Procedure

We begin our exploration of RPC programming by converting a simple program with a single local function call into a client–server configuration with a single RPC. Once generated, this RPC-based program can be run in a distributed setting whereby the server process, which will contain the function to be executed, can reside on a host different from the client process. The program that we will convert (Program 9.2) is a C program[4] that invokes a single local function, print_hello, which generates the message Hello, world. As written, the print_hello function will display its message and return to the function main the value returned from printf. The returned value indicates whether printf was successful in carrying out its action.[5]

Program 9.2 A simple C program to display a message.

```
File : hello.c
   |    /*
   |         A C program with a local function
   |    */
   |    #include <stdio.h>
   +    int print_hello( );
```

[4] Up to this point, our examples have been primarily C++-based. Due to the inability of the compiler to handle full blown C++ code in conjunction with **rpcgen**-generated output, we will stick to C program examples in this section. Think of this as an opportunity to brush up on your C programming skills!

[5] Many programmers are not aware that printf returns a value. However, a pass of any C program with a printf function through the **lint** utility will normally return a message indicating that the value returned by printf is not being used.

```
 |        int
 |        main( ){
 |          printf("main : Calling function.\n");
 |          if (print_hello())
10            printf("main : Mission accomplished.\n");
 |          else
 |            printf("main : Unable to display message.");
 |          return 0;
 |        }
 +        int
 |        print_hello( ) {
 |          return printf("funct: Hello, world.\n");
 |        }
```

In its current configuration, the `print_hello` function and its invocation reside in a single source file. The output of Program 9.2 when compiled and run is shown in Figure 9.5.

Figure 9.5 Output of Program 9.2.

```
linux$ hello
main : Calling function.
funct: Hello, world.
main : Mission accomplished
```

The first step in converting a program with a local function call to an RPC is for the programmer to create a protocol definition file. This file will help the system keep track of what procedures are to be associated with the server program. The definition file is also used to define the data type returned by the remote procedure and the data types of its arguments. When using RPC, the remote procedure is part of a remote program that runs as the server process. The RPC language is used to define the remote program and its component procedures. The RPC language is actually XDR with the inclusion of two extensions—the `program` and `version` types. Appendix C addresses the syntax of the RPC language. For the diligent, the manual pages on `xdr` provide a good overview of XDR data type definitions and syntax.

Figure 9.6 contains the protocol definition file for the `print_hello` function. Syntactically, the RPC language is a mix of C and Pascal. By custom, the extension for protocol definition files is `.x`.

The keyword `program` marks the user-defined identifier DISPLAY_PRG as the name of the remote procedure program.[6] The program name, like the

---

[6] Most often, the identifiers placed in the protocol definition file are in capitals. Note that this is a convention, not a requirement.

Figure 9.6 Protocol definition file `hello.x`.

```
File : hello.x
   |      /*
   |          This is the protocol definition file. The programmer writes
   |          this file using the RPC language. This file is passed to the
   |          protocol generator rpcgen. Every remote procedure is part of
   +          a remote program. Each procedure has a name and number. A
   |          version number is also supplied so different versions of the
   |          same procedure may be generated.
   |      */
   |      program DISPLAY_PRG {
  10        version DISPLAY_VER {
   |          int print_hello( void ) = 1;
   |        } = 1;
   |      } = 0x20000001;
```

program name in a Pascal program, does not need to be the same as the name of the executable file. The program block encloses a group of related remote procedures. Nested within the program definition block is the keyword `version` followed by a second user-generated identifier, `DISPLAY_VER`, which is used to identify the version of the remote procedure. It is permissible to have several versions of the same procedure, each indicated by a different integer value. The ability to have different versions of the same procedure eases the upgrade process when updating software by facilitating backward compatibility. If the number of arguments, the data type of an argument, or the data type returned by the function change, the version number should be changed.

As this is our first pass at generating a remote procedure, the version number is set to 1 after the closing brace for the version block. Inside the version block is the declaration for the remote procedure (line 11).[7] A procedure number follows the remote procedure declaration. As there is only one procedure defined, the value is set to 1. An eight-digit hexadecimal program number follows the closing brace for the program block. The program, version, and procedure numbers form a triplet that uniquely identifies a specific remote procedure. To prevent conflicts, the numbering scheme shown in Table 9.2 should be used in assigning version numbers.

Protocol specifications can be registered with Sun by sending a request (including the protocol definition file) to `rpc@sun.com`. Accepted specifications will receive a unique program number from Sun (in the range 00000000–1FFFFFFF).

---

[7] If the procedure name is placed in capitals, the RPC compiler, **rpcgen**, will automatically convert it to lowercase during compilation.

Table 9.2 RPC Program Numbers.

Numbers	Description
00000000 - 1FFFFFFF	Defined by Sun
20000000 - 3FFFFFFF	User-defined
40000000 - 5FFFFFFF	User-defined for programs that dynamically allocate numbers
60000000 - FFFFFFFF	Reserved for future use

A check of the file /etc/rpc on your system will display a list of some of the RPC programs (and their program numbers) known to the system.

As shown below, the name of the protocol definition file is passed to the RPC protocol compiler, **rpcgen**, on the command line

```
$ rpcgen -C hello.x
```

The **rpcgen** compiler produces the requisite C code to implement the defined RPCs. There are a number of command-line options for **rpcgen**, of which we will explore only a limited subset. A summary of the command-line options and syntax for **rpcgen** is given in Figure 9.7.

Figure 9.7 Command-line options for **rpcgen**.

```
usage: rpcgen infile
    rpcgen [-abkCLNTM][-Dname[=value]] [-i size] [-I [-K seconds]] [-Y path]
    infile
    rpcgen [-c | -h | -l | -m | -t | -Sc | -Ss | -Sm] [-o outfile] [infile]
    rpcgen [-s nettype]* [-o outfile] [infile]
    rpcgen [-n netid]* [-o outfile] [infile]
options:
-a              generate all files, including samples
-b              backward compatibility mode (generates code for SunOS 4.1)
-c              generate XDR routines
-C              ANSI C mode
-Dname[=value]  define a symbol (same as #define)
-h              generate header file
-i size         size at which to start generating inline code
-I              generate code for inetd support in server (for SunOS 4.1)
-K seconds      server exits after K seconds of inactivity
-l              generate client side stubs
-L              server errors will be printed to syslog
-m              generate server side stubs
-M              generate MT-safe code
-n netid        generate server code that supports named netid
```

```
-N              supports multiple arguments and call-by-value
-o outfile      name of the output file
-s nettype      generate server code that supports named nettype
-Sc             generate sample client code that uses remote procedures
-Ss             generate sample server code that defines remote procedures
-Sm             generate makefile template
-t              generate RPC dispatch table
-T              generate code to support RPC dispatch tables
-Y path         directory name to find C preprocessor (cpp)
```

9-1 EXERCISE

Other than standard C comments, **rpcgen** will attempt to interpret all of the lines in the protocol definition file. How do you notify **rpcgen** that you would like to have a statement passed on without having it interpreted? *Hint*: Read the manual page for **rpcgen** carefully.

In our invocation, we have specified the -C option requesting **rpcgen** output conform to the standards for ANSI C. While some versions of **rpcgen** generate ANSI C output by default, the extra keystrokes ensure **rpcgen** generates the type of output you want. When processing the hello.x file, **rpcgen** creates three output files—a header file, a client stub, and a server stub file. Again, by default **rpcgen** gives the same name to the header file as the protocol definition file, replacing the .x extension with .h.[8] In addition, the client stub file is named hello_clnt.c (the **rpcgen** source file name with _clnt.c appended), and the server stub file is named hello_svc.c (using a similar algorithm). Should the default naming convention be too restrictive, the header file as well as the client and server stub files can be generated independently and their names uniquely specified. For example, to generate the header file with a uniquely specified name, **rpcgen** would be passed the following options and file names:

```
linux$ rpcgen -C -h -o unique_file_name  hello.x
```

With this invocation, **rpcgen** will generate a header file called unique_file_name.h. Using a similar technique, unique names for the client and server stub files can be specified with the -Sc and -Ss options (see Figure 9.7 for syntax details).

---

[8] This can be a troublesome default if, per chance, you have also generated your own local header file with the same name and extension.

The contents of the header file, hello.h, generated by **rpcgen** is shown in Figure 9.8.

Figure 9.8 File hello.h generated by **rpcgen** from the protocol definition file hello.x.

```
File : hello.h
  |      /*
  |       * Please do not edit this file.
  |       * It was generated using rpcgen.
  |       */
  +
  |      #ifndef _HELLO_H_RPCGEN
  |      #define _HELLO_H_RPCGEN
  |
  |      #include <rpc/rpc.h>
 10
  |
  |      #ifdef __cplusplus
  |      extern "C" {
  |      #endif
  +
  |
  |      #define DISPLAY_PRG 0x20000001
  |      #define DISPLAY_VER 1
  |
 20      #if defined(__STDC__) || defined(__cplusplus)
  |      #define print_hello 1
  |      extern  int * print_hello_1(void *, CLIENT *);
  |      extern  int * print_hello_1_svc(void *, struct svc_req *);
  |      extern int display_prg_1_freeresult (SVCXPRT *, xdrproc_t, caddr_t);
  +
  |      #else /* K&R C */
  |      #define print_hello 1
  |      extern  int * print_hello_1();
  |      extern  int * print_hello_1_svc();
 30      extern int display_prg_1_freeresult ();
  |      #endif /* K&R C */
  |
  |      #ifdef __cplusplus
  |      }
  +      #endif
  |
  |      #endif /* !_HELLO_H_RPCGEN */
```

The hello.h file created by **rpcgen** is referenced as an include file in both the client and server stub files. The #ifndef _HELLO_H_RPCGEN, #define _HELLO_H_RPCGEN, and #endif preprocessor directives prevent the `hello.h` file from being included multiple times. Within the file `hello.h`, the inclusion of the file `<rpc/rpc.h>`, as noted in its internal comments, "... *just includes the billions of rpc header files necessary to do remote procedure calling.*"[9] The variable `__cplusplus` (see line 20) is used to determine if a C++ programming environment is present. In a C++ environment, the compiler internally adds a series of suffixes to function names to encode the data types of its parameters. These new "mangled" function names allow C++ to check functions to ensure parameters match correctly when the function is invoked. The C compiler does not provide the mangled function names that the C++ compiler needs. The C++ compiler has to be warned that standard C linking conventions and non-mangled function names are to be used. This is accomplished by the lines following the `#ifdef __cplusplus` compiler directive.

The `program` and `version` identifiers specified in the protocol definition file are found in the `hello.h` file, as defined constants (lines 17 and 18). These constants are assigned the value specified in the protocol definition file. Since we indicated the `-C` option to **rpcgen** (standard ANSI C), the `if` branch of the preprocessor directive (i.e., `#if defined (__STDC__)`) contains the statements we are interested in. If the remote procedure name in the protocol definition file was specified in uppercase, it is mapped to lowercase in the header file. The procedure name is defined as an integer and assigned the value previously given as its procedure number. Note that we will find this defined constant used again in a `switch` statement in the server stub to select the code to be executed when calling the remote procedure.

Following this definition are two `print_hello` function prototypes. The first prototype, `print_hello_1`, is used by the client stub file. The second, `print_hello_1_svc`, is used by the server stub file. The naming convention used by **rpcgen** is to use the name of the remote procedure as the root and append an underscore (_), version number (1), for the client stub, and underscore, version number, underscore, and `svc` for the server. The `else` branch of the preprocessor directive contains a similar set of statements that are used in environments that do not support standard C prototyping.

Before we explore the contents of the client and server stub files created by **rpcgen**, we should look at how to split our initial program into client and server components. Once the initial program (for example `hello.c`) is split, and we have run `rpcgen`, we will have the six files shown in Figure 9.9 available to us.

We begin with writing the client component. As in the initial program, the client invokes the `print_hello` function. However, in our new configuration, the code for the `print_hello` function, which used to be a local function,

---

[9] While this comment is somewhat tongue-in-cheek, it is not all that farfetched (check it out)!

329

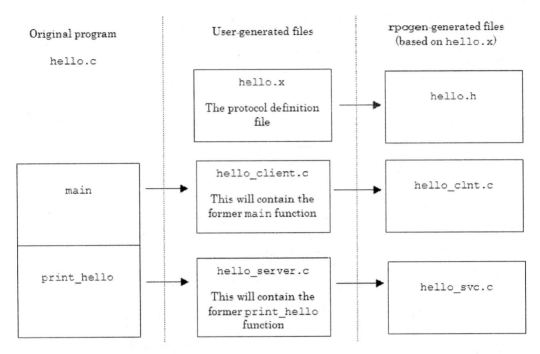

Original program

hello.c

User-generated files

rpcgen-generated files
(based on hello.x)

hello.x

The protocol definition
file

hello.h

main

hello_client.c

This will contain the
former main function

hello_clnt.c

print_hello

hello_server.c

This will contain the
former print_hello
function

hello_svc.c

Figure 9.9 Client-server files and relationships.

resides in a separate program that is run by the server process. The code for the client component program, which has been placed in a file named hello_client.c, is shown in Program 9.3.

Program 9.3 The client program hello_client.c.

```
File : hello_client.c
   |      /*
   |           The CLIENT program:  hello_client.c
   |           This will be the client code executed by the local client process.
   |      */
   +      #include <stdio.h>
   |      #include "hello.h"                 /* Generated by rpcgen from hello.x   */
   |      int
   |      main(int argc, char *argv[]) {
   |        CLIENT          *client;
  10        int             *return_value, filler;
   |        char            *server;
   |      /*
   |           We must specify a host on which to run.  We will get the host name
   |           from the command line as argument 1.
   +      */
```

```
  |          if (argc != 2) {
  |            fprintf(stderr, "Usage: %s host_name\n", *argv);
  |            exit(1);
  |          }
 20          server = argv[1];
  |        /*
  |            Generate the client handle to call the server
  |        */
  |          if ((client=clnt_create(server,       DISPLAY_PRG,
  +                             DISPLAY_VER, "tcp")) == (CLIENT *) NULL) {
  |            clnt_pcreateerror(server);
  |            exit(2);
  |          }
  |        printf("client : Calling function.\n");
 30        return_value = print_hello_1((void *) &filler, client);
  |        if (*return_value)
  |          printf("client : Mission accomplished.\n");
  |        else
  |          printf("client : Unable to display message.\n");
  +        return 0;
  |      }
```

While much of the code is similar to the original `hello.c` program, some changes have been made to accommodate the RPC. Let's examine these changes point by point. At line 6 the file `hello.h` is included. This file, generated by **rpcgen** and whose contents were discussed previously, is assumed to reside locally.

In this example, we pass information from the command line to the function `main` in the client program. Therefore, the empty parameter list for `main` has been replaced with standard C syntax to reference the `argc` and `argv` parameters. Following this, in the declaration section of the client program, a pointer to the data type CLIENT is allocated. A description of the CLIENT data type is shown in Figure 9.10.

The CLIENT **typedef** is found in the include file `<rpc/clnt.h>`. The reference to the CLIENT data structure will be used when the client handle is generated. Following the declarations in Program 9.3 is a section of code to obtain the host name on which the server process will be running. In the previous invocation, this was not a concern, as all code was executed locally. However, in this new configuration, the client process must know the name of the host where the server process is located; it cannot assume the server program is running on the local host. The name of the host is passed via the command line as the first argument to **hello_client**. As written, there is no checking to determine if a valid, reachable host name has been passed. The

Figure 9.10 The CLIENT data structure.

```
struct CLIENT {
  AUTH  *cl_auth;                                      /* authenticator         */
  struct clnt_ops {
    enum clnt_stat (*cl_call) (CLIENT *, u_long, xdrproc_t, caddr_t, xdrproc_t,
                             caddr_t, struct timeval);
                                                       /* call remote procedure */
    void (*cl_abort) (void);                           /* abort a call          */
    void (*cl_geterr) (CLIENT *, struct rpc_err *);
                                                       /* get specific error code */
    bool_t (*cl_freeres) (CLIENT *, xdrproc_t, caddr_t);
                                                       /* frees results         */
    void (*cl_destroy) (CLIENT *);                     /* destroy this structure */
    bool_t (*cl_control) (CLIENT *, int, char *);
                                                       /* the ioctl() of rpc    */
  } *cl_ops;
  caddr_t cl_private;                                  /* private stuff         */
};
```

client handle is created next (line 24). This is done with a call to the **clnt_create** library function. The **clnt_create** library function, which is part of a suite of remote procedure functions, is summarized in Table 9.3.

Table 9.3 Summary of the `clnt_create` Library Call.

Include File(s)	`<rpc/rpc.h>`		Manual Section	**3N**
Summary	`CLIENT *clnt_create(char *host,  u_long prog,` `                    u_long vers, char *proto );`			
	Success	Failure	Sets `errno`	
Return	A valid client handle	NULL	Yes	

The **clnt_create** library call requires four arguments. The first, host, a character string reference, is the name of the remote host where the server process is located. The next two arguments, prog and vers, are, respectively, the program and version number. These values are used to indicate the specific remote procedure. Notice the defined constants generated by **rpcgen** are used for these two arguments. The proto argument is used to designate the class of transport protocol. In Linux, this argument may be set to either tcp or udp. Keep in mind that UDP (Unreliable Datagram Protocol) encoded messages are limited to 8KB of data. Additionally, UDP is, by definition, less

Table 9.4 Summary of the `clnt_pcreateerror` Library Call.

Include File(s)	`<rpc/rpc.h>`		Manual Section	**3N**
Summary	`void clnt_pcreateerror(char *s);`			
Return	Success	Failure		Sets `errno`
	Print an RPC create error message to standard error.			

reliable than TCP (Transmission Control Protocol). However, UPD does require less system overhead.

If the **clnt_create** library call fails, it returns a NULL value. If this occurs, as shown in the example, the library routine **clnt_pcreateerror** can be invoked to display a message that indicates the reason for failure. See Table 9.4.

The error message generated by **clnt_pcreateerror**, which indicates why the creation of the client handle failed, are appended to the string passed as **clnt_pcreateerror**'s single argument (see Table 9.5 for details). The argument string and the error message are separated with a colon, and the entire message is followed by a newline. If you want more control over the error messaging process, there is another library call, **clnt_spcreateerror** (`char *s`), that will return an error message string that can be incorporated in a personalized error message. In addition, the `cf_stat` member of the

Table 9.5 `clnt_creat` Error Messages.

#	**Constant**	`clnt_pcreate` error **Message**	**Explanation**
13	RPC_UNKNOWNHOST	Unknown host	Unable to find the referenced host system.
17	RPC_UNKNOWNPROTO	Unknown protocol	The protocol indicated by the `proto` argument is not found or is invalid.
19	RPC_UNKNOWNADDR	Remote server address unknown	Unable to resolve address of remote server.
21	RPC_NOBROADCAST	Broadcast not supported	System does not allow broadcasting of messages (i.e., sending to all **rpcbind** daemons on a network).

external structure `rpc_createerr` may be examined directly to determine the source of the error.

Returning to the client program, the prototype for the `print_hello` function has been eliminated. The function prototype is now in the `hello.h` header file. The invocation of the `print_hello` function uses its *new* name, `print_hello_1`. The function now returns not an integer value but a pointer to an integer, and has two arguments (versus none). By design, all RPCs return a pointer reference. In general, all arguments passed to the RPC are passed by reference, not by value. As this function originally did not have any parameters, the identifier `filler` is used as a placeholder. The second argument to `print_hello_1`, `client`, is the reference to the client structure returned by the **clnt_create** call. The server component, which now resides in the file `hello_server.c`, is shown in Program 9.4.

Program 9.4 The `hello_server.c` component.

```
File : hello_server.c
   |      /*
   |          The SERVER program: hello_server.c
   |          This will be the server code executed by the "remote" process
   |      */
   +      #include <stdio.h>
   |      #include "hello.h"              /* is generated by rpcgen from hello.x   */
   |      int *
   |      print_hello_1_svc(void * filler, struct svc_req * req) {
   |        static int  ok;
  10        ok = printf("server : Hello, world.\n");
   |        return (&ok);
   |      }
```

The server component contains the code for the **print_hello** function. Notice that to accommodate the RPC, several things have been added and/or modified. First, as noted in the discussion of the client program, the **print_hello** function now returns an integer pointer, not an integer value (line 7). In this example, the address that is to be returned is associated with the identifier `ok`. This identifier is declared to be of storage class `static` (line 9). It is *imperative* that the return identifier referenced be of type `static`, as opposed to local. Local identifiers are allocated on the stack, and a reference to their contents would be invalid once the function returns. The name of the function has had an additional `_1` appended to it (the version number). As the `-C` option was used with **rpcgen**, the auxiliary suffix `_svc` has also been added to the function name. Do not be concerned by the apparent mismatch of function names. The mapping of the function invocation as `print_hello_1` in the client program to `print_hello_1_svc` in the server program is done by the code found in the stub file `hello_svc.c` produced by **rpcgen**.

The first argument passed to the `print_hello` function is a pointer reference. If needed, multiple items (representing multiple parameters) can be placed in a structure and the reference to the structure passed. In newer versions of **rpcgen**, the `-N` flag can be used to write multiple argument RPCs when a parameter is to be passed by value, not reference, or when a value, not a pointer reference, is to be returned by the RPC. A second argument, `struct svc_req *req`, has also been added. This argument will be used to communicate invocation information.

The client component (program) is compiled first. When only a few files are involved, a straight command-line compilation sequence is adequate. Later we will discuss how to generate a **make** file to automate the compilation process. The compiler is passed the names of the two client files, `hello_client.c` (which we wrote) and `hello_clnt.c` (which was generated by **rpcgen**). We specify the executable to be placed in the file `client`. Figure 9.11 shows details of the compilation command.

Figure 9.11 Compiling the client component.

```
linux$ gcc hello_client.c hello_clnt.c -o client
```

The server component (program) is compiled in a similar manner (Figure 9.12).

Figure 9.12 Compiling the server component.

```
linux$ gcc hello_server.c hello_svc.c -o server
```

9-2 EXERCISE

Is the `filler` variable really needed? Try commenting out the references to `filler` in the `hello_client.c` and `hello_server.c` files. Adjust the `hello.x` protocol definition file as well. Run **rpcgen** and recompile the modified components. What happens? Why?

9-3 EXERCISE

Modify the server component of the hello application so that the server will remove itself if it has not been referenced over a specified period of time (say, 5 minutes). Use the **signal** system call to associate the receipt of an **alarm** with a terminating function. Note that you will need to place code in both the hello_server.c and hello_svc.c files to accomplish this task.

Initially, we test the program by running both the client and server programs on the same workstation. We begin by invoking the server by typing its name on the command line. The server process is not automatically placed in the background, and thus a trailing & is needed.[10] A check of the **ps** command will verify the server process is running (see Figure 9.13).

Figure 9.13 Running the server program and checking for its presence with **ps**.

```
linux$ server &
[1] 21149
[linux$ ps -ef | grep server
. . .
gray      21149 15854  0 08:09 pts/5     00:00:00 server
gray      21154 15854  0 08:10 pts/5     00:00:00 grep server
```

The **ps** command reports that the server process, in this case process ID 21149, is in memory. Its parent process ID is 15854 (in this case the login shell) and its associated controlling terminal device is listed as pts/5. The server process will remain in memory even after the user who initiated it has logged out. When generating and testing RPC programs, it is important the user remember to remove extraneous RPC-based server type processes before they log out.

When the process is run locally, the client program is invoked by name and passed the name of the current workstation. When this is done, the output will be as shown in Figure 9.14. Notice that since our system has an existing program called client that resides in the /usr/sbin directory, the call to our client program is made with a relative reference (i.e., ./client).

---

[10] This is just the opposite of what happens in a Sun Solaris environment where no trailing & is needed, as the process is automatically placed in the background.

Figure 9.14 Running the client program on the same host as the server program.

```
linux$ ./client linux
client : Calling function.
server : Hello, world.
client : Mission accomplished.
```

While our client–server application still needs some polishing, we can test it in a setting whereby the server runs on one host and the client on another. Say we have the setting shown in Figure 9.15, where one host is called medusa and the other linux.

```
medusa$ ./client linux

client : Calling function.
client : Mission accomplished.
```

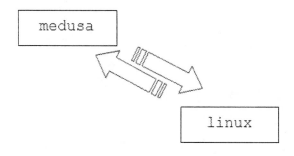

```
linux$ server : Hello, world.
```

Figure 9.15 Running the client program on a remote host.

On the host linux the server program is run in the background. On the host medusa the client program is passed the name of the host running the server program. Interestingly, on the host medusa the messages Calling function. and Mission accomplished. are displayed, but the message Hello, world. is displayed on the host linux. This is not surprising, as each program writes to its standard output, which in turn is associated with a controlling terminal (in our example this is the same terminal that is associated with the user's login shell). However, it is just as likely that the server program will write to its standard output, but what it has written will not be seen. This happens when there is no controlling terminal device associated with the server process. Remember that the server process remains in memory until removed.

337

It is not removed when the user logs out. However, when the user does log out, the operating system drops the controlling terminal device for the process (a call to **ps** will list the controlling terminal device for the process as ?). If, in a standard setting, there is no controlling terminal device associated with a process, anything the process sends to standard output goes into the bit bucket!

There are several ways of correcting this problem. First, the output from the server could be hardcoded to be displayed on the console. In this scenario, the server would, upon invocation, execute an **fopen** on the /dev/console device. The FILE pointer returned by the **fopen** call could then be used with the **fprintf** function to display the output on the console. Unfortunately, there is a potential problem with this solution: The user may not have access to the console device. If this is so, the **fopen** will fail. A second approach is to pass the console device of the client process to the server as the first parameter of the RPC. This is a somewhat better solution, but will still fail when the client and server processes are on different workstations with different output devices. A third approach is to have the server process return its message to the client and have the client display it locally.

9-4 EXERCISE

The following program uses the **ttyname** library function to display the output device associated with stdout.

```
File : ttyname.c
   |      #include <stdio.h>
   |      int
   |      main( ){
   |        char *dev = (char *)ttyname(fileno(stdout));
   +        if (dev)
   |          printf("My standard output device is %s\n", dev);
   |        else
   |          fprintf(stderr, "I don't know my standard output
   |                  device!\n");
   |        return 0;
  10      }
```

Modify the client and server programs so the output device associated with stdout is determined by the client and passed to the server as the first argument to the **print_hello** function. The server will open the device for writing to display the Hello, world message. *Hint*: The output device must be stored as an array of characters by the client so that it may be passed to the server. The **void** argument in the protocol definition file must be changed to reflect the passing of the character array. However, when making this change, you cannot use the data type **char** *, as it is ambiguous—it could be a reference to a single character or an array of characters. In the RPC language, the data type **string** is used to indicate a NULL-terminated array of characters.

9-5 EXERCISE

Write an RPC-based "time" server. When contacted by the client, the server should return the time. When displayed, the output should be in a user-friendly format.

We should also examine the two RPC stub files generated by **rpcgen**. The hello_clnt.c file is quite small (Figure 9.16). This file contains the actual call to the **print_hello_1** function.

Figure 9.16 The hello_clnt.c file.

```
File : hello_clnt.c
    |      /*
    |       * Please do not edit this file.
    |       * It was generated using rpcgen.
    |       */
    +
    |      #include <memory.h>              /* for memset */
    |      #include "hello.h"
    |
    |      /* Default timeout can be changed using clnt_control() */
 10      static struct timeval TIMEOUT = { 25, 0 };
    |
    |      int *
    |      print_hello_1(void *argp, CLIENT *clnt) {
    |             static int clnt_res;
    +             memset((char *)&clnt_res, 0, sizeof(clnt_res));
    |             if (clnt_call (clnt, print_hello,
    |                           (xdrproc_t) xdr_void, (caddr_t) argp,
    |                           (xdrproc_t) xdr_int,  (caddr_t) &clnt_res,
    |                           TIMEOUT) != RPC_SUCCESS) {
 20                    return (NULL);
    |                    }
    |             return (&clnt_res);
    |      }
```

As we are using **rpcgen** to reduce the complexity of the RPC, we will not formally present the **clnt_call**. However, in passing, we note that the **clnt_call** function (which actually does the RPC) is passed, as its first argument, the client handle that was generated from the previous call to **clnt_creat**. The second argument for **clnt_call** is obtained from the hello.h include file and is actually the print_hello constant therein. The third and fifth arguments are references to the XDR data encoding/decoding routines. Sandwiched between these arguments is a reference, argp, to the initial argument that will be passed to the remote procedure by the server process. The sixth argument for **clnt_creat** is a reference to the location where the return data will be stored. The seventh and final argument is the TIMEOUT value. While the cautionary comments indicate you should not edit this file, and in general you should not, the TIMEOUT value can be changed from the default of 25 to some other reasonable user-imposed maximum.

The code in the hello_svc.c file is much more complex and, in the interest of space, not presented here. Interested readers are encouraged to enter the protocol definition in hello.x and to generate and view the hello_svc.c file. At this juncture it is sufficient to note that the hello_svc.c file contains the code for the server process. Once invoked, the server process will remain in memory. When notified by a client process, it will execute the **print_hello_1_svc** function.

9.5 Debugging RPC Applications

Because of their distributed nature, RPC applications can be very difficult to debug. One easy way to test and debug an RPC application with, say, **gdb**, is to link the client and server programs *without* their **rpcgen** stubs. To do this, comment out the RPC reference in the client program. If the -C option was passed to **rpcgen**, then you must adjust the name of the function call appropriately (i.e., add the _svc suffix). In addition, you may need to cast the function call argument with the client reference to the correct type (i.e., struct svc_req *). Incorporating these changes with

preprocessor directives, our `hello_client.c` file now would be as shown in Figure 9.17.

Figure 9.17 A "debug ready" version of `hello_client.c`.

```
File : hello_client_gdb.c
  |      /*
  |          The CLIENT program:  hello_client.c
  |          This will be the client code executed by the local client process.
  |      */
  +      #include <stdio.h>
  |      #include "hello.h"              /* Generated by rpcgen from hello.x  */
  |      int
  |      main(int argc, char *argv[]) {
  . . .                                 /* SAME AS LINES 9-20 in hello_client.c */
  |      /*
  |          Generate the client handle to call the server
  |      */
  |      #ifndef DEBUG
  +          if ((client=clnt_create(server,       DISPLAY_PRG,
  |                                  DISPLAY_VER, "tcp")) == (CLIENT *) NULL) {
  |          clnt_pcreateerror(server);
  |          exit(2);
  |          }
30          printf("client : calling function.\n");
  |          return_value = print_hello_1((void *) &filler, client);
  |      #else
  |          printf("client : calling function.\n");
  |          return_value = print_hello_1_svc((void *) &filler,
  |                                  (struct svc_req *)client);
  +      #endif
  |          if (*return_value)
  |            printf("client : Mission accomplished\n");
  |          else
  |            printf("client : Unable to display message\n");
40          return 0;
  |      }
```

We would compile this modified version with the command sequence shown in Figure 9.18. As none of the network libraries are referenced, the `libnsl` library does not need to be linked (for most versions of **gcc**, this is not a concern). The compiler is passed the `-g` flag (to generate the symbol table information for **gdb**) and `-DDEBUG` is specified to define the DEBUG constant the preprocessor will test.

Figure 9.18 Debugging the client–server application with gdb.

```
linux$ gcc -DDEBUG -g hello_client_gdb.c hello_server.c    ◄──  Compile with gcc.
                                                                 Define the DEBUG
                                                                 constant and generate the
linux$ gdb -q a.out                                              symbol table information.
(gdb) list 25,35
25          if ((client=clnt_create(server,        DISPLAY_PRG,
26                              DISPLAY_VER, "tcp")) == (CLIENT *) NULL) {
27            clnt_pcreateerror(server);
28            exit(2);
29          }
30         printf("client : calling function.\n");
31         return_value = print_hello_1((void *) &filler, client);
32      #else
33         printf("client : calling function.\n");
34         return_value=print_hello_1_svc((void *) &filler,(struct
           svc_req *)client);
35      #endif
                                                            Set a break point at line 34
(gdb) break 34                              ◄──────────────  in the client program.
Breakpoint 1 at 0x804853f: file hello_client_gdb.c, line 34.

(gdb) run kahuna
Starting program: /home/faculty/gray/revision/09/hello_files/a.out kahuna
client : calling function.

Breakpoint 1, main (argc=2, argv=0xbffffc34) at hello_client_gdb.c:34
34          return_value=print_hello_1_svc((void *)&filler,(struct
            svc_req *)client);
                                                            Step into what was formerly
(gdb) step                                  ◄──────────────  the remote procedure.
print_hello_1_svc (filler=0xbffffbbc, req=0x80497ec) at hello_server.c:10
10          ok = printf("server : Hello, world.\n");
                                                            This is now the code for the
(gdb) list                                  ◄──────────────  server.
5       #include <stdio.h>
6       #include "hello.h"          /* is generated by rpcgen from hello.x  */
7       int           *
8       print_hello_1_svc(void * filler, struct svc_req * req) {
9         static int  ok;
10        ok = printf("server : Hello, world.\n");
11        return (&ok);
12      }

(gdb) quit
The program is running.  Exit anyway? (y or n) y
```

9.6 Using RPCGEN to Generate Templates and a MAKEFILE

The **rpcgen** command has additional functionality to assist the developer of RPC applications. If the -a flag (see Figure 9.7) is passed to **rpcgen**, it will generate, in addition to the client and server stub files and header file, a set of template files for the client and server and a makefile for the entire application. Unlike the -C flag, which will cause **rpcgen** to overwrite preexisting stub files, the -a flag will cause **rpcgen** to halt with a warning message if the template files (with the default names) are present in the current directory. Therefore, it is best to use the -a flag only when you are positive the protocol definition file is accurate; otherwise, you must manually remove or rename the previously generated template files.

For example, suppose we have a program called fact.c (Program 9.5) that requests an integer value and returns the factorial of that value if it is within the range of values that can be stored in a long integer; otherwise, it returns a value of 0.

Program 9.5 The original factorial program, fact.c.

```
File : fact.c
   |      /*
   |          A program to calculate Factorial numbers
   |       */
   |      #include <stdio.h>
   +      int
   |      main( ){
   |        long int        f_numb, calc_fact(int);
   |        int             number;
   |        printf("Factorial Calculator\n");
  10        printf("Enter a positive integer value ");
   |        scanf("%d", &number);
   |        if (number < 0)
   |          printf("Positive values only!\n");
   |        else if ((f_numb = calc_fact(number)) > 0)
   +          printf("%d! = %d\n", number, f_numb);
   |        else
   |          printf("Sorry %d! is out of my range!\n", number);
   |        return 0;
   |      }
  20      /*
   |          Calculate the factorial number and return the result or return 0
   |          if value is out of range.
   |       */
```

```
|      long int
+      calc_fact(int n){
|        long int        total = 1, last = 0;
|        int             idx;
|        for (idx = n; idx - 1; --idx) {
|          total *= idx;
30       if (total <= last)                  /* Have we gone out of range? */
|            return (0);
|          last = total;
|        }
|        return (total);
+      }
```

We would like to turn the factorial program into a client–server application whereby the client could make a request for a factorial value from the remote *factorial* server. To accomplish this, we begin by writing the protocol definition file shown in Figure 9.19.

Figure 9.19 The protocol definition file for the factorial program.

```
File : fact.x
|      /*
|          The protocol definition file for the factorial program.
|          The programmer generates this file.
|      */
+      program FACTORIAL {
|        version ONE {
|          long int CALC_FAC( int ) = 1;
|        } = 1;
|      } = 0x20000049;
```

We then use **rpcgen** with the -a and -C flags to generate the header file, the client and server stub files, the client and server template files, and the application Makefile. The details of and output from this process are shown in Figure 9.20.

Figure 9.20 Using **rpcgen** with the -a and -C flags.

```
linux$ ls
fact.x

linux$ rpcgen -a -C fact.x

linux$ ls -x
fact_client.c  fact_clnt.c  fact.h  fact_server.c  fact_svc.c  fact.x
Makefile.fact
```

As shown, passing **rpcgen** the protocol definition file with the -a and -C flags generates six files: the header file, fact.h, and the RPC stub files, fact_clnt.c and fact_svc.c, which are similar in content and nature to those in the previous example. The three *new* files created by **rpcgen** bear further investigation. The client template file is fact_client.c. Again, **rpcgen** has used the file name of the protocol definition file as the root for the file name and added the _client.c suffix. The contents of the fact_client.c file are shown in Figure 9.21.

Figure 9.21 The fact_client.c template client file generated by **rpcgen**.

```
File : fact_client.c
   |      /*
   |          This is sample code generated by rpcgen.
   |          These are only templates and you can use them
   |          as a guideline for developing your own functions.
   +      */
   |      #include "fact.h"
   |      void
   |      factorial_1(char *host) {
   |        CLIENT *clnt;
  10        long  *result_1;
   |        int   calc_fac_1_arg;
   |
   |      #ifndef DEBUG
   |        clnt = clnt_create (host, FACTORIAL, ONE, "udp");
   +        if (clnt == NULL) {
   |          clnt_pcreateerror (host);
   |          exit (1);
   |        }
   |      #endif                                  /* DEBUG */
  20        result_1 = calc_fac_1(&calc_fac_1_arg, clnt);
   |        if (result_1 == (long *) NULL) {
   |          clnt_perror (clnt, "call failed");
   |        }
   |      #ifndef DEBUG
   +        clnt_destroy (clnt);
   |      #endif                                  /* DEBUG */
   |      }
   |      int
   |      main (int argc, char *argv[]) {
  30        char *host;
   |
   |        if (argc < 2) {
   |          printf ("usage: %s server_host\n", argv[0]);
   |          exit (1);
   |        }
   +      }
```

345

```
|        host = argv[1];
|        factorial_1 (host);
|        exit (0);
|    }
```

In the template file **rpcgen** has created a function called factorial_1 (lines 7 through 27). The function name is derived from the program name given in the protocol definition file with a suffix of _1 (the version number). As shown, the factorial_1 function is passed the host name. This function is used to make the RPC **clnt_create** call and the remote calc_fac_1 function call. Notice that variables for the correct argument type and function return type have been placed at the top of the factorial_1 function. By default, the transport protocol for the **clnt_create** call is specified as udp (versus tcp, which was used in the previous example). The call to the remote cal_fac_1 function is followed by a check of its return value. If the return value is NULL, indicating a failure, the library function **clnt_perror** (Table 9.6) is called to display an error message.

Table 9.6 Summary of the clnt_perror Library Call.

Include File(s)	<rpc/rpc.h>		Manual Section	**3N**
Summary	void clnt_perror(CLIENT *clnt, char *s);			
Return		Success	Failure	Sets errno
	Print message to standard error indicating why the RPC call failed.			

The **clnt_perror** library call is passed the client handle from the **clnt_create** call and an informational message string. The **clnt_perror** message will have the informational message prefaced with an intervening colon.

A call to the library function **clnt_destroy** is also generated (Table 9.7).

The **clnt_destroy** function is used to return the resources allocated by the **clnt_create** function to the system. As would be expected, once a client RPC handle has been destroyed, it is undefined and can no longer be referenced.

To facilitate testing, **rpcgen** has also placed a series of preprocessor directives in the template file. However, it seems to overlook the fact that the call to **clnt_perror** requires the network library and thus may also need to be commented out when debugging the application. As in the previous example, if the -C option for **rpcgen** has been specified and a call to the remote factorial

Table 9.7 Summary of the clnt_destroy Library Call.

Include File(s)	<rpc/rpc.h>		Manual Section	**3N**
Summary	void clnt_destroy(CLIENT *clnt);			
Return		Success	Failure	Sets errno

function (calc_fac_1) is to be made in a debug setting, the function name should have the string _svc appended, and the clnt argument should be cast to the data type (struct svc_req *).

We can now edit the fact_client.c program and add the appropriate code from the function main in our initial fact.c example. The modified fact_client.c program is shown in Figure 9.22. Note the change in the call to the calc_fact function to the factorial_1 function.

Figure 9.22 The fact_client.c template file with modifications.

```
File : fact_client.c
  |     /*
  |        This is sample code generated by rpcgen.
  |        These are only templates and you can use them
  |        as a guideline for developing your own functions.
  +     */
  |     #include "fact.h"
  |     long int                              /* Returns a long int   */
  |     factorial_1(int  calc_fac_1_arg, char *host) {
  |       CLIENT *clnt;
 10       long  *result_1;
  |                                           /* int  calc_fac_1_arg;*/
  |
  |     #ifndef DEBUG
  |       clnt = clnt_create (host, FACTORIAL, ONE, "udp");
  +       if (clnt == NULL) {
  |         clnt_pcreateerror (host);
  |         exit (1);
  |       }
  |     #endif                                /* DEBUG */
 20       result_1 = calc_fac_1(&calc_fac_1_arg, clnt);
  |       if (result_1 == (long *) NULL) {
  |         clnt_perror (clnt, "call failed");
  |       }
```

347

```
  |     #ifndef DEBUG
  +        clnt_destroy (clnt);
  |     #endif                                    /* DEBUG */
  |        return *result_1;                      /* return value to main */
  |     }
  |     int
30    main (int argc, char *argv[]) {
  |        char *host;
  |        long int f_numb;                       /* Own declarations    */
  |        int       number;
  |        if (argc < 2) {
  +           printf ("usage: %s server_host\n", argv[0]);
  |           exit (1);
  |        }
  |        host = argv[1];
  |                                               /* factorial_1 (host);  */
40         /*
  |           Replace canned call with code from previous main in program fact.c
  |        */
  |        printf("Factorial Calculator\n");
  |        printf("Enter a positive integer value ");
  +        scanf("%d", &number);
  |        if (number < 0)
  |           printf("Positive values only!\n");
  |        else if ((f_numb = factorial_1(number, host)) > 0)
  |           printf("%d! = %d\n", number, f_numb);
50         else
  |           printf("Sorry %d! is out of my range!\n", number);
  |        exit (0);
  |     }
```

In order, the modifications to the client program were as follows. First, the return type of the generated function (factorial_1) is changed from void to a long int. Second, the factorial_1 argument list is adjusted to include the numeric value that is passed. The data type and other information for this argument was listed at the top of the function. Note that to prevent the overshadowing of the parameter, this previous declaration must be deleted or commented out (as done in line 11). Third, the return type for the factorial_1 function is added at the foot of the function. Fourth, in main the appropriate declarations are added (see lines 32 and 33). Fifth, and last, the bulk of the code from main in the fact.c is copied into the main of this program. When this is done, the canned call to factorial_1 must be removed (or commented out) and, most importantly, the name of the function to be invoked must be changed from its original calc_fact to factorial_1.

Figure 9.23 Server template file fact_server.c generated by **rpcgen**.

```
File : fact_server.c
   |      /*
   |          This is sample code generated by rpcgen.
   |          These are only templates and you can use them
   |          as a guideline for developing your own functions.
   +      */
   |
   |      #include "fact.h"
   |      long *
   |      calc_fac_1_svc(int *argp, struct svc_req *rqstp) {
  10        static long  result;
   |        /*
   |         * insert server code here
   |         */
   |
   +        return &result;
   |      }
```

The server template file generated by **rpcgen** is shown in Figure 9.23.

As with the client template file, we now can modify the server template to incorporate the code for the remote procedure. The modified fact_server.c file is shown in Figure 9.24.

Figure 9.24 The fact_server.c template file with modifications.

```
File : fact_server.c
   |      /*
   |          This is sample code generated by rpcgen.
   |          These are only templates and you can use them
   |          as a guideline for developing your own functions.
   +      */
   |
   |      #include "fact.h"
   |      long *
   |      calc_fac_1_svc(int *argp, struct svc_req *rqstp) {
  10        static long  result;
   |        /*
   |         * insert server code here
   |         */
   |      long int          total = 1, last = 0;
   +      int               idx;
   |      for (idx = *argp; idx - 1; --idx) {
   |        total *= idx;
```

```
  |          if (total <= last) {          /* Have we gone out of range? */
  |              result = 0;
 20              return (&result);
  |          }
  |          last = total;
  |      }
  |      result = total;
  +      return &result;
  |  }
```

The changes for the server program are more straightforward than those for the client program. Essentially, the function code is pasted into the indicated location. The only coding adjustment occurs in line 17 where idx is initialized. As the argument passed to this function is as reference (versus a value) it must be dereferenced.

The Makefile generated by **rpcgen** is shown in Figure 9.25.

Figure 9.25 Makefile.fact, generated by **rpcgen**.

```
File : Makefile.fact
  |
  |      # This is a template Makefile generated by rpcgen
  |
  |      # Parameters
  +
  |      CLIENT = fact_client
  |      SERVER = fact_server
  |
  |      SOURCES_CLNT.c =
 10      SOURCES_CLNT.h =
  |      SOURCES_SVC.c =
  |      SOURCES_SVC.h =
  |      SOURCES.x = fact.x
  |
  +      TARGETS_SVC.c = fact_svc.c fact_server.c
  |      TARGETS_CLNT.c = fact_clnt.c fact_client.c
  |      TARGETS = fact.h   fact_clnt.c fact_svc.c fact_client.c fact_server.c
  |
  |      OBJECTS_CLNT = $(SOURCES_CLNT.c:%.c=%.o) $(TARGETS_CLNT.c:%.c=%.o)
 20      OBJECTS_SVC = $(SOURCES_SVC.c:%.c=%.o) $(TARGETS_SVC.c:%.c=%.o)
  |  # Compiler flags
  |
  |      CFLAGS += -g
  |      LDLIBS += -lnsl
  +      RPCGENFLAGS =
  |
  |      # Targets
```

```
 |
 |      all : $(CLIENT) $(SERVER)
30
 |      $(TARGETS) : $(SOURCES.x)
 |              rpcgen $(RPCGENFLAGS) $(SOURCES.x)
 |
 |      $(OBJECTS_CLNT) : $(SOURCES_CLNT.c) $(SOURCES_CLNT.h) $(TARGETS_CLNT.c)
 +
 |      $(OBJECTS_SVC) : $(SOURCES_SVC.c) $(SOURCES_SVC.h) $(TARGETS_SVC.c)
 |
 |      $(CLIENT) : $(OBJECTS_CLNT)
 |              $(LINK.c) -o $(CLIENT) $(OBJECTS_CLNT) $(LDLIBS)
40
```

While the makefile can be used pretty much as generated, you may want to modify some of the entries in the compiler flag section. For example, you may want to add the -C flag to RPCGENFLAGS, or indicate that the math library should be linked by adding -1m to LDLIBS. If a compiler other than the default compiler (**gcc** on most systems) is to be used, you would add the notation in this section (e.g., CC = **cc** for Sun's C compiler or CC = **CC** for Sun's C++ compiler). The **make** utility will assume the Makefile it is to process is called makefile. As **rpcgen** creates a Makefile whose name is makefile with a period (.) root name of the protocol definition file (fact) appended, the user is left with two remedies. First, rename the generated Makefile to makefile by using the **mv** command, or second, use the -f flag for **make**. If the -f flag is used with **make**, then the name of the file for **make** to use should immediately follow the -f flag.

Figure 9.26 presents the sequence of events on a local system when the **make** utility with the -f flag is used to generate the factorial application.

Figure 9.26 Using the Makefile.fact file.

```
linux$ make -f Makefile.fact
cc -g    -c -o fact_clnt.o    fact_clnt.c
cc -g    -c -o fact_client.o fact_client.c
cc -g       -o fact_client    fact_clnt.o    fact_client.o -lnsl
cc -g    -c -o fact_svc.o     fact_svc.c
cc -g    -c -o fact_server.o fact_server.c
cc -g       -o fact_server    fact_svc.o     fact_server.o -lnsl
```

Figure 9.27 shows a sequence for running the factorial client-server application.

In the previous example, the factorial server program is invoked on the workstation called linux. The **ps** command verifies the presence of the fact_server process. The factorial client program is invoked and passed

Figure 9.27 Running the factorial client-server application.

```
linux$ fact_server &              ◄───────────────────  Put the server in the background
[1] 24366                                              on the host called linux.

linux$ ps -ef | grep fact
gray     24366 24036  0 14:30 pts/2   00:00:00 fact_server
gray     24368 24036  0 14:30 pts/2   00:00:00 grep gray

linux$ fact_client linux          ◄───────────────────  Run the client program and pass
Factorial Calculator                                   it the host name linux.
Enter a positive integer value 11
11! = 39916800

linux$ fact_client linux
Factorial Calculator
Enter a positive integer value 15                      On a different host (medusa)
Sorry 15! is out of my range!                          verify the server program is not
                                                       running.
medusa$ ps -ef | grep fact_server ◄
gray     28332 28192  0 15:17 pts/1   00:00:00 grep fact_server

medusa$ fact_client linux         ◄───────────────────  Run the client program and pass
Factorial Calculator                                   it the host name linux.
Enter a positive integer value 12
12! = 479001600
```

the name of the host that is running the factorial server process. The client process requests the user to input an integer value. The user enters the value 11. The client process makes a remote call to the server process, passing it the value 11. The server process responds by calculating the factorial value and returning it to the client. The client process displays the returned result. The client process is invoked a second time and passed a value of 15. The value 15 ! is beyond the storage range for an integer on the server. Thus, the server returns the value 0, indicating it was unable to complete the calculation. The client displays the corresponding error message. Next, the user has logged onto another workstation on the same network (medusa) and changes to the directory where the executables for the factorial application reside. The **ps** command is used to check if the factorial server process is present on this workstation—it is not. The factorial client is invoked again and passed the name of the workstation running the server process (linux). The client program requests an integer value (entered as 12). This value is passed, via the RPC, to the server process on the workstation linux. The factorial value is calculated by the server process on linux and returned to the client process on medusa, which displays the results to the screen.

9-6 EXERCISE

Write an RPC-based client–server application that evaluates, in a single pass in left to right order (*ignoring operator precedence*), a simple expression that consists of a series of single-digit operands and the binary operators +, −, / (integer division), and *. The client should process the expression and call the server application to perform the needed arithmetic operations. The server should have a *separate* procedure for each of the four operations. Try your application with the following input sequences (be sure to check for division by 0):

```
2 * 3 / 2 + 5 - 8
6 + 8 - 4 / 3
7 - 9 / 0
```

Hint: To pass multiple parameters, you should either make use of the -N option for **rpcgen** or place the parameters to be passed in a structure and then pass the reference to the structure.

9.7 Encoding and Decoding Arbitrary Data Types

For RPCs to pass data between systems with differing architectures, data is first converted to a standard XDR format. The conversion from a native representation to XDR format is called *serialization*. When the data is received in XDR format, it is converted back to the native representation for the recipient process. The conversion from XDR format to native format is called *deserialization*. To be transparent, the conversion process must take into account such things as native byte order,[11] integer size, representation of floating-point values, and representation of character strings. Some of these differences may be hardware-dependent, while others may be programming language-dependent. Once the data is converted, it is assumed that individual

---

[11] For example, with a 4-byte (32-bit) number, the most significant byte (MSB) is always leftmost and the least significant byte (LSB) rightmost. If the sequence of bytes composing the number is ordered from left to right, as in the SPARC, the order is called big endian. If the byte sequence is numbered from right to left, as in the i80x86 processor line, the order is called little endian.

bytes of data (each consisting of eight bits) are in themselves portable from one platform to another. Data conversion for standard simple data types (such as integers, floats, characters, etc.) are implemented via a series of pre-defined XDR primitive type library routines,[12] which are sometimes called **filters**. These filters return the simple data type if they successfully convert the data; otherwise, they return a value of 0. Each primitive routine takes a pointer to the result and a pointer to the XDR handle. The primitive routines are incorporated into more complex routines for complex data types, such as arrays. The specifics of how the data conversion is actually done, while inter-esting, is beyond the scope of a one-chapter overview of RPC. However, it is important to keep in mind that such routines are necessary and that when passing data with RPCs, the proper conversion routines must be selected. Fortunately, when using **rpcgen**, the references for the appropriate XDR conversion routines are automatically generated and placed in another C source file the application can reference. This file, containing the conversion routines for both the client and server, will have the suffix _xdr.c appended to the protocol definition file name.

To illustrate how data conversion is done, we will create an application that performs a remote directory tree listing. When the server for this application is passed a valid directory name, it will traverse the indicated directory and produce an indented listing of all of the directory's underlying subdirectories. For example, say we have the directory structure shown in Figure 9.28.

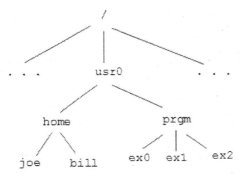

Figure 9.28
A hypothetical directory structure.

If we request the application to produce a directory tree of the direc-tory /usr0, the output returned from the directory tree application would be similar to that shown in Figure 9.29.

[12] For more details, see the manual pages on **xdr**.

Figure 9.29 The directory tree listing of /usr0.

```
/usr0:
   home
        joe
        bill
   prgm
        ex0
        ex1
        ex2
```

The directory traversed is listed with a trailing colon. Following this, each subdirectory displayed is indented to indicate its relationship to its parent directory and sibling subdirectories. The subdirectories home and prgm are at the same level and thus are indented the same number of spaces. The subdirectories joe and bill, which are beneath the home directory, are indented to the same level as are the subdirectories ex0, ex1, and ex2, which are beneath the prgm directory.

As written, the application will pass from the client to the server the name of the directory to be traversed on the server. The server will allocate an array of a fixed size[13] to store the tree directory listing and will return the contents of the array if it is successful. If the server fails, it will return a NULL value. The server using the following high-level algorithm fills the array with the directory tree information.

The passed directory reference is opened. While the directory reference is not NULL, each entry is checked to determine if it is accessible. Note that if the server process does not have root privileges, this may cause some entries to be skipped. If the entry is accessible and is a directory reference (versus a file reference) but not a dot entry (we are looking to skip the "." and ".." entries for obvious reasons), the entry is stored with the proper amount of indenting in the allocated array. For display purposes, each stored entry has an appended newline (\n) to separate it from the following entry. Since directory structures are recursive in nature, after processing an accessible directory entry, the **tree** display routine will call itself again, passing the name of the *new* directory entry. Once the entire contents of a directory have been processed, the directory is closed. When all directories and subdirectories have been processed, the array, with the contents of the directory tree, is returned to the client process, which will display its contents. The partial contents of the array returned for the previous example is shown in Figure 9.30.

---

[13] I know, I know, this is *not* the *best* way to do this—a dynamic allocation would be more appropriate here, as we do not know in advance how much storage room we will actually need. What is presented is a pedagogical example. The modification of the text example to use dynamic memory allocation is addressed in the exercise section.

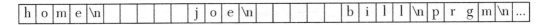

Figure 9.30 A partial listing of the directory tree array for /usr0.

The protocol definition file tree.x for the tree program is shown in Figure 9.31.

Figure 9.31 The protocol definition file, tree.x.

```
File : tree.x
  |     /*
  |              Tree protocol definition file
  |     */
  |     const    MAXP  = 4096;   /* Upper limit on packet size it 8K.     */
  +     const    DELIM = "\n";   /* To separate each directory entry.     */
  |     const    INDENT= 5;      /* # of spaces to indent for one level.  */
  |     const    DIR_1 = 128;    /* Maximum length of any one directory
  |                                 entry.                                */
  |
  |     typedef char line[MAXP]; /* A large storage location for all the
  |                                 entries                               */
 10     typedef line *line_ptr; /* A reference to the storage location.  */

  |                              /* If no errors return reference else
  |                                 return void                           */
  |     union dir_result
  |       switch( int errno ) {
  |       case 0:
  +           line *line_ptr;
  |       default:
  |           void;
  |       };
  |     /*
 20      *   The do_dir procedure will take a reference to a directory and
  |          return
  |      *   a reference to an array containing the directory tree.
  |      */
  |     program TREE {
  |       version one{
  +          dir_result do_dir( string ) = 1;
  |       } = 1;
  |     } = 0x2000001;
```

In the protocol definition file there is a series of constants. These constants will be mapped into #define statements by the **rpcgen** compiler. Following the constant section are two type declarations. The first, typedef char line[MAXP], declares a *new* type called line that is an array of MAXP

number of characters. To translate this type, **rpcgen** creates a routine named
xdr_line, which it places in the `tree_xdr.c` file. The contents of this routine are shown in Figure 9.32.

Figure 9.32 The `xdr_line` XDR conversion routine created by **rpcgen**.

```
File : tree_xdr.c
   |       /*
   |        * Please do not edit this file.
   |        * It was generated using rpcgen.
   |        */
   +
   |       #include "tree.h"
   |
   |       bool_t
   |       xdr_line (XDR *xdrs, line objp)
  10       {
   |               register int32_t *buf;
   |
   |               if (!xdr_vector (xdrs, (char *)objp, MAXP,
   |                   sizeof (char), (xdrproc_t) xdr_char))
   +                       return FALSE;
   |               return TRUE;
   |       }
   . . .
```

The generated **xdr_line** routine calls the predefined **xdr_vector** routine, which in turn invokes the **xdr_char** primitive. It is the **xdr_char** primitive that is found in both the client and server stub files that does the actual translation. A similar set of code is generated for the line pointer (`line_ptr`) declaration and the discriminated union that declares the type to be returned by the user-defined remote `do_dir` procedure. If we examine the `tree.h` file produced by **rpcgen** from the `tree.x` file, we find the discriminated union is mapped to a structure that contains a union (as shown in Figure 9.33). The single argument for the `do_dir` procedure is a string (a special XDR data type), which is mapped to a pointer to a pointer to a character. The argument to `do_dir` will be the directory to *examine*.

Figure 9.33 Structure, found in `tree.h`, generated by **rpcgen** from the discriminated union in `tree.x`.

```
File : tree.h
   |       /*
   |        * Please do not edit this file.
   |        * It was generated using rpcgen.
```

```
   |        */
   +
   |        #ifndef _TREE_H_RPCGEN
   |        #define _TREE_H_RPCGEN
   |
   |        #include <rpc/rpc.h>
   ...
   |        typedef line *line_ptr;
   |
   +        struct dir_result {
   |                int errno;
   |                union {
   |                        line *line_ptr;
   |                } dir_result_u;
  30        };
   |        typedef struct dir_result dir_result;
   ...
```

The code for the client portion (`tree_client.c`) of the tree program is shown in Program 9.6, and the server portion (`tree_server.c`) is shown in Program 9.7.

Program 9.6 The directory tree client program `tree_client.c`.

```
File : tree_client.c
   |      /*
   |
   |      #####  #####   ######  ######   ####   #       #  ######  #    #  #####
   |      #    #  #    # #       #       #    #  #    #  #  #       ##   #  #
   +      #    #  #    # #####   #####   #       #       #  #####   # #  #  #
   |      #    #  #####  #       #       #       #       #  #       #  # #  #
   |      #    #  #    # #       #       #    #  #    #  #  #       #   ##  #
   |      #    #  #    # ######  ######   ####   ######  #  ######  #    #  #
   |      */
  10  #include "local.h"
   |  #include "tree.h"
   |
   |  void
   |  tree_1(char *host, char *the_dir ) {
   +    CLIENT        *client;
   |    dir_result    *result;
   |
   |  #ifndef DEBUG
   |    client = clnt_create(host, TREE, one, "tcp");
```

```
20        if (client == (CLIENT *) NULL) {
|           clnt_pcreateerror(host);
|           exit(2);
|         }
|         result = do_dir_1(&the_dir, client);
+     #else
|         result = do_dir_1_svc(&the_dir, (svc_req *) client);
|     #endif                          /* DEBUG */
|         if (result == (dir_result *) NULL) {
|     #ifndef DEBUG
30          clnt_perror(client, "call failed");
|     #else
|           perror("Call failed");
|     #endif                          /* DEBUG */
|           exit(3);
+       } else                        /* display the whole array    */
|           printf("%s:\n\n%s\n",the_dir,result->dir_result_u.line_ptr);
|     #ifndef DEBUG
|         clnt_destroy(client);
|     #endif                          /* DEBUG */
40    }
|     int
|     main(int argc, char *argv[]) {
|       char      *host;
|       static char directory[DIR_1]; /* Name of the directory      */
+       if (argc < 2) {
|         fprintf(stderr, "Usage %s server [directory]\n", argv[0]);
|         exit(1);
|       }
|       host = argv[1];               /* Assign the server          */
50      if (argc > 2)
|         strcpy(directory, argv[2]);
|       else
|         strcpy(directory , ".");
|       tree_1(host, directory);    /* Give it a shot!            */
+       return 0;
|     }
```

The bulk of the `tree_client.c` program contains code that is either similar in nature to previous RPC examples or is self-documenting. The one statement that may bear further explanation is the `printf` statement that displays the directory tree information to the screen. Remember that the remote procedure returns a pointer to a *string*. This string is already in display format in that each directory entry is separate from the next with a newline. The reference to the string is written as `result->dir_result_u.line_ptr`. The proper syntax for this reference is obtained by examining the `tree.h` file produced by **rpcgen**.

Program 9.7 The directory tree client program `tree_server.c`.

```
File : tree_server.c
  |   /*
  |   #####  #####  ######  ######  ####  ######  #####  #   #  ######  #####
  |   #   #  #   #    #        #   #         #      #    #   # #   #     #   #
  |   #   #  #   #    #     #####  #####  ####   #####   #   # #   #   #####   #   #
  +   #   #####   #        #       #  #       #####  #   # #        #####
  |   #   #   #   #        #       #  #  #    #      #   # # #   #    #        #   #
  |   #   #   #   ######  ######  ####  ######  #   #   ##   ######  #    #
  |   */
  |   #include "local.h"
10  #include "tree.h"
  |
  |   static int cur = 0,                          /* Index into output array   */
  |          been_allocated = 0,                   /* Has array been allocated? */
  |          depth = 0;                            /* Indenting level           */
  +
  |   dir_result    *
  |   do_dir_1_svc( char **f, struct svc_req * rqstp) {
  |     static dir_result result;                  /* Either array or void      */
  |     struct stat       statbuff;                /* For status check of entry */
20  DIR               *dp;                         /* Directory entry           */
  |     struct dirent     *dentry;                 /* Pointer to current entry  */
  |     char              *current;                /* Position in output array  */
  |     int               length;                  /* Length of current entry   */
  |     static char       buffer[DIR_1];           /* Temp storage location     */
  +
  |     if (!been_allocated)                       /* If not done then allocate */
  |       if ((result.dir_result_u.line_ptr=(line *)malloc(sizeof(line))) == NULL)
  |         return (&result);
  |       else{
30        been_allocated = 1;                      /* Record allocation         */
  |     } else if ( depth == 0 )       {           /* Clear 'old' contents.     */
  |       memset(result.dir_result_u.line_ptr, 0, sizeof(line));
  |       cur = 0;                                 /* Reset indent level        */
  |     }
  +     if ((dp = opendir(*f)) != NULL) {          /* If successfully opened    */
  |       chdir(*f);                               /* Change to the directory   */
  |       dentry = readdir(dp);                    /* Read first entry          */
  |       while (dentry != NULL) {
  |         if (stat(dentry->d_name, &statbuff) != -1)      /* If accessible    */
40          if ((statbuff.st_mode & S_IFMT) == S_IFDIR &&   /* & a directory    */
  |              dentry->d_name[0] != '.') {                 /* & not . or ..    */
  |           depth += INDENT;                               /* adjust indent    */
  |             /*
  |                 Store the entry in buffer - then copy buffer into larger array.
  +             */
  |             sprintf(buffer, "%*s %-10s\n", depth, " ", dentry->d_name);
```

```
|              length = strlen(buffer);
|              memcpy((char *)result.dir_result_u.line_ptr + cur, buffer, length);
|              cur += length;                        /* update ptr to ref next loc */
50            current = dentry->d_name;             /* the new directory          */
|              (dir_result *)do_dir_1_svc(&current, rqstp);  /* call self          */
|              chdir("..");                          /* back to previous level     */
|              depth -= INDENT;                      /* adjust the indent level    */
|          }
+      dentry = readdir(dp);                         /* Read the next entry         */
|      }
|    closedir(dp);                                   /* Done with this one          */
|  }
|  return (&result);                                 /* Pass back the result        */
60 }
```

In the `tree_server.c` program, there are several static integers that are used either as counters or flags. The `cur` identifier references the current offset into the output array where the next directory entry should be stored. Initially, the offset is set to 0. The `been_allocated` identifier acts as a flag to indicate whether or not an output buffer has been allocated. Initially, this flag is set to 0 (FALSE). The last static identifier, `depth`, is used to track the current indent level. It is also set to 0 at the start.

The `do_dir_1_svc` procedure is passed a reference to a string (actually a character array) and a reference to an RPC client handle. Within the procedure, a series of local identifiers are allocated to manipulate and access directory information. Following this is an `if` statement that is used to test the `been_allocated` flag. If an output buffer has not been allocated, a call to **malloc** generates it. The allocated buffer is cast appropriately and is referenced by the `line_ptr` member of the `dir_result_u` structure. Once the buffer has been allocated, the `been_allocated` flag is set to 1 (TRUE). If the output buffer has already been allocated and this is the first call to this procedure (i.e., depth is at 0; remember this is a recursive procedure), a call to **memset** is used to clear the previous output contents by filling the buffer with NULL values. When the contents of the output buffer are cleared, the `cur` index counter is reset to 0.

The procedure then attempts to open the referenced directory. If it is successful, a call to **chdir** is issued to change the directory (this was done to eliminate the need to construct and maintain a fully qualified path when checking the current directory). Next, the first entry for the directory is obtained with the **readdir** function. A `while` loop is used to cycle through the directory entries. Those entries for which the process has access permission are tested to determine if they reference a directory. If they do, and the directory does not start with a dot (.), the `depth` counter is incremented. The formatted directory entry is temporarily constructed in a buffer using the **sprintf** string function. The format descriptors direct **sprintf** to use the depth value as a dynamic indicator of the number of blanks it should insert prior to the directory entry. Each entry has a newline appended to it. The formatted entry is then copied (using **memcpy**) to the proper location in the output buffer using the value of cur as an offset. The directory name is then passed back to the do_dir_1_svc procedure via a call to itself. Upon return from parsing a subdirectory, the procedure returns up one level via a call to **chdir** and decrements the depth counter accordingly. Once the entire directory is processed, the directory file is closed. When the procedure finishes, it returns the reference to output buffer.

An output sequence for the directory tree client–server application is shown in Figure 9.34. In this example, the directory tree server, tree_server, is run on the host called kahuna. The user, on host medusa, runs the tree_client program, passing the host name kahuna and the directory /usr/bin. The output, shown on the host medusa, is the directory tree found on kahuna (where the tree_server program is running in the background).

Figure 9.34 A sample run of the directory tree application.

```
medusa$ tree_client kahuna /usr/bin
/usr/bin:
      X11
      man
            man1
            man4
            man5
            man7
            man6
            man3
```

9-7 EXERCISE

On most UNIX-based systems the **spell** utility uses a file of words as a base for its spell checking. On our Linux system this file is in the /usr/share/dict directory. Write an RPC-based client–server application in which the client sends a word or partial word to the server. To process the request, the server returns all the words that contain the requested word (partial word) or the message "Nothing appropriate" if no match can be made.

Modify the directory tree example so that the server process allocates, on the fly, a node (structure) for each directory entry. A list of the nodes should be returned to the client (versus the fixed array in the example). Be sure to dispose of all allocated memory once the application is finished with it.

9.8 Using Broadcasting to Search for an RPC Service

It is possible for a user to send a message to all **rpcbind** daemons on a local network requesting information on a specific service. The request is generated using the **clnt_broadcast** network call. The broadcast requests are sent to all locally connected broadcast nets using connectionless UDP transport. When sent, multiple responses may be obtained from the same server and from multiple servers. As each response is obtained, the **clnt_broadcast** call automatically invokes a predefined routine. Table 9.8 provides the syntax details of the **clnt_broadcast** call.

Table 9.8 Summary of the `clnt_broadcast` Library Call.

Include File(s)	`<rpc/rpc.h>`		Manual Section	**3N**

Summary	`enum clnt_stat clnt_broadcast(`
	`        u_long prognum, u_long versnum, u_long procnum,`
	`        xdrproc_t inproc,  char *in,`
	`        xdrproc_t outproc, char *out,`
	`        resultproc_t eachresult      );`			

Return	Success	Failure	Sets `errno`	
	An enumerated type value RPC_SUCCESS indicating the success of the broadcast call.	Use `clnt_perrno` for error message.	Yes	

The **clnt_broadcast** call is similar in nature to the **callrpc** function (another call used to invoke a remote procedure). The first three arguments for **clnt_broadcast** are the program, version and procedure numbers of the service. The parameters inproc and in reference the encoding procedure and the address of its argument(s) while outproc and out reference the decoding procedure and the address of where to place the decoding output if it is successful. Every time the **clnt_broadcast** call receives a response, it calls the function referenced by the eachresult argument. The eachresult function has two arguments. The first is a char * that references the same value as the out argument used in the **clnt_broadcast** call. The second argument is a reference to a structure, struct sockaddr_in *, that has the address information from the host that responded to the broadcast request. Keep in mind that the system supplies these values when the function is invoked. Every time the eachresult referenced function returns a 0 (FALSE), the clnt_broadcast call continues to wait for additional replies. The **clnt_broadcast** call will eventually time out (the user has no control over the amount of time).

Program 9.8 demonstrates the use of the **clnt_broadcast** call.

Program 9.8   Program broad.c, sending a broadcast request.

```
File : broad.c
   |      #include <stdio.h>
   |      #include <rpc/rpc.h>
   |      #include <rpc/pmap_clnt.h>                    // For resultproc_t cast
   |
   +      u_long    program_number, version;      // Note: These are global
   |      static bool_t
   |      who_responded(char *out, struct sockaddr_in *addr) {
   |        int my_port_T, my_port_U;
   |        my_port_T = pmap_getport(addr, program_number, version, IPPROTO_TCP);
  10      my_port_U = pmap_getport(addr, program_number, version, IPPROTO_UDP);
   |        if ( my_port_T )
   |          printf("host: %s \t TCP port: %d\n",inet_ntoa(addr->sin_addr),
   |                  my_port_T);
   |        if ( my_port_U )
   +          printf("host: %s \t UDP port: %d\n",inet_ntoa(addr->sin_addr),
   |                  my_port_U);
   |        return 0;
   |      }
   |      int
  20      main(int argc, char *argv[]) {
   |        enum clnt_stat   rpc_stat;
   |        struct rpcent   *rpc_entry;
   |        if (argc < 2) {
   |          fprintf(stderr, "usage: %s RPC_service_[name | #] version\n", *argv);
```

```
+            return 1;
|        }
|        ++argv;                              // Step past your own prog name
|        if (isdigit(**argv))                 // Check to see if # was passed
|           program_number = atoi(*argv);     // If # passed use it otherwise
30       else {                               // obtain RPC entry information
|           if ((rpc_entry = getrpcbyname(*argv)) == NULL) {
|              fprintf(stderr, "Unknown service: %s\n", *argv);
|              return 2;
|           }                                 // Get the program number
+           program_number = rpc_entry->r_number;
|        }
|        ++argv;                              // Move to version #
|        version = atoi(*argv);
|        rpc_stat = clnt_broadcast(program_number, version, NULLPROC,
40                       (xdrproc_t)xdr_void, (char *) NULL,
|                        (xdrproc_t)xdr_void, (char *) NULL,
|                        (resultproc_t) who_responded);
|        if (rpc_stat != RPC_SUCCESS)
|         if (rpc_stat != RPC_TIMEOUT) {      // If error is not a time out
+           fprintf(stderr, "Broadcast failure : %s\n", clnt_sperrno(rpc_stat));
|           return 3;
|         }
|        return 0;
|     }
```

The program checks the command line for the number of arguments. It expects to be passed the name (or number) of the service to check and its version number. The first character of the first argument is checked. If it is a digit, it is assumed that the number for the service was passed and the **atoi** function is used to convert the string representation of the number into an integer value. If the name of the service was passed, the **getrpcbyname** network call is used (line 31) to obtain details about the specified service. Table 9.9 summarizes the **getrpcbyname** network call.

Table 9.9 Summary of the getrpcbyname Network Call.

Include File(s)	`<rpc/rpc.h>`		Manual Section	**3N**
Summary	`struct rpcent *getrpcbyname(char *name);`			
Return	Success	Failure	Sets errno	
	A reference to the rpcent structure for the service.	NULL		

365

The **getrpcbyname** call has one parameter, a reference to a character array containing the service name. If successful, the call returns a pointer to the **rpcent** structure for the service (as found in RPC program number database stored in the file /etc/rpc). The **rpcent** structure is defined as

```
struct rpcent {
                char *r_name;        /* name of this rpc service */
                char **r_aliases;    /* zero-terminated list of
                                       alternate names */
                long r_number;       /* rpc program number */
        };
```

In line 38 the program then converts the second command-line argument into a version number. The **clnt_broadcast** call is used to garner responses. Each time a server responds to a broadcast request, the user-defined function who_responded is automatically invoked.

The who_responded function contains two other function calls, **pmap_getport** and **inet_ntoa**. The **pmap_getport** library function is used to obtain the port associated with the service. Table 9.10 provides the syntax specifics for the **pmap_getport** library function.

Table 9.10 Summary of the **pmap_getport** Library Function.

Include File(s)	<rpc/rpc.h>		Manual Section	**3N**
Summary	u_short pmap_getport(struct sockaddr_in *addr, u_long prognum, u_long versnum, u_long protocol);			
Return	Success	Failure	Sets errno	
	The associated port number.	0	No, it sets rpc_createerr, query with clnt_pcreateerror( )	

The first argument for this call is a reference to an address structure. This structure is as follows:[14]

---

[14] In the **gdb** debugger the command ptype TYPE can be used to display definition of the type of the value for TYPE (assuming, of course, the type is referenced in the current code).

```
struct sockaddr_in {
    sa_family_t   sin_family;                // address family
    in_port_t     sin_port;                  // port
    struct        in_addr    sin_addr;       // reference to the address structure
    unsigned char sin_zero[8];               // unused
};
```

The prognum and versnum arguments are the program and version number of the service. The last argument, protocol, should be set to either IPPROTO_TCP for TCP or IPPROTO_UDP for UPD. If the call is successful, it returns the port number; otherwise, it sets the variable rpc_createerr to indicate the error. If an error occurs, the library function **clnt_pcreateer-ror** should be used to retrieve the associated error message.

At this point some should be asking, why use **pmap_getport** at all? Couldn't we just call **htons**(addr->sin_port) in the who_responded function to get the port number? The answer is, we could if we wanted only the UDP-associated port for the service.

The second function used in who_responded is the network function inet_ntoa. This function takes an encoded four-byte network address and converts it to its dotted notation counterpart. A sample run of the program requesting information about the status service, version 1, is shown in Figure 9.35.

Figure 9.35 Output of the broad.c program showing servers providing status service.

```
medusa$ broad status 1
host: 137.49.6.1          TCP port: 32768
host: 137.49.6.1          UDP port: 32768      ◄————  Same host, same ports.
host: 137.49.52.2         TCP port: 32782
host: 137.49.52.2         UDP port: 32791
host: 137.49.9.27         TCP port: 751
host: 137.49.9.27         UDP port: 749        ◄————  Different host, different ports.
host: 137.49.52.152       TCP port: 984
host: 137.49.52.152       UDP port: 982
host: 137.49.240.157      TCP port: 1024
host: 137.49.240.157      UDP port: 1025
host: 137.49.6.1          TCP port: 32768
host: 137.49.6.1          UDP port: 32768      ◄————  Hosts continue to respond.
host: 137.49.52.152       TCP port: 984
host: 137.49.52.152       UDP port: 982
host: 137.49.240.157      TCP port: 1024
host: 137.49.240.157      UDP port: 1025
host: 137.49.52.2         TCP port: 32782
host: 137.49.52.2         UDP port: 32791
. . .
```

Notice that before the broadcast call timed out, some servers responded more than once. Also note that the service can be associated with different ports on different hosts. This output should be somewhat similar to the output produced by the **rpcinfo** command when called as

```
medusa$ rpcinfo -b status 1
```

9-9 EXERCISE

Modify the broad.c program to display the name (versus the IP address) of the host that responds to the broadcast. *Hint*: Check into the **gethostbyaddr** network function that, when passed an address, will return a structure that contains a reference to the host name.

9.9 Summary

Programming with RPC allows the programmer to write distributed applications whereby a process residing on one workstation can request another "remote" workstation to execute a specified procedure. Because of their complexity, most RPC-based programs make use of a protocol compiler such as Sun Microsystems's **rpcgen**. A protocol compiler provides the basic programming framework for the RPC-based application. In RPC applications the client and server processes do not need to know the details of underlying network protocols. Data passed between the processes is converted to/from an external data representation (XDR) format by predefined filters. Beneath the covers, RPC-based programs make use of the socket interface to carry out their communications. While not discussed in this chapter, RPC does support authentication techniques to facilitate secure client – server communications.

9.10 Key Terms and Concepts

<netdb.h> header
<netinet/in.h> header
<rpc/pmap_clnt.h> header

<rpc/rpc.h> header
client process
client stub

CLIENT `typedef`
`clnt_broadcast` library call
`clnt_create` library call
`clnt_destroy` library call
`clnt_pcreateerror` library call
`clnt_perror` library call
deserialization
`gdb` debugging of RPC programs
`gethostbyaddr` network function
`gethostbyname` network call
`getrpcbyname` network call
`hostname` command
`htons` network call
`inet_ntoa` network call
LDLIBS
`make` utility
mangled function names
`memset` function
`pmap_getport` library call
protocol definition file
public–private key authentication
`readdir` library function
`rexec` library function
`rexecd` remote execution server
RPC (remote procedure call)
RPC filters
RPC makefile

RPC program number
RPC template file
RPC version number
RPC_NOBROADCAST
RPC_UNKNOWNADDR
RPC_UNKNOWNHOST
RPC_UNKNOWNPROTO
`rpcent` structure
`rpcgen` command
`rpcgen` utility
RPCGENFLAGS
`rpcinfo` command
`rsh` (remote shell command)
serialization
server process
server stub
`ssh` (Secure Shell command)
`ssh-keygen` command
TCP (Transmission Control Protocol)
transport protocol
`ttyname` library call
UDP (Unreliable Datagram
  Protocol)
XDR (External Data Representation)
`xdr_char` function
`xdr_line` function
`xdr_vector` function

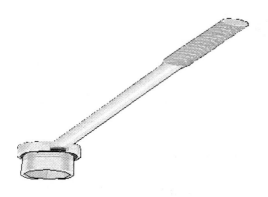

Chapter 10

SOCKETS

10.1 Introduction

One of the nice things about UNIX and its variants is that they use a common interface for the access of files and devices that reside on a single host. By using a file descriptor generated by an **open** system call, the user can easily read data from and write data to the file descriptor. This can be done without being overly concerned with the underlying mechanics of the process and without knowing to which device the descriptor has been mapped (e.g., the screen, a file on disk, etc.). When we discussed the use of **pipes**, we saw a similar approach. With pipes, we could have two-way (duplex) communications using **read** and **write** system calls as long as the processes involved were related. Again, the processes communicated by using **read** and **write** system calls as if they were dealing with files. When we discussed System V-based message queues, semaphores, and shared memory as interprocess communication techniques, we began to stray from the read/write paradigm. We also found that while we could use some of these techniques for interprocess communication, even with unrelated processes, each technique had its own special method for sending and receiving information. Unfortunately, while these techniques are powerful, and certainly

371

have their place, their arcane syntax is somewhat restrictive. In the last chapter, we examined remote procedure calls. We noted that RPC mechanisms are used for interprocess communications. The RPC API (application program interface) was developed to ease the burden of writing applications that required communication between unrelated processes residing in a distributed environment. In attempting to make things easier, the developers of RPCs have, in some cases, made things more complex and restrictive. RPC applications, by nature, have a large number of ancillary files whose contents and relationships may at times obscure their functionality. In an RPC-based application, it is easy to lose touch with and control of the mechanics of the communication process. It would seem that what is needed is an extension of the basic read/write paradigm with the inclusion of sufficient networking semantics to permit unrelated processes on different hosts to communicate as if they were reading and writing to a local file. This type of intermediate level of interprocess communications would lie somewhere in between pipes, message queues, shared memory techniques, and RPC applications. Fortunately, in UNIX there are several application interfaces that support this type of communication and are in fact the underlying basis for the RPC interface.

The most common APIs that provide remote interprocess communications are the Berkeley socket interface, introduced in the early 1980s, and Transport Level Interface (TLI) programming implemented by AT&T in the mid-1980s. There is much discussion as to which of these offers the better solution for remote interprocess communication. As the Berkeley socket interface preceded TLI, a majority of existing remote interprocess communication coding is done with sockets. However, Berkeley sockets are not transport-independent and must be used with caution in a multithreaded processing environment. On the other hand, TLI is designed to be transport-independent (i.e., applications can access transport specifics in a protocol-independent manner). Unfortunately, to date, not all transport protocols support every TLI service. Unlike sockets, TLI is STREAMS-based and requires that the application push a special module on the stream before performing reads and writes. The concept of privileged ports (a Berkeley concept) is not supported with TLI. In addition, broadcasting (the ability to send the same message to a group of hosts) is not transport-independent. Recently, TLI has begun to be replaced by the X/Open Transport Interface (XTI).

In this chapter we explore the Berkeley socket interface. Conceptually, a socket is an abstract data structure that is used to create a channel (connection point) to send and receive information between unrelated processes. Once a channel is established, the connected processes can use generalized file-system type access routines for communication. For the most part, when using a socket-based connection, the server process creates a socket, maps the socket to a local address, and waits (listens) for requests from clients. The client process creates its own socket and determines the location specifics (such as the host name and port number) of the server. Depending upon the type of transport/connection specified, the client process will begin to send and receive data either with or without receiving a formal acknowledgment (acceptance) from the server process.

10.2 Communication Basics

To understand how sockets work, a basic understanding of some of the details of process communications in a networked environment and its associated terminology is needed.

10.2.1 Network Addresses

Every host on a network has, at a minimum, two unique addresses. The first unique address is a 48-bit[1] media access control (MAC) address that is assigned to its network interface card (NIC). The manufacturer of the card assigns this address. The MAC address (sometimes called its Ethernet or hardware address) is written in hexadecimal notation. The address is broken into six 8-bit numbers with intervening colons (:). When using hexadecimal, each 8-bit number will be, at most, two digits, each consisting of 0–9, A–F. The case of the alphabetic digits is not important, and leading 0s are often not included. The first three groupings (bytes) of this number identify the hardware manufacturer. A variety of sites exist on the Internet that map manufacturer identifier values to their corresponding vendor. One such table can be found at http://www.iana.org/assignments/ethernet-numbers.

On some UNIX-based systems the file /etc/ethers contains the MAC addresses for local hosts. Additionally, the file /proc/net/arp contains recently resolved addresses (Internet addresses and their corresponding hardware address). On a Linux host the **ifconfig** utility can be used to display the

---

[1] In IPv4 (Internet Protocol version 4, which has been around for about 20 years) these addresses are 48-bit. In IPv6 (originally called IPng: Internet Protocol—the next generation) these addresses are 64-bit.

hardware address of its NICs. Figure 10.1 shows the output of the **ifconfig** command when passed the -a (all) option.

Figure 10.1 Displaying the MAC addresses on a Linux host.

```
linux$ /sbin/ifconfig -a
eth0  Link encap:Ethernet   HWaddr 00:B0:D0:AB:7C:96
      BROADCAST MULTICAST  MTU:1500  Metric:1
      RX packets:0 errors:0 dropped:0 overruns:0 frame:0
      TX packets:0 errors:0 dropped:0 overruns:0 carrier:0
      collisions:0 txqueuelen:100
      Interrupt:16  Base address:0xecc0 Memory:e08fc000-
                    e08fcc40

eth1  Link encap:Ethernet   HWaddr 00:02:B3:35:9E:21
      inet addr:137.49.6.1  Bcast:137.49.255.255  Mask:255.255.0.0
      UP BROADCAST RUNNING MULTICAST  MTU:1500  Metric:1
      RX packets:471693034 errors:2 dropped:0 overruns:27398 frame:2
      TX packets:2147483647 errors:0 dropped:0 overruns:0 carrier:0
      collisions:0 txqueuelen:100
      Interrupt:26 Base address:0xd4c0 Memory:e08fe000-e08fec40

lo    ink encap:Local Loopback
      inet addr:127.0.0.1  Mask:255.0.0.0
      UP LOOPBACK RUNNING  MTU:16436  Metric:1
      RX packets:95939986 errors:0 dropped:0 overruns:0 frame:0
      TX packets:95939986 errors:0 dropped:0 overruns:0 carrier:0
      collisions:0 txqueuelen:0
```

This host has two network cards. As shown, only eth1 is active

The second unique address for a host is a 32-bit[2] Internet (IP) address. Internet addresses used to be assigned by the Internet Network Information Center (InterNIC). At present, the process is a bit more complicated. At the uppermost level ICANN (the Internet Corporation for Assigned Names and Numbers) assigns blocks of addresses on a regional basis. At the regional level the American Registry for Internet Numbers (ARIN) allocates IP address space in North and South America, the Caribbean, and sub-Saharan Africa; APNIC (Asia Pacific Network Information Center) allocates addresses for Asia and the Pacific; RIPE (Réseaux IP Européens) handles European addresses. At a local level Internet service providers (ISPs) obtain their addresses from their regional authority. At the next level users request their addresses from the ISP. A 32-bit IP address is broken into four 8-bit numbers, each separated by a dot (.). Written in dotted decimal notation (DDN), each of the four subnumbers can range from 0 to 255 (although the numbers 0 and 255 in the

[2] With IPv6, the 32-bit IP addresses will become 128-bit.

last grouping often have a special meaning, such as a local loopback or broadcast address).

An IPv4 Internet address may be subdivided into a network and local portion. The network portion, or `netid`, occupies the leftmost portion of the IP address, and the local portion, or `hostid`, the rightmost portion. Using the leading bits of the `netid` value, networks can be divided into five classes, A through E. We will look at the first three classes.[3] In a Class A network bit 0 is 0; in a Class B the first two bits are 10, and in a Class C the first 3 bits are 110. The `netid` portion of the address is assigned by the ISP and indicates your network association. The content of the `hostid` portion is determined by the local network administrator and specifies the individual host (workstation) within your network. As can be seen in Figure 10.2, the range of `hostid`s that a local network administrator can assign is directly related to the class of the network. In general, small sites have Class C network addresses, larger sites Class B, and so on. When this numbering scheme was initiated, it was not anticipated that the range of available network addresses would be restrictive, as it allowed for 2^7 Class A networks, 2^{14} Class B networks, and 2^{21} Class C networks (see Exercise 10.1 for more on this topic).

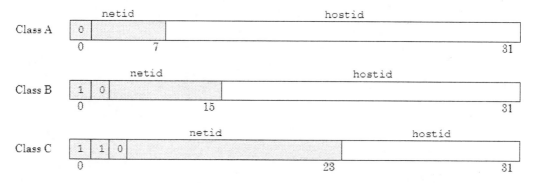

Figure 10.2 Network class numbering scheme.

It is the responsibility of the host to map a specific Internet address to its corresponding Ethernet (hardware) address. This process, called address resolution, uses its own protocol called address resolution protocol (ARP). The command `/sbin/arp -a` displays a listing of recently resolved Internet/Ethernet

---

[3] Classes D and E are special network classes. Class D is used for multicasting, and Class E is reserved for experimental use. Neither of these classes has an inherent host-addressing scheme.

address pairs on the current host. In discussing sockets, when we refer to an address, unless otherwise noted, we are referring to its Internet (IP) address.

The long-term solution to providing sufficient IP addressing space will be to move to 128-bit IPv6 addresses. In the interim Classless Interdomain Routing (CIDR) is being offered as a solution. What is CIDR, and why is it a more efficient method for assigning 32-bit IP addresses?

10.2.2 Domains—Network and Communication

While IP addresses are a handy way to reference a specific host, we often map a dotted IP address into a more easily understood symbolic notation using the Domain Name System (DNS). In this schema, all Internet addresses are divided into a set of high-level organizational and geographical domains. Each organizational domain (sometimes called a top-level domain) has an identifying code (usually three lowercase letters), such as com (commercial), edu (education), and gov (government). Each geographical domain consists of a two-letter country code, such as fi (Finland), ca (Canada), and us (United States).[4] Within each high-level domain are subdomains. For example, within the edu domain is the subdomain hartford (for the University of Hartford). Within the hartford domain there may be further subdomains (such as cs for Computer Science), or just an individual host's name. While there appears to be no established limit, usually the maximum number of levels for domain names is four to five. By using the domain naming system we can now reference a host as, for example, morpheus.cs.hartford.edu instead of 137.49.52.1. When reading names in this format, the domain with the broadest scope is listed on the far right. As you move to the left, each domain found is within the domain to its right. The last name in the sequence (the leftmost) is usually the name of the host. Most networks run software (such as BIND [Berkeley Internet Name Domain system]) that, using distributed DNS database information will dynamically map a domain-name reference to its corresponding Internet (IP) address.

---

[4] The Web site site http://www.iana.org/cctld/cctld-whois has a complete list of the two-letter country codes.

Explore the **dig** (Domain Information Groper), **nslookup**, and **host** commands by reading their manual pages. Pass **dig** your domain name (e.g., **dig** ucla.edu). Check the returned AUTHORITY SECTION information. What is the symbolic name of the DNS server for your domain? Given this symbolic name what is the IP address of this server (try using the command **host** -a with the symbolic name)? If **nslookup** is supported on your system (it is deprecated but still in wide use) invoke the command and set the server to be the appropriate DNS server. Then issue the command **ls** for the domain. What does the command display?

The term *domain* is utilized again in reference to the communication type for a socket interface. When we create the socket, we specify its **communication domain**. The two types of socket communication domains that we will discuss are

1. **UNIX domain**. In this domain, when sockets are created, they have actual file (path) names. These sockets can be used only with processes that reside on the same host. UNIX domain sockets are sometimes used as the first step in the development of socket-based communications because, due to their locality, they are somewhat easier to debug.

2. **Internet domain**. These sockets allow unrelated processes on different hosts to communicate.

While it should be clear by the context of the discussion, most often when we speak of domain, we will be talking about the communication domain of the socket, not the domain name of a host.

10.2.3 Protocol Families

Processes must also agree upon a set of rules and conventions for their communications. A set of such rules and conventions is called a **protocol**. Protocols, which can be quite complex in their entirety, are designed in layers. The layering of protocols facilitates a certain degree of isolation that permits changes to one layer to not affect the functionality of adjacent layers. The International Standards Organization (ISO) Open Systems Interconnect (OSI) reference model is often used as a generalized guide for how this layering should occur.[5] Figure 10.3 shows the standard seven-layer OSI model.

Figure 10.3 The ISO/OSI layer cake.

	Layer	Functionality
Higher Level	Application	Provides processes access to interprocess facilities.
	Presentation	Responsible for data conversion—text compression and reformatting, encryption.
	Session	Addresses the synchronization of process dialog—establishes, manages, and terminates connections.
Protocol Family	Transport	Responsible for maintaining an agreed-upon level of data exchange. Determines type of service, flow control, error recovery, and so on.
	Network	Concerned with the routing of data from one network to another—establishing, maintaining, and terminating connections.
Lower Level	Data Link	Insures error-free transmission of data.
	Physical	Addresses physical connections and transmission of raw data stream.

A grouping of layers, most commonly the transport and network layers of the OSI model, forms a **protocol family** or suite. As can be seen, a protocol family encompasses such things as data formats, addressing conventions, type of service information, flow control, and error handling. There are a number of protocol families, including the following:

- **SNA**—IBM's Systems Network Architecture
- **UUCP**—UNIX-to-UNIX copy
- **XNS**—Xerox Network System
- **NETBIOS**—IBM's Network Basic Input/Output System
- **TCP/IP**—DARPA (Defense Advanced Research Projects Agency) Internet

---

[5] Some protocols, such as TCP, preceded the OSI model and thus do not cleanly map to its layering. TCP/IP accomplishes the same functionality with four conceptual layers: application, transport, Internet, and network interface (data link). The transport and network layers of TCP/IP are roughly equivalent to the transport and network access layers of the OSI model except TCP/IP supports UDP, an unreliable protocol.

Our discussion centers on the TCP/IP protocol family (PF_INET), Internet domain, which is composed of

- **TCP**—Transmission Control Protocol. TCP is reliable, full duplex and connection-oriented. Data is transmitted as a byte stream.
- **IP**—Internet Protocol. Provides delivery of packets. TCP, UDP and ICMP usually call IP.
- **ARP/RARP**—Address/Reverse Address Resolution Protocol. These protocols are used to resolve Internet/hardware addressing.
- **UDP**—User Datagram Protocol. UDP is nonreliable, full duplex, and connectionless. Data is transmitted as a series of packets.
- **ICMP**—Internet Control Message Protocol. Used for error handling and flow control.

Within the TCP/IP family, we focus on TCP and UDP. When we create a socket, we will specify its protocol family to be either PF_UNIX (UNIX)[6] or PF_INET (TCP/IP). For the curious, the protocol definition file /etc/protocols contains the list of DARPA Internet protocols available with the TCP/IP subsystem.

10.2.4 Socket Types

For processes to communicate in a networked setting, data must be transmitted and received. We can consider the communicated data to be in a **stream** (i.e., a sequence of bytes) or in **datagram** format. Datagrams are small, discrete packets that, at a gross level, contain header information (such as addresses), data, and trailer information (error correction, etc.). As datagrams are small in size, communications between processes may consist of a series of datagrams.

When we create a socket, its type will determine how communications will be carried on between the processes using the socket. Sockets must be of the same type to communicate. There are two[7] basic socket types the user can specify:

1. **Stream sockets**. These sockets are **reliable**. When these sockets are used, data is delivered in order, in the same sequence in which it was sent. There is no duplication of data, and some form of error checking

---

[6] Technically, UNIX is not a true communications protocol, but will be treated as such for our socket discussions.

[7] Again, a slight fudge—there are other socket types, such as raw and sequenced packet sockets. Raw sockets are for those with superuser access that wish to design and implement their own network protocol. We will not address using raw or sequenced packet sockets.

and flow control is usually present. Stream sockets allow bidirectional (full duplex) communication. Stream sockets are **connection-oriented.** That is, the two processes using the socket create a logical connection (a virtual circuit). Information concerning the connection is established prior to the transmission of data and is maintained by each end of the connection during the communication. Data is transmitted as a stream of bytes. In a very limited fashion, these sockets also permit the user to place a higher priority urgent message ahead of the data in the current stream.

2. **Datagram sockets**. Datagram sockets are potentially **unreliable.** Thus, with these sockets, received data *may* be out of order. Datagram sockets support bidirectional communications but are considered **connectionless.** There is no logical connection between the sending and receiving processes. Each datagram is sent and processed independently. Individual datagrams may take different routes to the same destination. With connectionless service, there is no flow control. Error control, when specified, is minimal. Datagram packets are normally small and fixed in size.

There is an often-given analogy that compares stream socket communication to that of a phone conversation (address of sender and receiver determined when the connection is established) and datagram communication with communication (correspondence) via postcards (each card packet has its own address information). While the analogy is not entirely accurate, it does capture the spirit of the two types of communication.

10.3 IPC Using `Socketpair`

As a warmup, we begin our exploration of sockets with the generation of a pair of UNIX domain sockets. The **socketpair** call, shown in Table 10.1, is used to create the pair of sockets.

The **socketpair** call takes four arguments. The first argument, d, is an integer value that specifies the domain. In general, the domains for socket-based calls should be specified as one of the protocol family-defined constants found in the header file <bits/socket.h>. As in previous examples, the programmer does not directly include this file, since the <sys/socket.h> file, which must be included, includes this more system-specific header file. When we look in the <bits/socket.h> file, we find two sets of similar defined constants. One set of constants begins with AF_ (denoting address

Table 10.1 Summary of the socketpair System Call

Include File(s)	`<sys/socket.h>`		Manual Section	**2**
Summary	`int socketpair( int d,      int  type,` `             int protocol, int  sv[2] );`			
Return	Success	Failure	Sets `errno`	
	0 and two open socket descriptors	−1	Yes	

family) and the second set begins with PF_ (indicating protocol family). At one time the PF_ constants were defined in terms of the AF_ constants. Now the AF_ set of constants is defined in terms of the PF_ constants. This mishmash occurs as the concept of address families preceded that of protocol families. As we are heading toward the use of protocol families, the PF_ designated constants are more appropriate to use when generating a socket. The current set of all defined protocol families, as found in the `<bits/socket.h>` file, is shown in Table 10.2.

Table 10.2 Protocol Family Constants.

Constant	Value	Reference
PF_UNSPEC	0	Unspecified.
PF_LOCAL	1	Local to host (pipes and file-domain).
PF_UNIX	PF_LOCAL	Old BSD name for PF_LOCAL.
PF_FILE	PF_LOCAL	Another nonstandard name for PF_LOCAL.
PF_INET	2	IP protocol family.
PF_AX25	3	Amateur Radio AX.25.
PF_IPX	4	Novell Internet Protocol.
PF_APPLETALK	5	Appletalk DDP.
PF_NETROM	6	Amateur radio NetROM.
PF_BRIDGE	7	Multiprotocol bridge.
PF_ATMPVC	8	ATM PVCs.
PF_X25	9	Reserved for X.25 project.

Continued

Table 10.2 (Continued)

Constant	Value	Reference
PF_INET6	10	IP version 6.
PF_ROSE	11	Amateur Radio X.25 PLP.
PF_DECnet	12	Reserved for DECnet project.
PF_NETBEUI	13	Reserved for 802.2LLC project.
PF_SECURITY	14	Security callback pseudo AF.
PF_KEY	15	PF_KEY key management API.
PF_NETLINK	16	
PF_ROUTE	PF_NETLINK	Alias to emulate 4.4BSD.
PF_PACKET	17	Packet family.
PF_ASH	18	Ash.
PF_ECONET	19	Acorn Econet.
PF_ATMSVC	20	ATM SVCs.
PF_SNA	22	Linux SNA Project
PF_IRDA	23	IRDA sockets.
PF_PPPOX	24	PPPoX sockets.
PF_MAX	32	For now.

Note that most of the socket-based calls only work with a limited subset of address/protocol families. The **socketpair** call is only implemented for the PF_LOCAL (PF_UNIX) family, thus restricting it to same-host communications.

The second argument for the **socketpair** call, `type`, indicates the socket type. The defined constant SOCK_STREAM can be used to indicate a stream socket or the defined constant SOCK_DGRAM to indicate a datagram-based socket. The third argument, `protocol`, is used to indicate the protocol within the specified family. In most cases, this argument is set to 0, which indicates to the system that it should select the protocol. With Internet domain communications, the system will use, by default, UDP for connectionless sockets and TCP for connection-oriented sockets. If necessary, the IPPROTO_TCP or IPPROTO_UDP constants found in the header file `<netinet/in.h>` can be used to directly select the protocol within a specific family. The fourth argument, `sv`, is the base address of an integer array that references the two socket descriptors that are created if the call is successful. Each descriptor is bidirectional and is available for both reading and writing. If the **socketpair** call fails, it returns a −1 and sets errno. The value errno may take, and an interpretation of each value, is shown in Table 10.3.

Table 10.3 socketpair Error Messages.

#	Constant	perror **Message**	Explanation
14	EFAULT	Bad address	sv references an illegal address.
24	EMFILE	Too many open files	This process has reached the limit for open file descriptors.
93	EPROTONOSUPPORT	Protocol not supported	Requested protocol not supported on this system.
95	EOPNOTSUPPORT	Operation not supported	Specified protocol does not support socket pairs.
97	EAFNOSUPPORT	Address family not supported by protocol	Cannot use the indicated address family with specified protocol family.

Program 10.1 creates a socket pair, forks a child process, and uses the created sockets to communicate information between the parent and child processes.

Program 10.1   Creating and using a socket pair.

```
File : p10.1.cxx
  |     /*
  |          Creating a socket pair
  |      */
  |     #include <iostream>
  +     #include <cstdio>
  |     #include <unistd.h>
  |     #include <sys/socket.h>
  |     using namespace std;
  |     const int BUF_SZ = 10;
 10     int
  |     main( ) {
  |       int          sock[2],          // The socket pair
  |                    i;
  |       static char  buf[BUF_SZ];       // Temporary buffer for message
  +       if (socketpair(PF_LOCAL, SOCK_DGRAM, 0, sock) < 0) {
  |         perror("Generation error");
  |         return 1;
  |       }
```

```
   |        switch (fork( )) {
  20        case -1:
   |          perror("Bad fork");
   |          return 2;
   |        case 0:                              // The child process
   |          close(sock[1]);
   +          for (i = 0; i < 10; i += 2) {
   |            sleep(1);
   |            sprintf(buf, "c: %d", i);
   |            write(sock[0], buf, sizeof(buf));
   |            read( sock[0], buf, BUF_SZ);
  30            cout << "c-> " << buf << endl;    // Message from parent
   |          }
   |          close(sock[0]);
   |          break;
   |        default:                             // The parent process
   +          close(sock[0]);
   |          for (i = 1; i < 10; i += 2) {
   |            sleep(1);
   |            read( sock[1], buf, BUF_SZ);
   |            cout << "p-> " << buf << endl;   // Message from child
  40            sprintf(buf, "p: %d", i);
   |            write(sock[1], buf, sizeof(buf));
   |          }
   |          close(sock[1]);
   |        }
   +        return 0;
   |      }
```

The program starts by creating, with a single call in line 15, a pair of local UNIX datagram sockets. The program then forks, producing a child process. When in the child, the program closes the socket descriptor referenced as sock[1]. It then enters a loop, from 0 to 9, counting in steps of 2, where it does the following. The process sleeps for one second to slow down its output display sequence. It then creates, in a temporary buffer, a message to be sent to the parent process. The message contains the character sequence c:, to label it as from the child, followed by the current integer loop counter value. The contents of the temporary buffer are then written to socket descriptor 0 (sock[0]) using the **write** system call. Following the write to the socket, the child process reads from the *same* socket descriptor to obtain the message generated by the parent process. The child process then displays the message from the parent on the screen.

The parent process follows a similar set of steps. However, it closes sock[0] and does its socket reading and writing from sock[1]. When this program is run, it will produce the output as shown in Figure 10.4.

Figure 10.4 The output of Program 10.1.

```
linux$ p10.1
p-> c: 0
c-> p: 1
p-> c: 2
c-> p: 3
p-> c: 4
c-> p: 5
p-> c: 6
c-> p: 7
p-> c: 8
c-> p: 9
```

Before the process forks, both sock[0] and sock[1] descriptors are available in the parent for reading and writing. After the fork, the child process closes sock[1] and reads and writes using sock[0]. The parent process closes sock[0] and reads and writes using sock[1]. At the kernel level the sockets are still one and the same. Thus, what the child process writes to sock[0] can be read by the parent process from sock[1] and vice versa. Figure 10.5 presents a diagrammatic representation of this relationship.

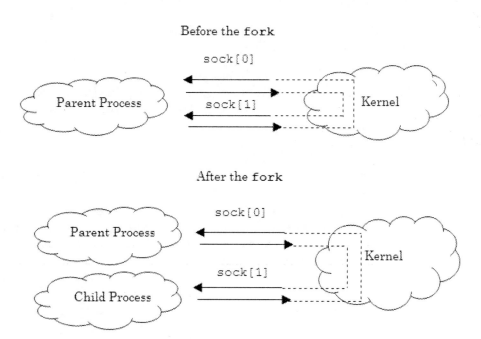

Figure 10.5 The socketpair before and after the process forks.

What happens when you adjust the **sleep** times in the child/parent processes in Program 10.1? Will the parent/child processes wait for each other no matter what the time differential? Why? Why not? Now edit the p10.1.cxx file and change both **sleep** times to 3 seconds. Recompile the source as p10.1. Read the manual page on **netstat**. Issue the following command sequence:

```
linux$ p10.1 &  netstat -p -x | grep p10.1
```

What information is returned by the **netstat** command? Once the p10.1 program is finished reissue just the **netstat** command with the -p -x options. What does this tell you about what the system is doing?

10.4 Sockets: The Connection-Oriented Paradigm

When using sockets for interprocess communications, we can specify the socket type as either connection-oriented (type SOCK_STREAM) or connectionless (type SOCK_DGRAM). The sequence of events that must occur for connection-oriented communications is shown in Figure 10.6. In this setting, the process initiating the connection is the client process and the process receiving the connection is the server.

As shown, both the client and server processes use the **socket** call to create a new instance of a socket. The socket will act as a queuing point for data exchange. The summary for the **socket** system call is shown in Table 10.4

The **socket** system call takes three arguments. The arguments parallel those for the **socketpair** call without the fourth integer array/socket pair reference. In short, the **socket** call takes an integer value (one of the defined constants in the <sys/sockets.h> file) that indicates the protocol family as its first argument. At present, the protocol families shown in Table 10.5 are supported.

The second argument, type, denotes the socket type (such as SOCK_STREAM or SOCK_DGRAM). The third argument, protocol, is the specific protocol to be used within the indicated address/protocol family. As with the **socketpair** call, we will most often set this value to 0 to

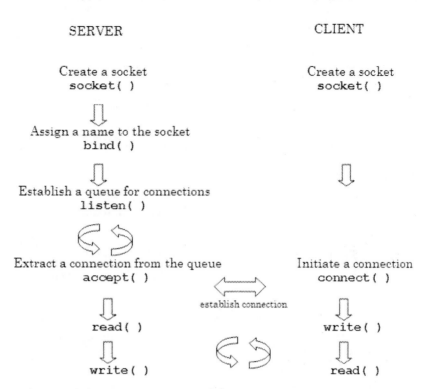

SERVER   CLIENT

Create a socket   Create a socket
socket( )   socket( )

Assign a name to the socket
bind( )

Establish a queue for connections
listen( )

Extract a connection from the queue   Initiate a connection
accept( )   connect( )

        establish connection

read( )   write( )

write( )   read( )

Figure 10.6 A connection-oriented client–server communication sequence.

Table 10.4 Summary of the `socket` System Call.

Include File(s)	`<sys/types.h>` `<sys/socket.h>`		Manual Section	**2**
Summary	`int socket( int domain, int type, int protocol );`			
Return	Success		Failure	Sets `errno`
	0 and an open socket descriptor.		−1	Yes

let the system choose the protocol based on the protocol family. If the **socket** call is successful, it will return an integer value that can be used to reference the socket descriptor. If the call fails, it returns a −1 and sets `errno`. The value for `errno`, and an interpretation of the error message, is shown in Table 10.6.

Table 10.5 Supported Protocol Families.

Constant	Protocol Family
PF_APPLETALK	Appletalk
PF_ATMPVC	Access to raw ATM PVCs
PF_AX25	Amateur radio AX.25 protocol
PF_INET	IPv4 Internet protocols
PF_INET6	IPv6 Internet protocols
PF_IPX	IPX - Novell protocols
PF_NETLINK	Kernel user interface device
PF_PACKET	Low-level packet interface
PF_UNIX, PF_LOCAL	Local communication
PF_X25	ITU-T X.25 / ISO-8208 protocol x25(7)

When a `socket` call is made in a program in some, but not all, development settings, the socket library must be specifically linked at compile time using the option `-lsocket`.

Table 10.6 `socket` Error Messages.

#	Constant	`perror` **Message**	Explanation
12	ENOMEM	Cannot allocate memory	When creating a socket, insufficient memory available.
13	EACCES	Permission denied	Cannot create a socket of the specified type/protocol.
22	EINVAL	Invalid argument	Unknown protocol or protocol family is not available.
23	ENFILE	Too many open files in system	Insufficient kernel (system) memory for socket allocation.
24	EMFILE	Too many open files	This process has reached the limit for open file descriptors.
93	EPROTONOSUPPORT	Protocol not supported	Requested `protocol` not supported on this system or within this domain.
105	ENOBUFS	No buffer space available	Socket cannot be created until resources are freed.

Read the manual page on **netstat**. Issue the following command to determine all listening sockets and their associated port numbers on your system:

```
linux$ netstat -l -n      # alt_cmd$  netstat -a -n | grep LISTEN
```

How many sockets are listening for connections? If the system is listening on port 80, issue the command sequence (note the back tics):

```
linux$ telnet 'hostname' 80
```

When the system responds, type GET /. What happens? What information is returned to the screen? What does the / stand for?

Initially, when the socket is created, it is unbound (i.e., there is no name or address/port number pair associated with the socket). If the process creating the socket is to act as a server, the socket must be bound. This is similar in concept to the assignment of a phone number to an installed phone or a street name and number to a mailing address. The **bind** system call is used to associate a name or address/port pair with a socket. If the socket is to be used in the UNIX domain, a file name must be provided, and we say the address resides in *local namespace*. In the Internet domain, an address/port pair must be assigned—the address resides in *Internet namespace*. Table 10.7 provides a summary of the **bind** system call.

Table 10.7 Summary of the `bind` System Call

Include File(s)	`<sys/types.h>` `<sys/socket.h>`		Manual Section	2
Summary	`int  bind(int sockfd, struct sockaddr *my_addr,` `            socklen_t addrlen);`			
Return	Success		Failure	Sets `errno`
	0		−1	Yes

The first argument for **bind** is an integer value that has been returned from a previous successful **socket** call. The second argument, a reference to a `sockaddr` structure, is a real gem. The short explanation is the `my_addr` argument references a generic address structure of the type:

```
/* Structure describing a generic socket address.                 */
struct sockaddr  {
    __SOCKADDR_COMMON (sa_);    /* Common data: adr family and length. */
    char sa_data[14];           /* Address data.                 */
};
```

We will use this structure definition as a starting point for our address references. In a few paragraphs we will come back to the use of this structure. For those who enjoy a syntactical challenge, a more detailed explanation of the definition of the `sockaddr` structure, as well as the definition of the `SOCKADDR_COMMON` macro, can be found in the first 100 or so lines of the include file `<sys/socket.h>`.

Again, **bind** can be used for both UNIX and Internet domain sockets. For UNIX domain sockets, a reference to a file must be bound to the socket. A UNIX socket domain address is defined in the header file `<sys/un.h>`[8] as

```
#define UNIX_PATH_MAX    108
struct sockaddr_un {
    sa_family_t  sun_family;                  /* AF_UNIX  */
    char         sun_path[UNIX_PATH_MAX]; /* pathname */
};
```

When this structure is used, the `sockaddr_un.sun_family` member is usually assigned the defined constant AF_UNIX to indicate UNIX addressing is being used. The second member, `sun_path`, is the path (absolute or relative) to the file name to be bound to the socket. In the UNIX domain, **bind** creates a file entry for the socket. If the file is already present, an error occurs. When listing a directory in long format with the **ls** command, a file that is bound to the socket will have the letter p or s as its file type, indicating it is a pipe or socket. The number of bytes in the file will be listed as 0. The maximum length for the `sun_path` member, including the NULL terminator, is 108 characters.

If the socket is to be used in the Internet domain, the addressing structure found in the file `<netinet/in.h>` is used. As with UNIX domain sockets, if we are working with Internet domain sockets, this file must be in the include list of the program. This address structure is defined as

---

[8] If we are working with UNIX domain sockets, this file *must* be in the include list of the program. If you do some spelunking, you will find the full definition of the UNIX sock structure is actually found in one of the files included by the `<sys/un.h>` file.

```
struct sockaddr_in {
  sa_family_t    sin_family;     /* address family: AF_INET          */
  u_int16_t      sin_port;       /* 16 bit port in network byte order    */
  struct in_addr sin_addr;       /* internet address structure          */
};

struct in_addr {
  u_int32_t      s_addr;         /* 32 bit address in network byte order */
};
```

Keep in mind that in Internet namespace, we must map the socket to an Internet address/port number pair. To accomplish this, we use the sock-addr_in structure shown above. The first member of the structure, like the sockaddr_un structure, is an integer value that indicates the address family. In this scenario, this member is assigned the value AF_INET. The second member, sin_port, indicates the port number for the service. The port number is a 16-bit value that acts as an offset[9] to the indicated Internet address and references the actual endpoint for the communication. A list of assigned port numbers can be obtained by viewing the contents of the /etc/services file. A partial excerpt from a local /etc/services file is shown in Figure 10.7.

Figure 10.7 Partial contents of a local /etc/services file.

```
linux$ cat /etc/services

# /etc/services:
# $Id: services,v 1.17 2001/02/28 20:11:31 notting Exp $
#
# Network services, Internet style
. . .

# Each line describes one service, and is of the form:
#
# service-name  port/protocol  [aliases ...]   [# comment]
tcpmux          1/tcp                          # TCP port service multiplexer
tcpmux          1/udp                          # TCP port service multiplexer
rje             5/tcp                          # Remote Job Entry
rje             5/udp                          # Remote Job Entry
echo            7/tcp
echo            7/udp
discard         9/tcp          sink null
discard         9/udp          sink null
systat          11/tcp         users
systat          11/udp         users
. . .
```

---

[9] Sticking with our phone system analogy for connection-oriented protocol, this would be similar to an extension for a given phone number.

As can be seen, each service has a name, such as **echo**, is associated with a specific port (e.g., 7), and uses a specific protocol (e.g., tcp). Ports with values less than 1024 are reserved (can only be used by processes whose effective ID is root). Many of these low-numbered ports are considered to be **well-known**; that is, they consistently have the same value and are always associated with the same type of service using the same protocol. A port can be associated with more than one protocol.

The third member of the sockaddr_in structure, sin_addr, is a reference to an in_addr structure. This structure, with just one member, holds the actual 32-bit host Internet address value (with adjustments for byte-orderings; i.e., little endian versus big endian). We present the details of how to fill in the sockaddr_in structure in the example section.

We are now ready to return to the *generic* sockaddr structure, which is the second argument of the **bind** call. There are two members in the generic sockaddr structure. The first member, the macro __SOCKADDR_COMMON (sa_), is used to indicate the address family information. The second member, sa_data, is a reference to the actual address. To make **bind** work, we first populate the appropriate addressing structure (sockaddr_un or sockaddr_in) with correct values. Then, when passing the structure as an argument to **bind**, cast the reference as (struct sockaddr *) to convince **bind** that we are passing a reference to the proper structure type. The third argument to **bind**, which provides the size of the address structure, helps to resolve things such as being able to pass a UNIX domain address with a 108-byte file/path reference. Again, the details of how to calculate the size of the address structure are presented in the example section.

If **bind** is successful, it returns a 0; otherwise, it returns a -1 and sets the value of errno. Table 10.8 summarizes the errors associated with a failure of **bind** for both local (UNIX) and Internet namespace.

Table 10.8 bind Error Messages.

#	Constant	perror **Message**	**Explanation**
2	ENOENT	No such file or directory	Component of the path for the file name entry does not exist.
9	EBADF	Bad file descriptor	sockfd reference is invalid.
12	ENOMEM	Cannot allocate memory	Insufficient memory.
13	EACCES	Permission denied	• Cannot create a socket of the specified type/protocol. • Search access denied for part of the path specified by name.

Continued

Table 10.8 *(Continued)*

#	Constant	`perror` **Message**	**Explanation**
14	EFAULT	Bad address	`my_addr` references address outside user's space.
20	ENOTDIR	Not a directory	Part of the path of `my_addr` is not a directory.
22	EINVAL	Invalid argument	• `addrlen` is invalid. • `sockfd` already bound to an address.
30	EROFS	Read-only file system	File would reside on a read-only file system.
36	ENAMETOOLONG	File name too long	`my_addr` name is too long.
40	ELOOP	Too many levels of symbolic links	Too many symbolic links in `my_addr`.
63	ENOSR	Out of streams resources	Insufficient STREAMS resources for specified operation.
88	ENOTSOCK	Socket operation on non-socket	`sockfd` is a file descriptor, not a socket descriptor.
98	EADDRINUSE	Address already in use	Specified address already in use.
99	EADDRNOTAVAIL	Can't assign request address	The specified address is not available on the local system.

While our primary concern is with Internet domain protocols, a UNIX domain socket may also be bound. In the UNIX domain, an actual file entry is generated that should be removed (unlinked) when the user is done with the socket.

Continuing with the server process in the connection-oriented setting, the next system call issued is to **listen**. This call, which only applies to sockets of type SOCK_STREAM or SOCK_SEQPACKET, creates a queue for incoming connection requests. If the queue is full and the protocol does not support retransmission, the client process generating the request will receive the error ECONNREFUSED from the server. If the protocol does support retransmission, the request is ignored, so a subsequent retry can succeed. The summary for **listen** is given in Table 10.9.

The first argument of the **listen** system call is a valid integer socket descriptor. The second argument, `backlog`, denotes the maximum size of the queue. Originally, BSD-based documentation indicated that there was no limit to the value for `backlog`. However, in many versions of BSD-derived UNIX, the limit was set to five for any `backlog` value greater than five. As of

Table 10.9 Summary of the `listen` System Call.

Include File(s)	`<sys/types.h>` `<sys/socket.h>`		Manual Section	**2**
Summary	`int listen(int s, int backlog);`			
	Success	Failure	Sets `errno`	
Return	0	−1	Yes	

Linux 2.2 the `backlog` value is for completely established sockets waiting for acceptance versus incomplete connection requests. If needed, the maximum queue size for incomplete socket requests can be set with the `/sbin/sysctl` command using `tcp_max_syn_backlog` variable.

Should the **listen** call fail, it sets `errno` and returns one of the values shown in Table 10.10.

Table 10.10 `listen` Error Messages.

#	**Constant**	`perror` **Message**	**Explanation**
9	EBADF	Bad file descriptor	`s` reference is invalid.
88	ENOTSOCK	Socket operation on non-socket	`s` is a file descriptor, not a socket descriptor.
95	EOPNOTSUPP	Operation not supported	Socket type (such as SOCK_DGRAM) does not support **listen** operation.

At this point, the server process is ready to accept a connection from a client process (which has already established a connection-based socket). By default, the **accept** call will block, if there are no pending requests for connections. The summary for the **accept** system call is given in Table 10.11.

The first argument is a socket descriptor that has been previously bound to an address with the **bind** system call and is currently **listen**ing for a connection. If one or more client connections are pending, the first connection in the queue is returned by the **accept** call. The second argument for **accept**, `*addr`, is a pointer to a generic `sockaddr` structure. This structure is returned to the server once the connection with the client has been established. Its actual format, as in the **bind** system call, is dependent upon the domain in which the communication will occur. The structure the `addr` pointer references contains the client's address information. The third argument, `*addrlen`, initially contains a reference to the length, in bytes, of the previous `sockaddr` structure. When the call returns, this argument

Table 10.11 Summary of the `accept` System Call.

Include File(s)	`<sys/types.h>` `<sys/socket.h>`		Manual Section	**2**
Summary	`int accept( int s, struct sockaddr *addr,` `                   socklen_t *addrlen );`			
Return		Success	Failure	Sets `errno`
	Positive integer **new** socket descriptor value		−1	Yes

references the size (in bytes) of the returned address. If **accept** is successful, it returns a new connected socket descriptor with properties similar to the socket specified by the first argument to the **accept** system call. This new socket can be used for reading and writing. The original socket remains as it was and can, in some settings, still continue to **accept** additional connections. If the **accept** call fails, it returns a value of −1 and sets the value of `errno` to one of the values shown in Table 10.12.

Table 10.12 `accept` Error Messages.

#	Constant	`perror` **Message**	**Explanation**
1	EPERM	Operation not permitted	Firewall software prohibits connection.
4	EINTR	Interrupted system call	A signal was received during the **accept** process.
9	EBADF	Bad file descriptor	The socket reference is invalid.
11	EWOULDBLOCK, EAGAIN	Resource temporarily unavailable	The socket is set to non-blocking, and no connections are pending.
12	ENOMEM	Cannot allocate memory	Insufficient memory to perform operation.
14	EFAULT	Bad address	Reference for `addr` is not writeable.
19	ENODEV	No such device	Specified protocol family/type not found in the `netconfig` file.

Continued

Table 10.12 *(Continued)*

#	Constant	`perror` **Message**	**Explanation**
22	EINVAL	Invalid argument	Invalid argument passed to `accept` call.
24	EMFILE	Too many files open	Process has exceeded the maximum number of files open.
63	ENOSR	Out of streams resources	Insufficient STREAMS resources for specified operation.
71	EPROTO	Protocol error	An error in protocol has occurred.
85	ERESTART	Interrupted system call should be restarted	`accept` call must be restarted.
88	ENOTSOCK	Socket operation on non-socket	The socket is a file descriptor, not a socket descriptor.
93	EPROTONOSUPPORT	Protocol not supported	Invalid protocol specified.
94	ESOCKTNOSUPPORT	Socket type not supported	Invalid socket type specified.
95	EOPNOTSUPP	Operation not supported	`s` is not of type SOCK_STREAM.
103	ECONNABORTED	Software caused connection abort	Connection aborted.
105	ENOBUFS	No buffer space available	Insufficient memory to perform operation.
110	ETIMEDOUT	Connection timed out	Unable to establish connection within specified time limit.

It is interesting to note that the Linux manual pages indicate that when called, `accept` will also pass on pending network errors as if they were from `accept`. This behavior is different from straight BSD socket implementations that do not have this quirk.

In the connection-oriented setting, the client process initiates the connection with the server process with the `connect` system call. The summary of the `connect` call is shown in Table 10.13.

The first argument is a valid integer socket descriptor. The second argument, `*serv_addr`, is handled differently depending upon whether the referenced socket is connection-oriented (type SOCK_STREAM) or connectionless (type

Table 10.13 Summary of the `connect` System Call

Include File(s)	`<sys/types.h>` `<sys/socket.h>`		Manual Section	**2**

Summary	`int connect(int sockfd,`
	`            const struct sockaddr *serv_addr,`
	`            socklen_t addrlen);`			

	Success		Failure	Sets `errno`
Return	0		-1	Yes

SOCK_DGRAM). In the connection-oriented setting, `*serv_addr` references the address of the socket with which the client wants to communicate (i.e., the serving process's address). For a connectionless socket, `*serv_addr` references the address to which the datagrams are to be sent. Normally, a stream socket is **connect**ed only once, while a datagram socket can be **connect**ed several times. Further, if the protocol domain is UNIX, `*serv_addr` will reference a path/file name, while in the Internet domain (i.e., AF_INET) `*serv_addr` will reference an Internet address/ port number pair. In either case, the reference should be cast to a generic `sockaddr` structure reference. Clear as mud, right? Hopefully, the section with the client – server examples will help to clarify the details of the **connect** system call. The third argument, `addrlen`, conveys the size of the `*serv_addr` reference.

As there are a number of ways in which the **connect** call can fail, the list of errors that **connect** can generate is quite extensive. A list of **connect** errors is found in Table 10.14.

Table 10.14 connect Error Messages.

#	Constant	`perror` **Message**	**Explanation**
1	EPERM	Operation not permitted	• Attempt to broadcast without having broadcast flag set. • Request failed due to firewall.
4	EINTR	Interrupted system call	A signal was received during **connect** process.
9	EBADF	Bad file descriptor	`sockfd` reference is invalid.
11	EAGAIN	Resource temporarily unavailable	No more free local ports.

Continued

Table 10.14 *(Continued)*

#	Constant	`perror` **Message**	**Explanation**
13	EACCES	Permission denied	Search permission denied for part of path referenced by `*serv_addr`.
14	EFAULT	Bad address	Address referenced by `*serv_addr` is outside the user's address space.
22	EINVAL	Invalid argument	`namelength` is not correct for address referenced by `*serv_addr`.
63	ENQSR	Out of streams resources	Insufficient STREAMS resources for specified operation.
88	ENOTSOCK	Socket operation on non-socket	`sockfd` is a file descriptor, not a socket descriptor.
91	EPROTOTYPE	Protocol wrong type for socket	Conflicting protocols, `socketfd` versus the `*serv_addr` reference.
97	EAFNOSUPPORT	Address family not supported by protocol family	Address referenced by `*serv_addr` cannot be used with this socket.
98	EADDRINUSE	Address already in use	Local address referenced by `*serv_addr` already in use.
99	EADDRNOTAVAIL	Cannot assign requested address	Address referenced by `*serv_addr` not available on remote system.
101	ENETUNREACH	Network is unreachable	Cannot reach specified system.
106	EISCONN	Transport endpoint is already connected	`sockfd` already connected.
110	ETIMEDOUT	Connection timed out	Could not establish a connection within time limits.
111	ECONNREFUSED	Connection refused	Connect attempt rejected; socket already connected.
114	EALREADY	Operation already in progress	Socket is non-blocking, and no previous connection completed.
115	EINPROGRESS	Operation now in progress	Socket set as non-blocking, and connection cannot be established immediately.

Once the connection between the client and server has been established, they can communicate using standard I/O calls, such as **read** and **write**, or one of a number of specialized send/receive type calls covered in Section 10.5. When the processes are finished with the socket descriptor, they issue a standard **close**, which by default will attempt to send remaining queued data should the protocol for the connection (such as TCP) specify reliable delivery.

10.4.1 A UNIX Domain Stream Socket Example

In the following example, programs 10.2 and 10.3, we create a server process and a client process that each use a UNIX domain, connection-oriented (SOCK_STREAM) socket for communication. The server will create the socket, bind it to an address, generate a wait queue, accept a connection, and when data is available, **read** from the socket and display the results to the screen. The client process will create a socket, connect to the server, and obtain from the user 10 expressions, each of which it writes to the socket. The server reads the data passed (the expression) and processes the expression by passing it, via a pipe, to the **bc** utility for evaluation. The output of the **bc** utility is read by the server and sent back, using the socket, to the client process where it is displayed.

Program 10.2 UNIX domain connection-oriented **server**.

```
File : p10.2.cxx
   |      /*
   |              Server - UNIX domain, connection-oriented
   |      */
   |      #define _GNU_SOURCE
   +      #include <iostream>
   |      #include <cstdio>
   |      #include <unistd.h>
   |      #include <sys/types.h>
   |      #include <sys/socket.h>
  10      #include <sys/un.h>                // UNIX protocol
   |      using namespace std;
   |
   |      const char *NAME = "./my_sock";
   |      const int  MAX = 1024;
   +      void clean_up( int, const char *); // Close socket and remove
   |      int
   |      main(  ) {
   |        socklen_t        clnt_len;       // Length of client address
   |        int              orig_sock,      // Original socket descriptor
  20                         new_sock;       // New socket descriptor from connect
   |      static struct sockaddr_un          // UNIX addresses to be used
```

399

```
|                        clnt_adr,               // Client address
|                        serv_adr;               // Server address
|    static char    clnt_buf[MAX],               // Message from client
+                   pipe_buf[MAX];               // output from bc command
|    FILE *fin;                                  // File for pipe I/O
|                                                // Generate socket
|    if ((orig_sock = socket(PF_UNIX, SOCK_STREAM, 0)) < 0) {
|      perror("generate error");
30     return 1;
|    }                                           // Assign address information
|    serv_adr.sun_family = AF_UNIX;
|    strcpy(serv_adr.sun_path, NAME);
|    unlink(NAME);                               // Remove old copy if present
+                                                // BIND the address
|    if (bind( orig_sock, (struct sockaddr *) &serv_adr,
|            sizeof(serv_adr.sun_family)+strlen(serv_adr.sun_path)) < 0) {
|      perror("bind error");
|      clean_up(orig_sock, NAME);
40     return 2;
|    }
|    listen(orig_sock, 1);                       // LISTEN for connections
|    clnt_len = sizeof(clnt_adr);                // ACCEPT connection
|    if ((new_sock = accept( orig_sock, (struct sockaddr *) &clnt_adr,
+                            &clnt_len)) < 0) {
|      perror("accept error");
|      clean_up(orig_sock, NAME);
|      return 3;
|    }
50                                               // Process 10 requests
|    for (int i = 0; i < 10; i++) {
|      memset(clnt_buf, 0x0, MAX);               // Clear client buffer
|      read(new_sock, clnt_buf, sizeof(clnt_buf));
|                                                // build command for bc
+      memset(pipe_buf, 0x0, MAX);
|      sprintf(pipe_buf, "echo \'%s\' | bc\n", clnt_buf);
|      fin = popen( pipe_buf, "r" );
|      memset(pipe_buf, 0x0, MAX);
|      read(fileno(fin), pipe_buf, MAX);
60     cout << clnt_buf << " = " << pipe_buf << endl;
|    }
|    close(new_sock);
|    clean_up(orig_sock, NAME);
|    return 0;
+  }
|  void
|  clean_up( int sd, const char *the_file ){
|    close( sd );                                // Close socket
|    unlink( the_file );                         // Remove it
70 }
```

When a connection is accepted, a new socket is generated—similar in form to the original socket.

Notice the call to **bind** in the server program (program p10.2.cxx, lines 36 and 37). As written, the third argument, which is the length of the address structure, is an expression. The expression calculates the total size by adding the size of the sun_family member of the address structure to the string length of the sun_path member. If we just applied the **sizeof** operator to the whole address structure, on most platforms the value returned would be 110 (say, 2 bytes for the sun_family member plus the 108 bytes for the sun_path member).

The client program is shown in Program 10.3.

Program 10.3   UNIX domain connection-oriented client.

```
File : p10.3.cxx
  |     /*
  |          Client - UNIX domain, connection-oriented
  |      */
  |
  +     #define _GNU_SOURCE
  |     #include <iostream>
  |     #include <cstdio>
  |     #include <unistd.h>
  |     #include <sys/types.h>
 10     #include <sys/socket.h>
  |     #include <sys/un.h>                  // UNIX protocol
  |     using namespace std;
  |
  |     const char *NAME = "./my_sock";
  +     const int  MAX = 1024;
  |     int
  |     main(  ) {
  |       int              orig_sock;        // Original socket descriptor
  |       static struct sockaddr_un
 20                      serv_adr;           // UNIX address of the server process
  |       static char     buf[MAX];          // Buffer for messages
  |                                          // Generate the SOCKET
  |       if ((orig_sock = socket(PF_UNIX, SOCK_STREAM, 0)) < 0) {
  |         perror("generate error");
  +         return 1;
  |       }
  |       serv_adr.sun_family = AF_UNIX;
  |       strcpy(serv_adr.sun_path, NAME);
  |                                          // CONNECT
 30       if (connect( orig_sock, (struct sockaddr *) &serv_adr,
  |             sizeof(serv_adr.sun_family)+strlen(serv_adr.sun_path)) < 0) {
  |         perror("connect error");
  |         return 2;
  |       }
  +                                          // Prompt for expressions
  |       cout << "Enter an expression and press enter to process." << endl;
```

```
|       for (int i = 0; i < 10; i++) {
|         memset(buf, 0x0, MAX);
|         cin.getline(buf, MAX-1, '\n');
40        write(orig_sock, buf, sizeof(buf));
|       }
|       close(orig_sock);
|       return 0;
|     }
```

We run the client–server pair by placing the server process in the background. We then run the client process in the foreground. The compilation sequence and some sample output generated by the client–server programs are shown in Figure 10.8.

Figure 10.8 UNIX domain client–server program compilation and run.

```
linux$ g++ p10.2.cxx -o server      ◄── Compile each program into an executable.
linux$ g++ p10.3.cxx -o client

linux$ ./server &                    ◄── Place server in background.
[1] 4739
                                     ◄── Check for presence of the socket.
linux$ ls -l my_sock
srwxr-xr-x    1 gray       faculty          0 May  9 15:35 my_sock
                                     ◄── Run client in the foreground.
linux$ ./client
Enter an expression and press enter to process.
78 * 92
78 * 92 = 7176

89 % 6 + 34 - 2 * -9
89 % 6 + 34 - 2 * -9 = 57

1 && 0 || 1
1 && 0 || 1 = 1

!( 1 && 1 || 0 )
!( 1 && 1 || 0 ) = 0

. . .
```

On the command line, the presence of the socket can also be confirmed by using the **netstat** command. This command, which has numerous options, can be used to display information about socket-based communications. Figure 10.9 shows part of the output of **netstat** on a local system after the UNIX domain server program has been placed in the background.

Figure 10.9   Sample output from the `netstat` command.

```
linux$ netstat -x -a
Active UNIX domain sockets (servers and established)
Proto RefCnt Flags    Type    State       I-Node Path
unix  13     [ ]      DGRAM               1384   /dev/log
unix  2      [ ACC ]  STREAM LISTENING    1681   /var/lib/mysql/mysql.sock
unix  2      [ ACC ]  STREAM LISTENING    2202   /tmp/.font-unix/fs7100
unix  2      [ ACC ]  STREAM LISTENING    5914   /opt/ARCserve/data/ds_callback
unix  2      [ ACC ]   STREAM   LISTENING    65439   ./my_sock
 . . .
```

10-5   EXERCISE

If we place the server process in the background and open, say, three windows on the same host and attempt to run multiple client processes, we find that one client will work correctly but the other clients will not. Rewrite the server program (p10.2.cxx) so that it will accept and process multiple client connections (each in their own window) correctly. *Hint*: Should the server **fork** a child process to handle each connection?

10.4.2   An Internet Domain Stream Socket Example

In the Internet domain, processes must have address and port information to communicate. An application may know the name of a host (such as `linux`, `kahuna`, or `morpheus`) with which it wants to communicate but lack specifics about the host's fully qualified name, Internet address, services offered (on which ports), and other information. There are a number of network information calls that can be used to return this information.

The **gethostbyname** call will return information about a specific host when passed its name. Table 10.15 presents a summary of the **gethostbyname** call.

The **gethostbyname** call takes a single character string reference that contains the name of the host. The call queries the local network database[10] to obtain information about the indicated host. If the host name is found, the call

---

[10] Information may come from any of the sources for services specified in the `/etc/nsswitch.conf` file (see `nsswitch.conf` in Section 5 of the manual pages for details).

Table 10.15 Summary of the `gethostbyname` Library Function.

Include File(s)	`#include <netdb.h>`
	`#include <sys/socket.h>`
	`extern int h_errno;`
		Manual Section	**3**

Summary	`struct hostent *gethostbyname(const char *name);`		

Return	Success	Failure	Sets errno
	Reference to a `hostent` structure	NULL	NO, sets `h_errno`

returns a reference to a `hostent` structure. The `hostent` structure is defined in the include file `<netdb.h>` as

```
struct hostent {
    char *h_name;                       /* Official name of host.            */
    char **h_aliases;                   /* Alias list.                       */
    int h_addrtype;                     /* Host address type.                */
    int h_length;                       /* Length of address.                */
    char **h_addr_list;                 /* List of addresses from name server. */
    #define h_addr  h_addr_list[0]      /* Address, for backward compatibility. */
};
```

If the host name is not found, the **gethostbyname** call returns a NULL. Should the call encounter an error situation, it sets a global variable called h_error (not errno) to indicate the error. The values h_error can take and the associated defined constants (found in the include file `<netdb.h>`) are shown in Table 10.16. An obsolete error messaging function called **h_error** (similar in spirit to **perror**) can be called to generate an error message.

Table 10.16 `gethostbyname` Error Messages.

#	Constant	Explanation
0	NETDB_SUCCESS	No problem.
1	HOST_NOT_FOUND	Authoritative answer not found/no such host.
2	TRY_AGAIN	Nonauthoritative host not found or SERVERFAIL.
3	NO_RECOVERY	Nonrecoverable error.
4	NO_DATA	Valid name but no data record of requested type.

In some development environments the object code for the **gethostbyname** network call resides in the `libnsl.a` archive. In these settings, when using this call, the switch -lnsl must be added to the compilation line. Program 10.4 uses the **gethostbyname** call to obtain information about a host.

Program 10.4 Obtaining host information with gethostbyname.

```
File : p10.4.cxx
   |      /*
   |           Checking host entries
   |      */
   |      #include <iostream>
   +      #include <cstdio>
   |      #include <netdb.h>
   |      #include <sys/socket.h>
   |      #include <netinet/in.h>                    // for inet_ntoa
   |      #include <arpa/inet.h>
  10      #include <string.h>                        // for memcpy
   |      extern int h_errno;
   |      using namespace std;
   |      int
   |      main(  ) {
   +        struct hostent *host;
   |        static char who[60];
   |        cout << "Enter host name to look up: ";
   |        cin  >> who;
   |        host = gethostbyname( who );
  20        if ( host != (struct hostent *) NULL ) {
   |          cout << "Here is what I found about " << who << endl;
   |          cout << "Official name : " <<  host->h_name  << endl;
   |          cout << "Aliases       : ";
   |          while ( *host->h_aliases ) {
   +            cout << *host->h_aliases << " ";
   |            ++host->h_aliases;
   |          }
   |          cout << endl;
   |          cout << "Address type  : " << host->h_addrtype << endl;
  30        cout << "Address length: " << host->h_length   << endl;
   |          cout << "Address list  : ";
   |          struct in_addr in;
   |          while ( *host->h_addr_list ) {
   |            memcpy( &in.s_addr, *host->h_addr_list, sizeof (in.s_addr));
   +            cout << "[" << *host->h_addr_list << "] = "
   |                 << inet_ntoa(in) << " ";
   |            ++host->h_addr_list;
   |          }
   |          cout << endl;
  40      } else
   |          herror(who);
   |        return 0;
   |      }
```

In Program 10.4, the **gethostbyname** call is used to obtain network database information about a host. When the program is run, the user is prompted for the name of a host (as written, the name can be at most 59 characters). If the **gethostbyname** call is successful, the official database entry name of the host is displayed. This is followed by a list of aliases (alternate names). The address type and length is displayed next. In an Internet domain setting, we can expect these values to be 2 (the value of AF_INET) and 4 (the number of bytes needed to store an integer value). The last part of the program displays the Internet address of the host. It uses an additional Internet address manipulation call, **inet_ntoa**, to translate the character-encoded network address referenced by the h_addr_list member into the more standard dotted notation. The manual page on **inet_ntoa** provides a good explanation of how the character string argument to the call is translated. A run of Program 10.4 is shown in Figure 10.10.

Figure 10.10 A run of Program 10.4.

```
linux$ p10.4
Enter host name to look up: www-cs
Here is what I found about www-cs
Official name : zeus.hartford.edu
Aliases       : www-cs.hartford.edu
Address type  : 2
Address length: 4                          The address list with and with-
Address list  : [14] = 137.49.52.2  ◀————  out inet_ntoa translation.
```

10-6 EXERCISE

There is a call similar to **gethostbyname** that returns host entry information when passed the dotted Internet address of the host. Write a program based on Program 10.4 that requests the Internet address of a host. Then use the **gethostbyaddr** call to display the host's information.

In addition to knowing the server's 32-bit Internet address, the client must also be able to make reference to a particular service at a given port on the server. As noted previously, there are some TCP- and UDP-based well-known ports that have standard services, such as **echo**, associated with them. The ports with numbers less than 1024 are reserved for processes with an effective ID of root. Ports 1024 and above are considered **ephemeral**, and may be used by any system user. Some further subdivide this upper range of ports into **registered** (1024–49151) and **dynamic** (49152 and greater) ports. An application can issue the **getservbyname** call (see Table 10.17) to obtain information about a particular service or port.

Table 10.17 Summary of the getservbyname Library Function

Include File(s)	`<netdb.h>`		Manual Section	**3**
Summary	`struct servent *getservbyname(const char *name,` `const char *proto);`			
Return	Success	Failure	Sets errno	
	Reference to a servent structure	NULL		

The **getservbyname** call is passed the name of the host and protocol (e.g., `tcp`). If successful, it returns a reference to a servent structure. The servent structure is defined in `<netdb.h>` as:

```
struct servent {
        char    *s_name;        /* official service name */
        char    **s_aliases;    /* alias list            */
        int     s_port;         /* port number           */
        char    *s_proto;       /* protocol to use       */
}
```

If the call fails, it returns a NULL value. Program 10.5 uses the **getservbyname** library function to return information about a selected service type for a given protocol.

Program 10.5 Obtaining service information on a host using getservbyname.

```
File : p10.5.cxx
   |    /*
   |         Checking service -- port entries for a host
   |    */
   |    #include <iostream>
   +    #include <cstdio>
   |    #include <netdb.h>
   |    using namespace std;
   |    int
   |    main( ) {
  10      struct servent *serv;
```

```
 |     static char protocol[10], service[10];        ◄─────── Arbitrary buffer sizes.
 |     cout << "Enter service to look up : ";
 |     cin  >> service;
 |     cout << "Enter protocol to look up: ";
 +     cin  >> protocol;
 |     serv = getservbyname( service, protocol );
 |     if ( serv != (struct servent *)NULL ) {
 |       cout << "Here is what I found " << endl;
 |       cout << "Official name  : " << serv->s_name << endl;
20       cout << "Aliases        : ";
 |       while ( *serv->s_aliases ) {
 |         cout << *serv->s_aliases << " ";
 |         ++serv->s_aliases;
 |         }
 +       cout << endl;
 |       cout << "Port number    : " << ntohs(serv->s_port) << endl;
 |       cout << "Protocol Family: " << serv->s_proto << endl;
 |     } else
 |       cout << "Service " << service << " for protocol "
30            << protocol  << " not found." << endl;
 |     return 0;
 |   }
```

Before the port number is displayed, it is passed to the **ntohs** function. This is one of a group of functions used to insure byte ordering is maintained when converting 16- and 32-bit integer values that represent host and network addresses. The summary for **ntohs** is shown in Table 10.18.

Table 10.18 Summary of the ntohs Library Function.

Include File(s)	<netinet/in.h>		Manual Section	**3**
Summary	unsigned short int ntohs(unsigned short int netshort);			
		Success	Failure	Sets errno
Return	The argument in proper byte order for the network.			

The inverse of the **ntohs** call is **ntohs** (notice the switch of the letters h and n). The letter s indicates the argument is a short (16-bit) integer, as is the returned value. There are two similar routines, **ntohl** and **htonl**, that accept and return long (32-bit) integers. If byte ordering is not necessary for a given platform, these calls act as a no-op.

A sample run of Program 10.5 and a copy of the corresponding /etc/ services entry are shown in Figure 10.11.

Figure 10.11   A run of Program 10.5.

```
linux$ p10.5
Enter service to look up : discard
Enter protocol to look up: tcp
Here is what I found
Official name  : discard
Aliases        : sink null
Port number    : 9
Protocol Family: tcp

linux$ grep discard /etc/services              ◄──────── Verify the information.
discard           9/tcp           sink null
discard           9/udp           sink null
```

10-7   EXERCISE

The manual page for **getservbyname** includes a description of a network function called **getservent**. The **getservent** call can be used to enumerate all the services on a host. Write a program that requests the protocol type and uses the **getservent** network call to display all the services on the host that use the indicated protocol. Be sure to call **setservent** prior to issuing the **getservent** call.

We now have most of the basic tools to write a client–server application that uses Internet protocol with a connection-oriented socket. In this next example, the server process receives messages from the client process. As each message is received, the server changes the case of the message and returns it to the client. Communication terminates when the client sends a string that has a dot (.) in column one. For each connection initiated by a client, the server process will **fork** a child process that runs concurrently and carries on communications.

All of the remaining client–server type socket examples share a common header file called local_sock.h. The content of local_sock.h file is shown in Figure 10.12.

Figure 10.12 The `local_sock.h` include file for all socket example programs.

```
File : local_sock.h
   |      /*
   |          Local include file for socket programs
   |      */
   |      #ifndef LOCAL_SOCK_H
   +      #define LOCAL_SOCK_H
   |      #define _GNU_SOURCE
   |      #include <iostream>
   |      #include <sys/ioctl.h>
   |      #include <cstdio>
  10      #include <string.h>
   |      #include <ctype.h>
   |      #include <unistd.h>
   |      #include <stdlib.h>
   |      #include <signal.h>
   +      #include <wait.h>
   |      #include <sys/types.h>
   |      #include <sys/socket.h>
   |      #include <sys/un.h>
   |      #include <netdb.h>
  20      const  int   PORT=2002;              // Arbitrary port programmer chooses
   |      static char buf[BUFSIZ];             // Buffer for messages
   |      const  char *SERVER_FILE="server_socket";
   |      #endif
   |      using namespace std;
```

The `local_sock.h` file contains references to the include files needed by both the server and client programs. The defined constant PORT is an arbitrary integer port number that we will use with this application. The value for the port should be one that is currently not in use and is greater than or equal to 1024. An alternate approach is to add an entry for the port in the /etc/services file. If the port is in the /etc/services file, the port information could then be obtained dynamically with the **getservbyname** network call. However, most users do not have the required root access to add an entry. The character array buf is used as a temporary storage location for characters.

The server program, Program 10.6, is presented first.

Program 10.6 The Internet domain, connection-oriented **server**.

```
File : p10.6.cxx
   |      /*
   |            Internet domain, connection-oriented SERVER
   |      */
   |      #include "local_sock.h"
```

```
   +      void signal_catcher(int);
   |      int
   |      main(  ) {
   |        int            orig_sock,         // Original socket in server
   |                       new_sock;          // New socket from connect
  10        socklen_t      clnt_len;          // Length of client address
   |        struct sockaddr_in                // Internet addr client & server
   |                       clnt_adr, serv_adr;
   |        int            len, i;            // Misc counters, etc.
   |                                          // Catch when child terminates
   +        if (signal(SIGCHLD , signal_catcher) == SIG_ERR) {
   |          perror("SIGCHLD");
   |          return 1;
   |        }
   |        if ((orig_sock = socket(PF_INET, SOCK_STREAM, 0)) < 0) {
  20          perror("generate error");
   |          return 2;
   |        }
   |        memset( &serv_adr, 0, sizeof(serv_adr) );         // Clear structure
   |        serv_adr.sin_family      = AF_INET;               // Set address type
   +        serv_adr.sin_addr.s_addr = htonl(INADDR_ANY);     // Any interface
   |        serv_adr.sin_port        = htons(PORT);           // Use our fake port
   |                                                          // BIND
   |        if (bind( orig_sock, (struct sockaddr *) &serv_adr,
   |                  sizeof(serv_adr)) < 0){
  30          perror("bind error");
   |          close(orig_sock);
   |          return 3;
   |        }
   |        if (listen(orig_sock, 5) < 0 ) {                  // LISTEN
   +          perror("listen error");
   |          close (orig_sock);
   |          return 4;
   |        }
   |        do {
  40          clnt_len = sizeof(clnt_adr);                    // ACCEPT a connect
   |          if ((new_sock = accept( orig_sock, (struct sockaddr *) &clnt_adr,
   |                          &clnt_len)) < 0) {
   |            perror("accept error");
   |            close(orig_sock);
   +            return 5;
   |          }
   |          if ( fork( ) == 0 ) {                           // Generate a CHILD
   |            while ( (len=read(new_sock, buf, BUFSIZ)) > 0 ){
   |              for (i=0; i < len; ++i)                      // Change the case
  50              buf[i] = toupper(buf[i]);
   |              write(new_sock, buf, len);                  // Write back to socket
   |              if ( buf[0] == '.' ) break;                 // Are we done yet?
   |            }
   |            close(new_sock);                              // In CHILD process
```

411

```
+            return 0;
|         } else
|            close(new_sock);                      // In PARENT process
|      } while( true );                             // FOREVER
|      return 0;
60   }
|    void
|    signal_catcher(int the_sig){
|      signal(the_sig, signal_catcher);            // reset
|      wait(0);                                     // keep the zombies at bay
+    }
```

The server program contains a few new bells and whistles that were not in our previous examples. The server process forks a child process to handle each connection. When the child process ends, the operating system will want to return the exiting status of the child to its parent. Normally, the parent process waits for the child. As multiple connections (producing multiple child processes) are possible, we do not want the parent (the server process) to block, which is the default for **wait**, for a given child process. To resolve this, we associate the receipt of a SIGCHLD signal (child process has terminated) with a signal-catching routine (see lines 15 to 18). When invoked, the signal-catching routine performs the **wait**. This arrangement prevents a child process from becoming a zombie while it waits for the parent process to retrieve its returned status information. Also, notice the use of the **memset** library function in line 23 to clear the address structure before its contents are assigned.[11] When assigning the address member of the server structure, the address is first passed to htonl. In this example, the server passes the defined constant INADDR_ANY, found in the header file <netinet/in.h>, to **htonl**. This constant, which is mapped to the value 0, indicates to the server that any address of socket type (SOCK_STREAM) will be acceptable. The client program is shown in Program 10.7.

Program 10.7   The Internet domain, connection-oriented **client**.

```
File : p10.7.cxx
|    /*
|         Internet domain, connection-oriented CLIENT
|    */
|    #include "local_sock.h"
+    int
|    main( int argc, char *argv[] ) {
|      int          orig_sock,              // Original socket in client
```

---

[11] An alternate approach is to use **bzero**, a strictly BSD string function, to fill the location with NULL bytes. However, **bzero** is a deprecated function and should not be used if portability is a concern. If **bzero** is used, the <string.h> file should be included.

```
  |                    len;                    // Misc. counter
  |        struct sockaddr_in
 10                       serv_adr;            // Internet addr of server
  |        struct hostent  *host;              // The host (server) info
  |        if ( argc != 2 ) {                  // Check cmd line for host name
  |          cerr << "usage: " << argv[0] << " server" << endl;
  |          return 1;
  +        }
  |        host = gethostbyname(argv[1]);      // Obtain host (server) info
  |        if (host == (struct hostent *) NULL ) {
  |          perror("gethostbyname ");
  |          return 2;
 20        }
  |        memset(&serv_adr, 0, sizeof( serv_adr));      // Clear structure
  |        serv_adr.sin_family = AF_INET;               // Set address type
  |        memcpy(&serv_adr.sin_addr, host->h_addr, host->h_length);
  |        serv_adr.sin_port   = htons( PORT );          // Use our fake port
  +                                             // SOCKET
  |        if ((orig_sock = socket(PF_INET, SOCK_STREAM, 0)) < 0) {
  |          perror("generate error");
  |          return 3;
  |        }                                   // CONNECT
 30        if (connect( orig_sock,(struct sockaddr *)&serv_adr,
  |                    sizeof(serv_adr)) < 0) {
  |          perror("connect error");
  |          return 4;
  |        }
  +        do {                                // Process
  |          write(fileno(stdout),"> ", 3);
  |          if ((len=read(fileno(stdin), buf, BUFSIZ)) > 0) {
  |            write(orig_sock, buf, len);
  |            if ((len=read(orig_sock, buf, len)) > 0 )
 40              write(fileno(stdout), buf, len);
  |          }
  |        } while( buf[0] != '.' );           // until end of input
  |        close(orig_sock);
  |        return 0;
  +      }
```

The client program expects the name of a server (host) to be passed on the command line. The **gethostbyname** network call is used to obtain specific host-addressing information. The returned information, stored in the hostent structure, is referenced by *host. This information is used in part to fill the server Internet address information stored in the serv_adr structure. Before its members are assigned, the serv_adr structure is cleared using the **memset** library function. The address family is set to AF_INET. The **memcpy** library function is used to copy the obtained host address to the server address member.

The **memcpy** function is used, as it will copy a specified number of bytes even if the referenced locations contain nonstandard strings (i.e., contain NULLs or do not end in a NULL). The assignment of the port number is similar to what was done in the server.

Next, a socket is created and a connection to the server process established. The client process then enters an endless loop. In the loop it requests user input with a > prompt. The user's input is read from the device mapped to standard input (most likely the keyboard). This input is then written to the socket where the server will read and process it (i.e., capitalize the string). The client process obtains the processed string by reading from the socket descriptor. The contents of this string (stored in the buf array) are written to the device mapped to standard output (usually the screen). The client continues to loop until a string that begins with a "." is entered.

A sample run of the Internet domain, connection-oriented client–server application is shown in Figure 10.13.

Figure 10.13 A run of the Internet domain, connection-oriented client–server application.

```
linux$ ps
  PID TTY         TIME CMD                          We check the system for the
21604 pts/0    00:00:00 csh                         server process—none is present.
23026 pts/0    00:00:00 3

linux ./server &                                    The server is placed in the
[1] 23028                                           background.

linux$ ./server &                                   The server has already bound the
bind error: Address already in use                  address.
[2] 23029
[2]  - Exit 2                    ./server

linux$ telnet medusa                                Run a terminal session on another
                                                    local host.
. . .
                                                    Run the client; pass the name of
medusa$ ./client linux                              the host (linux) that is running
                                                    the server process.
> this is a test of the system
THIS IS A TEST OF THE SYSTEM
> .
.

medusa$ ps
  PID TTY         TIME CMD
23095 pts/0    00:00:00 csh
23387 pts/0    00:00:00 ps
```

In this sequence, the user has logged onto the host `linux` and issued the `ps` command. The output of the command verifies that no server process is present. The server process is then invoked and explicitly placed in the background with the `&`. When the server is invoked a second time, the error message `bind error: Address already in use` is displayed. This message is generated by the call to **bind** because the previous invocation of the server program has already bound the port. The user then runs **telnet** to log onto another host on the network (`medusa`) and changes to the directory where the client–server application resides. The client program is invoked and passed the name of the host running the server program (in this example, `linux`). When the prompt appears, a line of text is entered. The client process passes the text to the server. The server, running on the host `linux`, processes the line of text and returns it to the client on host `medusa`. The client process displays the line (the initial line, which now is in all capitals). The application terminates with the entry of a line starting with a single period. A follow-up call to **ps** indicates the client process is gone.

10-8   EXERCISE

Modify Programs 10.6 and 10.7 to play a remote game of tic-tac-toe. The client (the user) will play against the server (the computer). The client (who goes first) requests the user enter a valid location. The location is stored in the representation of board. The board is then passed to the server. The server then generates a valid move [tries first to win; if it cannot win, then block; if no block is required, it moves randomly]. The server's move is stored in the board, the board is returned to the client, and so on. The client is responsible for validating a user's requested move, displaying the board, and determining a win, loss, or tie. The server should have separate routines to generate a winning, blocking, or random move. The server should always generate a valid move. The server should create a separate process for each connected client. *Note*: As a starting point, a PC platform executable version (authored by a former student: Mark Cormier) of this exercise can be found with the files for this chapter. The files are called `toe_server` and `toe_client`.

10-9 EXERCISE

Further modify the tic-tac-toe game to allow two users to play against one another by connecting to a separate tic-tac-toe arbitrator process (server). Offload some of the common functions, such as checking for a win, loss, or tie, who goes first, and whose turn is next, to the arbitrator process.

10.5 Sockets: The Connectionless Paradigm

The sequence of events for connectionless client–server communication has some common elements with connection-oriented communication. Both the client and server still generate sockets using the **socket** call. The server and, most often, the client, **bind** their sockets to an address. However, in the connection-oriented sequence, *only* the server performs this step. The client process does not use

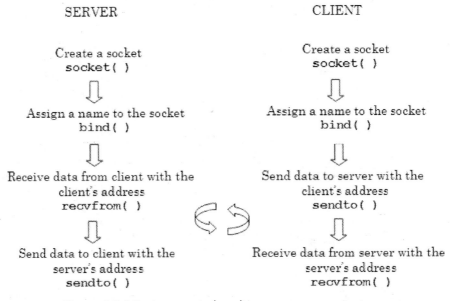

Figure 10.14 A connectionless client–server communication sequence.

connect to establish a connection with the server. Instead, both the server and client send and receive datagram packets to and from a specified address. The server process sends its packets to the client address, and the client sends its packets to the server address. These events are shown in Figure 10.14.

In this example, we have used the **sendto** and **recvfrom** system calls for data exchange. The **sendto** call in the client is somewhat similar in function to the **connect-write** sequence we saw in the initial Internet domain connection-oriented example. Similarly, the **recvfrom** call is analogous to the **accept-read** sequence we used for the server in the same example.

The **sendto** call is one of several alternate ways to write data to a socket. Table 10.19 provides a summary of three calls that can write data to a socket descriptor.

Table 10.19 Summary of the `send`, `sendto`, and `sendmsg` System Calls.

Include File(s)	`<sys/types.h>` `<sys/socket.h>`	Manual Section	**2**
Summary	<pre>int send (int s, const void *msg,size_t len, int flags); int sendto (int s,const void *msg, size_t len, int flags, const struct sockaddr *to, socklen_t tolen); int sendmsg(int s, const struct msghdr *msg, int flags);</pre>		

	Success	Failure	Sets `errno`
Return	Number of bytes sent.	−1	Yes

The **send** call, since it contains no destination addressing information, can only be used with connected (SOCK_STREAM) sockets. The **sendto** and **sendmsg** calls can be used with either socket type but are most commonly used with datagram sockets (SOCK_DGRAM). The **send** and **sendto** calls dispatch a sequence of bytes. The **sendmsg** call is used to transmit data that resides in noncontiguous (scattered) memory locations (such as in a structure).

In all three calls, the integer argument s is a valid socket descriptor. The *msg argument references the message to be sent. In the **sendmsg** call, the msg reference is to a structure of type msghdr that contains additional addressing/messaging information.[12] This structure is defined as

---

[12] As its use is rather complex, we will only mention **sendmsg** (and its reciprocal **recvmsg**) in passing (no pun intended!).

```
struct msghdr {
    void        *msg_name;      /* optional address          */
    socklen_t   msg_namelen;    /* size of address           */
    struct iovec *msg_iov;      /* scatter/gather array       */
    size_t      msg_iovlen;     /* # elements in msg_iov      */
    void        *msg_control;   /* ancillary data, see below */
    socklen_t   msg_controllen; /* ancillary data buffer len */
    int         msg_flags;      /* flags on received message */
};
```

where the type `iovec` is

```
struct iovec  {
    void *iov_base;    /* Pointer to data.  */
    size_t iov_len;    /* Length of data.   */
};
```

The `len` argument is the length of the message to send. Message size is limited by the underlying protocol. The **sendto** call contains an additional argument that references the address structure with the information of where to send the message. With **sendto** this argument is followed by an argument containing the size of the addressing structure. If **sendto** is used with a connection-oriented socket, these two arguments are ignored. All three calls have an integer-based `flag` argument. Bitwise ORing the value 0 with one or more of the defined constants in Table 10.20 generates the `flag` value.

Table 10.20 Flags for the `send`, `sendto`, and `sendmsg` Calls.

Flag	Meaning
MSG_OOB	Message out of band. At present this flag is valid only for Internet stream-based sockets. Specifying MSG_OOB allows the process to send *urgent* data. The receiving process can choose to ignore the message.
MSG_DONTROUTE	Bypass routing tables and attempt to send message in one hop. This is often used for diagnostics purposes.
MSG_DONTWAIT	Adopt non-blocking operation for operations that block return EAGAIN.
MSG_NOSIGNAL	On stream-based socket do not send a SIGPIPE error when one end of connection is broken.
MSG_CONFIRM	With SOCK_DGRAM and SOCK_RAW sockets, in Linux 2.3+, notify the link layer of successful reply from the other side.

In some settings when the above calls are used, the network and socket library must be specified. In such settings use the `-lnsl` and/or `-lsocket` compiler option to notify the linker. These calls return the number of bytes sent or, in case of error, a −1, setting `errno` to one of the values found in Table 10.21. Data sent to an unbound socket is discarded.

Table 10.21 `send`, `sendto`, and `sendmsg` Error Messages.

#	Constant	perror Message	Explanation
4	EINTR	Interrupted system call	A signal was received by the process before data was sent.
9	EBADF	Bad file descriptor	The socket reference is invalid.
11	EWOULDBLOCK, EAGAIN	Resource temporarily unavailable	The socket is set to non-blocking, and no connections are pending.
12	ENOMEM	Cannot allocate memory	Insufficient memory to perform operation.
14	EFAULT	Bad address	Argument references location outside user address space.
22	EINVAL	Invalid argument	`tolen` argument contains an incorrect value.
32	EPIPE	Broken pipe	Local end of a connection-oriented socket is closed.
88	ENOTSOCK	Socket operation on non-socket	The socket argument is a file descriptor, not a socket descriptor.
90	EMSGSIZE	Message too long	Socket type requires message to be sent to be atomic (all sent at once) and the message to send is too long.
105	ENOBUFS	No buffer space available	Output queue is full.

Other than **read**, there are three system calls comparable to send for receiving data from a socket descriptor. These calls are **recv**, **recvfrom**, and **recvmsg**. Unless otherwise specified (such as with **fcntl**), these calls will block if no message has arrived at the socket. Table 10.22 provides a summary of these calls.

Since it contains no sender address information, the **recv** network call should only be used with connection-oriented (SOCK_STREAM) sockets. The **recvfrom** and **recvmsg** calls can be used with connection-oriented or connectionless sockets. Usually, when data is written to a socket with **send**, **sendto**, or **sendmsg**, it is read with the corresponding **recv**, **recvfrom**, or **recvmsg** call.

Table 10.22 Summary of the `recv`, `recvfrom`, and `recvmsg` System Calls.

Include File(s)	`<sys/types.h>` `<sys/socket.h>`		Manual Section	**2**

Summary	`int recv(int s, void *buf, size_t len, int flags);`
	`int recvfrom(int s, void *buf, size_t len,`
	`    int flags, struct sockaddr *from, socklen_t`
	`    *fromlen);`
	`int recvmsg(int s, struct msghdr *msg, int flags);`			

	Success	Failure	Sets `errno`	
Return	Number of bytes received	−1	Yes	

In each call, the integer argument `s` is a valid socket descriptor. The `*buffer` argument references the location where the received message will be stored. The user is responsible for allocating the storage space for the received message. As with the **sendmsg** network call, the `*msg` argument for **recvmsg** references a `msghdr` structure. The `len` argument is the length of the receive message buffer. Remember that the message size is limited by the underlying protocol and exceedingly long messages may be truncated. The receive calls return the actual number of bytes received. If the `*from`

Table 10.23 Flags for the `recv`, `recvfrom`, and `recvmsg` Calls.

Flag	Meaning
MSG_ERRQUEUE	Receive error messages from the error message queue. The details of how to implement error message retrieval is beyond the scope of this text (see the manual page on **recv** for specifics).
MSG_NOSIGNAL	With a stream socket, do not raise a SIGPIPE error when the other end of the socket disappears.
MSG_OOB	Message out of band. At present, this flag is valid only for Internet stream-based sockets. Specifying MSG_OOB allows the process to read *urgent* out-of-band data.
MSG_PEEK	Look at the current data but do not consume it. Subsequent **read**-receive type calls will retrieve the same *peeked*-at data.
MSG_TRUNC	With datagram socket, return the real length of the message even if it exceeds specified amount.
MSG_WAITALL	Wait until the full request for data has been satisfied.

argument for the **recvfrom** call is not NULL, it should reference a sock-addr structure containing the address information of the host that sent the message. The *fromlen argument should reference the length of this addressing structure. ORing the value 0 with one or more of the defined flags shown in Table 10.23 forms the flag argument.

In cases of error, these calls will return a −1 and set errno to one of the values found in Table 10.24.

Table 10.24   recv, recvfrom, and recvmsg Error Messages

#	Constant	perror **Message**	**Explanation**
4	EINTR	Interrupted system call	A signal was received by process before data was received.
9	EBADF	Bad file descriptor	The socket reference is invalid.
11	EAGAIN	Resource temporarily unavailable	• The socket is set to non-blocking, and no connections are pending. • Timer expired before data was received.
14	EFAULT	Bad address	Argument references a location outside user address space.
22	EINVAL	Invalid argument	An argument contains incorrect value.
88	ENOTSOCK	Socket operation on non-socket	The socket argument is a file descriptor, not a socket descriptor.
107	ENOTCONN	Transport endpoint is not connected	A connection-oriented socket has not been connected.
111	ECONNREFUSED	Connection refused	Remote host has refused the connection request.

10.5.1 A UNIX Domain Datagram Socket Example

Our UNIX domain datagram socket example is somewhat similar in function to the stream socket example presented in Section 10.4. In this example, the server creates a datagram socket (SOCK_DGRAM) in the UNIX domain and binds it to an address (file name). The client also creates a datagram socket and binds it to an address (using a different file name, unique to each client process). The client and server use the **sendto** and **recvfrom** network calls for communication. The client generates 10 messages (the output of the /usr/games/ fortune utility), which are sent to the server. The server displays the messages that it has received. The code for the server process is shown in Program 10.8.

Program 10.8 The UNIX domain connectionless **server**.

```
File : p10.8.cxx
  |       /*
  |               SERVER - UNIX domain - connectionless
  |       */
  |       #include "local_sock.h"
  +
  |       void clean_up(int, const char *);       // Close socket and remove
  |       int
  |       main(  ) {
  |         socklen_t       clnt_len;             // Length of client address
 10       int             orig_sock;            // Original socket descriptor
  |       static struct sockaddr_un
  |                               clnt_adr,        // Client address
  |                               serv_adr;        // Server address
  |       static char       buf[BUFSIZ];          // Buffer for messages
  +                                               // Generate socket
  |       if ((orig_sock = socket(PF_UNIX, SOCK_DGRAM, 0)) < 0) {
  |         perror("generate error");
  |         return 1;
  |       }                                       // Assign address information
 20       serv_adr.sun_family = AF_UNIX;
  |       strcpy(serv_adr.sun_path,SERVER_FILE);
  |       unlink( SERVER_FILE);                   // Remove old copy if present
  |                                               // BIND the address
  |       if (bind(orig_sock, (struct sockaddr *) &serv_adr,
  +             sizeof(serv_adr.sun_family)+strlen(serv_adr.sun_path)) < 0) {
  |        perror("bind error");
  |         clean_up(orig_sock, SERVER_FILE);
  |         return 2;
  |       }                                       // Process
 30       for (int i = 1; i <= 10; i++) {
  |         recvfrom(orig_sock, buf, sizeof(buf), 0,
  |             (struct sockaddr *) &clnt_adr, &clnt_len);
  |         cout << "S receives " << buf;
  |       }
  +       clean_up(orig_sock, SERVER_FILE);
  |       return 0;
  |     }
  |     void
  |     clean_up( int sd, const char *the_file ){
 40       close( sd );                            // Close socket
  |       unlink( the_file );                     // Remove it
  |     }
```

The code for the client process is shown in Program 10.9.

Program 10.9 The UNIX domain connectionless **client**.

```
File : p10.9.cxx
 |      /*
 |              CLIENT - UNIX domain - connectionless
 |      */
 |      #include "local_sock.h"
 +
 |      void clean_up(int, const char *);      // Close socket and remove
 |      int
 |      main( ) {
 |        int            orig_sock;            // Original socket descriptor
10        static struct sockaddr_un             // UNIX addresses to be used
 |                       clnt_adr,              // Client address
 |                       serv_adr;              // Server address
 |        static char    clnt_buf[BUFSIZ],      // Message from client
 |                       pipe_buf[BUFSIZ],      // Output from fortune command
 +                       clnt_file[]="XXXXXX";// Temporary file name
 |        FILE           *fin;                  // File for pipe I/O
 |                                              // Assign SERVER address
 |                                              information
 |        serv_adr.sun_family = AF_UNIX;
 |        strcpy(serv_adr.sun_path, SERVER_FILE);
20        if ((orig_sock = socket(PF_UNIX, SOCK_DGRAM, 0)) < 0) {
 |          perror("generate error");
 |          return 1;
 |        }
 |        mkstemp(clnt_file);
 +        clnt_adr.sun_family = AF_UNIX;         // Assign CLIENT address
 |                                              information
 |        strcpy( clnt_adr.sun_path, clnt_file );
 |        unlink( clnt_file );                  // Remove
 |                                              // BIND the address
 |        if (bind(orig_sock, (struct sockaddr *) &clnt_adr,
30              sizeof(clnt_adr.sun_family)+strlen(clnt_adr.sun_path)) < 0) {
 |          perror("bind error");
 |          return 2;
 |        }                                     // Process
 |        for (int i=0; i < 10; i++) {
 +          sleep(1);                           // slow things down a bit
 |          fin = popen("/usr/games/fortune -s", "r");
 |          memset( pipe_buf, 0x0, BUFSIZ );   // clear buffer before reading
 |                                              cmd output
 |          read( fileno(fin), pipe_buf, BUFSIZ );
 |          sprintf( clnt_buf, "%d : %s", getpid(), pipe_buf );
40          sendto( orig_sock, clnt_buf, sizeof(clnt_buf), 0,
 |                  (struct sockaddr *) &serv_adr, sizeof(struct sockaddr) );
 |        }
 |        clean_up( orig_sock, clnt_file );
```

```
  |        return 0;
  +      }
  |      void
  |      clean_up( int sd, const char *the_file ){
  |        close( sd );
  |        unlink( the_file );
 50      }
```

In the client, the **mkstemp** library function is used to generate a unique file name to be bound to the client's socket. This function is passed a template of XXXXXX that is replaced by a unique file name. The function also opens the file. As only the file name is needed, the file itself can be removed (**unlinked**). If there are multiple clients communicating with the server, it is *imperative* that each has its own unique file name for binding.

A standard compilation/output sequence using this client–server pair is shown in Figure 10.15.

Figure 10.15 Compiling and running the UNIX domain connectionless client–server application.

```
linux$ g++ p10.8.cxx -o server
linux$ g++ p10.9.cxx -o client
linux$ ./server &
[3] 31801
linux$ ./client

S receives 31802 : Go to a movie tonight.  Darkness becomes you.
S receives 31802 : Out of sight is out of mind.
S receives 31802 : Q: What's tan and black and looks great on a lawyer?
                   A: A doberman.
. . .
[3]    Done                             server
```

Figure 10.16 shows what happens if we run two clients and use the **ls** command to check for the file names to which the client and server sockets are bound. Notice that the server still processes 10 messages. However, it receives half of the messages from one client and half from the other. No error message is generated when the clients continue to send their data to the unbound (closed) server socket.

Figure 10.16 Running the same application with multiple clients.

```
linux$ ./server &
[1] 32244
linux$ ./client & ./client & ls -l | grep ^s          Unique file names
[2] 32248                                             ╱generated for client sockets.
[3] 32249
srwxr-xr-x    1 gray     faculty      0 May 17 09:37 eUcOXq
```

```
srwxr-xr-x   1 gray    faculty    0 May 17 09:37 qOC0Tq
srwxr-xr-x   1 gray    faculty    0 May 17 09:37 server_socket

S receives 31754 : Anything worth doing is worth overdoing.
S receives 31755 : Marriage causes dating problems.
S receives 31754 : A handful of patience is worth more than a bushel of brains.
S receives 31755 : OK, so you're a Ph.D.  Just don't touch anything.
. . .

[3]  - Done                    ./client
[2]  - Done                    ./client
[1]  + Done                    ./server
```

10-10 EXERCISE

It was a slow night, and Frick and Frack were discussing UNIX domain connectionless sockets. Frick noted that he thought that the code for the client,
given as Program 10.9, was *excessive*. Frick's client code (about 20 lines less)
is shown below.

```
File : frick.cxx
  |      /*
  |             Frick's CLIENT - UNIX domain - connectionless
  |      */
  |      #include "local_sock.h"
  +
  |      int
  |      main( ) {
  |        int            orig_sock;
  |        static struct sockaddr_un
 10                       serv_adr;
  |        static char    clnt_buf[BUFSIZ],
  |                       pipe_buf[BUFSIZ];
  |        FILE           *fin;
  |
  +        if ((orig_sock = socket(PF_UNIX, SOCK_DGRAM, 0)) < 0) {
  |          perror("generate error");
  |          return 1;
  |        }
  |        serv_adr.sun_family = AF_UNIX;
 20        strcpy( serv_adr.sun_path, SERVER_FILE );
  |        for (int i=0; i < 10; i++) {
  |          sleep(1);
  |          fin = popen("/usr/games/fortune -s", "r");
  |          memset( pipe_buf, 0x0, BUFSIZ );
```

Continued

425

```
   +          read( fileno(fin), pipe_buf, BUFSIZ );
   |          sprintf( clnt_buf, "%d : %s", getpid(), pipe_buf );
   |          sendto( orig_sock, clnt_buf, sizeof(clnt_buf), 0,
   |                  (struct sockaddr *) &serv_adr, sizeof(struct
   |                  sockaddr) );
   |      }
  30      return 0;
   |  }
```

Does Frick's client code work with Program 10.8 as the server? If Frick's code works, what are its limitations? If it does not work, what must be done to make it work?

10.5.2 An Internet Domain Datagram Socket Example

In the next example, we create a client–server application that uses connectionless sockets. This application will act like a rudimentary **chat** program. A user running the server process can interactively **read** messages from and **write** messages to the user running the client program, and vice versa. When this application is run, the server program is invoked first and remains in the foreground. At startup, the server displays the port to which the client should **bind**. The client program, also run in the foreground, can be on a different host or in a separate window on the same host, and is passed on the command line the name of the host where the server process is executing and the port number. Once both processes are up and running, the user on the client enters a line of text and presses enter. The client's input is displayed on the screen of the server. The user running the server process then enters a response that in turn is displayed on the screen of the client, and so on. In a regimented lockstep, send and receive manner, the two users can carry on a very basic form of interactive communication.[13] The client process terminates when the user enters a ^D. The server, which is iterative, continues until removed with a **kill** command. The program for the server process is shown in Program 10.10.

Program 10.10 Internet domain connectionless **server**.

```
File : p10.10.cxx
   |    /*
   |          Program 10.10 - SERVER - Internet Domain - connectionless
   |    */
```

---

[13] Granted, this will never replace the **talk** utility, IRC, or some of the current instant messaging applications, but it could serve as a base for a more sophisticated application.

```
  |     #include "local_sock.h"
  +     int
  |     main(  ) {
  |       int                sock, n;
  |       socklen_t          server_len, client_len;
  |       struct sockaddr_in server,              // Internet Addresses
 10                          client;
  |                                               // SOCKET
  |       if ((sock = socket(PF_INET, SOCK_DGRAM, 0)) < 0) {
  |         perror("SERVER socket "); return 1;
  |       }
  +       memset(&server, 0, sizeof(server));  // Clear structure
  |       server.sin_family    = AF_INET;     // Set address type
  |       server.sin_addr.s_addr = htonl(INADDR_ANY);
  |       server.sin_port      = htons(0);
  |                                               // BIND
 20       if (bind(sock, (struct sockaddr *) &server,
  |           sizeof(server) ) < 0) {
  |         perror("SERVER bind "); return 2;
  |       }
  |       server_len = sizeof(server);        // Obtain  address length
  +                                           // Find picked port #
  |       if (getsockname(sock, (struct sockaddr *) &server,
  |           &server_len) < 0) {
  |         perror("SERVER getsocketname "); return 3;
  |       }
 30       cout << "Server using port " << ntohs(server.sin_port) << endl;
  |       while ( 1 ) {                             // Loop forever
  |         client_len = sizeof(client);          // set the length
  |         memset(buf, 0, BUFSIZ);               // clear the buffer
  |         if ((n=recvfrom(sock, buf, BUFSIZ, 0,    // get the client's msg
  +             (struct sockaddr *) &client, &client_len)) < 0){
  |          perror("SERVER recvfrom ");
  |          close(sock); return 4;
  |         }
  |         write(fileno(stdout), buf, n);              // display msg on
  |                                                     server
 40         memset(buf, 0, BUFSIZ);               // clear the buffer
  |         if ( read(fileno(stdin), buf, BUFSIZ) != 0 ){// get server's msg
  |           if ((sendto(sock, buf, strlen(buf) ,0,    // send to client
  |             (struct sockaddr *) &client, client_len)) <0){
  |             perror("SERVER sendto ");
  +             close(sock); return 5;
  |           }
  |         }
  |       }
  |       return 0;
 50     }
```

Keep in mind that for communications to occur between cooperating processes, a unique association must be established. In the Internet domain, the association is characterized by a quintuple consisting of

protocol, local address, local port, remote address, remote port

In the server program, a datagram (connectionless) socket is created with the **socket** call. The address family is set to AF_INET, and by default the protocol (which was set to 0) will be UDP. The addressing information for the server is assigned next. The defined constant INADDR_ANY, a wildcard address, indicates the server can use (receive messages at) any valid address for this protocol. Setting the port number to 0 (line 18) directs the system to select a port. When passed a 0 value, the system picks a port that is not in use and is greater than IPPORT_USERRESERVED. On our system this constant is set to 5000. Additional information about port numbers is stored in the file `ip_local_port_range` found in the `/proc/sys/net/ipv4` subdirectory. The first value stored in this file is the number of the first local port for TCP and UDP traffic on the system. The second value is the last local port number. On our system this files contains the values 32768 and 61000.

The **getsockname** call (line 26) is issued to determine which port the system selected. Note it is important to initialize the third argument of this call to the length of the address argument before the call to **getsockname** is made (see line 24). The server process displays the port number so a user running a client process will know which port to specify (a more elegant solution would be to store the port number in an environment varible). The server program then enters an endless loop. It clears a receiving buffer and issues a **recvfrom** call. The **recvfrom** call will, by default, cause the server process to block until information is received. Once information is received, the remaining parts of the association, the remote address and port, are realized, as this information is contained in the received data. The received message is written to standard output (the screen). The server then clears the buffer and collects the user's response with a call to **read**. Again, **read** will cause the serving process to block while awaiting input. If the user enters a non-null response, the **sendto** call is used to send the response to the address/port of the client from which the message was received. The server process remains active until removed with a **kill** command or an interrupt (^C) is entered from the keyboard.

As noted, when the client program is invoked, the name of the host running the server process and the port on the server is passed on the command line. The client then uses the **gethostbyname** call to obtain additional information about the server. This information, along with the passed port number, is stored in the server socket address structure of the client. In an Internet domain setting, a datagram socket is created next, the client addressing information is set, and a call to **bind** is issued. At this juncture, the client process has sufficient information to initiate communications with the server process. The client enters a loop. The **read** call is used to obtain user input. If user input does not indicate an end-of-file condition (i.e., the user has not entered ^D), the input is sent to the serving process with the **sendto** call. The receiving buffer is then cleared, and a call to **recvfrom** retrieves the response from the user running the server program. The response is displayed to the screen, the buffer cleared, and the loop repeated. If the user running the client process enters ^D, the processing loop is exited, the socket is closed, and the client process terminates.

In this example, the conventions for client–server communications are extremely regimented. The server process is always started first. The client process must be passed the name of the host running the server process and the proper port number. The client process obtains its user input first, which it then sends to the server. The user running the server process then responds. The user running the client responds to this response, and so on. As can be seen, there is a lot of room for improvement in this application! The code for the client is shown in Program 10.11.

Program 10.11 Internet domain connectionless **client**.

```
File : p10.11.cxx
   |    /*
   |          Program 10.11 - CLIENT - Internet Domain - connectionless
   |      */
   |    #include "local_sock.h"
   +    int
   |    main(int argc, char *argv[]){
   |      int           sock, n;
   |      socklen_t     server_len;
   |      struct sockaddr_in              // Internet addresses
  10                    server, client;
   |      struct hostent *host;           // For host information
   |      if ( argc < 3 ) {               // We need server name & port #
   |        cerr << "usage: " << argv[0] << "server_name   port_#" << endl;
   |        return 1;
   +      }                               // Server information
   |      if (!(host=gethostbyname(argv[1]))){
   |        perror("CLIENT gethostname ");  return 2;
   |      }                               // Set server address info
   |      memset(&server, 0, sizeof(server));  // Clear structure
  20      server.sin_family = AF_INET;        // Address type
   |      memcpy(&server.sin_addr, host->h_addr, host->h_length);
   |      server.sin_port   = htons(atoi(argv[2]));
   |                                          // SOCKET
   |      if ((sock=socket(PF_INET, SOCK_DGRAM, 0)) < 0 ) {
```

```
  +          perror("CLIENT socket "); return 3;
  |        }                                        // Set client address info
  |        memset(&client, 0, sizeof(client));   // Clear structure
  |        client.sin_family     = AF_INET;      // Address type
  |        client.sin_addr.s_addr = htonl(INADDR_ANY);
 30        client.sin_port       = htons( 0 );
  |                                                 // BIND
  |        if (bind(sock, (struct sockaddr *) &client,
  |            sizeof(client)) < 0) {
  |          perror("CLIENT bind "); return 4;
  +        }
  |        cout << "Client must send first message." << endl;
  |        while( read(fileno(stdin), buf, BUFSIZ) != 0 ){// get client's msg
  |          server_len=sizeof(server);                // length of address
  |          if (sendto( sock, buf, strlen(buf), 0,       // send msg to server
 40          (struct sockaddr *) &server, server_len) < 0 ){
  |             perror("CLIENT sendto ");
  |             close(sock); return 5;
  |          }
  |          memset(buf,0,BUFSIZ);                     // clear the buffer
  +          if ((n=recvfrom(sock, buf, BUFSIZ, 0,      // get server's msg
  |             (struct sockaddr *) &server, &server_len)) < 0){
  |           perror("CLIENT recvfrom ");
  |           close(sock); return 6;
  |          }
 50        write( fileno(stdout), buf, n );            // display msg on client
  |          memset(buf,0,BUFSIZ);                      // clear the buffer
  |        }
  |        close(sock);
  |        return 0;
  +      }
```

A sample compilation and run of this application is shown in Figure 10.17.

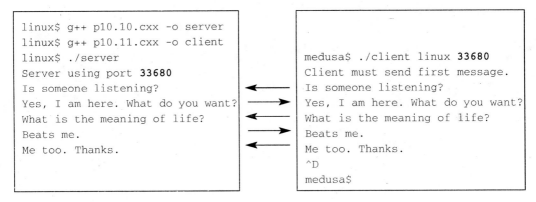

```
linux$ g++ p10.10.cxx -o server
linux$ g++ p10.11.cxx -o client
linux$ ./server                          medusa$ ./client linux 33680
Server using port 33680                  Client must send first message.
Is someone listening?              ◄──── Is someone listening?
Yes, I am here. What do you want?  ────► Yes, I am here. What do you want?
What is the meaning of life?       ◄──── What is the meaning of life?
Beats me.                          ────► Beats me.
Me too. Thanks.                    ◄──── Me too. Thanks.
                                         ^D
                                         medusa$
```

Figure 10.17 A run of Programs 10.10 and 10.11 using two different hosts.

Run the chat application presented in Program 10.10 and 10.11 with
multiple clients. To accomplish this, you will need either access to multiple hosts or the ability to create multiple windows on the same host.
Modify code for the client so that it initially requests a three-letter ID
(handle) from the user. To identify the source of each message, add the
handle to the beginning of all messages sent from the client to the server.

10.6 Multiplexing I/O with select

It is clear from the last example that when processes communicate, they need
a way to coordinate their activities other than blocking (waiting) for the recipient process to respond. One approach is to change the socket from its default
of blocking to non-blocking. The process could then perform its own
polling/checking at some designated interval to determine if I/O is pending.
This technique is shown in the modified server Program 10.12. The sections of
code that have been added or significantly modified are in bold in the gray
areas (lines 5, 6, 10, 18–20, and 42–49).

Program 10.12   Internet domain connectionless **server**, non-blocking.

```
File : p10.12.cxx
   |      /*
   |          Program 10.12 - SERVER Internet Domain - connectionless -
   |          NON-BLOCKING
   |      */
   |      #include "local_sock.h"
   +      #include <sys/ioctl.h>
   |      #include <errno.h>
   |      int
   |      main( ) {
   |        int                sock, n,
   10                          errcount=0, flag=1;
   |        socklen_t          server_len, client_len;
   |        struct sockaddr_in server,              // Internet Addresses
   |                           client;
   |                                                // SOCKET
```

```
  +       if ((sock = socket(PF_INET, SOCK_DGRAM, 0)) < 0) {
  |         perror("SERVER socket "); return 1;
  |       }
  |       if (ioctl(sock, FIONBIO, &flag) < 0 ) {
  |         perror("SERVER ioctl "); return 2;
 20       }
  |       memset(&server, 0, sizeof(server));   // Clear structure
  |       server.sin_family     = AF_INET;      // Set address type
  |       server.sin_addr.s_addr = htonl(INADDR_ANY);
  |       server.sin_port       = htons(0);
  +                                             // BIND
  |       if (bind(sock, (struct sockaddr *) &server,
  |           sizeof(server) ) < 0) {
  |         perror("SERVER bind "); return 3;
  |       }
 30       server_len = sizeof(server);          // Obtain address length
  |                                             // Find picked port #
  |       if (getsockname(sock, (struct sockaddr *) &server,
  |           &server_len) < 0) {
  |         perror("SERVER getsocketname "); return 4;
  +       }
  |       cout << "Server using port " << ntohs(server.sin_port) << endl;
  |       while ( 1 ) {                         // Loop forever
  |         client_len = sizeof(client);        // estimate length
  |         memset(buf, 0, BUFSIZ);             // clear the buffer
 40         if ((n=recvfrom(sock, buf, BUFSIZ, 0,     // get the client's msg
  |             (struct sockaddr *) &client, &client_len)) < 0){
  |           if ( errcount++ > 60 || errno != EWOULDBLOCK ) {
  |             perror("SERVER recvfrom ");
  |             close(sock); return 5;
  +           }
  |           sleep(1);
  |           continue;
  |         }
  |         errcount = 0;
 50         write( fileno(stdout), buf, n );              // display msg on
  |                                                        server
  |         memset(buf, 0, BUFSIZ);                       // clear the buffer
  |         if ( read(fileno(stdin), buf, BUFSIZ) != 0 ){// get server's msg
  |           if ((sendto(sock, buf, strlen(buf) ,0,     // send to client
  |             (struct sockaddr *) &client, client_len)) <0){
  +             perror("SERVER sendto ");
  |             close(sock); return 6;
  |           }
  |         }
  |       }
 60       return 0;
  |     }
```

In this example, the **ioctl** system call is used to change the socket to non-blocking. The **ioctl** call performs a wide variety of file control operations.[14] Its actions are described fully in two parts of the manual: **ioctl** and **ioctl_list**, both found in Section 2 of the manual pages. The **ioctl** call is not the only way to set the socket to non-blocking. An alternate approach is to use the fcntl (file control) system call. If **fcntl** is used, the syntax would be

```
#include <unistd.h>                          // include for fcntl call
#include <fcntl.h>
. . .
if (fcntl(sock, F_SETFL, FNDELAY) < 0 ) { // new lines 18-20
   perror("SERVER fcntl "); return 2;
   }
. . .
```

In Program 10.12, the file <sys/ioctl.h> is added to the include section. This file contains defined constants used by the **ioctl** system call. In the program we also reference errno and use one of the defined constants found in the include file <errno.h>. Once the socket is created, the **ioctl** call is employed to change the socket status to non-blocking. The **ioctl** call is passed the socket descriptor, the defined constant FIONBIO (signifying file I/O non-blocking I/O), and the address of an integer flag. If the **ioctl** call is successful, it returns a nonnegative value.

The processing loop of the server is modified to introduce a limited form of polling. If a message is not available, and fewer than 60 receive attempts have been made, the process will **sleep** and try again. When the socket is set to non-blocking, the **recvfrom** call returns immediately if no message is available. When this occurs, the external variable errno is set to EWOULDBLOCK, indicating the call would have blocked. As written, when the error code returned by **recvfrom** is EWOULDBLOCK, and the number of attempts to receive a message is less than 60, the process issues a call to **sleep** for one second. Once a message is received, the error count is reset to 0 and the message is processed as before. If **recvfrom** returns an error code other than EWOULDBLOCK, or the number of attempts to receive a message exceeds 60, an error message is generated and the process is exited. The number of times to retry and the amount of sleep time are arbitrary and can be adjusted by trial and error to meet specific needs.

While the above approach is both interesting and functional, it has all the drawbacks of any code that implements its own polling. It would seem that communication coordination would be greatly improved if a process could somehow notify a recipient process that a message was available. For example,

---

[14] I realize that this is a departure from the normal approach (i.e., a full explanation of the system call once it is encountered/used). The **ioctl** system call is complex, and as we will be using it only in passing, the details of its syntax and use have been omitted.

we could signal a process when a socket has data to be read. To do this, the process receiving the signal must establish a signal handler for the SIGIO signal. Second, it must associate its process ID with the socket. Third, the socket must be set to allow asynchronous I/O. While all this is possible (using the **signal** and **fcntl** system calls), it too is less than desirable. Signals can get lost, and should multiple processes be involved in the communication process, coding can become quite complex. When possible, it is best to allow the system to handle the details of notifying processes that I/O is pending. The **select** library call can be used for this purpose. The **select** call, as shown in Table 10.25, is fairly complex.

Table 10.25 Summary of the **select** System Call.

Include File(s)	`<sys/time.h>` `<sys/types.h>` `<unistd.h>`		Manual Section	2
Summary	`int select( int n, fd_set *readfds, fd_set *writefds, fd_set *exceptfds, struct timeval *timeout );`			
Return	Success		Failure	Sets errno
	Number of ready file descriptors		−1	Yes

The **select** system call uses a series of **file descriptor masks** to determine which files it should check for pending I/O. These references indicate file descriptors for reading (`*readfds`), for writing (`*writefds`), and those to be checked for exceptions (e.g., message out of band: `*exceptfds`). The initial argument, n, is the number of bits in the masks that should be processed. As these masks are 0-based, passing the value 4 indicates the first four bits, representing descriptors 0 to 3, are to be used. The final **select** argument, `*timeout`, references a `timeval` structure that contains information about the length of time the system should wait before completing the **select** call.

The read, write, and exception file descriptor[15] masks are actually arrays of long integers. On most Linux systems the number of file descriptors, FD_SETSIZE, that can be represented by a mask is 1024 (descriptors 0–1023). The first bit in the first element of the array is for file descriptor 0, the second bit

---

[15] These are file descriptors, not file pointers. When using **select**, a socket descriptor is treated the same as a file descriptor.

for file descriptor 1, and so on. If the process does not need to check any descriptors for pending reads, the read descriptor mask may be set to NULL. This also applies for the write and exception masks.

To simplify referencing a specific file descriptor represented by a single bit, several bit manipulation macros are offered. These macros, whose descriptions are usually found on the manual page for **select**, are

```
void FD_ZERO(fd_set *fdset);
void FD_SET(int fd, fd_set *fdset);
void FD_CLR(int fd, fd_set *fdset);
int  FD_ISSET(int fd, fd_set *fdset);
```

Each macro must be passed a reference to the address of the file descriptor mask to manipulate. The FD_ZERO macro will zero (set to all zeros) the referenced mask. The FD_SET macro will set the appropriate bit for the passed file descriptor value. The FD_CLEAR macro will clear the bit for the passed file descriptor. The FD_ISSET macro will return, without changing its state, the status of the bit for the passed file descriptor (0 for not set and 1 for set). In practice, the FD_ISSET macro is used when the **select** call returns to determine which descriptors are actually ready for the indicated I/O event.

The last argument for **select** specifies the amount of time the call should wait before completing its action and returning. This argument references a `timeval` structure, which is shown below:

```
struct timeval {
        long    tv_sec;         /* seconds */
        long    tv_usec;        /* and microseconds */
};
```

If this argument is set to NULL, the **select** call will wait (block) indefinitely until one of the specified descriptors is ready for I/O. If the `tv_sec` member and the `tv_usec` member are both set to 0, the **select** call will poll the specified descriptors and return immediately with their status. If the `timeval` members are nonzero, the system will wait the indicated number of seconds/microseconds for an I/O event to occur *or* return immediately if one of the indicated events occurs prior to the expiration of the specified time.[16] While the Linux version of the **select** call is fairly standard, it does differ in one very important way. Upon return, the `timeout` argument for **select** is modified to reflect the amount of time not slept. Thus, if the call to **select** is invoked multiple times (or in a loop), the timeout argument must be reinitialized before each call. This difference in behavior should be accounted for when porting code.

---

[16] If all the file descriptor masks are empty, the time specification for **select** can be used to fine-tune the amount of time a process should sleep.

If **select** is successful, it returns the number of ready file descriptors. If the call has timed out, it returns a 0. If the call fails, it returns a −1 and sets errno to one of the values shown in Table 10.26. The file descriptor masks are modified to reflect the current status of the descriptors when the **select** call is successful or has timed out. The masks are not modified in the event of an error.

Table 10.26 select Error Messages

#	Constant	perror **Message**	Explanation
4	EINTR	Interrupted system call	A signal was received by process before any of the indicated events occurred or time limit expired.
9	EBADF	Bad file descriptor	One of the file descriptor masks references an invalid file descriptor.
12	ENOMEM	Cannot allocate memory	System unable to allocate internal tables used by **select**.
22	EINVAL	Invalid argument	One of the time limit values is out of range or file descriptor is negative.

A closing note about **select**: The first argument, which indicates the number of bits that **select** will process in the file descriptor mask(s), must be assigned the value of the largest file (socket) descriptor value plus 1 (remember references are 0-based). Finally, **select**, while still widely used is on the deprecated call hit list in Linux. The system call **poll**, a variation of **select**, provides similar functionality.

Program 10.13, which shows how the **select** call can be used, is a modification of the original Internet domain connectionless server program (10.10). Modified statements and new lines of code are in bold and are placed in gray (lines 5, 9–11, 37–44, 54–65, 72, and 73).

Program 10.13 Using select to multiplex I/O in the server program.

```
File : p10.13.cxx
  |     /*
  |          Program 10.13 - SERVER - Internet Domain - connectionless
  |     */
  |     #include "local_sock.h"
  +     #include <sys/time.h>
  |     int
```

```
|      main(  ) {
|         int                 sock, n,
|                             n_ready, need_rsp;
10        fd_set              read_fd;
|         struct timeval      w_time;
|
|         socklen_t           server_len, client_len;
|         struct sockaddr_in server,          // Internet Addresses
+                            client;
|                                              // SOCKET
|         if ((sock = socket(PF_INET, SOCK_DGRAM, 0)) < 0) {
|           perror("SERVER socket "); return 1;
|         }
20        memset(&server, 0, sizeof(server));  // Clear structure
|         server.sin_family    = AF_INET;     // Set address type
|         server.sin_addr.s_addr = htonl(INADDR_ANY);
|         server.sin_port      = htons(0);
|                                              // BIND
+         if (bind(sock, (struct sockaddr *) &server,
|             sizeof(server) ) < 0) {
|           perror("SERVER bind "); return 2;
|         }
|         server_len = sizeof(server);         // Obtain  address length
30                                             // Find picked port #
|         if (getsockname(sock, (struct sockaddr *) &server,
|             &server_len) < 0) {
|           perror("SERVER getsocketname "); return 3;
|         }
+         cout << "Server using port " << ntohs(server.sin_port) << endl;
|         while ( 1 ) {                        // Loop forever
|           w_time.tv_sec = 5; w_time.tv_usec = 0;   // set the wait time
|           FD_ZERO( &read_fd );                      // zero all bits
|           FD_SET( sock, &read_fd );                 // indicate one to read
40          if ( (n_ready=select( sock + 1, &read_fd, (fd_set *) NULL,
|                           (fd_set *) NULL, &w_time)) < 0 ) {
|             perror("SERVER read socket select "); continue;
|           }
|           if ( FD_ISSET( sock, &read_fd ) ) {       // activity on socket
+             client_len = sizeof(client);            // estimate length
|             memset(buf, 0, BUFSIZ);                 // clear the buffer
|             if ((n=recvfrom(sock, buf, BUFSIZ, 0,   // get the client's msg
|                 (struct sockaddr *) &client, &client_len)) < 0){
|               perror("SERVER recvfrom ");
50              close(sock); return 4;
|             }
|             write( fileno(stdout), buf, n );        // display msg on server
|             memset(buf, 0, BUFSIZ);                 // clear the buffer
|             need_rsp = 1;
+           }
|           if ( need_rsp ) {
```

```
  |              w_time.tv_sec = 5; w_time.tv_usec = 0;      // set the wait time
  |              FD_ZERO( &read_fd );                        // zero all bits
  |              FD_SET( fileno(stdin), &read_fd );          // the one to read
 60              if ( (n_ready=select( fileno(stdin) + 1, &read_fd,
  |                   (fd_set *) NULL,(fd_set *) NULL, &w_time)) < 0 ) {
  |                perror("SERVER read stdin select "); continue;
  |              }                                           // get server's msg
  |                                                          // if activity stdin
  +              if ( FD_ISSET( fileno(stdin), &read_fd ) ) {
  |                if ( read( fileno(stdin),buf,BUFSIZ) != 0 ) {
  |                  if ((sendto(sock, buf, strlen(buf) ,0, // send to client
  |                      (struct sockaddr *) &client, client_len)) <0){
  |                    perror("SERVER sendto ");
 70                   close(sock); return 5;
  |                  }
  |                  need_rsp = 0;
  |                }
  |              }
  +            }
  |          }
  |          return 0;
  |        }
```

The modified server program adds the include file <sys/time.h>, since
it makes reference to the timeval structure. Two integer variables have also
been added. The n_read variable will be assigned the number of ready I/O
descriptors found by the **select** call. In this setting, this variable should only
contain the value 0 or 1. The second variable, need_rsp, is used as a flag to
keep track of whether or not the server has responded to a received message.
As the address of the process sending the message is included with the message, a **sendto** call to respond to the message cannot be issued until a message address pair has been received. The mask that represents the descriptors
for reading, read_fd, is allocated next. Following this, a structure to hold the
time to wait for the **select** call is allocated.

In the processing loop, the wait time is set arbitrarily to 5 seconds, the read
descriptor mask is zeroed, and the bit to indicate the socket to process is set. The
select call is used to determine the status of the socket. Since we are only interested in reading, the remaining descriptor masks are set to NULL (note that
each is cast appropriately). When the **select** call returns, the FD_ISSET
macro determines if the socket is actually available for reading. If the socket is
ready, the message is received, via **recvfrom**, and displayed. Once the message is displayed, the need_rsp variable is set to 1 to flag the reception.

After checking for received messages and having either received a message or
timed out waiting, the server looks to send a response. The need_rsp variable
is evaluated to determine if a response to a message should be generated. If

a response is needed, the wait time is reset, the `read_fd` mask is reset to reference **stdin**, and a call to **select** is made to determine if any input (in this setting, from the keyboard) is available for reading. If the user running the server process has entered information, it is **read** and sent to the client. After a message has been sent, the `need_rsp` variable is set to 0 to indicate a response was generated and sent.

While these changes help the server process to better handle asynchronous communications with the client process, it does not resolve all of the communication problems. The client process must also be changed in a similar manner to allow for non-blocking asynchronous communications. There are additional coordination problems to address. For example, say there are multiple clients and the user running the server is slow in responding. Once the user on the server does respond, how does the server process know (keep track of) to whom it should send the response if, in the interim, it has received additional messages from other clients?

10.7 Peeking at Data

The **recv**, **recvfrom**, and **rcvmsg** calls allow the user to look at received data without consuming it (the data will still be available for the next receive-type call). This is handy should the receiving process need to examine a message to, say, perhaps act upon it rather than pass it on to another process. To implement a nonconsumptive receive, the user must set the integer `flags` argument for the receive call to the defined constant MSG_PEEK. A modified Internet domain server program (Program 10.6) shows how this can be done. The processing loop of the program (where a child process is generated to handle the connection from the client) is modified to include a peek at the incoming message. These modifications are shown in Program 10.14.

Program 10.14 Internet domain connection-oriented **server** using MSG_PEEK.

```
File : p10.14.cxx
   |      /*
   |             Internet domain, connection-oriented SERVER - MSG_PEEK
   |      */
   .
   .      // Same as Program p10.6.cxx
   .
```

```
|          if ( fork ( ) ==0 ) {                            // Generate a CHILD
|             while ( (len==recv(new_sock, buf, BUFSIZ, MSG_PEEK)) > 0){
|                write( fileno(stdout), "Peeked and found: ",19);
50               write( fileno(stdout), buf, len);        // show peeked msg
|                if ( !strncmp(buf, ".done", len-1) ) break;
|                len=recv(new_sock, buf, BUFSIZ, 0 );     // retrieve same msg
|                write( fileno(stdout), "Re-read buffer  : ",19);
|                write( fileno(stdout), buf, len);
+             }
|             write( fileno(stdout),"Leaving child process\n",22);
|             close(new_sock);                            // In CHILD process
|             return 0;
|          } else close(new_sock);                        // In PARENT process
60      } while( true );                                  // FOREVER
.
.       // Same as Program p10.6.cxx
.
```

The modifications to the client program (Program 10.7) are shown in the partial listing in Program 10.15.

Program 10.15 Internet domain connection-oriented **client** using MSG_PEEK.

```
File : p10.15.cxx
|      /*
|          Internet domain, connection-oriented CLIENT
|      */
.
.       // Same as Program p10.7.cxx
.
+      do {                                        // Process
|         write(fileno(stdout),"> ", 3);
|         if ((len=read(fileno(stdin), buf, BUFSIZ)) > 0) {
|            write(fileno(stdout), "Sending ", 9);
|            write(fileno(stdout), buf, len);
40          send(orig_sock, buf, len, 0);
|         }
|      } while( strncmp(buf, ".done", len-1) );    // until end of input
.
.       // Same as Program p10.7.cxx
.
```

When these modified programs are compiled and run (as shown in Figure 10.18), it is easy to see that the server process can peek at the received data by specifying MSG_PEEK. When the second receive call is made, the peeked-at data is received again.

```
linux$ g++ p10.14.cxx -o server
linux$ g++ p10.15.cxx -o client
linux$ server
Peeked and found: George Orwell was
an optimist.
Re-read buffer  : George Orwell was
an optimist.
Peeked and found: Life is like a
simile.
Re-read buffer  : Life is like a
simile.
Peeked and found: .done
Leaving child process
```

```
perseus$ client linux
> George Orwell was an optimist.
Sending George Orwell was an
optimist.
> Life is like a simile.
Sending Life is like a simile.
> .done
Sending .done
perseus$
```

Figure 10.18 Peeking at messages—server and client running on separate hosts.

10.8 Out of Band Messages

There are occasions when a sending process needs to notify the recipient process of an urgent message. The MSG_OOB flag is used with the send and receive calls to indicate and process urgent messages. At present, only stream-based sockets support out of band messaging.

As with MSG_PEEK, we can modify Program 10.6 to show how the server process might process an urgent message that has been sent by a client. Since the modifications are somewhat more extensive, the entire server program is shown in Program 10.16. Modified sections of code are highlighted in bold (lines 5, 15, 16, and 42–68) and are in gray.

Program 10.16 Internet domain connection-oriented **server** using MSG_OOB.

```
File : p10.16.cxx
   |      /*
   |            Internet domain, connection-oriented SERVER - MSG_PEEK
   |      */
   |      #include "local_sock.h"
   +      #include <time.h>                    // For nanosleep
   |      void signal_catcher(int);
   |      int
   |      main(  ) {
   |        int          orig_sock,            // Original socket in server
  10                      new_sock;            // New socket from connect
   |        socklen_t    clnt_len;             // Length of client address
```

```
|        struct sockaddr_in              // Internet addr client & server
|                     clnt_adr, serv_adr;
|        int          len, i,            // Misc counters, etc.
+                     urg, mark;         // Flag reception of OOB msg and to
|                                        // note its location in the stream.
|                                        // Catch when child terminates
|        if (signal(SIGCHLD , signal_catcher) == SIG_ERR) {
|          perror("SIGCHLD");
20         return 1;
|        }
|        if ((orig_sock = socket(PF_INET, SOCK_STREAM, 0)) < 0) {
|          perror("generate error");
|          return 2;
+        }
|        memset( &serv_adr, 0, sizeof(serv_adr) );        // Clear structure
|        serv_adr.sin_family    = AF_INET;                // Set address type
|        serv_adr.sin_addr.s_addr = htonl(INADDR_ANY);    // Any interface
|        serv_adr.sin_port      = htons(PORT);            // Use our fake port
30                                                        // BIND
|        if (bind( orig_sock, (struct sockaddr *) &serv_adr,
|                   sizeof(serv_adr)) < 0){
|          perror("bind error");
|          close(orig_sock);
+          return 3;
|        }
|        if (listen(orig_sock, 5) < 0 ) {                 // LISTEN
|          perror("listen error");
|          close (orig_sock);
40         return 4;
|        }
|        struct timespec req, rem;                        // For nanosleep
|        do {
|          clnt_len = sizeof(clnt_adr);                   // ACCEPT a connect
+          if ((new_sock = accept( orig_sock, (struct sockaddr *) &clnt_adr,
|                             &clnt_len)) < 0) {
|            perror("accept error");
|            close(orig_sock);
|            return 5;
50         }
|          if ( fork( ) == 0 ) {                          // Generate a CHILD
|            urg = mark = 0;
|            do {
|              req.tv_sec = 5; req.tv_nsec = 0;           // set time to sleep
+              nanosleep( &req, &rem);                    // slow down the
                                                          //   server
|              if ( (len=recv(new_sock, buf, BUFSIZ, MSG_OOB)) > 0) {
|                write( fileno(stdout), "URGENT msg pending\n", 19);
|                urg = 1;
|              }
60             if ( urg ) ioctl(new_sock, SIOCATMARK, &mark);
```

```
|               if ( mark ) {
|                 write( fileno(stdout), " <-- the URGENT msg\n",20);
|                 mark = urg = 0;
|               }
+               if ((len=recv(new_sock, buf, BUFSIZ, 0)) > 0) {
|                 if ( !strncmp(buf, ".done", len-1) ) break;
|                 write( fileno(stdout), buf, len);
|               }
|            } while( 1 );
70           write( fileno(stdout),"Leaving child process\n",22);
|            close(new_sock);                          // In CHILD process
|            return 0;
|          } else
|            close(new_sock);                          // In PARENT process
+        } while( true );                              // FOREVER
|        return 0;
|      }
|      void
|      signal_catcher(int the_sig){
80       signal(the_sig, signal_catcher);              // reset
|        wait(0);                                      // keep the zombies at bay
|      }
```

In the server program (10.16), the integer variables urg and mark have been added to facilitate the processing of urgent messages. These variables act as flags to indicate when an urgent message has been received (urg) and actually processed (mark). In the processing loop of the server, these variables are initially set to 0. An inner do-while loop starts with a call to **nanosleep**. The **nanosleep** call is added to slow down server processing to clearly demonstrate the receipt sequence of client messages. The **nanosleep** call was chosen (rather than **sleep**), as it is standardized by POSIX, does not impact other signals, and provides a finer granularity for pausing.

Table 10.27 Summary of the nanosleep System Call.

Include File(s)	<time.h>	Manual Section	**2**
Summary	int nanosleep(const struct timespec *req, struct timespec *rem);		
	Success	Failure	Sets errno
Return	0	−1	Yes

The **nanosleep** call uses a reference to a timespec structure for each of its two arguments. The first argument, req, is the required sleep time (in seconds and nanoseconds). The second argument, rem, is the remaining time should the call be interrupted by a signal. When successful, the call returns a 0; if it fails, it returns a –1 and sets errno as shown in Table 10.28.

Table 10.28 nanosleep Error Messages.

#	Constant	perror Message	Explanation
4	EINTR	Interrupted system call	A non-blocked signal was received by process before the full time expired. The value in rem is the remaining time to sleep.
22	EINVAL	Invalid argument	One of the time limit values is out of range (0 to 999,999,999) or tv_sec value is negative.

When we run this program, we will see that the notification of the receipt of an urgent message is received prior to messages that have already been sent but not yet received. A **recv** call with the flags argument set to MSG_OOB is made next. If notification of an urgent message has been received, this call returns a value greater than 0 (i.e., 1). When the server receives notification, it displays, to standard output, the message URGENT msg pending and sets the urg variable to 1. Following this, the urg variable is checked. If it is set (i.e., is nonzero), a call to **ioctl** is made. With the addition of the **ioctl** call, we must include the header file <sys/ ioctl.h> in the local_sock.h file. The **ioctl** call is passed the socket descriptor, the flag SIOCATMARK,[17] and the address of the mark variable. With this argument set, the **ioctl** call assigns the variable mark a positive value if the next I/O call will process data that is beyond the urgent data; otherwise, it assigns mark a 0 value. The contents of the mark variable are tested next. If the server is beyond the processing of the urgent message data, the string <-- the URGENT msg is appended to the data currently displayed and the mark and urg variables cleared by resetting them to 0. In either event, a second call to **recv** is made to receive and process pending messages from the client. If a message is not the string .done, the message is displayed; otherwise, a message indicating the child process is exiting is generated, the socket descriptor is closed, and the child process exits.

The code for the client must be changed minimally. If the first character of the data entered by the user is an exclamation mark (!), the remaining data is

---

[17] This constant is defined in the <asm/ sockios.h> file (yet another one of the include files that is automatically drawn upon when including the standard include files for sockets).

considered urgent and sent with the flag argument set to MSG_OOB; otherwise, the data is sent with the flag argument set to 0. Program 10.17 shows the
modified client program (10.7).

Program 10.17   Internet domain connection-oriented **client** using MSG_OOB.

```
File : p10.17.cxx
  |     /*
  |         Internet domain, connection-oriented CLIENT - MSG_OOB
  |     */
  .
  .     // Same a Program 10.7
  .
  +     do {                                          // Process
  |       write(fileno(stdout),"> ", 3);              // Prompt the user
  |       if ((len=read(fileno(stdin), buf, BUFSIZ)) > 0) {
  |         if ( buf[0] == '!' ){
  |           write(fileno(stdout), "URGENT msg sent\n", 16);
 40          send(orig_sock, buf, len, MSG_OOB );
  |         } else
  |           send(orig_sock, buf, len, 0 );
  |       }
  |     } while( strncmp(buf, ".done", len-1) );      // until end of input
  .
  .     // Same as Program 10.7
  .
```

Figure 10.19 shows what occurs when this MSG_OOB client–server
application is run.

```
linux$ g++ p10.16.cxx -o server
linux$ g++ p10.17.cxx -o client
linux$ server                              perseus$ client linux
a                                          > a
b                                          > b
URGENT msg pending                         > c
c                                          > !help
!help <-- the URGENT msg                   URGENT msg sent
d                                          > d
e                                          > e
Leaving child process                      > .done
^C                                         perseus$
```

Figure 10.19   Using MSG_OOB in two separate windows on separate hosts.

The server process is established first, then the client is established. The user running the client program enters the letters a, b, c, the string !help followed by the letters d, e, and then the string .done. The server process begins to process the messages from the client (remember, we added a call to **nanosleep** in the server to slow it down). After it has processed the initial message, it receives notice that an urgent message is pending. However, it does not actually receive the urgent message at this time. The urgent message, which is eventually received and flagged by the server process with the words <-- URGENT msg, is received in its proper order. If we want to obtain the urgent message at the time of notification, we must either buffer the intervening messages or discard them.

10-12 EXERCISE

Further refine the chat program to allow multiple users on different clients to communicate with one another in a manner similar in function to a party line or conference conversation. In this implementation, each user chooses a chat name, which identifies all messages subsequently typed by that user. The chat name is prefaced by the host name. A chat conversation might look like this:

```
[beta:fred]  What did you think of the test yesterday?
[xi:zippo]   Ok, but I didn't like the question about efficiency!
[rho:joe]    Yeah, more or less efficient-we should have got
             the points on that one.
```

The options for invoking this version of chat are

chat   Invoke chat for eavesdropping (i.e., no talking allowed—just view messages)

chat fred   Invoke chat with the chat name fred

When in **chat**, the user should be able to issue commands that are acted upon rather than sent as a message to others. For example, some chat commands (lines beginning with either a . or !) might be

.re jokes   Read file jokes—contents appear in the conversation

.wr cstuff   Write a copy of the conversation in a file called cstuff

.ap cstuff   Append a copy of the conversation to a file called cstuff

.en   End recording of conversation to output file

`!cmd`	Escape chat temporarily and execute the command cmd
`.wn rho:joe`	Whisper (talk only) to chat name `joe` at host `rho`
`.wf`	Turn whisper off
`.lo`	Leave chat
`.wo`	Display the names of all chat participants

The chat program should make use of sockets. Implement some form of non-blocking I/O to prevent possible deadlock situations. To complete the assignment, you will need to write two programs: a server program, which facilitates communications between clients and runs continuously in the background, and a client program that runs in the foreground. You will need to decide whether or not the server should **fork** child processes to manage communications with individual clients or keep information in some sort of table arrangement. When the user invokes the client program, it connects to the chat server. As broadcasting is frowned upon, the client program should read the environment variable CHAT to find the name of the chat server. If the entry cannot be made in the `/etc/services` file for the chat port, an environment variable, such as PORT, should be used to hold the number of the port. You may want to use the MSG_PEEK option to peek at data to determine if it is a command or a message. Some commands should be processed locally by the client, while others might best be done by the server, with the information returned to the appropriate client.

10.9 Summary

Sockets provide the user with a means of interprocess communication whereby the processes involved can reside on different hosts across a network. The most common socket types are stream sockets, which provide a logical connection between processes and support the reliable exchange of data, and datagram sockets, which are connectionless and may be unreliable. The actual encoding of data and its transport are further dependent upon the selection of a specific transport protocol.

A series of socket system calls are used to establish socket-based communications. The **socket** system call is used to create a socket of a specific type using a particular protocol. The **bind** system call establishes a relationship between the socket and a system address. In a stream-based setting (connection-oriented), the serving process then creates a queue for incoming connections using the **listen** system call. When a connection from a client process is made, the server then uses the **accept** system call to generate a new socket, which will be used for actual communications. The connection-oriented client process creates its own socket and uses the **connect** system call to initiate a connection with the server process. Once a connection is established, the processes involved can use **read-write** system calls or specialized network send/receive calls to exchange data.

If the communication is datagram-based (connectionless), both the client and server processes generate a socket and bind it. Communication is carried out using a **connect-write** / **accept-read** sequence or with specialized send/receive network calls. In a connectionless setting, addressing specifics are incorporated within the message.

The **select** system call can be used to multiplex socket-based communications. In a stream-based setting a process can peek at arriving data without consuming it and can be notified of a pending urgent message.

10.10 Key Terms and Concepts

"local_sock.h" include file
__SOCKADDR_COMMON(sa_) macro
<arpa/inet.h> include file
<netdb.h> include file
<netinet/in.h> include file
<sys/ioctl.h> include file
<sys/socket.h> include file
<sys/time.h> include file
<sys/un.h> include file
<time.h> include file
accept system call
address resolution protocol (ARP)
AF_INET
AF_UNIX
American Registry for Internet Numbers (ARIN)
arp utility
ARP/RARP
Asia Pacific Network Information Center (APNIC)

BIND
bind system call
bzero library function
Class A network
Class B network
Class C network
communication domain
connect system call
connectionless communication
connection-oriented communication
datagram socket
dig utility
domain name system (DNS)
dotted decimal notation (DDN)
dynamic ports
ephemeral ports
Ethernet address
EWOULDBLOCK
fcntl system call
FD_CLR macro
FD_ISSET macro
FD_SET macro

FD_ZERO macro
file descriptor masks
fortune utility
gethostbyaddr library function
gethostbyname library function
getservbyname library function
getservent library function
host utility
hostent structure
hostid
ICANN (the Internet Corporation for Assigned Names and
  Numbers)
ICMP
ifconfig utility
in_addr structure
INADDR_ANY
inet_ntoa library function
International Standards Organization
  (ISO)
Internet (IP) address
Internet domain
Internet Network Information
  Center (InterNIC)
IPPORT_USERRESERVED
IPPROTO_TCP
IPPROTO_UDP
IPv4
ipv4 subdirectory
IPv6
listen system call
media access control (MAC)
  address
memcpy library function
memset library function
mkstemp library function
MSG_CONFIRM
MSG_DONTROUTE
MSG_DONTWAIT
MSG_ERRQUEUE
MSG_NOSIGNAL
MSG_NOSIGNAL

MSG_OOB
MSG_PEEK
MSG_TRUNC
MSG_WAITALL
msghdr structure
nanosleep system call
NETBIOS
netid
netstat utility
nslookup utility
ntohs library function
Open Systems Interconnect (OSI)
PF_INET
PF_LOCAL
PF_UNIX
protocol
protocol family
recv system call
recvfrom system call
recvmsg system call
registered ports
reliable connection
select system call
send system call
sendmsg system call
sendto system call
servent structure
services file
setservent library function
SNA
SOCK_DGRAM
SOCK_RAW
SOCK_SEQPACKET
SOCK_STREAM
sockaddr structure
sockaddr_in structure
sockaddr_un structure
socket interface
socket system call
socketpair system call
stream socket
sysctl utility

TCP/IP
timeval structure
Transport Level Interface (TLI)
UDP
UNIX domain

unreliable connection
UUCP
well-known ports
X/Open Transport Interface (XTI)
XNS

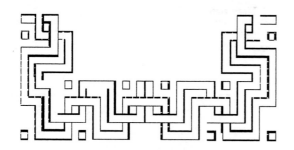

Chapter 11

THREADS

11.1 Introduction

A variety of techniques can be used to solve a problem. One common programming methodology is to divide the problem into smaller specific subtasks. Then, given the nature of the subtasks and the sequence in which they must be done, parcel them out to separate processes (generated via a **fork** system call). Then, if needed, have the processes communicate with one another using interprocess communication constructs. When each of the subtasks (processes) is finished, its solved portion of the problem is integrated into the whole to provide an overall solution. Indeed, this approach is the basis for distributed computation.

However, generating and managing individual processes consume system resources. As we have seen in previous chapters, there is a considerable amount of system overhead associated with the creation of a process. During its execution lifetime, the system must keep track of the current state, program counter, memory usage, file descriptors, signal tables, and other details of the process. Further, when the process exits, the operating system must remove the process-associated data structures and return the process's status information to its parent process, if still present, or to **init**. If we add to this the cost of the process communicating with other processes using standard interprocess communication facilities, we may find this approach too resource expensive.

Aware of such limitations, the designers of modern versions of UNIX anticipated the need for constructs that would facilitate concurrent solutions but not be as system-intensive as separate processes. As in a multitasking operating system where multiple processes are running concurrently (or pseudo-concurrently), why not allow individual processes the ability to simultaneously take different execution paths through their process space? This idea led to a new abstraction called a **thread**. Conceptually, a thread is a distinct sequence of execution steps performed within a process. In a traditional setting, with a UNIX process executing, say, a simple C/C++ program, there is a single thread of control. At any given time there is only one execution point (as referenced by the program counter). The thread starts at the first statement in main and continues through the program logic in a serial manner until the process finishes. In a multithreading (MT) setting, there can be more than one thread of control active within a process, each progressing concurrently. Be aware that some authors use the term multithreaded program to mean any program that uses two or more processes running concurrently that share memory and communicate with one another (such as what we did in Chapter 8). If the processes (with their threads) are executing and making progress simultaneously on separate processors, **parallelism** occurs.

There are certain problem types that lend themselves to a multithreaded solution. Problems that inherently consist of multiple, independent tasks are prime candidates. For example, monitor and daemon programs that manage a large number of simultaneous connections, concurrent window displays, and similar processes can be written using threads. Similarly, producer–consumer and client–server type problems can have elegant multithreaded solutions. Additionally, some numerical computations (such as matrix multiplication) that can be divided into separate subtasks also benefit from multithreading. On the other side of the coin, there are many problems that must be done in a strict serial manner for which multithreading may produce a less efficient solution.

Each thread has its own stack, register set, program counter, thread-specific data, thread-local variables, thread-specific signal mask, and state information. However, all such threads share the same address space, general signal handling, virtual memory, data, and I/O with the other threads within the same process. In a multithreaded process each thread executes independently and asynchronously. In this setting communication between threads within the same process is less complex, as each can easily reference common data. However, as expected, many tasks handled by threads have sequences that must be done serially. When these sequences are encountered, synchronization problems concerning data access—updating—can arise. Most commonly the operating system uses a priority-based, preemptive, non-time-slicing algorithm to schedule thread activities. With preemptive scheduling the thread executes until it blocks or has used its allotted time. The term sibling is sometimes used to denote other peer threads, as there is no inherent parent/child relationship with threads.

Figure 11.1 compares communications for multiple processes, each with a single thread, with that of a single process with multiple threads.

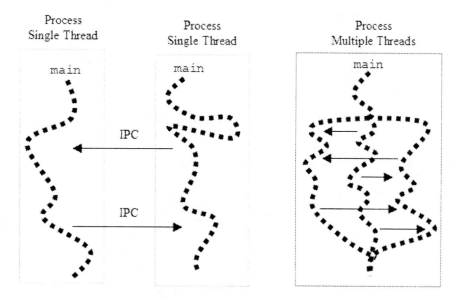

Figure 11.1 Conceptual communications—multiple single-threaded processes versus a single process with multiple threads.

At system implementation level there are two traditional approaches or models used to generate and manage threads. The first, the **user-level** model, runs on top of the existing operating system and is transparent to it. The operating system maintains a runtime system to manage thread activities. Library functions and system calls made within the thread are wrapped in special code to allow for thread run-time management.[1] Threads implemented in this manner have low system overhead and are easily extensible should additional functionality be needed. On occasion, the operating system may have difficulty efficiently managing a user-level-implemented thread that is not time sliced and contains CPU-intensive code. More importantly, user-level threads are designed to share resources with other threads within their process space when running on a single processor.

---

[1] For example, calls that would normally block (such as **read**) are wrapped in code that allows them to be non-blocking.

The second approach is the **kernel-level** model. In this implementation, the operating system is aware of each thread. While the management of kernel-level threads is less intensive than that of individual processes, it is still more expensive than user-level-based threads. A kernel that offers direct thread support must contain system-level code for each specified thread function. However, kernel-level threads can support parallelism with multiple threads running on multiple processors.

In an attempt to incorporate the best of both approaches, many thread implementations are composites (hybrids). In one implementation the system binds each user-level thread to a kernel-level thread on a **one-to-one** basis. Windows NT and OS/2 use this approach. Another approach is to have the system multiplex user-level threads with a single kernel-level thread (**many-to-one**). A more common composite model relies on the support of multiple user-level threads with a pool of kernel-level threads. The kernel-level threads are run as lightweight processes (LWP) and are scheduled and maintained by the operating system. In a multiprocessor setting some operating systems allow LWPs to be bound to a specific CPU.

Older versions of Linux supported user-level threads. In newer versions of Linux there are kernel threads. However, these threads are used by the operating system to execute kernel-related functions and are not directly associated with the execution of a user's program. Multithreaded support is offered through LWPs. Linux uses a system specific (non-portable) `clone` system call to generate an LWP for the thread. Threaded applications should use one of the standardized thread APIs described in the next paragraph. By comparison, Sun's Solaris uses a variation of the kernel-level scheme whereby the user can specify a one-to-one binding or use the default many-to-many mapping. While Sun's approach is more flexible, it is more complex to implement and requires the interaction of two scheduling routines (user and kernel).

From a programming standpoint, there is a variety of thread APIs. Two of the more common are POSIX (Portable Operating System Interface) Pthreads and Sun's thread library (UNIX International, or UI). By far, POSIX threads (based on POSIX 1003.1 standards generated by the IEEE Technical Committee on Operating Systems) are the most widely implemented thread APIs. The POSIX standard 1003.1c is an extension of the 1003.1 and includes additional interface support for multi-threading.

In current versions of Linux (such as Red Hat 5.0 and later) the POSIX 1003.1c thread API is implemented using the LinuxThreads library, which is included in the `glibc2` GNU library. In the Sun Solaris environment, both the POSIX and Sun thread libraries are supported, since Sun's effort at producing thread libraries predates the POSIX standards and many of the POSIX constructs have a strong Sun flavor. We will concentrate on POSIX threads, as they are guaranteed to be fully portable to other environments that are POSIX-compliant. The POSIX thread functions, except for semaphore manipulation, begin with the prefix `pthread`, while POSIX thread constants begin with the prefix PTHREAD_. The thread-related functions (over 100) are found in section **3thr** of the manual pages.

Note that all programs using POSIX thread functions need the preprocessor directive `#include <pthread.h>` for the inclusion of thread prototypes. If the code will contain **reentrant** functions,[2] the defined constant `#define _REENTRANT` should be placed prior to all includes and program code. A list of supported reentrant functions can be found by interrogating the `/usr/lib/libc.a` library. For example,

```
linux$  ar t /usr/lib/libc.a  |  grep '_r\.o'  |  pr -n -2 -t
```

1	random_r.o	32	getspnam_r.o
2	rand_r.o	33	sgetspent_r.o
3	drand48_r.o	34	fgetspent_r.o
4	erand48_r.o	35	getnssent_r.o
5	lrand48_r.o	36	gethstbyad_r.o
6	nrand48_r.o	37	gethstbynm2_r.o
7	mrand48_r.o	38	gethstbynm_r.o
8	jrand48_r.o	39	gethstent_r.o
9	srand48_r.o	40	getnetbyad_r.o
10	seed48_r.o	41	getnetent_r.o
11	lcong48_r.o	42	getnetbynm_r.o
12	tmpnam_r.o	43	getproto_r.o
13	strtok_r.o	44	getprtent_r.o
14	ctime_r.o	45	getprtname_r.o
15	readdir_r.o	46	getsrvbynm_r.o
16	readdir64_r.o	47	getsrvbypt_r.o
17	getgrent_r.o	48	getservent_r.o
18	getgrgid_r.o	49	getrpcent_r.o
19	getgrnam_r.o	50	getrpcbyname_r.o
20	fgetgrent_r.o	51	getrpcbynumber_r.o
21	getpwent_r.o	52	ether_aton_r.o
22	getpwnam_r.o	53	ether_ntoa_r.o
23	getpwuid_r.o	54	getnetgrent_r.o
24	fgetpwent_r.o	55	getaliasent_r.o
25	getlogin_r.o	56	getaliasname_r.o
26	ttyname_r.o	57	nscd_getpw_r.o
27	mntent_r.o	58	nscd_getgr_r.o
28	efgcvt_r.o	59	nscd_gethst_r.o
29	qefgcvt_r.o	60	getutent_r.o
30	hsearch_r.o	61	getutid_r.o
31	getspent_r.o	62	getutline_r.o

As shown, reentrant functions have _r appended to their non-reentrant name.

---

[2] A reentrant function supports access by multiple threads and maintains the integrity of its data across consecutive calls. Functions that reentrant should not in turn call a function that is non-reentrant.

The object code library for POSIX thread functions must be linked in at compile time using the compiler switch `-lpthread`. Additionally, `_POSIX_C_SOURCE`[3] should be defined if strict compliance to POSIX standards is required. For example,

```
linux$ cat demo.c

#define _REENTRANT
#include <pthread.h>
.
.
.
linux$ g++ demo.cxx -D_POSIX_C_SOURCE -lpthread
```

Threads and their use are a complex topic. This chapter presents the basics of POSIX threads—their generation, scheduling, synchronization, and use. Readers wishing to gain additional insight on the topic are encouraged to read current texts that address thread programming, such as Comer et al., 2001; Nichols et al., 1996; Kleiman et al., 1996; Mitchell et al., 2000; Norton et al., 1997; Lewis et al., 1996; Northrup, 1996; and Wall, 2000, as well as the online documentation (manual pages) and vendor-supplied system support documentation.

11.2 Creating a Thread

Every process contains at least one main or initial thread of control created by the operating system when the process begins to execute. The library function **pthread_create** is used to add a new thread of control to the current process. The new thread executes in concert with the other threads within the process and, if directed, with other threads of control in other processes. The syntax for **pthread_create** is shown in Table 11.1.

There are four pointer-based arguments for **pthread_create**.[4] The first, `*thread`, is a reference to a `pthread_t` type object (an unsigned integer that is `typedefed` as the data type `pthread_t`). Upon successful completion of the **pthread_create** call, `*thread` will reference a unique (to this process only) integer thread ID (TID) value. If this argument is set to NULL, the generated thread ID will not be returned. The second argument, indicated as `*attr`, references a dynamically allocated attribute structure. This

---

[3] On occasion, using the `-D_POSIX_C_SOURCE` flag will get us into trouble, as certain defined data types (such as **timeval**) do not seem to be officially defined when specifying ANSI C.

[4] This time the e is back in create!

Table 11.1 The `pthread_create` Library Function.

Include File(s)	`<pthread.h>`		Manual Section	**3**

Summary	`int pthread_create(pthread_t *thread,`
	`                    pthread_attr_t *attr,`
	`                    void *(*start_routine)(void *),`
	`                    void *arg);`			

	Success		Failure	Sets `errno`
Return	0		Nonzero	

structure contains a single `void` pointer (as shown in the code sequence below lifted from the `/usr/include/bits/pthreadtypes.h` file).

```
/*     Attributes for threads.   */

typedef struct __pthread_attr_s {
  int __detachstate;
  int __schedpolicy;
  struct __sched_param __schedparam;
  int __inheritsched;
  int __scope;
  size_t __guardsize;
  int __stackaddr_set;
  void *__stackaddr;
  size_t __stacksize;
} pthread_attr_t;
```

Attributes govern how the thread behaves. Attributes include stack size—address; scheduling policy—priority and detached state. If the `*attr` value is set to `NULL`, the new thread uses the system defaults for its attributes. If the user wants to modify the default attributes prior to thread creation, he or she should call the library function **pthread_attr_init**. The **pthread_attr_init** library function and related attribute setting functions are covered in a following section.

The third argument for **pthread_create** is a reference to a user-defined function that will be executed by the new thread. The user-defined function should be written to return a pointer to a `void` and have a single `void` pointer argument. If the return type of the user-defined function is a pointer, but it is not of type `void`, use a typecast (e.g., `(void * (*) ())`) to pass the function reference and keep the compiler from complaining. A reference to the actual argument to be passed to the user-defined function is the fourth argument for **pthread_create**. As with the user-defined function reference, this argument is also a `void` pointer. If multiple arguments are to be passed to the user-defined function, a structure containing the arguments should be **statically** allocated and initialized.[5] The reference to the structure should be cast to a void pointer when **pthread_create** is called.

Once a thread is created, it has its own set of attributes and an execution stack. It inherits its signal mask (which it then can alter) and scheduling priority from the calling program (the initiating thread). It does not inherit any pending signals. If needed, a thread can allocate its own storage for thread-specific data.

If the **pthread_create** call is successful, it returns a value of 0 and sets the `*thread` reference to a unique ID for this process. If the call fails, it returns a nonzero value. POSIX thread functions do not routinely set `errno` when they fail, but instead return a nonzero value, which indicates the source of the error encountered. However, `errno` is set when a library function **or** system call fails in a code segment being executed by the thread. In these cases the `errno` value is thread-specific. If the **pthread_create** call fails and returns the value EAGAIN (11), it indicates a system-imposed limit—for example, the total number of threads has been exceeded. A newly created thread (which in Linux is directly tied to an LWP) begins with the execution of the referenced user-defined function. The thread continues to execute until

- the function completes (implicitly or explicitly).
- a call is made to **pthread_exit**.
- the thread is canceled with a call to **pthread_cancel**.
- the process that created the thread exits (implicitly or explicitly).
- one of the threads performs an **exec**.

11.3 Exiting a Thread

The **pthread_exit** library call terminates a thread in much the same manner as a call to **exit** terminates a process. The **pthread_exit** library call is shown in Table 11.2.

The **pthread_exit** library call takes a single argument, a reference to a `retval` value. This reference is returned when a nondetached thread is exited. Upon termination, the thread releases its thread-specific (but not pro-

---

[5] As would be anticipated, locally allocated objects reside on the stack, and their value is undefined when we leave their scope.

Table 11.2 The `pthread_exit` Library Function

Include File(s)	`<pthread.h>`	Manual Section	**3**
Summary	`void pthread_exit (void * retval);`		
Return			

	Success	Failure	Sets `errno`
Return	This call does not return		

cess-specific) resources. If the thread was nondetached, its status information and thread ID are kept by the system until a join is issued or the creating process terminates. When the function being executed by the thread performs a return (implicitly or explicitly), the system implicitly calls **pthread_exit**.

In Chapter 3, Section 5, "Ending a Process," the **atexit** library function was presented. This function allows the user to specify one or more user-defined functions to be called in a LIFO (last-in, first-out) manner when the process exits. In a similar vein there is a small suite of `pthread` cleanup calls that can be used to specify and manipulate user-defined functions that are called when a thread exits. In this grouping are the calls **pthread_cleanup_pop**, which removes a function from the cancellation cleanup stack, and **thread_cleanup_push**, which pushes a function on the cancellation stack of the current thread. Additionally, nonportable versions of these functions (called **pthread_cleanup_pop_restore_np** and **pthread_cleanup_push_defer_np**) are provided. A full discussion of these functions is beyond the scope of this text.

11.4 Basic Thread Management

Once a thread is created, we can direct the calling process to wait until the thread is finished (it calls **pthread_exit** or is cancelled). This is accomplished with a call to the **pthread_join** library function shown in Table 11.3.

The first argument is a valid thread ID (as returned from the **pthread_create** call). The specified thread must be associated with the calling process and should not be specified as detached. The second argument, `**status`, references a static location where the completion status of the waited upon thread will be stored. The status value is the value passed to **pthread_exit**, or the value returned when the function code reaches a `return` state-

Table 11.3 The `pthread_join` Library Function.

Include File(s)	<pthread.h>		Manual Section	**3**
Summary	`int pthread_join( pthread_t target_thread,` `                   void **status );`			
Return	**Success**		**Failure**	**Sets errno**
	0		Nonzero	

ment.[6] If the second argument to **pthread_create** is set to NULL, the status information will be discarded.

There are some caveats associated with joining threads. A thread should be waited upon (joined) by only one other thread. The thread issuing the join does not need to be the initiating thread. If multiple threads wait for the same thread to complete, only one will receive the correct status information. The joins in competing threads will return an error. Should the thread initiating the join be canceled, the waited upon thread can be joined by another thread.[7] If the targeted thread has terminated prior to the issuing of the call to **pthread_join**, the call will return immediately and will not block. Last, but certainly not least, a nondetached thread (which is the default) that is not joined will not release its resources when the thread finishes and will only release its resources when its creating process terminates. Such threads can be the source of memory leaks. If **pthread_join** is successful, it returns a 0; otherwise, it returns a nonzero value. The return of ESRCH (3) means an undetached thread for the corresponding thread ID could not be found or the thread ID was set to 0. The return of EINVAL (22) means the thread specified by the thread ID is detached or the calling thread has already issued a join for the same thread ID. If EDEADLK (35) is returned, it indicates a deadlock situation has been encountered.

The process of joining a thread is somewhat analogous to a process waiting on a forked child process. However, unlike a forked child process, a thread can become detached with a single library call. When a detached thread finishes, its resources are automatically returned to the system. The **pthread_detach** library call (Table 11.4) is used to dynamically detach a joinable thread. In a later section the generation of a detached thread using a thread attribute object will be addressed.

---

[6] If the thread involuntarily terminates, its status information is not relevant.

[7] With POSIX threads the user can issue a cancellation of a specific thread. The thread may have had several cleanup routines associated with it. If one of the associated cleanup routines contains a call to **pthread_detach**, a subsequent call to **pthread_join** will fail.

Table 11.4 The `pthread_detach` Library Function.

Include File(s)	`<pthread.h>`	Manual Section	**3**
Summary	`int pthread_detach (pthread_t threadID);`		

	Success	Failure	Sets `errno`
Return	0	Nonzero	

The **pthread_detach** library function accepts a thread ID as its only argument. If successful, the call to **pthread_detach** detaches the indicated thread and returns a 0 value. If the call fails, the indicated thread is not detached, and a nonzero value is returned. The value EINVAL (22) is returned if an attempt to detach an already detached thread is made, or ESRCH (3) is returned if no such thread ID is found. Remember, once a thread is detached, other threads can no longer synchronize their activities based on its termination.

Program 11.1 uses the **pthread_create** and **pthread_join** library calls to create and join several threads.

Program 11.1   Creating and joining threads.

```
File : p11.1.cxx
    |     /*
    |              Creating and joining threads
    |     */
    |     #define _GNU_SOURCE
    +     #define _REENTRANT
    |     #include <iostream>
    |     #include <cstdio>
    |     #include <cstdlib>
    |     #include <pthread.h>
   10     #include <sys/types.h>
    |     #include <sys/time.h>
    |     #include <unistd.h>
    |     using namespace std;
    |     int MAX=5;
    +     inline int my_rand( int, int );
    |     void        *say_it( void * );
    |     int
    |     main(int argc, char *argv[]) {
    |       pthread_t        thread_id[MAX];
   20       int        status, *p_status = &status;
    |       setvbuf(stdout, (char *) NULL, _IONBF, 0);
```

```
       if ( argc > MAX+1 ){                    // check arg list
         cerr << *argv << " arg1, arg2, ... arg" << MAX << endl;
         return 1;
       }
     cout << "Displaying" << endl;
     for (int i = 0; i < argc-1; ++i) {     // generate threads
      if( pthread_create(&thread_id[i],NULL,say_it,(void *)argv[i+1]) > 0){
         cerr << "pthread_create failure" << endl;
         return 2;
       }
     }
     for (int i=0; i < argc-1; ++i){         // wait for each thread
       if ( pthread_join(thread_id[i], (void **) p_status) > 0){
         cerr << "pthread_join failure" << endl;
         return 3;
       }
       cout << endl << "Thread " << thread_id[i] << " returns "
            << status;
     }
     cout << endl << "Done" << endl;
     return 0;
   }
   //   Display the word passed a random # of times
   void *
   say_it(void *word) {
     int numb = my_rand(2,6);
     cout << (char *)word << "\t to be printed " << numb
          << " times." << endl;
     for (int i=0; i < numb; ++i){
       sleep(1);
       cout << (char *) word << " ";
     }
     return (void *) NULL;
   }
   //   Generate a random # within given range
   int
   my_rand(int start, int range){
     struct timeval t;
     gettimeofday(&t, (struct timezone *)NULL);
     return (int)(start+((float)range * rand_r((unsigned *)&t.tv_usec))
                 / (RAND_MAX+1.0));
   }
```

When Program 11.1 executes, it examines the number of arguments passed in on the command line. For each argument (up to a limit of 5), the program creates a separate thread. As each thread is created, its thread ID is saved in the thread_id array. As written, the program passes **pthread_create** a NULL value as its second argument; therefore, each thread created has the default set of attributes. The user-defined function `say_it` is passed as the starting point for each thread. The appropriate command-line argument is passed to the `say_it` function as the fourth argument of **pthread_create**.[8] Following the creation of the threads, the program waits for the threads to finish using the **pthread_join** library function call. The value returned from each thread and its thread ID is displayed.

The user-defined `say_it` function is used to display the passed-in sequence of characters a random number of times. At the start of the `say_it` function, a random value is calculated. The library functions **srand** and **rand** that we have used previously are not used, as they are not safe to use in a multiple thread setting. However, there is a library function, **rand_r**, that is multithread-safe. The **rand_r** library function is incorporated into a user-defined `inline` function called `my_rand`. In the `my_rand` function the number of elapsed microseconds since 00:00 Universal Coordinated Time, January 1, returned by the **gettimeofday**[9] library function, is used as a seed value for **rand_r**. The value returned by **rand_r** is then adjusted to fall within the specified limits. The calculated random value and the sequence of characters to be displayed are shown on the screen. Finally, a loop is entered, and for the calculated number of times, the function sleeps one second and then prints the passed-in sequence of characters. A compilation sequence and run of the program is shown in Figure 11.2.

Figure 11.2 A Compilation and run of Program 11.1.

```
linux$ g++  p11.1.c -o p11.1 -lpthread
linux$ p11.1 s p a c e
Displaying
s         to be printed 5 times.
p         to be printed 5 times.
a         to be printed 5 times.
c         to be printed 3 times.
e         to be printed 3 times.
s p a c e s p a c e s e p a c s p a a s p
Thread 1026 returns 0
Thread 2051 returns 0
Thread 3076 returns 0  ◄————  Each of these threads is supported by an LWP.
Thread 4101 returns 0          Each LWP has its own process ID as well as its
Thread 5126 returns 0          thread ID.
Done
```

---

[8] Note the type casting. If necessary, we can also use type casting when passing the function reference, using the less than intuitive typecast `(void * (*)())`.

[9] For **gettimeofday** the file `<sys/time.h>` must be included.

In this run, Program 11.1 was passed five command-line arguments: s, p, a, c, e. The program creates five new threads, one for each argument. The number of times each argument will be printed is then displayed. The request to print this information was one of the first lines of code in the user-defined function say_it (see line 48). As shown, all five threads process this statement prior to any one of the threads displaying its individual words. This is somewhat misleading. If we move the sleep statement in the for loop of the say_it function to be after the print statement within the loop, we should see the initial output statements being interspersed with the display of each word. If we count the number of words displayed, we will find they correspond to the number promised (e.g., letter s is displayed five times, etc). A casual look at the remainder of the output might lead one to believe the threads exit in an orderly manner. The **pthread_join**'s are done in a second loop in the calling function (main). Since the thread IDs are passed to **pthread_join** in order, the information concerning their demise is also displayed in order. Viewing the output, we have no way to tell which thread ended first (even though it would seem reasonable that one of the threads that had to display the fewest number of words would be first). When each thread finishes with the say_it function, it returns a NULL. This value, which is picked up by the **pthread_join**, is displayed as a 0. The return statement in the say_it function can be replaced with a call to **pthread_exit**. However, if we replace the return with **pthread_exit**, most compilers will complain that no value is returned by the say_it function, forcing us to include the return statement even if it is unreachable! If we run this program several times, the output sequences will vary.

As written, the display of each word (command-line argument) is preceded by a call to sleep for one second. In the run shown in Figure 11.3, sleep is called 19 times (7 for f, 5 for a, etc.). Yet, the length of time it takes for the program to complete is far less than 19 seconds. This is to be expected, as each thread is sleeping concurrently. We can verify the amount of time used by the program using the **/usr/bin/time**[10] utility. Several reruns of Program 11.1 using the **/usr/bin/time** utility confirms our conjecture.

Figure 11.3 Timing a run of Program 11.1.

```
linux$ /usr/bin/time -p p11.1 f a c e
Displaying
f        to be printed 7 times.
a        to be printed 5 times.
```

[10] In most versions of UNIX there are several utilities that provide statistics about the amount of time it takes to execute a particular command (or program). The most common of these utilities are **time**, **/usr/bin/time**, and **timex**. Most versions of Linux do not come with **timex**.

```
c        to be printed 3 times.
e        to be printed 4 times.
f a c e f a c e f e c a f e a af  f f
Thread 1026 returns 0
Thread 2051 returns 0
Thread 3076 returns 0
Thread 4101 returns 0
Done
real 7.07      ←──────────    Elapsed real time (in seconds).
user 0.00      ←──────────    CPU seconds in user mode
sys  0.02      ←──────────    CPU seconds in kernel mode
```

11-1   EXERCISE

The output of Program 11.1 shows the system assigns the thread ID 1026 to the first thread it creates, 2051 to the next, and so on (incrementing each time by 1025). To explore the generation of threads by the program, compile p11.1.cxx with the -g option and load it into the **gdb** debugger (linux$ gdb p11.1). Set a breakpoint at line 55 of the program at the return statement in the say_it function (to accomplish this, at the **gdb** prompt enter the command break 55). Now run the program with two arguments (i.e., at the **gdb** prompt enter run A B). When the program stops execution, at the **gdb** prompt enter the command info thread. How many threads are generated? Run the program with three arguments. Now how many threads are generated? How do you account for the extra thread(s)?

If your system supports the user command **strace**, try the command-line sequence

```
linux$ strace -c -f p11.1 A B C  > /dev/null
```

Is the number of calls to the **clone** system call the same as the number of threads generated? Why? Note that when threaded programs fail (or are interrupted), they may generate a core file for each thread. If space is at a premium, you may want to remove these files.

11.5 Thread Attributes

In a POSIX implementation, if we want to generate a thread that does not have the default attributes (obtained by setting the second parameter of the **pthread_create** call to NULL), an attribute object is used. To use an attribute object, it must first be initialized. This is accomplished using the library call **pthread_attr_init** (see Table 11.5).

Table 11.5 The `pthread_attr_init` Library Function.

Include File(s)	<pthread.h>	Manual Section	**3**
Summary	int pthread_attr_init (pthread_attr_t *attr);		
	Success	Failure	Sets errno
Return	0	Nonzero	

The **pthread_attr_init** library function has a single argument, a reference to a previously allocated `pthread_attr_t` type object. If the call is successful, it returns a 0 and initializes the referenced attribute object with the default value for each attribute (see Table 11.6). A return of ENOMEM (12) indicates the system does not have sufficient memory to initialize the thread attribute object.

Once initialized, individual attribute values can be modified (see the following discussion). The attribute object is passed as the second argument to the **pthread_create** call. The newly created thread will have the specified attributes. The attribute object is independent of the thread, and changes to the attribute object after a thread has been created are not reflected in existing threads. Once established, a thread attribute object can be used in the generation of multiple threads. Thread attributes and their default values are shown in Table 11.6.

Table 11.6 Thread Attributes and Default Settings.

Attribute	Default	Comments
detachstate	PTHREAD_CREATE_JOINABLE	A nondetached thread that can be joined by other threads. The thread's resources are not freed until a call is made to **pthread_join** or the calling process exits.
inheritsched	PTHREAD_EXPLICIT_SCHED	Indicates whether or not scheduling attributes are inherited from parent thread or set explicitly by the attribute object.

Continued

Table 11.6 *(Continued)*

schedparam	0	Scheduling parameters (priority).
schedpolicy	SCHED_OTHER	Scheduling is determined by the system (most often some sort of timesharing). Note the missing PTHREAD_ prefix.
scope	PTHREAD_SCOPE_SYSTEM	Scope of scheduling contention—with all threads in same process or all processes in the system.

As presented, if the user wants a thread to have different characteristics, he or she should first initialize the attribute object using the **pthread_attr_init** library call and then change the attributes he or she wants to be different. Each attribute listed in Table 11.7 has an associated **pthread_attr_setxxx** and **pthread_attr_getxxx** function call that will act upon the attribute object.

Table 11.7 Thread Attribute Set and Get functions

Attribute	set and get Calls	Defined Constants[11] for the 2nd setxxx parameter
detachstate	int pthread_attr_setdetachstate (pthread_attr_t *attr, int detachstate);	**PTHREAD_ CREATE_JOINABLE**
	int pthread_attr_getdetachstate (const pthread_attr_t *attr, int *detachstate);	PTHREAD_CREATE_ DETACHED
inheritsched	int pthread_attr_setinheritsched (pthread_attr_t *attr, int inheritsched	**PTHREAD_ EXPLICIT_SCHED**
	int pthread_attr_getinheritsched (const pthread_attr_t *attr, int *inheritsched) ;	PTHREAD_INHERIT_ SCHED

Continued

[11] The highlighted values are the default.

Table 11.7 *(Continued)*

schedparam	```int pthread_attr_setschedparam (
pthread_attr_t *attr,
const struct sched_param *param);```	0
	``int pthread_attr_getschedparam (
pthread_attr_t *attr,
const struct sched_param *param);```	Reference to valid sched_param[12] structure with its sched_priority member assigned a valid priority.
schedpolicy	```int pthread_attr_setschedpolicy (
pthread_attr_t *attr,
int policy);```	**SCHED_OTHER**[13] SCHED_FIFO SCHED_RR
	``int pthread_attr_getschedpolicy (
const pthread_attr_t *attr,
int *policy);```	
scope	```int pthread_attr_setscope (
pthread_attr_t *attr,
int contentionscope);```	**PTHREAD_ SCOPE_SYSTEM**
	``int pthread_attr_getscope (
const pthread_attr_t *attr,
int *contentionscope);```	PTHREAD_SCOPE_ PROCESS

If in Program 11.1 we wanted to use the thread attribute object to indicate our threads be detached (that is, the thread would exit as soon as it has completed its task rather than for a join to be done in the calling function), we would add and modify the following program statements:[14]

```
 .
 .
 .
|    int
|    main(int argc, char *argv[]) {
|      pthread_t       thread_id[MAX];
```

[12] The sched_param structure is found in the include file <sched.h>, which is included by the <pthread.h> file.

[13] Only processes with superuser privileges can specify SCHED_FIFO or SCHED_RR.

[14] While not shown, we would also remove the lines of code that implement the join. Of course, if the initial thread (process) terminates before all threads have finished, complete output will not be generated.

```
20      int     status, *p_status = &status;
 |      pthread_attr_t  attr_obj;                    // allocate attribute object
 |      setvbuf(stdout, (char *) NULL, _IONBF, 0);
 .
 .

 |      cout << "Displaying" << endl;
 |                                                   // Allocate & set atrib. obj
 |      pthread_attr_init( &attr_obj);
 |      pthread_attr_setdetachstate( &attr_obj, PTHREAD_CREATE_DETACHED );
 |      for (int i = 0; i < argc-1; ++i) {      // generate threads
 .
 .
 .
```

The set and get attribute calls return a 0 if they are successful. If they fail, they return EINVAL (22) if passed an invalid parameter or ENOTSUP (95)[15] if the parameter specifies an unsupported feature.

11-2   EXERCISE

Add a call to **pthread_attr_getschedparam** in Program 11.1 to determine the default priority (numeric value) for a thread on your system. Is it possible to modify the program to change the priority of each thread as it is created (use **pthread_attr_setschedparam**) so the display of the command-line arguments is always in an ordered inverse sequence? Notice the display starts with the last argument and proceeds to the first (see partial output below).

```
linux$  your_solution one two three four five
 .                                          ◄──── Five words are passed
 .          ╱ As the thread displaying the last word has      to the program.
 .        ╱   the highest priority, it displays first, etc.
five five four three two one five four three one four three
one three
```

If yes, run your program several times to confirm that it works correctly; if no, why not? *Note:* You may want to use the **pthread_getsched-param** library function within the code actually executed by a thread to verify the thread's priority has been set correctly.

---

[15] Linux does not support the constant ENOTSUP directly (which is usually assigned the value 48), but as a patch, defines ENOTSUP in terms of EOPNOTSUPP.

11.6 Scheduling Threads

We have alluded to scheduling in the previous sections. As a subject, scheduling is complex and is often the topic of an entire chapter or more in an operating systems text. *Understanding the Linux Kernel* provides an excellent in-depth presentation of Linux scheduling. Essentially, scheduling is used to determine which ready-to-run task the CPU will execute next. A check of any good operating systems text will reveal a variety of scheduling policies, some of the more common of which are

- First come, first served—first to request service is processed first (also called a FIFO arrangement).
- Shortest job first—the task requiring least amount of processing is done first.
- Priority-based—tasks with higher priority are done first.
- Round-robin—each task gets a small time slice; tasks reside in a circular queue until they are finished.

Furthermore, many of these strategies can be implemented as **nonpreemptive** (once the task begins, it goes to completion) or as **preemptive** (the task can be removed by a task of a higher priority). In current operating systems preemption is the norm. Keep in mind, as noted in Chapter 1, processes can be in user mode or kernel mode. Traditionally, a process running on a single processor system is nonpreemptive when it is in kernel mode.

Similar to processes, threads can be in one of several states. A very simplified thread state diagram is shown in Figure 11.4. As shown, a thread can be ready to run (able to run if selected); running (active); or blocked (waiting on some other event, say I/O or a wake-up, to occur).

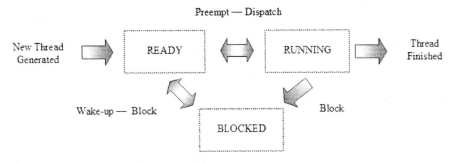

Figure 11.4 High-level thread state diagram.

In Linux the scheduling of a POSIX thread is determined by two factors: priority and scheduling policy.

The system uses the static priority value of a thread to assign it to a ready-to-run list. The static priority values for a Linux system range from 0 to 99, with 0 being the lowest priority. When dealing with a POSIX thread, higher priority threads are scheduled before those with a lower priority. Usually, the priority of a thread is inherited from its creating thread. However, the priority of a thread can be set at creation time by modifying the thread attribute object before the thread is created. Conceptually, the system maintains a separate list for each static priority value. The library calls **sched_get_priority_max** and **sched_get_priority_min** can be used to determine the actual priority limits for a specific scheduling policy.

POSIX specifies three scheduling policies for threads. The first policy, SCHED_OTHER, is used for normal (conventional) processes. The remaining two policies, SCHED_FIFO and SCHED_RR, are for real-time (time-dependent) applications. Implementation-wise, as all scheduling is basically preemptive, these policies are used by the system to determine where threads are inserted in a list and how they move within the list.

- SCHED_OTHER—the system default. This is a time-sharing policy where competing threads with the same static priority (0) are multiplexed (each receiving a time slice) according to their dynamic priority. A thread's dynamic priority is based on its nice level, which is established at runtime. The nice level can be changed using the setpriority system call. The thread's dynamic priority is increased each time it is ready to run but is denied access to the CPU.

- SCHED_FIFO—a first in, first out scheduling policy. SCHED_FIFO threads have a static priority greater than 0. The highest priority, longest waiting thread becomes the next thread to execute. The thread will execute until it finishes, is blocked (such as by an I/O request), is preempted, or yields (calls **sched_yield**). Initially, ready-to-run SCHED_FIFO scheduled threads are placed at the end of their list. If a SCHED_FIFO thread is preempted, it remains at the head of its list and resumes its execution when all higher priority threads have finished or blocked. A SCHED_FIFO thread that yields the processor is placed at the end of its list.

- SCHED_RR—Round-robin scheduling. This is similar to SCHED_FIFO with a time slicing factor (quantum) added in. When a thread has run for a period of time equal to it quantum (and has not finished) it is placed at the end of its list. If a SCHED_RR scheduled process is preempted, as with SCHED_FIFO, it stays at the head of its list, but when recalled, only gets to complete the remaining portion of its quantum.

A scheduling policy and priority of a thread that already exists can be set with the **pthread_setschedparam** library function, detailed in Table 11.8.

Table 11.8 The `pthread_setschedparam` Library Function.

Include File(s)	`<pthread.h>`		Manual Section	**3**

Summary	`int pthread_setschedparam(`
	`    pthread_t target_thread, int policy,`
	`    const struct sched_param *param );`			

Return	Success	Failure	Sets errno	
	0	Nonzero		

The first argument of **pthread_setschedparam** is a valid thread ID. The second argument should be one of the following defined constants: SCHED_OTHER, SCHED_FIFO, or SCHED_RR (see previous discussion). The third argument for this call is a reference to a `sched_param` structure (examine the include file `<sched.h>` for definition details).

If successful, the **pthread_setschedparam** library returns a 0; otherwise, it returns one of the following values: EPERM (1), the calling process does not have superuser privileges; ESRCH (3), the specified thread does not exist; EFAULT (14), `param` references an illegal address; or EINVAL (22), invalid `policy` or `param` value or priority value is inconsistent with scheduling policy. Again, it is important to note that only the superuser can specify SCHED_FIFO or SCHED_RR scheduling (and thus change a thread's static priority to something other than 0); others are left with the system default SCHED_FIFO with a static priority of 0.

Program 11.2 demonstrates the use of the **pthread_setschedparam**, **pthread_getschedparam**, **sched_get_priority_max**, and **sched_get_priority_min** functions. In `main` a scheduling policy is specified and the system's maximum and minimum priority values for the policy are displayed. The policy and an arbitrarily calculated priority are assigned to a `parameter` structure, which is passed to the `threadfunc` function. When a new thread is created, the `threadfunc` function calls **pthread_setschedparam** to set the scheduling policy and priority. To confirm the changes have actually been made, the **pthread_getschedparam** library function is used to retrieve the current scheduling and thread priority settings. The returned results are displayed.

Program 11.2 *Manipulating scheduling parameters.*

```
File : p11.2.cxx
  |     /*
  |        Changing scheduling parameters.
  |     */
  |     #define _GNU_SOURCE
  +     #define _REENTRANT
  |     #include <iostream>
  |     #include <cstdio>
  |     #include <cstring>
  |     #include <pthread.h>
 10     #include <sched.h>
  |     #include <unistd.h>
  |     using namespace std;
  |     char *p[] = {"OTHER ","FIFO ","RR "};
  |     struct parameter {                         // data to pass
  +       int    policy;                           // new policy
  |       int    priority;                         // new priority
  |     };
  |     void *threadfunc( void *);
  |     int
 20     main( ) {
  |       pthread_t          t_id;
  |       struct parameter parm;
  |       int                status;
  |       setvbuf(stdout, (char *)NULL, _IONBF, 0);   // non-buffered output
  +       for( int i=0; i < 3; ++i ){                 // display limits
  |         cout << "Policy SCHED_" << p[i] << "\t MAX = "
  |              << sched_get_priority_max(i);
  |         cout << " MIN = " << sched_get_priority_min(i) << endl;
  |         parm.policy  = i;                        // assign data to pass
 30         parm.priority= (i+1) * 2;                // make up a priority
  |         status=pthread_create( &t_id, NULL, threadfunc, (void *)&parm );
  |         sleep(1);
  |       }
  |       return 0;
  +     }
  |     void *
  |     threadfunc( void *d ) {
  |       struct    sched_param  param;             // local to this function
  |       int       policy;
 40       parameter *p_ptr=(parameter *)d;          // cast to access
  |       param.sched_priority = p_ptr->priority;   // passed data value
  |                                                 // set new scheduling
```

473

```
  |        pthread_setschedparam(pthread_self(), p_ptr->policy, &param );
  |        memset(&param, 0, sizeof(param));               // clear
  +                                                         // retrieve
  |        pthread_getschedparam(pthread_self(), &policy, &param );
  |        cout << "In thread with policy = SCHED_" << p[policy]
  |             << " \tpriority = " << (param.sched_priority)
  |             << " effective ID = " << geteuid() << endl;
 50        return NULL;
  |     }
```

Figure 11.5 shows two runs of Program 11.2. In the first the effective ID of
the user is 0 (that of the superuser). As a result, the requested scheduling
changes are implemented. In the second run the effective ID of the user is
500. The requested changes are not made in the thread and default remains
in effect.

Figure 11.5 Running Program 11.2 as root and as a regular user.

```
linux#  p11.2                                          Run program as root (eid = 0)—
Policy SCHED_OTHER        MAX = 0 MIN = 0              requested changes are implemented.
In thread with policy = SCHED_OTHER     priority = 0 effective ID = 0
Policy SCHED_FIFO         MAX = 99 MIN = 1
In thread with policy = SCHED_FIFO      priority = 4 effective ID = 0
Policy SCHED_RR           MAX = 99 MIN = 1
In thread with policy = SCHED_RR        priority = 6 effective ID = 0
.
.
.                                                      Run program as regular user—
linux$ p11.2                                           requested changes are not implemented.
Policy SCHED_OTHER        MAX = 0 MIN = 0
In thread with policy = SCHED_OTHER     priority = 0 effective ID = 500
Policy SCHED_FIFO         MAX = 99 MIN = 1
In thread with policy = SCHED_OTHER     priority = 0 effective ID = 500
Policy SCHED_RR           MAX = 99 MIN = 1
In thread with policy = SCHED_OTHER     priority = 0 effective ID = 500
```

By now I am sure you have noticed the similarities between the
pthread_setschedparam library call and the **pthread_attr_**
setschedpolicy and **pthread_attr_setschedparam** library calls.
The **pthread_setschedparam** call combines the functionality of the at-
tribute-based calls and allows the user to modify scheduling policy and priority
on the fly for an existing thread.

Find the file `sched.h` that is part of the *source code* for your version of Linux. Its location is somewhat system-specific. The command

```
linux$ find /usr/src -name sched.h -print
```

should reveal its location. On our system this file resides in the `/usr/src/linux-2.4.18-3/include/linux` directory. Examine the `sched.h` file and find the `INIT_TASK(tsk)` macro that is used to establish a variety of scheduling parameters. What starting value is assigned to each of the following: dynamic priority, static priority, scheduling policy, and time slice?

11.7 Using Signals in Threads

In a POSIX multithreaded setting, signals are delivered to the process. If a signal is synchronous (the result of the action of a particular thread), the operating system passes the signal on to the thread that generated the exception. Thus, synchronous signals such as SIGFPE (divide by zero), SIGSEGV (addressing violation), and SIGPIPE (broken pipe) would be passed on to the offending thread (which only makes sense). If a synchronous **pthread_kill** call (see Table 11.9) is used to send a signal, the specified thread also receives the signal. According to POSIX standards, if a signal is asynchronous (not related to a particular thread's activity), such as SIGHUP (hang-up) or SIGINT (interrupt), generated by, say, the **kill** system call, the decision as to which thread should handle the signal is based upon the signal mask configuration of the threads within the process. If more than one thread has not blocked the received signal, there is no guarantee as to which thread will actually receive the signal. To maintain mutex lock integrity, signals handled by threads that cause the thread to terminate, stop—continue will cause the process associated with the thread to also terminate, stop—continue. The details of mutex locking are covered in Section 11.8, "Thread Synchronization." The handling of asynchronous signals by threads in Linux (using the LinuxThreads library implementation) departs somewhat from the POSIX standard. LinuxThreads are LWPs that have their own process IDs. Thus, a signal is always directed to a specific thread.

Table 11.9 The `pthread_kill` Library Function.

Include File(s)	`<pthread.h>` `<signal.h>`		Manual Section	3
Summary	`int pthread_kill(pthread_t thread, int signo);`			
	Success	Failure	Sets errno	
Return	0	Nonzero		

The **pthread_kill** library function accepts a thread ID (of a sibling) as its first argument and an integer signal value as its second argument. Similar to the **kill** system call, the existence of a given thread can be checked by setting the signal argument for **pthread_kill** to 0 and examining the return value of the call. If **pthread_kill** is successful, the signal is sent, and the function returns a 0. If the call fails, a nonzero value is returned, and the signal is not sent. The return of ESRCH (3) means the specified thread does not exist, while the return of EINVAL (22) means an invalid signal was specified. The **pthread_kill** call cannot be used to send a signal to a thread in another process.

All the threads within the process share a common table of information specifying what action should be taken upon receipt of a specific signal. Each thread can alter its action for a particular signal (with certain constraints) by using a signal mask. When a thread is created, it inherits its signal mask and priority from its creating thread. The new thread starts with a clean slate and does not inherit any pending (not acted upon) signals from its creator. The signal mask can be manipulated with the **pthread_sigmask** library function (Table 11.10).

As we are working with signals, an additional header file `<signal.h>` is required when using this call. The first argument for **pthread_sigmask**

Table 11.10 The `pthread_sigmask` Library Function.

Include File(s)	`<pthread.h>` `<signal.h>`		Manual Section	3
Summary	`int pthread_sigmask(int how, const sigset_t *newmask, sigset_t *oldmask);`			
	Success	Failure	Sets errno	
Return	0	Nonzero		

should be one of the defined constants below. These constants indicate how the signal mask should be changed.

Constant	Value	Meaning
SIG_BLOCK	1	Block (ignore) the indicated signal(s).
SIG_UNBLOCK	2	Remove the indicated signal(s).
SIG_MASK	3	Replace the current mask with the referenced mask.

The second argument, `newmask`, is a reference to a `sigset_t` type object. If we track down the `sigset_t` data type, which is usually found in the include file `<sys/signal.h>`, we should find that it is a reference to an array of `unsigned long` integers. The array is used as a bit mask for signals. If we are modifying the signal mask, the `newmask` argument should reference the new signal mask. While we can hand-craft the new signal mask, most prefer to use the appropriate POSIX signal mask manipulation functions shown in Table 11.11.

Table 11.11 Signal Mask Manipulation Functions.

Signal Mask Function	Functionality
`int sigemptyset(sigset_t *set)`	Initialize the signal set to *exclude* all defined signals.
`int sigfillset(sigset_t *set)`	Initialize the signal set to *include* all defined signals.
`int sigaddset(sigset_t *set, int signo)`	Add the indicated signal to the signal set.
`int sigdelset(sigset_t *set, int signo)`	Remove the indicated signal from the signal set.
`int sigismember(sigset_t *set, int signo)`	Returns a nonzero value if the indicated signal is a member of the referenced signal set.

When using the signal mask manipulation functions, be sure to initialize a signal mask before attempting to manipulate it.

The third argument of **pthread_sigmask** references the current signal mask (a returned value). Thus, if the second argument is set to NULL, making the how argument a don't-care, the function returns the current signal mask via the third argument, `*oldmask`.

If the **pthread_sigmask** call is successful, it returns a 0. It returns EFAULT (14) when passed an invalid address for newmask or oldmask. Otherwise, it returns the value EINVAL (22) if the how argument was not SIG_BLOCK, SIG_UNBLOCK, or SIG_MASK.

Program 11.3 demonstrates the use of the **pthread_sigmask** call and several of the signal mask manipulation calls.

Program 11.3 Using pthread_sigmask.

```
File : p11.3.cxx
   |     /*
   |          pthread_sigmask example
   |     */
   |     #define _GNU_SOURCE
   +     #define _REENTRANT
   |     #include <iostream>
   |     #include <cstdio>
   |     #include <cstring>
   |     #include <cstdlib>
  10     #include <pthread.h>
   |     #include <unistd.h>
   |     #include <signal.h>
   |     using namespace std;
   |     const int MAX=3;
   +     void  trapper( int );
   |     int   global_i = 0;
   |     int
   |     main(int argc, char *argv[]) {
   |       struct sigaction  new_action;
  20       new_action.sa_handler = &trapper;
   |       new_action.sa_flags = 0;
   |       sigset_t       my_sigs;              // Signal mask
   |       int            sig_in;
   |       setvbuf(stdout, (char *)NULL, _IONBF, 0);
   +       if ( argc > 1 && argc < MAX+2 ) {
   |         sigemptyset(&my_sigs);                 // Clear it out, set to all 0's
   |         while( argc-- > 1 )                    // Add signal #'s passed in
   |           sigaddset(&my_sigs, atoi(argv[argc]));
   |       } else {
  30         cerr << *argv << " SIG1 ... SIG" <<  MAX << endl;
   |         return 1;
   |       }
   |       for (int i=1; i < NSIG; ++i)           // Attempt to trap all signals
   |         sigaction(i, &new_action, NULL);
   +                                              // BLOCK signals in mask
   |       pthread_sigmask(SIG_BLOCK, &my_sigs, NULL);
   |       cout << "Signal bits turned on" << endl;
   |       for (int i=1; i < NSIG; ++i)
```

```
   |          putchar( sigismember(&my_sigs, i) == 0 ? '0' : '1');
40            cout << "\nWaiting for signals\n";   // Wait for a few signals
   |          while (global_i < MAX){
   |            if ( (sigwait(&my_sigs, &sig_in)) != -1 )
   |              cout << "Signal " << sig_in
   |                  << " in mask - no signal catcher" << endl;
   +            ++global_i;
   |          }
   |          return 0;
   |        }
   |        void
50          trapper( int s ){
   |          cout << "Signal " << s << " not in mask - in signal catcher" << endl;
   |          ++global_i;
   |        }
```

Program 11.3 uses its command-line values (assumed to be numeric values representing valid signal numbers) to build a signal mask. The **sigemptyset** call clears the array representing the signal mask. Each value passed on the command line is added to the signal mask by a call to **sigaddset** (line 28). After the signal mask is created, the program uses the **sigset** call to replace the default action for the receipt of each signal with a call to the user-defined trapper function. The sole purpose of the trapper function is to print a message displaying the numeric value of an incoming signal. The call to **pthread_sigmask** blocks the receipt of the signals in the constructed signal mask. The specified signals will not be handled by the thread (keep in mind that even though we have not made a call to **pthread_create**, we are still dealing with a single thread within main). The content of the signal mask is displayed using the **sigismember** function (line 39) to verify the presence or absence of specific signals in the signal mask.

The program then waits for the receipt of signals. In a loop the **sigwait** call (Table 11.12) is used to wait for signals.

Table 11.12 The sigwait Library Function.

Include File(s)	`<pthread.h>` `<signal.h>`		Manual Section	**3**
Summary	`int sigwait(const sigset_t *set, int *sig);`			
	Success	Failure	Sets errno	
Return	0	Nonzero		

The POSIX version of **sigwait** takes two arguments: a reference to the signal set and a reference to a location to store the returned signal value. If successful, **sigwait** returns a 0 and a reference to the signal as its second argument (remember, this call waits for any signal, not just those in the signal mask). If the call is not successful, it returns a nonzero value, sets its second argument to −1, and returns the value EINVAL (22), indicating an unsupported signal number was found in the signal set, or EFAULT (14) if passed an invalid signal set address.

It is unwise to use **sigwait** to manage synchronous signals, such as floating-point exceptions that are sent to the process itself. Additionally, the Linux-Threads library implementation of **sigwait** installs a dummy signal-catching routine for each signal specified in the signal mask. A sample run of Program 11.3 is shown in Figure 11.6.

Figure 11.6 Output from Program 11.3.

```
linux$ p11.3 2 3
Signal bits turned on
011000000000000000000000000000000000000000000000000000000000000
Waiting for signals
Signal 20 not in mask - in signal catcher    ◄────────  User enters ^Z from keyboard.
Signal 3 in mask - no signal catcher         ◄────────  User enters ^\ from keyboard.
Signal 2 in mask - no signal catcher         ◄────────  User enters ^C from keyboard.
```

In the output shown, produced from a run of Program 11.3, the user passed the program the values 2 and 3 on the command line. The program uses these values to create a signal mask. When signal 2 or 3 is received, the initial thread, generated when `main` executes, does not handle the signals (that is, the `trapper` function is not called). When a non-blocked signal is received (for example the ^Z), the default action occurs: A call to the user-defined function `trapper` is made.

11-4 EXERCISE

Program 11.3 can be run in the background so signals that cannot be generated at the keyboard can be sent to the process. For example,

```
                                        Program is placed in the background.
linux$ p11.3 32 33 19 &    ◄────────    The system returns the process ID.
[1] 5414
linux$
Signal bits turned on
0000000000000000010000000000000110000000000000000000000000000000
Waiting for signals
```

```
linux$ kill -32 5414                    ◄──────────── Send signal 32 to process.
```

When Program 11.3 is passed the set of signal values 32 33 19, what
output is produced when, in turn, each of these signals is sent to the
process? Why do you get this output?

In a multithreaded setting most authors advocate using a separate thread to
handle signal processing. An example of how this can be done is shown in
Program 11.4.

Program 11.4 Using a separate thread to handle signal processing.

```
File : p11.4.cxx
   |      /*
   |              Handling signals in a separate thread
   |      */
   |      #define _GNU_SOURCE
   +      #define _REENTRANT
   |      #include <pthread.h>
   |      #include <iostream>
   |      #include <csignal>
   |      #include <cstdlib>
  10      #include <unistd.h>
   |      using namespace std;
   |      void       *sibling(void *);
   |      void       *thread_sig_handler(void *);
   |      sigset_t   global_sig_set;
   +      int        global_parent_id;
   |      int
   |      main( ){
   |        pthread_t  t1,t2,t3;
   |        sigfillset( &global_sig_set );                    // set of all signals
  20                                                          // BLOCK all in set
   |        pthread_sigmask(SIG_BLOCK, &global_sig_set, NULL);
   |                                                          // Create 3 threads
   |        pthread_create(&t1, NULL, thread_sig_handler, NULL);
   |        pthread_create(&t2, NULL, sibling, NULL);
   +        pthread_create(&t3, NULL, sibling, NULL);
   |        global_parent_id = getpid( );
   |        while (1){
   |          cout << "main thread \t PID: " << getpid() << " TID: "
   |               <<  pthread_self() << endl;
  30          sleep(3);
   |        }
   |        return 0;
   |      }
```

```
 |      void *
 +      sibling(void *arg){
 |        while(1){
 |          cout << "sibling thread \t PID: " << getpid() << " TID: "
 |               << pthread_self() << endl;
 |          sleep(3);
40 |        }
 |        return NULL;
 |      }
 |      void *
 |      thread_sig_handler(void *arg) {
 +        int  sig;
 |        cout << "signal thread \t PID: " << getpid() << " TID: "
 |             << pthread_self() << endl;
 |        while(1){
 |          sigwait( &global_sig_set, &sig );
50 |          if ( sig == SIGINT ){
 |            cout << "I am dead" << endl;
 |            kill( global_parent_id, SIGKILL );
 |          }
 |          cout << endl << "signal " << sig << " caught by signal thread "
 +               << pthread_self() << endl;
 |        }
 |        return NULL;
 |      }
```

In line 21 the program generates and fills a signal mask (indicating all signals). A call to **pthread_sigmask** blocks the signals (except, of course, those signals that even when requested cannot be blocked). Any threads that are subsequently generated will inherit this information. Next, a thread to handle signal processing is created. This thread runs the code in the thread_sig_handler function. This function identifies itself and enters an endless loop. In the loop the call **sigwait** causes this thread to block, waiting for the receipt of one of the signals in the signal mask. When a signal is received, it is examined. If the signal is SIGINT, the thread sends the parent process (running the main thread) a SIGKILL signal, which terminates all processing. Notice that due to their declaration placement in the program code, the signal mask and PID of the initial thread (process) are global. Once the signal-processing thread is established, two additional threads are generated. Both of these threads run the code found in the sibling function. This function contains another endless loop. Every couple of seconds the thread running this code identifies itself and displays its process and thread IDs. When all threads have been generated, main also enters a loop where every few seconds it identifies itself (process and thread IDs). A run of this program (shown in Figure 11.7) is very informative.

Figure 11.7 Output from Program 11.4.

```
linux$ p11.4
signal thread     PID: 15760 TID: 1026
sibling thread    PID: 15761 TID: 2051
main thread       PID: 15758 TID: 1024
sibling thread    PID: 15762 TID: 3076

signal 3 caught by signal thread 1026

signal 20 caught by signal thread 1026
sibling thread    PID: main thread       PID: 15758 TID: 1024
sibling thread    PID: 15761 TID: 2051
15762 TID: 3076
I am dead

signal 2 caught by signal thread 1026
Killed
```

Four threads are generated: main, a signal thread and two sibling threads. Each has its own thread ID and is run as a separate process.

User enters ^\ and ^Z from the keyboard. These signals are handled by the signal-processing thread.

While output is not buffered, it is still interleaved as threads compete.

Entering a ^C (from the keyboard) terminates processing. The signal-processing thread is able to slip in one last message.

11-5 EXERCISE

First, modify Program 11.4 to remove the global reference to the signal mask and parent process ID (check Program 11.2 for one way this can be done). Second, the threads running the sibling function should be passed a signal value that they (the threads) will be responsible for catching and processing. The first sibling should be passed SIGUSR1 and the second sibling passed SIGUSR2. The sibling threads should *not* make use of **sigwait** (think **sigaction**). Run the modified program in the background. Then use the user command **kill** to send SIGUSR1 and SIGUSR2 signals to the main and sibling threads. Record your output using the **script** command. Verify that each thread handles the receipt of signals properly. Is a signal-catching routine established in one thread shared by the others? Note that in older (2.1 or earlier) kernel implementations SIGUSR1 and SIGUSR2 were used by LinuxThreads for thread management. In these settings try using SIGINT and SIGQUIT in place of SIGUSR1 and SIGUSR2.

11.8 Thread Synchronization

It is a given that to fully utilize threads, we need to reliably coordinate their activities. A thread's access to critical sections of common code that modify shared data structures must be protected in a manner such that the integrity of the data referenced is not compromised. POSIX thread activities can be synchronized in a variety of ways.

11.8.1 Mutex Variables

One of the easiest methods to ensure coordination is to use a **mut**ual **ex**clusion lock, or **mutex**. Conceptually, a mutex can be thought of as a binary semaphore with ownership whose state either allows (0, unlocked)[16] or prohibits (nonzero, locked) access. Unlike a binary semaphore, any thread within the scope of a mutex can lock a mutex, but only the thread that locked the mutex *should* unlock it. Again, while it should not be done, unlocking a mutex that a thread did not lock does not generate an error. However, such action results in undefined behavior—forewarned is forearmed. Threads unable to obtain a lock are suspended. As actions on a mutex are atomic, and only one thread at a time can successfully modify the state of a mutex, it can be used to force the serialization of thread activities. If threads associated with multiple processes are to be coordinated, the mutex must be mapped to a common section of memory shared by the processes involved.

The manner in which a mutex is created and initialized determines how it will be used. A mutex is of data type `pthread_mutex_t`. Examining the include file `<bits/pthreadtypes.h>`, we find this data type to be the following structure:

```
typedef struct {
    int __m_reserved;                    /* Reserved for future use        */
    int __m_count;                       /* Depth of recursive locking     */
    _pthread_descr __m_owner;            /* Owner thread (if recursive or
                                            errcheck)                      */
    int __m_kind;                        /* Mutex kind: fast, recursive or
                                            errcheck                       */
    struct _pthread_fastlock __m_lock;   /* Underlying fast lock           */
} pthread_mutex_t;
```

[16] I know, I know—thinking semaphore-wise, you might expect a 1 to indicate unlocked and 0 locked. If the mutex is owned, it is considered locked.

Keep in mind that `pthread_mutex_t` is what is known as an **opaque data type**. That is, its specific structure is implementation-dependent. Thus, a POSIX threads implementation for the `pthread_mutex_t` data type for Linux might well be different from Sun's implementation. When in doubt, check it out!

A mutex, like a thread, can have its attributes specified via an attribute object, which is then passed to the **pthread_mutex_init** library function. Not to be outdone, the mutex attribute object also has its own initialization function, **pthread_mutexattr_init**, a deallocation function, and library functions (such as **pthread_mutexattr_settype**) for modification of the attribute settings once the object has been created. Changing the settings of the mutex attribute object will not change the settings of those mutexes previously allocated. We will restrict this section of our discussion to the following library calls: **pthread_mutexattr_init**, **pthread_mutexattr_settype**, and **pthread_mutex_init** (tables 11.13, 11.14, and 11.15).

Table 11.13 The `pthread_mutexattr_init` Library Function

Include File(s)	<pthread.h>		Manual Section	**3**
Summary	`int pthread_mutexattr_init( pthread_mutexattr_t *attr );`			
	Success	Failure	Sets `errno`	
Return	0	Nonzero		

The **pthread_mutexattr_init** call, which initializes the mutex attribute object, is passed a reference to a `pthread_mutexattr_t` structure. The definition of this structure, shown below, is found in the `/usr/include/bits/pthreadtypes.h` file.

```
typedef struct {
  int __mutexkind;
} pthread_mutexattr_t;
```

At present, the LinuxThreads implementation of POSIX threads provides support only for the attribute specifying the mutex kind. In LinuxThreads a mutex can be one of the following three kinds, with the default being the type fast. The kind (type) of a mutex determines the system's behavior when a thread attempts to lock the mutex (Table 11.14).

Table 11.14

Mutex Kind	Constant	Behavior
fast	PTHREAD_MUTEX_FAST	If the mutex is already locked by another thread, the calling thread blocks. If the thread that owns (locked) the mutex attempts to lock it a second time, the thread will *deadlock*! The thread that unlocks the mutex is assumed to be the owner of the mutex. Unlocking a nonlocked mutex will result in undefined behavior.
recursive	PTHREAD_MUTEX_RECURSIVE	The system will the record number of lock requests for the mutex. The mutex is unlocked only when an equal number of unlock operations have been performed.
error-checking	PTHREAD_MUTEX_ERRORCHECK	If a thread attempts to lock a locked mutex, an error (EDEADLK) is returned.

If the **pthread_mutexattr_init** call is successful, it returns a 0 and a reference to a default pthread_mutexattr_t object; otherwise, it returns the value ENOMEM (12) to indicate there was insufficient memory to perform the initialization. One final note: A fast mutex (the default) is POSIX-based and thus portable. The mutex kinds recursive and error-checking are nonstandard and thus nonportable.

The **pthread_mutexattr_settype** library function is used to modify a mutex attribute object.

Table 11.15 The `pthread_mutexattr_settype` Library Function

Include File(s)	<pthread.h>		Manual Section	3

Summary	`int`
	`pthread_mutexattr_settype(pthread_mutexattr_t *attr,`
	`                           int                     kind );`			

	Success	Failure	Sets errno	
Return	0	Nonzero		

The **pthread_mutexattr_settype** library call is passed a valid reference to a `pthread_mutexattr_t` object (presumably previously initialized by a successful call to **pthread_mutexattr_init**) and an integer argument (defined constant) indicating the mutex kind. The mutex kind is specified by one of the previously discussed PTHREAD_MUTEX_xxx constants. For example, the code sequence

```
pthread_mutexattr_t       my_attributes;
pthread_mutexattr_init( &my_attributes );
 . . .
pthread_mutexattr_settype( &my_attributes, PTHREAD_MUTEX_RECURSIVE);
```

would allocate a mutex attribute object, set the default attributes, and then at a later point change the mutex kind to recursive.[17] If the **pthread_muexattr_settype** call is successful, it returns a 0; otherwise, it returns the value EINVAL (22), indicating it has found an invalid argument.

At this point, we must keep several things in mind. First, initializing a mutex attribute object does not create the actual mutex. Second, if the mutex attribute object is to be shared by threads in separate address spaces, the user is responsible for setting up the mapping of the mutex attribute object to a common shared memory location. Third, if a mutex is shared across processes, it must be allocated dynamically, and therefore a call to **pthread_mutex_init** and/or **pthread_init** would be needed. The mechanics of how to set up a shared mutex for threads sharing the same process space and those in separate process spaces can be found in Program 11.5.

Next, let's look at initializing a mutex using the **pthread_mutex_init** library call. Table 11.16 provides the details for **pthread_mutex_init**.

Table 11.16 The `pthread_mutex_init` Library Function

Include File(s)	`<pthread.h>`		Manual Section	3

Summary	`int`
	`pthread_mutex_init(pthread_mutex_t   *mutex,`
	`                   const pthread_mutexattr_t`
	`                   *mutexattr);`			

Return	Success		Failure	Sets `errno`
	0		Nonzero	

---

[17] Older version LinuxThreads may not support the **pthread_mutexattr_settype** call. An equivalent but deprecated call would be

```
thread_mutexattr_setkind_np(&my_attributes, PTHREAD_MUTEX_RECURSIVE_NP);
```

The **pthread_mutex_init** library function initializes a mutex. Its first argument, *mutex, is a reference to the mutex, and the second argument, *mutexattr, is a reference to a previously initialized mutex attribute object. If the second argument is NULL, the mutex will be initialized with the default attributes. Thus, with **pthread_mutex_init**, we can generate a mutex with the default characteristics. For example, with the statements

```
. . .
pthread_mutex_t        my_lock;
. . .
pthread_mutex_init( &my_lock, NULL );
```

pthread_mutex_init returns a 0 and a reference to the mutex if successful. If the **pthread_mutex_init** call fails, it returns the value EINVAL (22) to indicate an invalid value for either the mutex or mutexattr argument.

While this approach (if we use an attribute object) is somewhat circuitous, it does allow greater freedom over the allocation of the mutex object. An alternate approach is to use a predefined constant PTHREAD_MUTEX_INIIALIZER[18] to initialize the mutex. The code sequence for this is:

```
pthread_mutex_t        my_lock = PTHREAD_MUTEX_INITIALIZER;
```

Additionally, LinuxThreads supports similar initializers for its two nonstandard mutex types: PTHREAD_RECURSIVE_MUTEX_INITIALIZER_NP and PTHREAD_ERRORCHECK_MUTEX_INITIALIZER_NP.

Once the mutex has been created and initialized, there are four library functions that operate on the mutex, listed in Table 11.17.

Table 11.17 The **mutex** Manipulation Library Functions.

Include File(s)	<pthread.h>		Manual Section	**3**

Summary	`int pthread_mutex_lock(     pthread_mutex_t *mutex );`
	`int pthread_mutex_trylock(  pthread_mutex_t *mutex );`
	`int pthread_mutex_unlock(   pthread_mutex_t *mutex );`
	`int pthread_mutex_destroy(  pthread_mutex_t *mutex );`			

	Success	Failure	Sets errno	
Return	0	Nonzero		

[18] In <pthread.h> we find this constant to be defined as {0, 0, 0, PTHREAD_MUTEX_TIMED_NP, __LOCK_INITIALIZER}.

Each function takes a single argument, *mutex, a reference to the mutex. The library functions **pthread_mutex_lock** and **pthread_mutex_unlock** are used to lock and unlock a mutex. A **pthread_mutex_lock**, issued on a previously locked mutex, causes the issuing thread to block until the lock is free. If the mutex is unlocked, **pthread_mutex_lock** locks the mutex and changes the ownership of the mutex to the thread issuing the lock. The manual pages on this function note that should the owner of a mutex issue a second lock on mutex that it has previously locked, deadlock will result. The **pthread_mutex_unlock** library function is used to unlock a mutex. The thread issuing the unlock call should be the same as the thread that locked the mutex; otherwise, the resulting behavior is unspecified. Again, it is very easy to break the rules, as with the default fast type mutex, the concept of ownership is not enforced. The call **pthread_mutex_ trylock** is similar to **pthread_mutex_lock** (i.e., it will lock an unlocked mutex); however, it will not cause the thread to block if the indicated mutex is already locked. The library function **pthread_mutex_destroy** causes the referenced mutex to become uninitialized. However, the user must explicitly free the memory referenced by the mutex for it to be reclaimed by the operating system. In general, if two or more resources are to be acquired by multiple threads and each resource is protected by a mutex, a locking hierarchy should be established to reduce the chance of deadlock. That is, each thread should attempt to gain access to each resource in the same order, and when done, release the associated mutexes in the reverse order of their acquisition.

When these functions are successful, they return a 0; otherwise, they return a nonzero value. Both **pthread_mutex_trylock** and **pthread_mutex_destroy** return the value EBUSY (16) if the mutex is already locked. All functions return the value EINVAL (22) if the mutex argument is invalid.

We use two programs to demonstrate the use of a mutex. The programs are adaptations of an earlier producer–consumer example described in some detail in the chapter on semaphores (Chapter 7). As both programs use the same section of produce and consume logic, this code along with a small driver routine called do_work has been placed in a separate file. For similar reasons, code for includes and declarations have been placed in a common header file called local_mutex.h. Program 11.5 uses a mutex to coordinate the activities of multiple nondetached threads. Each thread executes a series of calls to the produce and consume routines. These routines access a shared file that acts as a common buffer. Access to the buffer is controlled by the mutex. The include file for Program 11.5 is shown below.

Program 11.5 Header file for mutex example.

```
File : local_mutex.h
   |      /*
   |            Common local header file: local_mutex.h
   |      */
   |      #ifndef LOCAL_MUTEX_H
   +      #define LOCAL_MUTEX_H
   |      #define _GNU_SOURCE
   |      #define _REENTRANT
   |      #include <iostream>
   |      #include <cstdio>
  10      #include <pthread.h>
   |      #include <fstream>
   |      #include <stdlib.h>
   |      #include <unistd.h>
   |      #include <sys/types.h>
   +      #include <sys/wait.h>
   |      #include <sys/time.h>
   |                                              // When we share a mutex
   |      #include <sys/ipc.h>                     // we will need these.
   |      #include <sys/shm.h>
  20      static const char *BUFFER="./buffer";
   |      static const int MAX=99;
   |      void do_work( void );
   |      using namespace std;
   |      #endif
```

Most of what we see in the header file is self-explanatory or has been covered in previous sections. However, there are some items of note. The first mutex program example contains multiple threads within one process space; the second example uses single threads, each associated with its own heavy-weight process. When interprocess coordination is required, the mutex and two additional common variables must be mapped to a shared memory location. To accomplish this, we need to use the IPC shared memory functions (discussed in Chapter 8), and thus must include their corresponding header files. The defined constant BUFFER is the name of a local file that will be used as a common shared location to store generated data.

The listing containing the common logic for the production and consumption of data is shown in Program 11.5.PC.

Program 11.5.PC Common producer–consumer code for mutex examples.

```
File : p11.5.PC.cxx
   |      /*
   |            Common producer & consumer code
   |      */
```

```
    |       #include "local_mutex.h"
    +       struct timespec some_time;
    |       fstream          fptr;                    // common buffer location
    |       extern pthread_mutex_t *m_LOCK;           // shared mutex
    |       extern int            *s_shm,             // setup flag
    |                             *c_shm;             // counter
 10     /*
    |          Generate a random # within specified range
    |       */
    |       int
    |       my_rand(int start, int range){
    +         struct timeval t;
    |         gettimeofday(&t, (struct timezone *)NULL);
    |         return (int)(start+((float)range * rand_r((unsigned *)&t.tv_usec))
    |                   / (RAND_MAX+1.0));
    |       }
 20     /*
    |            Produce a random # and write to a common repository
    |       */
    |       void
    |       produce( ) {
    +         int   err, *n;
    |         cout << pthread_self( ) << "\t P: attempting to produce \t"
    |             << getpid( ) << endl;
    |         cout.flush( );
    |         if (pthread_mutex_trylock(m_LOCK) != 0) {        // LOCK
 30           cout << pthread_self( ) << "\t P: lock busy           \t"
    |               << getpid( ) << endl;
    |           cout.flush( );
    |           return;
    |         }
    +         n  = new int;                            // allocate
    |         *n = my_rand(1,MAX);
    |         fptr.open(BUFFER, ios::out | ios::app);        // Open for append
    |         fptr.write( (char *) n, sizeof(*n) );
    |         fptr.close( );
 40       delete n;                                // release
    |         cout << pthread_self() << "\t P: The # [" << *n
    |             << "] deposited    \t" << getpid( )  << endl;
    |           cout.flush( );
    |         some_time.tv_sec = 0; some_time.tv_nsec = 10000;
    +         nanosleep(&some_time, NULL);                   // sleep a bit
    |         if ((err=pthread_mutex_unlock(m_LOCK)) != 0){  // UNLOCK
    |           cerr << "P: unlock failure " << err << endl;
    |           cout.flush( );
    |           exit(102);
 50       }
    |       }
    |       /*
    |            Consume the next random number from the common repository
```

```
    |      */
    +      void
    |      consume( ) {
    |        int              err, *n;
    |        cout << pthread_self( ) << "\t C: attempting to consume \t"
    |             << getpid( ) << endl;
   60        cout.flush( );
    |        if (pthread_mutex_trylock(m_LOCK) != 0) {         // LOCK
    |          cout << pthread_self( ) << "\t C: lock busy              \t"
    |               << getpid( ) << endl;
    |          cout.flush( );
    +          return;
    |        }
    |        fptr.open(BUFFER, ios::in);                       // Try to read
    |        if ( fptr ) {                                     // If present
    |          fptr.close( );
   70          fptr.open (BUFFER, ios::in|uis::out);           // Reopen for R/W
    |        }
    |        fptr.seekp( *c_shm * sizeof(int), ios::beg );
    |        n = new int;                                      // allocate
    |        *n = 0;
    +        fptr.read( (char *)n, sizeof(*n));
    |        if ((*n) > 0) {                                   // For positive values
    |          cout << pthread_self() << "\t C: The # [" << *n
    |               << "] obtained    \t" << getpid( )    << endl;
    |          cout.flush( );
   80          fptr.seekp( *c_shm * sizeof(int), ios::beg );
    |          *n = -(*n);
    |          fptr.write( (char *) n, sizeof(*n) );
    |          fptr.close( );
    |          ++*c_shm;                                       // increment counter
    +        } else {
    |          cout << pthread_self( ) << "\t C: No new # to consume     \t"
    |               << getpid( ) << endl;
    |          cout.flush( );
    |        }
   90        delete n;                                         // release
    |        fptr.close( );
    |        some_time.tv_sec = 0; some_time.tv_nsec = 10000;
    |        nanosleep(&some_time, NULL);
    |        if ((err=pthread_mutex_unlock(m_LOCK)) != 0){   // UNLOCK
    +          cerr<< "C: unlock failure " << err << endl;
    |          exit(104);
    |        }
    |      }
    |      /*
  100       Simulate some work, 10 iterations about half produce, half consume
    |      */
    |      void
    |      do_work( ) {
```

```
 |         if (!(*s_shm)) {                                  // Clear @ start
 +           pthread_mutex_lock(m_LOCK);                      // LOCK
 |           if (!(*s_shm)++) {
 |             cout << pthread_self( ) << "  \t  : clearing the buffer  \t"
 |                  << getpid() << endl;
 |             fptr.open( BUFFER, ios::out | ios::trunc );
110            fptr.close( );
 |           }
 |           pthread_mutex_unlock(m_LOCK);                    // UNLOCK
 |         }
 |         for (int i = 0; i < 10; ++i) {
 +           some_time.tv_sec = 0; some_time.tv_nsec = 10000;
 |           nanosleep(&some_time, NULL);                     // sleep a bit
 |           switch ( my_rand(1,2) ) {
 |           case 1:
 |             produce();
120            break;
 |           case 2:
 |             consume();
 |           }
 |         }
 +       }
```

Overall, the `produce` and `consume` code listed in Program 11.5.PC is very much the same as what we saw in the Chapter 7 example. Nonetheless, there have been some important changes and a few additions. At the top of the listing a `timespec` structure, `some_time`, is declared. The program uses the **nanosleep** real-time library function instead of **sleep** to suspend the current thread from execution.

Next is the declaration of a file stream pointer, `fptr`, which is used to reference the file where generated values will be stored and retrieved. Following this is a reference to a mutex (`m_LOCK`) and two references to integers (`s_shm` and `c_shm`). The first, `s_shm`, is used as a flag to indicate whether or not the file, used as a storage place for generated data, has been cleared (reset). The second, `c_shm`, is used as a counter–index offset for the current item to be retrieved from the file. As the variables `m_LOCK`, `s_shm`, and `c_shm` were initially declared in the source file with the code for the function `main`, they are qualified as `extern` (external) here.

As shown, the user-defined `produce` function attempts, using the **pthread_mutex_trylock** call, to lock the mutex referenced by `m_LOCK`. If it is not successful, a message is displayed and the function is exited. If the mutex can be obtained, a random value is generated. The random value is stored at a temporarily allocated memory location referenced by n. Once the value is stored in the file, the file buffer is flushed and the file closed. Next, the temporary location is freed, and a call to **nanosleep** is made to simulate some additional processing. As a last step, the mutex is released.

Conversely, the user-defined consume function tries to lock the mutex. If it is successful, it tries to consume (read) a number from the file. To accomplish this, the file is opened for reading and writing (ios::in | ios::out). The offset into the file is calculated using the current index referenced by c_shm multiplied by the sizeof of the data value written to the file. The **seekp** method is used to move the file pointer to the proper offset in the file where the value is to be retrieved. As in the produce function, a temporarily allocated location is used to store the retrieved value. The newly allocated location is initially cleared (set to 0) prior to the call to **read**. If the value obtained is positive, the value is displayed. The displayed value is written back to its same location in the file as a negative number. The **seekp** method is used to move the file pointer back to its proper location so the update process will overwrite the correct data item. Rewriting the value as a negative is used as a technique for keeping track of consumed values. Once the value is rewritten, the file buffer is flushed and the current index value is incremented. Whether or not a valid value is retrieved, the file is closed. A short **nanosleep** (again to simulate additional processing) is made, and the temporary storage location freed. Finally, the mutex is unlocked and made available to other threads.

The user-defined function do_work uses the s_shm reference to determine if the file that stores the output has been cleared. Upon first entry, *s_shm references a 0. In this case the if logic is entered. The mutex referenced by m_LOCK is used to bracket access to the code that opens the file for writing (ios::out), truncating (ios::trunc) its content. The value referenced by s_shm is incremented in this process, allowing the initialization to occur only once. Following this, the user-defined do_work function sleeps for a few seconds to permit random startup times, and then loops 10 times to simulate a series of production and consumption events. If the random number generator is decent, there should be a somewhat even split of the calls to produce and consume within the loop. The loop also contains a call to **nanosleep**.

Program 11.5.INTRA contains the code for the function main for an intraprocess mutex example. All threads in this example share a common address space and are associated with an underlying LWP.

Program 11.5.INTRA   Code for function main for intraprocess mutex example.

```
File : p11.5.INTRA.cxx
  |      /*
  |          INTRA process main (multiple threads - one process space)
  |          Compile: g++  p11.5.PC.cxx  p11.5.INTRA.cxx  -lpthread -o INTRA
  |      */
  +      #include "local_mutex.h"
```

```
  |     pthread_mutex_t LOCK,    *m_LOCK = &LOCK;
  |     int             setup,  *s_shm  = &setup,
  |                     current,*c_shm  = &current;
  |     int
10    main(int argc, char *argv[]) {
  |       int  i, n;
  |       pthread_t worker[MAX];                    // worker TID's
  |       if ( argc != 2 ) {
  |         cerr << "Usage: " << *argv << " n_workers" << endl;
  +         return 1;
  |       }
  |       pthread_mutex_init(&LOCK,  NULL);
  |       *s_shm = 0;                               // Start as NOT setup
  |       *c_shm = 0;                               // current index (offset)
20      n = atoi(argv[1]) < MAX ? atoi(argv[1]) : MAX;
  |                                                 // # of threads to create
  |       for( i=0; i < n; ++i)                     // create each thread
  |         pthread_create( &worker[i], NULL,
  |                     (void *(*)(void *))do_work, (void *)NULL );
  |                                                 // wait for all to finish
  |       for(i=0; i < n; ++i )
  +         pthread_join(worker[i], (void **) NULL);
  |                                                 // show contents of buffer
  |       cout << "Contents of " << BUFFER
  |            << " negative values were 'consumed'." << endl;
  |       fstream  fptr;
30      bool     done = false;
  |       fptr.open( BUFFER, ios::in );
  |       while ( !done ) {
  |         fptr.read( (char *)&n, sizeof(n) );
  |         if ( fptr.fail() )
  +           done = true;
  |         else
  |           cout << n << endl;
  |       }
  |       fptr.close( );
40      return 0;
  |     }
```

In Program 11.5.INTRA several static declarations are made (by their placement prior to the function `main`). These are a mutex called `LOCK` and a reference to the mutex called `*m_LOCK`. The variables `setup` (is the file setup—cleared) and `current` (the index into the file) are also statically allocated. In `main` the mutex is initialized (line 17). Remember that initialization should be done only once—re-initializing an already initialized mutex results in undefined behavior. As the value NULL is passed as the second argument to **pthread_mutex_init**, the mutex has the default characteristics. The next

495

two statements assign both the setup and current variables the value 0. Next, the program checks the value passed in on the command line. This value represents the number of threads to be produced. As written, the value should be less than MAX (set arbitrarily at 99 in the include file). A for loop is used to create the specified number of threads. The thread IDs are saved, and each thread is passed a reference to the do_work function. As the do_work function reference is not the required data type for this parameter, it must be cast to keep the compiler from complaining. Once all the threads are created, the program waits for all the threads to terminate. When all threads are done, the contents of the file (the common buffer used by the threads) is displayed.

A compilation and partial run of the program is shown in Figure 11.8.

Figure 11.8 A compile and partial run of Program 11.5 with intraprocess mutexes.

```
linux$ g++  p11.5.PC.cxx  p11.5.INTRA.cxx  -lpthread -o INTRA
linux$ INTRA 3
1026      : clearing the buffer        18353          Notice the different thread
1026      P: attempting to produce     18353          IDs. Each thread is mapped
1026      P: The # [94] deposited       18353  ◄──    to a separate LWP (that has
2051      C: attempting to consume     18354          its own PID).
2051      C: lock busy                 18354
3076      C: attempting to consume     18355
3076      C: lock busy                 18355
. . .
1026      C: attempting to consume     18353
3076      P: attempting to produce     18355
3076      P: lock busy                 18355
1026      C: The # [48] obtained       18353
2051      C: attempting to consume     18354
2051      C: No new # to consume       18354
. . .
1026      P: The # [51] deposited       18353
1026      P: attempting to produce     18353
1026      P: The # [30] deposited       18353
Contents of ./buffer negative values were 'consumed'.
-94
-48
-50
-58
-98
-49
51
30
```

While the output of this program tends to be somewhat voluminous, it is very informative. With all the cout statements, it is easy to see what individual threads are doing. In this case there are three threads, with the thread IDs of 1026, 2051, and 3076. The mutex forces the competing threads to access the shared data structure in a manner that prevents data loss. If we rerun the program and pass the output to **grep** and keep only the lines containing the # symbol, we should find the output to be well behaved and furthermore note that the values placed in the file by one thread can be consumed by a different thread. A sample of this type of output is shown in Figure 11.9.

Figure 11.9 Filtering the output of Program 11.3.

```
linux$ INTRA 3 | grep '#'
1026     C: No new # to consume          18321
3076     P: The # [51] deposited         18323
2051     P: The # [77] deposited         18322
3076     C: The # [51] obtained          18323
2051     P: The # [61] deposited         18322  ←
3076     P: The # [86] deposited         18323          Deposited by thread 2051 and
2051     C: The # [77] obtained          18322          consumed by thread 1026
1026     C: The # [61] obtained          18321  ←
3076     C: The # [86] obtained          18323
1026     C: No new # to consume          18321
2051     P: The # [33] deposited         18322
3076     P: The # [96] deposited         18323
2051     C: The # [33] obtained          18322
3076     P: The # [91] deposited         18323
```

11-6 EXERCISE

In the Chapter 7 example we used two semaphores (MADE and READ) to coordinate activities. How is it that in this example we were able to coordinate activities using just one mutex?

Edit the source file p11.5.PC.cxx and comment out all references to **nanosleep**. Recompile the program. Run the INTRA executable several times with a varying number of threads. Redirect the output to **grep** and have it search for the word *obtained*. Pass this output to **wc -1** to find the number of actual values obtained. For example,

```
linux$ INTRA 5 | grep obtained | wc -1
        18
linux$ INTRA 10 | grep obtained | wc -1
        40
```

Is there any relationship between the number of threads specified and the number of overall values obtained? (It's best to run each sequence a number of times and obtain an average.) If yes, what is the relationship (graphs are acceptable)? If no, why is there no relationship?

The section of code containing `main` can be rewritten to support multiple heavyweight processes using a mutex mapped to a shared memory location. In this implementation the `setup` and `current` variables, which must be accessible across processes, are also mapped to a shared memory location. Program 11.5.INTER displays the code to accomplish this.

Program 11.5.INTER   Code for function `main` for interprocess mutex example.

```
File : p11.5.INTER.cxx
  |      /*
  |          INTER process main (multiple processes - 1 thread each)
  |          Compile: g++  p11.5.PC.cxx  p11.5.INTER.cxx  -lpthread -o INTER
  |      */
  +      #include "local_mutex.h"
  |      pthread_mutex_t  *m_LOCK;                    // Shared memory pointer
  |      int              m_shmid, i_shmid,           // Shared memory IDs
  |                       *s_shm, *c_shm;             // Shared setup and counter
  |      int
 10      main(int argc, char *argv[]) {
  |        pthread_mutexattr_t  the_attr_obj;                    // attribute object
  |        int  i, n;
  |        if ( argc != 2) {
  |          cerr << "Usage: " << *argv << " n_workers" << endl;
  +          return 1;
  |        }
  |        n = atoi(argv[1]) < MAX ? atoi(argv[1]) : MAX;
  |        if((m_shmid=shmget(IPC_PRIVATE,sizeof(pthread_mutex_t),IPC_CREAT|
  |                      0666))<0){
  |          perror("shmget fail mutex");
 20          return 2;
  |        }
  |        if ((m_LOCK=(pthread_mutex_t *)shmat(m_shmid,0,0)) == (pthread_
  |            mutex_t *) -1){
  |          perror("shmat fail mutex");
  |          return 3;
  +        }
  |        if ((i_shmid=shmget(IPC_PRIVATE,sizeof(int)*2,IPC_CREAT|0666))<0){
  |          perror("shmget fail ints");
  |          return 4;
```

498

```
  |        }
 30        if ((s_shm=(int *) shmat(i_shmid, 0, 0)) == (int *) -1){
  |          perror("shmat ints");
  |          return 5;
  |        }
  |        c_shm  = s_shm + sizeof(int);            // reference  correct loc
  +        *s_shm = *c_shm = 0;                     // start counter (offset)
  |        pthread_mutexattr_init( &the_attr_obj);  // initialize attrib obj
  |        for( i=0; i < n; ++i)
  |          if ( fork() == 0 ){                    // generate child process
  |            do_work( );                          // child process does work
 40            exit( 2 );
  |          }
  |        while( (n = (int) wait( NULL)) && n != -1 )  // wait for child
  |                                                          processes
  |                       ;
  |        shmdt((char *) m_LOCK);                  // cleanup shared memory
  +        shmdt((char *) s_shm);
  |        shmctl(m_shmid, IPC_RMID, (struct shmid_ds *) 0);
  |        shmctl(i_shmid, IPC_RMID, (struct shmid_ds *) 0);
  |        cout << "Contents of " << BUFFER         // show contents of buffer
  |            << " negative values were 'consumed'." << endl;
 50        fstream   fptr;
  |        bool      done = false;
  |        fptr.open( BUFFER, ios::in );
  |        while ( !done ) {
  |        fptr.read( (char *)&n, sizeof(n) );
  +          if ( fptr.fail() )
  |            done = true;
  |          else
  |            cout << n << endl;
  |        }
 60        fptr.close( );
  |        return 0;
  |      }
```

While some of the code is similar to the preceding intraprocess example, additional steps are taken to create and manipulate the shared mutex as well as the shared data values (setup and current). First, a shared memory segment large enough to hold a mutex is allocated (line 18), and a reference to the segment is to m_LOCK. Second, a shared memory segment large enough to hold two integers is allocated. The first part of the second segment, which will hold the value for setup, is referenced by s_shm. The second half of the segment, used to hold the value of current, is referenced by c_shm. The sizeof operator is used to find the proper offset for the second integer reference (see line 34). The shared memory locations for setup and current are set to 0. The for loop that generated the threads is replaced with a loop to generate child processes (using

499

fork). The child process, which by default has a single thread of control, executes the do_work function. The initial process waits for all the child processes to terminate. Once the child processes are finished, the shared memory is removed and the contents of the common buffer (the file) are displayed. This program segment can be compiled with the statement

```
linux$ g++ p11.5.PC.cxx p11.5.INTER.cxx -lpthread -o INTER
```

The output of this interprocess mutex example should be similar to the intraprocess example with the thread IDs remaining constant at 1024. A sample output sequence is shown in Figure 11.10.

Figure 11.10 A run of Program 11.3 with inter-process mutexes.

```
linux$ INTER 3 | grep #
1024      P: The # [76] deposited        18755
1024      P: The # [25] deposited        18754
1024      C: The # [76] obtained         18755
1024      P: The # [68] deposited        18754       Notice all the thread IDs are
1024      C: The # [25] obtained         18755       the same. Each thread is
1024      C: The # [68] obtained         18754  ◄─── associated with a heavyweight
1024      C: No new # to consume         18753       (standard) process—not with
1024      C: No new # to consume         18755       a LWP
1024      C: No new # to consume         18754
1024      C: No new # to consume         18755
1024      P: The # [17] deposited        18754
1024      C: The # [17] obtained         18755
```

11-7   EXERCISE

Which example (the INTRA or the INTER) seems to be able to process the greatest number of values for the number of threads and processes involved? Run the two versions with **/usr/bin/time** to obtain CPU time-usage data. You may want to redirect the output of the programs to /dev/null to reduce the volume of output. Why are the results so different?

11.8.2 Condition Variables

Sometimes we need to coordinate the activities of threads using the current value of mutex-protected data. Say, for example, we want to notify a reader thread once a writer thread has filled its data set. The counter for the number of items in the data set and the access to the data is protected by a mutex. The POSIX implementation of threads provides a construct called a **condition variable** that can be used for this purpose. A condition variable is associated with a specific mutex and predicate (condition). Similar to a mutex, a condition variable should be global and can be mapped to shared memory if it is to be used by threads in more than one process space. A thread uses the condition variable to either notify other cooperating threads (with access to the same condition variable) that the condition (predicate) has been met or to block and wait for the receipt of notification. When a thread blocks on a condition variable, it atomically releases the associated mutex, allowing other threads access to the mutex. Several threads can be blocked, waiting for the same notification. The thread that generates the notification does so by signaling the associated condition variable.

The majority of what was discussed concerning the creation and initialization techniques of a mutex also applies to the creation and initialization of a condition variable. The corresponding library functions have the occurrences of the string _mutex_ replaced with _cond_.

As with a mutex, a condition variable attribute object can be created, set, and then referenced when creating a condition variable. However, at present the LinuxThreads implementation of POSIX threads does not support condition variable attributes, and the reference to the cond_attr object (the second parameter to the **pthread_cond_init** function) is ignored. Like a mutex, a condition variable can be created and initialized in a single statement:

```
pthread_cond_t my_condition = PTHREAD_COND_INITIALIZER;
```

When a thread wants to notify others, it uses the library function **pthread_cond_signal** (signal one thread) or **pthread_cond_broadcast** (signal all threads). The specifics for the condition variable notification functions can be found in Table 11.18.

Table 11.18 The Condition Variable Notification Library Functions.

Include File(s)	<pthread.h>		Manual Section	3
Summary	`int pthread_cond_signal(   pthread_cond_t *cond );` `int pthread_cond_broadcast(pthread_cond_t *cond );`			
	Success	Failure	Sets errno	
Return	0	Nonzero		

The argument *cond is a reference to a condition variable of the type pthread_cond_t. When **pthread_cond_signal** is used, one thread blocked on the same condition variable will be unblocked. If several threads are blocked, the thread receiving notification is not specified. If **pthread_cond_broadcast** is called, all threads blocked on the condition variable are notified. Once awakened, a thread must still acquire the associated mutex. Either call essentially becomes a no-op if there are no threads waiting for notification. The value EINVAL (22) is returned if *cond references an illegal address.

The library functions **pthread_cond_wait** and **pthread_cond_timedwait** cause the calling thread to wait and block on a condition variable. Under the covers these functions atomically unlock the associated mutex (which must be locked prior to the call), suspend the thread's execution, and relock the mutex (by issuing a **pthread_lock_mutex**). The waiting thread does not consume CPU time.

Table 11.19 The Condition Wait Library Functions.

Include File(s)	<pthread.h>		Manual Section	3
Summary	`int pthread_cond_wait(pthread_cond_t *cond, pthread_mutex_t *mutex); int pthread_cond_timedwait(pthread_cond_t *cond, pthread_mutex_t *mutex, const struct timespec *abstime);`			
	Success	Failure	Sets errno	
Return	0	Nonzero		

The first argument, *cond, is a reference to a condition variable. The second argument, *mutex, is a reference to the associated mutex. The **pthread_cond_timedwait** function is similar to **pthread_cond_wait** except it will time out and return an error, ETIME (62), if the value referenced by *abstime is met or exceeded. The *abstime argument for **pthread_cond_timedwait** references a timespec structure that can be tracked down to the following structure:

```
typedef struct timespec {
         time_t      tv_sec;     /* seconds        */
         long        tv_nsec;    /* and nanoseconds */
    } timespec_t;
```

If a signal or **fork** interrupts either of these calls, the value EINTR (4) is returned. If any of the arguments are invalid, the value EFAULT (14) is returned.

Program 11.6, a variation of a bounded buffer producer-consumer problem, demonstrates the use of a condition variable. In this program, a reader thread continually reads data from standard input and fills a small data buffer. When the buffer is full, the reader thread notifies a writer thread to empty (display) the buffer so that it may be filled again. When an end-of-file is encountered, notification is sent to the writer thread to write out any partial data left in the buffer. A finished flag is set, notifying both the reader and writer that processing is complete.

Program 11.6 Using a condition variable.

```
File : p11.6.cxx
   |      /*
   |            Using a condition variable
   |      */
   |      #define _GNU_SOURCE
   +      #define _REENTRANT
   |      #include <iostream>
   |      #include <cctype>
   |      #include <pthread.h>
   |      using namespace std;
  10      const int MAX=5;
   |                                                          // global
   |      pthread_mutex_t lock_it  = PTHREAD_MUTEX_INITIALIZER;
   |      pthread_cond_t  write_it = PTHREAD_COND_INITIALIZER;
   |      typedef struct {                               // a small data buffer
   +         char              buffer[MAX];              // the buffer
   |         int               how_many;                // # of chars in buffer
   |      } BUFFER;
   |      BUFFER          share = {"", 0};               // start as empty
   |      void            *read_some (void *),
  20                      *write_some(void *);
   |      bool            finished = false;using namespace std;
   |      int
   |      main( ) {
   |      pthread_t       t_read,
   +                      t_write;                       // TID's
   |                                                     // create the threads
   |         pthread_create(&t_read,  NULL, read_some, (void *) NULL);
   |         pthread_create(&t_write, NULL, write_some,(void *) NULL);
   |                                                     // wait for the writer
  30         pthread_join(t_write, (void **) NULL);
   |         pthread_mutex_destroy( &lock_it  );         // clean up
   |         pthread_cond_destroy( &write_it );
```

```
  |      return 0;
  |    }
  +    //       Code to fill the buffer
  |    void *
  |    read_some(void * junk) {
  |      char  ch;
  |      cout << "R " << pthread_self( ) << "\t: Starting" << endl;
 40    while (!finished) {
  |        pthread_mutex_lock(&lock_it);
  |        if (share.how_many != MAX) {                    // buffer not full
  |          cin.get(ch);
  |          if ( cin.fail( ) ) {                          // end-of-file
  +            share.buffer[share.how_many] = (char)NULL;
  |            share.how_many = MAX;
  |            finished     = true;                // we are all done
  |            cout << "R " << pthread_self( ) << "\t: Signaling done" << endl;
  |            pthread_cond_signal(&write_it);        // signal condition var
 50            pthread_mutex_unlock(&lock_it);
  |            break;
  |          } else {                                  // sanitize input chars
  |            share.buffer[share.how_many] = isalnum(ch) ? ch : '#';
  |            cout << "R " << pthread_self( ) << "\t: Got char ["
  +                        << share.buffer[share.how_many++] << "]" << endl;
  |            if ( share.how_many == MAX ) {        // if full
  |              cout << "R " << pthread_self( ) << "\t: Signaling full"
  |                                                    << endl;
  |              pthread_cond_signal(&write_it);
  |            }
 60          }
  |        }
  |        pthread_mutex_unlock(&lock_it);
  |      }
  |      cout << "R " << pthread_self( ) << "\t: Exiting" << endl;
  +      return NULL;
  |    }
  |    //    Code to write (display) buffer
  |    void *
  |    write_some(void *junk) {
 70    int i;
  |      cout << "W " << pthread_self( ) << "\t: Starting" << endl;
  |      while (!finished ) {
  |        pthread_mutex_lock(&lock_it);
  |        cout << "W " << pthread_self( ) << "\t: Waiting" << endl;
  +        while (share.how_many != MAX)              // while not full
  |          pthread_cond_wait(&write_it, &lock_it);    // wait for notify
  |        cout << "W " << pthread_self( ) << "\t: Writing buffer" << endl;
  |        for( i=0; share.buffer[i] && share.how_many;
  |             ++i, share.how_many--)
  |          cout.put(share.buffer[i]);
```

```
80          cout.put('\n');
 |          pthread_mutex_unlock(&lock_it);
 |      }
 |      cout << "W " << pthread_self( ) << "\t: Exiting" << endl;
 |      return NULL;
 +      }
```

In this program a mutex, `lock_it`, and a condition variable, `write_it`, are allocated and initialized to their default settings prior to `main`. Their location, prior to `main` and to the functions that will reference them, guarantees they will be global in scope and accessible by all threads associated with this process space. A small buffer consisting of five locations and an indexing counter is defined, and a buffer of this type, called `share`, is allocated and initialized. A Boolean flag called `finished` is set to `false` before processing begins. In `main`, two threads are created: one to be the reader (consuming data from an input source) that executes the `read_some` function and another to be the writer (producing output) that executes the `write_some` function. After the threads are created, the program waits for the thread executing the `write_some` function to terminate. When this occurs, the mutex and condition variables are removed and the program terminates.

The `read_some` function loops while the `finished` flag is `false`. The mutex `lock_it` is used to serialize access to the code that manipulates the shared buffer. Once the mutex is obtained, the count of the number of characters in the buffer (the predicate) is checked. If the buffer is full, the mutex is released (the assumption being the buffer will be processed by a writer, which will need to gain access via the mutex). If the buffer is not filled, an additional character is obtained from standard input. The new character is checked; if it is not an end-of-file value, the character is added to the buffer and the character count is incremented. If the character fills the buffer, a call to **pthread_cond_signal** is made to notify the condition variable `write_it`. If the input character was an end-of-file value, a NULL value is inserted in the buffer in place of the end-of-file value. Next, the character counter is set to its maximum value to satisfy the predicate check in the writer, the `finished` flag is set to `true`, and **pthread_cond_signal** is used to notify the writer, so the remaining contents of the buffer can be processed.

The thread executing the writer code also loops, while the `finished` flag is set to `false`. Like the reader, it uses the `lock_it` mutex to gain access to the shared code and data. The inner `while` statement checks the count of the number of characters stored in the buffer. As long as the count is less than the maximum, the thread executing this code continues to block due to the call to **pthread_cond_wait**. When notified by the reader (when the character count is at the maximum), the `while` loop is exited, and the writer displays the contents of the common buffer. As the contents of the buffer are displayed, the character counter is decremented accordingly.

A compilation and run of Program 11.6 on a local system is shown in Figure 11.11.

Figure 11.11 A compile and run of Program 11.6.

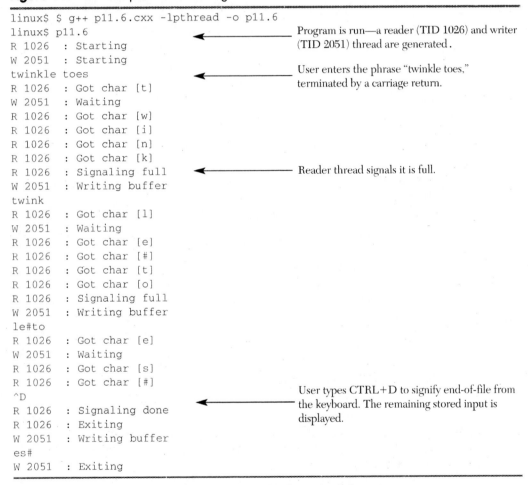

```
linux$ $ g++ p11.6.cxx -lpthread -o p11.6
linux$ p11.6                              Program is run—a reader (TID 1026) and writer
R 1026  : Starting                        (TID 2051) thread are generated.
W 2051  : Starting
twinkle toes                              User enters the phrase "twinkle toes,"
R 1026  : Got char [t]                    terminated by a carriage return.
W 2051  : Waiting
R 1026  : Got char [w]
R 1026  : Got char [i]
R 1026  : Got char [n]
R 1026  : Got char [k]
R 1026  : Signaling full                  Reader thread signals it is full.
W 2051  : Writing buffer
twink
R 1026  : Got char [l]
W 2051  : Waiting
R 1026  : Got char [e]
R 1026  : Got char [#]
R 1026  : Got char [t]
R 1026  : Got char [o]
R 1026  : Signaling full
W 2051  : Writing buffer
le#to
R 1026  : Got char [e]
W 2051  : Waiting
R 1026  : Got char [s]
R 1026  : Got char [#]
^D                                        User types CTRL+D to signify end-of-file from
R 1026  : Signaling done                  the keyboard. The remaining stored input is
R 1026  : Exiting                         displayed.
W 2051  : Writing buffer
es#
W 2051  : Exiting
```

When the program is run, its input is obtained from the keyboard. The user enters the string *twinkle toes*, and the program responds by displaying each character as it is obtained. Display by individual threads is labeled as either R for reader or W for writer, and the thread's ID is given. After the fifth character is processed, the reader thread signals the condition variable.

As there is only one writer thread (in this case thread ID 2051), it "wakes up" and processes (displays) the contents of the buffer. Nonalphanumeric characters are displayed as #. When a CTRL+D is entered to indicate end-of-file, the remaining contents of the buffer are displayed and the program terminates.

A little experimentation with this program produces some interesting output. For example, if we duplicate the writer **pthread_create** statement in main (line 28) so we have two writers, each with its own thread of control, the program on our system produces the output shown in Figure 11.12.

Figure 11.12 A run of Program 11.6 with two writers, using signal notification.

```
linux$ p11.6
R 1026  : Starting                        This time there are two writer threads, TID
W 2051  : Starting         ◄───────────   2051 and 3076.
W 3076  : Starting
twinkle toes
R 1026  : Got char [t]
W 2051  : Waiting
W 3076  : Waiting
R 1026  : Got char [w]
R 1026  : Got char [i]
R 1026  : Got char [n]
R 1026  : Got char [k]
R 1026  : Signaling full                  Writer TID 2051 is notified first that the
W 2051  : Writing buffer    ◄───────────  buffer is full.
twink
R 1026  : Got char [l]
W 2051  : Waiting
R 1026  : Got char [e]
R 1026  : Got char [#]
R 1026  : Got char [t]
R 1026  : Got char [o]
R 1026  : Signaling full                  Writer TID 3076 is notified second that the
W 3076  : Writing buffer    ◄───────────  buffer is full.
le#to
R 1026  : Got char [e]
W 3076  : Waiting
R 1026  : Got char [s]
R 1026  : Got char [#]
^D
R 1026  : Signaling done                  Writer TID 2051 is notified this time. Buffer
R 1026  : Exiting                         is written out and this thread exits. Remaining
W 2051  : Writing buffer    ◄───────────  writer thread does not exit until CTRL+C is
es#                                        entered.
W 2051  : Exiting
^C
```

The output shows the writer threads alternating the task of displaying the output. At the end of the input sequence, CTRL+D causes the reader thread to signal the condition variable that termination is necessary. The thread to act upon the signal is the writer thread 2051 (2051 and 3076 are alternating). Writer thread 3076 (the thread ID passed to the single call to join) is unaware of the change, continues looping, and must be terminated with a CTRL+C.

If we keep two writer threads and change the two **pthread_cond_signal** calls to **pthread_cond_broadcast** (lines 49 and 58), we obtain the output shown in Figure 11.13.

Figure 11.13 A run of Program 11.6 with two writer threads, using broadcast notification.

```
linux$ p11.6
R 1026  : Starting
W 2051  : Starting
W 3076  : Starting
twinkle toes
R 1026  : Got char [t]
W 2051  : Waiting
W 3076  : Waiting
R 1026  : Got char [w]
R 1026  : Got char [i]
R 1026  : Got char [n]
R 1026  : Got char [k]
R 1026  : Signaling full
W 3076  : Writing buffer
twink
R 1026  : Got char [l]
W 3076  : Waiting
R 1026  : Got char [e]
R 1026  : Got char [#]
R 1026  : Got char [t]
R 1026  : Got char [o]
R 1026  : Signaling full
W 3076  : Writing buffer
le#to
R 1026  : Got char [e]
W 3076  : Waiting
R 1026  : Got char [s]
R 1026  : Got char [#]
^D
R 1026  : Signaling done
R 1026  : Exiting
W 2051  : Writing buffer
es#
W 2051  : Exiting
^C
```

In this example, when all threads are awakened with the call to **pthread_cond_broadcast** and placed in contention, the thread with the ID of 3076 is always the first to act on the signal until the last (exiting) broadcast is made. Keep in mind that the actual thread chosen by the operating system is not specified. While our example seems robust, there are still some conditions we did not try (see Exercise 11.9).

11-8 EXERCISE

To some, the second while statement on line 75 in the user-defined writer function write_some appears to be superfluous. Can this while statement be replaced with an if statement? Why, or why not?

11-9 EXERCISE

Three computer science students, Alice, Kumar, and Rocco were experimenting with the original version of Program 11.6 on a Linux system. They wanted to see if the program would process information correctly if there were multiple reader threads with a single writer thread and multiple reader threads with multiple writer threads. Also, they were curious as to whether or not starting the writer thread(s) before the reader thread(s) would cause the program to fail. What did these students find (and why)? Be sure to compile, run, and record the program's output to document what you found.

11.8.3 Read/Write Locks

When writing programs, it is not unusual to run into a situation, such as with a database, where the data involved is read more often than it is modified (written). In these situations a locking mechanism that permits simultaneous reading of data if no writing is occurring and the writing of data if no reading or writing of data is needed. Until fairly recently, a POSIX thread implementation of read/write locks was not available and users were left to write their own.

Fortunately, newer versions of LinuxThreads contain support for POSIX-based read/write locks.

A read/write lock should always be set before it is used. A read/write lock is initialized with the library function **pthread_rwlock_init** (Table 11.20).

Table 11.20 The `pthread_rwlock_init` Library Function.

Include File(s)	`<pthread.h>`		Manual Section	**3**

Summary	`int`
	`pthread_rwlock_init( pthread_rwlock_t      *rwlock,`
	`              const pthread_rwlockattr_t *attr );`			

	Success	Failure	Sets `errno`	
Return	0	Nonzero		

The data type of the first argument of this call, `pthread_rwlock_t`, is defined as

```
typedef struct _pthread_rwlock_t {
struct _pthread_fastlock __rw_lock;  /* Lock to guarantee mutual exclusion */
int __rw_readers;                    /* Number of readers */
_pthread_descr __rw_writer;          /* Identity of writer, or NULL if none */
_pthread_descr __rw_read_waiting;    /* Threads waiting for reading */
_pthread_descr __rw_write_waiting;   /* Threads waiting for writing */
int __rw_kind;                       /* Reader/Writer preference selection */
int __rw_pshared;                    /* Shared between processes or not */
} pthread_rwlock_t;
```

The argument `*rwlock` is a reference to the read/write lock to be initialized. The argument `attr` is used to reference an attribute object (similar to previously presented `pthread` functions). If this argument is set to NULL, the read/write lock is set to the default.

A typical read/write lock initialization sequence for use with multiple threads in a single process is.[19]

```
pthread_rwlock_t  rw_lock;
. . .
pthread_rwlock_init( &rw_lock, NULL );
```

[19] As in previous initialization discussions, the explicit call **pthread_rwlock_init** can be skipped when we use the single statement approach; that is,

```
pthread_rwlock_t rw_lock = PTHREAD_RWLOCK_DEFAULT_NP; .
```

If the **pthread_rwlock_init** call is successful, it returns a 0. If the call fails, a nonzero value is returned. The return of EINVAL (22) indicates an invalid argument.

As with mutexes, there is a suite of read/write lock manipulation functions. A summary of some of the more commonly used functions is shown in Table 11.21. All the functions take a single reference to an allocated read/write lock. We restrict our discussion to the basics: locking and unlocking a read/write lock.

Table 11.21 Some Common Read/Write Lock Library Functions.

Function Prototype	Description
int pthread_rwlock_rdlock(pthread_rwlock_t *rwlock);	Locks the referenced read/write lock for *reading*. If the lock is currently held for writing, the calling thread blocks. Multiple threads can hold the lock for reading.
int pthread_rwlock_wrlock(pthread_rwlock_t *rwlock);	Locks the referenced read/write lock for *writing*. If the lock is currently held for reading or writing, the calling thread blocks. Only one thread can hold the lock for writing.
int pthread_rwlock_unlock(pthread_rwlock_t *rwlock);	Unlock a read/write lock held by the calling thread. If other threads are blocked on the read/write lock, one of them will be unblocked. At present, the implementation favors blocked writers over blocked readers. If the calling thread does not hold a lock for reading or writing but issues this unlock call, the program's behavior is undefined.
int pthread_rwlock_tryrdlock(pthread_rwlock_t *rwlock);	Try to lock the referenced read/write lock for *reading*. If the lock is not held for writing, it returns a read lock. If the lock is currently held for writing, it returns the error value EBUSY (16).
int pthread_rwlock_trywrlock(pthread_rwlock_t *rwlock);	Try to lock the referenced read/write lock for *writing*. If the lock is not held for reading or writing, return a write lock. If the lock is currently held for reading or writing, return the error value EBUSY (16).

Program 11.7 uses read/write locks to allow multiple threads read/write access to a stack of characters stored as a singularly linked list. Each thread can push (add) a character to the list, pop (remove) a character from a non-empty list, display the list, sleep, or quit. A random number generator drives the activities of each thread. Threads compete with one another for access to the list. The header file for Program 11.7 is shown below.

Program 11.7 Header file for read/write lock example.

```
File : local_stack.h
  |       /*
  |              Common local header file: local_stack.h
  |       */
  |       #ifndef  LOCAL_STACK_H
  +       #define  LOCAL_STACK_H
  |       #define  _GNU_SOURCE
  |       #define  _REENTRANT
  |       #include <iostream>
  |       #include <cstdlib>
 10       #include <pthread.h>
  |       #include <unistd.h>
  |       #include <sys/time.h>
  |       using namespace std;
  |       const int MAX=6;
  +       class Stack {
  |         public:
  |                   Stack      ( ) : head( NULL ) {}
  |                   ~Stack     ( );
  |           bool    StackEmpty( void ) const { return (head == NULL); }
 20         void    Display    ( void ) const ;
  |           void    Push       ( const char );
  |           char    Pop        ( void );
  |         private:
  |           struct node {
  +             char         item;
  |             struct node *next;
  |           };
  |           node *head;
  |       };
 30       #endif
```

User-defined Stack class implemented as a linked list.

As might be expected, the content of this file is similar to that of the header file for the previous example. However, some new items have been added. This example uses a user-defined Stack class. The definition of the class is found at the bottom of the header file. Code for the more complex Stack methods is found in the Program 11.7B. Additionally, Program 11.7B contains the code each

Program 11.7B Stack class methods and common list manipulation
functions for read/write lock example.

```
File : p11.7B.cxx
    |      #include "local_stack.h"
    |                                              // previously declared
    |      extern pthread_rwlock_t  *rw_ACCESS;    // RW lock
    |      extern Stack    *S;                     // Stack
    +                                              // remaining Stack methods
    |      Stack::~Stack( ){                       // List destructor
    |        node *curr = head, *next;
    |        while( curr ){
    |          next = curr->next;
   10          delete curr;
    |          curr = next;
    |        }
    |        head = NULL;
    |      }
    +      void                                    // Display the list
    |      Stack::Display( void ) const {
    |        node *temp = head;
    |        cout << "\t" << pthread_self() << " [head]" << endl;
    |        while( temp != NULL ){
   20          cout << "\t" << pthread_self() << " [" << temp->item
    |                  << "]" << endl;
    |          cout.flush( );
    |          temp = temp->next;
    |          sleep(1);                           // slow things down
    +        }
    |        cout << "\t" << pthread_self( ) << " [tail]" << endl;
    |      }
    |      void                                    // Add an item
    |      Stack::Push( const char item ){
   30        node *temp = new node;
    |        temp->item = item;
    |        temp->next = head;
    |        head       = temp;
    |      }
    +      char                                    // Remove an item
    |      Stack::Pop( void ){
    |        char item;
    |        node *temp = head;
    |        item = temp->item;
   40        head = temp->next;
    |        delete temp;
    |        return item;
    |      }
    |      int                                     // Random # in range
    +      my_rand(int start, int range){
```

```
   |       struct timeval t;
   |       gettimeofday(&t, (struct timezone *)NULL);
   |       return (int)(start+((float)range * rand_r((unsigned *)&t.tv_usec))
   |                 / (RAND_MAX+1.0));
50 }
   |   void *
   |   do_stack( void *junk ) {                        // Activity for thread
   |     char  item;
   |     sleep( my_rand(1,3) );                        // random start up time
 + do {
   |       switch ( my_rand(1,10) ) {                  // choose value 1-10
   |        case 1: case 2:                            // Display 2/10
   |          pthread_rwlock_rdlock(rw_ACCESS);        // read lock - block on W
   |          cout << pthread_self( ) << " Display:" << endl;
60         if ( S->StackEmpty( ) )
   |            cout << pthread_self( ) << " Empty list" << endl;
   |          else
   |            S->Display();
 +         pthread_rwlock_unlock(rw_ACCESS);         // unlock
   |          break;
   |        case 3: case 4: case 5:                    // Add item 3/10
   |          item = my_rand(1,25) + 64;
   |          pthread_rwlock_wrlock(rw_ACCESS);        // write lock - block on W|R
   |          cout << pthread_self( ) << " Push   : " << item << endl;
70       S->Push( item );
   |          pthread_rwlock_unlock(rw_ACCESS);        // unlock
   |          break;
   |        case 6: case 7: case 8:                    // Remove item 3/10
 |         pthread_rwlock_wrlock(rw_ACCESS);        // write lock - block
   |                                                              on W|R
 +         if (S->StackEmpty( ))
   |            cout << pthread_self( ) << " Underflow" << endl;
   |          else {
   |            cout << pthread_self( ) << " Pop    : ";
   |            item = S->Pop( );
80         cout << pthread_self( ) << " " << item << endl;
   |          }
   |          pthread_rwlock_unlock(rw_ACCESS);        // unlock
   |          break;
   |        case 9:                                    // Sleep 1/10
 +         cout << pthread_self( ) << " Sleep  :" << endl;
   |          sleep( my_rand(1,3));
   |          break;
   |        case 10:                                   // Quit 1/10
   |          cout << pthread_self( ) << " Quit   :" << endl;
90       return NULL;
   |        }
   |     } while ( 1 );
   |   }
```

thread will execute. This code consists of a driver function called do_stack that randomly chooses an activity for the thread on each pass through the loop.

In the do_stack loop, a random value from 1 to 10 is generated. This value determines the thread's activity. Given a good distribution of random values, approximately 20 percent of the time the thread executing this code should display the current list. About 30 percent of the time the thread should generate a new character and push the character onto the list. Roughly 30 percent of the time the thread should pop a character off the top of the list (if it is not empty). The remaining 20 percent of the thread will either sleep a few seconds or quit its activity.

The activities other than sleep or quit are bracketed with the appropriate read/write lock calls. As the display (reading) of the list can be done by multiple threads, a call to **pthread_rwlock_rdlock** is made before the display to obtain a read lock, and a call to **pthread_rwlock_unlock** is made once the display is completed to release the read lock. The Push and Pop methods, which cause the list contents to be modified, are bracketed with a call to **pthread_rwlock_wrlock** and **pthread_rwlock_unlock** calls. Thus, only one thread at a time is allowed to modify the linked list. It is important to note that all critical code was bracketed with the read/write locks. For example, if we were to move outside the bracketed area and check for an empty stack found in the section of code that calls Pop (line 75), we would on occasion find our program failing due to race conditions. This could occur when we have one item in our list. For example, say a thread calls Stack_Empty, finds the stack is not empty, and attempts to Pop (remove) the item. At the same time, a second thread (also finding the list to be not empty) also attempts to remove an item. While both consider the list to be not empty, one of the threads will draw an error, as the competing thread will have beaten it to the punch.

Each line of output identifies the underlying thread that generated it. The code for main is found in Program 11.7C.

Program 11.7C Code for function main for read/write lock example.

```
File : p11.7C.cxx
|       #include "local_stack.h"
|                                                       // global by placement
|       pthread_rwlock_t  *rw_ACCESS=new pthread_rwlock_t;
|       Stack             *S=new Stack;
+       void *do_stack( void * );
|       int
|       main( int argc, char *argv[] ){
|         int   i, n;
|         pthread_t worker[MAX];
```

```
10          pthread_rwlock_init(rw_ACCESS, NULL);
 |          if ( argc != 2) {
 |            cerr << "Usage: " << *argv << " n_workers" << endl;
 |            return 1;
 |          }
 +          n = atoi(argv[1]) < MAX ? atoi(argv[1]) : MAX;
 |          for( i=0; i < n; ++i )                      // create threads
 |            pthread_create(&worker[i],NULL,do_stack,(void *) NULL);
 |          for( i=0; i < n; ++i )                      // wait
 |            pthread_join(worker[i], (void **) NULL);
20          return 0;
 |        }
```

Figure 11.14 shows a portion of the output generated from a run of Program 11.7 when four threads are competing for access to the list. As can be seen, multiple threads can display the list, but only one thread at a time can modify the list.

Figure 11.14 A compilation and run of Program 11.7 with four competing threads.

```
linux$ g++ p11.7B.cxx p11.7C.cxx -o p11.7 -lpthread
linux$ p11.7   4
2051 Push    : A
2051 Sleep   :
3076 Pop     : 3076 A
3076 Push    : L
3076 Push    : L
3076 Push    : L
3076 Push    : K
3076 Push    : K
3076 Push    : F
3076 Quit    :
1026 Pop     : 1026 F
1026 Quit    :
4101 Push    : J
4101 Pop     : 4101 J
4101 Display:
       4101 [head]
       4101 [K]
2051 Display:
       2051 [head]
       2051 [K]
       4101 [K]
       2051 [K]
       4101 [L]
       2051 [L]
       4101 [L]
       2051 [L]
```

A series of letters are pushed onto the list by several different threads.

Thread 4101 begins to display the list. Shortly, thereafter, thread 2051 displays the list as well. This is perfectly acceptable, as more than one thread can access the list concurrently for reading. Their output is interspersed on the screen.

```
        4101 [L]
        2051 [L]
        4101 [tail]
4101 Display:
        4101 [head]
        4101 [K]
        2051 [tail]
        4101 [K]
        4101 [L]
        4101 [L]
        4101 [L]
        4101 [tail]
  . . .
```

Eventually, each thread finishes its display of the list.

11-10 EXERCISE

Adjust the `switch` statement in the user-defined `do_stack` function of Program 11.7 so approximately 70 percent of the thread's activity will be the display of the list. Recompile and run the program using the maximum number of threads. Direct the output to a temporary file (say output.txt). Use the **grep**, **sort**, and **uniq** utilities to obtain information on the number of times push, pop, and display were done. For example, the sequence

```
linux$ p11.7  6  > output.txt
linux$ grep  Push  output.txt | sort | uniq -c
```

would tally the number of times the word *Push* (printed each time push was called) was displayed by each thread. The sequence

```
linux$ grep  :  output.txt | wc -1
```

can be used to find the total number of activity lines displayed (each tagged with a :1).

Do you consistently find that percentage you specify is what is actually being done? Why, or why not? Does removing the **sleep** call in the user-defined `Display` method of the `Stack` class make a difference in the distribution of activities—the total number of activities before all threads terminate? Generate output to support your answer. You should run each sequence multiple times to be sure you are obtaining an accurate view of the program's activities.

517

11.8.4 Multithread Semaphores

The activities of threads may also be coordinated with semaphores. A semaphore is similar in function to a mutex. However, a semaphore can act as either a binary entity similar to a mutex or as a counting entity. Counting semaphores can be used to manage multiple resources. As they are somewhat more complex, semaphores are more system-intensive than mutexes. Semaphore concepts and operations were presented in some detail in Chapter 7. However, the Chapter 7 semaphore operations are System V-based and are not multithread safe. POSIX 1003.1b defines semaphores that can be used with threads. As these semaphore operations were written prior to the creation of the POSIX thread library calls, their interface has a slightly different flavor. Most notably, these operations do not begin with the sequence `pthread_` and do set `errno` when they fail. All programs that contain POSIX semaphore operations must include `<semaphore.h>`.

Conceptually, a POSIX semaphore is a nonnegative integer value that can be used to synchronize thread activities. Increment (post) and decrement (wait) operations are performed on the semaphore. A decrement issued on a 0 valued semaphore will cause the issuing thread to block until another thread increments the semaphore. Unlike a mutex, for which there is a sense of ownership, a semaphore does not need to be acquired (decremented) and released (incremented) by the same thread.

A semaphore must be initialized before it is used. The library call **sem_init**, shown in Table 11.22, is used to initialize a semaphore.

Table 11.22 The `sem_init` Library Function.

Include File(s)	`<semaphore.h>`		Manual Section	**3**

Summary	`int`
	`sem_init( sem_t *sem, int pshared,`
	`            unsigned int value );`			

		Success	Failure	Sets `errno`
Return		0	−1	Yes

The `sem_t` data type referenced by `sem` is declared in `<semaphore.h>` as

```
/* System specific semaphore definition. */
typedef struct {
  struct _pthread_fastlock __sem_lock;
```

```
    int __sem_value;
    _pthread_descr __sem_waiting;
} sem_t;
```

The `sem` argument references the semaphore to be initialized. The `pshared` argument is used to indicate if the semaphore will be shared between processes. A value of 0 indicates the semaphore is not to be shared between processes, while a nonzero value indicates the semaphore is shareable. If the semaphore is to be shared between processes, the programmer is responsible for mapping the semaphore to a shared memory location or to a memory-mapped file. At present, the LinuxThreads implementation of POSIX threads does not support process-shared semaphores. Given this limitation, this argument should always be set to 0. The argument `value` is a nonnegative integer that specifies the starting value of the semaphore. A successful **sem_init** call returns a 0 and sets the referenced semaphore to the indicated initial value. If the call fails, it returns a value of −1 and sets `errno` to indicate the source of the error (see Table 11.23). In a multithreaded setting a semaphore should be initialized only once.

Table 11.23 `sem_init` Error Messages.

#	Constant	`perror` Message	Explanation
22	EINVAL	Invalid argument	The `value` argument exceeds the value of SEM_VALUE_MAX.
89	ENOSYS	Function not implemented	The `pshared` argument is not 0.

Once created, a semaphore can be locked using the library call **sem_wait** or **sem_trywait**. Keep in mind that underneath locking, a semaphore is an atomic decrement operation against the value of the semaphore.

Both calls require a reference to a semaphore of type `sem_t`. If the referenced semaphore is nonzero, the call decrements (by one) the referenced semaphore. If the semaphore is 0, the **sem_wait** call blocks until the semaphore becomes greater than zero. If the semaphore is 0, the **sem_trywait** call does not block and returns immediately. Both calls return a 0 if they are successful; otherwise, **sem_trywait** returns a −1 and sets `errno` to the value shown in Table 11.25. Unsuccessful calls do not change the state of the semaphore.

Table 11.24 The `sem_wait` and `sem_trywait` Library Functions.

Include File(s)	`<semaphore.h>`		Manual Section	**3**
Summary	`int sem_wait( sem_t * sem );` `int sem_trywait( sem_t * sem );`			
	Success	Failure	Sets errno	
Return	0	−1	`sem_trywait` only	

Table 11.25 `sem_wait` and `sem_trywait` Error Message.

#	Constant	`perror` Message	Explanation
11	EAGAIN	Resource temporarily unavailable	The `sem_trywait` found the semaphore to be 0.

Semaphores are unlocked (i.e., incremented) using the **sem_post** library call (Table 11.26).

Table 11.26 The `sem_post` Library Function.

Include File(s)	`<semaphore.h>`		Manual Section	**3**
Summary	`int sem_post(sem_t *sem);`			
	Success	Failure	Sets errno	
Return	0	−1	Yes	

The **sem_post** call unlocks the referenced semaphore. If the semaphore was previously at 0 and there are other threads or LWPs blocking on the semaphore, they will be notified using the current scheduling policy (most often, the highest priority, longest waiting thread or LWP is scheduled next). If the semaphore was not previously at 0, its value is incremented by one. If successful, **sem_post** returns a value of 0; otherwise, it returns a value of −1 and sets errno to the value in Table 11.27 to indicate the error condition. The **sem_post** call is asynchronous-signal-safe (able to be called from within a signal handler).

Table 11.27 sem_post Error Message.

#	Constant	perror Message	Explanation
34	ERANGE	Numerical result out of range	If the semaphore were incremented, its value would exceed SEM_VALUE_MAX.

Chapter 7 provides a number of semaphore examples that can be readily adapted to a multithreaded setting by changing the nonmultithreaded semaphore operations to their POSIX multithread equivalents. Rather than duplicate these previous examples, in Program 11.8 I have used a semaphore to coordinate the activity of cooperating threads to determine when the threads have carried on their activities in a specific sequence.

Program 11.8 Using POSIX Semaphores with Threads

```
File : p11.8.cxx
     |    /*
     |            Using semaphores with threads
     |    */
     |    #define _GNU_SOURCE
     +    #define _REENTRANT
     |    #include <pthread.h>
     |    #include <iostream>
     |    #include <cstdio>
     |    #include <cstdlib>
    10    #include <cstring>
     |    #include <unistd.h>
     |    #include <sys/time.h>
     |    #include <semaphore.h>                    // for POSIX semaphores
     |    using namespace std;
     +    const int BUF_SIZE= 15;
     |    const int MAX     = 4;
     |    int    world_state = 1;
     |    sem_t check_state;
     |    typedef struct {
    20            char word[BUF_SIZE];
     |            int  my_state;
     |    } Info;
     |    void *speaker( Info * );
     |    //    Generate a random # within given range
     +    int
     |    my_rand(int start, int range){
     |      struct timeval t;
     |      gettimeofday(&t, (struct timezone *)NULL);
```

```
   |      return (int)(start+((float)range * rand_r((unsigned *)&t.tv_usec))
   30                    / (RAND_MAX+1.0)));
   |      }
   |    int
   |    main( int argc, char *argv[] ){
   |      pthread_t t_ID[MAX];
   +      Info      words[MAX];
   |      if ( argc != MAX+1 ) {
   |        cerr << "Usage " << *argv << " word1 ... word" << MAX << endl;
   |        return 1;
   |      }
   40     sem_init( &check_state, 0, 1 );         // start semaphore at 1
   |      for (int i = 0; i < MAX; ++i){
   |        strcpy( words[i].word, argv[i+1] );
   |        words[i].my_state = i+1;
   |        if ( (pthread_create( &t_ID[i],NULL,
   +          ( void *(*)(void *) )speaker,(void *) &words[i])) != 0 ) {
   |          perror("Thread create speaker");
   |          return i;
   |          }
   |      }
   50     pthread_join( t_ID[MAX-1], (void **) NULL);
   |      cout << "!" << endl;
   |      return 0;
   |    }
   |    /*
   +      Display the passed in word
   |    */
   |    void  *
   |    speaker( Info * s ){
   |      while( true ) {
   60       sleep(my_rand(1,3));
   |        sem_wait( &check_state );            // obtain & decrement else block
   |        cout << s->word << " ";
   |        cout.flush( );
   |        if ( s->my_state == world_state ) {
   +          ++world_state;
   |          if ( world_state > MAX ) break;
   |        } else {
   |          cout << endl;
   |          world_state = 1;
   70       }
   |        sem_post( &check_state );            // release & increment
   |      }
   |      return( (void *) NULL );
   |    }
```

In Program 11.8 the file <semaphore.h> is included, as POSIX semaphores are used. A global integer, world_state (declared before main), is allocated and set to 1. This variable is used by the cooperating threads to determine when processing should stop (i.e., when this variable exceeds the value MAX). Access to the `world_state` variable is controlled by the semaphore `check_state`. A `typedef` is used to create a user-defined type called `Info`. Items of this type will have storage for 15 characters and an integer value. The character array will hold a short sequence of characters (a word), and the integer, a value indicating the current state of output. In `main` two arrays are allocated. The first, `t_ID`, is used to store the thread IDs. The second array, called `words`, stores the word and state information that is passed to each thread. The **sem_init** call is used to set the allocated semaphore to 1. As the second argument of this call is 0, only threads within the same process space can share the semaphore. A loop is used to create additional threads and pass each a value obtained from the command line (stored in the elements of the `words` array) and its state value. Each thread is directed to execute the user-defined function `speaker`. The thread in `main` then waits (by way of a **pthread_join**) for the last thread generated to exit. When the **pthread_join** is completed, the program concludes.

The `speaker` function loops continuously. It **sleep**s for a random number of seconds (1–3), and then attempts to lock (obtain) the semaphore. Once it is successful, the thread displays the word it was passed. It then checks its state value against the current state value for the process (stored as `world_state`). If its state value is equivalent to the current value of `world_state`, the `world_state` is incremented, as progress is being made toward the printing of the words in the proper (command line) order. If the thread's state value is not equivalent to the `world_state` value, out-of-order processing has occurred, and the `world_state` variable is reset to 1 to indicate a restarting of the sequence. Once the evaluation and manipulation of `world_state` is complete the semaphore is released.

A run of Program 11.8 and its output are shown in Figure 11.15.

Figure 11.15 A run of Program 11.8.

```
linux$ p11.8 once upon a time
upon
a
once time                    ←——————————    Each time progress is no longer being
upon                                         made, the output sequence restarts.
a
once time
upon
once time
a
time
once upon a once
time
```

```
a
a
once upon a time !    ◄─────────    All command-line arguments are
                                     displayed in order; processing stops.
```

As can be seen, the threads do not finish their activity until they successfully display the sequence in the same order that it was passed on the command line.

The function **sem_getvalue**, which retrieves the current value of the semaphore, is also supported (Table 11.28).

Table 11.28 The sem_getvalue Library Function.

Include File(s)	<semaphore.h>		Manual Section	3
Summary	int sem_getvalue(sem_t * sem, int * sval);			
	Success	Failure	Sets errno	
Return	0	−1		

This function stores, in the location referenced by sval, the current value of the semaphore referenced by sem. The returned value should not be used by the program to make decisions, as it is transient and its use in a decision construct could result in race conditions.

11-11 EXERCISE

Write a program that implements a multithreaded bubble–merge sort. Have the initial process generate 10,000 random numbers—writing the numbers in groups of 1,000 each to 10 separate temporary files. Then create 10 threads and pass each a reference to one of the temporary files and a common bubble-sorting routine. As each thread finishes, its sorted results should be returned to the initial thread that performs a merge of sorted results (i.e., the temporary 1,000 number file) with a final, fully sorted file. Where appropriate, use semaphores and/or mutexes or condition variables to coordinate activities. Run your solution several times to be sure it works correctly. Once all the data is ordered, display every 100th value in the final data set to attempt to establish if the data was truly sorted. All temporary files and other data structures should be removed once processing is complete.

If time permits, keep the total number of values to be sorted constant (let's say 10,000) and attempt to determine empirically if there is a lower bound for the size of the list (e.g., 1,000 values per starting list with 10 files versus 100 values per starting list with 100 files, etc.) that is passed to the bubble–merge sort routines whereby no appreciable decrease in processing time is discernible. To maintain your sanity, keep the granularity of the list sizes you try fairly large. The executable file **grays_mbms**, found with the program files for this chapter, will allow you to compare your solution to that of the author. This program takes two command-line arguments: the number of values to sort and the number of files.

11.9 Thread-Specific Data

Sometimes we need to be able to maintain data that is specific to a given thread but is referenced in a section of code that will be executed by multiple threads. Data of this nature, stored in a memory block private to the thread, is usually termed thread-specific data, or TSD. This data is referenced using a thread-specific pointer and the associated key. The keys for TSD are global to all the threads within the process. To make use of TSD, a thread must allocate and bind (associate) the key with the data. The library call **pthread_key_create** (Table 11.29) is used to allocate a new key. Only one thread should issue the create call for a TSD item.

Table 11.29 The `pthread_key_create` Library Function.

Include File(s)	`<pthread.h>`		Manual Section	3

Summary	`int pthread_key_create( pthread_key_t *key,`
	`                        void(*destr_function)`
	`                        (void *) );`			

Return		Success	Failure	Sets `errno`
		0	−1	

As its first argument, the **pthread_key_create** library call is passed a reference, *key, to a pthread_key_t data type. The pthread_key_t data type is typedefed as an unsigned int. If the call to **pthread_**

key_create is successful, the *key argument references the newly allocated key. There is a system limit on the number of keys per thread. The limit is designated by the defined constant PTHREAD_KEYS_MAX.

The second argument for **pthread_key_create** is a reference to a destructor function. If this argument is non-NULL, the referenced function is called and passed the associated TSD when the thread exits (i.e., calls **pthread_exit**) or is cancelled. If TSD is allocated within the destructor function, the system attempts to repeat destructor calls until all keys are NULL. As might be expected, this behavior could lead to some interesting recursive situations. Some thread implementations, such as LinuxThreads, limit the number of calls to resolve the removal of TSD; some do not. In LinuxThreads these calls are limited by the defined constant PTHREAD_DESTRUCTOR_ITERATIONS. If the call to **pthread_key_create** is successful, it returns a value of 0; otherwise, it returns the value EAGAIN (11) if the limit for the number of keys has been exceeded or ENOMEM (12) if insufficient memory is available to allocate the key.

The **pthread_key_delete** library function (Table 11.30) is used to remove the storage associated with a specific key (versus the data associated with the key).

Table 11.30 The **pthread_key_delete** Library Function.

Include File(s)	<pthread.h>		Manual Section	**3**
Summary	int pthread_key_delete(pthread_key_t key);			
	Success	Failure	Sets errno	
Return	0	−1		

A valid TSD key is **pthread_key_delete**'s only argument. If the key value is non-NULL, it is removed. While it would seem reasonable, the **pthread_key_delete** function does not automatically call the key's associated destructor function. If the function is passed an invalid key, it returns the value EINVAL (22); otherwise, it returns a 0, indicating successful removal of the key.

TSD is manipulated with the **pthread_setspecific** and **pthread_getspecific** library calls (Table 11.31).

Both functions accept a globally allocated key argument. The key, created by a call to **pthread_key_create**, is used by the **pthread_setspecific** library function to store the data referenced by the pointer argument. By definition, each calling thread can bind a different data value with the key. Most often, pointer references memory that has been dynamically allocated by the

Table 11.31 The TSD manipulation Library Functions.

Include File(s)	<pthread.h>		Manual Section	**3**

Summary	`int`
	`pthread_setspecific(pthread_key_t  key,`
	`                    const void      *pointer);`
	`void`
	`*pthread_getspecific(pthread_key_t key);`			

Return	Success	Failure	Sets `errno`	
	0	−1		

calling thread. Once bound, the associated values are individually maintained on a per-thread basis. The **pthead_setspecific** function will fail and return the value ENOMEM (12) if there is insufficient memory to associate a value with a key. If successful, **pthread_setspecific** returns a 0. The **pthread_getspecific** library function uses the key argument to retrieve (return) a reference to the TSD. If the key is not bound, a NULL (0) is returned.

Program 11.9 demonstrates one approach for using TSD.

Program 11.9 Using TSD.

```
File : p11.9.cxx
   |     /*
   |        Using thread specific data
   |     */
   |     #define _GNU_SOURCE
   +     #define _REENTRANT
   |     #include <iostream>
   |     #include <pthread.h>
   |     #include <stdlib.h>
   |     #include <unistd.h>
  10     using namespace std;
   |     const int MAX=20;
   |     void *TSD( int ),                        // manipulates TSD
   |           free_me( void *  );                // destructor
   |     static pthread_key_t  key;               // global TSD key
   +     int
   |     main( int argc, char *argv[] ) {
   |       pthread_t thr_id[MAX];
   |       int inc;
   |       if ( argc  < 2 || atoi(argv[1]) > MAX){
```

```
20        cerr << *argv << " num_threads" << endl;
 |        return 1;
 |      }
 |                                            // generate key (once)
 |      pthread_key_create(&key, (void(*)(void*))free_me);
 +      for(int i=0; i < atoi(argv[1]); ++i){
 |       inc = i+1;                            // can't cast an expr
 |       if (pthread_create(&thr_id[i],NULL,(void *(*)(void *))TSD,
 |       (void *)inc) > 0){
 |         cerr << "pthread_create failure" << endl;
 |         return 2;
30        }
 |      }
 |                                            // wait for all threads
 |      for(int i=0; i < argc-1; ++i)
 |        pthread_join(thr_id[i], NULL);
 +      sleep( 1 );
 |      return 0;
 |    }
 |    /*
 |       TSD routine - passed a value that it will keep private
40    */
 |    void *
 |    TSD( int private_stuff ){
 |      static pthread_mutex_t   the_lock;
 |      void    *tsd = NULL;
 +      tsd = pthread_getspecific(key);         // initially NULL
 |      if (tsd == NULL) {
 |        tsd = new pthread_key_t;              // create storage
 |        tsd = &private_stuff;                 // make the association
 |        pthread_setspecific(key, tsd);
50        cout << pthread_self( ) << " TSD starts at \t "
 |             <<  *(int *)pthread_getspecific(key) << endl;
 |      }
 |      for( int i=0; i < 3; ++i ){
 |        sleep(1);
 +        pthread_mutex_lock(&the_lock);         // enter critical region
 |        cout << pthread_self( ) << " incrementing" << endl;
 |        *(int *)pthread_getspecific(key) *= 2;  // double private value
 |        cout << pthread_self( ) << " yielding" << endl;
 |        pthread_mutex_unlock(&the_lock);       // exit critical region
60        sched_yield();                         // notify scheduler
 |      }
 |      cout << pthread_self( ) << " TSD finishes at \t "
 |           << *(int *)pthread_getspecific(key) << endl;
 |      cout.flush( );
 +      pthread_exit(NULL);
 |      return NULL;
 |    }
```

```
 |      /*
 |            Dummy destructor routine
70      */
 |      void
 |      free_me( void *value ){
 |        cout << pthread_self( ) << " free reference to \t "
 |              << *(int *) value  << endl;
 +      }
```

The prototype for the user-defined function TSD that will manipulate the
TSD and the user-defined function free_me that will act as a destructor are
placed prior to main. In addition, the key that will be used to access TSD is
allocated prior to main. Its placement assures it will be global in scope. In
main, a call is made to **pthread_key_create** (line 24), and the addresses
of the key and the destructor function are passed. A cast is used to keep the
compiler from complaining about argument type mismatch. In the first for
loop in main, the value of the loop counter plus one is assigned to the variable
inc.[20] As each thread is created, it is passed a reference to the user-defined
TSD function and the value stored in inc. Again, the cast operator is used to
keep the compiler from flagging what it would consider to be mismatched
arguments. Once the threads have been generated, main uses a second for
loop with a call to **pthread_join** to wait for the threads to finish their activities. A call to **sleep** follows the **pthread_join** loop to allow the final terminating thread sufficient time to flush its output buffer.

In the user-defined function TSD a mutex, the_lock, and a void pointer,
tsd, are allocated. The storage class for the_lock is static, while the
storage class for tsd is auto (the default). A call is made to **pthread_
getspecific**, and the value returned is assigned to tsd. If the key passed
to **pthread_getspecific** has not been associated with a TSD value, the
pthread_getspecific call will return a NULL value. If the returned
value is NULL (which it should be upon initial entry), a storage location is
allocated using the **new** operator (line 47). The TSD is associated with the key
using the **pthread_setspecific** library function. Next, a for loop is used
to simulate activity. Within the loop, a mutex called the_lock is used to
bracket a section of code where we would like to keep our display messages
from being interleaved with those of other threads that will be executing
the same code. In this section of code the TSD is multiplied by 2. A cast is used
to coerce the void * to an int *. A call to library function **sched_yield**
causes the current thread to yield its execution to another thread with the same

---

[20] Note that the inc variable is used as a temporay storage location, as in this setting it is not legal to
pass a reference to an expression.

or greater priority. At different points within the program, informational messages tagged with the thread ID are displayed.

A run of Program 11.9 is shown in Figure 11.16.

Figure 11.16 A run of Program 11.9 with four competing threads.

```
1026 TSD starts at        1        ◄────   Each thread has a different starting value for
2051 TSD starts at        2                its data.
3076 TSD starts at        3
4101 TSD starts at        4
1026 incrementing
1026 yielding
4101 incrementing
4101 yielding
3076 incrementing
3076 yielding
2051 incrementing         ◄────             Each thread accesses its private data,
2051 yielding                               increments it and then yields three times for
1026 incrementing                           each tread.
1026 yielding
4101 incrementing
4101 yielding
3076 incrementing
3076 yielding
2051 incrementing
2051 yielding
1026 incrementing
1026 yielding
1026 TSD finishes at      8        ◄────    As each thread finishes, it releases its
1026 free reference to    8                 reference to the TSD. The order of
4101 incrementing                           processing is determined by the scheduler
4101 yielding                               and may vary across multiple invocations.
3076 incrementing
3076 yielding
2051 incrementing
2051 yielding
4101 TSD finishes at      32
4101 free reference to    32
3076 TSD finishes at      24
3076 free reference to    24
2051 TSD finishes at      16
2051 free reference to    16
```

As can be seen in Figure 11.16, each thread maintains its own TSD value. The call to the destructor function free_me is made as each thread finishes its execution.

In Program 11.9 we allocated the key for the TSD prior to `main` and created the key in `main`. We can, if we are careful, allocate and create the `key` within the code segment shared by multiple threads. For example, in Program 11.9 we can remove (comment out) the statement prior to `main` that allocates the `key` (line 14)

```
// static pthread_key_t  key;
```

and the **pthread_key_create** statement (line 24) within `main`

```
// pthread_key_create(&key, (void(*)(void*))free_me);
```

and add the following statements (lines 45 to 53) to the user-defined TSD function.

```
     /*
        TSD routine - passed a value that it will keep private
40   */
     void *
     TSD( int private_stuff ){
       static pthread_mutex_t  the_lock;
       void    *tsd = NULL;
                                                      // do once
       static pthread_key_t    key;
       static int              done_once = 0;
       if ( !done_once ) {
         pthread_mutex_lock(&the_lock);               // bracket code
50       if ( !done_once++ )                          // re-check & inc
           pthread_key_create(&key, (void(*)(void*))free_me);
         pthread_mutex_unlock(&the_lock);             // end bracket
       }
       tsd = pthread_getspecific(key);                // initially NULL
```

In this second approach the storage class qualifier `static` is used in the user-defined TSD function when allocating the `key`. An integer flag variable called `done_once`, specified as `static`, is also allocated and initially set to 0 (which with the `static` qualifier should be its default value anyway). The mutex is used to bracket the inner check of the content of the `done_once` variable. Only one thread will find the `done_once` variable at 0, increment the variable, and create the `key`. After the `done_once` variable is incremented, the outer `if` will prevent further access to this section of code. This is by no means the only way in which this can be done. Another approach is to use the **pthread_once** library function.[21]

---

[21] If this were a text on just threads, an examination of **pthread_once** would be in order. However, as this is only an introduction, we will skip the details concerning **pthread_once** at this time and direct the interested reader to the associated manual page on **pthread_once**.

This section ends with a final program example, Program 11.10, that uses TSD and incorporates a number of the previously discussed thread-related functions. In this example the program is passed the name of a file to store its output and the number of threads (1–10) to generate. Each thread, represented by a different uppercase letter of the alphabet, is responsible for moving about within a common two-dimensional grid. As the thread moves, its path is displayed on the screen. The starting point for a thread is marked by an @ symbol. When the thread moves to a new location, its previous location is changed to lowercase. As written, a thread can move in one of four directions: left, right, up, or down. Moves that run off the grid are wrapped, in a modular fashion, to the next valid row–column location. If a thread moves to a location that is boxed in (i.e., a location where its neighbors on the left, right, top, and bottom are occupied), the thread expires. The program terminates when all threads have been boxed in.

To make the output a bit more interesting, the current state of the grid is displayed using basic vt100 escape codes.[22] The vt100 escape codes are incorporated in the user-defined functions LOCATE (used to place the cursor at a specific screen coordinate) and CLS (used to clear the screen). The display is updated dynamically, and in vt100 supported settings, produces a rough appearance of animation. The header information for Program 11.10 is placed in the file local_TSD.h. The contents of local_TSD.h are shown in Figure 11.17.

Figure 11.17 The local_TSD.h file for Program 11.10.

```
File : local_TSD.h
   |      /* local header file for example p11.10.cxx
   |       */
   |      #define _REENTRANT
   |      #define _GNU_SOURCE
   +      #include <pthread.h>
   |      #include <iostream>
   |      #include <cstdio>
   |      #include <cstdlib>
   |      #include <cstring>
  10      #include <fcntl.h>
   |      #include <unistd.h>
   |      #include <sys/types.h>
   |      #include <sys/time.h>
   |      #include <sys/stat.h>
   +      #include <sys/mman.h>
   |      using namespace std;
   |      const int  ROW=20, COL=42, MAX=10;
```

[22] I am aware that using vt100 emulation–escape codes will limit the range of platforms on which the example may run. However, as vt100 emulation is fairly ubiquitous, the actual number of platforms excluded should be minimal.

```
|       const char ESC='\033';
|       inline
20      void LOCATE(int row, int col){
|          cout << ESC << "[" << row << ";" << col << "H";
|       }
|       inline
|       void CLS( ){
+          LOCATE(1, 1);
|          cout << ESC << "[2J";
|       }
|       int
|       my_rand(int start, int range){
30         struct timeval t;
|          gettimeofday(&t, (struct timezone *)NULL);
|          return (int)(start+((float)range * rand_r((unsigned *)&t.tv_usec))
|                  / (RAND_MAX+1.0));
|       }
+       typedef struct {
|          int left, right, top, bot;
|       } DIRECTION;
|       static char    guys[] = "ABCDEFGHIJ";
|       int            n_dead = 0;
40      char           *the_file;
|       pthread_mutex_t scrn_lock;
|                                                    // function prototypes
|       void           display_screen(char *);
|       bool           boxed(char *, int, int);
+       void           move(char *, int *, int *, char);
|       void           neighbors( int , int , DIRECTION * );
|       void           *play( void * );
```

Along with the vt100 functions, the local_TSD.h file contains a type definition for a DIRECTION structure that will hold the indices of neighbor locations. Within the program the two-dimensional grid is treated as a vector. Five user-defined functions are prototyped. The display_screen function, passed a reference to the grid, displays the current contents of the grid at a set location on the screen. The boxed function, passed a reference to the grid and a row and column location, returns a true if the neighbors of the row–column location are all occupied; otherwise, it returns false. The move function finds and moves to a new location. The move function is passed a reference to the grid and the row–column location, as well as a copy of the current letter associated with a given thread. Upon completion of move, the grid and the row–column location are updated. The neighbors function is passed a copy of a row–column location and returns a DIRECTION structure containing the indices of the neighbor locations. The play function, passed to each thread, serves as a driver routine for the activities of the thread.

Program 11.10 Animating threads.

```
File : p11.10.cxx
   |      /*
   |             p11.10.cxx: Thread animation
   |             Compile   : g++ -o p11.10  p11.10.cxx  -lpthread
   |      */
   +      #include "local_TSD.h"
   |      int
   |      main(int argc, char *argv[]) {
   |        char       the_screen[ROW][COL];
   |        pthread_t  thread_id[MAX];
  10        int        fd0, n_threads;
   |        struct stat buf;
   |        if (argc != 3) {                              // check cmd line
   |          cerr << "Usage " << *argv <<  " file_name #_threads" << endl;
   |          return 1;
   +        }
   |        if ((n_threads = atoi(argv[2])) > MAX ) {
   |          cerr << "# threads must be < " <<  MAX+1 << endl;
   |          return 2;
   |        }
  20        setbuf(stdout, NULL);
   |        guys[n_threads] = '\0';
   |        memset(the_screen, ' ', sizeof(the_screen));   // clear screen
   |                                                             array
   |                                                       // open file for
   |                                                             mapping
   |        if ((fd0 = open(argv[1], O_CREAT | O_RDWR, 0666)) < 0) {
   +          cerr << "Open error on file " << argv[1] << endl;
   |          return 3;
   |        }                                             // write screen
   |                                                             to file
   |        write(fd0, the_screen, sizeof(the_screen));
   |        if (fstat(fd0, &buf) < 0) {                   // stats on mapped
   |                                                             file
  30        cerr << "fstat error on file " << the_file << endl;
   |          return 4;
   |        }                                             // establish the
   |                                                             mapping
   |        if ((the_file =(char *) mmap(0, (size_t) buf.st_size, PROT_READ |
   |            PROT_WRITE,
   |                           MAP_SHARED, fd0, 0)) ==  NULL) {
   +          cerr << "mmap failure" << endl;
   |          return 5;
   |        }
   |        CLS( );                                       // clear the display
   |        for (int i=0; i < n_threads; ++i) {           // generate the
   |                                                             threads
```

```
40          pthread_create( &thread_id[i], NULL, play, (void *)i);
          }
          do {                                          // in main thread
            sleep(1);                                   // pause a bit
            pthread_mutex_lock( &scrn_lock);
              display_screen(the_file);                 // display screen
            pthread_mutex_unlock( &scrn_lock);
          } while (n_dead < n_threads);                 // while threads left
          for(int i=0; i < n_threads; ++i)
            pthread_join( thread_id[i], (void **) NULL);
50        LOCATE(25, 1);
          close(fd0);
          return 0;
        }
        /*
              Play the game by moving a character around the grid
        */
        void *
        play( void *numb ){
          static pthread_mutex_t  the_lock;             // single copy of these
60        static pthread_key_t    the_key;
          static int              first_time = 1;
          int                     row, col;             // local to each
                                                        //   invocation
          char                    pch;
          void                    *my_let = NULL;       // thread specific
                                                        //   data
          if ( first_time ) {
            pthread_mutex_lock( &the_lock );
            if ( first_time ) {
              pthread_key_create( &the_key, NULL );
              first_time = 0;
70          }
            pthread_mutex_unlock( &the_lock );
          }
          if ( (my_let = pthread_getspecific( the_key )) == NULL ) {
            my_let = (int *) &numb;
            pthread_setspecific( the_key, my_let );     // associate with key
          }
          row=my_rand(1,ROW)-1;                         // start at random
                                                        //   location
          col=my_rand(1,COL)-1;
          pch = (char) (65+*(int *)pthread_getspecific(the_key));
80        do {
            move(the_file, &row, &col, pch);            // move around
          } while( !boxed( the_file, row, col));        // while not boxed in
          n_dead++;                                     // update terminated
                                                        //   threads
          guys[*(int *)pthread_getspecific(the_key)] = '*';
          pthread_mutex_lock( &scrn_lock );
```

```
 |          LOCATE(1, 1);
 |          cout << "Dead = " << n_dead << "[" << guys << "]";
 |        pthread_mutex_unlock( &scrn_lock );
 |        return NULL;
90     }
 |     /*
 |            Find and move to new location.
 |     */
 |     void
 +     move(char *s, int *r, int *c, char pch) {
 |        int        old_offset = (*r * COL + *c),
 |                   new_offset = -1;
 |        DIRECTION d;
 |        neighbors( *r, *c, &d );                        // get neighbor
 |                                                           locations

100       do {
 |           if ( my_rand(1,3) == 1 ) sleep(1);           // 1/3 time sleep
 |                                                           first

 |           switch ( my_rand(1,4) ) {
 |           case 1:
 |              if ( *(s + d.left ) == ' ' ) new_offset = d.left;
 +              break;
 |           case 2:
 |              if ( *(s + d.right ) == ' ' ) new_offset = d.right;
 |              break;
 |           case 3:
110            if ( *(s + d.top  ) == ' ' ) new_offset = d.top;
 |              break;
 |           case 4:
 |              if ( *(s + d.bot  ) == ' ' ) new_offset = d.bot;
 |              break;
 +           }
 |        } while( new_offset == -1 );
 |        *r = new_offset / COL;
 |        *c = new_offset % COL;
 |        *(s + new_offset) = pch;                        // assign new
 |                                                           location
120       if ( *(s + old_offset) != '@' )                 // if its not a
 |                                                           start loc
 |           *(s + old_offset) += 32;                     // change old loc
 |                                                           to LC

 |     }
 |     /*
 |            Display the screen using VT100 escape codes for cursor
 |            placement.
 +     */
 |     void
 |     display_screen(char *s) {
 |        static int    pass = 1;
 |        static char   buffer[COL + 1];
```

```
130          LOCATE(1, 33);
 |           cout << "Thread World";
 |           LOCATE(2, 18);
 |           cout << "+---------------------------------------------+";
 |           for (int i=3; i < 23; ++i) {
 +             LOCATE(i, 18);                                    // move to screen
                                                                   location
 |             strncpy(buffer, (s + (i - 3) * COL), COL);       // get output
                                                                   segment
 |             cout << "|" << buffer << "|";
 |           }
 |           LOCATE(23, 18);
140          cout << "+---------------------------------------------+";
 |           LOCATE(24, 20);
 |           cout << "Pass " << ++pass;
 |         }
 |         /*
 +              Check neighbors to see if any free locations are left
 |         */
 |         bool
 |         boxed(char *s, int r, int c) {
 |           DIRECTION d;
150          neighbors( r, c, &d );                             // get my neighbors
 |           return ( *(s+d.left) != ' ' && *(s+d.right) != ' ' &&
 |                    *(s+d.bot ) != ' ' && *(s+d.top ) != ' ');
 |         }
 |         /*
 +              Calculate the surrounding locations
 |         */
 |         void
 |         neighbors( int row, int col, DIRECTION *d ){
 |           d->left  =  row * COL + (col > 0 ? col - 1 : COL - 1);
160          d->right =  row * COL + (col > COL - 2 ? 0 : col + 1);
 |           d->top   =  (row > 0 ? row - 1 : ROW - 1) * COL + col;
 |           d->bot   =  (row > ROW - 2 ? 0 : row + 1) * COL + col;
 |         }
```

In `main`, a character array, `the_screen`, is allocated along with an array to hold the thread IDs. The command-line contents are examined. The user must pass the name of a file and the number of threads to be generated. The number of threads, stored as `n_threads`, is used as an index to place a NULL in the `guys` array. The `guys` array is a list of uppercase letters that represent the active threads. A series of statements are used to map the `the_screen` display to the file name passed on the command line. While mapping the display to a file is not integral to the overall functionality of the example, it does show how this can be done and would allow, should the user so desire, a means for archiving the program's output. A loop is used to create the threads, and each is passed a reference to the user-defined function `play`. The initial thread, executing `main`, then loops until all threads have finished their activities. As it loops, after each one-second **sleep**, the screen is redisplayed.

The user-definded `play` function allocates the `key`. The logic to accomplish this is a variation of our previous example. The TSD *my_let reference, local to each invocation of `play`, is associated with the `key` by checking the return from the **pthread_getspecific** library function. If a NULL value is returned, as in the initial pass-through, the loop value from `main` (passed in as numb) is assigned to `my_let` and associated with the `key` via a call to **pthread_setspecific**.

A random location is chosen as the starting point for the thread. The character to be displayed is retrieved with a call to **pthread_getspecific**. Using a `do-while` loop, the thread moves about the grid while it is not boxed in. Once boxed in, the thread exits the activity loop. It then increments a global value representing the number of inactive (expired) threads and marks the appropriate location in the `guys` array with an *. Finally, it updates the display of terminated threads and exits.

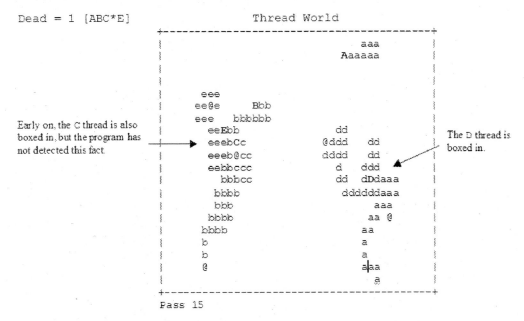

Figure 11.18 Partial output from Program 11.10.

As written, this example *usually* produces rather entertaining output. However, as the program contains some *oversights* in logic, it will on occasion not work as advertised.[23]

Figure 11.18 contains an output display of a partial run of Program 11.10 with five competing threads (letters A–E).

In the run shown, five threads were generated. Thread D was terminated when it became boxed in (in this case surrounded by its own previous movements shown by the lowercase d's). The upper left corner of the output shown has an * in place of the letter D (indicating its termination). As shown, thread C has also become boxed in. However, either the program has somehow missed this fact (the previously mentioned oversight) or it was interrupted before it had a chance to fully update the screen. The remaining threads are active. As shown, the thread executing main had completed its 15th pass.

11-12 EXERCISE

If we run Program 11.10 several times, we should occasionally notice the program does not terminate properly. When this happens, the program appears to believe one or more threads are still active, even though the display clearly indicates that they are boxed in. Find, and correct, the source of this "problem."

11-13 EXERCISE

The logic for the user-defined move function is simplistic. Modify Program 11.10 to incorporate two (or more) different move functions. These new move function(s), each run by a separate thread, should attempt to move in such a manner as to keep the thread from being boxed in for as long as possible. Where practical, they should also attempt to block in (thus terminate) other threads. Gather data to show your move function is superior to the initial simplistic version. If time permits, try pitting your move function against the move functions written by others. If you do not want to share your source for the function, just supply the unique move function name for its invocation in main and link the object code for your move function at compile time.

---

[23] The oversights are the basis for the exercises associated with this program.

11-14 EXERCISE

Using the code in Program 11.10 as a base, write a threaded version of Conway's Game of Life, whereby each thread manages a starting configuration of cells. Establish your own rules for what happens when competing threads attempt to access the same cell location.

11.10 Debugging Multithreaded Programs

Writing multithreaded programs that execute correctly can be quite a challenge. Fortunately, there are some tools available to help with the task. Many current C, C++ compilers are bundled with thread-aware debuggers. For example, newer versions of the GNU C, C++ compiler **gcc**, **g++**, come with **gdb**, and Solaris' C, C++ compiler comes with **dbx**. Thread-aware debuggers automatically recognize multithreaded code. Such debuggers can be used to step through multithreaded programs and examine the contents of mutexes and TSD.

We will use Program 11.11 as source for our thread-debugging example. The debugger presented will be GNU's **gdb** (version 5.1.90CVS-5.)[24] As presented, this program is syntactically correct but contains logic errors pertaining to the access and manipulation of common data by the multiple detached threads.

Program 11.11 Debugging multithreaded programs.

```
File : p11.11.cxx
   |    /*
   |         Debugging multithreaded prgrms - WITH LOCKING ERRORS
   |         Compile: g++ p11.11.cxx -lpthread -o p11.11
   |    */
   +    #define _REENTRANT
   |    #define _GNU_SOURCE
   |    #include <iostream>
   |    #include <cstdio>
   |    #include <cstdlib>
```

[24] Only the command-line version of the debugger will be addressed. GNU also provides a graphical interface for its debugger called **xxgdb** for those who are working in a windowing environment.

```
10      #include <pthread.h>
 |      #include <unistd.h>
 |      #include <sys/time.h>
 |      using namespace std;
 |      const int   MAX=5,
 +                  HOME=25;
 |      int
 |      my_rand(int start, int range){
 |        struct timeval t;
 |        gettimeofday(&t, (struct timezone *)NULL);
20        return (int)(start+((float)range * rand_r((unsigned *)&t.tv_usec))
 |                  / (RAND_MAX+1.0));
 |      }
 |      typedef struct {
 |        int increment;
 +        char *phrase;
 |      } argument;
 |      void  step( void * );
 |                                              // common to all threads
 |      pthread_t       thread_id[MAX];
30      bool            alive = true, home = false;
 |      int             position,total=0;
 |      char   walk[] = "    |     | ";
 |      int
 |      main(int argc, char *argv[]) {
 +        argument right={ +1, "ZOINK! Stepped off the RIGHT side.\n"},
 |                 left =={ -1, "SPLAT! Stepped off the LEFT side.\n"};
 |        pthread_attr_t attr_obj;
 |        if (argc < 2) {                        /* check arg list      */
 |          cerr <<  *argv << " start_position" << endl;
40          return 1;
 |        }
 |        position = atoi(argv[1]);
 |        if ( position < 1 )
 |          position = 1;
 +        else if ( position > MAX )
 |          position = MAX;
 |        walk[position+5] = '*';
 |        setvbuf(stdout, (char *) NULL, _IONBF, 0);
 |        cout << "The drunken sailor walk" << endl << endl;
50        cout << "     +12345+" << endl;
 |        cout << walk << endl;
 |        pthread_attr_init( &attr_obj );
 |        pthread_attr_setdetachstate( &attr_obj, PTHREAD_CREATE_DETACHED );
 |        pthread_create(&thread_id[0], &attr_obj,
 +                    (void *(*) (void *)) step, (void *) &right);
 |        pthread_create(&thread_id[1], &attr_obj,
 |                    (void *(*) (void *)) step, (void *) &left );
 |        pthread_exit(NULL);
 |        return 0;
```

541

```
60      }
 |      void
 |      step( void *a ) {
 |        argument *my_arg=(argument *)a;
 |        do {
 +          sleep( my_rand(1,3) );                    // pause a bit
 |          walk[position+MAX] = ' ';                 // clear old position
 |          position += my_arg->increment;            // calculate new position
 |          alive = bool(position > 0  && position <= MAX);
 |          walk[position+MAX] = alive ? '*' : '$';
70          cout << walk << endl;
 |          home = bool(++total >= HOME);
 |          if ( !alive || home ) {
 |            if ( !alive )
 |              cout << my_arg->phrase;
 +            else
 |              cout << "The sailor made it home safely this time!\n";
 |            pthread_kill(thread_id[ (position < 1 ? 1 : 0)], 9);
 |          }
 |          sched_yield( );
80        } while ( alive && !home );
 |      }
```

Program 11.11 contains an assortment of POSIX thread calls. The program, which is purely pedagogical in nature, implements a version of the "drunken sailor" problem. In this version, a drunken sailor is given a starting position on a boardwalk that is five steps wide. The program traces the path of the sailor as he or she progresses down the boardwalk toward home (located an arbitrary number of steps from the start). If the sailor steps off either side of the boardwalk, he or she perishes. If the sailor is still on the boardwalk after a set number of steps he or she is considered to have made it home. The sailor's position on the boardwalk is stored in a variable called position. Two threads manipulate this data. One thread executes a user-defined function, step, moving the sailor to the right, while a second thread executes the same function, moving the sailor to the left (the movement is based on the argument passed to the step function). Both threads are detached from the initiating thread. When the sailor perishes or reaches the end of the walk, the detached threads are terminated. Typical output from Program 11.11 is shown in Figure 11.19.

In the first run it appears that the program is working pretty much as would be expected. However, the second and third run produces somewhat unexpected results. In the second run it looks as if there might be two sailors on the boardwalk (I suppose one could be seeing double—but this is not the case). In the third run the right side of the boardwalk seems to have disappeared.

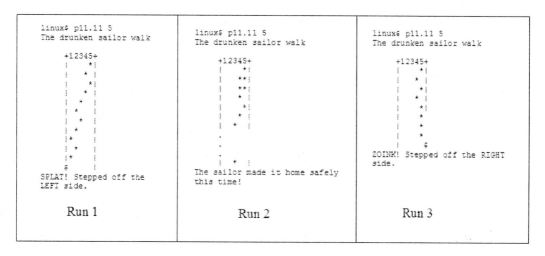

```
linux$ p11.11 5          linux$ p11.11 5          linux$ p11.11 5
The drunken sailor walk  The drunken sailor walk  The drunken sailor walk

  +12345+                     +12345+                  +12345+
  |    * |                    |   *|                   |   *|
  |    * |                    |  **|                    |  *  |
  |    * |                    |  **|                    |  *  |
  |    * |                    |   *|                     |  *
  |   *  |                    |   *|                     |  *
  |  *   |                    |  * |                     | *
  | *    |                    |    |                     |  $
  |*     |                  .                        ZOINK! Stepped off the RIGHT
  | *    |                  .                        side.
  |*     |                  |  * |
  $                       The sailor made it home safely
SPLAT! Stepped off the    this time!
LEFT side.
```

| Run 1 | Run 2 | Run 3 |

Figure 11.19   Several runs of Program 11.11.

Clearly, something funny is going on! The problem is tied to the unrestricted access of common data by competing threads. One way to check on what is happening is to run the program in the debugger.

To prepare the program for the debugger, pass the -g argument at compilation time to prevent the automatic removal of additional symbol table information from the executable. For example, the command sequence

```
linux$ g++ -g p11.11.cxx -lpthread -o p11.11
```

produces an executable, p11.11, that can be loaded and run in the debugger. When the debugger is invoked, it is passed the name of the executable. For our example this would be

```
linux$ gdb p11.11
GNU gdb Red Hat Linux (5.1.90CVS-5)
Copyright 2002 Free Software Foundation, Inc.
GDB is free software, covered by the GNU General Public License, and you are
welcome to change it and/or distribute copies of it under certain conditions.
Type "show copying" to see the conditions.
There is absolutely no warranty for GDB.  Type "show warranty" for details.
This GDB was configured as "i386-redhat-linux"...
(gdb)
```

Suppose we want the debugger to stop in the user-defined function step. We can use the list command in **gdb** to show us a given sequence of lines (with their line numbers). For example,

```
(gdb) list 61,81
61      void
62      step( void *a ) {
63         argument *my_arg=(argument *)a;
64         do {
65            sleep( my_rand(1,3) );                    // pause a bit
66            walk[position+MAX] = ' ';                 // clear old position
67            position += my_arg->increment;            // calculate new position
68            alive = bool(position > 0  && position <= MAX);
69            walk[position+MAX] = alive ? '*' : '$';
70            cout << walk << endl;
71            home = bool(++total >= HOME);
72            if ( !alive || home ) {
73               if ( !alive )
74                  cout << my_arg->phrase;
75               else
76                  cout << "The sailor made it home safely this time!\n";
77               pthread_kill(thread_id[ (position < 1 ? 1 : 0)], 9);
78            }
79            sched_yield( );
80         } while ( alive && !home );
81      }
```

Or, we can also use the list command and pass the name of the user-defined function we would like to see listed (such as step). If we do this, the debugger will show the first N (usually 10) lines of the referenced function. The listing usually begins a line or two prior to the actual function.

```
(gdb) list step
57                        (void *(*) (void *)) step, (void *) &left );
58         pthread_exit(NULL);
59         return 0;
60      }
61      void
62      step( void *a ) {
63         argument *my_arg=(argument *)a;
64         do {
65            sleep( my_rand(1,3) );                    // pause a bit
66            walk[position+MAX] = ' ';                 // clear old position
```

To stop at line 66, we establish a breakpoint.

```
(gdb) break 66
Breakpoint 1 at 0x8048b61: file p11.11.cxx, line 66.
```

To execute (run) the program, the run command is used. Any values that would normally be passed on the command line are placed after the run command.

```
(gdb) run 5
Starting program: /home/faculty/gray/revision/11/sailor/p11.11 5
[New Thread 1024 (LWP 3176)]
The drunken sailor walk
     +12345+
     |    *|
[New Thread 2049 (LWP 3193)]
[New Thread 1026 (LWP 3194)]
[New Thread 2051 (LWP 3195)]
[Switching to Thread 1026 (LWP 3194)]
Breakpoint 1, step (a=0xbffffb48) at p11.11.cxx:66
66          walk[position+MAX] = ' ';                      // clear old position
```

General program output.

When the debugger stops at the indicated line, the command `info`
`thread` can be issued to obtain a wealth of thread information.

```
(gdb) info thread
  4 Thread 2051 (LWP 3195)  0x420b4b31 in nanosleep () from
/lib/i686/libc.so.6
* 3 Thread 1026 (LWP 3194)  step (a=0xbffffb48) at p11.11.cxx:66
  2 Thread 2049 (LWP 3193)  0x420e0037 in poll () from /lib/i686/libc.so.6
  1 Thread 1024 (LWP 3176)  0x420292e5 in sigsuspend () from /lib/i686/libc.so.6
```

The astute reader will notice a number of things. Thread 1 (the initiating
thread) was directed to exit (line 58, `pthread_exit(NULL);`) but at this
juncture still appears to be active. At present, there are four threads associated
with the program. The current active thread, identified with an asterisk, is
thread ID 3, which is associated with LWP 3194.

The command `display variable_name`, where `variable_name`
is the name of the variable of interest, directs the debugger to display the current contents of the variable each time a breakpoint is encountered. In the
sequence below we have directed the debugger to display the contents of the
global variables `alive`, `position`, and `home` before we issue `run`.

.
.
.

```
Starting program: /home/faculty/gray/revision/11/sailor/p11.11 5
[New Thread 1024 (LWP 3274)]
The drunken sailor walk

     +12345+
     |    *|
[New Thread 2049 (LWP 3291)]
[New Thread 1026 (LWP 3292)]
[New Thread 2051 (LWP 3293)]
[Switching to Thread 1026 (LWP 3292)]
```

```
Breakpoint 1, step (a=0xbfffb48) at p11.11.cxx:66
66          walk[position+MAX] = ' ';                    // clear old position
3: home = false
2: position = 5                                          At this point the sailor, at position 5, has not
1: alive = true                                          reached home and is still alive.
(gdb) cont
Continuing.
        |     $
ZOINK! Stepped off the RIGHT side.
[Switching to Thread 2051 (LWP 3293)]

Breakpoint 1, step (a=0xbfffb40) at p11.11.cxx:66
66          walk[position+MAX] = ' ';                    // clear old position
3: home = false                                          Now the sailor is at position 6. He or she has
2: position = 6                                          not reached home and is no longer alive. The
1: alive = false                                         program should stop here, but it does not.
(gdb) cont
Continuing.
        |   *


Breakpoint 1, step (a=0xbfffb40) at p11.11.cxx:66
66          walk[position+MAX] = ' ';                    // clear old position
3: home = false
2: position = 5                                          Suddenly, the sailor is at position 5. While still
1: alive = true                                          having reached home, the sailor is now alive!
.                                                        Clearly, the thread doing the decrement to the
.                                                        position has performed its activity before the
.                                                        test for being alive was done.
```

A specific thread can be referenced with the command thread N, where N is the number of the appropriate thread. As shown below, information specific to the thread can be referenced once the thread is loaded.

```
(gdb) thread 4
[Switching to thread 4 (Thread 2051 (LWP 3342))]#0  step (a=0xbfffb40) at
p11.11.cxx:66
66          walk[position+MAX] = ' ';                    // clear old
                                                            position
(gdb) print *my_arg
$24 = {increment = -1, phrase = 0x8048da0 "SPLAT! Stepped off the LEFT
    side.\n"}                                      This is the thread that does the decrement.
(gdb) thread 3
[Switching to thread 3 (Thread 1026 (LWP 3341))]#0  step (a=0xbfffb48) at
p11.11.cxx:66
66          walk[position+MAX] = ' ';                    // clear old
                                                            position
(gdb) print *my_arg
$25 = {increment = 1, phrase = 0x8048d60 "ZOINK! Stepped off the RIGHT
    side.\n"}
```

Anytime the debugger is stopped, the contents of a mutex can be displayed (assuming it is within the current scope). For example, if we had a mutex called `my_lock`, its contents before it is acquired would be

```
(gdb) print my_lock
$1 = {__m_reserved = 0, __m_count = 0, __m_owner = 0x0, __m_kind = 0,
  __m_lock = {__status = 0, __spinlock = 0}}
```

and after it is acquired

> This member is set to 1 when the mutex is locked.

```
(gdb) print my_lock
$2 = {__m_reserved = 0, __m_count = 0, __m_owner = 0x0, __m_kind = 0,
  __m_lock = {__status = 1, __spinlock = 0}}
```

The `quit` command is used to leave the debugger. An abbreviated listing of **gdb** commands can be displayed in **gdb** using the command `help`. The manual pages on **gdb** contain a more detailed explanation of how to invoke **gdb**. On the command line, `info gdb` provides a wealth of information on how to use **gdb** (including a fairly detailed sample session).

11-15   EXERCISE

Modify Program 11.11 to support two (or more) sailors walking down the boardwalk at the same time (you may need to increase the width of the boardwalk). Use a different symbol for each sailor. No two sailors should occupy the same location at the same time (it's the law!). The program should end when either, all sailors have expired, or one or more sailors have reached their goal, say a set number of steps.

11.11 Summary

A thread is a distinct sequence of steps performed by one or more processes. By definition, all programs contain a single thread of control. Threads, which are created dynamically and execute independently, can be used to provide concurrency at a minimal cost (both in system resources and programming effort). Problems that consist of multiple individual tasks lend themselves to a threaded solution, while problems that are serial in nature do not.

Thread libraries (such as the POSIX thread library) provide programmers with a means for generating and coordinating multiple threads. These threads can be contained within a single process or spread across multiple processes. Threads within a process share most of the process's state information. At a system-implementation level, a thread can be bound (directly associated with an underlying LWP) or unbound. Unbound threads are mapped on an as-needed basis to an LWP from a pool maintained by the system. Threads can be specified as detached. A detached thread cannot be waited upon and exits once it has finished its processing. A nondetached thread can be waited upon (often by its creating thread) and its exiting status obtained. When a thread is created, it is passed a reference to the code it is to execute. Each thread has an associated priority and scheduling algorithm that is used by the system to determine how and when the thread will receive processing time. The actual scheduling of a thread is done by the thread library (if unbound) or by the kernel (if bound). Threads can send and receive signals. In a multithreaded setting, often one thread is designated as the signal catcher. A signal mask is used to specify whether or not a thread will act upon or ignore a particular signal.

Thread activity can be coordinated with mutexes (mutual exclusion locks), condition variables, and semaphores. A mutex is used to lock a specific section of code (often called the critical section) where the integrity of the data accessed must be maintained. The term monitor is sometimes used when the section of code to be locked encompasses the entire module to be executed. Some thread libraries support read/write mutexes. A read/write mutex allows any number of threads to read protected data, but only one thread at a time to write or modify the data. Read/write mutexes are considerably slower than their less complicated brethren. Mutexes that are used by threads in different processes must be mapped to a shared memory location. Condition variables are used to force a thread to block on an arbitrary condition. Multithread-safe semaphores, based on a POSIX4 implementation, can be binary or counting. Semaphores can be used to manage multiple resources. Usually, it is best to lock the minimal number of lines of code needed to maintain data consistency.

If needed, it is possible to have data items in common sections of code that contain a value specific to each thread. Such data, called thread-specific data (TSD), is accessible to all threads but is maintained on a per-thread basis. The system uses a unique key value to determine the data value in a given thread.

11.12 Nomenclature and Key Concepts

/usr/bin/time utility
_POSIX_C_SOURCE defined
  constant
_REENTRANT defined constant
<pthread.h> include file
<semaphore.h> include file
<signal.h> include file
clone system call
condition variable
gdb utility
heavyweight process
kernel-level thread
lightweight process (LWP)
multithreaded
mutex
nanosleep real-time library
  function
nonpreemptive scheduling
opaque data type
parallelism
POSIX 1003.1 standard
POSIX 1003.1c standard
preemptive scheduling
pthread_attr_getschedparam
  library function
pthread_attr_init library
  function
**pthread_attr_setsched-
  param** library function
pthread_cleanup_pop library
  function
**pthread_cleanup_pop_
  restore_np** library function
pthread_cleanup_push
  library function
**pthread_cleanup_push_
  defer_np** library function

PTHREAD_COND_ INITIAL-
  IZER defined constant
pthread_cond_broadcast
  library function
pthread_cond_signal library
  function
pthread_cond_timedwait
  library function
pthread_cond_wait library
  function
pthread_create library
  function
PTHREAD_CREATE_DE-
  TACHED defined constant
PTHREAD_CREATE_JOINABLE
  defined constant
PTHREAD_DESTRUCTOR_
  ITERATIONS defined constant
pthread_detach library
  function
PTHREAD_ERRORCHECK_
  MUTEX_INITIALIZER_NP
pthread_exit library function
PTHREAD_EXPLICIT_SCHED
  defined constant
pthread_getschedparam
  library function
pthread_getspecific library
  function
PTHREAD_INHERIT_SCHED
  defined constant
pthread_join library function
pthread_key_create library
  function
pthread_key_delete library
  function
pthread_kill library function

Appendix A

USING LINUX MANUAL PAGES

A.1 Manual Page Sections

The online manual pages found in Linux provide a wealth of information. The manual pages are loosely grouped by category into the following sections:

1 User commands and application programs.
2 System calls. A complete list of system calls can be found at the end of this appendix.
3 Library functions—these functions do not directly invoke kernel primitives.
4 Devices.
5 File formats.
6 Games and demonstrations.
7 Special conventions and protocols, character set standards, the standard file system layout, and a variety of other miscellaneous things.
8 Administrative and privileged commands available only to the superuser.
9 Device drivers and kernel interfaces.
n New.

There are a variety of ways to access manual page information. The most standard approach is to use the **man** utility on the command line. For example, almost every section has a manual page called `intro` that provides an overview of the section. To obtain the proper `intro` manual page for a section, the section number is passed on the command line when the **man** command is invoked. For example, the `intro` manual page for Section 2 (system calls) is specified as

```
linux$ man 2 intro
```

On the command line a manual page can be sent to the printer using the command sequence

```
linux$ man 2 intro | col -b | lp
```

In this sequence the output of the **man** command is piped to the **col** utility. This utility, when passed the `-b` option, filters out any backspaces and outputs only the last character written to each column position. The output of the **col** utility is then piped to **lp** for printing.

Another approach is to use the **info** utility. This program, which is a document-reading utility, helps to facilitate manual page navigation and access to related topics. The command line sequence

```
linux$ info info
```

brings up the manual page on the **info** utility. On our Linux system this brings up the following screen.

```
File: info.info, Node: Top, Next: Getting Started, Up: (dir)

Info: An Introduction
*********************

   Info is a program, which you are using now, for reading documentation of
computer programs. The GNU Project distributes most of its on-line manuals
in the Info format, so you need a program called "Info reader" to read the
manuals. One of such programs you are using now.

   If you are new to Info and want to learn how to use it, type the
command 'h' now. It brings you to a programmed instruction sequence.

   To learn advanced Info commands, type 'n' twice. This brings you to
'Info for Experts', skipping over the 'Getting Started' chapter.

* Menu:

* Getting Started::        Getting started using an Info reader.
* Advanced Info::          Advanced commands within Info.
* Creating an Info File::  How to make your own Info file.
* Index::                  An index of topics, commands, and variables.
```

Entering the letter h at this first screen displays the basics of how to use this utility. Entering the letter q quits (exit) the **info** utility.

Even another approach is to use **xman**, the X Window System manual browser. For example, on our Linux system entering the command sequence

```
linux$ setenv MANPATH /mit/kit/man:/usr/share/man
linux$ xhost+
linux$ xman &
```

assigns the environment variable MANPATH (used by **xman**) the directory locations to be searched,[1] disables access control (allowing X Window clients to connect from any host), and invokes **xman**, placing it in the background. On the client a small X Window similar to the one below is displayed.

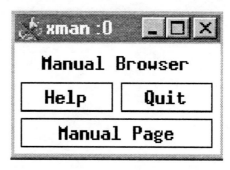

Selecting [Help] displays a window with online help, [Quit] terminates service, and [Manual Page] displays a window containing a manual page browser. Entering [Ctrl] + [S] after selecting [Manual Page] generates a text entry box where the name of a specific command can be entered.

The file /etc/man.config is a text based file that holds the default customization specifications for the **man** utility. Contained in this file are a variety of uppercase identifiers which are assigned values. These identifiers parallel corresponding environment variables used by the **man** utility. The values assigned to the identifiers in the man.config file act as the default values if the corresponding environment variable has not been set. Aside from MANPATH another item of passing interest is the value assigned to MANSECT. MANSECT stipulates which manual sections are to be searched and their order. On our system when initially configured MANSECT is set to:

```
MANSECT   1:8:2:3:4:5:6:7:9:tcl:n:l:p:o
```

This is fine from an administrative viewpoint. However, if you are doing a great deal of programming you might want to change the default order by moving

---

[1] Things get a bit dicey here as they vary somewhat from system to system. Check the file /etc/ man.config for specifics about the content of the MANPATH variable. In any case, when using **xman**, be sure to add /mit/kit/man to the directories to be searched.

section 8 (administrative and privileged commands) further back in the sequence and placing section 2 (system calls) and 3 (library functions) nearer the front. One such rearrangement would be:

```
MANSECT   3:2:1:4:5:6:7:8:9:tcl:n:l:p:o
```

A.2 Manual Page Format

Individual manual pages, as viewed with the **man** command, follow a somewhat standard format. A typical manual page (**perror** found in Section 3) is shown below.

```
PERROR(3)              Library functions           PERROR(3)
NAME
    perror - print a system error message
```
A brief summary-often is the same information returned by the **apros** or **man** -k command.

```
SYNOPSIS
    #include <stdio.h>
    void perror(const char *s);

    #include <errno.h>
    const char *sys_errlist[];
    int sys_nerr;
```
Syntactical information—include files, external variables, function prototype, function return data type, parameter data types, and so on. This is a key section. Special attention should be paid to arguments passed as a reference.

```
DESCRIPTION
    The routine perror() produces a message on the standard error output, de-
    scribing the last error encountered during a call to a system or library
    function. First (if s is not NULL and *s is not NUL) the argument string
    s is printed, followed by a colon and a blank. Then the message and a new-
    line.
         .
         .
         .
```
A detailed narration of what this system call or library function does.

```
    that errno is undefined after a successful library call: this call may well
    change this variable, even though it succeeds, for example because it in-
    ternally used some other library function that failed. Thus, if a failing
    call is not immediately followed by a call to perror, the value of errno
    should be saved.
CONFORMING TO
    ANSI C, BSD 4.3, POSIX, X/OPEN
```
As provided, the standards this system call or library function meets.

```
SEE ALSO
    strerror(3)
```
Other related system calls and/or library functions.

```
    Last update.  ——▶ 2001-12-14                      PERROR(3)
```

Across the top of the manual page is a title line. Following the title line is a series of subdivisions delineated by uppercase labels. The subdivisions common to most (but not all) system call and library function manual pages are

NAME

The name of the item is followed by a brief description. The description is often similar to, if not the same as, the description returned when a **man** -k (know) query for a specific topic is made.[2] The **man** -k pipe command returns all manual page summaries for any item (system call, library function, etc.) that contains the term pipe. For example,

```
linux$   man    -k pipe
fifo      (4)   - first-in first-out special file, named pipe
funzip    (1)   - filter for extracting from a ZIP archive in
                  a pipe
IO::Pipe (3pm)- supply object methods for pipes
mkfifo    (1)   - make FIFOs (named pipes)
mkfifo    (3)   - make a FIFO special file (a named pipe)
open      (n)   - Open a file-based or command pipeline channel
perlipc   (1)   - Perl interprocess communication (signals,
                  fifos, pipes, safe subprocesses, sockets,
                  and semaphores)
pipe      (2)   - create pipe
```

On most systems, **man** -k is equivalent to using the **apropos** utility, (i.e., **man** -k pipe returns the information as **apropos** pipe).

SYNOPSIS

This provides the syntactical information for the correct use of the item. In the case of a system call or library function, the requisite include file(s), external variables referenced, and prototype are given. The data type of the return value of the system call or library function can be obtained from the prototype definition. For example, the manual page for the **perror** library function has the following SYNOPSIS:

```
#include <stdio.h>
void perror(const char *s);

#include <errno.h>
const char *sys_errlist[];
int sys_nerr;
```

This indicates that to use **perror**, the header file stdio.h must be included. The **perror** call accepts a single argument, s, which is a pointer to a constant of type char. The return value for **perror** is of

---

[2] The -k command option for **man** uses the windex database, which is created by running the **catman** program. If the system administrator has not run this program, or the windex database is out of date, the -k option for **man** will not work correctly.

type void, indicating it does not return a value. Additionally, the SYNOPSIS indicates that if we want to make use of the external list of errors referenced by sys_errlist or the external variable sys_nerr (that has the number of possible errors), we should include the file errno.h. Be sure to note arguments that are pointers (references). These arguments must reference the correct data type (e.g., char, int, etc.). If information is to be passed to the system call or library function, the referenced object must be set to the proper initial value. In addition, if information is to be returned via the reference, the programmer must allocate sufficient space for the referenced item prior to the call.

DESCRIPTION   This subdivision contains a detailed narration of what the system call or library function does.

RETURN VALUE   The value(s) the system call or library function returns and how to interpret them. The RETURN VALUE entry should indicate whether or not errno is set.

CONFORMING   The standard(s) to which the system call or library function conforms.
TO   Typically the standards are abbreviated, such as SVr4, SVID, POSIX, X/OPEN, or BSD 4.3. On occasion a specific option for compilation and/or the definition of a specific constant (such as _GNU_SOURCE) is noted.

ERRORS   When present (i.e., errno is set), this entry lists the error codes generated by the system call or library function if it fails. A short explanation of how to interpret each error code is given.

FILES   Files accessed or modified by the system call or library function.

SEE ALSO   Other items of interest, such as related system calls or library functions.

NOTES   A catchall containing additional pertinent information that does not fall into any particular category.

LINUX NOTES   Notes specific to the Linux implementation.

AUTHORS   A list of authors (often with their email address).

There are several other manual page divisions that surface on an infrequent basis. These, like those above, are usually self-explanatory (e.g., OPTIONS, EXAMPLE, BUGS, HISTORY, WARNINGS, DIAGNOSTICS, etc.). On occasion, small flashes of self-deprecating humor are encountered. The following is from the manual page on the system command **tune2fs** (used for tuning a second extended file system in Linux) "*We haven't found any bugs yet. That doesn't mean there aren't any. . . .*" Unfortunately, as things become more standardized, such frivolities are becoming less common.

A.3 Standard Linux System Calls

_llseek	init_module	sched_setaffinity
_newselect	ioctl	sched_setparam
_sysctl	ioperm	sched_setscheduler
access	iopl	sched_yield
acct	ipc	security
adjtimex	kill	select
afs_syscall	lchown	sendfile
alarm	lchown32	sendfile64
bdflush	lgetxattr	setdomainname
break	link	setfsgid
brk	listxattr	setfsgid32
capget	llistxattr	setfsuid
capset	lock	setfsuid32
chdir	lremovexattr	setgid
chmod	lseek	setgid32
chown	lsetxattr	setgroups
chown32	lstat	setgroups32
chroot	lstat64	sethostname
clone	madvise	setitimer
close	madvise1	setpgid
creat	mincore	setpriority
create_module	mkdir	setregid
delete_module	mknod	setregid32
dup	mlock	setresgid
dup2	mlockall	setresgid32
execve	mmap	setresuid
exit, _exit	mmap2	setresuid32
fchdir	modify_ldt	setreuid
fchmod	mount	setreuid32
fchown	mprotect	setrlimit
fchown32	mpx	setsid
fcntl	mremap	settimeofday
fcntl64	msync	setuid
fdatasync	munlock	setuid32
fgetxattr	munlockall	setxattr
flistxattr	munmap	sgetmask
flock	nanosleep	sigaction

fork
fremovexattr
fsetxattr
fstat
fstat64
fstatfs
fsync
ftime
ftruncate
ftruncate64
futex
get_kernel_syms
getcwd
getdents
getdents64
getegid
getegid32
geteuid
geteuid32
getgid
getgid32
getgroups
getgroups32
getitimer
getpgid
getpgrp
getpid
getpmsg
getppid
getpriority
getresgid
getresgid32
getresuid
getresuid32
getrlimit
getrusage
getsid
gettid
gettimeofday
getuid
getuid32
getxattr
gtty
idle

nfsservctl
nice
oldfstat
oldlstat
oldolduname
oldstat
olduname
open
pause
personality
pipe
pivot_root
poll
prctl
pread
prof
profil
ptrace
putpmsg
pwrite
query_module
quotactl
read
readahead
readdir
readlink
readv
reboot
removexattr
rename
rmdir
rt_sigaction
rt_sigpending
rt_sigprocmask
rt_sigqueueinfo
rt_sigreturn
rt_sigsuspend
rt_sigtimedwait
sched_get_priority_max
sched_get_priority_min
sched_getaffinity
sched_getparam
sched_getscheduler
sched_rr_get_interval

sigaltstack
signal
sigpending
sigprocmask
sigreturn
sigsuspend
socketcall
ssetmask
stat
stat64
statfs
stime
stty
swapoff
swapon
symlink
sync
sysfs
sysinfo
syslog
time
times
tkill
truncate
truncate64
ugetrlimit
ulimit
umask
umount
umount2
uname
unlink
uselib
ustat
utime
vfork
vhangup
vm86
vm86old
wait4
waitpid
write
writev

Appendix B

UNIX ERROR MESSAGES

Errors generated by the failure of a system call or library function, can be displayed using the **perror** or **strerror** library function calls (see "Managing Failures" Section 1.5, "Managing System Call Failures"). For example, the error messages returned by **strerror** on a Linux system can be displayed in their entirety using Program B.1.

Program B.1 Displaying `strerror` messages.

```
File : errors.cxx
    |       #include <iostream>
    |       #include <cstring>
    |       #include <errno.h>
    |       extern int sys_nerr;
    +       using namespace std;
    |       int
    |       main( ){
    |         for (int err=0; err < sys_nerr; ++err )
    |           cout << err << '\t' << strerror(err) << endl;
   10         return 0;
    |       }
```

As the output of the program will fill more than one screen, it may be helpful to redirect the output to either a file, for future reference, or to the **more** command to permit viewing of the output at a controlled pace. To compile the source file and capture the output of the program in a file called emessages, the command sequence is

```
linux$  g++ errors.cxx -o errors
linux$  errors > emessages
```

If, after compilation, you want the program output to be piped to **more**, the command sequence is

```
linux$   errors | more
```

Note that the error message returned by **strerror** (and **perror**) in a C/C++ program is the same message that is returned by the Linux command-line utility called **perror**. A command-line sequence to determine the error message associated with error number 13 is

```
linux$ perror 13
Error code  13:  Permission denied
```

A Bourne shell script that uses the command-line **perror** utility to display all error messages is shown in Program B.2.

Program B.2 Bourne shell script that uses **perror** to generate error messages.

```
File : errors_script
   |      #! /bin/bash
   |      err=0
   | .    while test $err -lt  125; do
   |        echo -n "$err     "
   +        perror -s $err
   |        err='expr $err + 1'
   |      done
```

Table B.1 lists the error number, its symbolic name, and the actual message generated by **strerror**.

Table B.1 Error messages.

Error #	Symbolic Constant	Message Generated by `strerror`
0		Success
1	**EPERM**	Operation not permitted
2	**ENOENT**	No such file or directory
3	**ESRCH**	No such process
4	**EINTR**	Interrupted system call
5	**EIO**	Input/output error
6	**ENXIO**	No such device or address
7	**E2BIG**	Argument list too long
8	**ENOEXEC**	`exec` format error
9	**EBADF**	Bad file descriptor
10	**ECHILD**	No child processes
11	**EAGAIN**	Resource temporarily unavailable
12	**ENOMEM**	Cannot allocate memory
13	**EACCES**	Permission denied
14	**EFAULT**	Bad address
15	**ENOTBLK**	Block device required
16	**EBUSY**	Device or resource busy
17	**EEXIST**	File exists
18	**EXDEV**	Invalid cross-device link
19	**ENODEV**	No such device
20	**ENOTDIR**	Not a directory
21	**EISDIR**	Is a directory
22	**EINVAL**	Invalid argument
23	**ENFILE**	Too many open files in system
24	**EMFILE**	Too many open files
25	**ENOTTY**	Inappropriate `ioctl` for device
26	**ETXTBSY**	Text file busy
27	**EFBIG**	File too large
28	**ENOSPC**	No space left on device
29	**ESPIPE**	Illegal seek

Continued

Table B.1 *(Continued)*

Error #	Symbolic Constant	Message Generated by `strerror`
30	**EROFS**	Read-only file system
31	**EMLINK**	Too many links
32	**EPIPE**	Broken pipe
33	**EDOM**	Numerical argument out of domain
34	**ERANGE**	Numerical result out of range
35	**EDEADLK**	Resource deadlock avoided
36	**ENAMETOOLONG**	File name too long
37	**ENOLCK**	No locks available
38	**ENOSYS**	Function not implemented
39	**ENOTEMPTY**	Directory not empty
40	**ELOOP**	Too many levels of symbolic links
41	**EWOULDBLOCK**	Unknown error 41
42	**ENOMSG**	No message of desired type
43	**EIDRM**	Identifier removed
44	**ECHRNG**	Channel number out of range
45	**EL2NSYNC**	Level 2 not synchronized
46	**EL3HLT**	Level 3 halted
47	**EL3RST**	Level 3 reset
48	**ELNRNG**	Link number out of range
49	**EUNATCH**	Protocol driver not attached
50	**ENOCSI**	No CSI structure available
51	**EL2HLT**	Level 2 halted
52	**EBADE**	Invalid exchange
53	**EBADR**	Invalid request descriptor
54	**EXFULL**	Exchange full
55	**ENOANO**	No anode
56	**EBADRQC**	Invalid request code
57	**EBADSLT**	Invalid slot
58	**EDEADLOCK**	Unknown error 58
59	**EBFONT**	Bad font file format
60	**ENOSTR**	Device not a stream

Table B.1 *(Continued)*

Error #	Symbolic Constant	Message Generated by `strerror`
61	**ENODATA**	No data available
62	**ETIME**	Timer expired
63	**ENOSR**	Out of streams resources
64	**ENONET**	Machine is not on the network
65	**ENOPKG**	Package not installed
66	**EREMOTE**	Object is remote
67	**ENOLINK**	Link has been severed
68	**EADV**	Advertise error
69	**ESRMNT**	Srmount error
70	**ECOMM**	Communication error on send
71	**EPROTO**	Protocol error
72	**EMULTIHOP**	Multihop attempted
73	**EDOTDOT**	RFS-specific error
74	**EBADMSG**	Bad message
75	**EOVERFLOW**	Value too large for defined data type
76	**ENOTUNIQ**	Name not unique on network
77	**EBADFD**	File descriptor in bad state
78	**EREMCHG**	Remote address changed
79	**ELIBACC**	Can not access a needed shared library
80	**ELIBBAD**	Accessing a corrupted shared library
81	**ELIBSCN**	`.lib` section in `a.out` corrupted
82	**ELIBMAX**	Attempting to link in too many shared libraries
83	**ELIBEXEC**	Cannot exec a shared library directly
84	**EILSEQ**	Invalid or incomplete multibyte or wide character
85	**ERESTART**	Interrupted system call should be restarted
86	**ESTRPIPE**	Streams pipe error
87	**EUSERS**	Too many users
88	**ENOTSOCK**	Socket operation on nonsocket
89	**EDESTADDRREQ**	Destination address required

Continued

Table B.1 (Continued)

Error #	Symbolic Constant	Message Generated by strerror
90	**EMSGSIZE**	Message too long
91	**EPROTOTYPE**	Protocol wrong type for socket
92	**ENOPROTOOPT**	Protocol not available
93	**EPROTONOSUPPORT**	Protocol not supported
94	**ESOCKTNOSUPPORT**	Socket type not supported
95	**EOPNOTSUPP**	Operation not supported
96	**EPFNOSUPPORT**	Protocol family not supported
97	**EAFNOSUPPORT**	Address family not supported by protocol
98	**EADDRINUSE**	Address already in use
99	**EADDRNOTAVAIL**	Cannot assign requested address
100	**ENETDOWN**	Network is down
101	**ENETUNREACH**	Network is unreachable
102	**ENETRESET**	Network dropped connection on reset
103	**ECONNABORTED**	Software caused connection abort
104	**ECONNRESET**	Connection reset by peer
105	**ENOBUFS**	No buffer space available
106	**EISCONN**	Transport endpoint is already connected
107	**ENOTCONN**	Transport endpoint is not connected
108	**ESHUTDOWN**	Cannot send after transport endpoint shutdown
109	**ETOOMANYREFS**	Too many references: cannot splice
110	**ETIMEDOUT**	Connection timed out
111	**ECONNREFUSED**	Connection refused
112	**EHOSTDOWN**	Host is down
113	**EHOSTUNREACH**	No route to host
114	**EALREADY**	Operation already in progress
115	**EINPROGRESS**	Operation now in progress
116	**ESTALE**	Stale NFS file handle
117	**EUCLEAN**	Structure needs cleaning
118	**ENOTNAM**	Not a XENIX named type file
119	**ENAVAIL**	No XENIX semaphores available

Table B.1 (Continued)

Error #	Symbolic Constant	Message Generated by `strerror`
120	**EISNAM**	Is a named type file
121	**EREMOTEIO**	Remote I/O error
122	**EDQUOT**	Disk quota exceeded
123	**ENOMEDIUM**	No medium found
124	**EMEDIUMTYPE**	Wrong medium type

Keep in mind that in C/C++ programs it is always best to reference a specific error by its symbolic constant, as the underlying numeric value for an error can change from one implementation of UNIX to another (and even from one version of the same implementation to the next). For example, in Solaris 2.8 (EBADR—Invalid request descriptor) is associated with error number 51; in Red Hat Linux 7.3 this same error is associated with error number 53. Likewise, EIDRM—Identifier removed, is error number 43 in Red Hat Linux 7.3 but is error number 37 in Solaris 2.8.

In addition to error messages the command-line **perror** utility returns MyISAM/ISAM[1] table-handler error codes and messages. These codes and their associated messages are shown in Table B.2. Again, as with other error messages, these are mostly system-dependent.

Table B.2 MyISAM/ISAM Error Messages.

Error #	MyISAM/ISAM Message Generated by `perror`
120	Didn't find key on read or update
121	Duplicate key on write or update
122	
123	Someone has changed the row since it was read
124	
126	Index file is crashed/wrong file format
127	Record file is crashed
131	Command not supported by database
132	Old database file

Continued

[1]ISAM is short for Indexed Sequential Access Method a technique for storing and retrieving data.

Table B.2 (Continued)

Error #	MyISAM/ISAM Message Generated by `perror`
133	No record read before update
134	Record was already deleted (or record file crashed)
135	No more room in record file
136	No more room in index file
137	No more records (read after end of file)
138	Unsupported extension used for table
139	Too big row (>= 16 M)
140	Wrong create options
141	Duplicate unique key or constraint on write or update
142	Unknown character set used
143	Conflicting table definition between MERGE and mapped table
144	Table is crashed and last repair failed
145	Table was marked as crashed and should be repaired
146	Lock timed out; retry transaction
147	Lock table is full; restart program with a larger lock table
148	Updates are not allowed under a read-only transaction
149	Lock deadlock; retry transaction

Appendix C

RPC Syntax Diagrams

C.1 Introduction

The correct syntax for the RPC language (XDR with the addition of the **program** and **version** types) can be obtained by tracing through the syntax diagrams[1] following the flow indicated by the arrows. In each diagram, the words or symbols that are listed in boxes with rounded corners should be entered exactly as shown. Items in boxes with square corners that contain entries that are not italicized reference further syntax diagrams. *Italicized* entries reference "common" items. These items consist of

- identifiers (e.g., const-ident, type-ident, etc.), which adhere to standard syntax for C identifiers;
- types, which reference standard C data types (e.g., `int`, `double`, etc.) with the addition of three special XDR language data types: `bool` (boolean), `string` (a sequence of characters terminated by a NULL), and `opaque` (untyped data); and
- values, which reference standard C values (e.g., integer constants, literals, etc.).

[1] While I would like to be able to note that these syntax diagrams follow defined standards, they do not exactly. However, they are close enough in format and style that most readers should find no difficulty interpreting them.

The **rpcgen** compiler converts all RPC definitions into standard C. Statements that have a % in the first column are passed through without interpretation.

The RPC language consists of a series of RPC definitions delineated by semicolons:

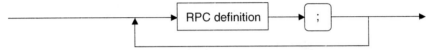

The RPC definition is divided into six categories or definitions.

C.2 RPC Definitions

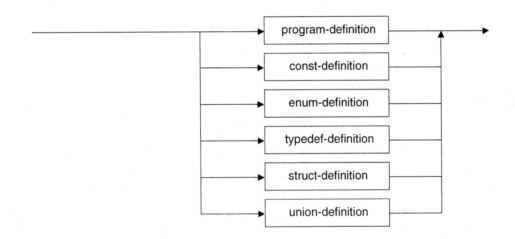

C.2.1 Program-Definition

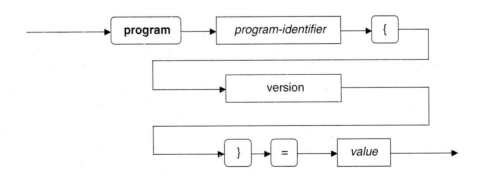

C.2.1.1 Version

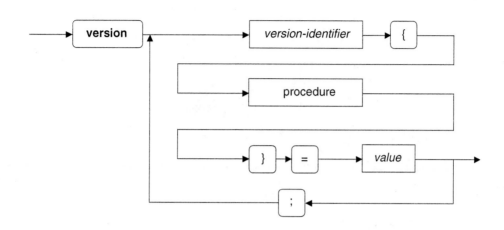

C.2.1.2 Procedure

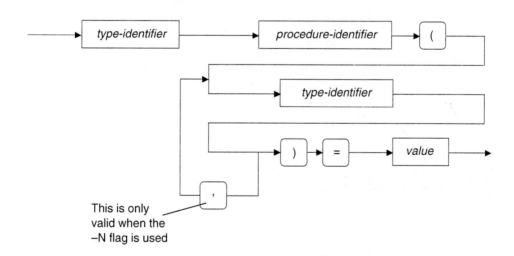

This is only
valid when the
−N flag is used

C.2.2 Const-Definition

C.2.3 Enum-Definition

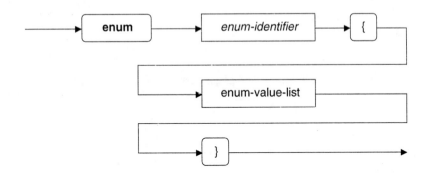

C.2.3.1 Enum-Value-List

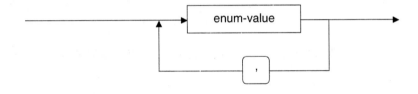

C.2.3.2 Enum value

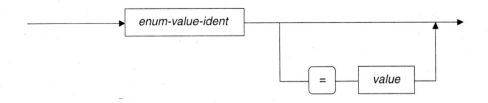

C.2.4 Typedef-Definition

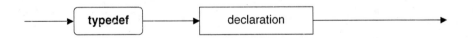

C.2.4.1 Declaration[2]

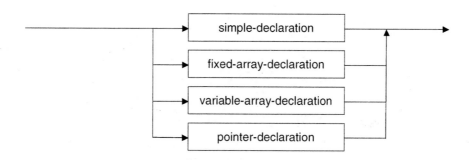

C.2.4.2 Simple Declaration

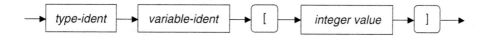

C.2.4.3 Fixed-Array Declaration

C.2.4.4 Variable-Array Declaration[3]

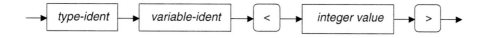

C.2.4.5 Pointer Declaration[4]

---

[2] These are type declarations, not variable declarations (e.g., `int my_number`), which are unsupported by **rpcgen**.

[3] The integer value in angle brackets indicates a maximum size or, if empty, an array of any size.

[4] Not actually an address. Technically called optional-data; often used for references to linked structures.

C.2.5 Structure-Definition

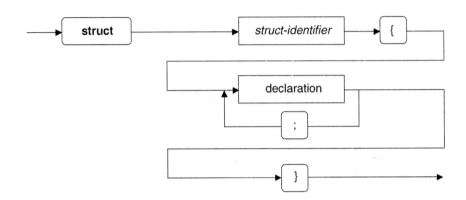

C.2.6 Union-Definition[5]

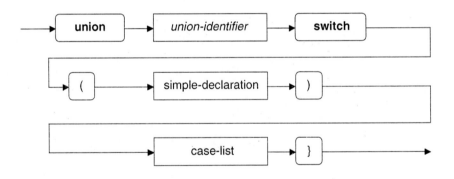

C.2.6.1 Case-List

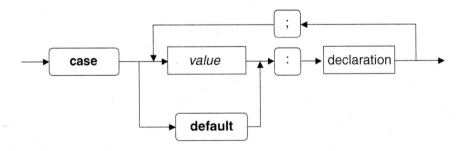

---

[5] In RPC, unions are closer in syntax (and spirit) to variant records in Pascal are than standard C/C++ unions.

C.3 RPC Keywords

The following RPC keywords have special meaning and cannot be used as identifiers.

bool	const	enum	int	string	typedef
char	double	hyper	quadruple	switch	unsigned
void	case	default	float	struct	union

C.4 Some RPC Examples

In the examples below, each set of entries in an RPC .x file is followed by a sequence of statements in gray, which are those produced by the **rpcgen** compiler.

```
/*
 ****************       const      ********************
 */
const MAX = 1024;
const DELIMITER = "@";
/* is converted to:                     */
#define MAX 1024
#define DELIMITER "@"
/*
 ****************       enum      ********************
 */
enum primary { red, yellow = 4, blue  };
/* is converted to:                     */
enum primary {
        red = 0,
        yellow = 4,
        blue = 4 + 1
};
typedef enum primary primary;
/*
 ****************       typedef ********************/
typedef colors strange;        /* simple                    */
typedef char line[80];         /* fixed length array        */
typedef string var_line<80>;   /* variable len array with max */
typedef int some_ints< >;      /* variable len array - NO max */
typedef var_line  *line_ptr;   /* pointer                    */
/* is converted to:                          */
```

The equal sign and semicolon are removed, and const is replaced with #define

Notice how the assignment of each color is handled. The duplicate use of primary is acceptable, as the C/C++ compiler stores these identifiers in a different namespace.

```
typedef colors strange;
typedef char line[80];
typedef char *var_line;
typedef struct {
    u_int some_ints_len;
    int  *some_ints_val;
} some_ints;
typedef var_line *line_ptr;
/*
 ***************         struct   ********************
 */
struct record {
        var_line  name;
        int       age;
};
/* is converted to:                    */
struct record {
        var_line name;
        int age;
};
typedef struct record record;
/*
 ***************         union   ********************
 */
union ret_value switch( extern errno ) {
case 0:
        line answer;
default:
        void;
};
/* is converted to:                    */
struct ret_value {
        extern errno;
        union {
                line answer;
        } ret_value_u;
};
typedef struct ret_value ret_value;
```

The variable length array is mapped to a structure with two members. The first stores the number of elements in the array. The second references the base address of the array. Note how the members are named incorporating the base name of the array.

This conversion is pretty much what one would expect. Again, because of namespace, there is no conflict with using record twice in the typedef.

The union is mapped to a structure containing a reference to the externally declared errno value and a union whose element is the larger (storage-wise) of the initially listed members.

Appendix D

PROFILING PROGRAMS

D.1 Introduction

One way to obtain useful information about the execution of a program is to use the GNU profiler utility **gprof**. This utility, which is part of most standard Linux installations, provides information on functions your program calls. By analyzing the data it provides, you can often improve the execution speed of a program by revising slow, inefficient sections of code. Additionally, profiling may illuminate bugs that may not have surfaced. The following sections present an overview of how to use **gprof**. Interested readers seeking additional information on this utility are encouraged to read the manual page for the utility and to visit the official GNU website (*www.gnu.org*) and peruse the full set of on-line documentation on **gprof**.

Profiling a program is a three-step process:

1. The program is compiled and linked with profiling enabled.
2. The executable version of the program is run to generate a special profile data file.
3. The **gprof** utility is used to analyze and display the profiling data.

D.2 Sample Program for Profiling

A selection sort program is used to demonstrate the profiling process. A selection sort is a general-purpose sort that is a variation of an exchange sort. Basically, this sort passes through a list of elements and finds the index (location) of the smallest (least) element. It exchanges the data at this index with the data stored in the first element of the list. It then repeats the selection process with the remaining list to find the second smallest element, and exchanges the data at this index with the data stored in the second element of the list. The process is repeated until the list is ordered.

There are numerous ways to code a selection sort. Below is a C++ version of this sort.

```
File : ss.cxx
   |      #include <iostream>
   |      using namespace std;                 // Function prototypes
   |      void Get_Data  ( int [], int );
   |      void Display   ( int [], int );
   +      void Do_S_Sort ( int [], int );
   |      int  Find_Least( const int [], int, int );
   |      int  Compare   ( const int & , const int & );
   |      void Swap      ( int &, int & );
   |      int
  10      main( ) {
   |        const int max = 10;
   |        int List[max];
   |        Get_Data ( List, max );            // Obtain data
   |        cout << "Initial list" << endl;
   +        Display  ( List, max );            // Show it
   |        Do_S_Sort( List, max );            // Sort it
   |        cout << "Sorted list" << endl;
   |        Display  ( List, max );            // Show it again
   |        return 0;
  20      }
   |      // Obtain data to sort from standard input
   |      void
   |      Get_Data(int a[], int n) {
   |        cout << "Please enter " << n << " integers" << endl;
   +        for(int i=0; i < n; ++i)
   |          cin >> a[i];
   |      }
   |      // Display the current contents of list
   |      void
  30      Display(int a[], int n) {
   |        for(int i=0; i < n; ++i)
   |          cout << " " << a[i];
```

```
 |        cout << endl;
 |      }
 +      //  Do the Selection Sort, Display after each pass
 |      void
 |      Do_S_Sort( int a[], int n ){
 |        int index;
 |        for (int i=0; i < n-1; ++i){
40          index=Find_Least( a, i, n );
 |          if ( i != index )
 |            Swap( a[i], a[index] );
 |          cout << "After pass " << i+1 << " : ";
 |          Display( a, n );
 +        }
 |      }
 |      //  Find the index of the least element in list
 |      int
 |      Find_Least( const int a[], int start, int stop ){
50        int Index_of_Least = start;
 |        for (int i=start+1; i < stop; ++i )
 |          if ( Compare(a[i], a[Index_of_Least]) )
 |            Index_of_Least = i;
 |        return Index_of_Least;
 +      }
 |      //  Compare two data elements
 |      int
 |      Compare( const int &a, const int &b ){
 |        return ( a < b );
60      }
 |      //  Exchange two data elements
 |      void
 |      Swap( int &a, int &b ){
 |        int temp;
 +        temp = a;
 |        a    = b;
 |        b    = temp;
 |      }
```

As shown, six functions are used to implement the sort.

FUNCTION	PURPOSE
Get_Data	Obtains the data to be sorted from standard input.
Display	Prints the current contents of the list to standard output.
Do_S_Sort	Performs the selection sort routine.

Continued

577

FUNCTION	PURPOSE
Find_Least	Traverses a portion of the list to find (and ultimately return) the index of the smallest element.
Compare	Compares two list elements and returns a nonzero value if the first element is less than the second element.
Swap	Exchanges the data for two elements in the list.

At first glance, using so many functions for such a simple algorithm may seem to be overkill. However, coding some statements (such as the compare in line 52) as a function call will facilitate referencing when generating profile information with **gprof**.

A good portion of the work done by the selection sort is actually performed by the Find_Least function (see line 49). This function is passed the list and two integer values. The first integer value is the starting point for the search through the remainder of the list. The second value is the size of the list (which in this case reflects its end or stopping point). This function works by storing, in the variable Index_of_Least, the index of the element having the smallest value. Initially, this is the index of the current start of the list (see line 50). It then uses a for loop to pass through the reminder of the list, checking each location against the current smallest value to determine if it has found a lesser value. Each check is carried out by the Compare function. If the value is less, the index (not the value) of the location is stored. When the loop finishes, the index of the element with the smallest value is returned to the calling function. If the returned index is not the index of the current head of list, the two values are exchanged by calling the Swap function. If the current value is already in order, no exchange is needed.

D.3 Generating Profile Data

To collect profiling information, a program must be compiled and linked with profiling enabled. To accomplish this, the command-line option -pg is passed to the compiler. For example, if our source program was ss.cxx, we would use the following command:

```
linux$ g++ ss.cxx -pg -o ss
```

If your program consists of separate source files, which are compiled individually, each intermediate compilation should be passed the -pg option if you want to profile the functions found in the source file. If the debug command-line option -g is also specified, the **gprof** utility will generate additional line-by-line profiling information. This technique is discussed in detail at the end of this appendix.

Once successfully compiled, the program is run using its normal arguments, input files, and so on. The profiling data generated by the program's execution is stored in a file called gmon.out in the current directory. Should there be an existing gmon.out file, it is overwritten. Note that the gmon.out file will not be produced if the program does not exit normally (i.e., does not return from main or call **exit**).[1] The gmon.out file is a data file not a plain text file and as such should not be directly printed or displayed on the screen.

D.4 Viewing and Interpreting Profile Data

The profile data stored in the gmon.out file is analyzed and displayed using the **gprof** utility. If called with no options or command-line arguments, **gprof** assumes that the executable it is working with is a.out and that the profile data for this executable is in the file gmon.out. Also, unless directed otherwise, **gprof** generates and displays a fully annotated flat profile and a call graph using the collected data. Like most utilities, **gprof** supports an extensive set of options. We will examine a small subset of its options.

Staying with our selection sort example, as shown previously, the command-line sequence

```
linux$ g++ ss.cxx -pg -o ss
```

compiles the source file ss.cxx into the executable file ss. The program is then run. In this example the program obtains its input, via command-line redirection, from a data file called data_reverse. The data file contains the numbers 1 through 10 in reverse order. The output from the program's execution is displayed on the screen.

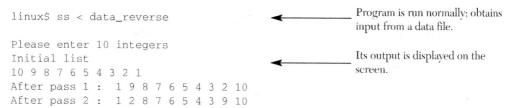

```
linux$ ss < data_reverse                          ◄──────  Program is run normally; obtains
                                                            input from a data file.
Please enter 10 integers
Initial list                                       ◄──────  Its output is displayed on the
10 9 8 7 6 5 4 3 2 1                                        screen.
After pass 1 :   1 9 8 7 6 5 4 3 2 10
After pass 2 :   1 2 8 7 6 5 4 3 9 10
```

---

[1] In this case calling **_exit** would not work, as it does not perform the cleanup activities that a call to **exit** does.

```
After pass 3 :  1 2 3 7 6 5 4 8 9 10
After pass 4 :  1 2 3 4 6 5 7 8 9 10
After pass 5 :  1 2 3 4 5 6 7 8 9 10        ◄──────
After pass 6 :  1 2 3 4 5 6 7 8 9 10
After pass 7 :  1 2 3 4 5 6 7 8 9 10
After pass 8 :  1 2 3 4 5 6 7 8 9 10
After pass 9 :  1 2 3 4 5 6 7 8 9 10
Sorted list
1 2 3 4 5 6 7 8 9 10
```

Given the unique nature of the input data (it starts in descending order) and the algorithm's logic, the data is actually sorted before the program terminates!

Once the program is run, the **gprof** utility is used to analyze and view the profile data. If options are to be passed to **gprof**, they should be specified individually on the command line following the call to the utility. The name of the executable file comes after the options. If not specified, the default is a.out. The executable file name is optionally followed by the profile file name, which, if not given, defaults to gmon.out. In the example below the -b option (for brief) is specified.

```
linux$ gprof -b ss    ◄──────
```

Call **gprof** and pass it the -b option and the name of the executable file (ss). The profile data file, which is not specified, is assumed to be gmon.out.

The output generated by this invocation is divided into two sections, the first of which is a flat profile. This section shows how much time the program spent in each function and how many times the function was called. Sorting 10 items is a trivial task even with the somewhat inefficient selection sort. Therefore, to produce a more instructive data set, the number of values to be sorted was increased to 1,000 and the program recompiled and rerun. To reduce the time needed for display, the output of the executable was discarded by directing it to /dev/null.

```
linux$ ss < data_reverse > /dev/null
```

The **gprof** output below is based on sorting 1,000 values.

```
Flat profile:

Each sample counts as 0.01 seconds.
  %   cumulative  self              self     total
 time   seconds   seconds   calls  us/call  us/call  name
100.00    0.04      0.04      999   40.04    40.04   Find_Least(int const *, int,
                                                       int)
  0.00    0.04      0.00   499500    0.00     0.00   Compare(int const &, int
                                                             const &)
  0.00    0.04      0.00     1001    0.00     0.00   Display(int *, int)
  0.00    0.04      0.00      500    0.00     0.00   Swap(int &, int &)
  0.00    0.04      0.00        1    0.00  40000.00   Do_S_Sort(int *, int)
  0.00    0.04      0.00        1    0.00     0.00   Get_Data(int *, int)
```

In the flat profile section each function is listed in decreasing order based on its runtime (if the runtime is too small to be recorded, it is reported as 0). The meaning of each field in the flat profile is listed in the following table.

FIELD NAME	MEANING
% time	The percentage of total execution time.
cumulative seconds	Total seconds executing this function and all those listed above it in the table.
self seconds	Total seconds executing just this function (the primary sort key).
calls	The number of times this function was called (blank if not called).
self Ts/call	Average number of T seconds spent in this function (m = milli, u = micro, n = nano, etc.).
total Ts/call	Per call, the average number of T seconds in this function and its descendants.
name	Function name (acts as the secondary sort key)

As might be anticipated with a list of 1,000 elements, the Compare function in our example is called 499,500 times (the summation of $999 + 998 + 997 \cdots + 1$, the series representing the number of compares). Clearly, the Find_Least function is the most time intensive of the group.

The flat profile is followed by a call graph that details the amount of time spent in each function. The output in this section is divided into a series of entries, one per function. Each entry, which is one or more lines in length, is separated from the next by a series of dashes. Within each entry there is one primary line. The primary line indicates the function associated with the entry data. The primary line is easily identified, as it begins with an index number surrounded by set of square brackets. In each entry lines that precede the primary line are functions that call the function, while lines that follow the primary line are functions that are called by the function (in call graph-speak, its children). If the caller of a function cannot be determined, <spontaneous> is printed instead.

Here is the call graph for our selection sort program when it sorts a list of 1,000 values, which were initially in inverse order. For ease of reference, each primary line has been highlighted.

```
                         Call graph
granularity: each sample hit covers 4 byte(s) for 25.00% of 0.04 seconds

index % time    self  children    called     name
                0.04    0.00     999/999         Do_S_Sort(int *, int) [2]
[1]    100.0    0.04    0.00     999           Find_Least(int const *, int, int) [1]
                0.00    0.00  499500/499500    Compare(int const &, int const &) [4]
```

```
-----------------------------------------------------
              0.00      0.04       1/1        main [3]
[2]   100.0   0.00      0.04        1         Do_S_Sort(int *, int) [2]
              0.04      0.00     999/999      Find_Least(int const *, int,
                                                            int) [1]
              0.00      0.00    999/1001      Display(int *, int) [5]
              0.00      0.00     500/500      Swap(int &, int &) [6]
-----------------------------------------------------
                                             <spontaneous>
[3]   100.0   0.00      0.04               main [3]
              0.00      0.04       1/1        Do_S_Sort(int *, int) [2]
              0.00      0.00     2/1001       Display(int *, int) [5]
              0.00      0.00       1/1        Get_Data(int *, int) [7]
-----------------------------------------------------
              0.00      0.00  499500/499500   Find_Least(int const *, int,
                                                            int) [1]
[4]    0.0    0.00      0.00    499500        Compare(int const &, int const &) [4]
-----------------------------------------------------
              0.00      0.00     2/1001       main [3]
              0.00      0.00    999/1001      Do_S_Sort(int *, int) [2]
[5]    0.0    0.00      0.00     1001         Display(int *, int) [5]
-----------------------------------------------------
              0.00      0.00     500/500      Do_S_Sort(int *, int) [2]
[6]    0.0    0.00      0.00      500         Swap(int &, int &) [6]
-----------------------------------------------------
              0.00      0.00       1/1        main [3]
[7]    0.0    0.00      0.00        1         Get_Data(int *, int) [7]
-----------------------------------------------------
Index by function name
[4] Compare(int const &, int const &)  [2] Do_S_Sort(int *, int)
[7] Get_Data(int *, int)               [5] Display(int *, int)
[1] Find_Least(int const *, int, int)  [6] Swap(int &, int &)
```

The meaning of each field is based on its context (i.e., the line's designation): primary, function's callers (call this function), or called functions (called by this function).

FIELD	PRIMARY	FUNCTION'S CALLERS	CALLED FUNCTIONS
index	Index number of this function.		
% time	Percent of total time spent in this function and its children.		

self	Total amount of time just spent in this function (same as `self seconds` value in flat profile).	Estimate of time spent in this function when invoked by the .caller function.	Estimate of time spent in called function.
children	Total amount of time spent in the function calls made by this function.	Estimate of time spent in calls to its children.	Estimate of time spent in the children of the called function.
called	Number of times this function was called. A +is used to separate recursive calls.	Number of times this function is called; the total number of nonrecursive calls.	Number of times this function is called; the total number of nonrecursive calls.
name	The name and index number of the function.	The name and index number of the function.	The name and index number of the function.

If we look at the first entry in the call graph output, we note that the primary line is flagged by `[1]`. The associated function, Find_Least, is called by the Do_S_Sort function 999 times. In turn, the Find_Least function calls the Compare function 499,500 times.

The **gprof** utility can be directed to display an annotated source code listing where it identifies the number of calls for the function. To produce this output, the source program must be compiled with the -g option, and **gprof** passed the -A option (indicating annotated source). Using our same source program, this sequence would be

```
linux$ g++ -g ss.cxx -pg -o ss
linux$ ss < data_reverse > /dev/null
linux$ gprof -A ss
```

As shown below, **gprof**'s output lists the program source code and indicates the number of times each function is called. At the end of the listing, it displays a top 10 list indicating the top 10 lines based on their execution activity. Following the top 10 list is an execution summary.

```
*** File /home/faculty/gray/revision/profile/ss.cxx:
                #include <iostream>
                using namespace std;                    // Function prototypes
                void Get_Data  ( int [], int );
                void Display   ( int [], int );
                void Do_S_Sort ( int [], int );
                int  Find_Least( const int [], int, int );
                int  Compare   ( const int &, const int & );
```

```
          void Swap       ( int &, int & );
          int
##### -> main( ) {
             const int max = 1000;
             int List[max];
             Get_Data ( List, max );                // Obtain data
             cout << "Initial list" << endl;
             Display   ( List, max );               // Show it
             Do_S_Sort( List, max );                // Sort it
             cout << "Sorted list" << endl;
             Display   ( List, max );               // Show it again
             return 0;
          }
          // Obtain data to sort from standard input
          void
     1 -> Get_Data(int a[], int n) {
             cout << "Please enter " << n << " integers" << endl;
             for(int i=0; i < n; ++i)
                cin >> a[i];
          }
          // Display the current contents of list
          void
  1001 -> Display(int a[], int n) {
             for(int i=0; i < n; ++i)
                cout << " " << a[i];
             cout << endl;
          }
          //  Do the Selection Sort, Display after each pass
          void
     1 -> Do_S_Sort( int a[], int n ){
             int index;
             for (int i=0; i < n-1; ++i){
               index=Find_Least( a, i, n );
               if ( i != index )
                 Swap( a[i], a[index] );
               cout << "After pass " << i+1 << " : ";
               Display( a, n );
             }
          }
          //  Find the index of the least element in list
          int
   999 -> Find_Least( const int a[], int start, int stop ){
             int Index_of_Least = start;
             for (int i=start+1; i < stop; ++i )
               if ( Compare(a[i], a[Index_of_Least]) )
                 Index_of_Least = i;
             return Index_of_Least;
          }
          //  Compare two data elements
          int
```

```
  499500 -> Compare( const int &a, const int &b ){
              return ( a < b );
            }
            //  Exchange two data elements
            void
     500 -> Swap( int &a, int &b ){
              int temp;
              temp = a;
              a     = b;
              b     = temp;
   ##### -> }
```

```
Top 10 Lines:
    Line       Count
      58     499500
      30       1001
      49        999
      63        500
      23          1
      37          1

Execution Summary:
       8   Executable lines in this file
       8   Lines executed
  100.00   Percent of the file executed
  502002   Total number of line executions
62750.25   Average executions per line
```

While the **gprof** utility is helpful in analyzing the execution of programs, the current Linux version of this utility does have a serious limitation. As implemented, the utility uses a signal handler to collect profile information. The signal handler is invoked by the periodic generation of a SIGPROF (27) signal. When a child process is generated via a **fork** or a new thread is created with a call to **pthread_create**, they do not, by default, receive these signals. As a result, no profile data is collected for the child process or new thread.

Appendix E

BIBLIOGRAPHY

Bach, M. J., *The Design of the UNIX Operating System*. Englewood Cliffs, NJ: Prentice Hall, 1986.

Bloomer, J., *Power Programming with RPC*. Sebastopol, CA: O'Reilly & Associates, Inc., 1992.

Brown, C., *UNIX Distributed Programming*. Englewood Cliffs, NJ.: Prentice Hall, 1994.

Bovet, B. P., and Cesati, M., *Understanding the Linux Kernel*. Sebastopol, CA: O'Reilly & Associates, Inc., 2001.

Comer, D. E., and Stevens, D. L., *Internetworking with TCP/IP, Vol. III: Client-Server Programming and Applications, Linux/Posix Sockets Version 1/E*. Upper Saddle River, NJ: Prentice Hall, 2000.

Dijkstra, E. W., "Cooperating Sequential Processes," Technological University, Eindhoven, Netherlands, 1965.

Ditel, H. M., *Operating Systems*. Reading, MA: Addison-Wesley, 1990.

Johnson, M. K., and Troan, E. W., *Linux Application Development*. Reading, MA: Addison-Wesley, 1998.

Kernighan, B. W., and Pike, R., *The UNIX Programming Environment*. Englewood Cliffs, NJ: Prentice Hall, 1984.

Kleiman, S., Shah, D., and Smaalders, B., *Programming with Threads*. Upper Saddle River, NJ: SunSoft Press—Prentice Hall, 1996.

Kochan, S. G., and Wood, P. H., *UNIX Networking*. Indianapolis, IN: Hayden Books, 1989.

Leach, R. J., *Advanced Topics in UNIX, Processes, Files, and Systems*. New York: John Wiley & Sons, Inc., 1994.

Leffler, S. J., McKusick, M. K., and Quarterman, J. S., *The Design and Implementation of the 4.3 BSD UNIX Operating System*. Reading, MA: Addison-Wesley, 1989.

Lewis, B., and Berg, D. J., *Threads Primer: A Guide to Multithreading Programming*. Upper Saddle River, NJ: SunSoft Press—Prentice Hall, 1996.

Matthew, N. and Stones, R., *Beginning Linux Programming*. Chicago, IL: Wrox Press, 1999.

Matthew, N. and Stones, R., *Professional Linux Programming*. Chicago, IL: Wrox Press, 2000.

Maxwell, S. A., *Linux Core Kernel Commentary*. Scottsdale, AZ: Coriolis, 2001.

Mitchell, M., Oldham, J., and Samuel, A., *Advanced Linux Programming*. Boston, MA: New Riders, 2001. (note: available for free download at: `http://www.advancedlinuxprogramming.com/`).

Mitchell, M., Oldham, J., and Samuel, A., *Advanced Linux Programming*. Indianapolis, IN: New Riders, 2001.

Nichols, B., Buttlar, D., and Farrell, J. P., *Threads Programming*. Sebastopol, CA: O'Reilly & Associates, Inc., 1996.

Northrup, C. J., *Programming with UNIX Threads*. New York: John Wiley & Sons, Inc., 1996.

Norton, S. J., and Dipasquale, M., *Threadtime: The Multithreaded Programming Guide*. Upper Saddle River, NJ: Prentice Hall, 1997.

Nutt, G., *Operating Systems: A Modern Perspective, Lab Update*, 2nd ed. Reading, MA: Addison-Wesley, 2002.

Rago, S. A., *UNIX System V Network Programming*. Reading, MA: Addison-Wesley, 1993.

Rieken, B., and Weiman, L., *Adventures in UNIX Network Applications Programming*. New York: John Wiley & Sons, Inc., 1992.

Rochkind, M. J., *Advanced UNIX Programming*. Englewood Cliffs, NJ: Prentice Hall, 1985.

Silberschatz, A., and Peterson, J. L., *Operating System Concepts*. Reading, MA: Addison-Wesley, 1989.

Stallings, W., *Operating Systems: Internals and Design Principles*, 4th ed. Upper Saddle River, NJ: Prentice Hall, 2001.

Stevens, W. R., *Advanced Programming in the UNIX Environment*. Reading, MA: Addison-Wesley, 1992.

Stevens, W. R., *UNIX Network Programming, Volume 2: Interprocess Communications*. Upper Saddle River, NJ: Prentice Hall, 1999.

Tanenbaum, A. S., *Modern Operating Systems*, 2nd ed. Upper Saddle River, NJ: Prentice Hall, 2001.

Wall, K., *Linux Programming Unleashed*, 2nd ed. Indianapolis, IN: SAMS, 2000.

There are countless sites on the Internet that deal with Linux and all its variants. It is virtually impossible to generate a list of these sites without leaving out at least one (or more) URLs for which someone will take you to task. This aside, the table below (in no particular order of importance) provides a good starting point. For additional locations and supporting sites, try searching the Internet for the terms GNU, GNU/Linux, Linux, and so on, using any one of the high-powered search engines (e.g., www.google.com, www.dogpile.com, etc.).

URL	Description
gcc.gnu.org	The GNU compiler's home page.
linuxtoday.com	Linux Today magazine Web site.
www.debian.org	Home base for Debian GNU/Linux
www.gnome.org	GNOME is a free desktop environment for Linux.
www.gnu.org	Home of the GNU Project.
www.kde.org	KDE is the other free desktop environment for Linux.
www.kernel.org	Linux kernel archive site with Linux kernel source code.
www.li.org	International nonprofit site for promotion and growth of Linux.
www.linux.com	Linux information and resources.
www.linux.org	Provides information on and resources for the Linux operating system.

URL	Description
www.linuxdoc.org	Linux documentation development projects.
www.linuxgazette.com	An online Linux journal.
www.linuxhq.com	Catalogs Linux patches, distribution indices, and links.
www.linuxjournal.com	Linux Journal Web site.
www.linux-mag.com	Linux Magazine Web site.
www.linuxworld.com	Provides hands-on technical information and product reviews.
www.redhat.com	Home base for Red Hat Linux software.
www.suse.com	Home base for SuSE Linux.

INDEX

U

W

X

Z